MW01194093

"As a contributor to the Theology for the People of God series, I am delighted to recommend this introductory volume, *A Handbook of Theology*. In about a dozen pages for each topic, this readily accessible volume ranges widely over theology and its method and history, core doctrines, and Christian living and cultural engagement. From responsible handling of biblical affirmations on nearly fifty topics, to tracing their development historically, and including practical counsel for their application, this *Handbook* is a comprehensive guide that will be consulted many times and on many occasions."

—**Gregg R. Allison**, professor of theology,
The Southern Baptist Theological Seminary

"This is a book you can confidently place in the hands of church leaders and students to introduce them to an array of different kinds of theology (biblical theology, historical theology, and so forth), and especially to an outline of systematic theology. Most of the contributors have sought to forge connections between their respective chapters and the life and vitality of the church. Confessionally, the work is conservative and baptistic but will doubtless serve readers from a wide range of backgrounds."

—**D. A. Carson**, theologian-at-large, The Gospel Coalition

"This handbook successfully addresses a wide range of subjects: theological foundations, theology, history, geography, doctrines, Christian living, and engagement with culture. The chapters are short enough to be digestible but long enough to inform. The essays are very competently written by scholars and practitioners in their fields. Both men and women as well as younger scholars and seasoned theologians are contributors to this very readable and worthy volume."

—**Graham A. Cole**, dean emeritus, Trinity Evangelical
Divinity School and emeritus principal, Ridley College

"A massive work. So much here to read, enjoy, immerse yourself in, and use as teaching tools for others. Let no one say Baptists don't know how to do theology!"

—**Josh Moody**, senior pastor, College Church in Wheaton,
and president, God Centered Life Ministries

"This handbook treats classic and contemporary topics in theology in a way that is biblically faithful, ecclesially rooted, and solidly evangelical. Written by both leading and emerging Baptist scholars, the chapters are insightful, succinct, edifying, and timely. The editors are to be commended for this significant achievement."

—**Christopher W. Morgan**, dean and professor of theology at the School of Christian Ministries, California Baptist University

"In a day when theology as the 'queen of the sciences' has been challenged, *A Handbook of Theology* joyfully reminds us of the enduring power and proper place of theology in Christian discourse. In this remarkable guide, dozens of respected theologians have laid a proper foundation of the broad contours of Christian theology, upon which a lifetime of study can be built. I heartily recommend it."

—**Timothy C. Tennent**, president and professor of World Christianity, Asbury Theological Seminary

A
HANDBOOK
OF
THEOLOGY

THEOLOGY for the PEOPLE of GOD

A
HANDBOOK
OF
THEOLOGY

EDITORS

Daniel L. Akin | *David S. Dockery* | *Nathan A. Finn*

ACADEMIC
BRENTWOOD, TENNESSEE

Published by B&H Academic
Brentwood, Tennessee

ISBN: 978-1-0877-0087-8

Dewey Decimal Classification: 230
Subject Heading: THEOLOGY / DOCTRINAL
THEOLOGY / CHRISTIANITY--DOCTRINES

This book is part of the Theology for the People of God series.

The web addresses referenced in this book were live and correct at the
time of the book's publication but may be subject to change.

Cover design by B&H Publishing Group. Cover image: Icon of the First Ecumenical
Council of Nicaea, by Michael Damaskinos (c.1591) Wikimedia Commons/C Messier

Printed in the United States of America

28 27 26 25 24 23 VP 1 2 3 4 5 6 7 8 9 10

CONTENTS

PREFACE

The apostle Paul, writing to the church at Thessalonica, urged the followers of Jesus Christ to stand firm and hold to the tradition that they were taught (2 Thess 2:15). Similarly, the apostle exhorted Timothy, his apostolic legate, to keep the pattern of teaching (2 Tim 1:13). In his letter to Titus, the apostle noted that leaders need to hold to the faithful message as taught in order to be able to encourage with sound doctrine and to refute those who contradict it (Titus 1:9). In what represents a summary of these various exhortations, Paul instructed Timothy to commit the teachings he had heard to faithful Christ followers so that they will be able to teach others also (2 Tim 2:2).

These important priorities continue to be the focus of ecclesial theologians, those Christian thinkers who understand that their calling and work should be carried out in service to the church, the people of God. Ecclesial theology, among other things, must be grounded in the Scriptures; it must be trinitarian, Christ-centered, Spirit-enabled, and doxological; it must be informed by the thinking of God's people throughout church history; and it must be ministry- and mission-focused.

The contributors to *A Handbook of Theology* understand the importance of speaking to both minds and hearts, seeking also to provide application for hands and feet. Ecclesial theologians in the twenty-first century must make every effort to help people develop a theologically informed way of seeing and understanding the world in order to engage the great ideas of the past and current issues in our context and culture. Such a theological framework will provide right motivations for Christian living and Christian ministry. This handbook in many ways serves as both an introduction to and a summary for the new multiauthored and multivolume series called Theology for the People of God, which is grounded in a calling to serve the church.

The more than four dozen contributors to this volume believe there must be a place for the true intellectual love of God, for Jesus has commanded us to love God with our heart, soul, strength, and mind, and to love our neighbor as well (Matt 22:37–39). This, however, should not lead to some cold, intellectual approach to the faith unaccompanied by affection. For too many people, the work of theologians seems to be characterized by a kind of intellectual aloofness or uncommitted intellectual curiosity.

Those contributing to *A Handbook of Theology* heartily affirm a commitment to the truthfulness of the Bible, the transformational power of the gospel, and the centrality of the church. In this way, those participating in this volume seek to be faithful to the best of our evangelical heritage. It is our prayer that this volume will render service to the church in many ways, satisfying the mind and heart so that we can know God (Jer 9:23–24) and lovingly follow the living and exalted Christ (Phil 3:10–14). We fully believe that theology is necessary to strengthen the church's worship as well as its tasks of evangelism, discipleship, teaching, service, and missions.

While the contributors to this volume have attempted to be faithful to the best of the Baptist and evangelical heritage, they have also sought to engage the issues of the day and prepare followers of Christ for the challenges of tomorrow. That said, our goal in this work has not been to be caught up in the latest movement, trend, or fad, always seeking that which is novel based on the newest thought or proposal in the theological world. The kind of maturity pictured in Ephesians 4 calls for a more carefully articulated theological foundation that will speak in a fresh way while not falling into the ill-suited paths leading to gullibility, instability, or heterodox thinking. The participants in this volume have written with the goal of providing a renewed vision for the relationship of theology, church, worship, ministry, and missions. They do this with an awareness that the health of the church requires a solid theological foundation.

Our hope is that this volume will serve as a helpful resource for students, pastors, and church leaders. We ask that readers join with us in asking God to use this volume as a source of strength, renewal, and revitalization for the church in the days to come. We trust that this will take place as people better understand what they believe and why they believe it. We believe that the sound, reliable theology found in these pages will serve as a source of strength and hope for God's people for decades to come.

The three of us have been working on this project for a few years. We now pray that it will serve as an instrument of grace for readers and those who will be influenced by the faithful efforts of the contributors who have collaborated with us. We are grateful for each author and the dedication, experience, skills, and gifts each person brings to this shared effort. We want to express our gratitude for our friends at B&H and the Lifeway administration for their wholehearted support, guidance, and patience, as well as for the assistance from colleagues and staff members at our institutions, especially Devin Moncada and Chris Kim. We are genuinely thankful for our families, who have encouraged us through the process of yet another writing project. We ultimately thank our great God for the privilege to work together on this project, trusting the Lord that it will strengthen the people of God in many and multifaceted ways.

Soli Deo Gloria
Daniel L. Akin, David S. Dockery, and Nathan A. Finn

INTRODUCTION TO THEOLOGY FOR THE PEOPLE OF GOD

At the heart of this volume is an understanding that the study of theology matters for the life and health of the church. The term "theology," however, often scares people. For some it sounds formidable, esoteric, technical, and abstract. Others believe theology to be irrelevant to our life with God, even suspicious that theology is some sort of human presumption that provides a distraction from genuine ministry. Most of us have encountered this kind of thinking. You might be surprised to hear us say that the suspicions are at least partly well-founded because theology has too often been studied in the wrong way. That has led to misthinking or even hurtful thinking in some contexts.

Guidance from the Apostle Paul

It will be helpful for us to take a step back and look at a passage from the apostle Paul in Ephesians 4. Here we see the goals of the teaching ministry for the people of God as threefold: (1) to build up the church; (2) to lead the church to maturity in faith; and (3) to lead the church to unity. Theology at its best aims to do these three things, equipping and strengthening God's people in a holistic way, addressing heads, hearts, and hands. If those involved in the work of theology focus only on the head, we will at best have followers of Christ who are well informed but not conformed to the character of Christ. It is our prayer that this volume will serve as a resource to help people develop (1) a theologically informed way of seeing the world (the head), (2) Christian responses in our experience and our affections (the heart), and (3) Christian strategies and motivations for ministry (the hands). We believe

1

that a full-orbed understanding of these things can only be addressed when we understand that theology finds its focus in the church, recognizing that head, hearts, and hands should not be separated.

Guidance from Church History

In the history of the church, both church leaders and church members were called to ongoing study (2 Tim 2:15) in order to provide oversight for the ministry of the Word of God in worship services, as well as to disciple new converts (2 Tim 2:2; Titus 1:9). Even during the time of Augustine in the fifth century, personal mentorship, guidance, and teaching from older pastors and bishops remained the primary model for doing theology for the people of God. By the time of the Reformation, Martin Luther, Philip Melanchthon, and John Calvin gave themselves to the work of theology and the teaching of theology. From their work came a threefold approach to the study of theology, which included (1) the study of the Bible and its interpretation in the history of the church; (2) the study of doctrine; and (3) the application of these subjects with special attention to the practical administration of churches, preaching, worship, and ministry. In many ways, the shape of this volume follows this pattern.

Enlightenment and Post-Enlightenment Challenges

It needs to be recognized that even in the twenty-first century, we still wrestle with the residual effects of the vast influence of Enlightenment and post-Enlightenment thought, which challenged the very heart of the Christian faith. While the purpose of this volume is not primarily one of apologetics or polemics, the contributors to this book do not share the approaches of Enlightenment thinking and its questions about supernaturalism, biblical authority, Christian tradition, and the role of reason. The Enlightenment, which blossomed in the eighteenth century, was a watershed in the history of Western civilization. The Christian consensus that had existed from the fourth through the seventeenth centuries was hampered by a radical secular spirit. Enlightenment emphases were characterized by a stress on the primacy of nature and reason over special revelation. Along with this elevated view of reason, the movement reflected a low view of sin, an antisupernatural bias, and an ongoing questioning of the place of authority and tradition.

In the nineteenth century, Friedrich Schleiermacher led the various attempts to synthesize the Christian faith with both Romantic and Enlightenment ideas. His attempt to translate the Christian faith to those changing times, as articulated in works such as *On Religion: Speeches to Its Cultured Despisers* (1799), was not just an attempt to make the Christian faith relevant or to bring Christianity to a place where it could be heard afresh. Rather, his work transformed the Christian faith into something quite different. Schleiermacher's thinking was formed in the context of pietism; yet, in his attempt to save the spiritual by divorcing theology from spirituality, he wound up losing both. Schleiermacher initiated a trajectory that created a disruption between the study of theology and the congregations, bringing about a separation of head and heart.

Theology for the People of God

Our desire in providing *A Handbook of Theology* is to help us all think afresh about bringing together to the people of God the study of theology, the importance of spiritual formation, and service. Thus, when we speak of theology, we are not merely echoing Schleiermacher's understanding of theology as an attempt to articulate our feelings about our dependence on God. On the other hand, we do not wish to overswing the pendulum by defining theology only in objective terms of putting truth in proper order. Faithful to our free church heritage, we suggest that theology involves both the developing of our minds for truth so that we indeed articulate "the faith once for all delivered to the saints" and developing a heart for God so our lives are built up in the faith. Ultimately, a theology for the people of God seeks to serve the church by building up the body of Christ so that it may grow up into the Head, which is Christ himself, in order to bring maturity in thought and in life (Eph 4:13–16).

For too many people, however, the province of theology has not been the church but has been limited to the realm of specialists in the academic world. We certainly believe that Christian theology should be a part of the academic world and should engage the academy as well as society-at-large. We affirm that there is a rightful place for academic and public theology.

Ultimately, however, we believe theology should have its focus on serving the church, building up believers in the faith. This does not mean that all Christ followers are to be theologians uniquely summoned to the task of leading in theological thought. It does mean, however, that all believers are responsible before God to think lofty thoughts about the triune God and to live according to his revealed Word to us. It is our prayer that the articles found in this volume will help men and women to see and understand the revelation of God for their foundational beliefs while integrating these beliefs into their life and practice.

In no way do we wish to suggest that theology is the whole of church life. But there must be a place for the true intellectual love of God, for Jesus taught us to love God with our heart, soul, strength, and mind, while loving our neighbors as well. This should not lead to some cold, intellectual approach to the faith unaccompanied by affection. For too many, theology is a kind of intellectual aloofness, merely a detached academic pursuit.

We believe theology renders service to the church in many ways. It satisfies the mind so that we can know God and know the living Christ. Theology is necessary for the church's teaching and apologetic tasks (1 Pet 3:15). Theology is important as a touchstone for understanding what the church believes and for recognizing the principles by which the allegiance of its members will be judged. Such beliefs and practices come from serious theological reflection. Such an understanding recognizes that the Christian faith is more than a personal and subjective experience; it is also the body of truth "delivered to the saints once for all" (Jude 1:3). It certainly includes "belief in," but it also must be understood in terms of "belief that." Moreover, theology points to ethics. Certainly, it is possible to act one way and think another, but it is not logically possible for one to do so for long, for as persons think in their hearts, so they will live (Prov 23:7). If the church is to live in the world with a lifestyle that issues forth in glory to God, it must think deeply about personal ethics as well as the implications of the biblical faith for society, culture, and marketplace. Such necessities touch the heart of the church's life and mission; they are not just matters on the periphery of options from which we can pick and choose.

One of the main problems the church faces in the twenty-first century is a failure to recognize one of the primary purposes of the church, which is articulated for us in Eph 3:10. God's intent is that, through the church, the manifold wisdom of God is to be made known. The history of the Christian church and the unfolding drama of redemption has been called a graduate school for the rulers and authorities in the heavenly realm. The church is central to God's working in history as well as to the gospel and Christian living. Thus, theology is more than God's words for us as individuals, for God is not just saving individuals; he is saving a people for himself. We suggest that theology is best understood as theology for the church, the community of faith. If the church is central to God's plan, then we cannot push to the periphery what is central for God. We need a framework for understanding a theology of the church before we can talk about doing theology for the church.

In Ephesians, Paul seems to advance the understanding of the church beyond that of a local body of believers to include the people of God on earth at any one time, plus all believers in heaven and on earth, which is often referred to as the universal church. At Pentecost, God inaugurated the church as his new society (Acts 2), founded on Christ's finished work (Acts 2:22–24) and the baptizing work of the Holy Spirit (1 Cor 12:13). The church is a mystery (Eph 3:1–6) that Christ prophesied (Matt 16:18) and that was revealed at the Spirit's coming at Pentecost. The church has apostles and prophets as its foundation and Christ as the cornerstone (Eph 2:20–21). In origin and in purpose, the church is God's church. The church is not created by our efforts, but received as God's gift, constituted by him and for him.

Membership in the community of faith is by divine initiative, for we love him because he first loved us (1 John 4:10). God creates a fellowship of people indwelt by the Holy Spirit. The New Testament presents the church as the household of faith (Gal 6:10), the fellowship of the Spirit (Phil 2:1), the family of God (Eph 3:14–15), the pillar of truth (1 Tim 3:15), the bride of Christ (Rev 19:7), the body of Christ (Eph 1:22–23), the new creation (Eph 2:15), and the temple of the Holy Spirit (Eph 2:21). More than a human organization, the church is a visible and tangible expression of the people who are reconciled to Christ and to one another.

Joining with the church's confession throughout the ages, we can maintain that the church is one—holy, universal, and apostolic. All four markers are vitally important and must be taken seriously, even as we live with the tensions inherit within them. The people of God must seek to pursue unity, to reflect holiness, and to remain in continuity with the past, primarily the apostolic doctrine and practice made known to us in Christian Scripture (Eph 2:20; 3:2–13), while seeking to live a commitment to the communion of saints across all generational, social, ethnic, and economic boundaries. The church must take seriously the work of doing theology as an aspect of its overall purpose and mission, for the role of the "Rule of Faith" since the church's earliest generations has served a shaping role.

Carrying out the image of the pillar of truth (1 Tim 3:15), we believe that the first responsibility in the work of theology is the equipping or building up of the church (Eph 4:13–16). Equipping involves moving believers toward (1) the unity of faith and (2) a maturity of the faith that involves the full knowledge of God's Son. When the church is equipped, the people of God will evidence stability in precept and practice, growing up in every way into Christ, with each member supporting the other, fitted together in harmony and built up in love. The church should not be characterized as unstable, always caught up in the latest movement, trend, or fad, always seeking the new and novel. A commitment to apostolicity and the Christian tradition provides an anchor for the church.

The kind of maturity described in Ephesians 4 needs a carefully articulated theological foundation that will lead the church away from instability and gullibility. The church must always be aware of deceptions and counterfeits to the truth, which can only be known when we learn to think wisely in theological categories. Theological maturity often comes by being able to recognize genuine heresy as found in Marcion, Arius, Pelagius, Abelard, and the denial of cardinal Christian doctrines. Almost all heresies throughout the history of the church have been adaptions of these four wrongheaded thinkers. Heresy must be rejected while we recognize that mere disagreement over secondary or tertiary matters must not be characterized as heresy.

Careful theological thought leading to the building up of the people of God results in the advancement of the gospel mission among the nations (Rev 5:7). In actualizing that mission, the church is called to be faithful, to discern, to interpret, and to proclaim the gospel of Jesus Christ as the transforming power for the world. Unfortunately, the contemporary separations that we often find among theology, spirituality, and church ministry results in mutual suspicion of the work of theology. The church has at times not encouraged, and in fact at times seemingly has discouraged, the need for faithful and collaborative work of theologians. Sadly, the flip side of the coin is not much better.

What is needed is a renewed eschatological vision for the people of God with a recognition of the importance of the church in God's overall plan and a fresh appreciation of the significance of a theological foundation for the church. Our prayer is for faithful theologians who are also faithful churchmen, faithful teachers who are also faithful evangelists. Our goal in this volume is for the articles to be applicable to and for the people of God. Moreover, theology must be set before the church and the world as a system of truth that depends on the regenerated mind and exposes the radical differences between Christianity and the philosophies of the world.

Theology and the Church's Beliefs, Proclamation, and Ministry

Beliefs about God and his Word have ultimate consequences in this life. Our beliefs about God have significant consequences not only for this life but for all eternity. Christian theology then forms the foundation of the church's beliefs, proclamation, and ministry. It involves not only believing revealed truth but articulating it in such a way that calls the church to genuine spirituality, purity, and ethical holiness. If Christian theology is the study of God and his works, then it cannot be merely the work of specialists. Theology is the responsibility of the church seeking to communicate what the church believes, practices, and proclaims, primarily for the good of believers, but also for a watching world.

We sometimes hear voices suggesting that theology is too divisive and therefore should be deemphasized. Theology, however, serves as the backbone of the church. Without good theology the church cannot and will not mature in the faith and will be prone to be tossed back and forth by waves and blown here and there by every wind of teaching (Eph 4:14). Healthy theology that matures the head and the heart not only will enable believers to move toward maturity but will result in the praise and exaltation of God among all peoples (Psalm 96). Good theology should always lead to vibrant and faithful doxology. The apostle Paul—after expounding the doctrines of sin, justification, sanctification, and the future of Israel in the first eleven chapters of Romans—concludes the section by declaring,

Oh, the depth of the riches both of the wisdom and the knowledge of God! How unsearchable his judgments and untraceable his ways! "For who has known the mind of the Lord? Or who has been his counselor? And who has ever given to God, that he should be repaid?" For from him and through him and to him are all things. To him be the glory forever. Amen. (Rom 11:33–36)

Theology that does not lead to doxology may be intellectually helpful, but it falls short of the biblical vision of doxological reflection for God's glory and the flourishing of his people.

We honestly acknowledge some theologians have unduly complicated the Christian faith or distracted us from aspects of Christian living. We should not, however, conclude that theology in itself is distracting or divisive. Theology needs to be as much a part of the church as worship, evangelism, benevolence ministries, and missions. Indeed, it should inform each of these priorities. Ministry based on unsound theology will itself be unsound and even dangerous. Worship that does not see God for who he is and how he has revealed himself will not glorify God. Theology can help us better understand the faith we desire to share in our evangelistic efforts and, moreover, can help lead us to an awareness of the grandeur, the greatness, and the goodness of the one, true, and wise God we worship and serve.

Theology can also enable God's people to recover a true understanding of human life. In this sense God's people can once again gain a sense of the greatness of the soul. Theology can help us recover the awareness that God is more important that we are, that the future life is more important than this one, and that a right view of God gives genuine significance and security to our lives. We will understand that hope is the promise of heaven and that holiness is the priority here in this world.

The church can better understand what we believe and why we believe it. We can appreciate our heritage and enliven our future hope. When the church carries out this theological task, and when theologians do theology for the church, the truth content of the faith can be preserved. For it is the express task of theology to expound the whole counsel of God (Acts 20:7). When this takes place, the church can be strengthened. The gospel and its fullness can be proclaimed. Without the foundation of solid theology, there can be no effective long-term preaching, evangelism, discipleship, or missionary outreach. Those who would suggest that what you do not know cannot hurt you could find themselves in great difficulty if this approach is taken toward ultimate matters such as heaven and hell. On the other hand, sound, reliable theology, based squarely on God's Word, offers reassurance and hope.

Understanding theology in the context of the history of the church provides insight for today and guidance for the future. In this way theology can preserve the church from wrongheaded fads. Knowledge of the past keeps the church from confusing what is merely a contemporary expression from that which is enduringly relevant, keeping us from falling into the trap of presentism. Theology helps present to the church a valuable accumulation of enduring insights along with numerous lessons and warnings, both positive and negative. Thus, theology done for the church will always have one eye on the church's historical paths.

Such an awareness of the church's history provides a bulwark against the pride and arrogance that would suggest that "we" are the only group or tradition that carries on the orthodoxy of the apostles. Knowledge of such continuities and discontinuities in the past will help us focus on those areas of truth that are truly timeless and enduring while encouraging authenticity and humility, as well as dependency on God's Spirit. Hopefully, this awareness will encourage us not just to accept things in accordance with our tradition or to do things in accordance with our own "comfort zones," but will repeatedly drive us back to the New Testament with fresh eyes and receptive hearts. We will then rest our case there.

Finally, we believe that a theologically informed and equipped church will be better prepared for times of duress and trial, whether through means of persecution, in the face of faithless scholarship, or during the church's internal bickering and divisions. With hope the church can focus on the triumphal work of God in Jesus Christ, living in expectation of the glorious reign of the King of kings and Lord of lords.

The Editors

For Additional Study

Akin, Daniel L., editor. *A Theology for the Church.* Rev. ed. Nashville: B&H Academic, 2014.

Basden, Paul, and David S. Dockery, eds. *People of God: Essays on the Believers' Church.* Nashville: B&H, 1991.

Dockery, David S., ed. *New Dimensions in Evangelical Thought.* Downers Grove: IVP, 1998.

———. *Theology, Church, and Ministry.* Nashville: B&H Academic, 2017.

Duesing, Jason, and Nathan A. Finn, eds. *Historical Theology.* Nashville: B&H Academic, 2021.

Erickson, Millard J. *Christian Theology.* 3rd ed. Grand Rapids: Baker, 2013.

Finn, Nathan A., and Keith S. Whitfield, eds. *Spirituality for the Sent.* Downers Grove, IL: IVP, 2017.

Garrett, James Leo, Jr. *Systematic Theology.* 2 vols. Grand Rapids: Eerdmans, 1995.

Hannah, John. *Our Legacy.* Colorado Springs: NavPress, 2001.

Morgan, Christopher. *Christian Theology.* Nashville: B&H Academic, 2020.

Yarnell, Malcolm B., III. *Formation of Christian Doctrine.* Nashville: B&H Academic, 2007.

PART I
THEOLOGICAL FOUNDATIONS

1

God's Existence

JEREMIAH J. JOHNSTON

The question of the existence of God can be approached from different angles. Theologians and philosophers usually address forms of the "Cosmological Argument" (the argument for the existence of God based on the origin and nature of the universe), the "Teleological Argument" (the argument from purpose or design), the "Ontological Argument" (the argument from being and existence), the "Moral Argument" (the argument from moral or ethical necessity), or arguments based on design, intelligence, or consciousness.[1] The present essay will consider the evidence for the existence of God that arises primarily from experience as recounted in biblical literature, which supports and clarifies the reality of God's existence. The Scriptures are about the experience of God. This literature includes Israel's ancient Hebrew Scripture. Here we find secondhand stories of the experience of the patriarchs and other figures of antiquity as well as firsthand accounts of prophets who claim to have seen God or have heard his audible voice. This literature also includes the sacred literature of the Christian Church, which provides secondhand accounts of events in which God or a supernatural being (viz., an angel) is seen or otherwise experienced as well as firsthand accounts of persons, such as the apostles Paul or John, who see God or, in some sense, enter God's presence.

---

[1] See J. P. Moreland, Chad V. Meister, and Khaldoun A. Sweis, ed., *Debating Christian Theism* (Oxford: Oxford University Press, 2013).

Teleological and Spiritual Arguments
for the Existence of God

In biblical literature, we find teleological arguments for the existence of God based on what can be observed in nature or experienced in one's heart. Reflecting the former, the Psalter declares, "The heavens declare the glory of God; and the expanse proclaims the work of his hands. Day after day they pour out speech, and night after night they communicate knowledge" (Ps 19:1–2). The logic of this confession lies in the idea that nature reflects God's greatness.[2] Elsewhere the Psalter declares, "When I observe your heavens, the work of your fingers, the moon and the stars, which you set in place, what is a human being that you remember him, a son of man that you look after him?" (Ps 8:3–4). Reflecting the belief that God is in some sense known by what he impresses on one's heart, the Psalter speaks of God giving counsel (Ps 16:7) or of God writing his law on one's heart (40:8). We find a similar idea in the prophets. In anticipation of future restoration, the prophet Jeremiah, speaking the words of God, says, "I will give them a heart to know me, that I am the Lord" (Jer 24:7), and "I will give them integrity of heart and action so that they will fear me always" (Jer 32:39). In the context of the promise of a new covenant, God says through Jeremiah,

> "I will put my teaching within them and write it on their hearts. I will be their God, and they will be my people. No longer will one teach his neighbor or his brother, saying, 'Know the Lord,' for they will all know me, from the least to the greatest of them"—this is the Lord's declaration. "For I will forgive their iniquity and never again remember their sin." (Jer 31:33b–34)

To have God's law "within" or "written upon" the heart is to know God intimately and truly. This is why God through Jeremiah can say that "no longer shall each man teach his neighbor and each his brother, saying, 'Know the Lord,' for they shall all know me" (31:34 ESV). Because all will know God, it will not be necessary that they be taught. The old covenant was written on stone tablets (i.e., at Sinai) that required reading, interpreting, and teaching,

---

[2] See Hans-Joachim Kraus, *Psalms 1–59: A Continental Commentary*, trans. Hilton C. Oswald (Minneapolis: Fortress, 1993), 270.

so that one may know God and his law. The prophet envisions a time when knowledge of God and his law will be unmediated and therefore will require no reading, study, or teaching.[3] Similar ideas are expressed in Ezekiel, who promises that God's people will be given a "new heart" (Ezek 11:19; 36:26), and eschatologically in Isa 11:9 and Hab 2:14.

In his sharp critique of the pagan culture of his day, the apostle Paul declares,

> Since what can be known about God is evident among them, because God has shown it to them. For his invisible attributes, that is, his eternal power and divine nature, have been clearly seen since the creation of the world, being understood through what he has made. As a result, people are without excuse. For though they knew God, they did not glorify him as God or show gratitude. Instead, their thinking became worthless, and their senseless hearts were darkened. (Rom 1:19–21)

Paul here probably echoes elements of Greek philosophy, in which it is argued that though God is invisible, he is perceived by what he has made and what he does.[4] Paul's argument presupposes and, in some places, goes beyond the Psalter's confession that the heavens declare the nature and creative power of God. The truth of God is known, Paul says, "because God has shown it to them." They are, therefore "without excuse."

Patriarchal Experiences of God

In Genesis, we read stories of God speaking to the patriarchs. For example, we read, "Then God said to Noah" (Gen 6:13), but we are told nothing of what Noah actually experienced. Did he see God, and how did he hear him? So also, in the case of Abram (later Abraham), "The LORD said to Abram: 'Go from your land, your relatives, and your father's house to the land that I will show you'" (Gen 12:1). God repeatedly speaks to Abra(ha)m, but only once are we told that the patriarch sees something: "After these events, the word of

---

[3] Jack Lundbom, *Jeremiah 21–36* (New York: Doubleday, 2004), 470.

[4] cf. Ps.-Aristotle, *De mundo* 6 §399b; Diodorus Siculus, *Bibliothēkē Historikē* 2.21.7.

the Lord came to Abram in a vision" (Gen 15:1), but the vision that follows is strange and terrifying and occurs while Abram sleeps (Gen 15:12–21). The "angel of the Lord" appears to Hagar (Gen 16:7–11; 21:17). Afterward Hagar asks herself, "In this place, have I actually seen the one who sees me?" (Gen 16:13). The "angel of the Lord" also appears to Abraham (Gen 22:11, 15). Three mysterious men meet Sarah and Abraham, and one of them, identified as "the Lord," speaks to Abraham and Sarah (Gen 18:13–15). Angels appear to Lot, Abraham's nephew, warning him to flee from Sodom (Gen 19:1, 15).

Another strange story involves Jacob, the "supplanter," who was swindled by his uncle and father-in-law Laban and then later swindled him in return. When Jacob and his family arrive at a place called Mahanaim, he is met by "God's angels" (Gen 32:1–2). There is no further explanation. The terse statement is probably intended to set the context for what happens later in the night, when Jacob, alone, encounters a mysterious man with whom he wrestles through the night (Gen 32:24–32). The man tells Jacob, "Your name will no longer be called Jacob. . . . It will be Israel because you have struggled with God . . ." (Gen 32:28). Jacob names the place Peniel ("Face of God"), explaining, "I have seen God face to face . . . yet my life has been spared" (Gen 32:30). Jacob's grateful acknowledgment that his life has been preserved (or lit. "was spared") reflects the widespread belief that seeing God was dangerous, for "to see God meant death."[5]

Perhaps one of the most celebrated encounters with God narrated in the Old Testament is found in the story of Moses and the burning bush. The relevant portions of this passage read,

> Then the angel of the Lord appeared to him in a flame of fire within a bush. As Moses looked, he saw that the bush was on fire but was not consumed. So Moses thought, "I must go over and look at this remarkable sight. Why isn't the bush burning up?" . . . Then he continued, "I am the God of your father, the God of Abraham, the God of Isaac, and the God of Jacob." Moses hid his face because he was afraid to look at God. (Exod 3:2–3, 6)

---

[5] Gerhard von Rad, *Genesis: A Commentary*, rev. ed. (Philadelphia: Westminster, 1972), 323; cf. Exod 33:20; Deut 4:33; 5:24, 26; 18:16; Judg 6:22–23; 13:22; and Isa 6:5.

Moses both hears and sees God, yet in what sense he sees God is not clear. We are only told that he sees "a flame of fire." Presumably that is all that Moses could see of God. In any case, his fiery encounter adumbrates the many appearances of God to come.

The depiction of God as fire is a commonplace in biblical literature. Already mentioned is Abram's terrifying vision, or dream, of God as "a smoking fire pot and a flaming torch" (Gen 15:17). During Israel's wilderness wanderings, God "went ahead of them in a pillar of cloud to lead them on their way during the day and in a pillar of fire to give them light at night" (Exod 13:21; cf. 14:24; Num 14:14; Neh 9:12, 19). When God descended on Mount Sinai to make his covenant with Israel, we are told that "the Lord came down on it in fire. Its smoke went up like the smoke of a furnace" (Exod 19:18), and that "the appearance of the LORD's glory to the Israelites was like a consuming fire on the mountaintop" (Exod 24:17). When the tabernacle was completed and the "glory of the LORD filled the tabernacle" (Exod 40:34), from that time on "the cloud of the LORD was over the tabernacle by day, and there was a fire inside the cloud by night, visible to the entire house of Israel" (Exod 40:38; cf. Num 9:15–16).

On one occasion when Israel angered God, "and fire from the LORD blazed among them, and consumed the outskirts of the camp. Then the people cried out to Moses, and he prayed to the LORD, and the fire died down. So that place was named Taberah, because the LORD's fire had blazed among them" (Num 11:1b–3). Similarly, men offering pagan incense were destroyed by fire that "came out from the LORD" (Num 16:35; cf. 26:10). Hearkening back to this event, Moses reminds Israel that "your God is a consuming fire, a jealous God" (Deut 4:24). Indeed, Israel is promised that God will go before them as a "consuming fire" that will destroy their enemies (Deut 9:3; cf. Ps 50:3). The prophet Isaiah warns that God will come in judgment, "like a consuming fire" (Isa 30:27, 30; 66:15–16). It is not surprising that the author of the book of Hebrews declares that "our God is a consuming fire" (Heb 12:29). Several times in Deuteronomy Israel is reminded of God's fiery presence at Mount Sinai/Horeb (Deut 4:11–12, 15, 36; 5:4–5, 22–25; 9:10, 15; 10:4 "the LORD had spoken to you on the mountain out of the midst of the fire" ESV). Indeed, says the psalmist, "The voice of the LORD flashes flames of fire" (Ps 29:7). According to Daniel, God's chariot throne has wheels of fire, and "a river of fire was flowing, coming out from his presence" (Dan 7:9–10).

In what is probably meant to be a parallel to the fiery divine presence in the tabernacle (and perhaps, too, a nod to Elijah's dramatic triumph over the prophets of Baal), the Chronicler tells us that "when Solomon finished praying, fire descended from heaven and consumed the burnt offering and the sacrifices, and the glory of the Lord filled the temple" (2 Chr 7:1). The Chronicler adds that "all the Israelites were watching when the fire descended and the glory of the Lord came on the temple. They bowed down on the pavement with their faces to the ground. They worshiped and praised the Lord: 'For he is good, for his faithful love endures forever'" (2 Chr 7:3).

Seeing God Was Believed to Be Fatal

To hear the voice of God or in some way sense his presence was not considered necessarily dangerous (though see below), but to see God could well mean death. The biblical tradition, however, is complex. When Moses first encountered God at the burning bush, he "hid his face because he was afraid to look at God" (Exod 3:6). Later, as leader of Israel in the wilderness, Moses frequently met with God, and God spoke to Moses "face to face, just as a man speaks to his friend" (Exod 33:11; cf. Num 14:14; Deut 5:4; 34:10). As a result of these encounters with God, Moses's face began to shine, which frightened the people (Exod 34:29–30, 35).

These encounters notwithstanding, Moses's request to see God's glory (Exod 33:18) is declined, for as God tells him, "You cannot see my face, for humans cannot see me and live" (Exod 33:20). If Moses regularly spoke with God "face to face"—and did so apparently without suffering injury— why can he not see God's face? The explanation lies in recognizing that the expression "face to face" is meant to denote intimacy, not theophany.[6] God spoke to Moses as a man would speak to his friend. But when Moses requests to see God's "glory" (his *kabōd*), he asks to see the very being and essence of God. Moses cannot see in his mortal body; to do so would be fatal.

In Deuteronomy's review of Israel's exodus and the giving of the law, Moses asks the people, "Has a people heard God's voice speaking from the fire as you have, and lived?" (Deut 4:33; cf. 5:24, 26). Usually, it is in *seeing* God that brings danger, but in *hearing* God speak at Mount Sinai (or

---

[6] John Durham, *Exodus* (Waco: Word, 1987), 443.

Horeb), the people fear they will die.[7] The refrain "out of the midst of the fire" (ESV) could explain why close encounters with God were sometimes fatal, which seems to be implied when Moses reminds the people that at the mountain they said, "Let us not continue to hear the voice of the LORD our God or see this great fire any longer, so that we will not die!" (Deut 18:16).

Seeking a sign from God, Gideon prepares an offering (Judg 6:11–18). The sign is given when "the angel of the LORD . . . touched the meat and the unleavened bread. Fire came up from the rock and consumed the meat and the unleavened bread. Then the angel of the LORD vanished from his sight" (Judg 6:21). Gideon perceives that it was the angel of the Lord and cries out, "'Oh no, Lord GOD! I have seen the angel of the LORD face to face!' But the LORD said to him, 'Peace to you. Don't be afraid, for you will not die'" (Judg 6:22–23). Here again God seems in some sense to be present in the fire. Although the divine being is described as "the angel of the LORD," ancients such as Gideon might well have assumed that God was himself present. Indeed, it is God who speaks and reassures his servant, "Peace to you. Don't be afraid, for you will not die." The word of peace reassures the frightened Gideon that all is well in his standing before God. His encounter with God will not result in his death.

We find a similar story later in the book of Judges. Manoah entreats God on behalf of his childless wife (Judg 13:8–14). A mysterious "man" appears, who, as it turns out, is identified as "the angel of the LORD" (Judg 13:13). Like Gideon before him, Manoah prepares an offering, and a "flame went up from the altar toward heaven," and "the angel of the LORD went up in its flame" (Judg 13:20; cf. Ps 104:4; Heb 1:7). It is then that Manoah perceives who the "man" truly was and so says to his wife, "We're certainly going to die, because we have seen God!" (Judg 13:22). This time, however, it is not God who reassures the frightened human; it is his wife, who rightly reasons that God would not have accepted the offering if he desired to kill them (Judg 13:23).

One of the most dramatic descriptions of an encounter with God is found in the book of Isaiah. While in the temple, Isaiah says, "I saw the Lord seated on a high and lofty throne, and the hem of his robe filled the temple" (Isa 6:1). The prophet, assuming he is a dead man, cries out, "Woe is me for I am ruined

---

[7] Exod 20:19; A. D. H. Mayes, *Deuteronomy* (Grand Rapids: Eerdmans, 1979), 157.

because I am a man of unclean lips and live among a people of unclean lips, and because my eyes have seen the King, the Lord of Armies" (Isa 6:5). In this case an explanation is offered: Isaiah is lost (Heb. *dāmah*, "lost" or "ruined") because he is a man of "unclean lips" and lives among a people of unclean lips. From this confession we should infer that mortals risk death in the presence of God because they are sinful and therefore spiritually estranged from God. This might well have been the point when the awestruck Peter, seeing the great catch of fish and perceiving more fully who Jesus truly is, says to Jesus, "Go away from me, because I'm a sinful man, Lord!" (Luke 5:8).

From these encounters with God, we may infer that the ancients believed humans were in mortal danger because of God's fiery and holy nature and because mortal humans were sinful. These stories are early and widespread. Although not always well understood, they attest to the ancient belief that, on occasion, a human being encountered God and that such an encounter sometimes resulted in death. It is no surprise, then, that such encounters were not sought out. They were accordingly as rare as they were unwelcome.

Experiencing God in Prophetic Visions

The existence of God in biblical literature is also seen in prophetic visions, which often were not visions in the sense of seeing things but hearing the divine voice. The voice of God is revelatory and experiential. Young Samuel hears the voice of God (1 Sam 3:1–14), which he first mistakes for Eli. At the fourth call from the Lord, Samuel responds, "Speak, for your servant is listening" (1 Sam 3:10). At the end of the chapter, we learn "the Lord continued to appear in Shiloh, because there he revealed himself to Samuel by that his word" (1 Sam 3:21). God frequently spoke to Samuel: (a) God revealed the people's desire for a king betrayed their rejection of God (1 Sam 8:7, 22); (b) The Lord spoke to Samuel with regard to where to find Saul, the first king of Israel, hiding among the supplies (1 Sam 10:22); and (c) in the scene anointing David King of Israel, the Lord appeared four times to Samuel (1 Sam 16:1–2, 7, 12). With divine omniscience, the Lord said "Do not look at his appearance or his stature because I have rejected him. Humans do not see what the Lord sees, for humans see what is visible, but the Lord sees the heart" (1 Sam 16:7). From a negative perspective, Saul is impacted by the reality that he no longer hears from the Lord: "God has turned away from me. He doesn't answer me anymore, either through the prophets or in dreams" (1 Sam 28:15); indeed, Samuel's spirit pronounces, "The LORD has turned away from you" (1 Sam 28:16). Saul's experience shows that if he inquired of the Lord, he could expect a reply, at least from an intermediary, but the communication was broken off. From this I infer the existence of God is known because God reveals himself in sight or, more commonly, in word.

In establishing the Davidic covenant, God spoke to Nathan the prophet "this entire vision" that David's house, kingdom, and throne would be established "forever" (2 Sam 7:4, 16–17). As the Lord spoke to David, so he spoke to his son, Solomon, in the temple dedication: "I will fulfill my promise to you, which I made to your father David" (1 Kgs 6:11–12). A discouraged Elijah hid in a cave at Horeb and witnessed a strong wind rend the mountains, then an earthquake, and then a fire; yet he heard the Lord, not in these "acts of God," but in a "still small voice" (KJV) as God revealed the faithful remnant numbering seven thousand who had not bowed to Ba'al (1 Kings 19). Following the vivid manifestation of divine victory over the prophets of Ba'al, Elijah discerned that God's transformational power is also revealed through the "still small [gentle] voice" (see 1 Kgs 17:8–9; 18:1; 19:15; 21:17–18).

Turning to the sacred Christian Scriptures, the two occurrences of God speaking in Mark's Gospel are at Jesus's baptism (Mark 1:9–11) and transfiguration (Mark 9:2–8). In both cases, God refers to his "beloved Son" (cf. Ps 2:7) and at the transfiguration appeals to those who are present to "listen to him." According to Mark, the theological point is that to listen to Jesus is to listen to God himself. God is experienced through his word. Paul is the most important New Testament witness to God's existence because of his firsthand testimony. Paul writes several letters, and he is rarely visionary. His style is prosaic and didactic, so we have great confidence that Paul has experienced God in 2 Corinthians 12 (see also 1 Cor 9:1; 15:8). Sometime before his first missionary journey (AD 43), Paul narrates an experience of visiting heaven and hearing things in the heavenly setting which come from God. Whether it is angels talking to God or God talking to angels, Paul has heard "inexpressible words, which a human being is not allowed to speak" (2 Cor 12:4), and he simply cannot communicate these things in human speech.

In another firsthand New Testament account, the author of Revelation sees the risen Christ (Rev 1:9–20) and nearly died: "I fell at his feet like a dead man" (Rev 1:17). To see Christ is to see God, for Jesus said, "The one who has seen me has seen the Father" (John 14:9). Additionally, John had the experience of visiting heaven itself (Revelation 4–5). John describes seeing the very throne on which God sits, which Ezekiel (chs. 1 and 10) and Daniel (ch. 7) also described. John sees the elders bowing before God. He hears the worship from an uncountable number and describes the continual "Amen" from the four living creatures. God is light. God is consuming. The exegetical point is that the existence of God is known not through argument but through experience. Therefore, the experiences of God described in biblical literature support and clarify the reality of the existence of God.

The ancients did not have a bias against experience, which is important to understand. Experience is a legitimate teacher. The word "science" (from *scientia* in Latin) means "knowledge," and one can acquire knowledge in a variety of ways. The Scriptures do not point to a committee of scientists, philosophers, and theologians reasoning through deductions related to the existence of God or surveying if the evidence is convincing. (This process is important to moderns, to be sure.) Throughout the Scriptures, the presence of God, both his existence and his benevolence with humanity, is experienced. From a biblical perspective, the experience of God is the prime proof for the existence of God in both the Old and New Testaments. God is unexpectedly encountered; to experience God is frightening. As we have seen, biblical characters (real people, real events, to be sure) are not necessarily eager to meet God because it could be deadly. Experiencing God shows that he exists, and he is different from the created order. This comparison establishes a contrast where the human being recognizes how small, weak, and vulnerable one is in dissimilarity to God. This leads to the study of what God has made in nature (which would include the human being, "remarkably and wondrously made," Ps 139:14), so deductions and inferences are made about the attributes of God (his skill, greatness, holiness, love, wisdom). As I have written elsewhere, the God of Israel—specifically his love, grace, and forgiveness—stood out in sharp contrast to the gods of the pagans, Greeks, and Romans. These gods felt no obligation toward humans and were viewed as potentially dangerous, jealous, and vindictive, which could have influenced the fear the biblical characters felt in entering God's presence.[8] The Hebrew

---

[8] Jeremiah J. Johnston, *Unimaginable: What Our World Would Be Like without Christianity* (Minneapolis: Bethany, 2017), 169–79.

people deduce the pagans have it wrong. The creation is such that the polytheistic pagan explanation is clearly inadequate. There is one Almighty God, who is all-wise, all-powerful, and he is the maker of the universe. The important point is God's nature and attributes are intelligently deduced based on observations, but God's existence is known through direct experience, which is not a deduction at all.

For Additional Study

Brierley, Justin. *Unbelievable? Why after Ten Years of Talking with Atheists, I'm Still a Christian.* London: SPCK, 2017.

Craig, William Lane. *Does God Exist?* Pine Mountain: Impact 360, 2014.

———. "The Kalam Argument," in J. P. Moreland, Chad V. Meister, and Khaldoun A. Sweis, eds., *Debating Christian Theism.* Oxford: Oxford University, 2013, 7–19.

Flew, Anthony. *There Is a God: How the World's Most Notorious Atheist Changed His Mind.* New York: HarperOne, 2007.

Guinness, Os. *God in the Dark: The Assurance of Faith Beyond a Shadow of Doubt.* Wheaton: Crossway, 1996.

Keller, Tim. *The Reason for God: Belief in an Age of Skepticism.* New York: Penguin: 2018.

McGrath, Alister. *A Fine-Tuned Universe: The Quest for God in Science and Theology.* Louisville: WJK, 2009.

Also see these articles: Revelation, The Trinity, God's Attributes, God's Covenants

2

Revelation

RHYNE R. PUTMAN

R evelation is the gracious self-disclosure of the triune God to his creatures in word and deed. Because God is infinite, transcendent, and
beyond the comprehension of finite human minds, knowledge of God is
only possible if he takes the initiative to reveal himself. Christians presume
that God exists, that he is a personal being who can be known, and that he
has acted to communicate his presence and will to his creatures in such a way
that they may know him and love him.

The biblical verbs frequently associated with "revelation" (Heb. *galah*; Gk.
apokaluptō) literally mean "to uncover" or "to unveil" a person or physical object.
They also figuratively describe the disclosure of previously unknown information. New Testament authors also use a closely related verb meaning "to
appear" or "to manifest" (Gk. *phaneroō*) to describe God's self-manifestation.
But the most prominent vocabulary for revelation in the Bible is the "word
of God" (Heb., *də-ḇar 'ĕ-lō-hîm*; Gk., *logos tou theou*). This word of God is
threefold: the verbal word expressed through human language and preserved
in Scripture, the word expressed through creation, and the word incarnate in
Jesus Christ. The word of God not only reveals the nature, character, and purposes of God; it also exposes people to their true selves. Only the word of God
"is able to judge the thoughts and intentions of the heart" (Heb 4:12b).

Christian theologians often distinguish between the *general revelation*
God has made available to all people everywhere and the *special revelation*

he has given specific persons at specific moments in time. While this theological distinction has practical and heuristic value, revelation in all its forms presents a single, unified witness to God. All forms of revelation—whether "natural" or "supernatural" in appearance, verbal or nonverbal, universal or particular—constitute a unified word from God.

General Revelation

God has made his existence, his power, and his eternal nature accessible to all people through general revelation, or what is sometimes called "natural revelation." This revelation is neither ambiguous nor the result of human intellectual efforts. God himself is the source of general revelation: "What may be known about God is *plain to them*, because *God has made it plain to them*" (Rom 1:19 NIV, emphasis mine). Some of God's attributes can be known through general revelation, but general revelation alone cannot reveal God's redemptive plan. This general revelation makes all people everywhere accountable to God but is insufficient to save them from their sins.

The Biblical Witness to General Revelation

God created all things by his powerful word, and everything he created testifies to his goodness. He made the skies, the sea, and the land teem with endless varieties of living creatures, but he created something unique with humanity. Only man and woman were created in the image and likeness of God (Gen 1:26a). As the image-bearers of God, men and women were themselves objects of revelation, imbued with an awareness of God from their creator.

Creation is a prominent theme in the book of Job. Job speaks of creation as a teacher who instructs us in the knowledge of the Lord (Job 12:7–9). Elihu claims everyone can recognize the work of God in creation (Job 36:24–25). The wonders of God in nature reveal God's power and justice (Job 37:1–24). When God finally breaks his silence with Job, he uses numerous illustrations from creation to demonstrate his wisdom and power (Job 38:39–41; 39:1–30).

Several psalms address God's word in creation. The works of God in creation stir the praises of his people (Ps 8:1–9; 89:11–12; 104:1–35; cf.

Neh 9:5b–6). Psalm 19 explicitly describes creation as a revelation which declares "the glory of God" and "the work of his hands" (Ps 19:1). In the theater of creation, no verbal words are used, and no literal voice is heard (19:3), but nature unceasingly "reveals knowledge" of God throughout the whole world (19:2–4 NIV). This word of God in nature perfectly coheres with his law (19:7–8).

Paul used creation as a starting point for preaching the gospel to Gentile audiences. At Lystra, Paul pled with the crowds to turn away from their false gods to the God "who made the heavens and the earth and the sea and everything in them" (Acts 14:15; cf. Exod 20:11). He asserts that God's provision of rain and crops is a "witness" to his mercy and kindness (Acts 14:16–17; cf. Lev 26:4). Paul begins his sermon at Mars Hill by acknowledging the piety of the Athenians (Acts 17:22–23) and the creative work of God evident to all (Acts 17:24–29) before preaching Christ and their need for repentance (Acts 17:30–31).

The clearest teaching on general revelation in Scripture comes from Paul's description of God's righteous judgment in Rom 1:18–32 and 2:1–16. He begins his letter to a church composed of Jewish and Gentile Christians with this harsh reality: Jews and Gentiles alike have squandered the revelation God has given them and suppressed the truth with unrighteousness (Rom 1:18, 21, 25), idolatry (Rom 1:22–23, 25), and lawlessness (Rom 1:24, 26–32; 2:12–14). Through creation, God has plainly revealed "his invisible attributes, that is, his eternal power and divine nature" (Rom 1:20). Through the human conscience, God has made what is morally right and good known to everyone, regardless of their religious or cultural backgrounds (Rom 2:15). Jews and Gentiles are both deserving of God's righteous judgment, with or without the law of Moses (Rom 1:18, 32; 2:15). Paul uses these circumstances to set the stage for the good news of Jesus's saving work in Romans 3–8.

General Revelation in Historical Theology

The church fathers agreed that God revealed himself in creation but disagreed about what role reason and philosophy played in discerning this revelation. Patristic theologians in the East such as Justin Martyr (c. 100–c. 165) and Clement of Alexandria (c. 150–c. 215) attempted to bridge Greco-Roman philosophy to general revelation. The Western theologian Tertullian (c. 155–c.

220) objected to moves like this by asking, "What does Jerusalem have to do with Athens, the Church with the Academy, or the Christian with the heretic?"[1]

Medieval theologians Anselm of Canterbury (1033–1109) and Thomas Aquinas (1225–1274) were among the first in the Christian tradition to develop natural theologies from general revelation. Anselm formulated an *ontological argument* by which he made the case for the necessary existence of God from his perfections. Aquinas distinguished between divine truths which can be known by reason and those which can only be known by special revelation. He claimed that the existence of God and some of God's attributes (e.g., simplicity, goodness, eternity, etc.) can be discovered by reason alone. Doctrines such as the Trinity, the incarnation, and the saving work of Christ can only be known through "articles of faith" or special revelation.

The Reformers affirmed the twofold distinction between God's general revelation and special revelation but rejected the natural theology of medieval Catholicism. For Luther and Calvin, general revelation was sufficient to hold human beings accountable for their sin but insufficient to save them from it. Calvin's unique contribution here was his concept of the "seed of religion" (*sensus divinitatis*) or an awareness of God sown in every person. Because of this awareness of God, "men cannot open their eyes without being compelled to see him."[2]

Following the Enlightenment, theologians in Deist and liberal Protestant traditions advanced new versions of natural theology, which conflated general and special revelation. Deists such as John Toland (1670–1722) and Matthew Tindal (1657–1733) sought to formulate a religion based on reason without any appeal to special revelation or Scripture. The liberal Protestants, led by Friedrich Schleiermacher (1768–1834), took a more existential approach to revelation, alleging that all people know God through a feeling of "absolute dependence."

Twentieth-century theologians varied greatly in their respective approaches to general revelation. Neoorthodox theologian Emil Brunner (1889–1966) claimed that redeemed individuals aided by grace could know something of God through creation. His theological counterpart, Karl Barth (1886–1968), emphatically denied this possibility, insisting that all revelation

---

[1] Tertullian, *Prescriptions Against Heretics* 7.
[2] John Calvin, *Institutes of Christian Religion* 1.5.1.

is the redemptive word of God in Christ. Dutch Reformed theologians such as G. C. Berkouwer (1903–1996) and Cornelius Van Til (1895–1987) affirmed general revelation in creation but maintained that the effects of sin on the mind blind the natural man in such a way that he is unable to know anything of God apart from a special work of grace.

General Revelation in Christian Belief and Practice

Christian theologians widely recognize three sources of general revelation: the external witness of God in *creation*, the internal witness of God in *human nature*, and the workings of God in *human history*. With creation, God has put his power (Rom 1:20; Heb 11:3), his glory (Ps 19:1–3), and his goodness (Gen 1:31; Jas 1:17) on display for all to see. The creatures and ecosystems of the earth attest to the infinite wisdom of God in their design (Ps 147:9; Prov 3:19–20; 30:4; Jer 27:5; Matt 6:26). Even the destructive forces of nature bear witness to his power and sovereignty (Ps 29:1–10; 89:9, 25).

Human nature also points to God because men and women are made in his image (Gen 1:26–28). Humanity is the pinnacle of creation and "crowned him with glory and honor" (Ps 8:5). Human beings have the capacity for reason, for moral judgment, and a relationship with God through Christ. People from every culture and walk of life know the basic difference between right and wrong because God has written his law on their hearts (Rom 2:12–15). Their consciences testify to God's existence and morality (Rom 2:15).

Human history is a witness to God's providential care over creation. This care can be seen in the formation of Israel (Acts 7:2–8) and its preservation through famines (Gen 50:20; Acts 7:11–15), slavery (Deut 6:10; 2 Kgs 17:36; Pss 78:1–29; 105:1–45), exile (Deut 30:1–6; Ezra 1:1–4; Ps 137:1–6; Isa 44:26–45:1; Jer 20:10–14), and the genocidal acts of modern history. God also presides over the affairs of Gentile nations, establishing and removing rulers (Dan 4:17, 25). God establishes and maintains order through human governments (Rom 13:1). God can also be seen in the events of history in which disasters were avoided (e.g., the Nazis never developing a hydrogen bomb) or where short-term evil and suffering produced long-term positive results (e.g., a global pandemic resulting in the discovery of vaccines).

General revelation prepares us to receive special revelation. As Paul makes clear, everyone *knows* about the existence of God from general revelation, even if they suppress that truth. This revelation grounds the arguments for God's existence used by philosophers and theologians throughout history. *Cosmological arguments* are arguments from causation that seek to explain why there is something rather than nothing: everything has a cause for its existence, and the ultimate cause of all things is God. *Teleological arguments* are arguments from design, purpose, or *telos*. If the material universe appears finely tuned for human life, then the evidence suggests that the material universe was designed with purpose and intentionality. These arguments might help remove intellectual hurdles that prevent some people from coming to saving faith, but they are not substitutes for sharing the gospel message rooted in God's special revelation. These arguments might provide rational support for the biblical God, but none of them necessarily lead to him (as they are equally applicable to gods from other faiths).

General revelation can provide partial knowledge of God's attributes. First, there is one God who "made the world and everything in it" (Acts 17:24a). Second, this God is an invisible spiritual being (John 4:24; Rom 1:20) who is not bound to the material world or contained in "shrines made by hands" (Acts 17:24b). Third, God has the attribute of aseity, meaning he is the source of his own life and needs nothing from anyone else (Acts 17:25a). Fourth, God is the source of life who "gives everyone life and breath and all things" (Acts 17:25b). Fifth, he rules providentially over all men, directing and guiding their lives to his sovereign purposes for them (Acts 17:26). Sixth, God has perfect power and knowledge. Seventh, God is the source of love (1 John 4:8), wisdom (Prov 2:6), righteousness (1 John 3:7), holiness, and judgment (Rom 1:28–32). Finally, God is a perfect being who is worthy of worship, gratitude, and service (Rom 1:21, 25).

General revelation also provides a foundation for all human morality. God is morally perfect and has written his moral law on every human heart (Rom 2:15a). Because of general revelation people from every worldview can affirm practices and policies which lead to human flourishing. God is a righteous judge who will hold men responsible for violating the moral law impressed on their consciences (Rom 2:15b–16).

General revelation explains why people from every culture are inherently religious. Every religion is a response to God's universal revelation. The failure of fallen human beings to glorify and thank God resulted in futile religious thinking (Rom 1:21). Paul directly connects the suppression of God's truth with idolatry (Rom 1:22) and sexual immorality (Rom 1:24). It follows that even idolatry and sexual sin are distorted reflections of God's nature and moral law made known through general revelation.

General revelation alone is incapable of fostering a redemptive relationship with God. Though all human beings may know of God through general revelation, all human beings stand condemned apart from Christ because they have suppressed this knowledge in unrighteousness. Even those who have never heard the gospel are held accountable because of what they know of God from creation and human nature. General revelation can only communicate the existence of an all-powerful creator and moral lawgiver, but special revelation is needed to tell us who this God is and how he has acted to redeem us.

Special Revelation

Special revelation includes the verbal revelation of God addressed to individuals and preserved in Scripture, as well as the personal revelation of God made manifest in dreams, visions, theophanies, and the incarnation of Christ. Though not all recipients of special revelation are saved, it is the sovereign means by which God draws specific individuals into a saving, life-changing relationship with him in Christ. For this reason, it is sometimes called *particular revelation*.

The Biblical Witness to Special Revelation

The Bible is both a revelation from God and a witness to God's unified revelatory activity throughout history. In their innocent state untainted by sin, Adam and Eve enjoyed a special fellowship with God, and he conversed with them directly (Gen 1:27–28; 2:15–16). But when the serpent tempted them and they disobeyed God's word, the natural fellowship humanity previously had with God was broken (Gen 3:8–24).

Human sin might have resulted in suffering, judgment, and death, but God mercifully continued to speak to the creatures he loved. During the age of the patriarchs, God personally addressed some individuals, and people began to call on the name he had revealed to them (Gen 4:26b). God made a covenant with Noah, vowing never to destroy the world by floodwaters again and reissued the command to multiply and fill the earth again (Gen 9:1–17). God made a special covenant with Abraham (Gen 15:1–21), promising him that all nations would be blessed through his offspring (Gen 22:18; cf. Gal 3:16–18). At Sinai, God made a covenant with Moses and the Israelites he freed from bondage in Egypt (Exod 24:3–8). God assured the Israelites that if they would obey him and keep his law, they would be his treasured possession (Exod 19:3–6). God also made a covenant with David, promising him his throne would be "established forever" through a future descendant (2 Sam 7:1–17). God chose Israel to be the people through whom he would reveal his name, his law, his covenants, his promises, and ultimately, his Son (Rom 9:4–5). He set Israel apart so they would be "a light for the nations, to be . . . salvation to the ends of the earth" (Isa 49:6; cf. 42:6).

God revealed himself to Israel "at different times and in different ways" (Heb 1:1). He spoke directly with individuals (1 Sam 3:2–21; Jer 1:4–15). God spoke "with Moses face to face, just as a man speaks with his friend" (Exod 33:11). He delivered his word through prophets (2 Kgs 21:10; Ezek 2:3–7; 3:1; Amos 3:7). He used dreams and visions to speak to believers and nonbelievers alike (Gen 28:10–17; 31:10–13; 40:4–8; Dan 1:17). God frequently delivered his word through angelic beings or heavenly messengers (Dan 4:13–17; 8:15–16; Zech 1:9–20).

Throughout the history of Israel, God used miracles to confirm his identity as the one true God (Exod 4:2–9; 1 Kgs 18:21–39). God provided visible manifestations of himself called theophanies (literally, "God-shows")—like the burning bush (Exod 3:2–6), the pillar of cloud by day and the pillar of fire by night (Exod 13:21–22), and the angel of the Lord (Gen 22:11, 15; Num 22:22–35; Josh 5:13–15). Occasionally, God revealed his will through objects such as the Urim and Thummim (Exod 28:30; Num 27:21), the fleece (Judg 6:33–39), and lots (1 Sam 14:41–42; Acts 1:24–26).

The most complete expression of God's nature came with the incarnation of Christ (Heb 1:1–3; 11:39–40). The Son displayed the Father with crystal clarity (John 1:18; 17:6; Col 1:15). No one can know the Father apart from the Son (Matt 11:25–27; John 14:6, 8–9). The Son disclosed "the mystery kept silent for long ages but now revealed" (Rom 16:25–26). The death of the Son on behalf of sinners revealed the magnitude of God's love (Rom 5:8; cf. 1 John 4:9). The Son was "revealed so that he might take away sins" (1 John 3:5) and so he could "destroy the devil's works" (1 John

3:8). Jesus's resurrection is a revelation of God's power (1 Pet 1:3, 21). When Jesus returns to earth in glory, "we will be like him because we will see him as he is" (1 John 3:2).

God spoke to the apostles through many of the same means he spoke to Israel before Christ: direct speech (Acts 9:4; 22:7–8), dreams and visions (Acts 10:1–15; 2 Cor 12:2–4), angelic messengers (Acts 5:19–20; Rev 22:6–9), and miracles (Acts 3:1–10; 9:17–19). Yet the church age is set apart by the permanent indwelling ministry of the Holy Spirit in every believer following Pentecost (Acts 2:1–13; 1 Cor 12:12–13). The Holy Spirit is "the Spirit of wisdom and revelation" (Eph 1:17; cf. 3:5–7). The Spirit leads individuals as well as churches (Rev 2:7, 11, 17, 29; 3:6, 13, 22).

The Spirit preserved God's revelation for all generations through the inspiration of Scripture (2 Tim 3:16–17; 2 Pet 1:20–21). Though the period of biblical inspiration has ended, the Spirit continues to guide believers in the truth he receives from the Son (John 14:16–17; 16:12–15) and the Father (Eph 1:17–18). The illuminating activity of the Spirit helps believers understand and apply divine truth to their lives (1 Cor 2:10–16; cf. Ps 119:18). The Spirit testifies to the Son (1 John 5:6) and protects believers from deception (1 John 4:6).

Special Revelation in Historical Theology

Before the Enlightenment, most Christian theologians simply presumed the authority and truthfulness of God's special revelation preserved in Scripture. Skepticism toward traditional conceptions of biblical inspiration and "supernatural" revelation came with modernity. The eighteenth-century Deists altogether stripped special revelation from religion, asserting that God's truth could be discovered by reason alone. Nineteenth-century liberal Protestants such as Friedrich Schleiermacher and Albrecht Ritschl (1822–1889) rejected the concept of the verbal inspiration of Scripture and essentially reduced all revelation to experiences with God in the private life of an individual. Consequently, the "revelation" received by the authors of Scripture was not qualitatively different from the experience religiously sensitive individuals can have today.

Pierre Teilhard de Chardin (1881–1955) and Paul Tillich (1886–1965) equated revelation with advances in human understanding. They viewed all history as an evolutionary process by which human beings attain deeper and more meaningful understandings of themselves and their world. Every stage of human progress comes with advances in human consciousness. For these so-called "new awareness" theologians, the formation of the biblical canon was only one stage in the ongoing development of human thought. This model gave lip service to the providential hand of God in human history, but it made human progress the focal point of "revelation," not God.

Neoorthodox theologians Barth and Brunner sought to forge a middle way between the traditional conception of Scripture as the word of God and the liberal Protestant notions of revelation as a feeling or experience. For Barth and Brunner, Christ, not the Bible, is the true word of God. One may "encounter" the word of God in the Bible, but the Bible is only a "witness" to the word of God. For Barth, calling the Bible the word of God is tantamount to revering creation as the creator. Barth and Brunner also maintained that revelation was personal, not propositional. In other words, God reveals his presence in Christ, not doctrinal truths.

Special Revelation in Christian Belief and Practice

Special revelation makes it possible for fallen men and women to be restored to fellowship with God through Christ Jesus. It supplies the disciple of Christ with a knowledge of the triune God richer than what general revelation alone can provide. Special revelation gives direction and guidance for obedient Christian living and mission. It also stirs affections, directing hearts away from sin and enabling creatures to love God with the totality of their being (Luke 10:27). Consequently, God's word becomes a source of delight for his people (Ps 119:16, 47, 70, 77).

As the history of Christian theology bears witness, there is a close correlation between one's doctrine of revelation and one's doctrine of God. Theologians who overemphasize the transcendence of God often conceive of God as distant and aloof, with little or no interest in giving a clear, intelligible word to men. Those who overemphasize the immanence of God often conflate ordinary human experiences with revelation, leaving no room for the distinctive voice of God. But when God's transcendence and immanence are in balance, God speaks to his creatures as one who is wholly other but capable of speaking to them on their level. The God who is transcendent and immanent can provide an objective revelation that is true, trustworthy, and life changing.

Revelation is both personal and propositional. It is propositional because it provides true knowledge about God, and it is relational because it makes fellowship with God possible. While revelation should not be reduced to statements of fact, no relationship with God is feasible without shared knowledge and understanding. Strictly speaking, "revelation" means the disclosure of new information, but God does many other things in relationship to his creatures with his verbal word, such as *blessing* (Gen 1:28; Deut 28:1–6), *commanding* (Exod 20:1–17; Deut 5:6–21), *covenanting* (Gen 9:11; 15:18), *comforting* (Isa 40:1–2; 2 Cor 1:3–4), *cursing* (Num 22:6; Gal 3:13–14), *promising* (Josh 21:44–45; 1 Kgs 8:56–57), *rebuking* (Hos 2:2–13; Mal 3:11), *forgiving* (Num 15:26; Mark 2:5), and *warning* (Lev 20:13; Gal 5:19–21; Rev 2:4–5).

All revelation is a testimony to Jesus Christ, but it is progressive in the sense that it has unfolded in various stages throughout history. Those who have read all the way to the end of the book of Revelation have a fuller and deeper understanding of God than those who are just beginning in Genesis! Special revelation provides people with everything needed to be saved and live in obedience to God, but it does not teach everything that can be known about God or his world. Even with special revelation, knowledge of God is still partial, and believers eagerly await the coming day in which this partial knowledge will be made complete. "For now, we see only a reflection as in a mirror, but then face to face. Now I know in part, but then I will know fully, as I am fully known" (1 Cor 13:12).

For Additional Study

Barth, Karl. *Church Dogmatics: The Doctrine of the Word of God*, I.2. Edited by G. W. Bromiley and T. F. Torrance. Translated by G. T. Thomson and Harold Knight. London: T&T Clark, 2004.

Bavinck, Herman. *Reformed Dogmatics*, vol. 1. *Prolegomena*. Edited by John Bolt. Translated by John Vriend. Grand Rapids: Baker, 2003.

Briggs, Richard S. *Words in Action: Speech Act Theory and Biblical Interpretation—Toward a Hermeneutic of Self-Involvement*. New York: T&T Clark, 2001.

Demarest, Bruce A. *General Revelation: Historical Views and Contemporary Issues*. Grand Rapids: Zondervan, 1982.

Dulles, Avery. *Models of Revelation*. 2nd ed. Maryknoll, NY: Orbis, 1992.

Frame, John M. *The Doctrine of the Word of God*. Phillipsburg, NJ: P&R, 2010.

Gunton, Colin E. *A Brief Theology of Revelation*. New York: Bloomsbury T&T Clark, 1995.

Johnston, Robert K. *God's Wider Presence: Reconsidering General Revelation*. Grand Rapids: Baker, 2014.

Tertullian. *Prescription Against Heretics*.

Wolterstorff, Nicholas. *Divine Discourse: Philosophical Reflections on the Claim that God Speaks*. New York: Cambridge University, 1995.

Also see these articles: Holy Scripture, Faith and Reason, The Trinity, Creation

3

Holy Scripture

J. MATTHEW PINSON

The Apostolic Witness

Scripture as Divine Speech

Christians have always believed in the divine inspiration of Holy Scripture. When the New Testament says that Scripture is inspired, it means something different from the common definition: "the process of being mentally stimulated to do or feel something, especially to do something creative."[1] Instead, the apostle Paul says that Scripture is *theopneustos*, "breathed out by God" (2 Tim 3:16 ESV). As much as such a view of Scripture grates against the sensibilities of modern theology, it is difficult to avoid Paul's simple statement: "Every Scripture is breathed out by God." Any divine writing originates from the *breath* of God, just as the universe and humanity originated from his creative breath (Gen 2:7; Ps 33:6). The use of "every" (*pasa*) led to what came to be known as the doctrine of "plenary" (full, complete) inspiration. Peter made a similar claim when he said that, in Scripture, God is *speaking*: "For no prophecy was ever produced by the will of man, but men spoke from God as they were carried along by the Holy Spirit" (2 Pet 1:21 ESV).

---

[1] *Oxford Dictionaries*, s.v. "inspiration (n.)," https://www.lexico.com/definition/inspiration.

The Traditional Interpretation of the Inspiration Texts

Traditionally, Christians took these texts at face value, conflating the divine breathing and the divine speaking. For example, the church father Ambrose of Milan said that the Holy Spirit is "the source of inspiration to the prophets. . . . For this reason, in the divine Scripture all is called *theopneustos*, because God inspires [breathes out] what the Spirit has spoken."[2] Thus, when early Christians encountered NT texts that said that the Holy Spirit spoke through the prophet Isaiah (Acts 28:25), or that God spoke, by the Holy Spirit, through David's mouth in the Psalms (Acts 4:25), they believed that meant when Scripture speaks, God speaks. An example of this universal understanding of the Christian tradition is seen in the Westminster Confession of Faith, which refers to "the Holy Spirit speaking in the Scripture."[3]

Inspiration of the Divine Writings as a Completed Work

Unlike much modern theology, which locates biblical inspiration in what God *is doing* in a living encounter with human beings in the here-and-now, the NT authors speak of inspiration as if it were an accomplished fact. Prophets *"spoke* from God" as the Spirit *"carried"* them. Peter and Paul see God's inspiration of Scripture as a finished work. The Spirit's ongoing work of illuminating believers' minds to understand Holy Scripture is different from his completed work of inspiration. Another thing one sees in the apostolic view of inspiration is that it is the *Scriptures* the apostles write that are inspired, not the persons of the apostles. The emphasis in the NT is on the divine writings themselves, the *graphai*, which are the object of divine inspiration. The Bible's emphasis is not as much on what God *is doing in people*, either the writers or hearers or readers of Scripture, as it is on what he *has done in the writings*.

Scripture as Divine Communication

The ancient Hebrews and Christians emphasized God as communicating himself and his divine will, as well as *ideas* about himself and his divine will,

---

[2] Ambrose, *On the Holy Spirit* 3.16.112.
[3] Westminster Confession of Faith (WCF), 1.10.

through writings rather than through images or ecstatic experiences. This teaching stood in marked contrast to ancient pagan conceptions of revelation and to modern ones that emphasize a subjective encounter. While this rabbinic and apostolic mentality does not sit well with modern theology, it resonated with traditional Christians. It was not at all inconceivable to them that the Hebrew Scriptures were the "oracles" of God—the very utterances of his mouth (see Rom 3:2). This belief led Clement of Rome to say, "Look carefully into the Scriptures, which are the true utterances of the Holy Spirit."[4]

Scripture's Divine Origin

Thus, the divine origin of Scripture is clear in the texts that deal with the sacred writings. They could not have originated from the human will, St. Peter said. Instead, they are God's speech (2 Pet 1:21). The scriptural authors "spoke from God," and that speech could not have occurred had the Spirit of God not borne them along. The last six verses of 2 Peter 1 delve into the divine origin of the "prophetic word" (a term that summarizes the whole of Scripture). Peter himself was an eyewitness to Jesus. He was face-to-face with Jesus when he saw him transfigured before his very eyes on the "holy mountain" and heard God's voice with his own ears (2 Pet 1:16–18). And he says that the prophetic word is *more certain*, more reliable (*bebaioteron*, 2 Pet 1:19), than these eyewitness experiences. The fact that the divine inscripturated Word is more certain than watching Jesus be transfigured or hearing the Father's own voice underscores its divine origin.

Paul and the author of the letter to the Hebrews agree with Peter on the divine origin of Scripture: in addition to being all God's breath (2 Tim 3:16), Paul says that it is God's utterance (Rom 3:2). Hebrews 1:1–2 says that same prophetic word constituted God's speaking in and through the prophets, just as he spoke in his Son. There was no biblical or theological reason apparent to traditional Christians to make them think these texts meant anything other than what they seemed to mean.

---

[4] Clement of Rome, *The First Epistle of Clement to the Corinthians* 55.

The New Testament as Scripture

The NT writers spoke as if their writings were a vehicle for divine speech in the same way the OT Scriptures were. The apostles saw their ministry as that of emissaries of Jesus deputized with apostolic authority to speak for him in "words not taught by human wisdom" but "revealed to us through the Spirit" (1 Cor 2:10, 13; cf. Heb 2:3–4; 1 Pet 1:10–12; 2 Pet 1:16–18; 3:1–2; 1 John 1:1–10; Rev 1:1–3). Peter refers to Paul's writings as Scripture, putting them on par with the OT Scriptures (2 Pet 3:15–16). Jesus had told his disciples that, just as he was speaking to them while he was still with them, the Father would send the Holy Spirit in Jesus's name for the purpose of teaching them "all things" and bringing to their memory "all that I have said to you" (John 14:25–26 ESV). Jesus promised that the "Spirit of truth" would guide them into "all the truth." The Spirit would declare the truth of the kingdom, not by his own authority, but through Jesus, who was sent by the Father and spoke for him (John 16:13–15).

Was the idea that all Scripture is breathed out, spoken, and uttered by God original to the apostles? Or did they share these ideas with Jesus? When one looks at what Jesus said about the nature and function of Scripture, one sees a consistency between his ideas and the apostolic teaching. Indeed, the churches received this doctrine from the apostles, who had learned it from Jesus himself.

Jesus's View of Scripture

In Jesus's day, when Jews used the word "Scripture," they were referring to the OT. Thus, when Jesus referred to Scripture, he meant the books of the Hebrew Bible commonly accepted as canonical in his day, to which he referred in Luke 24:44 as "the Law of Moses, the Prophets, and the Psalms." This passage also demonstrates the concordance of revelation in Christ (the incarnation) and in Scripture. Christians have always assumed that, because Jesus is God incarnate, his view of Scripture is accurate and authoritative.

Jesus's Assumption of the Truth of Hebrew Scripture

So what did Jesus think about the truth and authority of Holy Scripture? In both what he said explicitly and the way he alluded to the Hebrew Scriptures,

Jesus had the highest possible estimation of the truthfulness and authority of any writing considered divine Scripture.[5] In short, he believed that
when Scripture speaks, God speaks. As Thomas Oden said, Jesus acknowledged "God's Spirit as author of Hebrew Scripture [*sic*]."[6] Often, when Jesus
wanted to stress a truth to his Jewish interlocutors, he would simply quote
the OT, saying, "Have you not read . . . ?" or "It is written" (e.g., Matt 12:3;
21:13, 42 ESV).

Jesus assumed the understanding of Second Temple Judaism—including
his critics among the Pharisees and Sadducees—about the canonical Hebrew
Scriptures: that God was speaking in them. As the Jewish scholar Shaye J.
D. Cohen argues, "Many works of the Second Temple and rabbinic periods cite the Torah, and indeed other books of the Tanak, as the word of
God. 'Scripture says' and 'God says' are synonymous expressions. It is not
the human agent who is speaking in these pages but God."[7] Jesus said, for
example, that "not the smallest letter or stroke" would pass from the Torah
(Matt 5:18 NASB). In arguing with his Jewish interlocutors in John 10,
he cited Psalm 82 and reminded them of something on which he and they
would agree: "Scripture cannot be broken" (John 10:35).

Speaking in the Holy Spirit

When premodern Christians read Jesus saying that David, in writing Psalm
110, was speaking "in the Holy Spirit" (Mark 12:36; Matt 22:43), they
believed that Jesus was referring to a special, divine-human quality of communication. They took it for granted that he was saying the same thing Peter
later affirmed when he said in Acts 4:24–25 that Psalm 2 was God's speaking
through David's mouth by the Spirit. It did not occur to professed believers
before the Enlightenment that David's speaking *in* the third person of the
Holy Trinity could mean something different from the sort of divine inspiration Peter and Paul claimed for Holy Scripture. This plain reading of these

---

[5] See Daniel Akin, "Sermon: What Did Jesus Believe About the Bible? Matt
5:17–18," *SBJT* 5, no. 2 (Summer 2001): 80–88.

[6] Thomas Oden, *Classic Christianity* (New York: HarperOne, 2009), 553.

[7] Shaye J. D. Cohen, *From the Maccabees to the Mishnah, Library of Early
Christianity* (Philadelphia: Westminster, 1987), 203.

texts need not be seen as problematic today. It is rationally compelling to see this consistency between Jesus and the apostles.

Believing What the Incarnate Lord Believed

The Christian tradition taught that it makes perfect sense to believe as God incarnate believed about God's speaking in the Scriptures. This notion runs counter to that of some advocates of Kenotic Christology, who hold that Jesus could have had mistaken views about the inspired nature of Scripture. Other modern historical-critical authors contend that the early church was, in effect, putting words in Jesus's mouth. The historical Jesus did not make such claims, these scholars argue; early Christians interpolated their opinions into the Gospel accounts.

Yet even if one goes by the more radical critical interpretation of the "real Jesus" behind the Gospel texts, there is still enough material traceable to the pre-Gospel sources to substantiate that Jesus understood Scripture to be nothing less than divine speech.[8]

Inspiration of Words, Sentences, and Propositions

Verbal Inspiration

As seen above, classic Christianity, following St. Paul, taught that inspiration is plenary: It extends to all Scripture, every Scripture. Yet the NT also teaches that inspiration is verbal. That is, not just the ideas of Scripture but its very words are God's breath, his speech. In John 10:35 Jesus bases his argument on a single word, saying that that one word makes him right—that one word's being wrong would mean the Scriptures could be broken, which Jesus and his Jewish interlocutors agreed cannot happen. Similarly, in Gal 3:16, Paul distinguishes between the singular and plural of a single word to prove his theological point.

---

[8] See Craig L. Blomberg, "Reflections on Jesus's View of the Old Testament," in D. A. Carson, ed., *The Enduring Authority of the Christian Scriptures* (Grand Rapids: Eerdmans, 2016); and John Wenham, *Christ and the Bible*, 3rd ed. (Eugene, OR: Wipf and Stock, 2009).

God's breathing out of his Word is not limited to ideas. He breathed out words, and those individual words he spoke have meaning and give meaning to the whole. Some modern scholars, in speaking of inspiration, can, to quote D. A. Carson, "comfortably speak of God's Word, but never of God's words. Yet the biblical writers can oscillate between the two without a trace of embarrassment."[9]

Inspiration of Propositions, Sentences, and Words

Christian theology has traditionally taught that God's revelation in the Bible is propositional. He reveals himself personally in nature and conscience (general revelation) and in Christ and Scripture (special revelation). Yet biblical revelation is more propositional than the other forms of revelation. God uses the propositions of Scripture—the meaning of its words and sentences in their context, which includes their cultural and historical backgrounds and literary genres—to speak his mind, to communicate information about himself.

Some thinkers have portrayed this doctrine as being too cognitive and not emphasizing enough the personal nature of God's encounter with his people. However, classic Christian theologians thought that propositional revelation is precisely personal because that is how one person communicates to another person—using language to convey meaningful cognitive propositions.[10]

Significantly, however, traditional Christian theology goes beyond saying that God inspired the propositions of the Bible. He communicated those propositions by speaking the sentences of the Bible and the words that make up those sentences. That concept is natural, because he created humanity in his image as communicative beings who convey cognitive content in propositions. Yet the only way they can communicate that content effectively is in sentences, and the only way the meaning of a sentence can be determined is by looking at the words that comprise the sentence, and at the grammar and

---

[9] D. A. Carson, *Collected Writings on Scripture* (Wheaton, IL: Crossway, 2010), 248.

[10] See Ronald H. Nash, *The Word of God and the Mind of Man* (Grand Rapids: Zondervan, 1982) and Richard Swinburne, *Revelation: From Metaphor to Analogy* (Oxford: Oxford University Press, 2007).

syntax in which those words are arranged, which together help determine their meaning.

The Original Texts

Traditional Christian theology has always said it is the original Greek and Hebrew texts of Scripture that are inspired. Copies and translations of the Bible are inspired insofar as they accurately copy and translate the original texts. The NT, for example, is represented by several thousands of manuscripts—many more than all other classical works like Homer's *Iliad* and *Odyssey*. The discipline of textual criticism, which seeks to establish the original text of the NT, has shown that "no Christian doctrine or practice— major or minor—is determined by a textually difficult passage."[11] "Neither the Christian faith nor the Bible's inspiration is threatened by textual variants."[12]

Divine-Human Confluence

The classic Christian view of inspiration must be distinguished from the "dictation" theory, as if the biblical writers were amanuenses taking dictation from God, as some church fathers and some modern fundamentalists have asserted. Scripture is suffused with the personalities, styles, and genres of the individual biblical authors themselves—their "idiosyncrasies," as Oden says.[13] It is not a textbook of doctrinal propositions handed down by God. Scripture's writers gathered information in different ways and wrote with their own particular backgrounds, socio-cultural settings, and communicative aims and goals, and in different literary genres. The writings are miraculously both God's words and human words. There is a divine-human confluence in the words of Scripture. God superintended the writing of Holy Scripture to ensure that the writers spoke from him. In a miraculous way, Scripture was authored by both God and human beings.

---

[11] Elijah Hixson and Peter J. Gurry, *Myths and Mistakes in New Testament Textual Criticism* (Downers Grove: IVP, 2019), 208.

[12] Hixson and Gurry, 209. On the reliability of the OT, see K. A. Kitchen, *On the Reliability of the OT* (Grand Rapids: Eerdmans, 2003).

[13] Oden, *Classic Christianity*, 553.

The Truthfulness and Authority of Holy Scripture

So how do questions of the infallibility, inerrancy, and authority of Holy Scripture relate to the doctrine of inspiration? The answer to that question depends on how one defines inspiration. If one believes that God is speaking in every word of Scripture, that entails that what Scripture affirms will be true and will also be authoritative for what the church teaches, what the church does, and how the church says people should live.

Deduction from Divine Inspiration

For the Christian tradition prior to the advent of theological liberalism, the complete truthfulness of the Bible followed naturally from the doctrine of plenary-verbal inspiration: If God is actually speaking through the words of all and every Scripture, then everything the scriptural authors assert as true must be true. The Bible teaches, as it assumes throughout, that "it is impossible for God to lie" (Heb 6:18; cf., e.g., Num 23:19; Rom 3:4; Titus 1:2). Because God is omniscient, if he says something that is inaccurate, he knows it is inaccurate. Thus, to assert it would constitute a lie, of which God is incapable. If God, therefore, is speaking in Scripture, and Scripture is inaccurate, God would be lying. In this sense the doctrine of inerrancy is a logical deduction from the doctrine of plenary-verbal inspiration.

The Teaching of Jesus

Jesus also teaches biblical inerrancy directly. As cited above, Matt 15:17–18 and John 10:35 directly assert the complete truthfulness of Scripture in all that it affirms. Its clearest affirmation occurs in John 17:17: "Your word is truth." What God says is true. That is precisely what Jesus, the apostles, the church fathers, and the Christian tradition believed. When God speaks, what he says is true, and in Scripture God is speaking. Christian believers throughout the centuries are simply proclaiming what they see as the teaching of Holy Scripture on its own truthfulness. They do not maintain that they have unassailable empirical proof for their belief that the biblical authors' assertions are accurate. Yet these Christians hold that they are rationally justified in that belief and that no one can prove that what the biblical authors assert is false.

What Constitutes Error

Sometimes Christians who have not studied the classic doctrine of Scripture will have encounters with skeptics who say things such as, "When the devil says something in the Bible, isn't that an error?" or, "Isn't saying the earth rests on pillars an error?" and so forth. Of course, false assertions the biblical authors quote do not disprove the truthfulness of the assertions the biblical authors themselves make.

Furthermore, the writers of Scripture are using everyday language, describing things as they see them (phenomenal language), not stating things in the language of precision used, for example, in modern mathematics (e.g., rounded numbers) or astronomy (e.g., "The sun rose"). They use figures of speech, hyperbole, and so forth (e.g., "the mustard seed is the tiniest of seeds"). Sometimes there are apparent contradictions, for example, in the Synoptic Gospels, because the writers are not using the precise chronological methods of modern historiography. Sometimes the writers are describing events from different perspectives and leave out details that other writers include. When this happens, their statements are inexhaustive, not false.

Infallibility, the Noumenal, and the Phenomenal

Some modern Christians say they believe in the infallibility of Scripture but not its inerrancy. They say that infallibility is simply the impossibility of something's failing to achieve its purpose—despite dictionaries still defining it as "the inability to be wrong."[14] Of course, more is involved in the concept of infallibility than mere inerrancy. Yet if one believes what premodern Christians believed about inspiration, that God is speaking in Scripture, then for God to assert things that are false would entail his speech's having failed to achieve its purpose.

Others say they believe that the Bible is inerrant in noumenal things that are unfalsifiable but not in phenomenal things that are falsifiable. They believe the Bible *can* assert, for example, that an event occurred that could not have occurred because it is scientifically impossible or did not occur

---

[14] *Oxford dictionaries*, s.v. "infallibility (*n.*)," https://www.lexico.com/definition /infallibility.

because the author got it wrong. Yet they hold that the Bible *cannot* assert things that are doctrinally and ethically false. However, this is to impose peculiarly modern categories on the biblical writers. When they said that Scripture is God's speech, and he cannot lie, it would not have occurred to them to think that he could state things he knew were inaccurate in phenomenal matters but could *not* state things he knew were inaccurate in theological and moral matters.

The Christian Tradition

Thus, it seemed logical to premodern Christians, who interpreted the Bible to teach that God was speaking in Holy Scripture, to believe in its inerrancy. The existence of apparent contradictions in the Bible is not what caused modern liberal thinkers to reject traditional doctrines of biblical inspiration, trustworthiness, and authority. Such seeming inconsistencies had been discussed for centuries. As early as the second century, church fathers had dealt with them. Justin Martyr, a second-century pagan philosopher who converted to Christianity, said, "I am entirely convinced that no Scripture contradicts another. I shall admit rather that I do not understand what is recorded and shall strive to persuade those who imagine that the Scriptures are contradictory, to be rather of the same opinion as myself."[15]

Augustine said, regarding how he dealt with apparent contradictions in Scripture, "I most firmly believe that the authors were completely free from error. And if in these writings I am perplexed by anything which appears to me opposed to truth, I do not hesitate to suppose that either the manuscript is faulty, or the translator has not caught the meaning of what was said, or I myself have failed to understand it."[16] This same approach to dealing with apparent contradictions is seen in Jewish rabbinical teaching.

A Modern Evangelical Creation?

Some modern scholars intimate that the approach to Scripture described here is an invention of nineteenth-century American evangelical Protestants

---

[15] Justin Martyr, *Dialogue with Trypho*, 65.
[16] Augustine, *Letter 83* 1.3

motivated by a commitment to Scottish Common Sense philosophy. This, however, is not quite accurate. Conservative Catholics and Eastern Orthodox writers also held and hold that biblical inspiration means God is speaking in Scripture, and thus it is free from error in all its affirmations. For example, the First Vatican Council (1870) said that the books of the Bible "whole and entire, with all their parts . . . contain revelation without errors . . . because having been written under the inspiration of the Holy Spirit, they have God for their author." The same can be seen in papal encyclicals throughout the nineteenth and twentieth centuries, which demonstrates that this approach to inspiration is not the creation of American evangelical Protestants.

Indeed, what modern conservative Protestants, Catholics, and Eastern Orthodox believers have professed concerning the trustworthiness of Holy Scripture is in keeping not just with patristic but also with medieval and Reformation thought. Thomas Aquinas stated, for example, "Nothing false can underlie the literal sense of Scripture,"[17] and Martin Luther said, "The Scriptures cannot err."[18]

The Canon of Scripture

The difference between Roman Catholicism and Eastern Orthodoxy on one hand and traditional Protestantism on the other is not their view of inspiration and inerrancy but of canon and *sola Scriptura*. The former teach that certain OT apocryphal books are canonical, and hence inspired Scripture, which the latter deny. The former generally believe that the church created the NT canon. The latter believe that the church affirmed or accepted the canonical books of the NT as inspired because they were received by the Spirit-led church universal as apostolic in origin and as teaching true doctrine consistent with apostolic teaching. As Oden has said, "as the New Testament became consensually received by the church, the worshipping community understood itself to stand under the norm of the apostolic proclamation, for apostolicity was the chief criterion of the New Testament canon."[19]

---

[17] Thomas Aquinas, *Summa Theologiae* I, 1, 10, ad 3.
[18] Martin Luther, "The Misuse of the Mass," in *Works*, 36:137.
[19] Oden, *Classic Christianity*, 555; see also Michael J. Kruger, *Canon Revisited* (Wheaton: Crossway, 2012).

Sola Scriptura

The Catholic and orthodox churches deny the *sola Scriptura* (Scripture alone) teaching of the Reformers. The former believe that Scripture must be supplemented by an authoritative, Spirit-guided church magisterium that can speak in such a way that the truths it asserts are infallible and on par in authority with canonical Scripture. The Reformers highly respected the consensual witness of the Christian tradition. Yet they affirmed that Scripture alone is the church's only infallible Rule of Faith and practice, or, as was cited earlier from the Westminster Confession, "the supreme Judge, by which all controversies of religion are to be determined, and all decrees of councils, opinions of ancient writers, doctrines of men, and private spirits, are to be examined, and in whose sentence we are to rest, can be no other but the Holy Spirit speaking in the Scripture."[20] Scripture alone is the *norma normans* (norming norm) for the doctrine, ecclesial practice, and ethical teaching of the Christian church.[21]

The Assumptions of Modernity

The presuppositions of modernity, not the existence of apparent contradictions, are what led to the rejection of the Bible's divine inspiration, truthfulness, and authority. If people already "know" that supernatural incursions into nature—things such as seas parting or virgins conceiving or people being possessed by devils—do not occur, that will affect their view of whether the assertions the biblical authors make are accurate. If they think evolutionary theory entails that religions inexorably develop from more-primitive to more-enlightened, and thus that more-enlightened things must have been inserted into the OT by later editors, that will affect their view as well. That the latter notion no longer holds sway in the academy further undermines the tendencies of Enlightenment thinking that led to this point. Such assumptions precipitated the development of theological liberalism and historical criticism in the nineteenth and twentieth centuries.

---

[20] *The Westminster Confession of Faith*, 1.10.
[21] See A. N. S. Lane, "Scripture, Tradition, and Church: An Historical Survey," *Vox Evangelica* 9 (1975): 37–55.

The Jettisoning of Biblical History

The first step in that process was assuming that one could affirm the *unreliability* of biblical history alongside the *reliability* of the biblical authors' doctrinal and ethical assertions. However, the dichotomy between what Jesus called "earthly things" and "heavenly things" (John 3:12 ESV: "If I have told you earthly things and you do not believe, how can you believe if I tell you heavenly things?") was not such a facile distinction to make. After all, biblical history was tethered inextricably to redemptive history and the spiritual and ethical life. Driving a wedge between the historical authenticity of assertions in the Bible (including miraculous ones) and the theological and moral ones became increasingly implausible.

The Jettisoning of Biblical Authority

This implausibility caused some critics to move back toward the classic position. But most moved inexorably forward, driving the wedge less and less between assertions regarding nature and history and those that touched theology and morality. This movement eventually advanced to the point that one could think of oneself as a Christian yet assume that many of the (noumenal) ethical and doctrinal commitments of the prophetic and apostolic writings were just as suspect as the (phenomenal) assertions regarding nature and history.

It just so happened that this jettisoning of the moral commitments of the biblical writers occurred at each progressive stage of secular culture's public shift away from traditional moral strictures. This included such issues as male and female roles, divorce, and abortion, then eventually monogamous homosexuality, and then finally illicit heterosexual conduct, bisexuality/homosexual polyamory, and transgenderism. Curiously, the liberal biblical critics' repudiation of the accuracy and authority of Scripture's pronouncements changed decade by decade precisely in step with secular culture's moral progress. As a result, some conservative prognosticators have wondered when biblical proscriptions of polygamy, bestiality, and pedophilia will be moved from the inerrant to the errant category.

Conclusion

Historically, professed Christian believers have universally acknowledged that Christ and the apostles affirmed that, when Scripture speaks, God speaks. Since God was speaking in Holy Scripture, the things the biblical authors asserted to be true were thought to be true. Such truth extended not only to noumenal matters such as ethics and theology, but also to empirical phenomena. The church thus received this divine speech as authoritative for its doctrine, practice, and ethical prescriptions. Modern presuppositions, worldviews, and visions of the moral life militate against such authority. However, Christians who espouse the consensual teaching of the Christian tradition see the affirmation that the Bible is inspired, makes no false affirmations, and is wholly authoritative for the church's thought and life as rationally consistent and compelling. They also see it as life-giving because it is infallible and thus consistent with the gospel of Christ's kingdom and fruitful for human flourishing.

For Additional Study

Carson, D. A., ed. *The Enduring Authority of the Christian Scriptures*. Grand Rapids: Eerdmans, 2016.

The Chicago Statement on Biblical Inerrancy (https://www.etsjets.org/files /documents/Chicago_Statement.pdf).

Dockery, David S. *Christian Scripture: An Evangelical Perspective on Inspiration, Authority and Interpretation*. Eugene, OR: Wipf and Stock, 2004.

Frame, John M. *The Doctrine of the Word of God*. Phillipsburg, NJ: P&R, 2010.

Henry, Carl F. H. *God, Revelation, and Authority*, vols. 1 and 4. Wheaton, IL: Crossway, 1999.

Packer, J. I. *"Fundamentalism" and the Word of God*. Grand Rapids: Eerdmans, 1958.

Wenham, John. *Christ and the Bible*. Eugene, OR: Wipf and Stock, 3rd ed., 2009.

Woodbridge, John D. *Biblical Authority: Infallibility and Inerrancy in the Christian Tradition*. Grand Rapids: Zondervan, 2015.

Also see these articles: Revelation, Hermeneutics, Biblical Theology, Holy Spirit

4

Faith and Reason

Owen Strachan

I was driven to Whipsnade one sunny morning. When we set out, I did not believe that Jesus Christ is the son of God, and when we reached the zoo I did."[1]

So said C. S. Lewis of his famous conversion to Christianity in 1931. Lewis was a brilliant man, an Oxford University scholar of Renaissance literature *par excellence*, one of the thinkers to whom it was given to shape the academic world in their image. Possessed of a booming voice, a glint in his eye, and a quicksilver wit, Lewis made short work of Christians throughout the first several decades of his life. Yet Lewis was destabilized as well. Great thudding crashes of trial and tragedy dented the walls of his intellectual fortress, even as Lewis experienced an unquenchable longing for life to have meaning. Beneath the mask, Lewis yearned for joy, true Joy, and beauty, true Beauty.

It took years, but Lewis finally confessed faith in Christ. He went to the zoo one sunny morning an unbeliever; he reached the zoo a convert. There are many subtleties to Lewis's story, yet this man's journey is one that speaks to many of us on the subject before us. Leading lights of the Christian tradition agree on the question, How do we reconcile the need to trust in a

---

[1] C. S. Lewis, *Mere Christianity* (1952; repr., New York: HarperCollins, 2012), 237.

crucified and resurrected Messiah we cannot see (faith) with the need to think critically and analytically about all of life (reason)? From this point, however, theologians and philosophers disagree. Over millennia of history, we discover several differing conceptions of the relation between faith and reason. Here are four of the most common framings of this pairing:

First, the Christian faith is reasonable—faith aligns with reason.

Second, reason leads to faith—faith accessible by reason.

Third, faith is the master of reason—faith above reason.

Fourth, faith should be preached and reason rejected—faith against reason.

We shall now take each of these in turn. In studying these generalized perspectives, our prayer is not unlike Lewis's famous *credo* statement: we seek to arrive at the gates of heaven a believer, confident in God, trusting in Christ, thoroughly trained in the Christian faith.

The Christian Faith Is Reasonable

The early church found itself in the unenviable position of being called blasphemers and rabble-rousers. In the second century AD, Justin Martyr took upon himself the task of demonstrating to the church, and beyond it, the reasonableness of Christianity. Justin went to great lengths in his writings to defend the church from accusations of misconduct and evil. He sought to vindicate the church from false charges of cannibalism and ribald sexuality and helped make converts by his careful and patient explanatory ministry.

Justin went further. He argued an early form of the "all truth is God's truth" argument that Dutch theologian Abraham Kuyper would make famous. He based this view in the *Logos* theology of John 1 and other texts:

Whatever all men have uttered aright is the property of us Christians. . . . For all writers through the implanted seed of the Logos which was engrafted in them, were able to see the truth darkly, for the seed and imitation of a thing which is given according to the capacity of him who receives it is one thing, and quite a different one is the thing itself of which the communication and the imitation are received according to the grace from God. For whatever either lawgivers or philosophers uttered well, they elaborated by finding and contemplating some part of the Logos.[2]

The essential idea here is, as mentioned, that God owns the truth. As a result, any sound idea or writing is funded by—made possible through—the personal God, which is to say the Christian God. Justin does not mean in the above passage that all who have engaged philosophy or law in the past were necessarily true followers of God. He does mean that God owns the Wi-Fi, and everyone is using his for free. In more traditional terms, all truth is grounded in the true God, and specifically in Christ the perfect image of God, the one who not only taught truth, but in his person *is* truth.

This was a common apologetic move within the early church. Justin's line of argument will recur throughout church history. So will the real need for Christians to articulate what they actually believe and practice as opposed to what they are said to believe and practice. Justin argued for what we can call a "reasonable faith," and in so doing he launched an ongoing conversation over this concept and how Christians present themselves in a world that is fundamentally—and unalterably—opposed to the Gospel. Several centuries later, Augustine would pay similar attention to the way in which Christianity alone accounts for the beauty, truth, and goodness we find in this world. In later centuries in the medieval period, thinkers like Anselm would engage Justin's project afresh. The faith delivered to the saints was a reasonable faith, and if played out through syllogisms and reasoned dialogues (Anselm loved nothing more than a lengthy dialogue) would point the curious and the damned to God.

Reason Leads to Faith

The most famous proponent of this second view was the thirteenth-century philosopher Thomas Aquinas. A brilliant man, Aquinas believed that the existence of God "is not self-evident to us," and so it must be "demonstrated from those of his effects which are known to us."[3] This conviction

---

[2] Justin Martyr, *Second Apology* 13.
[3] Thomas Aquinas, *Summa Theologica* 1.2.2.

enfranchised the development of what is called "natural theology," one of the least-understood and most-confused terms in Christian theology. Natural theology for Aquinas is not equated with general revelation (which can also be called natural revelation). Natural theology for Aquinas is the construction of a sound understanding of God based upon "sense."[4] Reason gets us to God, and once we get to God, the Bible opens our eyes to specific truths such as the person of Christ and the Trinity.

Aquinas does not begin with God to know God. He begins with the ordered world, assumes that he is called to reason his way to God, and deploys numerous concepts toward this end. The most famous of them are the "five proofs" (or "ways"), the logical arguments that he believed paved the way for Christian faith.[5] They are as follows:

The First Proof: God, the Prime Mover

The Second Proof: God, the First Cause

The Third Proof: God, the Necessary Being

The Fourth Proof: God, the Absolute Being

The Fifth Proof: God, the Grand Designer

These arguments have been widely studied and used, particularly among Catholics. Aquinas did not believe that these proofs or ways rated the status of infallible Scripture. He put these ideas on par with the findings of science. This move merits considerable attention. Aquinas effectively carved out a way of knowing God, or at least finding one's way to God, outside of direct biblical instruction. Using one's mind according to sense experience meant that one could find the pathway to God. In this way, Aquinas believed that "reason" could indeed yield "the knowledge of God." Many are not fit for such an arduous quest; still others are taken up with the cares of the world or are waylaid in their investigation by sin and weakness. But there are some "few" who can pursue pure "love of knowledge." These able thinkers travel the river of learning by the vessel of reason and arrive safely in the harbor of God. Aquinas hedges his language but nonetheless makes this conviction clear:

---

[4] Thomas Aquinas, *Summa Theologica* 1.1.9.
[5] Aquinas, *Summa Theologica* 1.2.3.

The knowledge of the truths that reason can investigate concerning God presupposes much previous knowledge. Indeed almost the entire study of philosophy is directed to the knowledge of God. Hence, of all parts of philosophy, that part stands over to be learnt last, which consists of metaphysics dealing with points of Divinity. Thus, only with great labour of study is it possible to arrive at the searching out of the aforesaid truth; and this labour few are willing to undergo for sheer love of knowledge.[6]

In the broadly Christian tradition, Aquinas stands out for his high confidence in the ability of the mind to reason its way to God. His project creates not only natural theology, but natural (or classical) apologetics, and it will help to promote natural law thinking as well. The common thread running through these systems is their strong confidence in the natural (unregenerate) mind to know truth, understand the world aright, and establish belief in God through philosophical means. This intellectual scheme, seemingly united and coherent as a body of knowledge, would have major effect in Catholic circles and beyond, suggesting that Christianity can be defended and even substantiated (in major form) on rational grounds.

Faith Is the Master of Reason

Three hundred years after Aquinas lived, the sixteenth-century Protestant Reformers reframed Aquinas's project. They substantially rebuilt the apologetics, epistemology, and doctrine of their movement on what they saw as an explicitly biblical foundation. The Reformers championed the view called in later centuries *sola Scriptura*, which means that Scripture alone is the church's ultimate authority. The church's doctrinal decrees and reasoning may well have value but are not on par with Scripture and cannot be on par with it.

This extended into the Reformers' treatment of reason. The two best-known magisterial Reformers, Martin Luther and John Calvin, were both quite suspicious of reason. Actually, Luther was more than suspicious. In several places in his corpus, Luther was censorious toward reason. He polemicized against it and no doubt had Aquinas's brand of theology in

---

[6] Aquinas, *Summa Contra Gentiles* 1.1.4.

his sights. Beyond this, Luther dismissed the idea that one could grasp Scripture's meaning through use of the intellect. Instead, one had to "despair" of such means:

> To begin with, it is absolutely certain that one cannot enter into the Scripture by study or innate intelligence. Therefore, your first task is to begin with prayer. You must ask that the Lord in his great mercy grant you a true understanding of his words, should it please him to accomplish anything through you for his glory and not for your glory or that of any other man. . . . You must therefore completely despair of your own diligence and intelligence and rely solely on the infusion of the Spirit. Believe me, for I have had experience in this matter.[7]

This did not mean that Luther disdained the mind, however. Though his comments on reason sometimes reached near lava-levels of intensity, he understood the gift of thinking well and said as much at different points. On reason, he once said, "It is the inventor and mentor of all the arts, medicine, laws, and of whatever wisdom, power, virtue, and glory men possess in this life. . . . It is a sun and a kind of god appointed to administer these things in this life."[8] Luther knew that God had not made men brainless, with only a heart able to be saved. Luther's burden, however, was to destroy the stronghold of Catholic soteriology. Though a gifted theologian, he knew in his soul what it was to be enslaved to corrupt ideas. He thus spent much energy in combating a wrong vision of the place of the mind in the knowledge of God.

John Calvin had a similar burden. He did not practice Aquinas's natural theology. Calvin did, though, make a considerable contribution on the matter of the *sensus divinitatis* in every person. By this he meant that there is a "sense of divinity" in every image-bearer:

> That there exists in the human minds and indeed by natural instinct, some sense of Deity [*sensus divinitatis*], we hold to be beyond dispute, since God himself, to prevent any man from pretending ignorance, has endued all men with some idea of his Godhead. . . . This

---

[7] Martin Luther, *Luther's Works*, 48:53–54.
[8] Luther, *Luther's Works*, 34:137.

is not a doctrine which is first learned at school, but one as to which every man is, from the womb, his own master; one which nature herself allows no individual to forget.[9]

Calvin's concept of the *sensus divinitatis* made possible a recovery of a right situating of reason within a Christian worldview. Reason could not save the sinner; it could not, of its own capacities, lead man to God. Nor did the sinner need to be taught certain ideas according to human learning in order to arrive at the previously uncommunicated knowledge of God. Rather, "from the womb" every human person knows that God exists. Every person knows that God is the Creator and Ruler of all things. No man or woman may follow such generally revealed truth to salvation; by contrast, humanity rebels against this immediate, untaught, and plainly accessible revelation (Rom 1:18–32). But this does not decimate reason. Instead, in salvation, God awakens reason. He transforms the mind, overturning the "noetic" (intellectual) effects of the fall such that the mind now works rightly (though surely not perfectly) according to God's design.

The Reformed tradition later developed this idea further, building off of it to establish what is called "presuppositional" apologetics. In this system, one must start with God in order to know God. One does not start with reason, or evidence, to know God. One starts with God, presupposing what the Bible shouts from every page: that God is not only *not dead* per modern ideology but is alive, the Creator of all, the sustainer of all things, the architect of the mind, the ground of truth, three real divine persons but one resplendent God. Of course, such theistic thinking would come under major fire in the period known as the "Age of Lights," the Enlightenment. Immanuel Kant would challenge the very unity of Christian truth, splitting up knowledge into two categories, the phenomenal (sense-provable) and the noumenal (unproveable and mystical).[10]

This division radically altered the way that many people thought about religion. Where it treated ethics and daily living, Christianity was considered reliable and even sound by many, but where it treated higher-order doctrines,

---

[9] John Calvin, *Institutes of the Christian Religion* 1.3.1.
[10] Francis Schaeffer, *Escape from Reason* (1968; repr., Downers Grove: IVP, 2014), 217–28.

Christianity existed in the realm of speculation, mysticism, and wishful thinking. When Darwin developed (or borrowed) his theory of human origins in naturalistic terms, the migration of Western society (at least among the upper crust) away from a religious worldview grounded in some form of Christianity picked up serious steam. Christians gave varied responses to Enlightenment ideas. Some, like Jonathan Edwards, both rejected and selectively adapted tenets of Enlightenment thought. In response to the Enlightenment's creeping atheism, Edwards built his entire system upon the premise that God had created all things for the display of his own glory. This was an intellectual masterstroke.

Yet Edwards also carefully adapted Lockean epistemology, leaving a clear place for the spiritual judgment of the converted individual in coming to faith. Later centuries only extended this lively interaction of faith and reason in the post-Enlightenment world. In the nineteenth century at Princeton Theological Seminary, theologians like Charles Hodge and B. B. Warfield used Common Sense Realism to defend the doctrine of revelation. The Bible in its plainspoken sense shaped reality; thus, the theologian's task was to convince the mind of the evident truthfulness of the Scriptures. Once established, such doctrine would convict the interlocutor.

In the twentieth century, debates arose among the heirs of Old Princeton over the role of proofs in apologetics and Christian faith, splitting Reformed Christians. The "classicalists" would build from the Princeton apologetic, citing Aquinas in the process, to show that the Christian faith is a reasonable faith, believing that such a move would help win sinners to Christ. The "presuppositionalists" led by Cornelius Van Til would argue that such an apologetic method relegated belief in the truthfulness of God and God's Word to a backseat role. Though disagreements persist into the current day, these debates would occur in the wake of the Reformational recovery of the authority of Scripture.

Faith Should Be Preached and Reason Rejected

We have already alluded to this view in quoting Luther. This perspective came into prominence in the early twentieth century among the group that would later be called "fundamentalists." In truth, many fundamentalists would use their minds to know God. But their camp boldly separated from thinkers and church groups that emphasized that reason played anything like a strong role in the knowledge of God. Not for nothing did Billy Sunday purportedly say, for example, that he knew as much about theology as a jackrabbit knew about ping-pong. Like many of his peers, Sunday found no confidence in the life of the secular mind. He saw, with considerable justification, that many Western institutions of higher learning were traveling into the darkness of studied unbelief, and he wanted no part of it. His mission was to stand upon the Word of God and the Word of God alone.

The movement majored in Protestant *sola Scriptura* theology but with an unvarnished feel in many places. As time went on, it became a badge of honor among some doctrinally conservative Christians to not engage the life of the mind. Thinking itself became suspect for some fundamentalists. One did not really need to study history; one did not need to know methods of exegesis and hermeneutics; one did not need formal training at all. Better to stay untainted by the academy and its siren song of credibility, academic respect, and cultural respectability. This kind of instinct became associated with the critique of "biblicism," so called. To be a biblicist as some understand it is to deny reason any role in the Christian faith. *God says it; I believe it; that settles it.*

Some Christians do hold such a view. For them, faith effectively swallows reason, and the life of the mind is largely ignored, at least in any conscious way. But others who earn such a label are more complicated. They might have been raised in the kind of circles mentioned here, but they are not hostile to sound thinking and the exchange of ideas. They want to grow mentally, intellectually, and theologically. They trust the Word of God and trust it absolutely. But they want and need further formation. They have been trained in some cases to reject or distrust thinking, when in truth they need to be trained to think, and to think biblically and carefully.

Brief Reflections on Faith and Reason for the People of God

The foregoing leaves us much to think through. For starters, we can see that Christianity is in fact a reasonable faith. After all, Christianity alone makes sense of the world according to revelation. It is not that we are in a secular realm making a brave but foolish stand for God; it is that we are in the

God-made world, and we thus celebrate and defend and proclaim the manifold excellencies of God in this place. Our faith, then, is the most reasonable brand of thought there is. We do well to try to guide unbelievers into this realization. We pray that scales will fall from their eyes as we do so, just as in some sense they once did for we who know Christ.

But we cannot expect to be applauded for our faith, reasonable though it is. The world hates us already, according to Christ (John 15:18–19). Amidst such opposition, we must make the case for Christianity. This is what Aquinas and the medievalists sought to do. They had a tremendous confidence in the human mind. It is not surprising that they should have such confidence, for Aquinas might well have been the most intellectually gifted man in history. Further, when we read of Aquinas's inquiry into the nature of God and the world God has made, we cannot help but be challenged. Aquinas undertook the task of explaining everything. That is worth doing. But with this noted, we need to work out how we incorporate clear evidence of the divine into our witness and apologetics. Should we use the theistic proofs? Some Christians will, to be sure. Others will have serious concerns about Aquinas's approach (not to mention the doctrine he held as a Catholic theologian). For them, it is one thing to take note of possible proofs of God's existence; it is another to reason our way to God and bring faith in to close the deal.

The Reformers made real and massive doctrinal recoveries. However else we understand their work, they attempted to rebuild Christianity from the Bible up. What a momentous and important project this was. The Reformers did not follow Aquinas in his synthesis of faith and reason; in many respects, they rejected it. Yet we cannot fail to note that the Reformers themselves differed on how precisely to situate reason in the Christian worldview. This is not surprising, for the relationship between faith and reason is easy to introduce but complex to sort out. The Reformers nonetheless guide us well in giving first place to faith and making reason the handmaiden to Christian thinking.

So, too, do we learn something vital from the fundamentalists. They saw the naturalistic tsunami coming, and they did what they could to shelter their movement. The fundamentalists were right to reject the pursuit of worldly approval and accomplishments; they knew how deadly pride is. But theirs was not a full-fledged intellectual program. They remind us not to dismiss a thinking Christianity but to frame it very carefully. We find ourselves in a moment quite similar to theirs about 100 years ago. We will do well to remember that Christianity is an offense to the natural man; indeed, the natural man cannot receive the things of God (1 Cor 2:14). Such a truth will provide ironic comfort to many of us as we offer faithful witness in an evil world.

Perhaps, going even further back, we are in a context not unlike that of Paul at Mars Hill. Yet our task is not first contextualization, as some characterize Paul's approach there. In actuality, Paul rebukes idolatry and false religious teaching at Mars Hill. He shows that he knows something of Greco-Roman intellectual culture, yes; he engages and values the life of the mind. But he uses his own brilliant mind to distinguish Christianity from every system, to show the antithesis between Christ and every ideology, to vindicate the truth of God over the opinions of man. As we see from his second letter to the Corinthians, he does not seek to leave non-Christian systems untouched in his engagement but to "destroy strongholds" (2 Cor 10:5).

The apostle Paul knows the systems he faces; he pays them a form of intellectual respect in learning them, but he does not embrace them. He seeks their demolition through his apostolic (biblical, that is) weaponry. Having launched the project of cultural deconstruction, he then undertakes the project of gospel reconstruction. He builds a Christian worldview from the ground up. This worldview is revelational in form. Carl F. H. Henry said it well: "Christianity adduces not simply mythical statements but factual and literal truth about God." This truth is found in "valid propositional information" that comes from God himself and thus creates a worldview that is grounded from start to finish in the Word of God.[11] This worldview is not small or confined but rather comprehends all things and gives authoritative shape and form to all of life. As Van Til said, "The Bible is thought of as authoritative on everything of which it speaks. Moreover, it speaks of everything."[12] As with Van Til, so with Paul: he stood upon Scripture and found there a solid rock. So shall we.

---

[11] Carl F. Henry, *God, Revelation, and Authority* (Wheaton: Crossway, 2003), 1:69.

[12] Cornelius Van Til, *Defense of the Faith* (Phillipsburg, NJ: P&R, 1972), 29.

Conclusion

Once converted, C. S. Lewis did not turn his back on the thinking life. Instead, Lewis did something far more dramatic and far more needed. He lived and acted and *thought* as a Christian. He helped many see that Christianity was not a blind leap into a spiritual gulf. No, Christianity meant knowing the world as it truly is, seeing the world as an enchanted realm, a realm ruined by sin but already claimed by Christ.

It was on a sunny morning that Lewis came to believe in Christ. Years later, reflecting on his Christian worldview, he once again brought the sun into his description of his faith: "I believe in Christianity as I believe that the Sun has risen, not only because I see it but because by it, I see everything else."[13] For all the people of God, the light of faith has arisen; we see God in his Word, and by his Word we see everything else.

For Additional Study

Anselm. *Cur Deus Homo.*

Aquinas, Thomas. *Summa Contra Gentiles.*

———. *Summa Theologica.*

Bahnsen, Greg L. *Van Til's Apologetic: Readings and Analysis.* Phillipsburg, NJ: P&R, 1998.

Cowan, Steven B., ed. *Five Views of Apologetics.* Grand Rapids: Zondervan, 2010.

Henry, Carl F. H. *God, Revelation, and Authority, Vol. 1. The God Who Speaks and Shows.* 1976. Reprint, Wheaton: Crossway, 2003.

Johnson, Jeffrey. *The Failure of Natural Theology: A Critical Appraisal of the Philosophical Theology of Thomas Aquinas.* Conway, AR: Free Grace Press, 2021.

---

[13] Lewis, "Is Theology Poetry?" (Address given on Nov 6, 1944, to the Oxford Socratic Club).

Lewis, C. S. *Mere Christianity.* 1952. Reprint, New York: HarperCollins, 2012.

———. *The Weight of Glory.* 1949. Reprint, New York: Harper Collins, 2013.

Justin Martyr. *First Apology.*

———. *Second Apology.*

Schaeffer, Francis. *Escape from Reason.* 1968. Reprint, Downers Grove: IVP, 2014.

Sproul, R. C., John Gerstner, and Arthur Lindsey. *Classical Apologetics: A Rational Defense of the Christian Faith and a Critique of Presuppositional Apologetics.* Grand Rapids: Zondervan, 1984.

Van Til, Cornelius. *The Defense of the Faith.* Phillipsburg, NJ: P&R, 1972.

———. *Introduction to Systematic Theology.* Phillipsburg, NJ: P&R, 1974.

Also see these articles: Revelation, Role of Tradition, Christian Experience, Philosophical Theology, Modern Theology

Hermeneutics

ANDREW STREETT

Introduction

Hermeneutics is the study of the theory and method of interpreting texts, which includes both determining and appropriating a text's meaning. Since the Bible is a collection of ancient texts, we must consciously attempt to understand them in their own contexts. On the other hand, since we take the Bible to be God's revelation of himself,[1] we must also consider how to responsibly appropriate the historical meaning of these texts in our own theological endeavors. Hermeneutics is foundational for all areas of theology to be treated in this volume.

Preunderstanding and the Hermeneutical Circle

No one begins the process of interpretation with a blank slate. Everyone has assumptions about reality arising from experience, which affect how we view the world in every area of life. These preunderstandings include assumptions about the nature and purpose of the Bible, genres of individual books, and the meaning of particular passages. Thus, the first task of conscientious interpretation is "Know thyself!" These assumptions are not in themselves negative; they allow us to read the Bible and enter the "hermeneutical circle,"

---

[1] *Baptist Faith and Message 2000*, Article I.

the repeated process where preunderstanding is shaped into new under-standing by engagement with the text. This adjusted understanding then becomes the basis for future textual engagement, in which it will be refined again, and so on. Some assumptions may be confirmed, while others are cor-rected. The preunderstandings with which we come to a text are valuable for beginning the process of interpretation but should never predetermine the meaning of a text for us; we must remain open to the text and its revision of our understanding.

The Meaning of Meaning

What then are we seeking in texts in general and the Bible in particular? To what do we refer when speaking about a text's meaning? While some propose that a text has meaning in itself apart from an author or that readers make meaning for texts in the act of reading, the time-honored and com-mon-sense approach is to seek the author's intention as communicated by the text.[2] This is the default mode of interpretation for any human act of communication. It is certainly important to study the way a text takes on a life of its own or how different readers have understood the text over time, but these are not the object of biblical interpretation. Unfortunately, some texts, even in the Bible, are difficult to understand because we lack sufficient information to determine the author's intention. In such cases we might be able to give several possible meanings, but we must approach the text with humility, with a recognition of our limitations as interpreters, and with open-ness to the understanding of others.

It is important to note that acts of communication are not limited to stating propositions to an audience. An author may intend to change the readers' minds, make them feel a particular emotion, force them into action, pass judgment on them, and so on. The action an author accomplishes with his text is also part of the intended meaning, and we must try to determine this as well.[3]

---

[2] Kevin Vanhoozer, *Is There a Meaning in This Text?* (Grand Rapids: Zondervan, 1998), 201–80.

[3] Jeannine Brown, *Scripture as Communication* (Grand Rapids: Baker, 2007), 100–19.

Thus, Christians do not read the biblical texts solely out of interest in the historical events of Israel's past or the literary significance of Paul's writings, but we seek also to understand and know the God who chose Israel and commissioned Paul. The biblical texts themselves are the locus of theological meaning expressed in the author's communication. To understand the author's intended meaning is also to ask what the texts say theologically.

The Need for Hermeneutics

People interpret countless texts daily, from stop signs to news articles, though they do not consciously have to think much about the meaning of these texts. Texts of many different types can be easily understood with a basic knowledge of the language and the genre of the communication. In such cases, the hermeneutical process is not absent; it simply goes unnoticed. Nonetheless, many issues can complicate acts of communication. Obviously, texts written in different languages require more interpretation, and ambiguity or confusion in an author's words or writing style require the reader to work harder to understand the meaning. Other barriers to easy understanding include literary complexity and variety, historical or political background, and differences in socioeconomic status and social values.

Linguistics

Since the biblical texts were written in Hebrew, Aramaic, and Greek, interpretation requires access to these languages, whether through learning the languages or through translations and basic tools such as concordances and interlinear Bibles. Even when studying through translation, knowledge of a few basic linguistic principles can help guard against common mistakes. For instance, most words do not have one simple meaning. Instead, they have a range of meanings, and the interpreter must depend on context to determine which meaning is intended. It would be a mistake either to assume a meaning that does not fit the context or to combine several of the available meanings of the word into one specific use in context.

Another related principle is that words do not have inherent meanings; instead, words come to have specific meanings as a result of social convention. In addition, the range of possible meanings for a word is not stable but shifts over time. Thus, instead of interpreting the Greek word "*charis*" with a theological definition of "salvific grace" each of the 140-plus times the word is used in the NT, we must recognize that at the time of the NT, average people used the word to indicate a gift, the thanks returned, and a disposition of goodwill, among many other possibilities. With knowledge of these and other principles, a careful use of lexicons and other linguistic tools can aid in responsible interpretation.[4]

Historical Context

Imagine trying to understand Martin Luther King Jr.'s "I Have a Dream" speech without adequate knowledge of slavery in America, Jim Crow laws, the broader Civil Rights movement, King's personal history, or the March on Washington. Certainly, we could understand some of it, but our grasp of the meaning and importance of the speech would be proportional to our knowledge of the historical context. Likewise, biblical texts are most fully understood when we know about both their general and specific historical context. For general historical context, an interpreter should understand (1) historical and political events in the centuries preceding a text's origin (e.g., succession of rulers or empires), (2) cultural and religious movements (e.g., Hellenism or varieties of Second Temple Judaism), and (3) cultural values in relevant periods and regions (e.g., honor/shame, kinship, or purity/impurity).[5]

The specific historical context for each text will also aid interpretation. For instance, we will gain a much more specific understanding of 1 Corinthians if we consider Paul's personal history and mission, education, temperament, and relationship with the Corinthian Christians. Furthermore, we ought to consider the makeup of the Corinthian assembly, the culture in Corinth, and recent events in their community. Dating the letter in the early AD 50s helps us to place it accurately in the timeline of Paul's life, mission, and thought. We may also be able to specify the occasion and purpose for writing. In the case of 1 Corinthians, Paul has received communication from Corinth in the form of a letter (7:1) and a personal report (1:11) about

---

[4] William W. Klein, Craig L. Blomberg, and Robert L. Hubbard Jr. et al., *Introduction to Biblical Interpretation* (Grand Rapids: Zondervan, 2017), 324–44.

[5] Brown, *Scripture as Communication*, 189–211.

issues that threaten the unity and holiness of the church. He writes to guide the Corinthians through these complex situations. Some books might lack information on author, audience, date, occasion, and purpose. For example, Hebrews and 1–2 Kings are anonymous, the Gospels and General Epistles give little evidence of their audience, and it is not clear whether Obadiah was written in the ninth or sixth century BC. In such cases where specific information is not available, we must rely more on general context.

Literary Context

Paying attention to literary context respects the author's intended meaning. Rarely did a biblical author write a sentence or even a paragraph as an isolated unit. They wrote whole letters, entire narratives, full poems, lengthy prophetic discourses. Sometimes, because evangelicals hold every part of the Bible to be inspired, we focus on smaller units—a sentence here, a paragraph there—without regard for the larger context. In doing so, however, we miss the inspired shape and meaning of the Scriptures themselves. To attempt to interpret a small part of a text aside from the whole is like trying to understand one of the disciples in da Vinci's *The Last Supper* painting without considering their relation to Jesus, interaction with other disciples, or setting at a meal. Thus, smaller passages are more likely to be misunderstood.[6]

The immediate context in preceding and following passages can help clarify interpretation. For example, 1 Corinthians 9 can be understood on its own as a meditation on foregoing apostolic rights and adapting to different situations. But when read in the context of Paul's discussion of eating meat sacrificed to idols in chapters 8 and 10, it is clear Paul is giving himself as an example to the Corinthians of how they should lay down their own rights and adapt their lifestyle so that they do not cause others to stumble. Mark 11 presents a narrative example of the same principle with the disruption in the temple (Mark 11:15–19) sandwiched between the cursing of the fig tree (Mark 11:12–14) and seeing it withered (Mark 11:20–21). Read by itself, the fig tree episode can be very confusing, but when read in conjunction with the scene in the temple, it can be understood as a metaphor for the temple establishment and Jerusalem leadership not bearing the fruit they

---

[6] Klein, Blomberg, and Hubbard, *Introduction to Biblical Interpretation*, 299–300.

should. Without recognizing these passages are connected, one might draw misguided theological conclusions about God's evaluation of fig trees that do not bear fruit out of season!

On a larger scale of literary context is the issue of genre. Letters communicate meaning differently than narratives or poetic works. Letters are occasional, addressed to specific recipients, and have recognizable structures. We would be mistaken if we expect an author of a letter to speak in the same way he would if giving a topical theological discourse. Similarly, biblical poetry deals in repetition, imagery, figure of speech—all of which we must first encounter on its own terms before asking the question of what it means. In addition, poetry is more to be experienced and felt than it is to be dissected for propositions. Narratives communicate through plot, setting, character development, conflict, and climax. We cannot understand the full meaning of Jesus's healing a blind man or teaching about the kingdom of God without reference to Jesus's actions and other events related in previous and subsequent parts of the Gospel narrative. Knowledge of genre helps us to understand both the means by which an author communicates as well as the possible relationships of smaller parts to the whole.[7]

The need to understand a whole work in light of its parts and vice versa is a narrower view of the hermeneutical circle introduced above. Most people approach a work with a general idea of what kind of work it is and what it is about, then this general impression can be tested and reformed as the reader approaches one part of the work after another. This revised understanding of the work as a whole will affect their reading of the text and its parts on their next trip around the hermeneutical circle. The hermeneutical circle is an important concept because it shows that the interpreter's task is never done; instead, we constantly reevaluate the meaning of a work through fresh engagement with both part and whole.

Biblical texts should also be understood in the larger context of contemporary literature, whether Jewish, Christian, or pagan. The effect of this comparative reading cannot be underestimated. Works of similar origin and content can shed light on the rhetoric, concepts, worldview, theology, and genre of biblical texts. For example, our understanding of Paul's thought with

---

[7] Craig Bartholomew, *Introducing Biblical Hermeneutics* (Grand Rapids: Baker, 2015), 414–30.

regard to the Law has been deepened and sharpened by comparisons with the Jewish literature of the Second Temple period. Furthermore, it is almost unimaginable at this stage to interpret Revelation apart from similar apocalyptic literature like 1 Enoch, 2 Baruch, or 4 Ezra. And there is a growing consensus that the Gospels were written in the form of ancient biographies, which sheds light on their content, structure, and purpose.

Canon and Story

So far, we have discussed how to determine the original meaning of a text, that is, the meaning that the author intended and that the original readers would have understood. These disparate texts often speak about God, his intentions for the world and humans, and many other theological topics. Thus, when we interpret biblical texts in their original context, we are already attempting to articulate the theological truth of each text as expressed in a specific situation (time, place, culture, occasion), for a specific purpose, and in a specific form. If, however, the biblical books have "God for [their] author,"[8] we must also ask how these diverse texts work together to speak as a unified revelation of God. While some readers ignore the diversity of the texts in order to affirm unity, this is unnecessary and distorts the texts. The diverse biblical books are unified by one continuous storyline centered on God's redemptive purpose for the world.[9] This unity is organic to the texts themselves, arises from historical and literary interpretation, and is discovered inductively by observing the way that the biblical authors explicitly and implicitly connect their works to an overarching narrative worldview and to other biblical texts.[10] Interpretation of the biblical books in the context of this unified redemptive-historical narrative is often called "biblical theology," though this term is applied to a variety of methods (see chapter 8).

This storyline is founded in the extensive, unified narrative of Genesis through 2 Kings. It is then rehearsed and extended in 1–2 Chronicles, beginning with the genealogy from Adam to David in chapters 1–8 and

---

[8] *Baptist Faith and Message (BFM) 2000*, Article I.

[9] See Craig Bartholomew and Michael Goheen, *The Drama of Scripture* (Grand Rapids: Baker, 2014).

[10] Bartholomew, *Introducing Biblical Hermeneutics*, 439–41.

ending with the return from exile. Ezra-Nehemiah picks up the story of 1–2 Chronicles as signaled by the repetition of the edict of Cyrus from 2 Chr 36:22–23 (Ezra 1:1–3). In the NT, the Gospels and Acts are presented as continuations of the OT story and explicitly appeal to it by means of citations, genealogies, and interpretive retellings by Stephen and the apostles. Revelation looks forward to the culmination of the entire story in the return of Christ, judgment, and New Creation. This narrative provides the context in which to understand the rest of the biblical books. Even those works that do not belong to the narrative genre are situated in the story by way of authors mentioned in the narrative books (e.g., prophecy, letters, Solomonic books), summaries of the overarching narrative (e.g., Psalms 78 and 105), or settings assigned to them either explicitly (Psalms) or implicitly (Lamentations) during the canonical process.[11]

The NT universally presents Jesus's life, death, resurrection, and ascension as the climax of the entire story. The resurrected Jesus himself teaches this explicitly in Luke 24:44–47 when he opens the disciples' minds to understand the Scriptures, that "the Messiah will suffer and rise from the dead the third day, and repentance for forgiveness of sins will be proclaimed in his name to all the nations." Paul also interprets the larger storyline of the OT in light of the climax of Jesus, most directly in Romans 3–5, Galatians 3–4, and 2 Corinthians 3. This climax comes as something of a surprise when approaching the narrative of Scripture from beginning to end, but Christian interpreters can then return to the OT for a second reading with full knowledge of NT events. This is similar to rereading a mystery novel after discovering the hidden facts that make sense of the whole story (Steinmetz, "Second Narrative"). This is an additional level of meaning born from reading the biblical texts within an expanded literary context.

Interpreters must consider how each text appeals to and is shaped by this overall narrative and ask how it affects their meaning. For instance, many NT authors appeal to their placement in the story between the climax of Christ's death and resurrection and the culmination of his second coming in order to encourage their audiences to holiness and readiness. Paul's unusual

---

[11] Richard Bauckham, "Reading Scripture as a Coherent Story," in *The Art of Reading Scripture*, ed. Ellen Davis and Richard Hays (Grand Rapids: Eerdmans, 2003), 38–53.

recommendations about marriage seem to be based on his understanding that, although marriage is good, it participates in the "form of this world" that is passing away and can be a distraction from total devotion to the Lord in this crucial period of history (1 Cor 7:25–31 ESV). That is, his position in redemptive history influences his practical and theological reasoning and leads him to make judgments that differ from those of Gen 2:18–25 and Jer 29:6.

Hermeneutics and Theology

The biblical texts as interpreted in their linguistic, historical, literary, and redemptive-historical contexts serve as the source and standard for the great variety of theological tasks. Whether systematizing the Bible's teaching, integrating theology and philosophy, discerning a faithful Christian ethic, developing disciples in community, or engaging culture, we must allow these pursuits to be guided by a continual encounter with the biblical texts. Because of the authoritative role of the Scriptures, it is tempting to describe the hermeneutical relationship of the Bible to theological work as a linear methodology from historical-literary interpretation, to biblical theology, to systematic theology, to ethics and practical theology, and so on. But this is not how texts shape thinking and worldview. Biblical interpretation and theological development are distinguishable but intrinsically related tasks whose weight and authority reside in the text itself.

No Interpretation without Theology

Within the theological hermeneutical circle, there is no such thing as interpretation of Scripture without theology. In the first place, theology and other fields provide an entry into the interpretive process. All Christians have a theological preunderstanding of the Bible and its contents stimulated by church tradition, influential teachers, and previous study, among other influences. This preunderstanding is both the result of prior interpretations and the impetus for new engagement with the Bible; without it, previous interpretation would have no result, and new engagement would have no starting point.[12] Moreover, because evangelicals hold that the Bible

---

[12] Bartholomew, *Introducing Biblical Hermeneutics*, 436–439.

is a theological document—it speaks about God and draws the reader into his life—if interpretation of the text does not translate into theological and practical reflection on all of life, then the interpretive process has been short-circuited.

In addition, the desire to understand the world theologically in concert with other fields of study (philosophy, arts, sciences) can open up new implications of biblical interpretation. For example, modern issues surrounding gender and sexuality send us back to Scripture to find meaningful applications that would not have arisen from a purely inductive process. Furthermore, "because integrating the biblical texts themselves obligates us to undertake conceptual analysis, philosophical/theological construction is integral to the process."[13]

Scripture as the Authority of Theology

Within the theological hermeneutical circle, there is no such thing as faithful theology without returning to interpret the text again in its historical, literary, and redemptive-historical contexts. All theological work must be judged by its faithfulness to the meaning of the biblical texts. For this reason, it is worth considering that the unified narrative character of the Bible might provide the shape of the theological task. Recognizing that we live within the biblical storyline (between climax and conclusion), Christian theology and practice might be imagined through the medium of drama. The biblical story may be seen as the incomplete script of a play. The church is a troupe of actors who must learn the extant parts of the play and improvise the penultimate act in line with the world of the play, the characters, the author, and the plot. In this view, theology is the creative analysis, interpretation, adaptation, rehearsal, and enactment of the Scriptures in order to live consistently with its narrative worldview.[14]

In addition, while theology can provide an entry to the interpretive process, as noted above, one cannot allow conclusions from theological work to

---

[13] Daniel J. Treier, "Biblical Theology and/or Theological Interpretation of Scripture?" *Scottish Journal of Theology* 61, no. 1 (2008): 31.

[14] N. T. Wright, *New Testament and the People of God* (Minneapolis: Fortress, 1992), 139–43; see Vanhoozer, *The Drama of Doctrine* (Louisville: WJK, 2005).

override the distinctiveness and diversity of the text; rather, the historical, literary, and theological "otherness" of the text should always be allowed to act correctively.[15] It is all too easy to develop arguments based on theological or philosophical presuppositions without once again approaching the texts to see if our work aligns with the authority. The biblical text must remain our priority. It is a mistake, for example, to focus our vision of Christ so strongly on his divinity, pre-existence, and ontological unity with the Father and the Spirit that we can no longer make sense of the Gospels' portrayals of a Galilean peasant crucified by Rome as a rebel.

Furthermore, it is important to recognize that with each step away from interpreting the biblical texts on their own terms, we are relying more and more on our own creative abilities to draw principles, fill in gaps, make extrapolations, organize systematically, apply ethically, and incorporate the meaning of biblical texts into many other fields. It can be tempting to portray theological descriptions or applications of the text as if they are exact representations of the text or bear the same authority as the text itself. This is hermeneutically naïve and misleading; it is essentially saying that no interpretation has happened, that the theologian was not personally involved in the process, that their theological formulation cannot be questioned. Theological formulations and applications must be held tentatively, always open to reformulation and critique through fresh engagement with the authoritative text.

Interpretation and Theology in Community

Although we like to imagine ourselves as independent interpreters and theologians, the truth is that we are heavily influenced by others, whether scholars, teachers, or fellow church members. Not only is this the fact of the matter, but it is also the way it should be. The more these interpretive practices take place in diverse communities, the more our limitations as interpreters are mitigated by the insights of others. The natural community in which both interpretation and theology belong is the church where groups of disciples study and live out Scripture together.

---

[15] Bartholomew, *Introducing Biblical Hermeneutics*, 437.

Conclusion

Though this description of the complex and circular hermeneutical process has no linear beginning or end, it does have a *telos*, a goal. With each lap around the circle, faithful interpreters fuse an understanding of life and text into an integrated whole renewed and refreshed by the author of life himself.

For Additional Study

Bartholomew, Craig. *Introducing Biblical Hermeneutics*. Grand Rapids: Baker, 2015.

———— and Michael Goheen. *The Drama of Scripture*. 2nd ed. Grand Rapids: Baker, 2014.

Bauckham, Richard. "Reading Scripture as a Coherent Story." In *The Art of Reading Scripture*, ed. Ellen Davis and Richard Hays, 38–53. Grand Rapids: Eerdmans, 2003.

Billings, J. Todd. *The Word of God for the People of God: An Entryway to the Theological Interpretation of Scripture*. Grand Rapids: Eerdmans, 2010.

Bray, Gerald. *Biblical Interpretation: Past and Present*. Downers Grove: IVP, 2000.

Brown, Jeannine. *Scripture as Communication*. Grand Rapids: Baker, 2007.

Gorman, Michael, ed. *Scripture and Its Interpretation*. Grand Rapids: Baker 2020.

Klein, William, Craig Blomberg, and Robert Hubbard Jr. *Introduction to Biblical Interpretation*. 3rd ed. Grand Rapids: Zondervan, 2017.

Mangum, Douglas, and Josh Westbury, eds. *Linguistics and Biblical Exegesis*. Bellingham, WA: Lexham, 2017.

Steinmetz, David. "Uncovering a Second Narrative." In *The Art of Reading Scripture*, ed. Ellen Davis and Richard Hays, 54–65. Grand Rapids: Eerdmans, 2003.

Thiselton, Anthony. *New Horizons in Hermeneutics*. Grand Rapids: Zondervan, 1992.

Treier, Daniel J. "Biblical Theology and/or Theological Interpretation of Scripture?" *Scottish Journal of Theology* 61, no. 1 (2008): 16–31.

Vanhoozer, Kevin. *Is There a Meaning in This Text?* Grand Rapids: Zondervan, 1998.

———. *The Drama of Doctrine*. Louisville: WJK, 2005.

Wright, N. T. *The New Testament and the People of God*. Minneapolis: Fortress, 1992.

Also see these articles: Scripture, Role of Tradition, Biblical Theology

6

The Role of Tradition

LUKE STAMPS

W hat comes to your mind when you hear the word "tradition"? Maybe you start singing the opening lines from the musical *Fiddler on the Roof:* "Tradition! Tradition!" Maybe you think of the Masters Tournament: "a tradition like no other." Maybe family holiday rituals come to your mind. Or perhaps you think of something more negative, like a church that is resistant to change or a culture that opposes any kind of progress. Many Christians, particularly Protestant Christians, and perhaps especially *Baptist* Christians, tend to think of tradition as something entirely negative, something that stifles the Spirit and displaces Scripture. But in reality, no one can escape tradition. Everyone is embedded within and shaped by some tradition or other. All humans are formed by the community of which they are a part and by the identity-shaping beliefs and practices that are handed down from one generation to another in that community. In other words, we are all *traditioned* creatures, whether we realize it or not.

But tradition is not just an unfortunate fact of human existence that needs to be mitigated, like a set of biases or blinders that needs to be set aside in order to attain a more objective perspective. No, tradition is actually a precondition for all creaturely thinking and acting. For example, we all inherit a culture and a language that makes human agency possible. Tradition even serves as a conveyor of truth. To turn now to the Christian tradition, everyone who comes to believe in Jesus Christ only does so because certain truths were preserved and handed down to them. As many have pointed out, faith is personal but never private. Christian faith has both an individual and a corporate or communal dimension. No one can believe for you. For Baptists, there is no such thing as proxy faith. But each Christian's faith is conceived, carried, born, and nurtured in the context of community, that is, in the context of the church. And that Christian community extended across time is what we call "tradition."

This chapter explores the role of tradition in the theological task.[1] Its central claim is that the "Great Tradition" of Christian doctrine serves as a derivative authority, subordinate to the foundational and supreme authority of Holy Scripture. Only Scripture possesses intrinsic divine authority as the inspired and inerrant written revelation of God. But to the degree that tradition conforms to the clear teaching of Scripture, as it has been interpreted by a consensus of believers across time and place, then tradition, too, has a kind of authority, namely, an interpretive authority that guides and directs the faithful reading of Scripture. The focus of this chapter is specifically on the *doctrinal* tradition of the church, but it is also worth noting that the tradition of the church is broader than doctrine. An appreciation for tradition also includes spirituality, worship, preaching, ethics, and more. In all these areas, but particularly in the area of doctrine, contemporary Christians have much to gain in rediscovering the riches of the Christian tradition. This does not mean that we follow the tradition blindly or that we supplant the ultimate authority of Scripture. But it does mean that we recognize our communion and continuity with the whole body of Christ throughout history. The tradition is, in this sense, our family history—indeed, it is *our* history.

What Is Tradition?

The English word "tradition" is derived from the Latin word *tradere*, which means "to deliver or hand over" (*trans* + *dare*, "give"). The Greek term for tradition has a similar meaning and etymology: *paradosis* (*para* + *didomi*, "give"). Most of the occurrences of *paradosis* in the Greek New Testament

---

[1] See also R. Lucas Stamps, "*Norma Normata*: The Role of Tradition in Analytic Theology," in *T&T Clark Handbook of Analytic Theology*, ed. James M. Arcadi and James T. Turner (London: Bloomsbury, 2021).

(translated "tradition" in most English versions) have a negative connotation: it is the "tradition of the elders" (e.g., Matt 15:2; Mark 7:3) or the "human tradition(s)" (Mark 7:8; Col 2:8). In these cases, tradition is a human construct that goes beyond and, indeed, stands in opposition to the revelation of God in Holy Scripture. Yet in other contexts, the word "tradition" is used in a positive light. Paul encourages the Thessalonians to "stand firm and hold to the traditions you were taught, whether by what we said or what we wrote" (2 Thess 2:15; cf. 3:6). Likewise, he commends the Corinthians for holding to "the traditions just as I delivered them to you" (1 Cor 11:2). Paul uses the verb form of the word to speak about a form of doctrine that was "delivered to" (*paradothēte*) the Romans (Rom 6:17). In this sense, "tradition" is simply the doctrinal and ethical content of the gospel message that the apostles and their associates delivered to the churches and that the churches, in turn, were expected to preserve, guard, and pass on to others.

Beyond these instances of the word "tradition," the New Testament also contains several passages that seem to summarize the Christian faith in creedal or hymnic form. These texts explain the Christian message in a brief form. We might think of Paul's summaries of the gospel in Rom 1:1–6 and 1 Cor 15:3–11, or the Christological hymns found in Phil 2:6–11 and Col 1:15–20. Another creed-like statement comes in 1 Tim 3:16 (NIV):

Beyond all question, the mystery from which true godliness springs is great:

He appeared in the flesh,
     was vindicated by the Spirit,
was seen by angels,
     was preached among the nations,
was believed on in the world,
     was taken up in glory.

This confession of faith has a rhythmic, memorizable form, indicating that it represented something that had perhaps been handed down to Paul, and that he expected his readers to guard and deliver to others as well. In short, the New Testament itself anticipates a role for tradition in this positive sense of handing on the faith to others.

The earliest Christians after the New Testament carried on this positive and formative sense of tradition. To pick just one of the most prominent examples, consider the case of Irenaeus of Lyons (c.120–c. 200), a disciple of Polycarp, who was himself a disciple of John the apostle and evangelist. Irenaeus sees tradition as a means of safeguarding the apostolic faith. In the church's confrontation with the various Gnostic heresies of the second century, the key question was this: Who has the proper interpretation of Jesus Christ and his gospel? Part of Irenaeus's answer to this question concerns the role of tradition: we know the proper interpretation of Christ because "the elders, the disciples of the apostles" have handed down to us the rule (Greek, *canon*) of faith, a summary of the Scriptures' main teaching.[2] The rule takes a decidedly trinitarian shape: the proper framework for interpreting the biblical story (God's "economy," that is, his plan for human history) is God's identity as Father, Son, and Holy Spirit. The revelation of God in Christ is the main point of this narrative (its "hypothesis"). The work of Christ recapitulates, or sums up, the whole of human history, including all of God's previous revelation in the Hebrew Scriptures.[3] For Irenaeus and other early church fathers, these interpretive keys to the biblical text are delivered by means of tradition.

Sola Scriptura and Tradition

So, tradition, in the sense that we have been describing it, is an interpretive guide to understanding the biblical revelation. Tradition is not a supplement to the *content* of Scripture but rather a guide to proper Christian *interpretation* of Scripture. Conceived in this way, tradition need not be seen as a rival to biblical authority, nor even to the Reformation principle of *sola Scriptura*, the belief that Scripture is the sole written revelation of God and thus the supreme authority on all matters of faith and practice.

But not everyone in Christian history has understood the tradition in this way. Reformation historian Heiko Oberman suggests that there are two main approaches to tradition in the history of Christian thought.[4] According

---

[2] Irenaeus, *On the Apostolic Preaching* 3.

[3] See John J. O'Keefe and R. R. Reno, *Sanctified Vision: An Introduction to Early Christian Interpretation of the Bible* (Baltimore: Johns Hopkins University Press, 2005).

[4] See Heiko A. Oberman, *Forerunners of the Reformation: The Shape of Late Medieval Thought* (New York: Holt, Rhinehart, and Winston, 1966).

to "Tradition I," the tradition is seen as an interpretive guide to understanding Scripture. This is the sense that we have been explicating from Irenaeus: the tradition does not give us new content in addition to the biblical revelation; instead, it provides the authoritative guide to interpreting Scripture's main message. According to the second view of tradition, "Tradition II," however, the tradition is seen as a second source of revelation alongside Scripture (or at least as a second aspect of the one revelation of God to the church). This view also has roots in the early centuries of the church, but it developed most fully in the medieval Roman Catholic Church. It is important to note that when the sixteenth-century Reformers argued so strongly against tradition and for *sola Scriptura*, it was this second sense of tradition that they had in view. The Reformers themselves often cited the early church fathers (especially Augustine) and certain revered medieval theologians as well (such as Bernard of Clairvaux). They had no interest in rejecting the ancient creeds of the church and were eager to demonstrate that their views had precedent in previous eras. The point of *sola Scriptura* was not to reject the authority of tradition altogether; it was simply to subordinate tradition to the supreme authority of Scripture itself. Scripture has intrinsic divine authority, but tradition has a kind of derivative authority to the degree that it conforms to the clear teaching of Scripture as it has been understood by faithful Christian interpreters through the centuries. In sum, it is a misunderstanding and distortion to assume that Protestantism is concerned only with Scripture and Catholicism is concerned mainly with tradition. Protestants have a different approach to the tradition, to be sure, but it is a mistake to conceive of Protestant theology as an utter rejection of the role of tradition in the theological task.

Sources of Tradition

On some doctrinal issues, the church has achieved a remarkable degree of unanimity. On other issues, opinions are more diverse. Regarding the former, we can rightly speak of *the* tradition of Christian doctrine, even the "Great Tradition," as some have called it.[5] Here, we might think of the cardinal

---

[5] See David S. Dockery and Timothy George, *The Great Tradition of Christian Thinking: Reclaiming the Christian Intellectual Tradition* (Wheaton: Crossway, 2012).

doctrines of the Christian faith as expressed in the ancient ecumenical creeds: the Trinity (one essence, three persons), the incarnation (one person, two natures), and the basic contours of the gospel message (the death, burial, descent, resurrection, ascension, session, and second coming of Christ). On more disputed doctrines, it is better to speak of *traditions*, plural, rather than *the* tradition, singular. Here, we might think of theories of the atonement, conceptions of the order of salvation, or views of the meaning of the church's ordinances. In both cases, contemporary Christian theologians should carefully attend to the history of Christian reflection. It would be folly to ignore this rich heritage and to attempt to reinvent the wheel, so to speak, by beginning from scratch in each new generation. Even on those points where we might feel compelled by Scripture to dissent from the tradition, we still do so from within the tradition and within its doctrinal history.[6] We stand on the shoulders of theological giants who have come before us and rely on countless faithful Christian interpreters, whose names we will never know this side of eternity. We respect their contributions even when we disagree. And on consensus doctrines, those beliefs that enjoy broad support among Christians across space and time and denomination, we gladly submit to the collective wisdom of the whole, Spirit-illumined church of Jesus Christ.[7]

Some sources of tradition command more authority than others. In other words, we can speak of a hierarchy of cascading authorities within the Christian tradition.[8] At the top of the hierarchy is, of course, Holy Scripture. Because Scripture alone is the inspired, written revelation of God, Scripture alone should be considered inerrant, infallible, and intrinsically authoritative. Scripture uniquely testifies to the definitive revelation of God in Jesus Christ and, indeed, *is* the written revelation of the mystery of Christ. Thus, Scripture is qualitatively different than subsequent Christian reflection on Scripture.

---

[6] See Stephen R. Holmes, *Listening to the Past: The Place of Tradition in Theology* (Carlisle, Cumbria, UK: Paternoster, 2002).

[7] See Thomas C. Oden, "The Faith Once Delivered: Nicaea and Evangelical Confession," in *Evangelicals and Nicene Faith: Reclaiming the Apostolic Witness*, ed. Timothy George (Grand Rapids: Baker Academic, 2011).

[8] See Oliver D. Crisp, *God Incarnate: Explorations in Christology* (London: Bloomsbury, 2009).

Ecumenical Creeds and Councils

But under Scripture's supreme authority are other sources of derivative authority that represent the standard Christian interpretations of Scripture's meaning and central message. In the next tier, then, are the *ecumenical creeds and councils.* *Ecumenical* in this context simply means "worldwide." There are three creeds (summary statements of belief) that have been received as ecumenical: the Apostles' Creed, the Nicene Creed, and the Athanasian Creed.[9] These creeds do not address every doctrinal matter, nor even every *important* doctrinal matter. But they do address the core or cardinal doctrines of the Christian faith, especially the Trinity, the Incarnation, and the gospel. Consider, for example, the Nicene Creed, which was originally formulated at the Council of Nicaea in 325 and further developed and finalized at the Council of Constantinople in 381:

> I believe in one God, the Father Almighty, Maker of heaven and earth, and of all things visible and invisible.
>
> And in one Lord Jesus Christ, the only-begotten Son of God, begotten of the Father before all worlds, God of God, Light of Light, very God of very God, begotten, not made, being of one substance with the Father; by whom all things were made; who for us men, and for our salvation, came down from heaven, and was incarnate by the Holy Ghost of the Virgin Mary, and was made man, and was crucified also for us under Pontius Pilate; He suffered and was buried; and the third day He rose again according to the Scriptures; and ascended into heaven, and sitteth on the right hand of the Father; and He shall come again with glory to judge the quick and the dead; whose kingdom shall have no end.
>
> And I believe in the Holy Ghost, the Lord and Giver of life, who proceedeth from the Father and the Son; who with the Father and the Son together is worshiped and glorified; who spake by the Prophets. And I believe in one holy catholic and apostolic Church. I acknowledge one Baptism for the remission of sins; and I look for the resurrection of the dead, and the life of the world to come. Amen.

---

[9] See Justin S. Holcomb, *Know the Creeds and Councils* (Grand Rapids: Zondervan, 2014).

Several elements are especially worthy of note in this classic statement of Christian belief. First, note the creed's trinitarian structure and content. The creed has three main articles—one on each of the three divine persons. Within this threefold structure, the main tenets of classical trinitarianism are explicated: essential sameness ("of one substance with the Father" and "who with the Father and the Son together is worshiped and glorified") and personal distinctions ("begotten of the Father" and "who proceeds from the Father and the Son"). In short, God is one in essence and three in persons. The three share all the same essential properties: all the divine attributes can be ascribed equally and eternally to all three divine persons. But the three are personally distinguished by their relations to one another; that is, by their so-called eternal relations of origin: the Father is begotten of no one; the Son is eternally begotten of the Father; and the Spirit eternally proceeds from the Father and the Son.

Second, note that the second article of the creed, the article on the Son, is the longest and most detailed. This partly reflects the nature of the fourth-century controversies that gave rise to the Nicene Creed. While the true deity of the Holy Spirit was an important element in the trinitarian controversy (especially debates with the heretical group known as Macedonians), the most seminal and sustained debates concerned the status of the Son in relation to the Father. Against the Arians, Eunomians, and other heretical groups, the creed clearly affirms the equality—indeed, the sameness—of the Son to the Father in terms of the divine essence. The Son is "of the same substance" (Greek, *homoousios*; Latin, *consubstantialis*) as the Father. But the second article also includes more detail because it explicates the main contours of the Christian gospel in the work of Christ. The creed recounts the great story of redemption, what John Calvin called "the whole course" of Christ's obedience: his conception, suffering, death, burial, descent, resurrection, ascension, session, and second coming.[10] This fulsome summary of the work of Christ would go a long way in our own day toward correcting certain truncated versions of the gospel.

Third, note that the final article of the creed frames the church's life in terms of the person and work of the Holy Spirit. The creed reminds us that life between the ascension of Christ and the world to come is Pentecostal

---

[10] See John Calvin, *Institutes of the Christian Religion*.

life—life enabled and enriched by the Spirit who is the Lord and Giver of life. To certain contemporary ears, the third article may sound like a grab bag of doctrines: the church, baptism, the resurrection, and eternal life. But its coherence lies in the work of the Holy Spirit: the Spirit applies the work of Christ to the church and sustains her until the final consummation.

Just as there are three ecumenical creeds, so there are seven ancient councils that have been accepted as ecumenical; their doctrinal decisions have been accepted by all branches of Christianity. Below is a tabular summary of the seven councils, the heresies that they addressed, and the doctrinal conclusions that they reached.

The Seven Ecumenical Councils

Council	Date	Result	Heresies Condemned
Nicaea	325	Affirmed that the Son is *homoousios* (of same substance) as the Father	Arianism
Constantinople	381	Reaffirmed Nicaea; fuller statement on the Holy Spirit	Arianism, Macedonianism
Ephesus	431	Affirmed Mary as *theotokos* (the God-bearer) and thus affirmed the unity of Christ's person	Nestorianism
Chalcedon	451	Defined the *hypostatic* (=personal) union; Christ is one person with two natures "without confusion, without change, without division, without separation"	Arianism, Apollinarianism, Eutychianism, Nestorianism

Constantinople II	553	Condemned the "Three Chapters" of the Nestorians; reaffirmed that the person of Christ is the Second Person of the Trinity	Nestorianism
Constantinople III	680–81	Affirmed that the Son has two wills, proper to his two natures	Monothelitism
Nicaea II	787	Affirmed the veneration of icons based on the true humanity of Christ; NOTE: This substance of this council would later be rejected by some Protestants	Iconoclasm

Space does not permit a full exposition of these doctrinal decisions, but the important thing to note is that the councils, like the creeds, address doctrines of primary importance, especially the Trinity and the incarnation.[11] In many ways, the first two councils settled the issue of the Trinity (culminating in the Nicene Creed), and the final five councils then turned to address the incarnation: How can the second person of the Trinity be both true God and true man?

In short, the ecumenical creeds and councils summarize the basic teaching of the historic Christian church on the cardinal doctrines of the faith. In this way, the creeds and councils function as a formalized "Rule of Faith," the accepted standard for any truly *Christian* interpretation of Scripture. This "Great Tradition" can also be expressed in the terms of the Vincentian Canon, the rule put forth by Vincent of Lerins (400–450): "Care must be taken, that we hold that faith which has been believed everywhere [*ubique*],

---

[11] See Leo Donald Davis, *The First Seven Ecumenical Councils (325–787): Their History and Theology* (Collegeville, MD: Liturgical Press, 1983).

always [*semper*], and by all [*ab omnibus*]."[12] We might wonder if any doctrine can meet such an exacting standard. But, in fact, there is remarkable unanimity on these core doctrinal commitments. Traditions as diverse as high church Anglicanism and low church Pentecostalism both affirm the doctrine of the Trinity and the two natures of Christ. All orthodox Christian denominations affirm the death, physical resurrection, and literal return of Christ. Some ecclesial communions might have the creedal language more ready at hand, but even communions that might not nevertheless affirm the core doctrinal judgments of the creeds and councils.

Confessions of Faith

A second tier of tradition comes in the form of *confessions of faith*. As I am using the terms, what distinguishes a confession from a creed is the particularity of the former and the universality of the latter. In other words, the creeds are affirmed by all Christians everywhere (e.g., Nicene Creed), but confessions are affirmed by specific churches or assemblies of churches (e.g., Westminster Confession of Faith). Confessions of faith have some doctrinal overlap with the creeds, but they tend to be more specific and detailed on secondary and tertiary matters (such as the specifics of soteriology, church polity, and eschatology). Confessions of faith still have a kind of authority over those who voluntarily subscribe to them. For example, the Baptist Faith and Message (2000) functions as a boundary marker for cooperation in some important ways within the Southern Baptist Convention. But (hopefully) no Southern Baptist would want to insist that the BF&M is a requirement for all Christians everywhere. Still, the great Baptist confessions of faith (e.g., the London Baptist Confessions of the Particular Baptists or the Orthodox Creed of the General Baptists) serve as important markers for the Baptist tradition.[13] Even if contemporary Baptist theologians do not strictly

---

[12] Cited in John A. Hardon, *Catholic Dictionary: An Abridged and Updated Edition of Modern Catholic Dictionary* (New York: Image, 2013).

[13] See William L. Lumpkin, ed. *Baptist Confessions of Faith* (Valley Forge, PA: Judson, 1959).

subscribe to one of these historic confessions of faith, they would still do well to study them with due respect to this rich Baptist heritage.

Respected Theologians

A step below both creeds and confessions are the works of what we might call the *theological masters* in the history of Christian thought. Luminaries such as Augustine, Thomas Aquinas, John Calvin, and John Wesley do not rise to the level of creedal or confessional authority. But their works have been profoundly influential and are widely recognized as deserving special honor and consideration. These are value judgments, obviously. The list of recognized authorities is not fixed or universally agreed upon. But generally, the theologians whose works have stood the test of time at least deserve some level of respect and interaction, even if we do not follow them on every point. Beyond these theological giants, we might simply list *learned theological opinions*. Trusted books and authors from the past (and even the present) also constitute a part of the rich tradition of the church. As with all authorities under the supreme authority of Scripture, we test these sources of tradition according to their conformity to the definitive revelation of God in the Bible. We ought to treat the tradition with respect and deference, but also, as the noble Bereans, we ought to examine the Scriptures daily to see if these things are so (Acts 17:11).

Conclusion

As we have noted, the Christian tradition possesses no intrinsic divine authority. It is not a source of divine revelation. It is not inspired and inerrant, as the Scriptures are. But the tradition does possess a kind of derivative authority to the degree it conforms to Scripture, as the consensus of the faithful have interpreted it throughout history. Not every part of the tradition possesses equal authority, however. The ancient creeds and councils represent the broadest consensus and therefore carry the most weight. Confessions of faith are narrower but still represent the consensus of certain churches and denominations. The works of respected individual theologians are also a part of the tradition but carry relatively less weight than these communal statements. Christians, including evangelicals and Baptists, have good biblical and theological reasons to appeal to the tradition, and we would do well to become more familiar with the rich resources it affords us. In sum, the Christian tradition plays a crucial role in the theological task because God has made us historical creatures, because he is providentially guiding the church throughout history, because he has covenantally united believers to one another in the body of Christ, and because he has promised to illuminate the whole Spirit-indwelt church in every age until Jesus returns. In these ways, the theologian attuned to the Great Tradition is, to use the words of our Lord, like a scribe trained for the kingdom, "like a master of a house, who brings out of his treasure what is new and what is old" (Matt 13:52 ESV).

FOR ADDITIONAL STUDY

Calvin, John. *Institutes of the Christian Religion.* 2 vols. Philadelphia: Westminster, 1960.

Crisp, Oliver D. *God Incarnate: Explorations in Christology.* London: Bloomsbury, 2009.

Davis, Leo Donald. *The First Seven Ecumenical Councils (325–787): Their History and Theology.* Collegeville, MD: Liturgical Press, 1983.

Dockery, David S., and Timothy George. *The Great Tradition of Christian Thinking.* Reclaiming the Christian Intellectual Tradition. Wheaton: Crossway, 2012.

Hardon, John A. *Catholic Dictionary: An Abridged and Updated Edition of Modern Catholic Dictionary.* New York: Image, 2013.

Holcomb, Justin S. *Know the Creeds and Councils.* Grand Rapids: Zondervan, 2014.

Holmes, Stephen R. *Listening to the Past: The Place of Tradition in Theology.* Carlisle, Cumbria, UK: Paternoster, 2002.

Irenaeus. *On the Apostolic Preaching.* Translated by John Behr. Crestwood, NY: St. Vladimir's Seminary Press, 1997.

Lumpkin, William L., ed. *Baptist Confessions of Faith*. Valley Forge, PA: Judson, 1959.

Oberman, Heiko A. *Forerunners of the Reformation: The Shape of Late Medieval Thought*. New York: Holt, Rhinehart, and Winston, 1966.

Oden, Thomas C. "The Faith Once Delivered: Nicaea and Evangelical Confession." In *Evangelicals and Nicene Faith: Reclaiming the Apostolic Witness*. Edited by Timothy George. Grand Rapids: Baker Academic, 2011.

O'Keefe, John J., and R. R. Reno. *Sanctified Vision: An Introduction to Early Christian Interpretation of the Bible*. Baltimore: Johns Hopkins University, 2005.

Stamps, R. Lucas. "*Norma Normata*: The Role of Tradition in Analytic Theology." In *T&T Clark Handbook of Analytic Theology*. Edited by James M. Arcadi and James T. Turner. London: Bloomsbury, 2021.

Also see these articles: Hermeneutics, Historical Theology

7

Christian Experience

Harry L. Poe

All people are created by God with the capacity for experience of the world. Made in the image of God, people also have the capacity for spiritual experience, often referred to as religious experience. Spiritual experience, however, should not be confused with what the New Testament regards as faith, repentance, conversion, or salvation, which are unique to Christian experience.

Experience

Human experience involves more than simply what happens to a human. Things happen to rocks and amoebas, but inanimate objects and the lowest forms of life do not have experience. Rocks and amoebas never learn from the things that happen to them. The ability to learn things, however, forms one of the marks of humanity. The Romans had three words to describe different aspects of knowledge. *Scientia*, from which we get the word "science," referred to knowledge in general. *Sapientia* referred to "wisdom." A person may have factual information without having the wisdom to act or respond in the face of that information. *Experientia*, from which we get the words "experience" and "experiment," refers to what we learn from the things that happen to us. *Experientia* deals with the knowledge people acquire from finding things out and putting matters to the test. By its nature, it is personal. Some people never learn from experience. Put another way, "The fear of the LORD is the beginning of knowledge; fools despise wisdom and discipline" (Prov 1:7).

The five senses provide humans with a large capacity for learning from experience. Empirical knowledge that comes from hearing, seeing, smelling, tasting, and touching provides humans with immediate information. Information, however, is not the same as knowledge. Information requires interpretation. The nerve endings provide the brain with information, but the brain must make sense of the data. Rational knowledge involves how the intellect understands the world. The intellect exercises reason to determine what the empirical data means. Over the course of the past three thousand years of Western civilization, the culture has vacillated between the options of whether empirical knowledge or rational knowledge should take priority.

Plato took the view that empirical data was the least reliable form of knowledge. People often misunderstand what their senses tell them. He took the view that human reason is the most reliable path to truth because he assumed that the human mind has a divine origin and that in its essence, the mind is an eternal aspect of the divine that will return to the divine. Plato's divine absolute, however, did not involve a personal God. Plato's student Aristotle, on the other hand, gave preference to empirical knowledge. The modern world is largely influenced by Aristotle's perspective, and our folk philosophy reflects it with such phrases as "seeing is believing" and "the proof is in the pudding."

The Greek philosophers, including Aristotle, assumed that rationalism would provide humans with perfect knowledge of the divine. The history of Greek philosophy is the history of the failure of rationalism to arrive at the knowledge of God. The Platonists, Aristotelians, Epicureans, Stoics, Pythagoreans, Sophists, and more arrived at their own views of God, but they all contradicted one another. Empiricism and rationalism provided imaginative alternative views of God but no certainty.

The insufficiency of empiricism and rationalism operating independently can be seen through the history of science. Empirical observation told our ancient forebears that the sun rises in the east in the morning, makes its way across the heavens in a slow arc, and then it sets in the west at the end of the day. Aristotle applied his reason to this empirical data and developed an elaborate explanation for how the universe works. Ptolemy worked out the math to explain how the sun and all the planets revolve around the earth. It was a highly complex system, but the math works to explain an earth-centered universe. Alas, the ancients were mistaken in their empirical observations and in their rationalistic explanations.[1]

At the beginning of his first letter to the Corinthians, Paul pointed out the shortcomings of empiricism and rationalism as ways to know God when he remarked, "Jews demand signs [empiricism] and Greeks look for wisdom [rationalism]" (1 Cor 1:22 NIV). In contrast to these two ways of knowing, Paul argued for the knowledge we may have of God through God's initiative to make himself known through the incarnation and sacrifice of Jesus. Paul did not repudiate empiricism and rationalism because, after all, they were not invented by humans. God endowed his creatures with these capacities. The frailty of humanity, however, means that the exercise of our ways of knowing never comes with certainty. Yet, the capacity for experiential knowledge has allowed humans to make extraordinary strides in our own daily well-being.

Spiritual Experience

Beyond the human experience of the world, humans also have the capacity for experiencing God. Very few people have ever been true atheists. Religion is a phenomenon in every culture. Even short-lived cultures like the communist state of the Soviet Union never succeeded in eradicating religion. Nonetheless, the tiny group of virulent atheists that springs up from time to time in many cultures has attempted to provide some explanation for the universal phenomenon of religion.

Karl Marx insisted that religion was an invention of the ruling class to keep the workers in subjugation. Sigmund Freud argued that the idea of God is a psychological projection of a good and loving father on the universe. Richard Dawkins simply declares that God is a delusion and religion is a great evil. The purpose of this essay is not to refute these views, but in acknowledging these adversaries of belief in God, a brief response is in order.

Marx's argument fails in the face of his own system. The full power and force of the communist state in China has attempted to erase religion, but in

---

[1] See Mi-Kyoung Lee, *Epistemology after Protagoras: Responses to Relativism in Plato, Aristotle, and Democritus* (Oxford: Clarendon, 2005).

the face of deadly persecution, Christianity has grown from approximately one million faithful followers of Christ in 1978 to more than 125 million by 2020. Religion is not the tool of the ruling class in China. People believe in Jesus Christ despite the power of the ruling class. Freud's argument fails in the face of logic. On the one hand, Freud and others argue that the idea of a loving father is a projection on the universe while at the same time arguing that the universe is full of danger, calamity, and death. The primitive religion of every continent saw the gods as dangerous and malevolent. A good God stands at odds with human experience of nature. A good and loving God is not a projection. That idea came from some other source than empirical experience of nature.[2] As for Dawkins, he does not really make an argument. He simply makes a complaint. He does not like the idea of God. He relies on the reliability of empiricism and insists that God should be treated like any other physical experiment.[3]

When we speak of the human spirit by which people have spiritual experience, we tend to be vague about what we mean. This vagueness can often lead to a misunderstanding of the very nature of spiritual experience. Humans do not have a consensus between cultures about the meaning of the human spirit and what it is. This short essay will not explore all the alternative views but will focus on what the Bible says about the human spirit. The spirit is the locus of a variety of human activities. In the discussions of the human spirit in the Bible, it is the seat of the intellect, the emotions, the character, the will, the imagination, and vitality itself. Furthermore, the human spirit is bound to the body as a psychosomatic whole, as a living soul (Gen 2:7). The glory of humans is that we are made in the image of God (Gen 1:27). The tragedy of humans is that we have fallen short of the glory of God (Rom 3:23). Though all humans have a spiritual dimension, the spirit is corrupted and flawed by sin. This corruption affects our thought processes, our emotions, our character, our will, our imagination, and ultimately our lives.

In creating the universe and in creating humans, God made everything in such a way that humans are aware of God (Rom 1:19–20; Acts 17:26–27).

---

[2] See Walter Davis, *Inwardness and Existence: Subjectivity in Hegel, Heidegger, Marx, and Freud* (Madison, WI: University of Wisconsin Press, 1989).

[3] See Richard Dawkins, *The God Delusion* (Boston: Houghton Mifflin, 2006).

Awareness of the existence of an eternal, divine being is not the same as faith or salvation, however, for the devil and his angels also know that God exists (Jas 2:19). The corruption of the human spirit means that humans not only have the capacity to know of God but also to distort that knowledge, just as we have the capacity to misrepresent the motion of the planets around the earth. While acknowledging universal spiritual experience, Paul declared that the history of religion is the history of the human distortion of the truth of God (Rom 1:21–23).

While our bodies make empirical observations of the physical world and its majesty, our spirits make sense of those observations, especially our imaginations. The imagination is that unusual aspect of the human spirit that allows us to transcend time and space. We are so accustomed to the imagination's operation that we rarely notice it. Our imaginations allow us to travel into the future and plan what we will do or say. Our imaginations allow us to see things we have not yet done. Every major scientific discovery comes from the imagination rather than from the calculating, reasoning intellect. The imagination sees things and hears things. Our daydreams are examples of this capacity. When a scientist such as Charles Townes suddenly knows that he can alter the behavior of light by stimulating it with emissions of radiation, thus inventing the laser, his imagination gives him immediate knowledge. This kind of knowledge is not a delusion. In contrast, a psychotic person sees things and hears things that are delusional. The human spirit, particularly in the domain of the imagination, is both the organ for experiencing God—think of the prophets and apostles receiving direct revelation from God—and for distorting that experience.[4]

In his study of the universality of spiritual experience, Rudolf Otto described three dimensions of the human encounter with God. He called it the *Mysterium, Tremendum, et Fascinans.* Spiritual experience is "mysterious."[5] It is not something that a human initiates, nor can the human repeat it by an exercise of the will. It is so different from all other human experience that it is unknown. No previous experience is like it. Spiritual experience is also

---

[4] See Charles Townes, *Making Waves* (Melville, NY: American Institute of Physics, 1995).

[5] See Rudolf Otto, *The Idea of the Holy,* 2nd ed. (Oxford: Oxford University Press, 1958).

"tremendous" in the sense that it is powerful and has a frightfulness about it that evokes fear. Human frailty becomes apparent in the midst of the experience that elicits a sense of danger. Yet, spiritual experience is also "fascinating," for we are drawn to the experience despite the danger. An example of what Otto describes can be seen when Moses came upon the burning bush (Exod 3:1–4:17).

Christian Experience

Christian experience of God goes beyond the spiritual experience common to all people. Beyond the physical endowments that people have in order to perceive the world around them through sensory experience, and beyond the way that God created humans and the universe so that humans could recognize the existence of God behind the physical world, God has also made himself known in particular ways. Christians believe in a God who created the universe and who exists as three persons simultaneously without division, a Trinity. God exists eternally outside of created time and space, all-powerful and all-knowing and everywhere present. Further, he exists throughout all of the universe from below subatomic particles to above galaxies. God not only created the universe, but he also took on human form and lived the full life of a human from cradle to grave in the person of Jesus Christ. In these ways, God is at once the eternal Father, the loving Son, and the life-giving Holy Spirit—three persons, yet one God.

The Holy Spirit came upon people known as prophets and caused them to know the message they would deliver to the people. Anyone can claim to speak for God, so God declared to Moses a simple empirical test to know if someone had actually been inspired by God. God would give his messenger a sign, and if the sign came to pass, then everyone would know that the prophet had had a true experience with God and the message spoken had come from God (Deut 18:21–22; cf. Judges 6–7; 1 Sam 10:9). The sign to Abraham that he was having a genuine experience and not a psychotic episode was the promise of a son by Sarah when she was too old to give birth (Gen 18:10). The sign to Joseph that he had a genuine experience with God and not a delusion was seven years of plenty followed by seven years of famine (Genesis 41). The sign to Gideon that God was speaking to him came in the form of a wet fleece on dry grass followed by a dry fleece on wet grass

(Judg 6:36–40). Jesus gave his generation the "sign of Jonah" (Matt 12:39). Just as Jonah lay in the belly of the great fish for three days, Jesus would lie in the belly of the earth for three days and then rise.

All humans have spiritual experience, but not all spiritual experience comes from God or is valid. John warned the early church of false prophets and the need to test the spirits to see if they are from God (1 John 4:1–3). The Spirit of the Lord "came upon" the prophets and the servants of God, and they suddenly had profound ability to do whatever God had charged them to do (Judg 6:34; 11:29; 14:6; 1 Sam 10:10; 16:13; 1 Kgs 18:46). Yet, the Holy Spirit was not a possession of the figures in the Old Testament, for the Holy Spirit came and went. The sign of the curse of God was that the Holy Spirit should depart (1 Sam 16:14). The purpose of occult practices, which are found in every culture, is to gain control of the unseen power of the universe. No one, however, can cause the Holy Spirit to act. No one uses the Holy Spirit. Instead, the Holy Spirit overshadows people to accomplish the will of God. Simon the sorcerer made the mistake of thinking he could bargain for the power to control the Holy Spirit (Acts 8:9–24).

Under the old covenant, God promised Israel that he would be their God and give them a land of their own where he would protect them (Exod 6:7–8). They would live out their lives and then die. He also warned that if Israel did not follow him, he would take away their land and the covenant would come to an end. Deuteronomy reminded Israel of both the blessings and the curses attached to the old covenant (Deuteronomy 28). Whenever God sent a prophet to foretell the doom of Israel and Judah, however, he also offered the promise of a new covenant written on the heart by the Holy Spirit that he would pour out on everyone, not just a few prophets (Jer 31:31–34; Joel 2:28–32). The new covenant would involve the removal of sin and the changing of the very nature of those faithful to God from children of the dust to children of God who share everlasting life (Zech 3:8–9; Mal 3:1–3; Isa 32:15). Under the new covenant, God destroys death itself and bestows everlasting life (Isa 25:8; 26:19).

At the Last Supper, Jesus explained that his death constituted the sacrifice that confirmed the new covenant when he took the cup and said, "This cup is the new covenant in my blood, which is poured out for you" (Luke 22:20). Though the new covenant involves factual information about God and the plan for the ages, the heart of the new covenant involves knowing and being known by God. In the Sermon of the Mount, Jesus warned that religious involvement is irrelevant apart from being known by him (Matt 7:23). The apostle Paul declared that everything on earth was rubbish compared with knowing Christ (Phil 3:8). The essence of the Christian faith is the present and everlasting experience that the believer has with Jesus Christ.

The Gospels of Matthew, Mark, and Luke were written before the Jewish War of AD 66 and the destruction of the temple that brought an end to the religion of the Old Testament in AD 70. These Gospels were written to churches with large Jewish memberships who would have known the prophecies of the new covenant. The Gospel of John, however, was written around the year AD 90 after the large influx of Jewish believers had come to an end. The Gentile Christians for whom John wrote had a pagan past and knew nothing of the Old Testament Scriptures or the prophecies of God. For the Gentiles, John devoted one-fourth of his entire Gospel to the conversation over the table at the Last Supper in which Jesus described what it means for the Holy Spirit to come.

Jesus explained that though he was leaving, the Holy Spirit would be with his disciples forever (John 14:16–17; 16:7). Jesus explained that when the Holy Spirit comes, he comes also (John 14:18). When the Holy Spirit takes up residence within a human heart, the Father and the Son also reside in that person (John 14:23). In this way, Jesus described in John 15:4 the relationship between him and believers as "abiding" (KJV; ESV) or "remaining" (CSB; NIV). The point is that Christianity involves a permanent relationship with Jesus Christ and not merely acknowledgment of information about Jesus. Satan accepts the information but trembles (Jas 2:19).

At the moment of faith, believers are immersed in and by the Holy Spirit who transfigures them from children of the dust to children of God (Gal 3:2, 26). This was what Jesus explained to Nicodemus about the need to be born again by the Holy Spirit and what he explained to the woman at the well about living water (John 3:3–8; 4:10–14). God had long ago explained to Moses that sinful humans cannot behold the glory of God and live. Human nature cannot exist in the presence of the holiness of God any more than paper can exist in the presence of fire. Sin is consumed by the holiness of God. By withholding himself from us, God protects us from destruction. Yet, God made us for fellowship with him. The nature of humans must be changed to exist in the presence of God. When someone believes in Jesus

Christ, he wraps them up in his own holiness as the Holy Spirit engulfs them. Baptist thinkers such as E. Y. Mullins and W. T. Conner emphasized the role of experience in shaping Christian theology, which represented both the best of pietism and the influence of F. D. E. Schleiermacher. Mullins defended the Bible on the basis of Christian experience both as to what was recorded in Scripture as well as what was confirmed by other believers through the centuries.[6]

The Life in Christ

God adopts the new believer at the moment of faith when the believer becomes enveloped by the Holy Spirit (Rom 8:14–17). Swallowed up by the Holy Spirit, Christians are "in Christ" and, thus, forever present with him. Through the Holy Spirit, eternally one with the Father and the Son, and across time and space, the new believer dies with Jesus Christ and rises with him, forever freed from the sinful flesh (Rom 6:1–11). The Greek word transliterated into English as "baptize" means to be completely immersed, covered over, or incorporated into something else. The practice of Christian baptism by which the believer goes under the water and then comes out of it provides a picture of what has happened to the believer at first salvation: immersed in the Holy Spirit, the believer is dead and buried with Christ and rises from the dead. From the moment of faith onward, the Christian is "in Christ." The apostle Paul could hardly write a sentence without using this phrase. It refers to the Christian's present relationship to the Lord Jesus Christ.

Not only are we crucified with Christ (present tense), but we are also seated (present tense) in Christ in the heavenly realms, where he is seated on the throne of majesty as King of kings and Lord of lords (Eph 2:4–7; Rev 19:16). Existing in Christ is not only the essence of salvation, but it is also the basis for the corporate experience of all Christians in the church, which Paul described as both the body of Christ and the temple of God (1 Cor 12:13; 2 Cor 6:16). Christ is the head of the body and the cornerstone of the temple (Eph 2:19–22; 4:15–16; Col 1:18).

---

[6] See E. Y. Mullins, *The Christian Religion in Its Doctrinal Expression* (Philadelphia: Judson, 1917), and W. T. Conner, *Revelation and God* (Nashville: Broadman, 1936).

Christians experience the immediate presence of Christ in many ways. Yet, weighed down by the cares of the world and its distractions, Christians do not necessarily have conscious awareness of their presence with Christ at all times. Jesus taught that the experience of his presence would be felt powerfully in certain situations. First, we may experience his presence when we gather with other believers in his name (Matt 18:20). Second, we may experience his presence when we minister to the needy as he did (Matt 25:40). Third, we may experience his presence when we partake of the Lord's Supper (1 Cor 10:16). We may also experience his presence when we bear witness to him (Matt 28:19–20). These are not the only ways, however, that Christians experience the presence of God.

At the Last Supper, Jesus made a number of clear promises about what it means to experience the indwelling of the Holy Spirit. First, Jesus said that the Holy Spirit would teach believers (John 14:26a). We see this promise fulfilled as Christians perceive guidance in personal and corporate decision-making and in grasping the implications of the gospel. Second, Jesus said that the Holy Spirit would call to our remembrance the things concerning him (John 14:26b). We see this promise fulfilled when Christians find themselves quoting or paraphrasing a passage of Scripture that they never memorized and that they do not even know in which book of the Bible it might be found. Third, Jesus promised that those who abide in him will bear much fruit (John 15:1–5). Paul explained that the Holy Spirit causes believers to gradually take on the character of Christ, which manifests itself in the fruit of the Spirit (Gal 5:22–25). This work of the Holy Spirit involves a gradual transformation of emotions, intellect, character, will, and imagination, along with immortality.

The experience of the Holy Spirit also involves illumination of knowledge and truth. Jesus promised that the Holy Spirit will convince the world there is such a thing as sin, there is such a thing as rightness, and there will be a judgment (John 16:8–11). It is the Holy Spirit, rather than philosophical speculation, that makes known spiritual reality. This fact relieves the believer of the burden of convincing anyone of these principles of spiritual reality. The Holy Spirit also guides the believer into truth (John 16:13). The Bible does not provide a rule for every decision a person may have to make in life. It is a divine resource in decision-making, but it does not contain a verse that explains which stocks I should buy or whether I should buy stocks at all. In decision-making, we have the Bible, but we also have immediate access to the Lord of glory through his Holy Spirit in prayer. Thus, Paul could explain to the Corinthians that we have access to the mind of Christ (1 Cor 2:16).

As Jesus consoled his disciples the night before his death, he promised another Comforter. Perhaps the hallmark of Christian experience is the comfort we find in Christ in times of trouble. In those moments, the distractions of the world fall away, and the presence of Christ becomes powerfully evident. At the Last Supper, Jesus stressed his intention to provide his disciples with joy, peace, and love (John 14:1; 15:11; 17:26).

For Additional Study

Augustine. *The Confessions of St. Augustine.* Translated by John K. Ryan. New York: Image, 1960.

Bunyan, John. *The Pilgrim's Progress: An Illustrated Edition.* Nashville: Thomas Nelson, 2019.

Mullins, E. Y. *The Christian Religion in Its Doctrinal Expression.* Philadelphia: Judson, 1917.

Packer, J. I. *Knowing God.* Downers Grove, IL: IVP, 1993.

Spener, Philip Jacob. *Pia Desideria.* Translated by Theodore Tappert. Philadelphia: Fortress, 1964.

Also see these articles: Revelation, Holy Scripture, Holy Spirit, Sanctification, Spiritual Formation

PART II
TYPES OF THEOLOGY

8

Biblical Theology

J. Scott Duvall

C hristians have always been interested in the theological message of the whole Bible and how that message affects the Christian life, both individually and corporately. This is the central concern of the discipline known as biblical theology (BT). In what follows we provide an overview of BT, both its theory and practice. Then we attempt to define BT by considering the essential elements of the discipline. We explore the relationship between BT and other theological disciplines such as historical, systematic, and practical theology. Next, we identify the guiding assumptions and overall methodology of BT. The goal of BT remains important to identify since it affects not only the academy but also the church. We finish our introduction to BT by explaining the various ways of doing BT and looking more closely at an explicitly evangelical approach to the discipline. If the Scriptures are inspired by God, one would expect an overarching message from the divine Author that is coherent and captivating. Many scholars turn to BT to help uncover just such a whole-Bible message.

Defining Biblical Theology

While there is disagreement among nonevangelicals about how to best define BT, evangelical biblical theologians find more in common and define BT in ways that incorporate the following essential elements:[1]

- Canonical—BT limits itself to the Scriptures and seeks a whole-Bible theology.
- Exegetical—BT draws its teachings from a careful analysis of the biblical texts.
- Theological/Christological—As to content, BT focuses on God's revelation of himself that centers in Jesus Christ.
- Historical and descriptive—BT emphasizes the progressive unfolding of God's revelation by never losing sight of the overarching storyline of Scripture.
- Synthetic—BT seeks to synthesize the Bible's teachings and themes in a coherent manner.
- Ecclesiological—BT is committed to reading Scripture in and for the church.

As Brian Rosner contends, BT is "principally concerned with the overall theological message of the whole Bible."[2] It is "the attempt to grasp Scripture in its totality according to its own, rather than imposed, categories."[3] For this reason, and as the above elements illustrate, BT involves the literary/linguistic, historical, and theological realities of the biblical text and how these relate within the canon of Scripture for Christian believers. For the biblical theologian, exegesis of the whole biblical text is foundational. The interpreter takes seriously not only the language and literature of Scripture but its historical context as well. The various themes and teachings of the Bible about God and his relation to the world are analyzed and synthesized

---

[1] Larry R. Helyer, *The Witness of Jesus, Paul and John: Explorations in Biblical Theology* (Downers Grove: IVP Academic, 2008), 21–22.

[2] Brian S. Rosner, "Biblical Theology," in *New Dictionary of Biblical Theology* (Downers Grove: IVP, 2000), 3.

[3] Craig Bartholomew, "Biblical Theology and Biblical Interpretation: Introduction," in Bartholomew et al., *Out of Egypt: Biblical Theology and Biblical Interpretation* (Grand Rapids: Baker, 2015), 4.

in their individual contexts and in light of the Bible's overarching storyline. This interpretation is done by the church and for the church.

The Relation of Biblical Theology to Other Theological Disciplines

BT is related to but distinct from other theological disciplines, specifically historical, systematic, and practical theology. Historical theology focuses on the development of Christian thought through the history of the church. It seeks to formulate the origin of the church's theology and show how it has developed by highlighting the creeds, confessions, doctrines, and traditions of the church. Historical theology provides a sense of historical context for evaluating current theological trends. BT is more focused on the exegesis and synthesis of biblical texts than on how they have been understood throughout Christian history.

Systematic theology attempts to organize and systematize biblical truth. Systematic theology orders its finding logically and topically according to the chosen system. The division of topics involve some or all of the following: Bible, God, angels, humanity, sin, Israel, Jesus, salvation, Holy Spirit, Church, and end times, all using proper theological designations, of course (e.g., eschatology or ecclesiology). Systematic theology is more concerned with logic and philosophical connections while BT centers more on the historical and literary contexts and the overall theological message of Scripture. While systematic theology can certainly be done in a way that is faithful to Scripture, it is one step removed from the biblical text when compared to BT.

Practical or pastoral theology gives priority to the application of biblical truths for the contemporary church. This aspect of theology focuses on the outworking of biblical thought for the life of the church, including evangelism, discipleship, missions, pastoral ministry, and the like. In many ways, practical theology is the "so what?" of the other theological disciplines. BT serves as foundational to practical theology.

Biblical exegesis serves as the foundation for all the theological disciplines, and exegesis, in turn, should be informed by continued theological reflection.

The final authority is the Bible, but our understanding of the Bible's teachings does not always come to us in a neat, clean, linear manner. The feedback loop illustrates the organic, dynamic process of constant interaction between the theological disciplines.

The Guiding Assumptions of Biblical Theology

BT has certain guiding assumptions.[4] These begin with the Bible itself. "All Scripture is inspired by God," Paul writes in 2 Tim 3:16, meaning among other things that God is the source of the entire Bible. BT should be whole-Bible biblical theology (see the emphasis on biblical storyline below). God has chosen to reveal himself in human language in the Scriptures, and here we find the essence of theology—a discourse about the God who has revealed himself. BT should never become disconnected from its grounding in faithful biblical exegesis.

The Bible is coherent in telling a single story, and while God has used different human authors in the process, the divine Author has not contradicted himself. There are tensions to be sure, and some parts of Scripture emphasize different aspects of a particular truth. But Scripture's essential unity is grounded in God himself. The coherence of the Bible's message is an important assumption of BT.

In addition, Scripture is also trustworthy, reliable, and beneficial for both the individual Christian and the entire church (cf. 2 Tim 3:16–17). As Larry R. Helyer says, "Biblical theology is thus not merely descriptive but rather is normative as well."[5] As we will discuss below, the goal of BT is to be found in the faith and practice of the church.

Along with a high view of Scripture's inspiration, unity, and reliability, BT presupposes the Christocentric (or perhaps Christotelic) nature of the Bible. BT sees Christ playing a central role in the Bible's theology, whether the vantage point is of anticipation or fulfillment. God's relationship to the world centers in Christ, and BT takes notice. The guiding assumptions of BT can be summed up using these terms: canonical and exegetical, coherent, church-related, and Christ-focused.

---

[4] Robert W. Yarbrough, "Biblical Theology," in Walter Elwell, ed., *Evangelical Dictionary of Biblical Theology* (Grand Rapids: Baker, 1996), 62.

[5] Helyer, *The Witness of Jesus, Paul, and John*, 22.

Methodology Used in Biblical Theology

The overarching methodology of BT involves a partnership between exegetical analysis and theological synthesis. We begin with the analytical phase.
BT is rooted and grounded in careful, responsible biblical exegesis. There
is no substitute for the unhurried exegesis of individual books/sections of
Scripture in their own historical and literary contexts. The temptation to
read one book in light of another should be resisted at this stage as each
book/section is understood on its own terms. The goal here is to listen to
what the Spirit is saying through the human author's intended meaning of
a particular book. Careful exegesis includes textual criticism, background
study, and literary analysis.

The result of exegetical analysis is theological synthesis. What are those
theological truths and principles that emerge from the text? What are the
leading theological ideas and themes that flow from the careful study of the
text? The same movement from analysis to synthesis that was applied to the
smaller units of sections and books is now applied to larger sections of all
the writings of a particular author (e.g., Paul's letters), an entire genre (e.g.,
the Gospels or OT Wisdom literature), each testament, and then the entire
canon of Scripture. Scholars have attempted theological synthesis in various
ways (see below on "Ways of Doing BT").

The Goal of Biblical Theology

The goal of BT is tied to the goal of the entire Bible, and this certainly moves
beyond a mere academic exercise to a spiritual/relational one. The point is
not simply to arrive at a deeper knowledge of the storyline of Scripture but
to know and love the divine Author more deeply. Helyer identifies the goal
of BT as three-dimensional: (1) the obedience and spiritual growth of the
individual believer, (2) the building up of the body of Christ, the church, and
(3) the glory of God.[6] This final aspect deserves additional comment.

Most readers likely understand "glory" as praise, but there is more to
"glory" than praise. When discussing the validity of formulating centers or

---

[6] Helyer, *The Witness of Jesus, Paul and John*, 42–43.

storylines in BT, G. K. Beale promotes the storyline approach but sees the glory of God as the "uppermost goal even within the storyline."[7] He writes, "God's glory should be seen as the major point in the storyline, since it is the ultimate goal . . . the ultimate goal, then, of this storyline hub is God's glory."[8] Earlier in the chapter Beale defines "God's glory" as both praise and presence: "God's glory, both his very essence and the glorious praise offered for who he is and what he has done, is the *goal* of the overall storyline that I have formulated."[9] Bauckham follows suit by understanding "glory" as (1) honor, prestige, and reputation (i.e., praise), and (2) visible splendor in the sense of glorious presence.[10]

In this context, Beale suggests that "divine presence is almost synonymous with God's glory." Danny Hays and I have argued elsewhere that God's relational presence is the cohesive center of BT.[11] This relates directly to the goal of BT. What is the relationship between praise and presence? We conclude, "We see glory (in the sense of praise) to be the result of glory (in the sense of presence). Presence precedes praise and makes it possible. Praise is the ultimate result of presence. Praise flows from presence, which makes presence even more central to the Bible's main message."[12] This is not to downplay the glorious praise deserved by our God but to emphasize an even more foundational goal—the experience of God's glorious, relational presence. Presence is the ultimate reason for creation. It lies at the heart of the covenant. Presence describes the result of the kingdom, supplies the goal of the gospel, and stands as the final chapter of God's salvation story. The goal of doing BT should be to understand and experience God's glorious presence in the life of discipleship in the context of the church, all resulting in praise and thanksgiving.

---

[7] G. K. Beale, *New Testament Biblical Theology: The Unfolding of the Old Testament in the New* (Grand Rapids: Baker Academic, 2011), 182.

[8] Beale, 183.

[9] Beale, 175.

[10] Richard Bauckham, *Gospel of Glory: Major Themes in Johannine Theology* (Grand Rapids: Baker Academic, 2015), 43–62, 72–74.

[11] J. Scott Duvall and Danny Hays, *God's Relational Presence: The Cohesive Center of Biblical Theology* (Grand Rapids: Baker Academic, 2019), esp. 1–11, 325–36.

[12] Duvall and Hays, 329.

Various Ways of Doing Biblical Theology

There are multiple ways of doing BT as a survey of publications will demonstrate.[13] Klink and Lockett define BT by describing various approaches to the discipline along a spectrum stretching from the more historical to the more theological.[14] They identify five main ways of doing BT. The five types include historical description, history of redemption, worldview-story, canonical approach, and theological construction. We will briefly survey their fivefold taxonomy.[15]

BT as historical description is concerned with "what it meant" and restricts itself to describing the theology of the biblical authors. There is no theological integration between the various books or between the testaments and no concern with the religious value of the message for today's readers. James Barr would represent this approach.

The history of redemption approach focuses on tracing God's redemptive acts throughout the Scriptures. This approach values and uses history but for theological purposes. Whole-Bible BT as seen through God's progressive revelation is given priority. A theological unity can be seen between the testaments through thematic-typological connections that grow out of solid biblical exegesis. "What it means" is added to "what it meant" as BT is ultimately done for the church. D. A. Carson represents this approach.

BT as worldview-story tries to balance history and theology by concentrating on the overarching narrative shape of the Bible. This "story" of Scripture represents the Bible's theology. This approach highlights a rich intertextual reading of the whole Bible. N. T. Wright would be a proponent of this approach.

The canonical approach attempts to connect the diverse teachings of Scripture under the umbrella of the Christian canon. This results in a unified theological witness to the true subject of the Bible: Jesus Christ. Since the canon is ultimately a confessional document, this approach is rooted in the

---

[13] Eckhard J. Schnabel, "Biblical Theology from a New Testament Perspective," *JETS* 62, no. 2 (June 2019): 225–44.

[14] See Edward W. Klink III and Darian R. Lockett, *Understanding Biblical Theology: A Comparison of Theory and Practice* (Grand Rapids: Zondervan, 2012).

[15] Schnabel, 20–25, 186–89.

church even while using the tools of the academy. Brevard Childs represents this approach.

BT as theological construction gives priority to the church's theology rather than the historical reconstructions of the academy. This position is often associated with the hermeneutical method known as the theological interpretation of Scripture as both emphasize BT as coming under owner-ship of the church. Francis Watson would be a proponent of this approach.

There are many ways of doing BT, but all of the above approaches wres-tle with two primary relationships. First, what is the relationship between history and theology, between what it meant and what it means? How one understands the unity and diversity of the Bible comes into play here. Second, what is the correlation between the academy and the church? Which body is the leading guardian and recipient of the Bible's theology?

An Evangelical Approach to Biblical Theology

The diversity of the Bible is self-evident given the numerous authors, genres, and situations. What is much harder to grasp is the unity of the Bible, and this is the chief evangelical contribution to BT.[16] To begin with, evangeli-cals presuppose the Bible's inspiration and authority stemming from its one divine Author (2 Tim 3:15–17; 2 Pet 1:20–21). As a result, evangelicals see BT as *theological*; that is, grounded in and flowing from God's nature. The Spirit's superintending authorship of Scripture ensures a coherent, unified message that makes BT possible for the whole Bible.

For evangelicals, BT is also thoroughly *trinitarian*. Along with the theo-logical and pneumatological foci of BT, the discipline is also thoroughly Christological. Jesus Christ unites the two testaments. The covenants, the storyline, and the central themes are all rooted in Christ. Whether the Bible should be read as Christocentric or Christotelic remains up for debate, but there is no doubt that Christ himself occupies a central place in unifying the Scriptures (Luke 24:25–27, 44–49; John 5:39). God has revealed himself as Father, Son, and Spirit, and this trinitarian shape of the Bible surfaces repeatedly in the doing of BT (see Matt 28:19–20).

---

[16] See Helyer, *The Witness of Jesus, Paul, and John*, 79–82.

The unity of the Bible can also be seen when it is read as a *single, redemptive story*. This one overarching story of redemption and restoration runs from Genesis to Revelation as promises that were made early on are fulfilled throughout the rest of the story. Promise-fulfillment plays a key role in how redemptive history unfolds as God's self-revelation progresses through the entire story. In the Bible we find not just scattered fragments of unrelated stories, but a single coherent metanarrative. At its core this unified storyline includes creation, fall, redemption, and consummation. Each of the four major movements in the story can be expounded in much greater detail, but the whole remains intact and informs and guides the various parts.

Evangelicals also see a role for *typology* or recapitulation in unifying the Bible. Typology may be defined as the parallels between people, events, institutions, and stories, and their later analogous fulfillment. The former elements symbolize or prefigure later Christian beliefs. This is normally a partnership between the Old and New Testaments (e.g., creation and new creation, the sacrificial system and the sacrifice of Christ, the exodus and deliverance through Christ, the first and second Adam), but it can also be seen within the OT. Typology assumes a coherence to the overall message and a progression in revelation so that what God has said and done in earlier times finds its ultimate fulfillment later and especially in Christ.

Closely related to typology is *intertextuality*, but intertextuality understood in a particular way. Evangelicals tend to see intertextuality as a tool for understanding how "Scripture interprets Scripture," rather than in the more postmodern sense of how later texts give new meanings to earlier texts. Understanding how biblical texts draw on other biblical texts involves studying how Scripture quotes, alludes to, and echoes other Scripture, and how these intertextual relationships run between testaments and between biblical books.

A final way that evangelicals find unity in Scripture is through its *unifying themes*. Which mega-theme drives the biblical story by providing cohesion across the canon for other major themes? Is such a unifying center even possible? There have been many leading candidates, including the kingdom of God, God's glory, Christ, covenant, redemption, restoration, and divine presence, to name a few. The most likely unifying theme should drive the biblical storyline, provide the most comprehensive explanation of the various parts of Scripture and best account for the other main themes.

The Bible's trinitarian nature, redemptive story, typology, intertextuality, and unifying themes are certainly not mutually exclusive and are normally seen as interdependent and complementary. What makes all this possible is a hermeneutic that prioritizes divine authorial intention communicated through the human authors of Scripture.

Conclusion

One way of estimating the value of a theological discipline is to ask what would be lost if the discipline were eliminated altogether. Despite BT's struggle to define itself, the role of BT within evangelicalism at present is crucial. While all the theological disciplines build on careful, responsible exegesis, the link with BT seems most direct. Before looking at the logical organization of the Bible's teachings through systematics, the development of doctrine through historical theology, or the application of biblical truths through practical theology, BT offers insight into understanding the parts of Scripture in light of the whole. It is the essential next step from exegesis to the world of theological reflection that leads to application in the Christian life. In systematics, the link with exegesis can be diminished unless the theologian remains intentional and does not become overly fascinated with building a system. The risk is even greater with historical theology disconnected from BT. Without BT, practical theology can easily begin to provide solutions from sources other than the Bible. Even though people can "apply it to their lives," if what is being applied is not grounded in the Bible's overall message, the practitioner will not be helped and could easily be hurt. Bad or no BT ultimately hurts people!

In holding fast to the guiding assumptions and goal articulated above, BT will prove to be just the countercultural nourishment that the church needs amidst growing fragmentation and polarization. Knowing and loving the God of the Bible means listening to his story from beginning to end and giving the benefit of the doubt to the unity of its message. We have seen the fruit of endless critical approaches that emphasize analysis. They offer less-direct benefit to the church, although indirectly they can be of great help. BT, on the other hand, offers fresh access to an old message through faithful synthesis. This holistic message of the Bible is welcomed, needed, and understood by the contemporary church.

For Additional Study

Alexander, T. Desmond. *From Eden to the New Jerusalem: An Introduction to Biblical Theology*. Grand Rapids: Kregel, 2009.

Bartholomew, Craig G. "Biblical Theology and Biblical Interpretation: Introduction." In Bartholomew et al., *Out of Egypt: Biblical Theology and Biblical Interpretation*. Grand Rapids: Zondervan, 2004.

———, Mary Healy, Karl Möller, and Robin Parry, eds. *Out of Egypt: Biblical Theology and Biblical Interpretation*. Grand Rapids: Zondervan, 2004.

Bauckham, Richard. *Gospel of Glory: Major Themes in Johannine Theology*. Grand Rapids: Baker Academic, 2015.

Beale, G. K. *A New Testament Biblical Theology: The Unfolding of the Old Testament in the New*. Grand Rapids: Baker Academic, 2011.

Duvall, J. Scott, and J. Daniel Hays. *God's Relational Presence: The Cohesive Center of Biblical Theology*. Grand Rapids: Baker Academic, 2019.

Gentry, Peter John, and Stephen J. Wellum. *Kingdom through Covenant: A Biblical-Theological Understanding of the Covenants*. Wheaton: Crossway, 2012.

Goldingay, John. *Biblical Theology: The God of the Christian Scriptures*. Downers Grove: IVP, 2016.

Hamilton, James M., Jr. *God's Glory in Salvation through Judgment: A Biblical Theology*. Wheaton: Crossway, 2010.

Helyer, Larry R. *The Witness of Jesus, Paul and John: Explorations in Biblical Theology*. Downers Grove: IVP Academic, 2008.

Klink III, Edward W., and Darian R. Lockett. *Understanding Biblical Theology: A Comparison of Theory and Practice*. Grand Rapids: Zondervan, 2012.

Rosner, Brian S. "Biblical Theology," in *New Dictionary of Biblical Theology*. Downers Grove: IVP, 2000.

Schnabel, Eckhard J. "Biblical Theology from a New Testament Perspective." *JETS* 62, no. 2 (June 2019): 225–44.

Schreiner, Thomas R. *The King in His Beauty: A Biblical Theology of the Old and New Testaments.* Grand Rapids: Baker Academic, 2013.

Yarbrough, Robert W. "Biblical Theology." In Walter Elwell, ed., *Evangelical Dictionary of Biblical Theology.* Grand Rapids: Baker, 1996.

Also see these articles: Scripture, Hermeneutics, Systematic Theology

9

Historical Theology

Jonathan Arnold

A t its core, historical theology is the academic pursuit of understanding how God has continued to work for and through his people after the closing of the canon of Scripture and without the direct revelation of God himself regarding his ongoing activity.

Defining the Field: A Brief History and Definition

Historical theology is the area of academic study that asks its practitioners to consider the obviously human elements of a given context alongside the constant search for truth and clarity of that truth that characterizes the work of Christians for all time. It recognizes the extraordinary, yet foundational, claim that God continues to use mere humans to teach his people and that he calls his people to continue plumbing the depths of what the apostle Paul calls "the mystery of godliness" (1 Tim 3:16).

This field of study takes seriously the now-famous claim attributed to Bernard of Chartres, the twelfth-century theologian who noted that "we see more and farther than our predecessors, not because we have keener vision or greater height, but because we are lifted up and borne aloft on their gigantic stature." We, Bernard was evidently fond of saying, are but "[puny] dwarfs perched on the shoulders of giants."[1] Historical theology, then, aims to understand how we dwarfs have found our way onto those shoulders, strives to consider what all the other dwarfs have seen from their disparate perches, and, ultimately, attempts to distill what the God of Abraham, Isaac, and Jacob could possibly be teaching his people—his dwarfs—through the myriad reports across the millennia of Christian thought.

For sources, the historical theologian must consider both the Scriptures— for the evangelical Christian, the closed canon of Scripture necessarily takes a position of absolute authority—and the writings about those Scriptures that have been preserved for the benefit of posterity. But the historical theologian must also consider the broader cultural context of the writings and thoughts in question. The idea of a creation from nothing—*creatio ex nihilo*—applies to a singular event at the beginning of the cosmos when God spoke everything into existence. Beyond that, every writing about Scripture, every pastoral insight, every theological musing, and every personal letter from trail-blazing missionaries develops in the midst of a cultural context. They are preceded by various conversations and complex conflicts. Thus, the historical theologian considers far more sources than those obvious and necessary documents. They also consider, for example, the broader publishing context, the political and economic climate, the academic milieu of the age, as well as the more obvious denominational and broader theological traditions. In other words, the historical theologian draws from a wide array of sources and must, if she is to take the project seriously, engage with a broad spectrum of academic genres. This makes the study both dauntingly complex and incomparably valuable for the church as a whole.

Any discussion of the concept of historical theology invites its participants into a lengthy conversation that proves to be far more involved than most people would anticipate. Most contemporary readers do not naturally struggle with the mere phraseology of "historical theology." The very existence of that phrase causes little consternation, and, in fact, many readers— even those immersed in theological discussions—would happily gloss over the phrase without so much as a second thought. That majority simply accepts historical theology as the study of the development of Christian doctrine across time. To them, the field of historical theology takes as her

---

[1] John of Salisbury, *Metalogicon*, trans. and ed. Daniel D. McGarry (1955), 167.

focus the way the church has read, interpreted, applied, and inculcated the teachings of Scripture and those concepts closely related to and deriving from that teaching.

At the most basic level, that contemporary reader would be correct in assuming that definition. It harmonizes well with the broad descriptions of historical theology provided by such significant figures as Adolf von Harnack,[2] Gregg Allison,[3] Jaroslav Pelikan,[4] and Alister McGrath[5]—a group of scholars that covers a wide swath of the spectrum of theological and historiographical positions. Such acceptance of the definition of historical theology was not always the case, however. In Pelikan's monumental work that dealt with the history of the field, he noted the struggle within the academy even to combine the two terms—*historical* and *theology*—into a single coherent label. "History," he said, "speaks of becoming; theology deals with being."[6] Those two concepts, in the eyes of at least some of Pelikan's colleagues, could rightly be seen as diametrically opposed, thus rendering the phrase meaningless. Thankfully, despite some reservations, the academic world did not ignore the field altogether, and since the publication of the

---

[2] Harnack saw the history of dogma as a subset of historical theology, arguing that "[t]he History of Dogma is a discipline of general Church History, which has for its object the dogmas of the Church. These dogmas are the doctrines of the Christian faith logically formulated and expressed for scientific and apologetic purposes, the contents of which are a knowledge of God, of the world, and of the provisions made by God for man's salvation." Adolf von Harnack, *History of Dogma* (New York: Russell & Russell, 1958), 1:1.

[3] Allison defined historical theology as "the study of the interpretation of Scripture and the formulation of doctrine by the church of the past." Gregg R. Allison, *Historical Theology: An Introduction to Christian Doctrine* (Grand Rapids: Zondervan, 2011), 23.

[4] Pelikan defined historical theology as "the genetic study of Christian faith and doctrine." Jaroslav Pelikan, *Historical Theology: Continuity and Change in Christian Doctrine* (London: Hutchinson, 1971), xiii.

[5] McGrath defined historical theology simply as "the branch of theological inquiry which aims to explore the historical development of Christian doctrines and identify the factors which were influential in their formulation and adoption." Alister E. McGrath, *Historical Theology: An Introduction to the History of Christian Thought* (Chichester, West Sussex: Wiley-Blackwell, 2013), 8.

[6] Pelikan, *Historical Theology*, xiii.

seminal work by S. G. Lange in 1796, the study has developed an academic guild of its own.

Historical theology as a distinct discipline, then, has the paradoxical position of being both notably ancient and remarkably young. On its face, the concept of considering the development of doctrine as it has passed from one generation to the next seems undoubtedly biblical. From the earliest days of the church, the leaders understood their charge as "contend[ing] for the faith that was delivered once for all to the saints" (Jude 3), a clear statement of the need not only to acknowledge the receipt of an historical doctrine but also to align the young community's teaching with that which had been received. That understanding could rightly be deemed the earliest version of an historical theology within the church, but even that arrived in the midst of a longer tradition that included the resurrected Christ teaching his followers about the ways in which the revelation of the Jewish writings always pointed to the God-in-the-flesh Messiah—no doubt a master course in the historical teaching of the community of faith.

Even by the first century, the concept of building theology on the foundation of the generations that came beforehand already had centuries, millennia even, of tradition. After all, the Exodus generation of Israelites undertook as a primary responsibility the role of teaching their offspring about the work of God in the life of the community, having received the divine command to do so (Deut 4:9; 6:7–9). Thus, the idea of teaching the theology of bygone generations has, itself, generations of tradition built into it.

To equate historical theology with the mere practice of discipling the next generation, however, would be doing a disservice to both the general call to discipleship and to the academic discipline as it has evolved in the more recent past. That overly distilled description would also do a disservice to the other categories of theological endeavors and to the practitioners involved in those projects as they, too, are at their best when they are an integral part of the discipleship process. In other words, in order to consider historical theology as a unique academic endeavor, something more must be included. That something more can be found in the concerted effort to understand the historical context of the various doctrinal discussions and the development of the teaching across the generations of Christ's followers. For the evangelical, the historical theologian recognizes that the same God who inspired the writing of the Bible, the same God who created the cosmos and interacted with humanity in biblical days, that same God continues to interact with his people even after the closing of the biblical canon.

Thus, at its most basic form, historical theology has been part of the work of the people of God since they first came into existence. In its more formal sense, however, the discipline of historical theology first arrived on the scene as an academic field only at the end of the eighteenth century. Since that time, the academy has developed an expertise specifically in the area of historical theology with scholars specializing in various historical eras as well as in different theological traditions. By focusing on understanding the development of the church's teaching in its historical context, the historical theologian seeks to clarify the specific meaning(s) of doctrines, to grasp the various conflicts that faced the church and her teaching, and to understand why disparate theological questions have been asked at different times in the life of the church.

One particular example should prove sufficient to demonstrate the aims of this field of study. During the first few generations after the death of the apostles, the church famously began wrestling with several major theological concepts, including the complexities of Christology and those associated with the doctrine of the Trinity. Because the Bible is not merely a theological reference work, those concepts did not have single passages of Scripture that could serve as authoritative definitions of belief. Instead, the church—following the biblically astute thinking of such theologians as Athanasius of Alexandria (c. 296–373), Basil of Caesarea (329–379), and Gregory of Nazianzus (330–389), among others—had to determine how to speak of and define the various concepts.

Needless to say, not all parties involved arrived at the same conclusion simultaneously. The resulting discussions—sometimes quite heated—left behind a veritable gold mine of theological thought and, millennia later, still provide the historical theologian with a helpful test case for understanding the development of Christian thought. Whether the church should refer to the Trinity using the term *homoousios* (Greek for "same substance") or *homoiousios* (Greek for "similar substance")—a difference in a single letter!—has probably not crossed the mind of many individual Christians in the twenty-first century. The very concept, however, stands at the core of the central doctrinal claims of Christendom and can be found in the oft-recited Nicene Creed, which was formalized at the Council of Constantinople in AD 381.

Understanding how the church came to express those doctrines in specific ways allows the twenty-first-century Christian to avoid the many pitfalls that lead into what the church has deemed to be heresy: in this specific example, either diminishing Christ's divinity by making him into something less than the Father or diminishing Christ's humanity by making him into something completely separate from the average human. In either case, the resulting deficient Christ undermines the biblical concept of salvation and leads the church away from the faith that has been once and for all delivered to the saints.

The job of the historical theologian is to consider both the *whats* and the *whys* of the development of that doctrine. The historical theologian must delve into the various conversations of the fourth century to understand the positions of each party involved in the conflict. She uses the tools of the historian to access the events of the past, and she utilizes the tools of the theologian to grasp the complexities of the various arguments as they developed. By so doing, the historical theologian makes the connection from past generations to the present, allowing contemporaries to understand how the church has come to her current stances, to learn from the many mistakes of those who have come before, to emulate the good examples that stand out from the crowd, and to recognize that the God of the Bible has not ceased working in and through his people in the intervening two millennia.

Benefits of Historical Theology

Even from that single example, several benefits of historical theology can easily be identified and should provide an encouragement for the church to appreciate the field. Perhaps the most obvious benefit is simply in the increased understanding of truth. Surely, the mysteries of God remain beyond humanity's complete comprehension, but they do not remain completely beyond humanity's comprehension. God's people have been called to know their God, and doing so requires much hard work. The written Word serves as the self-revelation of God to humanity, but even the reception of the truth about Scripture is enhanced by the contextualized understanding of various conversations, interpretations of that Scripture, and challenges posed both from within the church and from outside. The intricate work of historical theology allows the church not only to explore the mysteries of God that remain on the edge of comprehension, but it also anchors the church to historic truth. The very identification of orthodoxy and heresy falls within the purview of historical theology and helps the church maintain her good news message of truth and hope.

Closely connected to that better understanding of truth lies the realization that God has indeed been faithful to his people and to that message of truth and hope. Historical theology allows the church to see beyond the era of the New Testament to comprehend how God's faithfulness took shape. Reaching beyond the divinely inspired Word of God comes with inherent difficulties and obvious restrictions. Regardless, for a people who serve the living God who promised never "to leave nor forsake" them (Deut 31:6 NIV; Matt 28:20; 2 Cor 4:9; Heb 13:5), catching some glimpses of God's continued work cannot be anything but a buttress for the faith. The work of historical theology enhances those glimpses—inherently limited though they may be—and allows God's people to better understand his continuing faithful protection of them and of the good news message entrusted to them.

Additionally, the work of historical theology teaches the church—and the watching world—about the great cloud of witnesses, spoken of in Hebrews 11–12. That "cloud" not only includes the saints who had already lived and died by the time of the writing of that Scripture but also includes the many saints who have lived and died in the interim. By studying those saints—both well-remembered and those previously largely forgotten—and their unique struggles, the church can learn from them, even as God's people try to emulate the best examples of godliness. By learning the way the church has previously read Scripture and taught about God, the twenty-first-century believer can be inserted into that living tradition, gaining wisdom from that great cloud of witnesses and passing that wisdom onto the next generation of believers. With skill, faith, and divine guidance, the church can prayerfully avoid the many mistakes of previous generations even as she strives to attain to the godliness of those who have come before. At its best, historical theology helps the present generation to avoid the pitfalls of self-centered readings of history, stained as they are with the hubris that says, "This generation finally has everything figured out!" Rather, historical theology opens the eyes of the contemporary church to see that a perfect, golden age of the church has yet to exist and, simultaneously, that no struggles of the current age are unique—never before seen by believers. In other words, the church that utilizes historical theology well will learn from the past and will strive to walk in the righteous path that has been illuminated, even while being able to see more of the potential pitfalls thanks to the work of those who have come before.

Cautions of Historical Theology

Of course, the benefits of historical theology do not come without some amount of risk, and those risks have often, sadly, been realized in various eras of the church. The easiest pitfall for the church lies in the inherently human tendency either to idolize those who have been used in spectacular ways or to demonize those who have not. Historical theology done poorly can easily—if not certainly—lead to an unnecessarily pristine presentation of major figures. The resulting picture paints the historical figure as either a saint or a sinner, removing the obvious complexities of humans who are—even when regenerate—simultaneously saints and sinners. One of the beautiful aspects of the biblical stories is the consistent way the main figures are presented as complete personalities, warts and all. Rarely does the biblical record gloss over sinful behavior or turn three-dimensional human characters into simplistic representations of good or evil. Sadly, the church in general, and historical theologians in particular, have not always followed that example, choosing instead to present an either-or version of historical figures, resulting in an unhealthy idolization or demonization of the past.

In addition, while the critical and intentional use of historical theology can protect the church from becoming narcissistic and myopic in her outlook, the uncritical consideration of historical theology can actually lead to problems from the other direction. Specifically, the twenty-first-century believer who is not careful with historical theology can easily fall into the trap of seeing their own culture as being somehow more evolved, less sinful, or otherwise just better than the past they are studying.

None of these potential problems or any others that could be enumerated outweigh the clear benefits of practicing historical theology in the church. They merely exist as reminders of the potential downsides of an otherwise healthy and even essential endeavor. Indeed, if the church is going to do precisely what Bernard of Chartres suggested—stand on the shoulders of the giants who have come before us, or, even better, stand on the shoulders of the dwarfs who have come before us—she must learn to be a good student of historical theology.

Further Reading

Thankfully, the church in the twenty-first century has been blessed with a plethora of resources designed to help the conscientious reader benefit from the field of historical theology. Some of the more accessible works specifically designed to introduce the concept of historical theology have been published in the last decade. Gregg Allison's work, entitled *Historical Theology: An Introduction to Christian Doctrine*, intentionally follows the format of *Systematic Theology: An Introduction to Biblical Doctrine* by Wayne Grudem and can be read either alone or alongside that work. Alister McGrath, on the other hand, designed his work *Historical Theology: An Introduction to the History of Christian Thought* to be read as a standalone. Gerald Bray intriguingly used a trinitarian framework for his 1264-page tome, entitled *God Has Spoken: A History of Christian Theology*. Finally, editors Jason Duesing and Nathan Finn have designed *Historical Theology for the Church* to be accessible for a more general readership. Each of those works provides an excellent entry point into the field.

For older volumes that have stood the test of time, the works of Jaroslav Pelikan (5 volumes of *The Christian Tradition: A History of the Development of Doctrine* and *Historical Theology: Continuity and Change in Christian Doctrine*) and Adolf von Harnack (*History of Dogma*, 7 volumes) stand out. Neither are without their problems—not the least of which being their length. Both Pelikan and Harnack are intended for an academic audience and should be read with this in mind, but the treasures that can be found in their pages reward the diligent student handsomely. Another twentieth-century volume that has proven quite useful is that of the Dutch Reformed theologian, Louis Berkhof, entitled *The History of Christian Doctrines*. Of course, as with any field of study, the deeper one dives into it, the larger and more specific the bibliography becomes. Indeed, the twenty-first-century church finds herself at an incredible juncture of history—with more access to the history of theological thought than ever before. The eyes of mere dwarfs have never been able to see more.

For Additional Study

Allison, Gregg R. *Historical Theology: An Introduction to Christian Doctrine.* Grand Rapids: Zondervan, 2011.

Berkhof, Louis. *The History of Christian Doctrines.* London: Banner of Truth Trust, 1969.

Bray, Gerald. *God Has Spoken: A History of Christian Theology.* Wheaton: Crossway, 2014.

Duesing, Jason G., and Nathan A. Finn, eds. *Historical Theology for the Church.* Nashville: B&H Academic, 2021.

Harnack, Adolf von. *History of Dogma.* 7 vols. New York: Russell & Russell, 1958 (originally published in German, 1894–1898; in English, 1894–1899).

McGrath, Alister E. *Historical Theology: An Introduction to the History of Christian Thought.* 2nd ed. Chichester, West Sussex: Wiley-Blackwell, 2013.

Pelikan, Jaroslav. *Historical Theology: Continuity and Change in Christian Doctrine.* London: Hutchinson, 1971.

———. *The Christian Tradition: A History of the Development of Doctrine.* 5 vols. Chicago: University of Chicago Press, 1973–1990.

Also see these articles: Role of Tradition, Systematic Theology, Philosophical Theology

10

Philosophical Theology

R. L. Hatchett

Philosophical theology is used freely and often interchangeably with philosophy of religion. When distinguished, philosophy of religion addresses issues that are seen as ancillary and preparatory for the work of theology. This article focuses, with some liberty, on influential voices from history who used philosophy in the effort to articulate theology.

Gnosticism and Irenaeus (c. 130–c. 200)

Gnosticism is an umbrella term for several second-century cults. The movement is an early and enduring threat and rival to Christianity. Collectively they thought the material world was evil and in constant battle with pure, nonmaterial stuff. Some low-order being made the evil world. Some chosen persons had a spiritual dimension that was trapped in an evil body in the hostile, material world. Secret knowledge (*gnosis*) was instrumental in escaping from the world and undertaking a journey of the essential self. Gnostics habitually tempted Christians to repudiate the goodness of God and creation and the hope of resurrection and cosmic restoration. They also exchanged the incarnated Jewish Jesus for an other worldly teacher.

Irenaeus defended Christianity against this threat. He was a narrative thinker who discerned one grand story in the OT and emerging NT. He captured its plot and characters in a trinitarian summary, the Rule of Faith.

Christian theology, with God present and acting in the Son and Spirit, was the best antidote to Gnosticism.

Irenaeus pictured Adam and Eve as children who must grow to mature faith. God was a Father who oversaw their souls growing as they faced struggles and sin. Later theorists appropriated this insight and fashioned a "soul-building" theodicy. Irenaeus himself pictured God's triumph over evil happening in the unfolding of history.

Origen (c. 185–c. 254)

Origen left a legacy of joining the Greek reflections about God (eternal and unchanging) with the God seen in the narrative of the Bible. His answer to the famous critic Celsus is instructive (AD 170). Celsus claimed Christianity rested upon barbarians telling gross stories of God's entanglement with the physical world. Celsus demanded Christians logically demonstrate their teachings in order to be taken seriously. This challenge went unmet until Origen answered in AD 248, two years before his martyrdom. Origen argued the challenge was unfit for Christians because they arrived at their teaching by God's revelation in history and Scripture with its own proof in Spirit and power. Christians know what they know of God not because human minds had ascended but because God had descended. The appropriate challenge would examine revelation with reason and wisdom. Christianity proved superior to the teachings of the philosophers about God. Faith is not established by reason but can, with wisdom, be defended or even vindicated.[1]

Augustine (354–430)

Augustine's integration of ancient philosophy and Christian theology set the stage for most Catholics and Protestants. Augustine instructed "believe in order to understand." Was he advising that one must give serious plausible consideration to an idea before grasping it? More likely his answer was Catholic and personal; one must trust the faith revealed and captured in

---

[1] Robert Louis Wilken, *The Spirit of Early Christian Thought: Seeking the Face of God* (New Haven: Yale University Press, 2005), 10–14.

the creed. Only then would the insights of the philosophers come together as an ordered whole. Augustine acknowledged the world gives evidence of God. He is more famous for suggesting our sinful nature suppressed such knowledge. God overcomes by illumination—by placing these eternal truths or their general patterns (forms) within our minds.

Philosophy proved helpful to Augustine's journey. Cicero inspired him to seek an intellectual and moral integrity. Neoplatonism helped him abandon Manichaeism, a Gnostic-like dualism seeing the cosmic principles of good and evil at war. He came to see that God was nonmaterial. More importantly, he was helped to reconsider the nature of evil.

He rejected evil deriving from God and that evil is the opposite of good. Instead, evil is the privation or lacking in the good. God makes good things such as eyesight. But when something essential to seeing is removed or distorted, blindness occurs. These insights allowed Augustine to read Genesis and join the church in affirming that God is a good creator.

Evil emerged when Adam misused his freedom to rebel and disobey God. Many follow Augustine's teaching: evil is privation, sin grips the world when freedom is misused for sinning, and God desired and valued freedom to enable genuine love. Modern Free-Will theodicies appropriate these ideas.

Augustine articulated the Christian view of history for the Western church. Rome was shaken by conquering invaders and blamed Christianity's rise for its decline. Augustine answered the charge in *The City of God*. He distinguished Christianity from Rome to show how Christianity would survive the empire's demise. Augustine explained that the communities and political structures men build are rooted in love of self and contempt for God. The community that God is building is rooted in the love of God and contempt for self.[2] Human political projects will coexist with the city God builds, sometimes contributing and other times being hostile to God's purpose. History begins with an ideal creation of paradise. With the sin of the first couple, the entire human family falls into sin. The two cities will coexist until God brings the world to its conclusion when believers will then enter the eternal presence of God. Milton's titles capture the sweep of history—*Paradise Lost, Paradise Regained*.

---

[2] Augustine, *City of God* 14.28.

Anselm (c. 1033–1109)

Known today for his philosophy, Anselm was a spiritual director for monks and was best known for his book on prayer. He was likely the last person to have rock-star status in both monasticism and scholasticism (the life of schoolmen in emerging universities).

He had previously offered a cosmological argument, which he believed was implied in Augustine, but attention is given to what we call his "ontological argument" for the existence of God. This type of argument draws from the idea or concept of God, or perhaps the concept of BE-ING itself.

The audience and intention of the argument are greatly debated. The argument addresses the monks he sought to guide to maturity and is couched within a prayer. Some (Karl Barth) conclude the work intends to strengthen the faith of people who already believe. Previously, most theologians understood such arguments to reaffirm what they already knew by faith. Some serious readers believe Anselm intended his arguments as a logical exercise to precede faith.[3]

The argument rests on two assumptions granted by virtually every ancient reader. (1) When we think of God, we think of him maximally; specifically, he is "that than which nothing greater can be conceived." (2) A reality that exists in our minds and in "external" reality is greater than the very same idea if it were to exist only in our minds. We have the idea of the Empire State Building in our heads; it is greater, given it really stands in New York City. Granting these two convictions, Anselm said it proves impossible to defend the fool who says there is no God.

The argument has known great controversy. I will paraphrase simplified responses.

- Guanilo (against): you can prove everything this way . . . how about a perfect island?
- Thomas (against): you can't start from the concept of God; that's what we don't know.
- Descartes (for): can you not think of the idea of perfection? Why not? Must be a God.

---

[3] M. J. Charlesworth, *Philosophy of Religion: The Historic Approaches* (London: Macmillan, 1972), 56–57.

- Kant (against): these are word games; existence is different from other descriptive terms.
- Norman (for): well, Kant saying God is a "has-to-exist kind of being" is too descriptive.

Anselm is equally famous for recasting the doctrine of atonement in the book *Why the God-Man?* Here he starts with revelation, the story of God's Son coming to reconcile sinners. Anselm wanted to explain the drama of atonement as occurring between God and mankind and avoid earlier approaches that saw sinners in need of rescue from Satan's authority. Humans had insulted God's dignity and were unable to pay damages given God's greatness. The human predicament could only be remedied by a God-Man, one who has the status of God and who can also genuinely represent humanity. The classical doctrine of Christ as fully God and fully human was not merely how things happened to turn out; it was logically necessary.

Thomas Aquinas (1225–1274)

Scholars often say Thomas begins with reason, but his great work, *Summa Theologiae*, begins by grounding theology in God's necessary revelation. The revelation exceeds what is accessible to reason.[4] Thomas distinguished the rational *theology* of Aristotle and his craft of *holy teaching* rooted in Scripture. Thomas declared theology a science. Ancient science reasoned to new insights from known truths. Thomas's science of theology rested on the known truth of revelation, not reason.[5]

Thomas rejected the dualism of Plato and adopted a more integrated approach found in Aristotle. Thomas showed how the eternal God had left his order and rational imprint on the material creation. He also observed that revelation yielded saving truths beyond reason's grasp. But very importantly, reason exercised properly supports revelation. Thomas used a time-honored phrase, "Grace does not destroy nature but perfects it."[6] Faith in God's revealing completes what reason may render. But reason never contradicts

---

[4] Frederick Christian Bauerschmidt, *Holy Teaching: Introducing the Summa Theologiae of St. Thomas Aquinas* (Grand Rapids: Brazos Press, 2005), 31–33.

[5] Thomas Aquinas, *Summa Theologiae* 1.1.2.

[6] Thomas Aquinas, *Summa Theologiae* 1.1.8.

revealed teaching. Modern admirers of this insight reject the *divided mind* (where faith yields one truth and reason yields another) and embrace the *unity of truth* or declare *all truth is God's truth*.

Students of Thomas distinguish between natural theology and revealed theology. They differ in method. Natural theology arrives at knowledge by rational reflection (thinking like Aristotle) upon nature. Revealed theology arrives at the truth by trusting what God reveals. They also differ in content. Natural theology demonstrates that God exists, is one, and is good. Revealed theology includes the knowledge of natural theology but includes more, especially the twin mysteries of the Incarnation and Trinity.

Thomas offered five arguments for God's existence. Each observed a phenomenon in the world (thus the label "Cosmological"): motion, causation, contingency, ranking, and purposeful design. Each is incapable of explaining itself and requires a reality able to account for it. A world of things that move or change because something else moves them can't explain why everything is moving. Only an unmoved mover (who moves without need to be moved) could explain. One must decide between an inexplicable world or an external being. Yet Thomas was not primarily concerned to move his readers from unbelief to faith (that is our circumstance) but to show readers that the best of human thinking about God (like Aristotle) fits what God revealed about himself.

Thomas's view of religious language proved very influential. He distinguished metaphor from literal senses. The metaphorical could be identified by the informed believer because it was in a technical or tedious sense untrue. Thomas trusted Scripture, but he believed biblical authors wrote metaphorically when claiming God was their rock. God protects, but he is not limestone.

Literal language is more modest and direct, but special attention is required when speaking of God. We use the same set of words to speak of two domains—the divine and the human or natural. Words could be used in three different ways. We could (1) use words in precisely the same way (univocally, both Fido and Spot *bark*), (2) use words with completely different meanings (equivocally, Fido has a *bark,* and the tree has *bark*), or (3) use words recognizing a genuine similarity and distinctiveness. We can explore this example: "My father is wise, and God is wise." Thomas argues that only analogy is appropriate for speaking of God. Speaking univocally ignores our father's limits and imperfection and fails to acknowledge that God possesses a wisdom beyond our capacity to grasp. Speaking univocally would place our father and God on the same scale, dangerously close to idolatry. Speaking equivocally would sever the genuine connection between God and his world. Speaking analogically, we speak meaningfully but not exhaustively.[7] Thomas was defending God's boundaries—his distinctiveness and uniqueness. He worried theologians would presume to grasp or measure God in human terms.

For Thomas, the natural and supernatural touched. Analogy reveals their relationship. But Duns Scotus (1266–1308) and the nominalist tradition saw them as unconnected. God's ruling did not correspond to his ordered creation (as with Thomas) but was a sheer act of his mysterious will (voluntarist).

Martin Luther (1483–1546) and John Calvin (1509–1564)

Luther and Calvin emerge in this emphasis on God's untethered freedom. They were, however, committed to the incarnation and Trinity as articulated at Nicaea and Chalcedon. Luther railed against Catholic dependence upon Aristotle's ethics, which treated righteousness as an acquired virtue. Calvin taught that sin suppressed what was previously an immediate sense of God revealed in creation. General revelation (to all persons through creation) would precede special revelation (to persons at particular times, e.g., the Bible). Strangely, sin reversed the designed order. Trusting special revelation opened minds to the creation's witness to God's greatness. Calvin emphasized that accepting God's word rested upon the self-authenticating testimony of the Holy Spirit.

René Descartes (1596–1650)

Descartes is known as the father of modern philosophy. Several issues were problematic. He faced the challenge of skepticism, which held that knowledge rested on inadequate justification. He worried the volitional view of God had aided the Thirty Years' War. He faced the encroachment of materialistic explanations (generally science). His famous answer argues science

---

[7] Bauerschmidt, *Holy Teaching*, 66–70.

can master the workings of the human body (as physical) but not the human mind (as nonmaterial).

He sought a new course for philosophy and theology. He proposed an approach that can be compared to geometry with axiomatic starting points and subsequently flawless logic to produce conclusions that would be certain. The term "methodological doubt" conveys his subjecting every proposed truth to rigorous inspection. In his great thought experiment, he rejected any idea that could be doubted by a reasonable person. He rejected ideas that were noble and widely held. He was looking for a premise or foundation upon which to build. He came to the famous "I think; therefore, I am." He concluded his own sense or consciousness of being a thinking being is sufficient evidence that he exists.

Now Descartes could work logically from his foundation to affirm many of the ideas that he discarded when looking for ideas that were foundational (indubitable). He proposed an influential understanding of the mind-body problem. He also believed he had proved the existence of God. He focused on God's perfection. God's perfection made him appear less willful or fitful. The perfect God would make a stable world. Importantly, the human mind comes with the idea of perfection (a form of the ontological argument). A major innovation has occurred. Ancient and medieval thinkers had depended on Nature or timeless truth (forms) as the centerpiece for human deliberation. Christian theologians and philosophers built all thinking and deliberation to correspond to a transcendent God. Now Descartes could place the weight for knowing reality on the inner workings of the human mind. The workings of the conscious individual mind held the answer for securing knowledge. The modern self emerges. The soul of pagan and the Christian thinkers recedes.[8]

Descartes left a legacy for the modern or critical (subjected to inspection) age.

1. Building upon a foundation is the new path to certainty.
2. Tradition and community must be rejected as a source or resource for knowledge until its ideas are tested. In antiquity, one would

---

[8] Christopher Ben Simpson, *Modern Christian Theology* (New York: T&T Clark, 2016), 46–48.

find comfort in relying upon a master of spiritual and intellectual standing (an authority). Belonging to a tradition (an ongoing
conversation between wise masters) no longer seemed credible.
Communities likely shelter convictions and loyalties insufficiently
examined. Dependence upon an authoritative master seemed child-
like to modern minds.

3. The expression "individual rational autonomy" captures the new
    approach. A solitary person judges for himself or herself on rational
    grounds without being swayed by loyalties.
4. Certainty becomes the new standard or goal: it is not enough to
    know; now you must know that you know.

Blaise Pascal (1623–1662)

In 1654 Pascal left witness of his "definitive conversion" when he encountered the God of the patriarchs and of Jesus, not the God of the philosophers
and scientists. He spoke of "reasons of the heart," claiming there is more
to wise living than mechanical reasoning. His apologetics addressed human
experience, with its tensions and desire for happiness. Speaking of faith as a
wager differs boldly from Descartes's demand for logical certainty.

- If one affirms God—you have everything to gain and nothing to lose.
- If one denies God—you have nothing to gain and everything to lose.

Pascal did not think common arguments were wrong; they were impoverished, lacking applied wisdom.

Immanuel Kant (1724–1804)

Kant's work is as controversial and difficult as it is influential. I will describe
his legacy (more than his actual teaching) for the Anglo interpreters who
depend upon his first and second great *Critiques*. Several observations are
important for our topic.

1. Kant concluded we cannot reason from observations in the physical
world to conclusions concerning a realm beyond the material world.

2. Kant proposed a constructive role for the mind. He believed the
human mind came with pre-established ways of thinking that prove to work

when we address the tangible world. This mental "hardwiring" imposes order upon the world full of sensory impressions. For example, the mind only processes numbers belonging to one of three categories—individual, partial, and universal (my dog, some dogs, or all dogs). So we can know and share knowledge about the tangible world. Sadly, our minds do not have a suitable set of interpretive frameworks for the dimension beyond experience concerning topics such as God and moral and aesthetic judgment.

3. Kant attacked the traditional arguments for God's existence and his criticisms were widely embraced. The ontological argument (rooted in the concept or being of God) confused the idea of existence with a quality describing God. The cosmological arguments implied the same mistake in logic as the ontological. Additionally, the arguments mistakenly tried to move from the tangible world to make conclusions about a realm beyond.

4. While reason could not demonstrate the existence of God, Kant found promise in his "practical" deliberations. An exploration of his inner experience of moral obligation seemed to require a God who would reward someone trying to live up to their sense of oughtness. This is called a moral argument.

5. Kant believed ethics could not be rooted in religion, revelation, or doctrine. Morality found clarity and authority when directed by reason. Religious ethics could be divisive and dangerous but may move simple persons to better behavior.

6. Kant held religion functioned best in a pure abstract form (best for morality). When religion took on institutions and doctrines (called positive religion), they were compromised. For example, believing in the punishment of hell compromises one's ability to do the right thing because it is the right thing.

7. Kant's view that the mind shapes experience has inspired diverse interpretations. Some scholars assert Kant leads to the supremacy and objectivity of science since the mind is properly wired with the correct preset questions. Other scholars assert Kant leads to a modern form of relativism since each person's mind may constitute reality differently. Still others observe Kant makes the rational self the fulcrum for knowing. Kant assumed humans had knowledge and explored the inner mind for what had to be true for knowledge to occur. Even the notion of God rested upon moral intuition.

In this climate atheism and agnosticism were not uncommon. A half measure of sorts was called deism. Deists picture God as the world's designer and creator. Once finished, he never interfered but stayed distant though he likely would reward good behavior at the world's end. Some found the deist God more defensible. Others suspected revelation would prove unnecessary if it were redundant (duplicating what reason provided). Many believers found vibrancy in an experiential movement called Pietism and the Great Awakenings. Some liberals also found experience central.

Friedrich Schleiermacher (1768–1834)

Schleiermacher is known as the father of modern/liberal theology. His upbringing in Pietism marks his work even though he abandoned traditional Christian doctrines. He perceives real piety is not located in doctrine or deeds but in the awakening of an experiential connection or consciousness of God. The allure of Romanticism gives insight into his work. Romantics see the world as more than mechanical and mathematical explanations of lifeless bits of matter. The world manifests dynamic wholeness and energy that is as fascinating as it is dangerous. The infinite (divine) is present in the finite realities of the world. A person can intuitively become conscious and attuned to the enriched world. Romantics celebrate the artistic and human insights achieved by persons tapping into such creative potency.

Schleiermacher addressed these Romantic cultured elites in *On Religion: Speeches to Its Cultured Despisers* in 1799. Its important apologetic strategy is paraphrased thusly: "Your instincts to reject Christianity were correct in one sense. You discarded the awkward expression of tedious rationalist doctrine. Yet sadly you did not sense that Christianity gives powerful insight to the nature of true piety." The awareness or consciousness of being completely dependent upon God is the common religious experience for all persons. While the nature of religious experience is the same, it comes to expression in different ways (e.g., Buddhists and Baptists).

In 1821–22 Schleiermacher revised theology around the notion of religious experience in *The Christian Faith*. Each doctrine was assessed for its potential to illumine this awareness of the divine. He detected the doctrine of the Son's divine and human natures revealed that humans could be joined to the divine. Jesus became our pioneer who models for us a higher God consciousness.

Georg W. F. Hegel (1770–1831)

Scholars debate whether Hegel was anti-religious or hyper-religious. Art, religion, and philosophy each address vital questions. Art restricts itself to representation through mediums like paint or clay. Religion employs concepts but relies upon representations like Jesus. Philosophy employs only concepts (seeming superior). Parents may use Santa Claus to teach the concept of generosity. But the child will no longer need the representation of Santa Claus when mature. Yet later Hegel finds the Trinity illuminating.

Hegel believed that Geist or Spirit (more collective than holy) is pulling history toward its goal. History is unfolding to bring the Spirit or goal to more complete concrete expression. Ideas move history forward. What may appear as absolute opposing forces (thesis and anti-thesis) in a snapshot of history proves to be the dialectic process that brings together insights from both groups to form a new and better expression (syn-thesis).

Important voices respond to Hegel. (1) Theological liberals study representations like God becoming man and conclude that every human was part of the Spirit (man discovers his divinity rather than God becoming man). (2) Hegel inspires numerous types of "developmentalism." Everything from biology to theology grows from simple to complex. (3) Kierkegaard offers a corrective protest that genuine encounter with God is found in the contingencies of moments in history that call for obedience. Some truths (confusingly called "subjective") require commitment rather than assent. (4) Marx keeps Hegel's dialectic process but claims it is a person's material circumstance that causes his or her ideas and not his or her ideas driving the circumstances of history.

Karl Barth (1886–1968)

Barth controversially rejected natural theology (reasoning to truths about God). He thought natural theology was to blame for the liberalism prevalent in Europe and Nazism in Germany. Each affirm something in nature and conclude God must have sponsored it. They were making God in their image. He took another hard line toward other religions. He agreed in part with the atheist Ludwig Feuerbach (1804–72) that people create their gods.

Only Christianity is God revealing to humans below. Rejecting philosophical projects, he boldly returned to God's revelation. His progress in theology occurred when he came to see that Scripture must be read through the lens of the Trinity and incarnation.

In the 1960s, evangelical scholars were increasingly distinguishing themselves in biblical studies, theology, and philosophy. Philosophers especially were employing new approaches and exacting standards in logic. Christian practitioners now commonly demonstrated that best practices in philosophy required Christian claims to be taken seriously. Famously, Alvin Plantinga showed that belief in a good and powerful God is not disproven by the existence of evil. More recently evangelical theologians are employing this rigor to clarify Christian teaching in "analytic theology."

Christians will find philosophy a crucial tool in defending and articulating Christian beliefs such as reason's relationship to revelation, God's character in the face of evil, and God's governance of the world to a meaningful end.

FOR ADDITIONAL STUDY

Bauerschmidt, Frederick Christian. *Holy Teaching: Introducing the Summa Theologiae of St. Thomas Aquinas*. Grand Rapids: Brazos Press, 2005.

Charlesworth, M. J. *Philosophy of Religion: The Historic Approaches*. London: Macmillan, 1972.

Crisp, Oliver D., and Michael C. Rea, eds. *Analytic Theology: New Essays in the Philosophy of Theology*. New York: Oxford University Press, 2009.

McCall, Thomas H. *An Invitation to Analytic Christian Theology*. Downers Grove: IVP Academic, 2015.

Morris, Thomas. *Our Idea of God: An Introduction to Philosophical Theology*. Downers Grove: IVP, 1991.

Plantinga, Alvin. *God and Other Minds: A Study of the Rational Justification of Belief in God*. Ithaca, NY: Cornell University Press, 1990.

Simpson, Christopher Ben. *Modern Christian Theology*. New York: T&T Clark, 2016.

Wilken, Robert Louis. *The Spirit of Early Christian Thought: Seeking the Face of God*. New Haven: Yale University Press, 2005.

Also see these articles: Faith and Reason, Historical Theology, Systematic Theology, Modern Theology

11

Systematic Theology

John S. Hammett

The adjective in the title of this article, "systematic," does not enjoy universal favor in theological circles today. The most widely used systematic theology text among evangelicals, now in its third edition by Millard Erickson, is called *Christian Theology*, not Systematic Theology. The class in which systematic theology is taught in some evangelical *seminaries* is also called Christian theology rather than systematic theology. Perhaps postmodern sensibilities are suspicious of anything systematic as inherently oppressive and coercive. The desire to be systematic can lead to the exclusion of data that do not fit neatly into one's system. Moreover, when speaking of an infinite God, is anything systematic even possible? Is that not to attempt to put God in a box? Still, this article will argue that systematic theology is an accurate and useful phrase to describe an important and necessary theological task.

Definitions and Distinctions

Most definitions of systematic theology see it as seeking to give a rational or coherent or orderly exposition of the Christian faith, thus justifying the adjective "systematic." Though aware of the dangers entailed in the attempt to be systematic, theologians have believed that incoherence and confusion are not virtues, and thus think the attempt to be systematic is a risk worth taking. However, recognizing the infinite nature of theology's subject and the limited and fallen perspective of every practitioner of theology, it does seem that systematic theology should be conducted in a spirit of humility and should build some safeguards into its methodology to guard against the dangers inherent in seeking to be systematic, safeguards we will discuss in more detail shortly.

Most definitions of systematic theology also mention the sources or bases for systematic theology. Some approaches (Roman Catholic) give tradition an equal place with Scripture as sources for theology; the famous Wesleyan quadrilateral incorporates reason, tradition, and experience along with Scripture. But most definitions of systematic theology, especially those in the evangelical tradition, give Scripture a privileged place as the sole normative source for systematic theology. Other sources may serve a secondary role, but Scripture is the principal source for systematic theology and the sole normative source.

What has been said thus far serves to distinguish systematic theology from some other branches of theology. Philosophical theology differs from systematic theology in terms of its tools, tasks, and sources. It utilizes philosophical reasoning, argumentation, and concepts in its work, and assists systematic theologians in the tasks of defending various claims of the Christian faith, sharpening the arguments for those claims, and at times contributing concepts to help systematic theologians articulate their message. Philosophical theology differs most sharply from systematic theology in terms of its sources. Systematic theologians, especially those in the evangelical tradition, take Scripture as their sole normative source; philosophical theologians may wrestle with key Christian claims drawn from Scripture, but they do not draw directly from Scripture as a normative source in their work.

Historical theology focuses upon works by and about certain figures in church history and illuminates their claims and contributions. It is of value to systematic theologians, and systematic theology should incorporate the contributions of historical theology, but again, the tasks and sources differ. Historical theologians discuss how past theologians interpreted Scripture; systematic theologians seek to expound what Scripture itself teaches. But here is where systematic theologians can build in one of the safeguards mentioned above. They can seek to expound what Scripture teaches in dialogue with twenty centuries of figures who sought to do the same thing. Utilizing the insights of previous generations should guard us against being prisoners of our own context, and when repeated generations see the same truths in Scripture, it lessens the chance that they are all in error on this point. By contrast, any systematic theologian proposing an understanding of Scripture contrary to all those ever found in the history of theology bears a weighty burden of proof. At times there have been some relatively novel interpretations that have been able to supply such proof. Luther's doctrine of justification by grace alone through faith alone in Christ alone might be one such example. For Baptists, their views of believer's baptism and congregational government had not been advanced in more than a thousand years when first reintroduced. But if new views can be defended cogently from Scripture, they may be accepted, as Scripture is normative while history is not. Still, history is a useful guide we would be sinfully arrogant to ignore.

A more recent companion to historical theology is global theology. If historical theology seeks to illuminate the understandings of figures in other chronological contexts, global theology seeks to present the understandings of those in other geographical, racial, ethnic, and cultural contexts. This is one of the newer branches of theology, but one that is needful. It is being conducted with the recognition that systematic theology has, for most of its history, operated with typically Western cultural assumptions and has been written mostly by white male Westerners. Such a context has inevitably shaped the questions asked and the answers received from the study of Scripture. And just as historical theology can guard us from mistakes due to the limitations of our age, incorporating the voices of women and those from various racial, ethnic, and cultural groups can guard us from mistakes due to the limitations and blind spots of theologians who all come from the same sexual, racial, and cultural context. One recent example of the contributions of global theology to systematic theology is Timothy Tennent's *Theology in the Context of World Christianity*, in which the insights of world Christianity are applied to the various doctrines studied by theologians.

What about biblical theology? With the evangelical emphasis on the Bible as the sole normative source for systematic theology, is systematic theology just biblical theology? While the data provided by biblical theologians provide the foundation for systematic theology, there are also important differences. One is their differing approaches to Scripture. Biblical theologians will trace a theme through the whole of Scripture, paying careful attention to the metanarrative of creation, fall, redemption, and consummation, or will focus on one portion of Scripture, with subdivisions such as Pauline theology or Old Testament theology. Systematic theology approaches Scripture with doctrinal categories in mind, seeking to give an orderly presentation of all Scripture teaches on a given doctrine. An even more important difference is the integrative nature of systematic theology. It begins with the findings of biblical theologians, but then checks those findings against the interpretations of those from other eras (historical theology) and other cultures (global theology). It utilizes philosophical theology to check the cogency of its conclusions, the logic of its arguments, and even the accuracy of its terms. By contrast, biblical theology, strictly speaking, operates independently of these other disciplines.

The integrative nature of systematic theology is also seen in its relationship to practical theology, which may be simply defined as the practice of theology, as seen in worship, evangelism, preaching, discipling, and counseling. For all these practices and more, systematic theology serves as the basis. Because Christians believe the things they believe, they do the things they do. Practical theology also provides a feedback loop, contributing to the development of systematic theology, by checking its adequacy for practical application. Systematic theology is never intended to be speculative but to be intentionally integrated with practical theology. As one systematic theology textbook puts it, "Theology *arises from* and *issues forth* in mission."[1]

This intended practical outworking of systematic theology adds a further element to our definition of systematic theology. Most definitions of *systematic* make mention of its inescapably contextual nature. It is intended to address the questions and concerns of a particular cultural context. This is why systematic theology must be an ongoing enterprise. There will never be one systematic theology textbook that will be good for all times and places, as the concerns and questions of one context will not be those of another.

Finally, systematic theology should impact the life of the theologian. As Kevin Vanhoozer puts it, a practitioner of systematic theology "seeks to know and love the God of the gospel and to demonstrate its understanding

---

[1] Daniel L. Akin, ed., *A Theology for the Church*, rev. ed. (Nashville: B&H Academic, 2014), 50.

in forms of obedient speech and practice."[2] The nineteenth-century Baptist theologian John L. Dagg is even more emphatic. He writes,

> The study of religious truth ought to be undertaken and prosecuted from a sense of duty, and with a view to the improvement of the heart. When learned, it ought not to be laid on the shelf, as an object of speculation; but it should be deposited deep in the heart, where its sanctifying power ought to be felt. To study theology, for the purpose of gratifying curiosity, or preparing for a profession, is an abuse and profanation of what ought to be regarded as most holy.[3]

Putting all these elements together, here is one possible definition of systematic theology: it is the attempt to give a systematic, coherent exposition of the Christian faith, based principally on the Scriptures, addressing the concerns and questions of a contemporary culture and leading to personal application in Christian life and ministry.

Historical Development

There is little resembling a systematic theology in the Bible itself. Much of the Bible is descriptive narrative, and even the intentionally prescriptive or didactic portions such as Paul's letters are often shaped by specific local issues. But the desire for doctrinal clarity and coherence soon pushed some to seek to articulate the faith more completely. Most see Origen's *On First Principles* as the first comprehensive presentation of the Christian faith, but it bears clear signs of its early third-century context, with consideration given to many issues not included in later works of systematic theology (see chapters on "The Perpetuity of Bodily Nature" and "The Just and the Good") and other doctrines important today given little or no attention (no chapter on ecclesiology, for example).

Augustine wrote prolifically, but mostly in response to pressing issues in the churches of his day or in sermons and expositions of the Bible, and

---

[2] Kevin J. Vanhoozer, ed., *Dictionary for Theological Interpretation of the Bible* (Grand Rapids: Baker Academic, 2005), 773.

[3] John Leadley Dagg, *Manual of Theology* (1858; Harrisonburg, VA: Gano Books, reprint 1982), 13.

he left nothing resembling a systematic theology. A full-length exposition of Christian doctrine awaited the thirteenth century and the work of Thomas Aquinas's *Summa Theologica*. This massive work, stretching sixty-one volumes in the Blackfriars English edition, is intended to be comprehensive, but the organization of topics and scholastic pattern of presentation is foreign to modern sensibilities, as is his extensive use of Aristotle and Aristotelian categories.

Among Protestants, many see the 1521 work of Philipp Melanchthon, *Loci Communes*, as the first orderly presentation of Reformation doctrine, but by far the landmark work of systematic theology from the Reformation is John Calvin's *Institutes of the Christian Religion*. Again, while the order of topics is quite different than most contemporary systematic theology textbooks, and while much of the content is polemic directed to individuals and issues specific to Calvin's day, this treatise continues to be widely read by many today, and in many ways it set the pattern for centuries to come. Friedrich Schleiermacher gave liberal theology its first "systematic theology" in his 1821 work, *The Christian Faith*, totaling more than 1,100 pages in a recent two-volume English translation. Charles Hodge's three-volume, 2,000-page *Systematic Theology* dominated Reformed theology for decades after its 1873 publication, and A. H. Strong gave Baptists a shorter but similar *Systematic Theology* (three volumes and more than 1,000 pages in the 1909 edition).

In the past generation, dozens of lengthy systematic theology texts have appeared, from the Arminian Thomas Oden (*Systematic Theology*), to the Catholic Richard McBrien (*Catholicism*), to the Charismatic J. Rodman Williams (*Renewal Theology: Systematic Theology from a Charismatic Perspective*). In addition to these full-length systematic theology texts, there are hundreds of shorter books on every conceivable doctrine within the field of systematic theology. Despite facing numerous challenges, interest in the field does not seem to be dying.

Theological Methodology

Of course, not all theologians do their theology in the same way. Mary Veeneman includes seven major categories in her recent work *Introducing Theological Method: A Survey of Contemporary Theologians and Approaches*, and even within those major categories, there is wide variation. To further explain what is involved in a theological method, one such method will be described here.

This method begins by openly acknowledging its presuppositions: that God exists; that he is both capable and desirous of revealing himself; that he has done so in creation, in Scripture, and in Jesus Christ; and that humans are capable of understanding this revelation from God, imperfectly, to be sure, and only with the assistance of the Holy Spirit, but nonetheless sufficiently capable to be subject to judgment based on their response to that revelation. These presuppositions may be justified on the basis of coherence and comprehensiveness; that is, they enable one to make as much sense of all of the observable reality of human life as any other set of presuppositions. Moreover, they argue that all humans operate with a set of presuppositions, recognized or not.

From these presuppositions, theologians following this method develop a Christian worldview, which includes a number of philosophical assumptions that undergird this theological method. For example, this method operates with the assumption that the physical creation exists; it is not an illusion. It also assumes that there is a real, unseen, supernatural realm. It assumes that time is linear, not cyclical. It draws these and other assumptions from the revelation given by God but welcomes the help of philosophical theology in articulating and defending these assumptions. These are very general assumptions shared by most Western readers of systematic theology texts, and so these philosophical assumptions do not need to be given lengthy treatment in the doing of systematic theology for Western readers. For the most part they can be simply assumed. But they must be much more explicitly addressed when theology is done in contexts not sharing these assumptions.

The first official step in this methodology is to begin with the Bible. For Wayne Grudem, this is the whole of systematic theology, which he defines as "collecting and understanding all the relevant passages in the Bible on various topics and then summarizing their teachings clearly so that we know what to believe about each topic."[4] The method advocated here sees this as the first and by far the most important step in formulating systematic

---

[4] Wayne Grudem, *Systematic Theology: An Introduction to Biblical Doctrine*, 2nd ed. (Grand Rapids: Zondervan Academic, 2020), 21.

theology. But in recognizing the fallibility of all biblical interpreters, it goes on to a second step.

In this second step, the method checks the understanding of biblical teaching derived from the previous step of biblical study by including two groups as dialogue partners in the interpretive process. From historical theology, one brings in the voices of the past twenty centuries of biblical interpretation. They provide a safeguard against interpretations unduly shaped by the current historical context. It also brings in voices from global theology to safeguard against interpretations unduly shaped by the current cultural context. This method recognizes that these Christians, though in other times and contexts, sought to understand the same Bible we seek to understand today and believes that the Holy Spirit has been active, throughout history and across cultures, in illuminating God's people to understand God's Word. With these dialogue partners available, it seems the height of arrogance to ignore and despise their help. Biblical interpretation is best done in a community of interpreters.

The next step in this method is systematic formulation. The understanding of biblical teaching derived from the first two steps is now summarized and presented in an orderly form, seeking to be as comprehensive as possible. It answers questions that obviously arise and argues why one formulation is better than others. What is being formulated in this step is what evangelicals regard as doctrine.

It can also be helpful at this point for systematic theologians to recognize different levels of doctrine. First-order doctrines are those beliefs that are regarded as essential to being a Christian. They are intrinsically related to the gospel and have been believed by most Christians down through history. Second-order doctrines are those that differentiate major theological traditions, such as Reformed or Arminian. Third-order doctrines may be called "denominational distinctives." The importance of this step, called by some "theological triage," is that it guides believers in responding to those with different positions on some point of theology. If one regards every point of doctrine as a first-order doctrine, she will have to divide with others who differ from her in any way. If one regards every doctrine as a fourth-order doctrine, he might be accepting of heretical beliefs on an essential point. One helpful byproduct of theological study should be a better awareness of the level of each individual belief.

Finally, in this methodology, systematic theology reaches its goal only when it leads to expression in practical theology. As one theology textbook argues, "theology is done for the purpose of knowing and loving God and participating in his mission in this world."[5] Contrary to some who think of systematic theology as a purely rational abstract enterprise, unrelated to the practical matters of everyday life, systematic theology, when defined, understood, and practiced properly, is intimately involved in life.

The Practical Importance of Systematic Theology

For every Christian, systematic theology is a practical necessity. Once a believer reads more than one verse in the Bible, she will inevitably begin to put biblical teaching together; in other words, she will begin to embark on the work of systematic theology. The only remaining question is whether she will be a good theologian or a poor one. Systematic theology is even involved in obeying the commandment Jesus identified as the greatest of all the commandments, for the rational effort involved in doing systematic theology is one way we love God with all of our minds (Matt 22:36–38).

Systematic theology is also essential to a believer's health. The devil attacks with lies, even lies that twist Scripture by taking a verse out of context. Systematic theology places individual verses in their larger biblical context and shows their place in an orderly summary of biblical teaching. That is essentially what Jesus did in his reply to Satan's Scripture-twisting temptation (Matt 4:6–7). What liberates and equips believers is Scripture rightly applied (2 Tim 3:16–17). But the right application of Scripture depends on a thorough knowledge of Scripture, and that type of work in the Scriptures is the foundation of systematic theology. Pastors, in particular, are to be those who "can encourage others by sound doctrine and refute those who oppose it" (Titus 1:9 NIV). How will pastors know what is sound doctrine? It comes from the study of systematic theology.

Systematic theology will be essential to every aspect of ministry to which believers are called. In evangelism, believers must confront people with a multitude of beliefs. Which beliefs leave one lost and in need of the gospel, and which beliefs are different from those of the one evangelizing but

---

[5] Akin, *A Theology for the Church*, 39.

not first-order beliefs? Without some of the understandings and categories supplied by systematic theology, believers might not recognize that some people might be religious but still in need of the gospel, while others might differ from some of the beliefs of other Christians but still fit within consensual Christianity. This need is especially keen when dealing with groups with many beliefs similar to those of orthodox Christianity. It is useful if not imperative to have a sound Christology in conversations with Mormons, Jehovah's Witnesses, and even Muslims. A sound doctrine of salvation is important to rightly evaluate when those who espouse the prosperity gospel, or the health and wealth gospel, cross the line into a false gospel.

Systematic theology is especially important to those involved in cross-cultural ministry, for they want to take the gospel into another culture, but if they are not careful, they will also bring elements of American culture. Elements of culture that are embedded in church life and practices and allow churches to fit in North America might be a hindrance to churches in other cultures. In particular, the doctrine of systematic theology called "ecclesiology" is necessary to separate what in a church is biblical and what is cultural.

Finally, systematic theology is important for every person. For example, the most important, life-shaping, destiny-defining question anyone will ever face is what they believe about Jesus Christ. That is essentially a systematic theology question. There is rational content about Jesus Christ that must be affirmed for one to exercise saving faith. The writer of Hebrews says the same about God: "Anyone who comes to him must believe that he exists and that he rewards those who earnestly seek him" (Heb 11:6 NIV). Saving faith is more than just intellectual belief, but it cannot be devoid of intellectual content. Stating that content is the task of systematic theology.

For Additional Study

Akin, Daniel L., ed. *A Theology for the Church*. Rev. ed. Nashville: B&H Academic, 2014.

Bird, Michael. *Evangelical Theology: A Biblical and Systematic Introduction*. 2nd ed. Grand Rapids: Zondervan, 2020.

Charry, Ellen T. *By the Renewing of Your Minds: The Pastoral Function of Christian Doctrine.* New York: Oxford University Press, 1997.

Clark, David. *To Know and Love God: Method for Theology.* Foundations of Evangelical Theology. Wheaton: Crossway, 2003.

Davis, John Jefferson. *The Necessity of Systematic Theology.* Grand Rapids: Baker, 1978.

Erickson, Millard. *Christian Theology.* 3rd ed. Grand Rapids: Baker Academic, 1998.

Garrett, James Leo. *Systematic Theology: Biblical, Historical & Evangelical.* 2 vols. Grand Rapids: Eerdmans, 1990–1995.

Grudem, Wayne. *Systematic Theology: An Introduction to Biblical Doctrine.* 2nd ed. Grand Rapids: Zondervan Academic, 2020.

Kapic, Kelly. *A Little Book for New Theologians: How and Why to Study Theology.* Downers Grove: IVP Academic, 2012.

Lints, Richard. *The Fabric of Theology: A Prolegomenon for Evangelical Theology.* Grand Rapids: Eerdmans, 1993.

Vanhoozer, Kevin. *The Drama of Doctrine: A Canonical-Linguistic Approach to Christian Doctrine.* Louisville: Westminster-John Knox, 2005.

Also see these articles: Revelation, Holy Scripture, Biblical Theology, Historical Theology, Philosophical Theology, Modern Theology, Pastoral Theology, Global Theology

12

Pastoral Theology

M. Justin Wainscott

Pastoral theology is that specific field of Christian theology that focuses its theological exploration on the identity and responsibilities of pastors. As such, it seeks to provide a theological framework for understanding the biblical office of pastor, giving theological meaning to who a pastor is and what a pastor does. It builds this framework by defining the pastorate—the nature of the office, the requirements of the office, and the functions of the office—from an intentionally biblical and theological perspective. Therefore, its goal is to establish a biblical and theological foundation or paradigm both for understanding and practicing pastoral ministry.

It should be mentioned, however, that pastoral theology can often be a misunderstood and even misused term. For instance, it can sometimes be described merely as the exercise of doing theology from the perspective of pastors, where pastors appropriate truths from various fields of theology and make them more accessible to laypeople. But as helpful (and needed) as this practice is, it would be misleading to label that as pastoral theology. Pastoral theology, then, is not to be thought of as theology from a pastoral perspective. Rather, it is thinking about the nature and work of pastoral ministry from an intentionally theological perspective. In other words, it is not a type of theology done *by* pastors, but a type of theology focused *on* pastors.

In addition, it can also be assumed that pastoral theology implies nothing more than an academic, ivory-tower approach to thinking about ministry.

It is considered to be entirely theoretical and completely removed from the real-life people and real-life situations that confront pastors. But while it is true that pastoral theology is not as concerned with the "how to" aspects of ministry, that is not to suggest it is unconcerned with the practice of ministry. Not only does pastoral theology include the exploration of the specific practices of pastoral ministry (preaching, counseling, caring for the sick and hurting, conducting public worship, etc.), it seeks to enhance the effectiveness of such practices by focusing on the theological motivations behind them and the theological significance of them. It is not intended to be an exercise in knowledge simply for knowledge's sake; it is intended to infuse the work and duties of pastors with theological meaning. Again, its goal is not only to establish a theological foundation for *understanding* ministry but also for *practicing* it.

Like any field of Christian theology, pastoral theology is informed by holy Scripture and derives its concepts, categories, and understandings from divine revelation. Indeed, this is what properly qualifies and legitimizes it as theology. Its fundamental starting point for understanding the role and responsibilities of pastors is what God himself says in his Word. Therefore, pastoral theology bases its view of ministry not on denominational trends, congregational expectations, or cultural stereotypes but on theological truths revealed in the Word of God. In short, it is the fruit of sustained theological reflection on the Bible's teaching about pastoral ministry.

As such, it rightly deserves its own distinct place among the different fields of Christian theology. It is no less theology than systematic theology or biblical theology. But while pastoral theology is its own distinctive field of theology, it is certainly not detached or disconnected from the other fields. Instead, pastoral theology intentionally draws insights from biblical theology, systematic theology, historical theology, and moral theology. It makes use of the traditional theological categories found in those other disciplines and applies the biblical, systematic, and historic doctrines of the Christian faith specifically to the pastorate. And those insights, categories, and doctrines greatly aid in the understanding of ministry that pastoral theology seeks to develop. Moreover, the other theological disciplines help inform and enhance the actual practice of ministry that pastoral theology seeks to cultivate. In this way, pastoral theology not only integrates the other theological disciplines, it depends upon them, serves them, and affirms them.

Historically speaking, though, pastoral theology did not begin as a specific academic discipline. Instead, it grew out of theological reflection on the task of shepherding God's flock. For that is the essence of pastoral ministry. In fact, the word "pastor" is derived from the word for "shepherd." Thus, the historical roots of pastoral theology extend as far back as the shepherding imagery used in the Bible. Of course, God himself is depicted in the Scriptures as the ultimate Shepherd of his people (e.g., Ps 23; Ezek 34:11–16), but he also chooses to use "undershepherds" (or pastors) to lead and care for his flock. This is why Jesus refers to himself as "the good shepherd" who "lays down his life for the sheep" (John 10:11). It is also why, prior to his ascension, he gives the apostle Peter the following pastoral charge: "Tend my sheep" (John 21:16 ESV). Those words, from the lips of the Good Shepherd himself, give pastoral ministry profound theological meaning. Though Jesus continues to be the "chief Shepherd" (1 Pet 5:4) and "the great Shepherd" (Heb 13:20), he now entrusts his appointed undershepherds with the weighty task of tending his sheep.

Unsurprisingly, then, later in the New Testament Peter is heard reinforcing the importance of this theological understanding of pastoral ministry when he gives fellow pastors a similar charge: "Be shepherds of God's flock that is under your care" (1 Pet 5:2 NIV). The apostle Paul also alludes to this imagery in his message to the Ephesian elders: "Keep watch over yourselves and all the flock of which the Holy Spirit has made you overseers. Be shepherds of the church of God, which he bought with his own blood" (Acts 20:28 NIV).

Pastoral theology, then, is historically rooted in this biblical metaphor for understanding and practicing ministry. Together with the three "pastoral epistles" that Paul writes to Timothy and Titus, which serve to put the metaphor in motion and show what it looks like for pastors to tend Christ's sheep, a consistent, biblical foundation for pastoral theology is firmly established in the apostolic era. And this foundation has continually been built upon throughout the history of the church.

In the Patristic era, some of the earliest examples of pastoral theology come from Ignatius of Antioch (110), Tertullian (220), and Cyprian (248), later followed by Ambrose (397) and Isidore of Seville (636). But three works from the church fathers, two Greek and one Latin, deserve special mention, both for their influence and for their content. The first comes from the pen of Gregory of Nazianzus (389), and it is titled *In Defense of His Flight to Pontus*, *and His Return, After His Ordination to the Priesthood, With an Exposition of the Character of the Priestly Office.* In this fourth-century work, Gregory provides a lasting metaphor for pastoral ministry, describing the work of pastors as "physicians of souls." In addition, he articulates some of the specific challenges of the pastorate, along with the moral requirements of those called to serve in this office. The second work, *Six Books on the Priesthood* by John Chrysostom (407), is a theological treatise in which Chrysostom expounds on the shepherding imagery used in the Scriptures to emphasize the serious responsibility entrusted to pastors to care for the flock of Christ. And a third work that deserves to be mentioned is the most influential, *Pastoral Care* by Gregory the Great (604). Gregory's *Pastoral Care* was not only the first work in the history of the church to approach something like a comprehensive textbook on pastoral care, but it also became Christianity's primary text on pastoral theology during this period (and remained so for roughly the next thousand years).

Theological reflection on pastoral ministry continued in the centuries following the patristic era, albeit on a much more limited basis. While evidence of such reflection can be seen in the works of figures such as Bede (735), Thomas Aquinas (1274), and Bonaventure (1274), pastoral duties were largely neglected or undervalued during much of the medieval period. Consequently, so was theological reflection related to the pastoral office. Not until the period of the Protestant Reformation did a renewed interest in pastoral theology arise.

While reformers such as Martin Luther, John Calvin, and Huldrych Zwingli all served as pastors and all modeled the significance of pastoral theology, it was the reformer of Strasbourg Martin Bucer (1551) who wrote the primary work of pastoral theology during this era. Bucer's *Concerning the True Care of Souls* remains the Reformation's most valued systematic treatment of pastoral theology. He takes as his primary biblical text Ezek 34:16 (yet another example of the significance of the shepherding metaphor), and he uses it to launch into a discussion on the responsibilities of pastors in caring for souls, responsibilities that include searching for lost sheep, bringing back straying sheep, binding up wounded sheep, strengthening weak sheep, as well as guarding and feeding healthy sheep.

Following on the heels of Bucer, the Puritan pastor Richard Baxter (1691) wrote *The Reformed Pastor*, which has become one of the most influential works on pastoral ministry ever published in the English language. The book is an extended exposition of Acts 20:28, emphasizing the high calling and utter seriousness of pastoral ministry, as well as challenging pastors to take to heart the need to provide spiritual care for the flock that has been entrusted to them. As for the evangelical period that came after Puritanism, resources such as *The Christian Ministry* by Charles Bridges (1869) and *Lectures to My Students* by Charles Spurgeon (1892) serve as commendable examples of pastoral theology written by the early generations of evangelicals.

Beginning in the nineteenth and twentieth centuries, however, and continuing down to the present day, two major shifts occurred in the field of pastoral theology. One was its emergence as a new academic discipline, becoming a regular part of the curriculum in theological education. The discipline has grown such that in 1985, the Society for Pastoral Theology was established as a community for scholars, educators, and practitioners. This Society also publishes *The Journal of Pastoral Theology*, which seeks to advance the discipline in the academic arena. The other, more troubling shift was that pastoral theology gradually began to lose its original meaning and purpose within much of Protestantism. No longer did it focus on theological exploration of the identity and responsibilities of pastors, and no longer did it look to the Bible as its source and guide. Instead, it took a decidedly psychological and therapeutic turn, focusing almost exclusively on counseling and the social sciences. This shift eventually gave rise to what is now known as the modern pastoral care movement, which has become the dominant emphasis in contemporary pastoral theology. Originally founded by Anton Boisen (1965) and later championed by Seward Hiltner (1984), the Clinical Pastoral Education movement completely reoriented the field of pastoral theology, moving the focus away from the biblical and theological to the psychological. Moreover, the primary locus of ministry was moved away from local church settings to clinical settings. As a result, much of what passes for pastoral theology in academic settings today is neither theological nor pastoral. It is driven more by psychology than theology, and many in the field are simply secular therapists rather than shepherds tending the flock of God.

A more recent trend influencing pastoral theology is its reliance on corporate leadership theory, which promotes practices borrowed from the realm of business. Increasingly, pastors are encouraged to see themselves and their work in light of the corporate world. The emphasis is much more organizational than theological. Accordingly, the new model for pastoral ministry has become the business-savvy CEO rather than the faithful shepherd of God's flock.

Therefore, if pastoral theology, as it has been understood for the majority of Christian history, is to be revived and is to flourish in our own day, then the following suggestions should be kept in mind. One, pastoral ministry should be seen as inherently theological. For too long now pastoral ministry has been viewed primarily through psychological, sociological, or managerial lenses. For the last century at least, most of the literature in the field has been focused predominantly on theories of counseling, providing a psychological rather than a theological emphasis. And even when resources free of psychological emphasis have been produced for pastors, they have largely focused on technical skills, business acumen, or purely pragmatic leadership concerns rather than theological truth. But shepherding God's flock is unavoidably theological by nature. Consequently, pastoral ministry should be seen, first and foremost, as theological work. To be a pastor is to be a theologian because to be a pastor is to be concerned with the things of God. It is to be entrusted by God with the mysteries of God for the sake of the people of God. Sociological, psychological, organizational, and pragmatic realities might be of benefit, but they are insufficient to provide a foundation for understanding and practicing pastoral ministry. For that, theology is essential. Preaching, praying, evangelizing, counseling, ministering to the sick—these are all deeply theological acts. Pastors must recapture a sense of the theological realities that are essential to their calling and work. Therefore, pastors should see their ministry as inherently theological.

Two, biblical identity should shape pastoral practice. Every pastor has an identity that shapes his practices. He might not consciously realize it, but it is there nonetheless, controlling and motivating how he spends his time and carries out the duties of his office. But that identity may be misplaced. And if it is, then his practices will likewise be misguided. If pastors do not rightly understand who they are, then they will not rightly understand what they are called to do. If they do not see themselves the way the Bible intends, which is primarily as shepherds tending to God's flock, then they will obviously not be involved in tasks that resemble shepherds tending to God's flock.

Sadly, this is the exact situation that confronts the church today. Large numbers of pastors no longer look to the Bible for their sense of identity. Their view of themselves is defined by something or someone else. It might be psychological theory, it might be the world of business, it might be ministerial pragmatism, it might be cultural or congregational assumptions, or it might be their own personality and giftedness. But as long as unbiblical substitutes give them their sense of identity, then their pastoral practices will be shaped in unbiblical ways as well. The solution is for pastors to return to seeing themselves in light of the biblical pattern (see especially Acts 20:17–35; 1 Tim 3:1–7; Titus 1:5–9; 1 Pet 5:1–4), which will have a profound effect on how they carry out their ministry. Moreover, it will have a profound effect on the flock that God has entrusted to them. Therefore, pastors should become well acquainted with the biblical texts that define the pastoral office, that detail the requirements of pastors, and that describe their specific responsibilities. This is the primary means by which a pastoral theology is developed and then implemented in the life and work of a pastor.

Third, pastoral theology should result in ministry marked by Christological and ecclesiological emphasis. That is, pastoral ministry should be practiced in such a way that Jesus Christ and his church are unmistakably central. A theology of shepherding that does not lead to a clear emphasis on the Chief Shepherd and his flock is a deficient theology. And yet Christ and his church are seen as largely irrelevant in much of contemporary pastoral theology. Very little mention is even made of Jesus—his person or his work. And as mentioned above, the modern pastoral care movement has shifted the context for pastoral ministry away from the local church and placed it in the counseling clinic. Admittedly, pastoral care and counseling are of great benefit and are unquestionably needed, but when they are completely divorced from Christ and his church, they cease to be either Christian or pastoral. Therefore, pastoral ministry must be rooted in the local church and undertaken by those whom God has called to shepherd his flock, faithfully laboring to point people to Jesus Christ for salvation, for sanctification, for healing, for peace, for hope, and for the grace to meet their every need.

Fourth, pastors should draw on the rich history of pastoral examples from the past to help them develop a deeper and more faithful pastoral theology. While the last few hundred years have not produced nearly as much in the way of a historic and faithful pastoral theology, that is not the case for the previous eighteen hundred years. Pastors have numerous examples to draw on and learn from, and they would be well served by making themselves familiar with these classic works of pastoral theology. If today's pastors would sit at the feet of previous generations of pastors—men like Gregory, Bucer, and Baxter—it would be time well spent. There will be differences for sure, both in terms of context and of theological emphasis, but there will also be much wisdom to glean from those who have labored faithfully before them. To ignore the theological treasures of the past is to impoverish the ministry of the present.

Conclusion

Pastors should keep in mind their accountability to the Chief Shepherd, Jesus Christ. After all, it is his flock that pastors are called to tend. And while it is true that they are caretakers, he is the owner. Therefore, to be a pastor, or an undershepherd, is "to be both *responsible for* (the flock) and *responsible to* (the Owner) . . . Those who are called to leadership in the covenant community are called to take care of those whom God calls '*my* sheep'" (John 21:15–17).[1] Such a reminder should instill in all pastors a sense of humility and a sense of gravity. Humility, because they remember that they are only undershepherds and Jesus Christ is the Chief Shepherd. Gravity, because they recognize that they will one day have to give an account for the sheep that he has placed under their care (Heb 13:17). This is a sobering reality, one that should demonstrate the serious nature of pastoral ministry and leave those who are pursuing this office, as well as those already in it, asking the appropriate question in response: "Who is sufficient for these things?" (2 Cor 2:16 ESV).

FOR ADDITIONAL STUDY

Akin, Daniel L., and Scott Pace. *Pastoral Theology: Theological Foundations for Who a Pastor Is and What He Does*. Nashville: B&H, 2017.

---

[1] Timothy Laniak, *Shepherds after My Own Heart* (Downers Grove: IVP, 2006), 248.

Baxter, Richard. *The Reformed Pastor*. London: Religious Tract Society, 1862.

Bridges, Charles. *The Christian Ministry*. Edinburgh: Banner of Truth Trust, 1980.

Bucer, Martin. *Concerning the True Care of Souls*. Edinburgh: Banner of Truth Trust, 2009.

Chrysostom, John. *Six Books on the Priesthood*.

Gregory of Nazianzus. *Oration II: In Defense of His Flight to Pontus, and His Return, After His Ordination to the Priesthood, with an Exposition of the Character of the Priestly Office*.

Gregory the Great. *Pastoral Care*.

Laniak, Timothy. *Shepherds after My Own Heart*. Downers Grove: IVP, 2006.

McNeill, John. *A History of the Cure of Souls*. New York: Harper & Bros., 1951.

Oden, Thomas. *Pastoral Theology*. San Francisco: Harper & Row, 1983.

Peterson, Eugene. *Five Smooth Stones for Pastoral Work*. Atlanta: John Knox, 1980.

Purves, Andrew. *Pastoral Theology in the Classical Tradition*. Louisville: Westminster John Knox, 2001.

Spurgeon, Charles. *Lectures to My Students*. Peabody, MA: Hendrickson, 2010.

Also see these articles: Systematic Theology, Church, Worship, Baptism, Lord's Supper, Preaching

PART III
THEOLOGY, HISTORY, AND GEOGRAPHY

13

Patristic Theology

D. Jeffrey Bingham

In the summer of AD 177, Pothinus, the bishop of Lyons, died giving witness to Christ, the Christian God.[1] To the name of Pothinus, among others, we could add that of Attalus, roasted alive in the amphitheater. Likewise,
Maturus and Sanctus succumbed to the flames while a bull fatally gored a
slave girl named Blandina. What fortified this slave girl in the face of Roman
accusers? Why did she not curse Christ? Why did she stand immovable as a
Christian? The answer is as simple as it is incredible: her theology.

Following the martyrdom of Pothinus, Irenaeus succeeded him as
bishop of Lyons. It is with him that our glance into the early Christian faith
begins—a biblical, ancient, and communal theology grounded in the earth-
shaking and earth-redeeming gospel of Christmas, Good Friday, and Easter.

Theological Controversies and Doctrinal Formulation

Eusebius (c. 314) lauded Irenaeus as a peacemaker, yet this irenic churchman,
writing *Against Heresies* c. 180, argued against two groups of false teachers—
the Valentinians and the Marcionites.[2] In early Christianity, much doctrinal

---

[1] *Letter of the Churches of Lyons and Vienne* in Eusebius of Caesarea, *Church
History* (5.1–3).
[2] Eusebius, *Church History* 5.24.

development took place in the face of heresy (cf. 1 Cor 15:12–33; Gal 1:6–9; 1 John 4:1–6; 2 John 7–11).

Both the heterodox and orthodox appealed to Scripture and elements of the church's established tradition for doctrinal construction. The fundamental question concerned how Scripture should be understood. Orthodoxy answered it by attending to the Bible's precise terminology, the literary context of a word or passage, the whole canonical context, and the symbiotic relationship between Scripture and tradition, with Christ as the center.

Fundamental Theological Issues

Scripture and Tradition

From the apostles to those they mentored and eventually down to Irenaeus himself and his successors, Irenaeus believed there existed an unbroken received line of apostolic teaching, a Rule of Faith. This established tradition provided the hermeneutical standard for accurately connecting all the various parts of the Bible into a coherent whole.[3] The trustworthy apostolic interpretation of *Scripture* had been deposited within the church and providentially passed down and preserved.[4] Heretics made connections as well, but theirs were disordered.[5] Their biblical theology may have at first appeared to be genuine, but it wove together a counterfeit theology.[6]

Irenaeus had been a disciple of Polycarp, the bishop of Smyrna and a pupil of the apostle John and others who had seen Christ.[7] This pedigree linked Irenaeus to the teaching of the apostles and illustrates the principle of apostolic succession. He taught what he received. The same convention holds on a conciliar creedal scale as well. The Council of Constantinople (381), for example, confesses "one holy, catholic, and apostolic church," and Chalcedon (451) follows "the holy fathers" and represents biblical teaching. Councils were not inventing doctrine. In the face of contemporary heresies,

---

[3] Irenaeus, *Against Heresies* 3.3.1–4; cf. 4.26.2; 4.33.8.
[4] Irenaeus, *Against Heresies* 3.1.1; 3.21.2; 4.1.1–2.
[5] Irenaeus, *Against Heresies* 1.8.1.
[6] Irenaeus, *Against Heresies* 1. Pref. 2; 1.8.1; 1.9.4; 3.16.4.
[7] Eusebius, *History of the Church* 5.20; Irenaeus, *Against Heresies* 3.3.4.

they were making explicit from Scripture and tradition what the church had received from the apostles but had not yet expressly stated.[8]

A generation before Irenaeus, Ignatius, bishop of Antioch, had applied the principle of apostolic succession to the trustworthiness of the bishop's protective teaching.[9] Hilary of Poitiers (359) remarks that the faith was once laid down, that it had persevered to his day, and that it remained steadfast.[10] Similarly, among the reasons he would never leave the one true universal church, Augustine (397) lists the succession of bishops from Peter.[11]

The early confidence in apostolic succession should not be taken to indicate the secondary or superfluous nature of Scripture to tradition. The church derived the principle from its reading of Scripture. The Scriptures furnished proof for the church's faith, and the whole of Scripture interpreted the bits of Scripture.[12] The Scriptures were the inspired, sufficient source and filter for theological truth. For clarity and accuracy in the face of heresy, it sometimes became necessary to introduce extra-scriptural theological terminology, yet such language had to faithfully represent and evoke Scripture.[13]

Faith and Understanding

The epistemology of the ancient church differed from a modern rationalism. Truth did not require contemporary, individualistic, rationalistic reexamination to verify its authenticity. For early Christians, the Scriptures and the Rule of Faith were authoritative as received from Jesus, his apostles, and his successors.

But neither did ancient Christianity reject metanarrative, a confidence in an overarching, foundational, absolute account of reality. Early Christians believed in a coherent, unified, perfect, and fixed rule of doctrine and the nonrelative message of the Bible with each part integral to the whole. Scripture

---

[8] See Hilary of Poitiers (356), *Against Valens and Ursacius* 1.8.7.

[9] Ignatius, *Letter to the Philadelphians* 2.

[10] Hilary, *Against Valens and Ursacius* 2.12.

[11] Augustine, *Against the Epistle of Manichaeus Called "Fundamental"* 4.5.

[12] Matt 16:18–19 and John 21:15–17; Irenaeus, *Against Heresies* 3.5.1; 3.12.9.

[13] Athanasius, *Festal Letter* 39; *Against the Heathen* 1; *Letter to the Bishops of Egypt* 1.1–10; *Defense of the Nicene Definition* 32; *On the Councils of Ariminum and Seleucia* 6.

and the Rule of Faith could be elucidated but were not fluid or mutable. There was heterodoxy. There was orthodoxy. One was false, the other true.

Explicit in Irenaeus, faith alone, simply put by the Lord to the Prophet Isaiah, is the singular basis for understanding.[14] Faith enables accurate reasoning: "If you do not believe, neither will you understand." Faith is grounded on the scriptural teaching handed down by the apostles and their disciples, the church's bishops and elders, in the Rule of Faith, the creed or theology received in baptism.[15] It is with this understanding that Hilary of Poitiers (c. 360) prayed that God would preserve his creedal faith confessed at his baptism in the name of the triune God.[16] This premodern theological orientation, which is commonly associated with Anselm of Canterbury in the late eleventh century, is a much earlier scripturally grounded driving principle.[17]

The Biblical Canon

Some early groups competed with orthodoxy by attempting to add to, subtract from, or hermeneutically deprecate the received Scriptures. The Valentinians denigrated the Old Testament by arguing that its teaching contradicted Christ and his apostles, and they deprecated the four Gospels by supplementing them with other texts. Marcion (c. 144), excommunicated by Papias and demonized by the martyrs Polycarp and Justin, erred in two ways: (1) he disparaged the Old Testament as the revelation of a merciless, legislative, evil deity inferior to the benevolent, gracious Father of Jesus Christ manifested in the New Testament; and (2) he put forth a corrupt version of the New Testament containing only distortions of Luke and Paul's letters. For Irenaeus, the church's Scriptures included Old and New, prophet and apostle, and only four Gospels with a harmonious theology. Stephen, the church's first martyr, believed this.[18]

---

[14] 7:9 LXX, Latin.T

[15] Irenaeus, *Demonstration* 3.

[16] Hilary, *On the Trinity* 12.57; cf. Clement of Alexandria, *Miscellanies* 5.11.71 (c. 200); Augustine, *On Christian Doctrine* 2.12; *Tractates on the Gospel of John* 29.6; *On Free Choice* 1.2.4–5.

[17] Anselm of Canterbury, *Proslogion* 1.

[18] Irenaeus, *Against Heresies* 1.27.2; 3.2.1; 3.11.1–15; 3.12.12.

For the apostolic church, the Old Testament was Christian Scripture inspired by the Spirit and in union with Jesus's words. Clement of Rome (late first century), probably martyred under the Roman emperor Trajan, demonstrated early Christian devotion to the Old Testament by liberally quoting it to teach essential Christian virtues, beliefs, and ecclesiastical polity.[19] Tertullian of Carthage (c. 200) addressed Marcion's teachings and those of his disciples (Marcionites) in five books (*Against Marcion*). The great number of early doctrinal works, homilies, and commentaries that cite or exposit the sacred Jewish writings point to Marcion's failure. Some New Testament books were disputed,[20] but none were rejected, and in 367 Athanasius of Alexandria listed all the canonical books without qualification.[21]

Although the premodern early church would be scripturally and traditionally based, tenets of the ancient common faith and communally held doctrine would be disputed. In response, the church might interpret or translate, the implicit might be made explicit, or the tacit might be spoken, but it did not alter the substance. What were some basic elements of that enduring substance received at baptism? Here, we return to focus on the ground of the martyr's witness, the God-man, Jesus.

God in Eternity and History

From at least the second century, the church faced challenges to its distinctive monotheistic faith. For the Valentinians, two gods existed: the supreme, spiritual Father of the heavenly world, revealed by Christ; and the vile demiurge, the creator of the material world identified with the ignorant, arrogant Old Testament deity.[22] Two dualisms resulted: the Father versus the creator and the good, heavenly world versus the abject, material world of earth, flesh, and blood. Marcion held to a similar theological dualism.[23] Irenaeus, representatively, declared that all of Scripture harmoniously revealed only one

---

[19] See Clement of Rome, *Letter to the Church of Corinth*.

[20] James, Jude, 2 Peter, and 2 and 3 John; Eusebius, *Church History* 3.25.1–7.

[21] Athanasius, *Festal Letter* 39.5.

[22] Irenaeus, *Against Heresies* 1.1–7; cf. *Tripartite Tractate*.

[23] Justin Martyr, *Apology* 1.26, 58; Tertullian, *Against Marcion* 1.6, 19; 4.6.

God who is Creator, Father, and Redeemer of his creation.[24] A symphonic *Christian* monotheism taught the canonical unity of Father and Creator. But early Christian monotheism confessed another reality.

Early Christian theology also included belief in one God: the Father, the Son, and the Holy Spirit. Unlike the Valentinians who believed the Son and Spirit were beings of a lesser substance than the Father's, the church confessed that the eternal, divine Spirit of God and the eternal Son of God were indivisible in essence from the Father's divine substance. They are what God is. The Son eternally co-existed with the Father although he is begotten of the Father, for the one who is begotten of God is God.[25]

Tertullian taught, too, that the Three (Father, Son, and Spirit) were one in substance, one God yet a "Trinity" of distinct "persons."[26] He refuted the modalistic monarchianism (modalism) of Praxeas (c. 206) that sought to defend monotheism against polytheism.[27] This early twisting of the Godhead taught one divine substance and conflated the three persons into the same person, the Father, who might simply manifest himself, circumstantially, as one of the other two. The three were not distinct persons unto themselves. What the Son was and did, the Father was and did. Praxeas taught the birth, crucifixion, and suffering of the Father, that the Father both comes from himself and returns to himself, and that the Father is Jesus Christ. Sabellianism, a leading form of modalism linked to Sabellius (c. 215) also taught one person in three modes, one being with simply three names.[28]

Valentinianism and Marcionism threatened monotheism. Modalism threatened God's existence as three, distinct persons. In the early fourth century, again in the name of monotheism, a presbyter in Alexandria, Arius, challenged God's triunity. Praxeas stole the Son's personhood; Arianism robbed him of deity.

---

[24] Irenaeus, *Against Heresies* 2.30.9; cf. Tertullian, *Against Marcion* 2.1–29.

[25] Irenaeus, *Against Heresies* 1.10.1; 2.13.8; 2.28.4–6; 5.12.2; *Demonstration* 5, 40, 47.

[26] Tertullian, *Against Praxeas* 1–2; Theophilus of Antioch, *To Autolycus* 2.15.

[27] Tertullian, *Against Praxeas* 1–3, 13, 23.

[28] Epiphanius, *Panarion* 62; Also, see Dionysius of Alexandria, *Against the Sabellians*.

Arius taught that the Son was created by the Father, was not eternal, and was different in essence from the Father.[29] To him, the Son as *begotten* was created, made. The Son had a beginning to his existence; only the Father was unbegotten, eternal.

Bishop Alexander rebuked his wayward presbyter, an empire-wide argument raged, and Constantine, pressured, called the council of Nicaea (325), where the Arians and Alexander's party (including the deacon Athanasius) met in theological argument. The creed condemned the Arian views and confessed that the Son was of divine nature with the Father, but he was not the Father. Christian monotheism lay neither in the direction of modalism or Arianism. The Son was begotten of the Father. He was from the Father but not made or created. Instead, the Son was "of the same essence as the Father." As true God the Son, he shared with the Father the glorious deity of the Father.

After establishing that the Son is consubstantial with the Father, the creed clarifies three of his ministries: (1) the divine Son was the agent of the Father's creative activity; (2) the divine Son, in order to save human beings, became human and fulfilled all aspects of his incarnate ministry from descent to ascent; and (3) the incarnate, divine Son will return as judge. Creation, salvation, and judgment are ministries of the divine Son. To believe Christianly and redemptively in the Son is to believe in the gospel of the incarnate, divine Son.

The creed, trinitarian in structure, affirmed the church's faith in the Holy Spirit without further elucidation. That would come in fifty-six years at Constantinople. Nicaea's ecumenical creed served archetypally: both biblical terminology and extra-biblical terminology, inspired by the Bible, were used to clarify the Bible's meaning.

Councils and creeds rarely solve doctrinal problems immediately. In 381, at Constantinople, the church would reaffirm and supplement the Nicene Creed. It made explicit, for instance, that the Son was eternally begotten; that both the Spirit and Mary participated in the incarnation; that the Spirit proceeds from the Father; that he is Lord, Life-giver, and

---

[29] See Arius, *Letter to Eusebius of Nicomedia* (c. 318); Alexander of Alexandria, *Encyclical Letter* (c. 318); Arius, *Letter to Alexander of Alexandria* (c. 320).

the one who inspired the prophets; and that he should be worshipped and glorified together with the Father and Son. The council took place only after much homiletical, theological, exegetical ministry and correspondence during the intervening years, in no small part by Athanasius and the three Cappadocians. Such theological-pastoral service strengthened the church's anti-Arian position on three fronts: (1) the Father, Son, and Spirit were consubstantial, of the same substance; (2) the real differences between them were hypostatic, that is, a matter of person, not substance; and (3) the Spirit was equal to the Father and Son in essence. A few of those ministerial works were Athanasius's *Against the Arians* and *Letter to Serapion*, Basil of Caesarea's *On the Holy Spirit* and *Epistle 38*, Gregory of Nyssa's *Against Eunomius*, and Gregory of Nazianzus's *Theological Orations*. Hilary of Poitiers provided the first comprehensive Latin response to anti-Nicene theology in *On the Trinity* (357/358).

Stirred by the reasserted Nicene theology, expository preaching and fresh contemplation of the biblical, trinitarian God would flourish. John Chrysostom (c. 390) provides an exemplary sermon on John 1:3.[30] In his *On the Trinity* (400), Augustine reminds his readers that such reflection always begins with faith, not reason (1.1.1). Then, mainly through analogies drawn from inner human aspects and virtues, he offers potentially illustrative, but not dogmatic, ways for understanding the oneness of the divine essence and the three separate persons.

Some forty-six years after Constantinople reaffirmed the Son's deity, Augustine concluded his *City of God* (22.6) by reminding his readers of the gravity of this doctrine. This theology determined how Christians live as strangers upon this earth. The martyrs had died rather than deny Christ's divinity. They despised a brief respite from temporal suffering when they, as peaceful citizens of Christ's city, preferred not retaliatory violence but the confession that yields eternal salvation: Christ is God.

Jesus Christ, Son of God Incarnate

While Jesus's earliest Jewish detractors might have questioned his deity (John 5:17–19), others denied his humanity, his fleshly incarnation (2 John 7). The

---

[30] John Chrysostom, *Homilies on John 5*.

latter issue became dominant in the second century. Valentinians taught that Christ must be separated from evil, unredeemable flesh. As a divine spirit-being from the heavenly realm, he did not really become flesh or really suffer. He only seemed to be human (Docetism) or temporarily inhabited a human named "Jesus" (Adoptianism). "Christ" and "Jesus" were divided. Marcion, too, viewed Christ in a Docetic-like manner.[31]

Before Irenaeus, the Bishop-martyr, Ignatius of Antioch (c. 110) wrote eloquently against Doceticism: "There is one Physician of flesh and spirit; born yet un-generated (not created); God in man (incarnate); true life in death; of Mary and of God; at first subject to suffering and then beyond suffering, Jesus Christ our Lord."[32]

For the faithful, those theologically sound, the eternal Son really became flesh, born of his virgin mother in order to save his creation. Jesus Christ, deity and humanity, secured the inherent preciousness of human flesh and promised salvation of the believer's flesh through bodily resurrection by the Holy Spirit. What the Son of God became, the Spirit raises.

The martyrs, including Polycarp, saw their real, fleshly suffering as imitation of the Lord's real, incarnate passion and his bodily resurrection as a guarantee of their own. Their theological faith in the Son of God's union with flesh was indivisible from their ultimate Christian faithfulness. Unity in Christology inspired unity in faith and practice.[33]

But controversy continued. Unbelievers greeted the gospel that God and flesh were compatible with incredulity. Christological argument troubled the later fourth and fifth centuries but ushered in the creed of Chalcedon (451).

One could simplify the debate that ensued as an argument over the meaning of the biblical teaching summarized in John 1:14 (and Phil 2:6–8): "the Word became flesh." Each term required theological definition. Nicaea had declared "the Word" as fully divine. But what about "became" and "flesh"? Typically, heresies developed. There were three.

---

[31] Irenaeus, *Against Heresies* 4.33.2; Tertullian, *Against Marcion* 1.19; 3.8; 4.7; *On the Flesh of Christ* 1.1–4.

[32] Ignatius, *Letter to the Ephesians* 7.

[33] *Martyrdom of Polycarp* 14, 17, 19; Irenaeus, *Against Heresies* 3.3.4; 3.16.1–9; 3.18.1–7; 3.19.1–3; 5.8.1–2; 5.9.1–4; 5.14.1; cf. Tertullian, *Against Marcion* 3.1–24.

First came Apollinarianism, promoted by Apollinaris, Bishop of Laodicea (c. 350/360). His view was condemned in AD 381 at the Council of Constantinople. Apollinaris claimed that the incarnate Son, insofar as it concerned his humanity, was only body. He was not fully human. He did not assume a human spirit, a human mind. The divine, eternal Word, the Son of God, had substituted himself for the human spirit and functioned as the rational and spiritual center of Jesus. "Flesh" meant only body, not "fully human." Sacrificing the humanity, he thought, preserved Christ's impeccability. Full humanity and deity were incompatible.[34] In reply, Gregory of Nazianzus argued that Jesus is both divine Son of God and fully human with spirit, soul, and body. The salvation of human beings necessitated Jesus being a complete human being.[35]

Nestorianism presented the second threat. Nestorius of Constantinople (428) was probably not ultimately guilty of the heresy (see *Bazaar of Heracleides*), but the label stuck. Nevertheless, in contrast to Cyril of Alexandria and the Council of Ephesus (431), he found it objectionable to apply the term *Theotokos* ("Mother of God") to Mary (Nestorius, *First Sermon Against Theotokos* [428]; Cyril, *Second Letter to Nestorius* [c. 429] 24e; Nestorius, *Second Letter to Cyril of Alexandria; Third Letter to Nestorius* [430] 75b-76a).

Theotokos had Christological force: Mary was the "mother of God" because the son conceived within her and delivered by her in Bethlehem, Jesus, was fully God the Word *and* fully human. Mary bore a whole person of two natures, not merely a human nature. *Theotokos* moved the church to affirm unswervingly, without halting qualification of the hypostatic union stressed by Cyril, the unity of the two natures (magisterial infinitude with frail finitude) in the one person of Jesus Christ.

Although Nestorius said that Christ is two natures, God and man, Cyril suspected he segregated the natures. Nestorius taught that "Christ," but not explicitly the Son of God, had assumed human nature, that God indwelt the

---

[34] Apollinaris, *On the Union* 7–10, 12; *According to the Faith* 2, 8–9, 11, 28, 30–31; *Fragments* 19, 22, 28, 41, 72, 129.

[35] Gregory of Nazianzus, *Epistle* 101.32, 51–52; cf. *Epistle* 102; *Oration* 45; Gregory of Nyssa, *Refutation of the Views of Apollinaris; To Theophilus: Against the Apollinarians*; Athanasius, *Letter 59 to Epictetus*; Ps-Athanasius, *On the Incarnation of Our Lord Jesus Christ: Against Apollinaris*.

human nature, that he divided the natures, that Christ was twofold, and that he linked the two by "conjunction."[36]

To Cyril (and the Council of Chalcedon), all this indicated an error in Nestorius's doctrine that compromised the union of the natures in the one person and taught that Christ was two loosely conjoined *persons*.[37] The incarnation did not result in a *personal* union, a *hypostatic* union, a union of the single person of the eternal, divine Son of the Father with a human nature so that one person, the Father's Son, was now also Mary's son, two complete natures in union in one *person*.[38]

The third Christological heresy, Eutychianism, was prominently associated with Eutyches of Constantinople. Originally condemned at Constantinople in November of 448, the Second ("Robber") Council of Ephesus restored Eutyches in 449.[39] That same year Leo I, bishop of Rome, denounced him again (*Letter to Flavian*), and Chalcedon (451) sealed his teaching as heretical.

Eutyches said that Jesus had only "one nature" after the union.[40] Uncorrectable in his own reading of the Bible and the fathers (like all false teachers), he refused to confess two natures in one person, terminology that had been received in Constantinople (448). His language seemed to deny Christ's full humanity. Consequently, the synod numbered him with Valentinus and Apollinaris. He also taught that the two natures were mixed and confused into one nature, thus failing to preserve the integrity of two complete, distinct natures in the incarnate union.[41]

Responding to this chaos of scriptural misinterpretation, the church took responsibility to bring order in its fourth ecumenical council at Chalcedon in 451. The international body of Christ acted to correct schismatic individuals gone rogue. The resulting statement of faith built upon Nicaea's (325) and

---

[36] Nestorius, *First Sermon Against Theotokos*; *Second Letter to Cyril of Alexandria* 6.

[37] Cyril, *Second Letter to Nestorius* 23b; 24d-e; *Third Letter to Nestorius* 70b, 70e-71d; 73b-d; 75b-c; 76a-c.

[38] Cf. Leo, *Letter (28) to Flavian of Constantinople (Leo's Tome)* 5–6.

[39] *Acts of the Synod of Constantinople* Sessions 3–7 (esp. Sessions 6–7) in the *Acts of the Council of Chalcedon* 354–552 (esp. 451, 488–89, 505–52).

[40] Leo, *Letter to Flavian* 6; *Synod of Constantinople* Session 7/*Council of Chalcedon* 527.

[41] *Synod of Constantinople* Session 7/*Council of Chalcedon* 545.

Constantinople's (381) received theology, faithfully represented the teaching of both Testaments, employed language from Cyril and Leo, and took direct aim at the three heresies.

Beginning with a confession that the Lord Jesus Christ, the Son of God, is perfect and complete in deity and humanity (only sin is excepted), consubstantial with both the Father (Nicaea) and human beings, it opposed Apollinarianism: Jesus was truly human with both a reasonable soul and body. Then, announcing the soteriological importance of the union of his deity and humanity, the creed affirmed, against Nestorianism, that Mary is *Theotokos*. Whether one calls him Christ or Lord, her son is the Father's divine Son (Nicaea). Against Eutyches and Nestorianism, Christ has two natures. In response to the former, the two are neither confused nor changed in the incarnate union, while in reply to the latter, they are not divided or separated. While each nature remains distinct in Jesus and the characteristics of each are preserved, the two natures concur in one person. There are not two persons as Nestorianism taught.

Jesus Christ and Discipleship

Faced with trial and death and searching for salvation, early Christians longed for deliverance, courage, and comfort. What they looked for, they discovered in Christian theology. They found it in the church's received teachings of the prophets, Christ, and the apostles. They found it in the waters of baptism as they put the dried-out pagan gods of stone behind them and received refreshment from God the Father, through God the Son, by God the Holy Spirit. They found it in the supper of the Eucharist as they feasted gratefully on the good news that God the Son, Jesus Christ, the God-man, in flesh and blood, endured suffering and mortality, triumphed over death, and would return to judge and raise them bodily to glory by the Spirit. They were not alone in their suffering; the Son of God in mortal flesh had preceded them. Death need not terrorize them; the Son of God in immortal flesh had preceded them in bodily resurrection. He, in incorruptible flesh, would come for them.

For Additional Study

Behr, John. *The Way to Nicaea*. Crestwood: St. Vladimir's Seminary, 2001.

———. *The Nicene Faith*. Crestwood: St. Vladimir's Seminary, 2004.

Bingham, D. Jeffrey, ed. *The Routledge Companion to Early Christian Thought*. London/New York: Routledge, 2010.

Burns, J. Patout, ed. *Theological Anthropology*. Minneapolis: Fortress, 1981.

Heine, Ronald. *Classical Christian Doctrine: Introducing the Essentials of the Ancient Faith*. Grand Rapids: Baker, 2013.

Kelly, J. N. D. *Early Christian Doctrines*. Rev. ed. New York: HarperCollins, 1978.

Norris, Richard A., ed. *The Christological Controversy*. Minneapolis: Fortress, 1980.

Rusch, William, ed. *The Trinitarian Controversy*. Minneapolis: Fortress, 1980.

Stevenson, J., ed. *Creeds, Councils and Controversies: Documents Illustrating the History of the Church, AD 337–461*. Rev. W. H. C. Frend. Grand Rapids: Baker, 2012.

———. ed. *A New Eusebius: Documents Illustrating the History of the Church to AD 337*. Rev. W. H. C. Frend. Grand Rapids: Baker, 2013.

Wilken, Robert Louis. *The Spirit of Early Christian Thought: Seeking the Face of God*. New Haven, Yale University, 2003.

Also see these articles: Role of Tradition, Historical Theology, Medieval Theology

14

Medieval Theology

Timothy George

T he early Middle Ages witnessed the fall of the old Roman Empire, the invasion of the barbarians, and the gradual emergence of a new political and social order known as feudalism. During this time, the bishop of Rome played an increasingly important role in the conversion of the barbarian tribes and the establishment of a new political order.

Although the title "pope" was not applied solely to the bishop of Rome until the eleventh century, a major papal figure had already emerged much earlier in the person of Pope Gregory I, who occupied the See of Peter from 590 until 604. Gregory was the first pope who had also been a monk. He welded a powerful alliance between papacy and monasticism. In 597 he sent one of his fellow monks, Augustine, on a missionary venture to Britain. From this mission, Roman Christianity spread to that important island kingdom. At the Synod of Whitby in 664, the authority of the pope was recognized over the older Celtic brand of Christianity. Within a few years, England became a beachhead of missionary activity, sending monastic evangelists such as Willibrord and Boniface to convert the peoples of northern Europe and to establish churches and monasteries loyal to the bishop of Rome.

A new era began on Christmas Day 800 when Pope Leo III crowned Charlemagne, the ruler of the Franks, as "the deputy of God . . . set to guard and rule all his members and . . . render an account for them on the day of judgment." This event, which would be replayed many times throughout the Middle Ages, marked the beginnings of the Holy Roman Empire.

Under Charlemagne, there was a minor revival of literature and religion led by the scholar Alcuin. The so-called "Carolingian Renaissance" stimulated new theological controversies over Christology, predestination, and the Lord's Supper. After Charlemagne, his empire was plunged into civil war, and the church was thoroughly corrupted by abuse. A fresh wave of barbarian attacks by the Vikings plunged Europe into what is known as the Dark Ages. Many people believed that the end of the world was near as the year 1000 approached.

The Eastern Church

In 330 Constantine had established a new capital city for the empire and named it after himself, Constantinople. This city became the center of a thriving civilization and the home of the Eastern Christian tradition. From this "New Rome" the emperor, seen as "the living image of Christ," exerted great influence over the life of the church. In the East, the emperor came to be seen as the earthly reflection of the heavenly potentate. The emperor controlled the election of high church officials and spoke with great authority on matters of theology and worship. The most famous of the Eastern emperors was Justinian (527–565), who built the great church Saint Sophia, expelled the barbarians, and established orthodoxy throughout his realm. He also consolidated the Roman Law in the Justinian Code, which became the basis for the medieval system.

In a sense, the Eastern church never went through the "Middle Ages," since Constantinople withstood all external invasions until 1453. The only exception was the sack of the city by the (Christian) crusaders in 1204. This meant that Eastern Christianity, also known as the orthodox church, became a bulwark of the historic Christian faith and a custodian of classical Christian culture. The orthodox church accepts the decisions of the first seven great church councils, concluding with Nicaea II in 787, as definitive and binding statements of Christian dogma. These important councils addressed significant questions such as how the Trinity should be believed and proclaimed, how Jesus Christ can be fully God and simultaneously be fully human, how to understand the two natures and two wills of Jesus Christ, and the meaning of the phrase "the Holy Spirit, the life giver."

Several of these councils dealt with controversial matters such as the nature of Christ's will and the role of icons, that is, images, in the church. In the eighth century, Emperor Leo III launched an attack on the use of icons, contending that such religious practice was idolatry. The use of icons was defended by the great theologian John of Damascus, who argued that to deny that Christ could be depicted on an image was, in reality, to deny the possibility of the incarnation. Still, he declared that icons should not be worshiped but simply honored and venerated as outward symbols of the faith.

The rise of Islam posed a tremendous threat both to the empire and the church. Based on the teachings of Muhammad, the Muslim faith is built around five "pillars," or basic doctrines: (1) There is no God but Allah, and Muhammad is his prophet. (2) The will of Allah is written down in the Qur'an, a divine book that shows the way to salvation. (3) There are six great prophets: Adam, Noah, Abraham, Moses, Jesus, and Muhammad, who surpasses all the others. (4) Prayer five times a day in the direction of the holy city of Mecca, along with almsgiving and fasting, are required of all true Muslims. (5) Pilgrimage to Mecca, either in person or by proxy, is an expected act of devotion. Armed with these beliefs, the followers of Muhammad fanned out from the deserts of Arabia in a series of violent holy wars capturing the ancient Christian centers of Jerusalem, Antioch, Alexandria, and Carthage. They entered Europe through the Iberian Peninsula (Spain) and were only turned back in France by Charles Martel at the famous Battle of Poitiers in 732. The interaction of Christianity and Islam is a major theme of the Middle Ages leading to the Christian efforts to recapture the holy land during the Crusades.

While the Eastern church was besieged by hostile forces during this entire period, it developed a vigorous spiritual life and displayed a missionary concern. The two brothers, Cyril and Methodius, carried the gospel to the Slavic peoples, giving them the Scriptures and liturgy in their own language. In 989 the Russian people embraced the orthodox faith, thus inaugurating a rich heritage of Christian life in that land. When Constantinople fell to the invading Turks in 1453, Moscow emerged as the "third Rome," that is, the new center and bulwark of Eastern Christianity. Even earlier, in

1054, the Eastern church had broken fellowship with the Christians of the West. To this day this schism remains one of the major divisions within the body of Christendom.

Monasticism

After the conversion of Constantine, when martyrdom was no longer likely, many zealous Christians retreated to the desert to embrace the "white martyrdom" of the monastic life. As successors to the martyrs, the monks registered a vigorous protest against the laxity and lukewarmness of "mainline" Christianity. The father of monasticism was Anthony, a third-century Egyptian hermit, whose biography by Athanasius influenced many others to take up the solitary life. The early monks lived alone and gave themselves to a life of prayer, fasting, and solitude. Most of them were laypersons, not priests, and their practice of strict discipline, called asceticism, was an important witness to the entire church.

After Anthony the three most important leaders of the monastic movement were Pachomius, Basil the Great, and Benedict of Nursia. Pachomius believed that monks should live and work together in community. While his ideas were rejected by those who preferred to retreat alone to the desert or remain perched high atop a stone pillar, in time cenobitic (from the Greek *koinos bias,* "life in common") life became the norm in both East and West.

In the East the monks followed the rule of Basil, which stressed obedience, prayer, and a life of service. Benedict is known as the "Patriarch of Western Monasticism." The rule of Benedict, drawn up around 480, became the normative guideline for monks throughout the Middle Ages. It set forth the ideals of obedience, humility, daily prayer, and manual labor. The motto of the Benedictine monastic life was *ora et labora,* pray and work. Benedict avoided some of the extreme asceticism of the early hermits, believing that the monastery should more resemble a family than a penitentiary. He also advised that "great care and concern should be shown in receiving poor people and pilgrims, because in them more particularly Christ is received."

Throughout the Middle Ages there were many forms of the monastic movement. One of the most important of these was associated with the influential monastery of Cluny in eastern France. Founded in 909, this monastery became the "mother house" of more than one thousand affiliated communities. A series of strong abbots, including Odo and Peter the Venerable, called for a stricter observance of the monastic life and imposed a uniform liturgy of prayer on the monks under their control.

Bernard of Clairvaux (1090–1153) was perhaps the leading monastic figure of the entire Middle Ages. Bernard founded a new order of monks, the Cistercians, and called for a return to a literal observance of Benedict's rule. He was a popular preacher and author of important works on Scripture and monasticism. Bernard was a great preacher whose eighty-six sermons on the Song of Solomon presented a beautiful picture of the soul's longing for God. Some of Bernard's hymns, such as "Jesus, The Very Thought of Thee," are still sung by Christians today. Bernard also wielded great power in the church politics of his day. He helped to place several popes in power and preached sermons urging knights to fight in the Second Crusade. Known for his devotional spirit, Bernard faithfully extended the work of the early church traditions to the extent that he was sometimes called "the last of the church fathers." He brought together Scripture, tradition, and reason in the practice of engaged and engaging Christian thinking.

The rise of the mendicant (beggar) orders in the thirteenth century marked a new stage in the spirituality of the Middle Ages. Whereas traditional monks were expected to stay in one place and devote themselves to manual labor and prayer, the mendicants, or friars (brothers) as they were also called, moved freely about in the world and depended on the charity of others for their survival.

The Dominican order was founded by a Spaniard, Dominic de Guzman (1170–1221), whose mission focused on winning heretics and heathen to the true faith through vigorous preaching and a lifestyle of poverty and simplicity. Because of their concern to ensure ecclesiastical orthodoxy, the Dominicans were known as "the Lord's dogs" (the literal meaning of their name in Latin, *domini cani*). The Dominicans produced many great scholars, the most notable of whom was Thomas Aquinas.

A very different legacy was forged by Francis of Assisi, who founded the Order of Friars Minor (lesser brothers) in 1209. The son of a wealthy cloth merchant, Francis abandoned a life of ease to identify himself with the deprived. Unlike Dominic, he was wary of too much "book learning," which he felt would lead to pride. Above all else, Francis's desire was to imitate his Lord, Jesus Christ. Near the end of his life, he was reported to have received the stigmata, bleeding wounds that resembled the nail and spear prints on Jesus's crucified body. Although Francis's order was approved by the pope, his way of life challenged the power and wealth of the church of his day. He was a great promoter of peace and made a missionary journey to the East, where he appeared before a Muslim sultan and sought to convert him to Christ. Shortly after his death in 1226, there was a major split in the Franciscan Order between the "spirituals," who insisted on following Francis's rule and example literally, and the more moderate majority, who accepted joint ownership of property and a liberal interpretation of the rule. In the sixteenth century, the Protestant reformers rejected monasticism as a valid Christian lifestyle. More recently, however, some Protestant groups, such as the church of England, have permitted the emergence of monastic orders within their ranks.

Scholasticism

Through their intense study of the Bible and their preservation of ancient manuscripts, the monks did much to keep the spirit of learning alive during the Dark Ages. The cathedral and monastic schools were centers of study that served as seed beds for the later universities. Scholasticism refers both to the revival of learning that occurred during the Middle Ages and the method of study by which it occurred: the process of careful, rational scrutiny; logical deduction; and the systematic ordering of truth.

Anselm (1033–1109) is known as the father of scholasticism. A devout monk and churchman, he became Archbishop of Canterbury in 1093. Building on the earlier work of Augustine, Anselm suggested three levels of theological insight: faith, where all Christian thinking begins; understanding, the effort to think and speak clearly about that which we believe; and vision, face-to-face communion with God, which is the ultimate goal of all our theology.

In his treatise *Proslogion*, Anselm put forth a simple proof for the existence of God known as the ontological argument, which he believed could be reduced to one sentence: God is that than which no greater can be conceived. The reality of God, he said, was bound up with this definition of his existence. It is significant, however, that Anselm's proof of the existence of God is contained in the form of a prayer. In other words, he had already been grasped in faith by the One he was seeking to understand. Anselm appealed to Scripture and to tradition as he attempted to bring together the roles of reason and faith. Again, echoing Augustine, he wrote, "I believe in order that I might understand."

Anselm is also remembered for setting forth a major understanding of the atonement in his treatise *Why God Became Man*. Since humans incurred an infinite debt to God when they sinned, and since only God could pay this great debt, God became human in Jesus Christ to offer satisfaction for sinful humanity through his death on the cross. The majority of God had been offended by sin. The death of Christ satisfies that offense by his sinless human life wedded to the divine. This understanding of the cross, later clarified by John Calvin, has remained an important part of the evangelical understanding of atonement.

Between the time of Anselm and Thomas Aquinas, two important teachers influenced the development of scholasticism. Peter Lombard (1100–1160) summarized the existing body of theology, which he arranged in four books on (1) the Trinity, (2) the creation and sin, (3) the incarnation and the virtues, and (4) the sacraments and last things. Lombard's *Books of Sentences*, as they were called, became the standard theological textbooks of the Middle Ages.

The second such teacher, Peter Abelard (1079–1142), was a brilliant scholar who emphasized the role of reason in understanding the Christian faith. His most famous work, *Sic et Non* (Yes and No), was a collection of apparently contradictory excerpts from the Scriptures and the church fathers on a large number of questions. Although he tried to resolve these differences by means of logic, Abelard's ideas went beyond the bounds of historic Christian orthodoxy on several important points. He rightly rejected the ransom to Satan theory, but he challenged Anselm's understanding of the atonement by claiming that the cross was more a moral display of divine love rather than a required satisfaction for human sin. In applying reason to the mystery of the Trinity, he also undermined this foundational principle. At the urging of Bernard of Clairvaux, among others, Abelard was condemned for heresy. Bernard exemplified serious apologetic work, using reason and argumentation at the Council of Sens in 1140 to refute the false teaching of Abelard.

Thomas Aquinas (1225–1274) was known as the "dumb ox" during his days as a schoolboy because he seldom spoke in class. However, he proved to be one of the most brilliant scholars of all time and the greatest theologian between Augustine and Martin Luther. A member of the Dominican Order, Thomas served as a professor at the universities of Cologne and Paris. His *Summa Theologica* and *Summa contra Gentiles* were masterful syntheses of Christian revelation set forth in the Scriptures and interpreted by the church fathers with the newly rediscovered philosophy of Aristotle. Thomas believed that reason could show us many truths about God such as his existence, his eternity, and his providence, while other fundamental truths such as the Trinity and the incarnation could only be known through revelation. The prominent place of reason in the thought of Thomas should not lead one to think that he downplayed the role of Scripture. Thomas sought to demonstrate that the spiritual sense of Scripture was always based on the literal sense and derived from it. He also suggested that the literal sense of the biblical text should be equated with the meaning intended by the biblical author.

Thomas accepted the Aristotelian maxim that "there is nothing in the mind which is not first in the senses." This led him to seek empirical proofs for the existence of God that he set forth in his famous "Five Ways." One could show, he believed, the existence of God by examining his effects in the external world in things such as motion, causation, contingency, degrees of perfection, and design. Nowhere is serious Christian engagement better seen in this medieval period than in the work of Aquinas, who has remained the most authoritative theologian for the Roman Catholic tradition. He was declared to be a saint in 1323 and a doctor of the church in 1557. In 1879, his writings were made required reading for all Catholic students of theology and philosophy. Other important scholastic theologians such as Bonaventure, Duns Scotus, and William of Ockham extended and developed Thomas's teachings in different directions. None of them could ignore the contribution he had made.

The Seven Sacraments

One of the most enduring contributions of scholastic theology was the systematizing of the seven sacraments of medieval Catholicism. Peter Lombard was the first theologian to insist that there were only seven sacraments. Other thinkers such as Hugh of St. Victor and Thomas Aquinas discussed the meaning of these sacraments and their role in the Christian life.

Two of the sacraments were for a restricted group within Christendom: ordination or holy orders for those who were called to a priestly ministry in the church and marriage for those who were wedded as husband and wife. The other five sacraments, which included baptism, confirmation, the Eucharist, penance, and extreme unction, were intended for everyone. The sacraments were believed to have a direct effect on salvation; they not only signified grace but contained and conferred it. Not all of the sacraments were of equal necessity. Baptism, the Eucharist, and penance contributed most directly to the process of salvation.

By the Middle Ages the rite of infant baptism had become almost universally practiced throughout the church. Augustine's doctrine of original sin, which implied that unbaptized babies dying in infancy went to limbo, the outer region of hell, contributed to this practice. It was believed that baptism removed the taint of original sin and disposed the one baptized to receive the grace of the other sacraments. The high rate of infant mortality prompted the practice of baptism by midwives when newborn infants were in danger of death. The doctrine of baptism was reflected in the structure of certain cemeteries: a section of hallowed ground for those dying in the state of grace, unconsecrated soil for those dying unrepentant of mortal sin, and a third parcel of ground for those infants dying without benefit of baptism.

The Eucharist or sacrament of the altar was called the crown of the sacraments and received extensive theological treatment. The Fourth Lateran Council in 1215 approved the dogma of transubstantiation. This teaching held that at the moment of consecration, the bread and wine of the Eucharist became the actual body and blood of Christ. This doctrine gave rise to new forms of eucharistic piety in the late Middle Ages: the saying of private masses, the veneration of the consecrated hosts outside the context of the Lord's Supper, and the denial of the cup to the laity (to prevent the spilling of the transubstantiated wine).

Baptism and the Eucharist were supplemented by the sacrament of penance, which was the means of removing the penalty of sin and preparing oneself for the full benefits of the sacrament of the altar. Penance consisted of four stages: (1) contrition, that is, being sorry for one's sin; (2) confession, the making known of sin to a priest, an act required at least once a year by the Fourth Lateran Council; (3) satisfaction, an act of compensation to God for offenses done against him; and (4) absolution, pronounced by the priest who, it was believed, had the authority of Christ to formally remit sins. During the late Middle Ages, the sacrament of penance was continually threatened by the abuse of indulgences, that is, the promise of forgiveness in exchange for a sum of money. In effect, this meant that absolution could be attained without contrition, confession, or satisfaction. It was Luther's protest against the abuse of the penitential system that triggered the Reformation in 1517.

The Quest for the True Church

The last two centuries of the Middle Ages were a time of ferment and upheaval. Popes and emperors vied with one another for control of Europe; the Crusades introduced new ideas and new social conditions to the world of feudalism; plagues such as the Black Death ravaged the countryside; and the church was beset by new forms of nationalism, heresy, and dissent. All of this presented a crisis of confidence in the identity and authority of the church.

The question of whether the pope or the emperor would be sovereign over the church went back to the eleventh century, when Pope Gregory VII had resisted the efforts of the emperor Henry IV to nominate bishops and induct them into office. He asserted papal supremacy and insisted that "the Roman church has never erred, nor ever, by witness of Scripture, shall err to all eternity." The pope who came closest to putting into effect Gregory's designs was Innocent III, who presided over a vast world empire from 1198 until 1216. Even more extravagant claims for papal sovereignty, however, were set forth by Boniface VIII in 1302. He declared that "it is altogether necessary to salvation for every human creature to be subject to the Roman pontiff." By the fourteenth century, however, these words sounded hollow since the papacy had been greatly weakened by its seventy-year exile in France, the so-called Babylonian Captivity (1309–1377).

In addition, there followed the shocking confusion of the Great Western Schism (1378–1417) when for a while two, and then three, popes claimed at once to be the supreme head of the church. The great schism was ended by the Council of Constance, which named a new pope, Martin V, and affirmed the supremacy of a general council over the papacy. By the end of the fifteenth century the papacy had lapsed again into great moral decadence and seemed unable to inaugurate reform.

In England, John Wycliffe attacked the abuses in the church. His followers, the Lollards, translated portions of the Bible into English and spread the ideas of their teacher across the land. A similar movement of Reform in Bohemia centered on the martyred John Hus, who had been burned at the stake at the Council of Constance. The Waldensians represented still another alternative to the established religious system. They met secretly in the mountain caves and valleys of Europe. They rejected the ministrations of worldly priests and called into question many rituals that were common to the Roman Church, such as indulgences, purgatory, relics, and pilgrimages.

There was a great hunger and thirst for God on the eve of the Reformation. One of the most popular books during this time was Thomas à Kempis's *The Imitation of Christ*. In Germany, mysticism was thriving, and from Italy the revival of learning known as the Renaissance was recovering the classical sources of Christian antiquity. The Dutch scholar Desiderius Erasmus, who transmitted much of the Renaissance spirit to northern Europe, believed that he could see "a golden age dawning in the near future." The Reformation, however, unleashed far more virulent energies than even Erasmus could foresee.

The medieval period saw the development of some of the first great universities. These institutions were largely established for the purpose of professional education, with some general education for the elite. Of the seventy-nine universities in existence during this time, Paris, Oxford, and Cambridge were best known for the study of theology. Established within medieval Christendom, where the Christian faith provided shape and illumination for the intellectual landscape, the central mission of the university generally focused on inquiry in pursuit of truth. Faith in the context of medieval Christendom was understood to be an indispensable ally, not an enemy, of reason and intellectual exploration.*

For Additional Study

Evans, G. R. *The Language and Logic of the Bible: The Earlier Middle Ages.* Cambridge: Cambridge University Press, 1984.

Houston, James, ed. *Bernard of Clairvaux: The Love of God and Spiritual Friendship.* Portland, OR: Multnomah, 1983.

Howard, Thomas, ed. *Christian Learning.* Grand Rapids: Brazos, 2008.

Lampe, G. W. H., ed. *The Cambridge History of the Bible: The West from the Fathers to the Reformation.* Cambridge: Cambridge University Press, 1969.

McGrath, Alister. *The Intellectual Origins of the European Reformation.* Oxford: Blackwell, 2004.

Smalley, Beryl. *The Study of the Bible in the Middle Ages.* Oxford: Blackwell, 1952.

Also see these articles: Role of Tradition, Patristic Theology, Reformation Theology

* Large portions of this article have been adapted from Timothy George, "Christian Faith in History," in the *Holman Bible Handbook*, ed. David S. Dockery (Nashville: B&H, 1992).

15

Reformation Theology

J. Andrew Dickerson and Stephen B. Eccher

In October 1529, several prominent Protestant Reformers met at Marburg, Germany, to establish an agreement regarding foundational matters of theology. Despite optimistic hopes for a unified theological consensus, an accord between them remained elusive. The Reformers present at the colloquy agreed on many points of theology but not all. Ironically, the sacrament most frequently connected with the principle of Christian unity, the Lord's Supper, proved to be what separated them. In a real sense, Marburg served as a microcosm of the era regarding Reformation theology: general agreement among the Protestant Reformers in overarching theological convictions contra Roman Catholicism alongside substantive disagreement in their developing Protestant theologies. This doctrinal division not only helped to establish the Protestant tradition but also set a trajectory for the various denominations that remain today.

Given such a complex history, this essay will introduce the reader to the major aspects of Reformation theology that emerged during the sixteenth century and to the Reformers who helped establish those unique convictions. Special attention will be given both to shared points of agreement among the Reformers and to those points of theological dissent that led to the fracture of Protestantism. This will include an examination of certain core beliefs relating to biblical authority and the gospel alongside theological disagreements on nuanced soteriological and ecclesiological differences. Lastly, the reader will be challenged to consider how understanding these Reformation theologies might better inform their own faith in the twenty-first century.

Reformation as Renewal and Recovery

When considering the genesis of Reformation theology, one must remember that Martin Luther and the other Protestant Reformers were not trying to split the church. Their goal was initially a Reformation of late-medieval Roman Catholicism. Despite this hopeful aspiration, schism became the unintended consequence of their work, mostly born of differing readings of Scripture and irreconcilable visions for Reformation. Both ultimately led to the unique Reformation theologies that emerged from the period. Undergirding their shared desire for change, the Reformers pursued both a renewal of what once was and a recovery of what had been.

For each of the Reformers, the renewal they sought, along with the figures and movements they hoped to recover, varied widely. For instance, Luther mostly labored to renew the Roman Catholic tradition by correcting what he perceived to be two great problems: (1) the church's unbiblical overreach of papal authority and (2) Rome's veiling of the gospel through its distortion of sacramental theology. According to Luther, both of those errors were rampant between the thirteenth and fifteenth centuries. As we shall soon see, this led to a Lutheranism that re-appropriated an Augustinian anthropology and theology of grace while also remaining thoroughly medieval in its theological underpinnings and liturgical sensibilities.

Luther's recovery of earlier medieval forms of theology stood in contrast to those individuals steeped in Renaissance humanism. Reformers committed to that intellectual movement believed the written sources of antiquity, including the Bible in the original languages, the early church fathers, and other historic writings, were the key to a *Christianismus renascens* ("Christian rebirth"). The Prince of the Humanists, Erasmus of Rotterdam, leveraged the rhetorical and literary tools of the past to challenge the Catholic Church's morality, though he never departed from Catholicism's main theological tenets or authority. Renewal for Erasmus related to morality alone, not to doctrine. Other Humanists, such as Huldrych Zwingli, used the argumentative forms and literary devices of Humanism to cast a covenantal vision for reform that positioned his Zürich community as a contemporary recasting of God's people, the Israelites. Ancient Israel served as his model for recovery.

The Swiss evangelical Anabaptists, a group once trained by Zwingli, looked elsewhere for renewal and recovery. They believed the wedding of church and state was a grievous mistake. This led them to a rigid separatism and the establishment of a believers' church. The Anabaptists sought a model for change rooted in Jesus's ethical teachings and a willingness to share his cross. These examples highlight how the hope for Reformation was not only applied differently in a variety of contextual settings but also led to incongruent theologies. These are a few examples that remind us how diverse the theological commitments and aspirations were from those of the era. Renewal and recovery never looked the same for the Reformers. Thus, the development of differing theologies during this era was not only inevitable, but it should have been expected.

The Root of Division

Although papal indulgences first sparked questions in Luther about Roman Catholic theology, these were symptomatic of a more foundational problem. In the wake of the *95 Theses* controversy, Luther realized, through the Leipzig Debate in 1519, that the Catholic Church had mistakenly over-elevated the authority of church tradition. Catholic apologists like Sylvester Mazzolini, called Prierias, and Cardinal Cajetan even believed that the pope's words superseded those of Holy Writ. Against this dual-fount view of authority (the Bible and church tradition), Luther and other Reformers began espousing *sola Scriptura*, a theological belief that positioned the Bible as the final, normative authority for establishing doctrine and church practice.

Bear in mind that the Reformers did not jettison church tradition altogether. Rather, they recast church tradition as a handmaiden to holy Scripture. The Latin term *sola* was employed here by Luther and others to denote primacy or supremacy, not exclusivity. For most of the Reformers, church tradition did not establish doctrine. Instead, it was a crucial hermeneutical tool that helped to preserve the core tenets of orthodoxy. Here, things such as ecumenical church councils and the early church fathers' writings served as important interpretive guardrails that helped the church to avoid veering into doctrinal heresy through misinterpretations of the text. Much like the *regula fidei* ("Rule of Faith") did during the Patristic period, these secondary sources helped to maintain the faith given once and for all.

The Reformers' decision to root ultimate authority in the Bible was based on the reality that individuals and institutions could and had made critical errors in theology and church practice. However, the Bible's authority was different because of its unique divine nature. As Luther argued in his *Lectures on the Psalms*, because of its origin, the divinely inspired Word of God transforms its reader, conforming people and institutions to its prescribed patterns. In this sense, not only was the Bible to be trusted, but it would also be the catalyst to reform, not the work or words of humanity.

Not all Reformers held to this particular understanding of authority. Radical Reformers such as Thomas Müntzer and Andreas Karlstadt not only abandoned the papacy's ecclesiastical oversight but began uncoupling doctrinal truth from the written text of Scripture as well. Accordingly, a Spirit-guided authority emerged that proved in application to be dangerously subjective and open to progressive forms of revelation. Karlstadt saw the Holy Spirit as the key to biblical interpretation, which meant anyone could interpret the text regardless of learning, ecclesiastical authority, or creedal boundaries. Müntzer went even a step further. He argued that absent the special revelation of Scripture, one could still obtain an authentic Christian faith directly through the Holy Spirit's teachings. The violent debacle at the German town of Munster in the 1530s, where a deadly form of Reformation was employed, demonstrated how dangerous following Spirit-led prophets such as Jan Mattijs or Jan van Leyden was. According to Rome, such instances were proof of the dangers undergirding Luther's scandalous theology. Catholicism's response came at the Council of Trent (1545–1563), where the Roman Curia's authority was reaffirmed, especially on matters where Scripture was silent.

The Hope of Heaven

The disagreements over authority eventually bore fruit in the form of divergent soteriological convictions. Luther's issues with papal indulgences were situated within his personal struggle to understand God's grace and the assurance of his salvation. The failings of late-medieval Roman Catholicism's sacramental theology dogged him in these pursuits. Ironically, the pathway toward a different understanding of salvation, especially on the issue of justi-fication, came via a Catholic saint, Augustine of Hippo. Luther's appropria-tion of an Augustinian view of the human will left him convinced humanity was impotent in all pursuits of reconciliation with God.

This particular anthropology, when viewed through a Pauline lens, led to Luther's theology of the cross. His theology positioned God as the sole active agent in regeneration based upon the completed work of Christ. Here, Augustine's basic predestinarian position was affirmed, though loosed from his sanative, sacramental language. Philipp Melanchthon, a young prodigy teaching at Wittenberg, later helped the Reformer to frame this develop-ing notion of justification in forensic legal terms. They contended that God does not make a person righteous by means of the sacramental rites of the Church. Instead, the Lord declares one to be righteous based on the work of Jesus. A *fröhlicher Wechsel* ("sweet exchange") takes place when Jesus's righ-teousness becomes the sinner's, while their sin becomes Christ's at Calvary. For Luther, the doctrine of justification by grace through faith alone was the essential Christian doctrine; every other doctrine was dependent upon it.

Several magisterial Reformers held similar positions on salvation but with their own particular locution based upon different life experiences and unique hermeneutical commitments. Zwingli's soteriology closely aligned with Luther's, but his understanding of justification was more commu-nally oriented, based on his covenantal reading of the Bible. The Zürich Reformer's commitment to Renaissance Humanism also left his understand-ing of justification with a much stronger ethical bent, thereby steering clear from the charges of antinomianism that plagued Luther. Similarly, Martin Bucer posited a double justification where an *iustitia inhaerens* ("inherent righteousness") worked symbiotically alongside a preceding *iustitia imputata* ("imputed righteousness"). This created a soteriological interdependence between God's declarative act of election and the human works that followed.

John Calvin oriented his soteriology around the idea of union with Christ. For the Genevan Reformer, the one who is given faith not only finds adoption into God's family but also true fellowship with God through their relational union with the Incarnate Christ. The consequence of this mysti-cal union, what Calvin called a *duplex gratia* ("double grace"), included both justification and sanctification. The Christian's growth in piety was a natural fruit of this relationship, not a result of the justification or an obligation required to secure the union. In each of these above models God was cast as the principal actor in the theatre of redemptive history. He alone secures salvation through Jesus's sacrificial work for those whom he grants faith. Moreover, a strong determinative view of election was maintained in each of these soteriologies. Yet this was tempered by unique ways of thinking about the Christian ethic that remains for those in Christ.

Other first-generation Reformers held synergistic views of salvation that stressed human cooperation in God's redemptive work. The Anabaptist theologian Balthasar Hubmaier affirmed a tripartite anthropology, similar to Erasmus's, that saw the human will as unaltered by the fall. God was still the first mover in the act of redemption. Yet Hubmaier's focus on a requisite repentant life, characterized by *Besserung* ("moral improvement"), more closely aligned justification and sanctification than most of the magisterial Reformers. Hubmaier also moved away from the static notion of justification embodied by Luther's soteriology as he framed salvation more in terms of process. Karlstadt went beyond Hubmaier on this. He argued that God's external grace makes an individual both aware of the gospel and empowers them with the choice to accept or reject that same gospel. For Karlstadt, humanity played a participatory role in regeneration through one's *Gelassenheit* ("submission" or "surrender") to the calling of God. Once again, action and confession afforded humanity more of a shared role in the work of regeneration than did the mainline magisterial Reformers.

In England, although Henry VIII's personal and political ambitions were the main cause for the Anglican Church's separation from Rome, soteriological issues proved deeply divisive as well. Anglicanism initially maintained a synergistic view of salvation with humanity gaining a knowledge of God via natural law. However, many of those forced into exile during Mary Tudor's reign in the mid-1550s later embraced a covenantal theology while abroad on the continent. When these exiles returned home during Elizabeth I's reign, they brought their new soteriology with them, which surfaced in both Puritanism and separatism. An additional soteriological shift came with John Smyth and Thomas Helwys, two separatists turned Baptists. Changes in their understanding of the nature of the church and baptism led them to a general view of the atonement, which birthed the distinction between the particular and general Baptists in England.

By the mid to late sixteenth century, others began crafting soteriologies based upon the work of the first- and second-generation Reformers, oftentimes modifying those earlier ideas. The divergent views that eventually emerged characterize the period, especially to those in modernity. Theodore Beza, Calvin's successor at Geneva, systematized and modified his mentor's soteriology. This ultimately begat a decretal theology that focused attention on God's divine election over the creation itself. Others, like Jacob Arminius, challenged Beza's supralapsarian theology and sought a more balanced approach to the relationship between divine sovereignty and human responsibility. He retained Beza's focus on a salvific divine decree, but Arminius situated that decree in terms of people groups. Here, God saves those who respond to the free gospel offer, not those who have election forced upon them. Arminius's successors championed his position until their condemnation at the Synod of Dordt in 1619. That Dutch assembly established a Dordtian Calvinism, whose soteriology is frequently distilled down to the famous "TULIP" acronym, though its ideas were substantively disconnected from Calvin, the Reformer from whom it drew inspiration.

The Bride of Christ

Ongoing disputes regarding authority and soteriology eventually culminated in a concern to locate the true church. In an era marked by religious schism, the veracity of any claim to be the bride of Christ had to be based upon something. But what would that be? Those loyal to Rome continued to view the authority of the papacy and the efficacy of the sacraments as those things that locate the one true church, outside of which there was no salvation. The Protestant Reformers collectively looked elsewhere, and a general consensus soon emerged. The true church was marked by gospel preaching and a non-Catholic administration of the sacraments. For most of the Reformers, this meant that the Roman Mass had to be abolished. Regrettably, this is where the agreement ended, and differing theologies emerged. These divergent convictions are what inevitably led the various Reformers in different directions.

Though Luther is often viewed as the cause of the church's fracture, his ecclesial vision departed the least from Rome's. His emphasis on the preached Word as a real means of grace was paired with a similar understanding of baptism and communion. As he clarified in his 1539 work *On the Councils and the Church*, "Wherever you hear or see [the] word preached, believed, professed, and lived, do not doubt that the true *ecclesia sancta catholica*, 'a Christian holy people,' must be there."[1] According to Luther, God works in the preached Word and the sacraments in a powerful and salvific way. Similarly, the Wittenberg Reformer's belief in what later came to be known as the normative principle of worship also meant that most of the external ceremonial aspects of Roman Catholic worship surrounded the preached and visual Word. Crucifixes and icons remained in the Lutheran Church, as did the use of clerical vestments.

Despite these aspects of continuity with Roman Catholicism, substantive distinctions were present as well. Luther's rejection of Rome's commitment to Augustine's *ex opere operato* ecclesial belief was chief among these. Accordingly, the sacraments did not work exclusively independent of a person's faith. For Luther, these liturgical rites were only of value if connected to genuine faith, a faith that the Lord alone can gift. In the case of Communion, Luther retained a corporeal understanding of Jesus's presence in the elements, much like Rome did. However, according to Luther, Jesus's presence was only of value to those who consumed his body and blood in faith.

Most of the mainline magisterial Reformers followed Luther in their mixed church ecclesiologies. Practically speaking, this meant that the invisible church of the elect was believed to be a future eschatological gathering presently hidden anonymously within the larger, visible state churches. Reformers such as Zwingli, Bucer, and Johannes Oecolampadius saw Israel as analogous, for as Paul once declared, not all from Israel were believing Israel. These mixed churches eventually faced challenges with the rise of Anabaptism in the 1520s. In response, many of the Swiss Reformers retained infant baptism to accommodate the fragile social relationship that existed between the church and state in Christendom. Thus, Israel's practice of circumcision became theologically linked with infant baptism in a New Covenant context. Calvin built on this idea but also highlighted the church's long-standing practice of infant baptism to validate his position.

---

[1] Martin Luther, *Luther's Works*, ed. Jaroslav Pelikan and Helmut T. Lehmann (Philadelphia: Fortress, 1966), 41:150.

In contrast, radical visions for Reformation emerged that saw the relationship between the church and state functioning toward dramatically different ends. After failed attempts at territorial forms of Reformation, the Swiss evangelical Anabaptists eventually adopted a Reformation "from below" model where reforms were enacted without the civil authorities' oversight. The Swiss Anabaptists' ecclesiology functionally loosed the church from the state. As Michael Sattler contended in the Schleitheim Confession from 1527, the church's separatism was required since "there is nothing else in the world and all creation than good or evil, believing and unbelieving, darkness and light, the world and those who are [come] out of the world."[2] Thus, a regenerate gathered church was required and established. A believer's baptism became the gateway to this regenerate church, which was then stringently disciplined to maintain its purity. Other radicals like Thomas Müntzer mixed the social ambitions of the German peasants with the church's eschatological hopes. His request that the civil magistrates help establish the kingdom of God by force led to a violent form of Reformation. Thus, as both examples show, a rejection of the typical church/state relations from the era could vary greatly in ecclesiological application.

As alluded to earlier, the sacraments, specifically the Supper, proved to be the era's most volatile and divisive area of concern. Most of the Reformers believed the sacraments provided assurance of salvation, since these were divinely appointed markers regarding one's incorporation into Christ's body. However, who was acting in the sacramental *Pfand* ("pledge"), God or humanity, remained a major point of division. Luther believed God acted, hence his belief that one's salvation was connected with baptism. Most of the other Protestant Reformers saw either humanity as the one acting exclusively in their pledge to Christ and his church or both acting symbiotically in their commitment to each other. Here Calvin argued that the sacraments are both an external sign denoting God's covenantal promise toward humanity and the recipient's parallel commitment to pursue piety. For the Genevan Reformer, both God and humanity have a shared role to play in this sacramental rite.

Understanding Jesus's statement "this is my body" from the Supper's institution further exacerbated the divide among the Reformers. Luther held

---

[2] John H. Yoder, *The Legacy of Michael Sattler* (Scottdale, PA: Herald, 1973), 38.

steadfastly to a corporeal understanding of Christ's presence in the elements, mostly based on Jesus's *promissio* ("promise") that he would be present in the bread and cup. Zwingli, Bucer, and Oecolampadius argued that Jesus was memorially present. A Humanist reading of the text, with a focus on the original historic context of Jesus's institution of the Supper, alongside Christ's current position at the Father's right hand, wouldn't allow for the word "is" to be understood corporeally. In the *Consensus Tigurinus* from 1549, Calvin and the Zürich Reformer Heinrich Bullinger argued for a mediating position that affirmed Jesus's spiritual presence. They agreed that for the communicant, "all those who embrace in faith the promises there offered, receive Christ spiritually."[3] Interestingly, one could trace the shifting language on the Supper in a place like Thomas Cranmer's *Book of Common Prayer* to see not only how important this question was for the era but how it was a marker identifying who was in control of each unique Reformation.

Our Reformation Heritage

For each of the Protestant Reformers, what they determined to be wrong with the church informed their subsequent correctives. The theological commitments undergirding their reforms helped establish the proliferation of confessional heritages that remains to this day. In this sense, modern believers continue the Reformers' work of maintaining and proclaiming the faith given once and for all. We do this while holding differing theological commitments based in large part on the past work of the Reformers. Given the shifting of culture and the expansion of secularism today, this is as weighty a task as ever. While we embrace this gospel trust, what the Reformation era reminds us is that our theologies will not be monolithic, nor should they be. That would assume far too much regarding the human condition and our application of the Bible's teachings. Yet how we collectively steward the Christian faith, while upholding deep commitments to our confessional heritages, will reveal much.

The Bible, guided by the Reformers' understanding of *sola Scriptura*, should be the foundational principle that helps us to determine our doctrine

---

[3] Jaroslav Pelikan and Valerie Hotchkiss, eds., *Creeds & Confessions of Faith in the Christian Tradition* (New Haven, CT: Yale University Press, 2003), 808.

and church practice. Yet *sola Scriptura* does not directly address the fact that Christians read the Bible differently. This was true for the Reformers and is true for us as well. Thus, *sola Scriptura*, as the Reformers understood it, equally affirmed the Bible's infallible, divine nature while also humbly confessing the human fallibility of our interpretations of the Scriptures due to our finitude. This is where our re-engagement with the early church's creeds, alongside the teaching of our individual confessions of faith in an ethnically diverse community of faith, should benefit the church in our contemporary context. The challenge in this is rightly discerning what are creedal, gospel issues and what are theological differences of confessional belief within the safe waters of orthodoxy. Admittedly, as examples like the German Peasants' War and the Anabaptist kingdom of Munster demonstrated, not all the Reformers maintained the true faith. And even for those who did, they were not always able to discern well between matters of orthodoxy and differences of belief within orthodoxy. Here, their failed examples should remind us of the importance of holding unwaveringly tight to gospel matters, while more loosely on issues of confessional distinction.

Much like at Marburg, evangelicals have often allowed pride and personality to needlessly exacerbate the theological divisions of today. In both the Reformers' and our historical theatres, dialogues over theological disagreement may be either corrosive or edifying in nature. We choose which of these two paths to walk in our discourse. As the Reformation demonstrated, unity in the one true gospel does not mean uniformity in secondary and tertiary theological commitments. Here modern believers might find benefit from the distinction between working together and worshipping together. All Christians, regardless of their confessional heritage, may labor alongside one another in shared areas of common theological agreement, such as the sanctity of human life and the value of religious liberty. Believers may also find worshipping alongside those who hold similar theological convictions to be freeing and more practical when gathering as a local body. Such confessional separation in worship might also be the best path forward on externally focused efforts such as missions and church planting. Such division is understandable and ceded in a preglorified era. Through it all, we may celebrate together that God is still working to change lives, regardless of which heritage has been the vessel of proclamation for the one true gospel.

In the end, the words of the irenic Reformer Martin Bucer offer a helpful perspective on our dealings with one another in an age of confessionalization. In his 1538 work, *Concerning the True Care of Souls*, Bucer responded to mistaken claims that he and others were allowing the weeds of false doctrine to grow in the true church by stating, "And yet, praise God, there are to be found on all sides many really faithful Christians, who have genuinely trusted in Christ and given themselves over to a heartfelt obedience to the Gospel through the doctrine of Christ which he has granted us to maintain."[4] Theological diversity may not only be accepted but should be celebrated by those who have a shared commitment to the one true gospel.

For Additional Study

Bagchi, David, and David C. Steinmetz, eds. *The Cambridge Companion to Reformation Theology.* Cambridge: Cambridge University Press, 2012.

Bucer, Martin. *Concerning the True Care of Souls.* Translated by Peter Beale. Edinburgh: The Banner of Trust, 2013.

George, Timothy. *Theology of the Reformers.* Rev. ed. Nashville: B&H Academic, 2013.

Lindberg, Carter. *The European Reformations.* 2nd ed. Oxford: Wiley-Blackwell, 2010.

MacCulloch, Diarmaid. *The Reformation: A History.* New York: Viking, 2004.

McGrath, Alister E. *Reformation Thought: An Introduction.* 4th ed. Oxford: Wiley-Blackwell, 2012.

Pelikan, Jaroslav and Valerie Hotchkiss, eds. *Creeds & Confessions of Faith in the Christian Tradition.* New Haven, CT: Yale University Press, 2003.

———— and Helmut T. Lehmann, eds. *Luther's Works.* Vol. 41. Philadelphia: Fortress, 1966.

---

[4] Martin Bucer, *Concerning the True Care of Souls*, xxxvii.

Yoder, John H. *The Legacy of Michael Sattler*. Scottdale, PA: Herald Press, 1973.

Also see these articles: Holy Scripture, Justification, Role of Tradition, Historical Theology, Medieval Theology, Systematic Theology, Modern Theology, Baptism, Lord's Supper

16

Modern Theology

W. Madison Grace II

The task of understanding the theology of those who have come before us is not *merely* an exercise in historical enquiry. Not only do we stand on their shoulders, but we live out their theology because their theology is also our theology. Their Bible is our Bible. Their concerns about God, humanity, salvation, and the end of time are our concerns as well. In this, I agree with Karl Barth: "We cannot be in the Church without taking as much responsibility for the theology of the past as for the theology of the present. Augustine, Thomas Aquinas, Luther, Schleiermacher, and all the rest are not dead, but living. . . . There is no past in the Church, so there is no past in theology."[1]

Every major era of church history has provided important and intriguing theology. The Fathers, the scholastics, and the Reformers all have their place, but so do those theologians who have engaged theology since the Enlightenment, with all its philosophical achievements. Though some still ask what Athens has to do with Jerusalem, every period of Christian history is shaped and molded by philosophical movements. Think of Neo-Platonism and Augustine or Aristotle and Aquinas. It is clear that the works of Kant, Hegel, and others affect the modern period of theology. Our task will be to investigate

---

[1] Karl Barth, *Protestant Theology in the Nineteenth Century: Its Background and History*, new ed. (Grand Rapids: Eerdmans, 2001), 3.

the major movements of this era beginning with Friedrich Schleiermacher (1768–1834) and moving to our present day. Though every era has more than enough material to investigate, the modern era has even more. We will not be looking at every theological turn over the last two centuries. Nor will we be able to engage movements outside of Protestant thought. The resources at the end of the chapter will aid the reader in diving into some of these works more deeply as well as the subject matter to which we now turn.

Modern Theology or What Is Modern?

The title of this chapter utilizes the term "modern," and it is important to note that it has a connotation of its own beyond that which is "contemporary" or "recent." Sometimes it is used for theology that developed after the Enlightenment. In other places, it particularly refers to liberal theology in Protestantism beginning with Schleiermacher. It is the theology of modernity, which is an era that is concerned with human reason and its ability to discern knowledge in itself, including knowledge of God. This turn to modernity did not happen overnight, but there are some important markers, one beginning with Descartes's *cogito*, wherein he surmised that there is one truth that can be known—one's own existence. This thought shifted philosophy's beginning point from God to a person's ability to think. Added to this philosophical thought is the work of Immanuel Kant, whose work led to the belief that we cannot know God since we cannot empirically experience him. This ultimately led to a divide between knowledge and faith, and it relegated religion to ethics or moral living.

Thus, the modern period, in which Schleiermacher begins his work, is one wherein experience and human rationality are privileged over against ecclesial tradition. Commitments to the authority of Scripture were less important during this period, especially with the growth of newer methodologies.

Liberal Theology

Since many correlate modern theology with liberal theology, and since its origin begins with Schleiermacher, who, as we will see, is the father of liberal theology, a good starting point of our discussion is here. However, it is important to define what we mean by "liberal." The term is popularly used to mean anyone that is "to the left of me" or "more progressive than I am," and it is especially utilized in politics and religion for those who are more progressive. However, in theology, it has a particular meaning that sets it against other groups that are to the left of conservatives (e.g., neo-orthodox or post-liberals). Two theologians are helpful in ascertaining what liberal theology is: Friedrich Schleiermacher and Albrecht Ritschl.

Friedrich Schleiermacher

Friedrich Schleiermacher was a professor of theology in the late eighteenth and early nineteenth centuries and is known as the father of liberal theology because his work changed the methodology of theology. Though he was reared in a Pietist household, Schleiermacher later came under the influence of the thought of Kant and began to question many historic Christian beliefs. In particular, he began to seek for the essence of religion, which was not to be found in tradition, reason, or even in the Bible. For Schleiermacher, religion is found in one's experience or feeling (*Gefühl*). This "feeling" is particularly related to the concept of a feeling of absolute dependence, which refers to the way in which humans find themselves completely dependent upon something higher or beyond themselves.

Schleiermacher initially presented this idea of theology based upon feeling in his *On Religion: Addresses in Response to Its Cultured Despisers* but continued his thought in his systematic theology published in 1821 entitled *The Christian Faith*. This work expounded the idea that one comes to know that God exists not because the church said so, or because of philosophical proofs for God's existence, or even because the Bible claims it. God exists because, inwardly, all humans experience or feel a dependence on a greater being. This dependence is not necessarily upon a concrete idea of God; rather, it is upon the feeling that is a God-consciousness. This understanding of the common God-consciousness, according to Schleiermacher, is best understood through the religion of Christianity. Any doctrinal formulation that one creates must be mediated through the understanding of this God-consciousness. Doctrines such as Christology are understood in terms of the ability to experience this God-consciousness more pristinely. Jesus is the ideal human, and he redeems humanity by the way in which he communicates his God-consciousness to others.

Schleiermacher stands at the head of a long line of thinkers who were attempting to find God in an environment that did not see any certain theological authority in the tradition of the church or in the Bible. Not all who followed after him approached theology exactly the same way, but most utilized his foundational approach of the experience of God being the ground of theological knowledge. Thus, Schleiermacher is commonly understood to be the father of the movement.

Albrecht Ritschl

If Schleiermacher is the father of liberal theology, Albrecht Ritschl (1822–1889) is the head of the liberal theology school of which there were many followers. Though his major theological work is not as accessible today as is Schleiermacher's, the effects of his work and his students' work are still felt. In the later part of the nineteenth century, when Ritschl was writing, the divide between science and religion was growing ever greater. In this environment, Ritschl approached theology as one that must distinguish between two types of knowledge: the scientific and the religious. The former is concerned with objective ideas, whereas the latter is concerned with value judgments. The religious knowledge one can gain is found in the idea of the kingdom of God, which he saw as the essence of Christianity. Ethics becomes more important to theology, which is most clearly seen in the idea that God is love. The end of this theology is the kingdom in which the love of God is most clearly realized: where selfishness is eradicated, and love of neighbor reigns. This reality can be obtained by looking to Jesus, who is the moral example of God's love and the ideal all humans should strive after.

Ritschl's followers helped establish liberal theology as a major force in theology for Europeans and Americans, evidenced in the work of persons such as Walter Rauschenbusch and his Social Gospel and Adolf von Harnack's work on the essence of Christianity. In summary, Stanley Grenz and Roger Olson provide a helpful analysis of the overall teaching and legacy of liberal theology underneath five major points. First, liberal theology is that which adapted its belief to modernity with all its scientific and philosophical formulations. Second, it highlighted the freedom of the individual, especially over against the tradition coming from the churches. Third, there is an emphasis on ethics and morality especially seen through the idea of the kingdom of God. Fourth, theological authority no longer rested upon the Bible. Rather, one was to find the essence of Christianity behind the text or to seek the kernel of the gospel apart from the husk that included tradition and the Bible. Fifth, liberal theology more and more became concerned with the immanence of God over against his transcendence.[2]

Neoorthodoxy

In the human person, liberal theology sees a goodness that minimizes the reality of sin in humanity. With the advent of World War I (1914–18), the question of human goodness and sinfulness was raised. God had become thought of as being immanent with the person and the rationality that person could employ to know truth. This position began to be challenged by thinkers such as Søren Kierkegaard but clearly came into force with the work of Karl Barth in a movement known as neoorthodoxy.

This new teaching was not exactly a *de novo* movement of theologians in the twentieth century. On the one hand, it is a critique of the methodologies of modernism in theology that could be found in both liberal and fundamentalist approaches. On the other hand, it was not a complete rejection of the Christianity in which these thinkers were born. In general, those who are connected with neoorthodoxy are to be applauded for rejecting a part of liberal theology, especially its adherence to natural theology. In response, these theologians looked to God as being a sovereign, transcendent being that was making himself known exclusively through the Word, which is Jesus Christ. They also adhered to an approach to theology that is *dialectical*, which tried to find truth by juxtaposing opposites against one another. Tensions can and do exist in the Bible and theology and do not need to be resolved.

In the early part of the twentieth century, these neoorthodox theologians were prominent in the United States with Reinhold and Richard Niebuhr, as well as Paul Tillich. However, it was in Germany that one sees much of this work in the thought of Karl Barth, Emil Brunner, Dietrich Bonhoeffer, and Rudolf Bultmann.

---

[2] Stanley J. Grenz and Roger E. Olson, *20th Century Theology: God & the World in a Transitional Age* (Downers Grove, IL: IVP, 1992), 52–53.

Karl Barth

The Swiss-born theologian Karl Barth took the world by storm when in 1919 he published his *Römerbriefe* (his commentary on Romans) that questioned the approach to the Bible by the historical-critical method. This initial work would go through six revisions for the next decade. Later, he would write in *The Word of God and the Word of Man* that "it is not the right human thoughts about God which form the content of the Bible, but the right divine thoughts about men. The Bible tells us not how we should talk with God but what he says to us; not how we find the way to him, but how he has sought and found the way to us; . . . It is this which is within the Bible. The word of God is within the Bible."[3]

Here one clearly sees that the internal reason of a human is not what is able to bring divine truth; rather, it is the work of God presenting his Word to humanity via the Bible.

Barth would serve as a professor at Göttingen, Münster, Bonn, and eventually Basel. The reaction to the optimism of liberal theology continued not only due to his fellow theologians' alignment with WWI but also due to the church's accommodation of Nazi Germany. Barth would align with the confessing church and lead in the forming of the Barmen Declaration of 1934 that delineated the centrality of Jesus Christ over against a church or state that would assume authority over that Word. This later work would eventually force him to leave Germany and move back to Switzerland, where he would live out the remainder of his days.

The *magnum opus* of Karl Barth is a thirteen-volume theology entitled *Church Dogmatics*. He began working on this system of theology while at Bonn and left it incomplete at the time of his death in 1968. The ability to know God is not found from within a person, but it must come to them from without. This place, for Barth, was the Bible, where the revelation of Jesus Christ is given to humanity. Barth grounded his whole theology Christologically. The centrality of the Word in Barth's theology does need some clarification. The way in which God presents revelation to humanity is by means of the Word in three senses. First, as the Word Jesus Christ.

---

[3] Karl Barth, *The Word of God and the Word of Man*, trans. Douglas Horton (Boston: Pilgrim, 1928), 100.

Second, as the Bible. Third, as the proclamation of the Bible in the churches. The latter two are mediations of the first when God uses them to bring revelation in Jesus Christ.

Much more can be said of Barth's approach to theology, but his work created a rift in the liberal approach to theology as can be evidenced even by his contemporaries such as Dietrich Bonhoeffer and Rudolf Bultmann.

Dietrich Bonhoeffer

The approach to theology as one centered in Christ is not something that was unique to Karl Barth. His younger friend and fellow confessing church pastor-theologian Dietrich Bonhoeffer also saw the importance and centrality of Jesus Christ in the theology of the church. Bonhoeffer was born into an intellectual and academic environment, especially given his father's work as a professor of psychiatry. Early on, Bonhoeffer declared that he wanted to devote his life's work to the church, which caused some concern for his family. However, Dietrich was committed and sought a career in the church and in the academy, completing his doctorate at the age of twenty-one and writing his first and seminal work, *Sanctorum Communio*. Here Bonhoeffer establishes the Christo-ecclesiology that would be central to the majority of his life's work.

Bonhoeffer's career took a different path than that of Barth's. The latter began in the church and finished in the academy, whereas Bonhoeffer began in the academy and completed his ministry in service to the confessing church. This was in part due to his youth at the time of his graduation and the requirements of older persons to be employed as clergy in his Lutheran tradition. Bonhoeffer was a friend of Barth's and likewise offered a critique of liberal theology. His approach in theology was to emphasize the nature of the church-community in relation to the work of Christ in the world. Central to this thinking is his usage of *Stellvertretung*, which is sometimes defined as "vicarious representative action." This action is what Christ has accomplished for humanity by means of his work, but it also is the ethical action that each Christian is intended to engage in this world. Two of his later writings, *Discipleship* and *Life Together*, exemplify this thought well. However popular these works have become in recent days, they are not what garnered attention to this Lutheran theologian.

Bonhoeffer's popularity comes posthumously given his execution by the Nazis in 1945 shortly before the end of WWII. In the years leading up to this unfortunate end, Bonhoeffer was imprisoned where he wrote letters to his friend Eberhard Bethge, who later published them in the now famous *Letters and Papers from Prison*. That work greatly intrigued the world as it grappled with Bonhoeffer's prison musings on "religionless Christianity" and a "world come of age." He was soon claimed by all religious groups, from death of God theology to evangelicals. His intrigue lies in his approach to an engagement with God in the world. Though often misunderstood, his call to a life that centered on Christ's work and called to responsible ethical action makes him one of the more popular theologians in the twentieth century. This is especially seen in the popularity of *Discipleship*, *Life Together*, and *Ethics*.

Rudolf Bultmann

The New Testament theologian Rudolf Bultmann is often considered alongside neoorthodox theologians, though he could more broadly be found in liberal theology. He was professor at the University of Marburg and engaged with the liberal theology and philosophy of his time, which can be seen in his work *The New Testament and Theology*. In particular, he was interested in applying Martin Heidegger's thought to Christianity.

Bultmann was interested in looking for the *kerygma* of the Bible, the central message of the Bible, to help people come to understand its true meaning. He also engaged in the existentialism of his time, which was a broad movement interested in individual experience in reality over against a rationalist view. Bultmann's dependence on Heidegger led him to focus on the importance of future decision and freedom for an individual so that one can come to an understanding of human existence. The dependence is applied in Bultmann's theology especially through his concept of *demythologization*, a teaching that is incredulous of miracles in the Bible to which he ascribed the term *myth*. In fact, Bultmann thought the Bible was historically conditioned and that the Jesus of history is impossible to know. However, Bultmann was not rejecting or removing these stories; rather, he was attempting to ascertain, or recover, the meaning that is found in them. For example, the fall of Adam is less about sin and more about finitude. This leads to a denial of a future coming of Christ, a reinterpretation of the resurrection, and a reinterpretation of Jesus himself, which he separates from the Christ of faith, all in the effort to make the Bible more palatable for modern, scientific sensibilities.

Liberation Theology

A final major movement that arose in modern theology is liberation theology. This movement is concerned with the groups of people that are structurally oppressed in sociopolitical or socioeconomic ways. This broad definition encompasses a variety of groups of people that identify along economic, ethnic, or gender categories, though it originates from the Latin American context. The theological focus of the movement is intended to provide liberation from the structures of sin that exist in the world by employing the teaching and work of Jesus to provide freedom, whether it be economic, societal, or political. Its purpose is to find a theological sense of solidarity with those who are oppressed and, as such, is often more activist in nature. The community takes precedence over the individual as the major social category. This makes the movement more open to ideas of communal or structural sin and salvation. Redemption is understood by means of the themes of the exodus and the cross, and there is an expectation that liberty will be realized in history. In what follows, we will briefly engage this by looking at Latin American liberation theology, Black liberation theology, and feminist theology.

The beginning of liberation theology can be found in the Latin American context with theologians such as the Dominican priest Gustavo Gutiérrez and his work *A Theology of Liberation*. Here the liberation of humanity is obtained by overcoming the economic system wherein the oppressed and the oppressors are freed from the system in which they are imprisoned. This work comes as the fruit of the *Consejo Episcopal Latinoamericano* (CELAM), which was a conference of Latin American priests who wanted to alleviate the plight of the poor. Jesus, for them, became the revolutionary who fought against the social ills of his time. God prefers the poor and impoverished because these are the ones in greatest need. Gutiérrez states this position clearly: "To know God is to work for justice. There is no other path to reach God."[4]

---

[4] Gustavo Gutierrez, *A Theology of Liberation*, trans. Caridad Inda and John Eagleson (Maryknoll, NY: Orbis Books, 1988), 156.

A similar form of liberation theology arose in the United States within both the Black Power movement and the Civil Rights movement of the 1950s and 1960s. In many presentations, black liberation theology is more simply called black theology and sometimes African-American theology. The origin of the movement is debated, but James Cone often stands as the initial interlocuter, at least academically. His thoughts can be found in his works *Black Theology and Black Power* and *A Black Theology of Liberation*. Like Latin American counterparts, black liberation theology provides a critique of the over-spiritualization of the work of God in the world. God's work, exemplified in the exodus, is a work that stands with the oppressed. Black liberation theology looks to Luke's Gospel and its specific mention of the poor and the liberation of captives as a basis for finding Jesus's work as one of solidarity with the oppressed. Cone presents this solidarity with the oppressed in the contemporary context with conception of "blackness" as those who are the oppressed; thus, "blackness" functions as a term for the set of experiences that often results in marginalization. In general, black liberation theology is interested in engaging in a social change that overcomes racism by addressing the structural injustices that exist in society.

A final movement in the twentieth century that often stands on its own, though has affinities with liberation theology, is feminist theology. In brief, feminist theology relates to the feminist movement and is interested in providing social liberation for women. Though connected to movements dating back to the nineteenth century, feminist theology (or rather theologies) finds its most recent expression in the latter part of the twentieth century with the work of scholars such as Mary Daly, Rosemary Radford Ruether, and Elisabeth Schüssler Fiorenza. The experience of being a woman is often seen as the starting point of feminist theology (or liberation theology). However, Ruether, in *Sexism and God-Talk*, clarifies that "the uniqueness of feminist theology lies not in its use of the criterion of experience but rather the use of *women's* experience, which has been almost entirely shut out of theological reflection in the past."[5] The movement wants to see an increase in the usage of the feminine in God-talk and gender inclusivity in theology

---

[5] Rosemary Radford Ruether, *Sexism and God-Talk: Toward a Feminist Theology* (Boston: Beacon, 1983), 13.

as a whole. It is also concerned with the equality of women in theology and the church. The general questions of how women can relate to God drive the varying forms of feminist theologies as differing experiences of women add to the movement. One example that comes from feminist theology is womanist theology, which looks at the African-American woman's perspective, in distinction from a white woman's perspective of much of early feminist theology.

Conclusion

Modern theology is a topic that is broad in scope as we have seen in the variety of approaches to theology during this period. Theologians from Schleiermacher to those of the twenty-first century have moved away from the classic approach in grounding theology in Scripture and tradition to allow one's experience (individually or corporately) to define one's theology. In the wide presentation of liberalism, neoorthodoxy, and liberation theology, we have seen this appropriation of experience. We could have presented many other theologians of this period as well, such as Jürgen Moltmann or Wolfhart Pannenberg to name a couple. Of course, there were others at this time writing theology from premodern perspectives that can be found in groups like the evangelicals with theologians such as Carl F. H. Henry. These theologians distinguish themselves from their counterparts in modern theology by utilizing a theological methodology that, while not shrugging off the reality of experience, is founded upon the supremacy and authority of the Bible.

For Additional Study

Barth, Karl. *Protestant Theology in the Nineteenth Century: Its Background and History.* New Edition. Grand Rapids: Eerdmans, 2001.

Grenz, Stanley J., and Roger E. Olson. *20th Century Theology: God & the World in a Transitional Age.* Downers Grove: IVP, 1992.

Livingston, James C. *Modern Christian Thought.* 2 Vols. 2nd ed. Minneapolis: Fortress, 2006.

MacGregor, Kirk R. *Contemporary Theology: An Introduction: Classical, Evangelical & Global Perspectives.* Grand Rapids: Zondervan, 2019.

Also see these articles: Faith and Reason, Hermeneutics, Philosophical Theology, Systematic Theology, Global Theology

17

Global Theology

CHRISTY THORNTON

O ver the last century, Christianity has grown exponentially outside
the West, a trend that seems sure to continue for years to come. As
Christianity's center creeps southeastward and technology advances, scholars in the West must reckon with how to engage our brothers and sisters
producing theology in a vast array of cultural contexts. Global theology has
emerged out of these relatively recent trends of growth and development in
the majority world.

Global theology has developed into its own academic discipline and
involves two central facets. On the one hand, scholars debate the methodological impact of including cross-cultural dialogue in theological construction. Even though Western theology has a longstanding tradition of
including intercontextual dialogue with historical sources, the concern in
global theology focuses on including contemporary cross-contextual dialogue, which is similar to but distinct from its historical counterpart. On
the other hand, global theology always involves understanding and dialogu-
ing with the voices of theologians from the majority world. To give a full
overview of the discipline, we will survey representative thinkers in global
theological methods and major theologians from Africa, Asia, and Latin
America before concluding with a proposal for the contemporary relevance
of global theology for American evangelical Christians.

Global Theological Method

Global theology as an academic discipline is an offshoot of systematic theology, which includes scholars from a diverse array of contemporary cultural contexts in its discourse. Global theology shares the same general methodological facets of systematic theology but adds cultural diversity in theological reflection as a necessary pillar of its theological project.

In the background of all global theological methods lies a basic commitment that theology is, to some extent, inherently contextual. The mere reality that theology requires articulation in a particular language at a particular time necessitates that it be contextual. Even so, the interplay between subjectively located conceptual language and objective theological reality (God and his Word) allows for differing proposals for precisely how theology should be intercontextual. One can distinguish between methodologies by recognizing how each theologian understands the nature of revelation and relates the contextual and universal, diverse and unified, aspects of theology. Timothy Tennent (b. 1959), Veli-Matti Kärkkäinen (b. 1958), and Henning Wrogemann (b. 1964) have each developed influential and representative approaches to global theological methods.

In 2007, American Timothy Tennent published *Theology in the Context of World Christianity*—one of the earliest global theological textbooks. Tennent argues the West has engaged with Christians in the majority world one-directionally—from the West to the rest, and that it would be beneficial for Western theologians to dialogue with theologians from other contexts to identify blind spots and correct biases. His text offers a model for such dialogue by including crucial theological questions from the majority world so that Christians might be more equipped for missional proclamation. Tennent aims to create a supplement to aid Western theology, as opposed to undertaking a constructive systematic theology. Methodologically, he ingrafts majority world voices through comparative engagement and careful appropriation of contextual, conceptual categories—all while maintaining an unwavering commitment to the primacy of Scripture. He sets narrow boundaries for his exposition of each major doctrine by considering just one question from one context in the majority world. By limiting his conversation partners, he stops short of a fully integrative theology with numerous voices. Tennent's project has proven to be one of the most widely read introductions to global thinkers.

Finnish theologian Veli-Matti Kärkkäinen brought an integrative global theology to the forefront of American evangelicalism. In his five-volume *A Constructive Christian Theology for the Pluralistic World*, and one-volume *Christian Theology in the Pluralistic World*, Kärkkäinen crafts an expansive global systematic theology which aims to provide "a coherent, inclusive, dialogical, and hospitable vision."[1] For Kärkkäinen, the object of theology is God and everything in relation to him. Thus, for theology to be coherent, one must consider how theological statements correspond not only to God, but all of creation. With this definition, Kärkkäinen casts the web of theological coherence to encompass every facet of knowledge, including all contextual Christian theology, world religions, and natural sciences. His commitment to wide coherence predicates his desire for inclusivity—where Christians welcome engagement with diverse Christian voices, dialogue—where Christians confessionally and comparatively construct theology with other religions, and hospitality—where Christians humbly give and receive from one another. Even with his broad and inclusive approach, Kärkkäinen still exalts Scripture as the highest authority and argues for the traditional categories of orthodoxy, like God's triune being and Christ's two natures. From Kärkkäinen's intentional inclusion of a myriad of voices, while maintaining Christian theological distinction, emerges an integrative global theology with a breadth of charitable dialogue across many times, contexts, and religions.

German theologian Henning Wrogemann, in his three-volume *Intercultural Theology* series, provides an intricate proposal for cross-contextual and interreligious dialogue in theological development. Wrogemann puts significant weight on semiotics and discourse between people from different cultures. He focuses on the role of linguistic signs in communication and the substantial level of understanding needed to interpret signs within a foreign context. This type of semiotic care is a prerequisite to meaningful

---

[1] Veli-Matti Kärkkäinen, *Christ and Reconciliation*, vol. 1 (Grand Rapids: Eerdmans, 2013), 13.

intercultural dialogue. However, while his nuanced approach to such dialogue can be practically helpful, Wrogemann focuses his project almost entirely on the subjective, contextual aspects of theological construction and the interaction between those contexts. In the process, he gives little attention to the objective aspects of theological construction. For Wrogemann, in contrast to both Tennent and Kärkkäinen, theology is entirely contextual with little, if any, objective mooring for theological reflection.

These scholars represent different approaches to account for cultural diversity in theological reflection. Tennent seeks to respect the contextual nature of theology while maintaining evangelical faith commitments. Kärkkäinen takes a broader approach, viewing intercontextual and inter-religious dialogue as revelatory, while maintaining clear commitments to orthodoxy. Wrogemann widens the net further, nearly losing categories of orthodoxy in favor of the contextual. Majority world theologians, like their Western counterparts, have a significant amount of diversity in their approaches to theology, as we will see below.

Global Theologians

Regardless of method, global theology draws its lifeblood from meaningful dialogue with theologians around the world. As these theologians take their seats around the theological table, they carry with them rich history and cultural complexity, just like their Western peers do. In the West, theological discourse requires one to understand the pioneering thinkers in our history, who come from a wide swath of confessional convictions, from John Calvin to Friedrich Schleiermacher to Rudolf Bultmann to Karl Barth. Each region of the world has its own set of groundbreaking theologians, many of whom have been influenced by theology in the West. In this section, we will introduce the seminal thinkers in Africa, Asia, and Latin America. Just like in the West, the most influential scholars from the majority world have not always shared evangelical convictions. Even so, much of the conversation in these regions today builds upon or reacts to these key thinkers.

Before surveying seminal scholars, one historical development bears consideration. Most of these theologians and their academic work arose out of the cataclysmic sociopolitical shifts in the twentieth century. The shift away from the colonizing West to indigenous leadership and independently governed nation states provides a cohesive thread running through all the theological trends mentioned below. In many places, Protestant missionary activity had been woven so closely to European imperialism that one would be hard-pressed to clearly differentiate the two. As the majority world rent the chains of the colonizers, indigenous leaders emerged with an effort to remove undue Western theological influence. As these postcolonial thinkers stake their claim to a contextually appropriate theology, they each incorporate church tradition, modern Western theology, and historical circumstances in a variety of ways. Many of these theologians journeyed to Europe to complete their academic training and returned with the presuppositions of their European mentors from whom they developed their contextual theology. As a result, some of their theological texts are disconnected from the ecclesial experiences of Christians in their context. The influence of postcolonialism lurks in the background for every thinker mentioned below.

Theologians from Africa

Theology in Africa has a long robust history from Tertullian, Athanasius, Augustine, and Zar'a Ya'qob to the Egyptian and Ethiopic churches, which continue to persevere in a region ravaged by centuries of oppression. In the nineteenth and twentieth centuries, Christianity experienced explosive growth in sub-Saharan Africa. Several African theologians have added their voices to this rich theological heritage, including John Mbiti (1931–2019), Charles Nyamiti (1931–2020), and Bolaji Idowu (1913–1993). These three scholars pioneered academic theological development as the first generation of African scholars in the modern era.

Kenyan-born Anglican priest John Mbiti has the longest list of publications among twentieth-century African theologians. Mbiti's works, such as *African Religions and Philosophy* and *Concepts of God in Africa*, focus on demonstrating the value and validity of integrating traditional African religion into Christian theology. He bases much of his work on the presupposition that God's work in the world necessarily extends beyond the Bible. Therefore, God has been working in traditional African religion since ancient times, and the exposition of African traditional religion has necessary import for Christian theological reflection. Mbiti claims God's preparatory work among African religions provided the tinder for Christianity to spread like wildfire across the continent. One would be hard-pressed to over-state Mbiti's influence among African theologians. He towers over twenty-first-century African theology, and his voice will undoubtedly continue to resound for years to come.

Tanzanian Roman Catholic priest Charles Nyamiti's widely read and appreciated *Christ as Ancestor* introduces Christology through the lens of African ancestor concepts. Nyamiti positions his Christology in compara-tive conversation with traditional African religion and a biblical Christology, demonstrating both similarities and necessary differences between the two. He introduces "Christ as ancestor" as a conceptual construct to explain the intra-trinitarian relationship of the Father and Son and the nature of the church in relationship to Christ, our brother. Nyamiti carefully employs ancestor language to explain basic Christian dogma, including the Son's eternal generation, Christ's two natures, substitutionary death, and glorious resurrection. Nyamiti's Christology is both contextually appropriate for an African audience and anchored in the Roman Catholic tradition. While oth-ers have appropriated the ancestor theme for African Christology, Nyamiti's work continues to be one of the most influential.

Nigerian Methodist Bolaji Idowu's work covers a significant span of missiological and theological topics. Idowu was an outspoken proponent for the indigenization of African Christianity for the well-being of the church, which he focused on in his work *Towards an Indigenous Church.* Theologically, he argued no conceptions of God are absolute, though experiential knowl-edge of God remains possible. For Idowu, God rules over the whole universe, and thus he has revealed himself universally in each culture's native concep-tions of God. His texts, such as *Olódùmarè: God in Yoruba Belief,* focus on the Yoruba conceptions of God and their inherent value for African Christianity. Idowu's work bears striking similarity to Mbiti's theology, though, with a focus on West African religion. Certainly, Idowu's work raises questions about the nature and extent of God's general self-revelation. Even so, his influence among African scholarship remains significant.

In addition to these seminal thinkers, new theologians continue to emerge. Scholars such as Kwame Bediako and Lamin Sanneh have their own significant influence. In addition, scholars more theologically near to evan-gelicalism, such as Tite Tiénou and Elizabeth Mburu, though less widely published, continue to shape the theological trajectory in Africa. Looking forward, as theological education continues to develop on the continent, we can expect to see more African scholars shaped by other African scholars. The founding in 2019 of the African Baptist Theological Education Network (ABTEN) provides an exciting opportunity for the development of African Baptist scholars to serve the church in Africa and around the world.

Theologians from Asia

Asia includes a wide swath of languages, cultures, religions, and sociopolitical structures, which result in numerous diverse theological proposals across the continent. In the twentieth century, a number of Asian theologians rose to prominence on the world stage. Choan-Seng Song (b. 1929), Ahn Byung-Mu (1922–1996), and Kosuke Koyama (1929–2009) each provided influential theological texts that continue to shape the course of Asian theology.

Taiwanese Choan-Seng Song remains one of the most widely published theologians from Asia. In his works such as *Third-Eye Theology: A Theology in Formation in Asian Settings* and *Jesus, The Crucified People*, Song endeavors to offer an Asian theology that listens to and addresses the struggles of Christians in his context. While he eschews unmitigated appropriation of Asian religion for Christian theology, he argues if scholars do not address Asian spirituality, their theology will deal only with abstract ideas and not engage the embodied lives of Christians in Asia. In emphasizing embodiment, he argues against using classic metaphysical categories as the centerpiece of his doctrine of God and Christology. Rather, Song focuses on God's present and active work and personal experience with him. Song argues that Christians know Jesus truly in their experiences and should orient their theology around those current theological encounters. Song's academic longevity and winsome style make him one of the most influential theologians in recent years.

Korean Ahn Byung-Mu provided the seminal scholarship in what would become Minjung Theology. He saw the plight of the Korean people suffering in the political turmoil of the 1960s and 1970s under Park Chung-Hee's dictatorship. In studying the Bible, Ahn recognized the significance of the poor masses (*ochlos*) in the Gospel of Mark. He connected the plight of the crowds in Mark to the pain of his people. Ahn then translated *ochlos* into

Korean as the politically and historically laden term "*minjung*" and argued that in Mark, Jesus identifies with the *minjung*—the poor and lowly. For Ahn, Christ is brother to and present with suffering people. He argues the inverse is also true—that the impoverished, downtrodden *minjung* are identified with Jesus. He makes this claim based on a corporate identity, which he sees as both Hebraic and Asian. Scholars around East Asia, such as Suh Nam-Dong, Koo Dong Yun, and Paul S. Chung, continue to appropriate Minjung Theology's conceptual framework.

Japanese Kosuke Koyama's best-known work, *Waterbuffalo Theology*, provides an audience-focused theology from below that addresses pressing questions from numerous Asian contexts with love and compassion. His style uses simple sentence structure and vocabulary to explain complex realities with ease. Koyama routinely begins his theology with the linguistic and conceptual framework of his hearers. He then discusses the Scripture passages in conversation with a myriad of Western and non-Western theologians to develop answers for the questions from his Asian readers. After engaging the biblical text and theological community, Koyama sometimes appropriates native conceptual categories and other times reorients them. While his conceptual categories will seem foreign to Western readers, he seeks to uphold a distinctly Christian theology in his conclusions. Many of his conclusions fit within traditional orthodoxy, though with different language, but others depart from evangelical theological commitments.

In addition, Asian theologians such as Arvind P. Nirmal, Kazo Kitamori, and S. J. Samartha have developed other influential theological texts. As the church in Asia continues in the twenty-first century, one can expect more engagement with indigenous religions. That gives voice and response to the suffering people in Asia but also more constructive approaches from Asian immigrants to the West, who provide a unique bridge to the majority world.

Theologians from Latin America

From the days of the Catholic conquistadors to the influx of Protestant missionaries and more recently the church's experience in political instability, theology in Latin America has had a long and convoluted history. To expose the current complexity of theology in the region, we will consider interdependent but unique contributions of Gustavo Gutiérrez (b. 1928), Justo González (b. 1937), and Samuel Escobar (b. 1934).

Peruvian Roman Catholic priest Gustavo Gutiérrez's 1971 publication, *Theology of Liberation*, is the fountainhead for most liberation theologies around the world. Gutiérrez builds his anthropologically oriented theology on the works of Yves Congar, Georg Hegel, and Karl Marx. For Gutiérrez, theology should reflect on human experience in the light of the Word of God. Christian theology presupposes orthodoxy but is centered around orthopraxy. In reflecting on the experience of his own people in Latin America, Gutiérrez recognizes the suffering of the impoverished. He sees poverty as the fruit of unjust sociopolitical structures and as inherently antithetical to Christianity. As a result, the church must engage in political action to remove the injustices and lead the impoverished to economic, political, and psychological liberation. Gutiérrez adds an eschatological orientation, arguing that liberation ushers the inbreaking now of the coming hope of the final age. Over the second half of the twentieth century, liberation theology developed into a diverse theological school with adherents both in the West and in the majority world. As a result, Gutiérrez remains one of the most influential Christian scholars of the twentieth century.

Cuban-born Methodist historian and theologian Justo González is best known for his texts *The Story of Christianity* and *Mañana: Christian Theology from a Hispanic Perspective*. González's theology emerges from a deep-seated commitment to the authority of Scripture and global theological dialogue that preserves the particularity of each contextual community. González's convictional and irenic tone makes space around the theological table for any number of diverse participants and, in doing so, lends his voice to the methodological conversation in global theology. As a trained historian, González provides beneficial historical analogies to explain contemporary theological development. For González, the dynamic shifts in twentieth-century theology were a macro-reformation, which will have a more wide-reaching impact than the Protestant Reformation. Latin American scholars contribute to this new reformation as a communal people acquainted with the guilt of their Spanish and indigenous ancestors, many of whom have personally experienced the plight of the sojourner. González takes these particularities and demonstrates their value for biblical interpretation and theological reflection. González continues to be a significant influence, particularly in the English-speaking world.

Peruvian Baptist minister Samuel Escobar's missiological theology, including his works *The New Global Mission* and *In Search of Christ in Latin America*, develops a biblical and historically informed theology that accounts for Christ's ongoing work in the world, including in Latin America. Escobar seamlessly weaves together Scripture, ecumenical creeds, and Latin American political and theological history in his theological reflection. His works have recognizable orthodox assertions, like using classical, metaphysical categories. At the same time, he includes Latin American voices and emphases that might be unfamiliar to many in the West. Escobar focuses on the holistic mission of Christ, in word and deed, in the church and the world, and follows other Latin American thinkers by emphasizing the poor. In this way, Escobar achieves his aim of creating a Latin American missiological theology.

Looking forward, we can expect to see the continued rise of Latin American voices in the theological academy as the Hispanic population in the United States continues to grow at a rapid pace. Along with such growth, Latin-American scholars in the United States are poised to connect the West and the majority world in a strategic way.

Contemporary Relevance for American Evangelical Christians

As American evangelicals participate in global theology, we celebrate the faithfulness of our God who is covering the earth with knowledge of himself and growing his church. We rejoice in God's providence, moving all things according to his good purposes, reconciling the world to himself in Christ, and making us his ambassadors. As we listen to majority world Christians, who work with diligence to reveal the relevance of the gospel for people in their contexts, we should be challenged to refine our own contextual theology by considering what language and concepts aid us in proclaiming Christ in the church and to the lost.

At the same time, the substantial diversity among global voices forces us to reflect on the meaning and reality of the church's unity in Christ. We must contemplate which theological commitments are necessary for orthodoxy and which ones leave room for legitimate differences. Where we discover beneficial diversity among our brothers and sisters, we celebrate the beauty of our differences and rejoice that the real unity we enjoy in Christ does not depend upon unanimous agreement. Where we discover departures from orthodoxy, we correct with compassion. Where we are discovered to be in error ourselves, we receive correction with humility as we spur one another on to love and good deeds.

Partaking in cross-cultural dialogue, we join in God's missional work as he increases the church not only in number and location, but in wisdom and understanding. While American evangelicals know God in Christ, we continue to grow in the knowledge of him. God invites us to participate with the global church and grow up together into the fullness of Christ. As we share in God's eschatological movement of self-revelation, we marvel at his infinite worth. All the people, in all the languages, in all the world could never exhaust the extent of his greatness or extol the measure of his grace. As we await the return of the Lord Jesus, we unite with our brothers and sisters from the majority world to continue the theological task of growing up into maturity until we all attain to the unity of the faith and the knowledge of the Son of God.

FOR ADDITIONAL STUDY

Greenman, Jeffrey P., and Gene L. Green, eds. *Global Theology in Evangelical Perspective: Exploring the Contextual Nature of Theology and Mission.* Downers Grove: IVP Academic, 2012.

Kärkkäinen, Veli-Matti. *A Constructive Christian Theology for the Pluralistic World.* 5 volumes. Grand Rapids: Eerdmans, 2013–2017.

Ott, Craig, and Harold Netland, eds. *Globalizing Theology: Belief and Practice in an Era of World Christianity.* Grand Rapids: Baker Academic, 2006.

Tennant, Timothy C. *Theology in the Context of World Christianity: How the Global Church Is Influencing the Way We Think about and Discuss Theology.* Grand Rapids: Zondervan Academic, 2007.

Wrogemann, Henning. *Intercultural Theology.* 3 volumes. Translated by Karl E. Böhmer. Downers Grove: IVP Academic, 2016–2019.

Also see these articles: Gospel, Evangelism and Missions, Systematic Theology, Modern Theology

PART IV
CHRISTIAN DOCTRINES

18

The Trinity

Malcolm B. Yarnell III

The one God, who is the Father and the Son and the Holy Spirit, created all that is, redeems believers, and will guide creation to its end. The eternal God of love, whom Christians hear, worship, and serve, is simply One and personally Three. This biblically imparted and historically received doctrine, known today as "the Trinity," remains simultaneously the greatest mystery of divine revelation and the fundamental dogma of Christian faith. That God is triune shapes our worship, our dogmatic systems, and our ethics. Explicit denial casts doubt upon one's salvation, while altering the dogma endangers the teacher's soul.

The Bible does not include the direct proposition "God is Trinity," though it repeatedly presents God as triune in his being and his actions, so we will first emphasize the biblical evidence. Second, we will summarize the historical responses to the Trinity before, third, sketching the contemporary contours of the doctrine.

The One Biblical God

There is only one true God, and he is triune throughout Scripture. The same God is revealed from Genesis at the beginning of the Old Testament to Revelation at the end of the New. Our understanding of God deepens with the historical narrative of the biblical revelation, yet he remains the same God throughout the Bible. The eternal ontology of God as Trinity is epistemologically unveiled to us in a progressive manner. According to Jesus, "the God of Abraham and the God of Isaac and the God of Jacob" is the one true God (Exod 3:6; Matt 22:32), and he is the same God in whose singular "name" Christians are baptized with "the Father and the Son and the Holy Spirit" (Matt 28:19). When rehearsing history and grammar, one must not surrender transcendent trinitarian theology. The Holy Spirit inspired both testaments and discloses the same truth about God in both, albeit progressively.

The Old Testament Basis: Only God

Hints or pointers that God is One yet Three are found as early as the first chapter of the first book of the first testament of the canon. In the first three verses of the Bible, the eternal God is implicated as initiating creation (Gen 1:1), the Spirit of God as performing creation (Gen 1:2), and the Word of God as commanding creation (Gen 1:3). The Word and the Spirit of God are likewise agents of creation in Psalm 33:6.

Orthodox commentators recognize that the triune nature of the eternal God becomes clearer with the Gospel of John. The apostle John grounded his doctrine of Christ in the prophet Moses's doctrine of God. Where Moses wrote, "In the beginning God" (Gen 1:1), John writes, "In the beginning was the Word, and the Word was with God, and the Word was God" (John 1:1; cf. 1 John 1:1). The New Testament portrayal of God fulfills the Old Testament outline.

Another hint for the complex yet simple nature of God in Genesis 1 is found in the creation of humanity in the image or likeness of God. God refers to himself three times with plural pronouns in verses 26–27. The same passage presents the human being as a mirror of God's plurality in unity. Mirroring the poetic description of God, three times humanity is referenced in the singular, while once humanity is referenced in the plural as "male and female." Later passages reiterate plural references to the only God (Gen 3:22; 11:7; 18:2–3; Isa 6:8).

Other Old Testament pointers to the triunity of God appear. For instance, the Lord allowed Abraham to offer worship to the three he called "Lord" in Genesis 18. Consider also the personalization of "Wisdom" alongside God as an eternal agent of creative action (Prov 8:22–31). Similarly, the Prophet Isaiah speaks of the "Word" of God as eternal (Isa 40:8). The Word comes from God into the world and exercises personal agency with divine authority (Isa 55:9–11). The Psalter treats the "Spirit" (Ps 104:30 NIV) and the Word in personal terms (Ps 147:15–18).

Especially suggestive is the internal dialogue within the Godhead relayed in a key messianic text: "The LORD says to my Lord" (NIV). Psalm 110 was, therefore, highlighted in the teaching of Jesus (Mark 12:35–37 and par.). The apostles later repeatedly cited this royal song to substantiate that Jesus is the Messiah, the eternal Priest-King, one with God (Acts 2:34–35; 1 Cor 15:25; Eph 1:20; Col 3:1; Heb 1:3; 7:17, 21; 1 Pet 3:22).

Jesus's favored self-designation of "Son of Man" recalled Daniel's prophecy of the One who approaches the "Ancient of Days" to receive eternal rule (Dan 7:9–14). When Jesus affirmed this claim about himself before the high priest, he was rejected and condemned to death for making himself equal with God (Mark 14:61–64). When Daniel's prophecy is paired together with the Lord's covenantal promise to David that he would have a descendant to rule an eternal throne, whom God will also call "my son" (2 Sam 7:12–16), the prophetic revelation of the Messiah as the incarnate Son of God achieves more definition (cf. Rom 1:1–4).

In numerous ways, the Old Testament thus includes plurality within divine unity, creating the impression of more than one person within the Godhead. However, passages regarding the plurality of God must be affirmed simultaneously with the numerous passages reserving worship for God alone (cf. Exod 20:3; Deut 6:4–5). There is room in the Old Testament for only one true God, and he is characterized by perfect simplicity alongside internal range. The Old Testament emphasizes the unity of the God who is transcendent, sovereign, and righteous Creator, while it simultaneously affirms the inner plurality of One who is immanent, loving, and gracious Redeemer.

Consider next the fuller disclosure of God available in the New Testament, a revelation centered on Jesus Christ, the eternal Son who became a human being. The New Testament also reveals the Holy Spirit as One to be honored together with God the Father and the Son.

First New Testament Pattern: The Son of God

Like the Old Testament, the New Testament emphasizes the unity of God. It condemns any who would worship someone other than God.

Jesus affirmed the *Shema*, which Jews often prayed as a reminder of their necessary devotion to the one true God (Deut 6:4–5). A Jewish scribe responded to Jesus, "Teacher, you have truly said that he is one, and there is no other but he" (Mark 12:32 RSV). The Greek adjective indicates both "one" (cardinal use) and "first" (ordinal use). Paul concurs with Jesus, "For there is one God and one mediator between God and mankind, the man Christ Jesus" (1 Tim 2:5).

On the firm canvas of the canonical call to worship only the true God, the New Testament authors paint a series of beautiful studies representing God as One and Three. We recall herein three patterns perceived from these biblical portraits. First, the Son of God is united with God the Father even while he is distinguished from him. Second, the Holy Spirit is identified with God the Father and the Son even while he is distinguished. Third, orthodox theologians discern a pattern of eternal divine relations through personal origin in the Father.

The first pattern concerns the unity and distinction of the Son with the Father. In the already quoted John 1:1, the Word is both equated with God and distinguished from God. He is simultaneously "God" and "with God." Moreover, this One who is distinct from the Father yet one with the Father became flesh in Jesus Christ (John 1:14). In Jesus the Messiah, the Word of God became man, attaching our human nature to his eternal divine person for eternity.

The incarnation of the Son of God was necessary for humanity to be reconciled to God through Christ's atoning death upon the cross and justifying resurrection from the dead. One may not mediate between hostile parties unless one shares a commonality with both (Col 1:19–20). This is why Paul claimed there is only "one mediator between God and mankind" (1 Tim 2:5). Our hope resides in the God-Man; our Savior is none other than Jesus Christ (Luke 2:11; 1 Tim 4:10).

The audacity of the teaching of Jesus with regard to his unity and equality with the Father created the legal excuse for the Sanhedrin to condemn him. The unity of the Son and the Father was, therefore, not an inconsequential claim. When he said, "Before Abraham was, I am" (John 8:58), Jesus affirmed his preexistence before Abraham and his unity with the God whose covenantal name is "I am." *Yahweh*, the covenantal name, was not even spoken by the Jews due to its holiness. Instead, they referred to him as *Adonai*, "the Lord." This is why Jesus's repeated self-designation of "I am" generated such a furor with unbelieving Jews (John 8:58–59).

Jesus's self-identification with the Lord also explains why the fundamental Christian confession has always been "Jesus is Lord" (Rom 10:9; 1 Cor 12:3). When Jesus said unequivocally, "I and the Father are one," the unbelieving Jewish leaders determined to kill him (John 10:30–39). But his Spirit-inspired disciples, the apostles, affirmed that Jesus Christ is the "exact expression" or "image" of the Father's "nature" (*hypostaseos*; Heb 1:3).

Alongside the unity of the Son with God is the distinction of the Son from the Father. Keep in mind we are speaking primarily of the divine nature of the Son, although his human nature cannot be divorced from his person. The Son is one with the Father and distinct from the Father. He is "with God" (John 1:1). He was "set apart" and sent into the world (John 10:36). He has come into the world "from the Father" and returns "to the Father" (John 16:28; cf. 13:3).

The Son possesses everything the Father possesses (John 16:15; Matt 11:27), but he was "forsaken" by the Father (Matt 27:46; cf. Psalm 22). Why did God the Father forsake his Son? So that God might present him "as the mercy seat by his blood" (Rom 3:25). The Son is equated fully with the Father yet distinguished personally from the Father.

Second New Testament Pattern: The Spirit of God

The second notable trinitarian pattern revealed by the New Testament concerns the unity and the distinction of the Holy Spirit with God. On the one hand, the Spirit is clearly one with Father and Son. The Christian's first act of public worship, when the believer makes known his or her new identity, is baptism in a name. This singular "name" indicates the character of the One God with whom the believer is united. The one name is threefold. The Lord explicitly commanded baptism should occur "in the name of the Father and the Son and the Holy Spirit" (Matt 28:19).

In another act of prayer, a canonical benediction still widely used in Christian liturgy, the Spirit is incorporated within the divine economy of the Father and the Son (2 Cor 13:13). Moreover, only the Spirit knows God internally (1 Cor 2:10–11). According to Paul, "the Lord is the Spirit" (2 Cor 3:17–18). The apostle hereby equates the Son directly with the Spirit.

On the other hand, the Holy Spirit is distinguished from the Father and the Son. Paul united and distinguished the Holy Spirit from the Son in the same passage: "The Lord is the Spirit" is also "the Spirit of the Lord." The pneumatological pattern of 2 Cor 3:17 hereby parallels the Christological pattern of John 1:1.

Moreover, not only is the Spirit distinguished from "the Lord" Jesus Christ, it is also the Spirit "of God" the Father (Rom 8:9, 11). In several places, the New Testament reinforces the distinction of the Spirit with the Father. Jesus said the Holy Spirit is "another Helper" alongside the Son and will be sent from the Father to reside with the believer forever (John 14:16).

The Father will send the Spirit in the name of the Son, and it will teach his disciples (John 14:26; 15:26). The Son himself gives the Spirit to the disciples (John 20:22). Through the personal presence of the Holy Spirit "with" and even "in" his disciples, the Son of God will be personally present "to" the disciples (John 14:17–18). Christ must, however, depart to the Father for the Spirit to come to them (John 16:7; cf. 7:39). Repeatedly, the Spirit is simultaneously identified with yet distinguished from the Father and the Son.

The presence of these first two patterns naturally prompts the question about the origin of these relations. How should we understand the unity of the Son with the Father along with his distinction from the Father? And how should Christians perceive the unity of the Spirit with the Father and the Son along with his distinction from the Father and the Son?

Third New Testament Pattern: Eternal Relations

The doctrine of the trinitarian relations of origin shows how the first two New Testament patterns may be maintained coherently. This third biblical pattern, the eternal relations of origin between the Father, the Son, and the Holy Spirit, also contributes a settled orthodox language for the unity and the distinction of the Three as One. The third pattern is apparent in several key prepositions, verbs, and nouns. We start with the prepositions.

The New Testament reveals the Father, the Son, and the Holy Spirit are "in" and "with" one another, just as the Son and the Spirit are generally "from" and "to" the Father. The Father and the Son are "in" one another (John 10:38; 17:21) and share everything eternally "with" one another (John 17:5). Moreover, the Spirit comes "from" the Father (John 15:26), just as the

Son comes "from" the Father (John 1:14; 6:46, 65; etc.) and returns "to" the Father (John 13:3; 16:28; 17:13).

The relation between the Son and the Spirit is, from the human perspective, so intertwined that to be "in the Spirit" is to have Christ "in you" and the Spirit "in you." This same Spirit is "of" God the Father, who raised Jesus from the dead (Rom 8:9–11). The complex "in," "with," "of," "from," and "to" pattern of the relations between the Three receives more clarity when we consider the verbs describing the eternal origin.

According to the Gospel of John and the Epistle to the Hebrews, the Son is "begotten" of the Father. The closely related verbs *gennao* and *genao* are applied to the Son regarding his eternal relation with the Father (*gennao* in Heb 1:5; 5:5; Acts 13:33; *genao* in John 1:14, 18; 3:16, 18; 1 John 4:9). In Heb 1:5, the begetting clearly occurs before the incarnation. In John 1:18, the begetting refers to the deity of Christ and his intimacy with the Father—he is "the only begotten God, which is in the bosom of the Father" (KJV). *Gennao/genao* may be translated into English as either "generated" or "begotten."

The generation of the Son from the Father is necessarily an eternal event, having neither beginning nor end, because the fatherhood of the Father is manifestly "eternal" (Isa 9:6; cf. 1 John 1:2). From these numerous biblical references, classical theologians conclude the Son's relation to the Father is one of "eternal generation." Generation must not be taken in a low crass or carnal sense, for divine perfection transcends, even while it is conveyed through, limited human metaphor.

If the relation between Father and Son is that of "eternal generation," how does Scripture portray the relation of the Holy Spirit? The key Greek term, *ekporeuomai*, "proceeds from," is used to describe the Spirit's personal relation in John 15:26: "When the Counselor comes, the one I will send to you from the Father—the Spirit of truth who proceeds from the Father—he will testify about me." *Ekporeuomai* may be translated as "to travel out" or "move out of" and is used elsewhere to depict words or spirits coming from human persons (Matt 15:11; Acts 19:12). John 15:26 applies it uniquely to God.

From this passage comes the classical Christian description of the relation of the Spirit to God as "eternal procession." Because the Spirit is unique to the eternal God, procession is necessarily eternal in quality (1 Cor 2:10–11). The eternal and personal procession of the Spirit ontologically "from the Father" must, moreover, be distinguished from his being "sent" economically into temporal creation from the Father and the Son (John 14:26; 15:26; 16:7).

If the relation of the Son to God is one of "eternal generation," and the relation of the Holy Spirit to God is "eternal procession," what is the proper description for the relation of God the Father? The Christian tradition has typically referred to God the Father as the "source" or "beginning" of the Son and the Spirit. The apostle John begins his first epistle in a way similar to that of his Gospel, recalling Genesis 1. However, rather than saying "in the beginning," he now states, "from the beginning." The Son of God who became flesh is "from the beginning," *ap' arches*. The Greek noun *arche* may indicate a beginning point in time, "first cause," "ruler," or "supernatural power." *Arche* refers to the Father simply in Revelation 21:6 and to the Father as the One from whom the Son derives in 1 John 1:1–3. Using a different term, *kephale*, to describe this relation, Paul states the Father is the Son's "source" or "head" (1 Cor 11:3).

The third New Testament pattern thus depicts the Trinity as comprised of three relations: the eternal Father is the "source" of the Trinity, while the Son is "generated" from the Father, and the Spirit "proceeds" from God. This basic biblical definition of the eternal relations of origin was discerned by the Cappadocian Fathers in the East and accepted in the West.

Alas, to complicate matters, following Augustine, the Roman church argued on the basis of the economic sending of the Spirit by both the Father and the Son that the Spirit proceeds ontologically from both the Father and the Son. (This author, like many theologians East and West, prefers to say the Spirit proceeds from the Father through the Son.) Since we have raised the development of classical orthodoxy, we now proceed to a summary of the historical doctrine of the Trinity, even while referring the reader to the scriptural basis of orthodoxy.

The Trinity in Church History

Theophilus of Antioch in the late second century first referred to God as *Trias* (Greek), while a few decades later Tertullian of Carthage used *Trinitas* (Latin), "Trinity." Latin Christians also differentiated the Three as *Personae*, "Persons," and described the unity as *Consubstantia*, "one substance." Greek

Christians similarly developed the terms *Tria Hypostaseis* and *Homoousios*. *Hypostasis*, which means "nature," was first applied to the Father in Hebrews 1:3. It subsequently became equivalent in use to the Latinate "person." The term *Homoousios* ("one essence") is manifestly extrabiblical but effectively preserves biblical ways of thought against pagan philosophical intrusion. The classical terms helpfully preserve scriptural truth.

As the early Christians continued explaining God as triune, they drew upon natural, psychological, and social analogies. Natural illustrations compared the Trinity to a root, tree, and its fruit or to a fountain, stream, and lake. Augustine of Hippo developed a complex psychological analogy in his famous *De Trinitatis* with the Father as memory, the Son as understanding, and the Spirit as will. The Cappadocians alluded socially to Adam, Eve, and Seth or Peter, James, and John sharing a common human nature. Augustine spoke of the Lover, the Beloved, and Love comprising the divine unity.

Karl Barth decried the use of these supposed "vestiges of the Trinity" from creation as illustrations, for the Creator is thereby conceptually reduced to the level of the creature. Human analogies and illustrations prove problematic when allowed to overwhelm the biblical and classical descriptions. While preachers and teachers inevitably use illustrations, we must heed Barth's warning and be careful not to limit God to our explanations.

The language of orthodoxy achieved a settled form only after responding to several early heresies, which endangered the church's worship of the true God. Three major forms of trinitarian heresy are identifiable, although individual heresies often reappear in various permutations. The first, modalistic monarchianism, preserved God's Oneness by redefining Threeness. According to this view, God merely reveals himself in three different modes or manners, usually related to an epoch. Modalism, or sabellianism, affirms the economic Trinity but denies the essential Trinity. Tertullian reported the heretic Praxeas believed the Father was crucified.

The second major form of heresy, unitarianism, preserves the Oneness of God through subordinating the Son and the Spirit. The premiere unitarian challenge was posed by Arius of Alexandria. He did not deny the Son should be worshiped; rather, the Son is less than the Father. Arians said the Son was of a different substance from the Father and "there was a time when he was not." The ecumenical Council of Nicaea, meeting in 325 to settle the dispute, unequivocally concluded the Son was "begotten from the Father before all the ages, light from light, true God from true God, begotten not made, one essence with [*homoousios*] the Father."

The third major form, Tritheism, separates the Three into many gods. Classical orthodoxy responded that God should be perceived as possessing one will rather than three. According to the sixth ecumenical council, Constantinople III (681), when Jesus prayed, "Not my will, but yours, be done" (Luke 22:42), he was contrasting his divine and human wills. God has one will. Jesus said he and the Father are "one" (John 10:30), and the Spirit is included therein.

Following the widespread liturgical use of the Apostles' Creed, the Nicene Creed, and the Athanasian Creed, controversies surrounding the doctrine of the Trinity began to settle down after the fourth century. The first two creeds contain three major articles, one each devoted to God the Father, God the Son, and God the Holy Spirit. The third creed is a sustained defense of the classical doctrine of the Trinity.

The second ecumenical council, Constantinople I (381), revised the Nicene Creed to strengthen the article on the Holy Spirit. Drawing upon biblical language, it affirmed the Spirit is "the Lord and Life-giver; who is proceeding from the Father; who with the Father and the Son is together worshiped and together glorified." The church of Rome later added *Filioque*, "and the Son," to the same creed to indicate a double procession of the Spirit, causing a split with the East at the dawn of the second millennium.

The Contemporary Doctrine

Whichever way a particular theologian today interprets the procession of the Holy Spirit, orthodox Western and Eastern theologians concur that the Son and the Spirit receive entire and undiminished deity from the Father. The eternal relations of origin, simply speaking, require the eternal participation of the Three in all the divine perfections. The Lord Jesus teaches in John 16:14–15 that "everything the Father has is mine," and the Holy Spirit has free access to the same. In the Great Commission, the Son asserts, "All authority has been given to me in heaven and on earth" (Matt 28:18).

Divine authority is not the only perfection explicitly identified as eternally shared. The divine perfection of love was shared "before the world's foundation" (John 17:24). And the divine perfection of glory was shared "before the world existed" (John 17:5). Similar affirmations of the full equality of the Three in all the divine attributes suffuse the biblical text and thus determine the orthodox affirmations of divine simplicity and Triune equality.

The ancient Athanasian Creed affirms there is only one God, one Lord, one Almighty. This One is Father and Son and Holy Spirit. There are not three Gods, nor three Lords, nor three Almighties. There can be no limitation in orthodox theology to any of the Three sharing in each of the divine attributes eternally by reason of the biblical pattern of the eternal relations of origin. There are not three levels of divine authority. The Baptist Faith and Message agrees: The "personal attributes" of the "eternal triune God" are "without division of nature, essence, or being." Like the Father, the Lord Jesus Christ is "fully God," and the Holy Spirit is "fully divine" (article II).

When theologians turn from considering Scripture's witness of God in his eternal being (trinitarian ontology) to considering God in his temporal actions toward creation (trinitarian economy), the ontological triune patterns manifest themselves appropriately. However, a word of caution about the logic of theology: Divine simplicity preserves our doctrine of God's triune perfection, asserting no unrealized potentiality nor parts in God. God's attributes are inseparable from his essence. The three persons likewise inhere in one another. Theological simplicity may not be compromised without compromising the biblical Trinity. God's being, moreover, grounds God's activity. God is pure act. His activities ought never be conceived without reference to his eternal perfections.

From the preceding biblical exegesis, historical developments, and theological logic, we garner five truths about God the Trinity in his being: First, there is one God, and he alone must be worshiped by his creatures, all of whom he perfectly transcends. Second, this one biblical God is three equal persons: Father, Son, and Holy Spirit. Third, the Father is the source from whom the Son is eternally generate and the Spirit eternally proceeds. Fourth, the Three completely share the one substance and every perfection, for they inhere in one another as God (known in Greek as *Perichoresis*). Fifth, the perfect triune God acts perfectly toward creation.

After triune being, we must consider trinitarian economy. Note three major truths about the Trinity's acts toward his creature. First, all God's works are performed together by all three persons. The Trinity works indivisibly. This can be seen, for instance, in the biblical descriptions of election, creation, redemption, and final consummation. In addition, while space limits our development of trinitarian anthropology, we affirm that because humanity was created in God's image and God is triune, human beings participate in his triune glory individually and communally.

Second, even as the Three work indivisibly, there remains a sense of order in their work. The "order" (Gk. *Taxis*) of the divine relations is manifested in the divine economy. The Father necessarily leads in election, creation, and providence. Some theologians speak of a "covenant of redemption" to describe the divine will for human redemption. The Son became a human being in order to reveal the mystery of our salvation performed through his incarnation, death, resurrection, ascension, heavenly reign, and Second Coming. The Holy Spirit sovereignly applies the will of God to his creatures, including the various graces that move the salvation of individual human believers.

Third, the unity and order, the harmony and melody, and the equality and diversity of the Triune being are patterned symmetrically in God's work of salvation. God the Trinity works from heaven for our journey to heaven. *From heaven*, God the Father sends the Son and the Spirit to accomplish redemption for us and reconciliation in us (Gal 4:4–6). *To heaven*, the Spirit unites all who believe in Christ through his convicting work by the gift of faith with the Son, who intercedes so we may enter the eternal presence of the Father (Eph 2:18). Eschatologically, we who believe shall joyfully worship God and the Lamb who sit as One on the eternal throne whence the Spirit proceeds, gifting us abundant life forevermore (Revelation 21–22).

FOR ADDITIONAL STUDY

Augustine. *The Trinity*. Hyde Park, NY: New City Press, 1991.

Gregory of Nazianzus. *On God and Christ: The Five Theological Orations*. Yonkers, NY: St. Vladimir's Seminary Press, 2002.

Reeves, Michael. *Delighting in the Trinity*. Downers Grove: IVP, 2012.

Swain, Scott R. *The Trinity: An Introduction*. Wheaton: Crossway, 2020.

Yarnell, Malcolm B., III. *God the Trinity: Biblical Portraits*. Nashville: B&H Academic, 2016.

Also see these articles: God's Existence, God's Attributes, God's Covenants, Creation, Person of Jesus Christ, Holy Spirit

19

God's Attributes

Adam Harwood

An attribute refers to the nature or characteristics of a person or thing. Thus, God's attributes describe his nature. Though no words can adequately describe God, it is right and proper to formulate statements to describe the God who reveals himself in nature, through Scripture, and in Jesus. Whatever one says about God—even if everything one says is true—is inadequate and falls short of communicating his greatness. Our knowledge of him is inadequate, partial, and fractured. Nevertheless, our glimpses of God reveal One who is more than worthy of our worship, commitment, and affection.

Before presenting various attributes, a few remarks are in order. First, Scripture provides neither a list nor definitions of divine attributes. Instead, God is revealed in Scripture, and the biblical authors make no attempt to categorize or classify the attributes. Readers of Scripture must decide which attributes will be identified and then define and possibly categorize them. When formulating and reflecting on God's attributes, one should be guided by descriptions of God in Scripture—as well as his names and actions revealed in the Bible. The attributes should describe God's character, and those definitions should never contradict the teachings in Scripture about God.

Second, every attribute is true of God simultaneously, and his attributes are not in competition with one another. For example, God does not cease to be loving in order to be just. Rather, he is simultaneously loving and just, as well as every other attribute. Similarly, attributes do not represent only one part of a larger whole. Instead, every attribute is a true statement about God's nature.

Third, God's attributes are (in Aristotle's terms) essential rather than accidental. Essential attributes belong to the essence of the thing in question; the addition or subtraction of the attribute would affect the nature of the person or thing. Accidental attributes, however, do not inhere in the nature of a person or thing and can be added or removed without changing its nature. Thus, all of God's attributes are essential attributes because the addition or removal of any attribute would result in a change in God's essence.

God's Attributes

Holy

Scripture explicitly says God is holy. Moses and the Israelites sang, "Lord, who is like you among the gods? Who is like you, glorious in holiness, revered with praises, performing wonders?" (Exod 15:11). God's ways are holy (Ps 77:13), and God is holy (Josh 24:19; Ps 99:9). Moses was required to remove his shoes at the burning bush because God's presence extended holiness to the ground on which he stood (Exod 3:5). Isaiah saw a vision of God high and lifted up, and seraphim called out a triple-declaration of God's holiness (Isa 6:3). In John's vision, creatures called out continuously, "Holy, holy, holy, Lord God the Almighty, who was, who is, and who is to come" (Rev 4:8). Jesus called God "Holy Father" in prayer (John 17:11), and Jesus taught us to say to God in prayer, "hallowed be thy name" (Matt 6:9 KJV).

In Scripture, God is holy, God's dwelling place is holy, and his people are called to be holy. The call to holiness is an ethical and religious standard for God's people to live separate from sin. God's people are called to holiness because they worship and serve a holy God. Peter wrote, "But as the one who called you is holy, you also are to be holy in all your conduct; for it is written, 'Be holy, because I am holy'" (1 Pet 1:15–16).

God's holiness is mentioned first among the attributes, not to imply that his holiness is more important than his love or justice. Rather, all of God's attributes are fully and equally true of God.

Love

God is love. The statement is not mere sentimentality. Scripture declares, "God is love" (1 John 4:8, 16). Also, the Bible provides a glimpse of the eternal relationship of love among the persons of the Trinity. For example, Jesus prayed to the Father, "You loved me before the world's foundation" (John 17:24). Though Scripture does not explicitly mention the Holy Spirit's love, Augustine called the Spirit the bond of love between the Father and the Son.[1]

God's act of creating all things flows from his free and loving choice. He created and sustains a world of people made in his image, who have the capacity for a loving relationship with their Creator and one another. God pursued a relationship with the first couple as well as with subsequent generations. He created out of one man a nation to be a blessing to the nations (Gen 12:2–3). He made a covenant with Abram and others, binding himself to a people who would be unfaithful to him. Israelites were commanded to love God with their heart, soul, and strength (Deut 6:5). God loved them, though they did nothing to deserve his love (Deut 7:7–8). Many of the statements about God's love in the Old Testament focus on the Israelites, who were his people and treasured possession. Such statements, however, should be read in light of God including non-Israelites among his people (such as Rahab the Canaanite and Ruth the Moabite) as well as the missionary call for Israel to be a light to the nations (Isa 42:6). God's love was focused *uniquely* on Israel, but it was not the case that he loved *only* Israel.

God's love is self-giving. At the incarnation and crucifixion of Christ, God acted out of concern for the welfare of people he created and loves, though they are sinners and his enemies. Paul explains, "God's love has been poured out in our hearts through the Holy Spirit" (Rom 5:5). Paul continues, "For while we were still helpless, at the right time, Christ died for the ungodly" (v. 6). Though people will rarely sacrifice their life for a good person (v. 7), the death of Christ is a demonstration of God's love for *sinners* (v. 8). We were reconciled (made right) with God through the death of his Son while we were God's enemies (v. 10). God did not wait for sinners to wave a

---

[1] Augustine, *On the Trinity* 6.5.

white flag of surrender before Jesus journeyed to the cross. Rather, God initiated reconciliation with sinners through his Son's self-sacrifice while we were God's enemies. It is not that we loved God, John explains, but God loved us and sent Jesus as a sacrifice for our sins (1 John 4:10).

Just

God and his ways are just, or righteous. Moses declared in song, "All his ways are just. A faithful God, without bias, he is righteous and true" (Deut 32:4). Moses affirmed that God's actions are right, never wrong. He is faithful, always doing what is just. Similar affirmations are found in other texts. David professed, "For the LORD is righteous" (Ps 11:7a). Daniel prayed, "Lord, righteousness belongs to you" (Dan 9:7). In the same verse, Daniel noted that the Israelites were scattered because of their unfaithfulness to God. Daniel continued, "So the LORD kept the disaster in mind and brought it on us, for the LORD our God is righteous in all he has done. But we have not obeyed him" (Dan 9:14). Daniel declared in the same breath that God is just and the people were scattered—he brought disaster due to their unfaithfulness and disobedience. These affirmations of God's just character include mention that *some*—though not *all*—instances of disaster on God's people resulted from unfaithfulness and disobedience to the God who is just.

The New Testament emphasizes that God justifies people through faith in Christ (Rom 1:17; 4:5; Gal 3:11), and the cross of Christ is the clearest view of God's justice. Jesus—who was innocent—willingly took on himself the punishment and judgment due to others—who were guilty. Paul explains, "God made him who had no sin to be sin for us, so that in him we might become the righteousness of God" (2 Cor 5:21 NIV). God's just requirements were fulfilled at the sacrifice of Christ on the cross because God punished the sin of all who would be justified by faith (Rom 3:25–26). God and his ways are just, and he justifies sinners through faith in Jesus.

Self-Existing

God is self-existing. This attribute is also called "aseity" (from Latin, *a se*, "from himself"). Unlike people, who require food, water, and oxygen to survive, God requires nothing outside of himself to exist. It is not the case that

God does not require those things only because he is spirit; otherwise, one might wrongly think angels, demons, and even Satan self-exist because they also exist without food, water, or oxygen. Rather, God exists from himself, which is not true of angels, demons, or Satan, all created beings. Before God created the heavens and the earth—if it is proper to refer to a time *before* he created time as we know it—God existed. Jesus said, "For as the Father has life in himself, so he has granted the Son also to have life in himself" (John 5:26). By Jesus's testimony, the Father and the Son have equal power to give others life. Jesus also said, "The Spirit is the one who gives life" (John 6:63). Also, Paul explained to the Areopagus at Athens, "The God who made the world and everything in it is the Lord of heaven and earth and does not live in temples built by human hands. And he is not served by human hands, as if he needed anything. Rather, he himself gives everyone life and breath and everything else" (Acts 17:24–25). The Creator does not depend on creation. Rather, the self-existing Creator gives life to and provides for creation.

Unchanging

Some Christians affirm God is unchanging because they conceive of God through "perfect being" theology. According to this view, God has every great-making property to the maximum extent. Thus, any change in any attribute would mean God was not already the greatest of all conceivable beings. If he were to become more loving, for example, then he would not be the God of maximal love.[2] Thus, there is no movement in God. This classical concept of God also affirms God is pure act (Lat. *actus purus*), a metaphysical claim that excludes any potentiality or change in God. For Aristotle, God is the unmovable prime mover. Some regard these ideas to be extra-biblical metaphysical concerns that originate outside the Bible and are contrary to the relational God portrayed in Scripture.

Scripture includes statements such as "I, the LORD, do not change" (Mal 3:6 NASB) and "Jesus Christ is the same yesterday, today, and forever" (Heb 13:8). Such statements should be interpreted as declarations of God's unchanging *nature*. God is, always has been, and always will be holy, loving, and just. In that sense, he is unchanging. If it were possible for God

---

[2] See Anselm, *Proslogion* 2–3.

to change in his character, then it would be possible for him to be unholy, unloving, or no longer the Father of the Lord Jesus Christ. If so, then God would no longer be who he revealed himself to be. However, God is who he revealed himself to be, and he will do what he has promised he will do. God is immutable, meaning he is unchanging in his nature.

Related issues are whether God is impassible, unchanging in his emotions, and whether God suffers. Though God's nature and purposes do not change, he suffers and is moved emotionally as he relates to people. In this sense, God is immutable and passible. Despite God's comprehensive knowledge of all things, including future possibilities and events, Scripture indicates God is sometimes emotionally moved. For example, God was "deeply grieved" over human sin in Noah's day (Gen 6:6). At times, God rejoices (Isa 62:5); at other times, he grieves (Ps 78:40; Eph 4:30). Jesus cried over the city of Jerusalem (Luke 19:41) and at the death of his friend Lazarus (John 11:35). Interpretation of such passages is key. We have analogous experiences when a relative or friend's illness brings them near death. Although we anticipate their death is imminent, the event of death results in tears and grief. We do not say, "I knew she would die, so I'm not sad." The knowledge of the imminent death does not remove the pain. Explorations of God's unchanging nature should include examples in Scripture of God's emotions.

Discussions of God's immutability and impassibility should account for the incarnation. Those who affirm God is unchanging also believe he has acted in the world at various times, decisively in the incarnation of the preexistent and eternal Son of God. God is *unchanging*, yet he *acts* in the world. Prior to the incarnation, the eternal Son had not been subject to change, such as those changes that occurred in the person of Jesus. When the Word became flesh, the incorporeal became corporeal. The eternal Son, who was and is truly and fully God, was born of a woman (John 1:14; Gal 4:4), grew (Luke 2:52), learned (Heb 5:8), suffered (Luke 22:15; Heb 5:8), and died (Rom 5:8; 1 Cor 15:3). The incarnation did not result in a change in the character or plans of God. Rather, the incarnation, cross, and resurrection *fulfilled* God's plan, which predates creation. The incarnation of Christ should inform any discussion of the Trinity and God's attributes because the incarnate Son is God. God is unchanging in his character and promises, though he suffers and is moved emotionally as he relates and responds to people.

Eternal

When the concept of eternity includes pre-existence, then it is proper to affirm that only God is eternal. Thomas Aquinas argued that only God could be eternal.[3] Against the view that the universe and some creatures existed from eternity, he argued God has always existed, God will always exist, and God created all things from nothing. God's existence extends eternally in both directions, before the beginning and after the end of time.

God's existence at creation is assumed in Gen 1:1, John 1:1, and other biblical texts. The psalmist declares God's existence before creation: "Before the mountains were born, before you gave birth to the earth and the world, from eternity to eternity, you are God" (Ps 90:2). He is "the everlasting God" (Isa 40:28) and "the eternal God" (Rom 16:26). God's eternity is also communicated without using the words everlasting or eternal. For example, Christ's kingdom "will have no end" (Luke 1:33), Jesus "remains forever" (Heb 7:24), and God "alone is immortal" (1 Tim 6:16), meaning he is not subject to death.

God's relationship to time is a dense topic. Historically, the majority view among Christians has been that the eternal God created time and is not bound by it. Yet he has manifested his presence at significant moments in time, such as creation, the exodus, the cross, Pentecost, and the future return of Christ. It is reasonable to affirm that God *was* timeless and *then* related to creation temporally when he created and acted in time, though he is in no way bound or constrained by time.

Omnipresent

God is omnipresent (all-present). More precisely, God is not limited by physical space. Though he is distinct from and should not be confused with creation, he is present in all places because he sustains all things, and he has manifested his presence at specific times in history.

Scripture speaks of God's presence. David, confessing his sinful acts against Bathsheba and Uriah, prayed, "Do not banish me from your presence" (Ps 51:11a). On another occasion, David prayed, "Where can I go to

---

[3] Thomas Aquinas, *Summa Theologica* 1.46.1.

escape your Spirit? Where can I flee from your presence?" (Ps 139:7). In the verses that follow, David answered that God would be present in the heavens, on the far side of the sea, and in darkness. Those verses do not affirm that God is everywhere because wherever you happen to go, God is already there. Rather, the verses affirm that wherever David goes—literally or metaphorically—God will be present with him. God never promises in Scripture that he will be present at all places and times in the same way in the present age. Though it would be improper to affirm that God could be *confined to* any place, it would be equally improper to affirm that God could be *kept from* any place. God can be present at any place and time.

Sometimes the question arises whether God will be present in hell. The question is built on a series of related assumptions. If God is present in a minimal way in every place (and if Col 1:17 means that God maintains properties such that places and things continue to exist in or by the power of Christ), then is God present in hell to maintain its existence? The question creates difficulty reconciling God's presence and holiness. God does not belong in hell, but how could it exist without his maintaining presence? In answer to this speculative question, if God is present for different purposes at various times, then perhaps God is present at some times to punish, other times to sustain, and still other times to bless. God is omnipresent, able to be present in any place and in no way bound by space.

Omnipotent

God is omnipotent (all-powerful). He has the power to do anything consistent with his nature, desires, and plans, as revealed in Scripture. God's power is evidenced by his creating all things from nothing and his title, God Almighty (*El Shaddai*). God's power can be regarded as either unlimited or limited in some way. If God's power were unlimited, then he could do everything, which would be problematic. God *cannot* do some things, not because of any lack of power but for other reasons. For example, God cannot sin because it would be a violation of his holy nature. He cannot lie or cheat for the same reason. James explains, "God is not tempted by evil, and he himself doesn't tempt anyone" (Jas 1:13). It seems prudent to view God's power as limited, not by anything external to God, but limited only by God to align with his nature, desires, and plans. God has the power, for example, to destroy the earth by a flood, but he chose to limit the use of his power when he promised never again to flood the earth (Gen 9:15). Just because God has the power to do something does not mean he will. God acts in ways consistent with his attributes. Thus, any act of his power will be consistent with his other attributes as well as his desires and plans.

Omniscient

God is omniscient (all-knowing). The psalmist remarked, "The LORD looks down from heaven; he observes everyone. He gazes on all the inhabitants of the earth from his dwelling place. He forms the hearts of them all; he considers all their works" (Ps 33:13–15). These verses use synonymous parallels to refer to God seeing and watching *all* humanity, *all* who live on earth.

God's "understanding is infinite" (Ps 147:5). The eyes of the Lord are everywhere, watching both evil and good people (Prov 15:3). Jesus remarked that God's knowledge extends to details such as sparrows falling to the ground and the number of hairs on one's head (Matt 10:29–30). Hebrews 4:13 states, "No creature is hidden from him, but all things are naked and exposed to the eyes of him to whom we must give an account." God knows everything.

Some biblical texts have been interpreted in ways that create doubt about God's comprehensive knowledge of the future. Those texts include 1 Sam 15:11 and 35; 2 Kgs 20:1–20; Gen 22:1–19; and Jer 7:31. 1 Samuel 15:11 quotes the Lord saying, "I regret that I made Saul king." Some interpret "regret" to mean God did not know the outcome of Saul's reign and thus regretted his decision to make him king. However, a better interpretation is that God regretted making Saul king because when Saul was given a choice, he continually disobeyed God, harming himself and Israel.

Second Kings 20 tells the story of God judging King Hezekiah by declaring he would not recover from his illness (2 Kgs 20:1). Hezekiah responded in repentance (2 Kgs 20:2–3), and the Lord replied, "I have heard your prayer; I have seen your tears. Look, I will heal you" (2 Kgs 20:5). God granted him another fifteen years (2 Kgs 20:15). Though some interpret this story to mean God changed his mind, a better interpretation is that God relates to people in accordance with their responses to him, regardless of his knowledge of how we will respond. God's knowledge of future events is clarified by his declaration that Hezekiah will live another fifteen years rather than an undetermined time.

Genesis 22 begins with the curious statement "God tested Abraham" (Gen 22:1). Though some interpret this to mean God did not know how Abraham would respond, a better interpretation is that the test revealed the extent of Abraham's faith in God to himself and others.

In Jer 7:31, the Lord indicts a group for sacrificing their children in the fire, "a thing I did not command; I never entertained the thought." Some interpret the last phrase to mean God did not know that the people would act in this sinful way. However, a better interpretation is that God was speaking in tautology language. In support of this interpretation, consider that God had previously forbidden such behavior (Lev 18:21; 20:2–6), and Manasseh had sacrificed his son to the flames, arousing the Lord's anger (2 Kgs 21:6). Thus, the idea that people would sacrifice their children to the flames had occurred to God. He was making a statement of outrage at their sin. These brief explanations illustrate some of the biblical texts that raise questions about interpreting texts about God's knowledge.

Creator

The first sentence of the Bible and the first line of the Apostles' Creed are united in their claim that God is Creator of heaven and the earth. For centuries, millions of Christians have affirmed the Apostles' Creed, an expanded version of the old Roman creed, which begins, "I believe in God the Father almighty, creator of heaven and earth." Karl Barth, a significant theologian of the twentieth century, was known for emphasizing the radical distinction between God and creation. This Creator-creature distinction is all-encompassing. One could categorize all of reality as either Creator or creation.

One might argue that Creator is not an essential attribute because the affirmation depends on something external to God—namely, creation. Thus, such a property is contingent and should not be considered an attribute of God. Though the affirmation "God is Creator" violates a philosophical-theological rule of what counts as an attribute, the Bible reveals and the church has confessed that God is Creator of all things. What would it mean to affirm that all people·at all times and places know from creation that there is a Creator but simultaneously deny that Creator is a faithful statement about God? Others can dispute whether one can affirm God's act (of creating) without also affirming something about his essential nature (as Creator). Despite this possible glitch in the theological method on attributes, it is proper to affirm God as Creator.

Suggestions for Contemporary Application

The attributes described above are not intended as a comprehensive list. Other attributes could be mentioned, some of which are subtopics of those listed above and others that might deserve consideration. Other possible attributes that could be discussed include grace, truth, mercy, wisdom, faithfulness, patience, and simplicity.

The events of life affect our view of God. Those with abusive fathers, for example, struggle to envision God as a good and loving Father. Those who have experienced injustice struggle to imagine a just God. These reactions to difficult circumstances are understandable. Nevertheless, they result in inadequate views of God. We must not construct our view of God based on our circumstances and experiences in the present and fallen world. Instead, we must construct our view of God from his revelation in Scripture, which culminated in the person and work of Christ. Only then can we rightly view God in a broken world. Those who experience abandonment by their parents, for example, learn from Scripture that though their father and mother forsake them, God will receive them (Ps 27:10). Those who experience injustice are assured that God is just and will one day make all things right (Rev 21:5). Our view of God's character is distorted when viewed through the lens of our experience. His character can be seen in biblical revelation and most clearly at the incarnation and cross of Christ.

When confronted with God's holiness, the proper response modeled in Scripture is to confess one's unholy condition and ask for God's forgiveness and mercy. Isaiah's response to the vision of God's holiness was to cry out, "Woe is me." He continued, "I am ruined because I am a man of unclean lips and live among a people of unclean lips, and my eyes have seen the King, the LORD of Armies" (Isa 6:5). His lips were touched with a hot coal, and Isaiah was declared free from guilt; his sins were atoned for (Isa 6:6–7). Similar responses of repentance and recognition of one's sinful status before God can be seen among individuals in the New Testament, such as Peter (Luke 5:8) and the tax collector (Luke 18:13). The holy God relates to and invites a response from sinful people.

God's love should prompt in his people a love for him and others. The degree of our love for God might correlate to an awareness of our forgiven sin. As Jesus explained to Simon the Pharisee, the one who has been forgiven much loves much (Luke 7:47). Jesus said his followers would be recognized by their love for others (John 13:35). Love is more than an idea to affirm. Rather, love expresses itself in good works on behalf of others. Pure and undefiled religion, James taught, expresses itself in acts of love, such as caring for widows and orphans (Jas 1:27).

God is just, though people do not fully experience justice on earth. Paul consoles believers that at the future revelation of Jesus, God will repay troublemakers with trouble and provide relief to those who are afflicted (2 Thess 1:6–7). Similarly, James counsels those enduring injustice to entrust themselves to God (Jas 5:1–6). They are to "be patient until the Lord's coming," which is "near" (Jas 5:7, 8). They are told, "The judge stands at the door!" (v. 9). Paul informed the meeting of the Areopagus that God "has set a day when he is going to judge the world in righteousness by the man he has appointed," a reference to Jesus (Acts 17:31). The New Testament implies that although things are not right in the world, God knows and plans to one day set things right. God and his ways are just and right—though we do not see it in our lifetime. True and final justice on earth will come at the future revelation of Jesus.

Only a self-existing God is worthy of worship, and only an unchanging God can be trusted. The God who has always been and always will be created all things, is present, has all power, and sees all things. This God desires a relationship with his creation, including you.

FOR ADDITIONAL STUDY

Anselm. *Monologion* 5–24.

———. *Proslogion* 5–26.

Augustine. *Confessions* 1.1–4; 11.10–28.

Barrett, Matthew. *None Greater: The Undomesticated Attributes of God*. Grand Rapids: Baker, 2019.

Craig, William Lane. *The Only Wise God: The Compatibility of Divine Foreknowledge and Human Freedom*. 1987. Reprint, Eugene, OR: Wipf & Stock, 2000.

Feinberg, John S. *No One Like Him: The Doctrine of God*. Foundations of Evangelical Theology. Wheaton: Crossway, 2006.

Fiddes, Paul S. *The Creative Suffering of God*. Oxford: Clarendon, 1988.

Ganssle, Gregory E., ed. *God & Time: Four Views*. Downers Grove: IVP Academic, 2001.

John of Damascus. *On the Orthodox Faith* 1.4, 14.

Matz, Robert, and A. Chadwick Thornhill, eds. *Divine Impassibility: Four Views*. Downers Grove: IVP Academic, 2019.

Peckham, John C. *The Doctrine of God: Introducing the Big Questions*. London: T&T Clark, 2020.

Tozer, A. W. *The Knowledge of the Holy*. 1961. Reprint, New York: HarperCollins, 1978.

Also see these articles: God's Existence, The Trinity, God's Covenants

20

God's Covenants

OREN R. MARTIN

G od's covenants with humanity occupy an important place throughout Scripture. For this reason, some assign to it theological pride of place. In any case, though most would agree with its importance, the question of the relationship among the covenants has been the subject of much debate throughout the centuries.

This article explores the topic of God's covenants by addressing several related issues. First, it defines the biblical concept of covenant. Second, it discusses the historical development of covenant in the Christian tradition. Third, it surveys covenantal development across Scripture as the biblical covenants progress toward their goal, Jesus Christ, the head of the new covenant. Finally, it offers some concluding thoughts on this key biblical theme.

Covenant Defined

For practical purposes, covenant can be defined as an initiated relationship between (at minimum) two parties that involves mutual obligations. Scripture includes a number of covenants between human beings in Scripture (e.g., Abraham and Abimelech in Gen 21:27, Jacob and Laban in Gen 31:44, David and Jonathan in 1 Sam 18:3). The biblical covenant(s) between God and humanity, however, are more important theologically. Covenant is crucial for describing God's relationship with his people.

Scripture presents numerous covenants at crucial times throughout salvation history that serve to (re)establish God's fellowship with humankind, reverse the curses of Eden, and progressively bring about the establishment and expansion of God's kingdom on earth. Each covenant serves, then, as a divinely orchestrated means by which the ordained end—a consummated kingdom—will come about. God's divinely initiated covenants get to the heart of his gracious plan to constitute a people for himself. This plan begins with Adam and ends with the people of the Last Adam from every tribe and language and people and nation (Rev 5:9).

Covenant in Christian History

While covenant is a biblical theme, there is no clear line of thinking on the subject that covers the entirety of the Christian tradition. There was no comprehensive treatment or systematic use of covenant in the patristic era, though early theologians such as Irenaeus and Augustine frequently used language and identified themes similar to what would be emphasized later by the Reformers. Medieval theologians such as Duns Scotus, William of Ockham, and Gabriel Biel blurred the lines between the law and covenant in various ways. This resulted in the idea that sinners are infused by and cooperate with grace in the process of justification, though they still retained the importance of God's covenants that enabled one to do the law.

It was not until the time of the Reformation, and especially the post-Reformation era, that the idea of covenant came to occupy an overarching place in theological reflection. Though Luther preferred the law/gospel distinction, Huldrych (or Ulrich) Zwingli and Heinrich Bullinger emphasized continuity between the Abrahamic covenant and the new covenant, which was an important Reformed defense for infant baptism. Bullinger wrote an early exposition on the covenant, *A Brief Exposition of the One and Eternal Testament or Covenant of God.* John Calvin employed covenants in his *Institutes of the Christian Religion* to emphasize the unity between the Old and New Testaments, predestination, and salvation. Seventeenth-century Dutch Reformed theologians Johannes Cocceius and Herman Witsius further advanced the covenant concept in federal theology, which distinguished between the idea of covenant, covenant theology (the one covenant of grace with different administrations), and federalism (the distinction between the covenant of redemption, covenant of works, and covenant of grace). Through this lineage, covenant theology was articulated in the Westminster Confession of Faith and related catechisms.

In the sixteenth and seventeenth centuries, Baptist theologians such as John Gill, Andrew Fuller, and Nehemiah Coxe, while agreeing with Anabaptists on believer's baptism, remained tethered to the covenant theology of the Calvinistic tradition. Although they emphasized in various ways the continuity of God's gracious plan across salvation history that reached its fulfillment in the person and work of Christ, they also saw sharper discontinuity between the Abrahamic covenant and the new covenant, from old covenant sign (physical circumcision) to new covenant sign (spiritual circumcision), and the newness of the new covenant in Christ. Thus, they held to a distinctively Baptist form of covenant theology that differed at several points from Reformed pedobaptists.

In the nineteenth century, a new scheme called "dispensationalism" arose among evangelicals in the English-speaking world. Like covenant theology, dispensationalism emphasized the importance of the biblical covenants in the narrative of Scripture. However, dispensationalism rejected the covenant of grace and advocated for significant discontinuity between each biblical covenant. The result was a sharp distinction between Israel and the church, each with its own role to play in salvation history. Many Baptists and other baptistic evangelicals found dispensationalism attractive because of its emphasis on the newness of the new covenant. In the late-twentieth century, progressive dispensationalists advocated for greater continuity among the biblical covenants and emphasized a singular people of God that includes both Israel and the church, though they still rejected several emphases in covenant theology related to the covenant of grace, federalism, and infant baptism.

More recently, a new iteration of baptistic covenantal theology has been advanced under the name progressive covenantalism. Like covenant theology, progressive covenantalism emphasizes continuity, including a single redemptive plan of God and one people of God, in Christ, who share in the same blessings, both now and forever. However, progressive covenantalism also affirms discontinuity, including the newness of the new covenant, the regenerate nature of the church, and the fulfillment of circumcision in regeneration, not baptism. The most significant advocates of progressive covenantalism are the biblical scholar Peter Gentry and the systematic theologian Steven Wellum. Progressive covenantalism is rooted in biblical theology. Its adherents believe it offers a more biblically faithful account of covenant than either covenant theology or dispensationalism do.

Covenant in Scripture

Scripture begins with God, continues through creation, and ends with the description of a more glorious new creation. Between these two creative accounts is the history of redemption. God's plan for his people begins with Adam and Eve (Genesis 1–2). Though some would argue that the term "covenant" should not be employed, it is not improper to see the relationship God initiated in the garden within a covenantal context. When looking at concepts and not strictly words, there is sufficient warrant for calling this relationship a covenant. First, the creation account is framed within a covenantal pattern or framework. That is, there is a title/preamble (Gen 1:1), historical prologue (Gen 1:2–29), stipulations (Gen 1:28; 2:16–17a), witnesses (Gen 1:31; 2:1), and blessings/curses (Gen 1:28; 2:3, 17). Second, although the term for covenant is not present, the essential relational elements of a covenant are there. God is clearly committed to his image-bearers, even after they disobey him. Third, the Noahic covenant in Genesis 6–9 appears not to be initiating something entirely new but rather confirming for Noah and his descendants God's prior commitment to humanity previously at creation (see also Isa 24:4–6; Hos 6:7). For Adam and Eve to enjoy God and his blessings, they must take him at his word (Gen 1:28–30; 2:16–17). However, they despised God's word and instead believed the serpent's lies, which led to their expulsion from God's blessed presence (Genesis 3). As a result, sin and death entered creation and separated man from God. But his plan did not end, for God made a promise that would, in time, undo the effects of sin by the serpent-crushing offspring of the woman (Gen 3:15). The rest of the story, then, focuses on how God will progressively reestablish his kingdom.

A crucial means the Lord uses to accomplish his redemptive ends is through the subsequent biblical covenants. A cursory overview will establish this point. Judgment and death reign after mankind's fall into sin, and the initial sign of Yahweh's reversing the curse is his covenant with Noah (Gen 6:18; 9:9–17), which reaffirms the covenant he initiated with Adam. Noah is

God's representative commissioned to rule the earth, be fruitful and multiply, and bring the Lord's blessing to the world (Gen 9:1–17). In other words, Noah is an Adam-like figure. But just as Adam failed, so also does Noah (Gen 9:18–29). Sin and death continue to reign, and, as a result, Yahweh judges the nations at the Tower of Babel (Gen 11:1–9). Yet God keeps his promise by calling out another—Abram—to fulfill his purposes.

God's covenant with Abraham provides *the way* in which God will fulfill his promises. Through Abraham and his offspring Israel, God will bring about universal and international blessing. But how, ultimately, will this blessing come? The answer is through a promised offspring (Gen 15:4–5; 22:17b–18; Galatians 3). And as Genesis 15 makes clear, God will make good on his promise. By passing between the pieces, Yahweh graciously pledges that he will fulfill his covenant commitment to Abram (Gen 15:17; cf. Jer 34:18). Thus, Abram believed the Lord, and he counted it to him as righteousness (Gen 15:6). And as glorious and gracious as the blessing of justification is (cf. Romans 4; Ps 32:1–2), this blessing was not the end but only the beginning of the story. Through Abraham, then, God sets out in programmatic form his plan to make a people for himself (Gen 17:8; Rev 21:3).

However, one problem remained. As time went on and history repeatedly demonstrated, sin plagued God's people and brought his curses. Though they were physically circumcised as a sign of belonging to God, they needed a deeper circumcision—circumcision of the heart (Deut 30:6). Whether it was Abraham, Isaac, Jacob, Moses, Israel, David, or Solomon, one thing was certain: the blood of bulls and goats could not permanently bring the forgiveness of sin (Heb 10:4). Furthermore, God's commands under the old covenant only exacerbated the problem, for through the law came the knowledge of sin (Rom 3:20). But thanks be to God who used the guardianship of the law until Christ came so that all might be justified by faith—both Jew and Gentile (Gal 3:23–29). It is the *new* covenant (Jer 31:31–34; Isaiah 54; Ezek 36:22–32) in Christ's blood that brings these blessings (Luke 22:20).

In the new covenant there is both continuity and discontinuity with the old covenant that precedes it. We see continuity in that the new covenant involves God's people (Jer 31:31), emphasizes obedience to God's law (Jer 31:33), focuses on offspring (Jer 31:36)—particularly on a royal seed (Isa 55:3; Jer 33:15–26; Ezek 37:24–25)—and, in the end, will fulfill the repeated covenant refrain: "I will be their God, and they will be my people" (Jer 31:33).

Despite its continuity, however, it is not like the previous (old) Mosaic covenant (Jer 31:32). First, the new covenant will not be broken (Jer 31:32). Israel's history was one of repeated covenant breaking, but in the new covenant Yahweh ensures this will not happen. In fact, look at Jeremiah's use of first-person pronouns that emphasizes God's effectual work: "*I* will put *my* law within them, and *I* will write it on their hearts" (Jer 31:33 ESV, emphasis added). "*I* will not turn away from doing good to them. And I will put the fear of me in their hearts, that they may not turn from me" (Jer 32:40 ESV, emphasis added). The new covenant discloses this infrangibility in the way Christ kept the law for those who are united to him by faith, resulting in God's counting Jesus's obedience to us (Rom 5:18–19; 8:4; 2 Cor 5:21). Furthermore, God's power is now guarding members of the new covenant for their future salvation (1 Pet 1:5).

Second, the new covenant transforms the heart and permanently supplies the indwelling of the Spirit so that obedience will flow from the inside out (Jer 31:33; Ezek 36:26–27). Rather than writing the law on stones and scrolls and exhorting the people to internalize it, the Lord now writes his law on his people's hearts.

Third, *every* member of the new covenant is regenerate—for they shall *all* know the Lord (Jer 31:33–34; Isa 54:13). Whereas under the previous covenants God urged the various members to know and follow him, most did not. However, the new covenant includes only those whom God teaches in the heart and who know him (John 6:44–45; 1 Thess 4:9; 1 John 2:20–21, 27). "But this man, after offering one sacrifice for sins forever, sat down at the right hand of God. . . . For by one offering he has perfected forever those who are sanctified" (Heb 10:12, 14).

Finally, all of these new covenant blessings will come because God has provided full and final forgiveness of sin (Jer 31:34; Ezek 36:29, 33). Through the inauguration of the new covenant, then, God fulfills his promises and secures his redemptive purposes for his people.

The new covenant makes clear that God always finishes what he starts. In fact, the ultimate fulfillment of the divine promises comes through a Suffering Servant, an "ideal Israel." Isaiah 42:6–7 says that Yahweh will give his servant as "a covenant for the people and a light to the nations, in order to open blind eyes, to bring out prisoners from the dungeon, and those sitting in darkness from the prison house." By being a covenant (Isa 42:6;

49:8; 55:3; 59:21), the servant will supply the means through which people will come into a covenant relationship with the Lord. The new covenant is grounded on better promises than the old because God's obedient Son would fulfill it (Hebrews 8–10).

Covenant in Life

So what do God's covenants teach us? First, they confront us with the reality of human sin and the necessity of salvation by faith in Christ. If we are to be right with God, we must rely on God's gracious provision in Christ—and Christ alone—for the forgiveness of our sins. Abraham is the father of all who believe—Jew and Gentile. Paul writes, "Now to the one who works, pay is not credited as a gift, but as something owed. But to the one who does not work, but believes on him who justifies the ungodly, his faith is credited for righteousness" (Rom 4:4–5). But how does faith come? Faith comes as a gift of God's grace through the proclamation and reception of the word of Christ (Rom 3:24–25; 10:17). May God strengthen his people to be faithful in proclaiming this gloriously good news to those who need to hear and be set free by it.

Second, circumcision in the old covenant was a shadow of spiritual cir- cumcision in the new (Rom 2:28–29; cf. Deut 10:16; 30:6). In this new covenant, God removes old hearts and gives believers in Christ new hearts wrought by the Spirit, thereby causing them to obey his Word (Ezek 36:26– 27), all of which is rooted in the final forgiveness of sin obtained by the better priest and sacrifice, Jesus Christ (Jer 31:31–34; Hebrews 7–10). As a result, the New Testament commands believers to be baptized in order to testify that one has died to sin and risen to new life in Christ, experienced the new birth and entered into the realities of the new covenant, received the gift and guarantee of the Spirit, joined to the body of Christ, and separated from the world unto God (Acts 2:40–41; Rom 6:1–11; 1 Cor 12:12–13; Gal 2:27–29; Col 1:11–15).

Third, since all new covenant members are regenerate, pastors and churches should diligently (though to be sure, imperfectly) work to ensure their church membership includes only those who give a credible profession of faith. Local churches are assemblies of men and women who give credible evidence of saving faith in Jesus Christ.

Finally, all of God's promises, including what he promised Abraham, find their Yes in Christ (2 Cor 1:20). Christ is the mediator of a new covenant, so that those who are called into fellowship with him may receive the promised eternal inheritance (Heb 9:15). Indeed, all of God's promises reach their goal when Jesus rises from the dead and by this fulfills God's saving plan, which will end in nothing less than a new creation for all of his redeemed people in Christ from every tribe and language and people and nation (Rev 5:9). And "he will live with them. They will be his peoples, and God himself will be with them and will be their God" (Rev 21:3).

Conclusion

The great and awesome triune God always keeps his covenant promises. "When the fullness of time had come, God sent forth his Son, born of woman, born under the law, to redeem those who were under the law, so that we might receive adoption as sons" (Gal 4:4–5). In his ministry, Jesus announced that God was working through him to fulfill his ancient promises and defeat sin, redeem sinners, and reestablish his worldwide kingdom. In this age, between the time when Christ inaugurated and will consummate those promises, we live as sojourners and exiles who seek a city that is to come, whose designer and builder is God (1 Pet 2:11; Heb 11:10, 13–14). We should in faith, therefore, anticipate the ultimate end in our minds, hearts, and words before others until that day "when the dwelling place of God is with man. He will dwell with them, and they will be his people, and God himself will be with them as their God" (Rev 21:3).

For Additional Study

Augustine. *The City of God.* Translated by William Babcock. Hyde Park, NY: New City, 2012.

Blaising, Craig A., and Darrell L. Bock. *Progressive Dispensationalism.* Grand Rapids: Baker, 1993.

Cocceius, Johannes. *The Doctrine of the Covenant and Testament of God.* Grand Rapids: Reformation Heritage, 2016.

Coxe, Nehemiah, and John Owen. *Covenant Theology from Adam to Christ.* Ed. R. D. Miller, J. M. Renihan, and F. Orozco. Palmdale, CA: Reformed Baptist Academic Press, 2005.

Fiddes, Paul, William Brackney, and Malcolm B. Yarnell III. *The Fourth Strand of the Reformation: The Covenant Ecclesiology of Anabaptists, English Spiritualists, and Early General Baptists.* Oxford: Centre for Baptist History and Heritage, 2018.

Gentry, Peter J., and Stephen J. Wellum. *Kingdom through Covenant: A Biblical-Theological Understanding of the Covenants.* 2nd ed. Wheaton: Crossway, 2018.

Golding, Peter. *Covenant Theology: The Key of Theology in Reformed Thought and Tradition.* Ross-Shire, Scotland: Mentor, 2004.

Horton, Michael S. *God of Promise: Introducing Covenant Theology.* Grand Rapids: Baker, 2006.

Irenaeus of Lyons. *On the Apostolic Preaching.* Trans. John Behr. Yonkers, NY: St Vladimir's Seminary Press, 1997.

Robertson, O. Palmer. *The Christ of the Covenants.* Phillipsburg, NJ: P&R, 1980.

Schreiner, Thomas R. *Covenant and God's Purpose for the World.* Wheaton: Crossway, 2017.

Wellum, Stephen J., and Brent E. Parker, eds. *Progressive Covenantalism: Charting a Course Between Dispensational and Covenant Theologies.* Nashville: B&H, 2016.

Williamson, Paul R. *Sealed with an Oath: Covenant in God's Unfolding Purpose.* New Studies in Biblical Theology. Downers Grove: IVP Academic, 2007.

Witsius, Herman. *The Economy of the Covenants between God and Man: Comprehending a Complete Body of Divinity.* 2 vols. Phillipsburg, NJ: P&R, 1990.

Also see these articles: God's Existence, The Trinity, God's Attributes, Last Things

21

Creation

KENNETH D. KEATHLEY

The Bible's opening sentence is brief and sublime: "In the beginning God created the heavens and the earth." With an economy of words, we are introduced to a fundamental truth: God created everything. The Christian doctrine of creation can also be summed up in one sentence: *God, without opposition or equal, called the world into existence out of nothing, for his own good purpose of glorifying his Son.* This definition is theologically dense and expresses at least five essential tenets: 1) creation out of nothing; 2) the freedom of God; 3) the contingency of nature; 4) the goodness of creation; and 5) the Christological purpose of creation.

Creation out of nothing (*creatio ex nihilo*): Modern readers often fail to realize that the original audience would have found the Genesis creation account radical. The ancient Egyptians, Babylonians, and Canaanites had their respective creation myths. Despite significant differences in the accounts, they all agreed about one thing: the ultimate primeval reality was an eternal, watery chaos. The Deep brought forth an initial god (or gods), who in turn fashioned other deities and then, finally, the world we presently see. When these deities made the heavens and the earth, they used whatever pre-existing materials were already at hand. Thus, the various creator deities never had complete control over what they made.

The Genesis account presents a completely different scenario. The eternal God speaks the universe into being out of nothing. He produces the watery deep, not the other way around. There are no competing deities. Everything immediately and completely obeys his spoken commands.

The freedom of God: Because God is sovereign, he is free. He created freely in that he experienced no outward coercion or inward compulsion to do so. He could have refrained from creating, or he could have created a different world from the one he in fact created.

The contingency of nature: God's freedom means that creation is contingent, and it is contingent in two ways. First, it is contingent in that it is completely dependent upon God's will and power. The world did not bring itself into existence, and it continues to exist only by the sustaining providence of God. Second, it is contingent in the sense that it could have been different. God could have created a world in which no genuinely free and thus morally responsible creatures ever existed. God chose to create this world for his own good reasons and for his own good pleasure.

The goodness of creation: Genesis 1–2 presents God as lovingly preparing a place for his image-bearers. The Bible declares that creation manifests God's nature and character (Psalm 19; Romans 1). God is good and glorious, so his creation is also. But these traits do not mean (to paraphrase C. S. Lewis) that either is safe. How evil could arise in a world created by a good God is a question with which the best biblical scholars, theologians, and philosophers have struggled. Even though creation has been tragically marred by the effects of the fall, it is still God's good world.

The Christological purpose of creation: The fact that God created freely does not mean he created arbitrarily. The New Testament makes clear what the Old Testament implies: God created the world for the purpose of glorifying his Son. The doctrines of *creatio ex nihilo* and the incarnation serve as bookends of Christian doctrine. God created the world—out of nothing—as something distinctively different from himself, but then he permanently wedded himself to creation by his Son's virgin conception in Mary's womb. Thus, God's ultimate goal is to unite Creator and creation in Jesus Christ (Eph 1:9–10).

The Biblical Witness

The missional approach of the OT. When Moses gave the Law to Israel, they had spent four hundred years immersed in Egyptian culture. So, in the creation account, Moses met his audience where they were. He spoke to them using their grammar. In other words, he used concepts and terminology with which they were familiar. This approach is why Genesis 1–2 has so many similarities to the other Ancient Near Eastern (ANE) creation accounts. He was not borrowing; he was doing mission work, even evangelism. Today we call this approach "contextualization."

ANE context of the OT. The inhabitants of the Ancient Near East believed the world to be made up of a multitude of deities. They seemed to have had little or no notion of transcendence. In the ANE worldview, almost everything was alive and divine—the air, the water, the sky. Moses subverts this worldview. Using language that they would understand, he leads them to a radically different understanding of God. Moses de-deifies nature by presenting the spaces of nature—water, land, and sky—as nonsentient things created by the sovereign will of God. He then populated those spaces with their respective inhabitants. The God of Israel is not a tribal deity, one parochial god among many. He is the I AM. Besides him there is no other.

Major Old Testament texts. The Old Testament gives a great deal of attention to creation in a number of texts. Often the purpose is to call attention to some aspect of God's nature or character. Some of the most notable are:

Genesis 1:1–2:3. Much debate has centered on the proper interpretation of the seven days of creation. The argument about the length of the days not only misses the point but also detracts from the point being made. Fixating on the meaning of "day" (*yom*) is similar to trying to understand Michelangelo's Sistine Chapel by mainly examining the paint pigments he used.

The seven days of creation serve as a prologue to what happens next in Genesis, the Pentateuch, and ultimately the whole Bible. The seven days function as a theological framework. Initially the world was "unformed and unfilled" (Gen 1:2). The forming and filling are accomplished in two sets of three days. Days 1–3 present God as forming and fashioning the water, sky, and land (1:3–13). Days 4–6 present God as filling that which he had formed (1:14–25). As God culminates his creative activity, he decides to make something very special: beings who bear his image. Thus, he creates man and woman. Moses teaches Israel that God made all spatial structures and everything that inhabits those structures and that humanity has a very special role in God's creation. On the seventh day God rests and, thus, takes his rightful throne over what he had made.

Genesis 2:4–25. Genesis 1 presents God as the transcendent Sovereign and humanity as imprints of the divine. By contrast, Genesis 2 zooms in to give a different down-to-earth picture. God "gets his hands dirty" by planting a garden. Adam ("the groundling") is fashioned from dirt. Eve is subsequently made from a portion of Adam. God blesses them in a priestly fashion. The various geographical references (Gen 2:10–14) are intended to anchor the narrative in history.

Scholars have long debated exactly how the first two chapters of Genesis relate to each other. Some see them as two different creation accounts—borrowed from earlier pagan sources—that have been poorly stitched together and are thus incompatible. Even among those who understand the chapters to be presenting a coherent narrative, the question of relationship remains. Is Genesis 2 a recapitulation of Genesis 1? If so, what's the point? Or are the events in Genesis 2 subsequent to those that take place in Genesis 1? And if so, does that mean that Adam's creation was also subsequent to the general creation of humanity?

When considering these questions, one feature seems especially noteworthy. Throughout Genesis, Moses uses the expression "These are the generations of" (i.e., the *toledot* formula) to signify the beginning of a new section, similar to chapter divisions. Moses uses this formula for the first time in Gen 2:4 ("These are the generations of the heaven and the earth" ESV), thus indicating that a sequential, temporal narrative is beginning in earnest. Thus, perhaps the best way to view the relationship of the two accounts is to understand Gen 1:1–2:3 as an atemporal, overarching prologue or preamble (much in the way John 1:1–18 serves as prologue to the Gospel of John) and Genesis 2 as the beginning of the chronological narrative.

Other significant OT texts. The Prophets regularly appeal to God's rule over creation to assure Israel of his faithfulness to his promises and of his ability to keep them. To assure Israel that God can and will deliver a new covenant with them, Jeremiah points to how God created the sun, the moon, and the stars, and gave them their respective orbits (Jer 31:31–35). Isaiah repeatedly directs Israel's attention to God's creation of the universe and his sovereign rule over it (see chaps. 40, 42, 43, 44, and especially 45).

The One who called the world into existence will call them back from exile, and he will eventually make all things new in a new heaven and a new earth (Isaiah 40–66).

One intriguing OT theme that perhaps does not get the attention it should is how much God delights in his creation. He enjoys what he has made, even (and perhaps especially) that which seems wild, mysterious, and beyond human comprehension—the world's origin, the oceans and the weather, the constellations, the places only he can see, even monsters such as the behemoth and the leviathan (Job 38–41). The world teems with innumerable wonders and myriad forms of life, great and small (Psalm 104). In a remarkable example of personification, the book of Proverbs presents God's wisdom as playfully rejoicing in everything he has made (Prov 8:22–31). God loves his world.

The New Testament witness. The New Testament gives a decidedly Christological focus to creation. God created the world through his Son. John declares, "He was with God in the beginning. All things were created through him, and apart from him not one thing was created that has been created" (John 1:1–3). Paul concurs: "For everything was created by him, in heaven and on earth . . . all things have been created through him and for him" (Col 1:15–17). The author of Hebrews opens by describing the Son as the One "appointed . . . heir of all things and (God) made the universe through him" (Heb 1:1–3).

This purposeful understanding of creation stands in stark contrast to the Greco-Roman thinking of the day. The pagan philosophers, almost without exception, believed that the world was eternal. Thus, they held to a cyclical notion of time. They were often fatalistic with no sense of *telos* or purpose. Since the pagan had no reason to expect improvement, they were typically pessimistic in their attitude toward nature.

The Good News of Jesus Christ presents a different story. The New Testament explicitly affirms creation out of nothing (Rom 4:17; Heb 11:3). The One who created all things took on flesh to redeem that which he had made (John 1:1–18; Col 1:15–23). All creation eagerly groans in anticipation of the Son's glorious return (Rom 8:18–25). God's ultimate plan and purpose is that at "the right time" he will "bring everything together in Christ, both things in heaven and things on earth in him" (Eph 1:7–10).

Historical Development

The early debate about creation from nothing and eternalism: For the most part, the pagan Greco-Roman philosophers believed in eternalism—that the world has eternally existed. Those who did accept some type of temporal creation taught that the present age was created out of some type of pre-existing chaotic substance. The slogan of the pagans was *ex nihilo nihil fit* ("Out of nothing comes nothing"). The result was a dualistic understanding of reality. The material world is an inferior reflection of the greater spiritual realm. This dualism is the way it always was and always shall be.

The patristic fathers uniformly rejected eternalism and instead argued for *creatio ex nihilo* ("creation from nothing"). They realized, as Augustine argued, that the doctrine of creation profoundly affects the doctrine of God. The Bible presents God as transcendent and sovereign. This means that the world is not a part of God, nor was it fashioned out of any type of competing, eternal "stuff." Therefore, God must have called the cosmos into existence from absolutely nothing. The pagans contended that creation out of nothing was impossible. "Impossible to everyone except almighty God," replied the church fathers.

The denigrating, Greco-Roman understanding of the cosmos manifested itself in Gnosticism, one of the first great heresies to confront the early church. The Gnostics viewed the material world as so irredeemably bad that they routinely rejected the physical reality of the incarnation (a heresy known as doceticism).

The medieval union of creation and Neoplatonism. By the beginning of the medieval era, belief in eternalism gave way to *creatio ex nihilo*. Most also accepted the ptolemaic cosmology—the earth is a sphere in the center of the universe, surrounded by concentric spheres containing the Sun, the planets, and the stars. Beyond the stars, God put the cosmos in motion as the unmoved Mover. This fit the Neoplatonic worldview that Spirit was ultimate and that the world below is a dim reflection of an ideal form that existed within the mind of God.

The challenge of Aristotle and nominalism. For whatever reason, during the medieval period, Christian Europe had mostly forgotten Aristotle. Then the Crusades occurred during the high medieval ages (the eleventh–thirteenth centuries). One result was that Christian scholars were brought into contact with Islamic scholars, who still studied Aristotle.

Concerning the ideal forms (or essences) existing within God's mind, Aristotle disagreed with his mentor Plato. Aristotle argued that the form of a thing is located within that thing itself. In other words, if one wants to understand the essential features of, say, a horse, don't try to plumb the mind of God. Instead, study a horse. The reintroduction of Aristotle, as exemplified in the work of Thomas Aquinas, brought about a renewed emphasis in the empirical approach to knowing creation.

Along with Aristotelianism came the rise of nominalism, the notion that God is pure will. Nominalists also argued against the futility of attempting to know God's mind by philosophical or logical means. In order to know God's mind, one must look at what God actually has done. Thus Christian doctrine, viewed through the bifocals of Aristotelianism and nominalism, set the stage for the rise of science.

Creation and the scientific revolution: Historians and philosophers of science generally agree that Christian doctrine played a crucial role in the development of modern science during the seventeenth and eighteenth centuries as a freestanding method for exploring and knowing the world. The doctrine of creation provided the unique and necessary framework that enabled Christian European thinkers to fuse Hellenistic philosophical categories with Islamic advances in mathematics. The Christian worldview gave them the robust conceptual structure and the ethical sanction to do science as we understand it today. Consequently, the scientific revolution occurred in Europe, primarily but not exclusively in northern post-Reformation Protestant Europe.

Though historians of science recognize that the Christian worldview played a pivotal role in modern science's development, they disagree as to how pivotal that role was. Some historians argue that the biblical worldview deserves virtually all the credit, while others are more reserved. But all generally agree that the biblical doctrine of creation provided the intellectual framework, the ethical justification, and the moral motivation needed for science to become a distinct and self-correcting discipline.

Darwinism and the creation/evolution debates. The rise of modern science might have been a triumph of the Christian doctrine of creation, but the same cannot be said about the response to Darwinism in the nineteenth and twentieth centuries. Jonathan Wilson argues that the church held to a shallow and rather naïve understanding of creation and, thus, was not ready to face the challenges posed by Darwin's theory of evolution.[1]

Darwin proposed that new species arise by means of natural selection. Neo-Darwinism added genetics as the engine for providing random variation and as the means for retaining helpful mutations. As a biological theory, Neo-Darwinism seems rather innocuous. But as a philosophical system or ideology, it is pernicious. Certain proponents quickly used the theory to deny divine providence, to deny purpose, and to see suffering, predation, and selfishness as essential features of nature. Social Darwinism was the deliberate attempt to apply the principles of natural selection to society.

The church's various responses to Darwinism can be placed on a spectrum. The more liberal Christians embraced Darwinism to the point of capitulation. The more conservative resisted to the point of rejecting mainstream science across the board, not just biology but also geology and astronomy. Most Christians landed somewhere in between the two extremes, typically accepting the scientific consensus but continuing to hold to humanity as the special creation of God. The dialogue is ongoing.

Systematic Formulation

The fundamental distinction. Scripture presents the Creator/creation distinction as the fundamental truth of reality. God is and he made us. This contrasts with other competing formulations such as the matter/spirit distinction of the Greco-Roman philosophers or the natural/supernatural distinction of the Enlightenment. The Creator/creation distinction is essential for a proper understanding of God and the world. This understanding is why theologians sometimes treat the doctrine of creation as a subsidiary of the doctrine of God. Grasping this distinction leads to the awareness of just how radical the claim of the incarnation really is. Creator and creation are united in the Lord Jesus Christ. It is no wonder why other monotheists (i.e., Jews

---

[1] See Jonathan Wilson, *God's Good World* (Grand Rapids: Baker Academic, 2013).

and Muslims) often accuse Christians of blasphemy. Our only defense is that the incarnation is true.

The grand narrative. Creation is the opening chapter of the grand story of the Bible. There is an arc to the biblical narrative. The storyline begins with the tree of life in the garden (Genesis 1–3) and ends with that same tree in the new Jerusalem (Revelation 22). Scripture presents us with the four-chapter narrative of creation, fall, redemption, and consummation. Each of the chapters is essential for understanding the biblical story. Take one out, and the plot line is lost. This progression to the narrative arc gives Christianity a distinctly linear understanding of time. We are not trapped in an eternal now or in endless cycles, nor is the universe doomed to a slow heat-death. He is "making all things new" (Rev 21:5).

The great themes. Creation serves as the central stage of the grand theo-drama. Four great themes are introduced at the beginning and then developed throughout the story: kingdom, mission, covenant, and temple.

Kingdom. The Bible presents the kingdom of God paradoxically in a "now but not yet" fashion. Genesis 1–2 introduces this tension. God is sovereign, but he also establishes his sovereignty. He rules directly, yet he sets up humanity as his vice-regents.

Mission. The mission of God is the full establishment of his kingdom. From creation to new creation, God moves purposefully to bring about his full beneficent rule over all. Marvelously, God commissions humanity to take part in his mission. As Bartholomew and Goheen point out, this commissioning is akin to Michelangelo offering an apprentice the opportunity to assist with the Sistine Chapel.[2]

Covenant. God is bringing his kingdom into full fruition through a series of covenants, beginning with the covenant he made with Adam. God's initial covenant with humanity was for us to serve as his vice regents ("have dominion," Gen 1:26–28) and his priests ("work it and watch over it," Gen 2:15–17).

Temple. One of the more exciting developments in biblical theology is recognition of the temple motif in Scripture. Genesis 1 presents the universe as a cosmic temple. Genesis 2 presents Adam and Eve as priests serving in the inner sanctuary. This temple imagery, begun in Genesis, is sustained

---

[2] See Craig Bartholomew and Michael Goheen, *The Drama of Scripture* (Grand Rapids: Baker, 2014).

throughout Scripture up through the final scenes in the book of Revelation (Rev 21:1–4). Thus, creation begins the story of redemption and provides the framework for understanding the age to come.

Creation and soteriology. Perhaps unsurprisingly, most Christians focus on the personal aspects of salvation. What comfort is it for a particular person if the whole world is saved but it personally ends badly for him or her? However, this individualistic emphasis tends to obscure the grander biblical account and lends itself to a type of low-grade Gnosticism. Scripture does not present salvation as an escape from the world but rather as the redemption of the world. Evangelicals rightly emphasize the necessity of personal repentance and faith, but by and large they struggle to successfully integrate salvation's individual and cosmic features.

Creation and eschatology. Creation has a goal, a *telos*, a reason for being. One must look at the world from the perspective of its end in order to fully understand its beginning. The Bible connects creation with the new creation (Isa 65:17–18). Many of the themes begun in the creation account of Genesis resurface in Revelation 21–22, especially the tree of life and the unencumbered presence of God. The tree of life disappears after Genesis 3, but it returns by the "river of the water of life," and its leaves will provide "healing for the nations" (Rev 22:1–2). God walked with the original couple "in the cool of the day" (Gen 3:8 ESV); once again God "will dwell with them" (Rev 21:3 ESV). Creation will be transformed into the new creation (Isa 66:22–23).

Certain passages, taken in isolation, can give the impression that the present universe will be obliterated. However, taken in context, the Bible makes clear that the present creation will give way to a new creation (2 Pet 3:12–13; Rev 20:11; 21:1–2). What God did for the Lord Jesus Christ on Easter, he intends to do for the whole cosmos. In this respect, the end of the age could be understood as the final stage of God's work of creation.

Christ as the central focus of creation. Creation was the divine act whereby God brought into being that which was other than him. This radically altered reality because previously the triune Godhead was the total of reality. Reality was expanded by God to include that which is not-God—dependent yet distinct. By the incarnation the Creator and his creation are united, a wedding of the human and the divine. Christ's two natures remain distinct, but he is one person. Thus the hypostatic union ultimately remains a mystery that leads us to gratitude, awe, and worship.

The reign of the incarnate Son of God is the *telos* of creation. Christ's incarnation accomplishes what was begun at creation, and his passion redeems the world he made. Creation was, on the part of God, a gratuitous act of condescension and self-giving grace. God's self-renunciation was completed in the incarnation. The Word became flesh, and in a sense "he can never go back." The incarnation is permanent. In order to redeem that which he made, the Son of God became man, gave his life as a man, and will forever rule as a man. The Second Person of the Trinity from now on will always be the man Jesus Christ.

Conclusion

When God commissioned humanity to be his vice-regents, he gave us a stewardship. We are to care for this world with the same loving care God shows to us. We have been given a royal role to play, and with it comes great responsibility.

History demonstrates that Christianity played a unique and crucial role in bringing about the scientific revolution and the rise of modern science as a stand-alone discipline. This historical fact raises a question: How did the church lose control of the narrative? Just as important, how do we go about the task (to borrow from Vern Poythress) of redeeming science?

Theologians have noted that the church has failed to give proper attention to developing a theology of creation. Compared to the efforts that have been expended on Christology, soteriology, and the doctrine of Scripture, the doctrine of creation has been given the short stick. In the academy, theology was once the queen of the sciences. But when theology failed to provide a vigorous answer to the Enlightenment's challenges concerning the created order, the academy began to raise serious questions about the place of theology. There are encouraging signs that a recovery is underway and that the church is taking steps to give creation its proper foundational role.

For Additional Study

Bartholomew, Craig G., and Michael W. Goheen. *The Drama of Scripture: Finding Our Place in the Biblical Story.* Grand Rapids: Baker, 2004.

Beale, G. K. *The Temple and the Church's Mission: A Biblical Theology of the Dwelling Place of God.* Downers Grove: IVP, 2004.

Collins, C. John. *Reading Genesis Well: Navigating History, Poetry, Science, and Truth in Genesis 1–11.* Grand Rapids: Zondervan, 2018.

Ferngren, Gary B. *Science and Religion: A Historical Introduction.* Baltimore: John Hopkins University Press, 2002.

Gunton, Colin. *The Triune Creator: A Historical and Systematic Study.* Grand Rapids: Eerdmans, 1998.

Keathley, Kenneth D., and Mark F. Rooker. *40 Questions about Creation and Evolution.* Grand Rapids: Kregel, 2014.

Levering, Matthew. *Engaging the Doctrine of Creation: Cosmos, Creatures, and the Wise and Good Creator.* Grand Rapids: Baker, 2017.

Ungureanu, James C. *Science, Religion, and the Protestant Tradition: Retracing the Origins of the Conflict.* Pittsburgh: University of Pittsburgh Press, 2019.

Wilson, Jonathan. *God's Good World: Reclaiming the Doctrine of Creation.* Grand Rapids: Baker, 2013.

Also see these articles: God's Existence, Revelation, The Trinity, Providence

22

Providence

R. Stanton Norman

All Christian doctrine in some way shapes and defines all other Christian beliefs. God's revelation reflects the unity of his being. As such, our beliefs about God and his purposes for his creation must be developed by and relate in a coherent way to all other Christian doctrines.

This unified understanding for Christian belief is especially true for the doctrine of providence. The providential work of God permeates both Old and New Testaments, encompassing all facets of God's purposes for and interactions with his creation. A robust, biblical understanding of this doctrine should shape and inform all Christian belief.

For example, one's understanding of providence will affect one's view of human freedom and responsibility. Also, one's view on this issue will influence one's view of sin, suffering, and evil. The doctrine of providence determines our understanding of the purpose of creation and the direction of history. Providence likewise encompasses the doctrines of salvation and the Christian life. Our beliefs about God's attributes will also determine our view of providence. When viewed this way, the Christian doctrine of providence becomes a fundamental issue of vital theological importance.

The word "providence" does not actually appear in the Bible (Acts 24:2 in the KJV is the exception). There is no Hebrew equivalent for "providence," and the Greek word *pronoia* is used only of human foresight (Acts 24:2; Rom 13:14; *pronoeo* in Rom 12:17; 2 Cor 8:21; 1 Tim 5:8–9). The English term is derived from the Latin *providere*, meaning "to see ahead, to be able to anticipate."

The absence of the actual word in the Bible, however, does not mean the concept is absent in Scripture. God's providential working runs the gamut of the entire biblical story, from creation to consummation. Orthodox Christianity has overwhelmingly defined providence to affirm that God provides, directs, sustains, and governs his creation. Broadly speaking, providence means God's control or direction of the universe toward the end he has chosen. Providence is a biblical doctrine essential to the Christian faith.

Thomas Oden notes that providence "concerns how God thinks ahead to care for all creatures, fitting them for contingencies, for the challenges of history, and for potential self-actualization to the glory of God." Yet providence is more than God's foreknowledge of the future or his foresight in divine planning. The word carries the idea of acting prudently or making preparation for the future. Oden defines God's providence as his governing activity of moving "all creatures, inorganic and organic, animal and rational creation, toward a purposeful end that exceeds the understanding of those being provided for."[1]

Providence and Creation

The doctrine of providence must be distinguished from the doctrine of creation. The upholding and directing of all things in the Bible is subsequent to and distinct from the bringing of all things into existence. Whereas creation is God's originating work with respect to the universe, providence is his continuing relationship to it. Creation is typically considered a finished act, but providence is an ongoing task. In providence, God keeps creation in existence and guides it to his intended purposes.

This distinction is essential for our understanding of evil and suffering. God's original creation was righteous and good. The fall of Adam and Eve into sin introduced a transformed spiritual reality—a reality of depravity, decay, disease, darkness, and death. The providence of God focuses on the history of creation and God's activity to bring redemption to a fallen, sin-sick world.

---

[1] Thomas C. Oden, *Systematic Theology*, vol. 1 (San Francisco: Harper Collins, 1987), 272–73.

Preservation and Guidance

God's provision for his creation can be categorized into two broad, unitary expressions: preservation (or sustenance) and guidance (or governance). God's preservation means that he sustains and cares for what he has created. Having brought the creation into being, God keeps it in being. The created order does not have an inherent power to sustain itself independently from God. God has neither imbued a self-preserving ability into his creation nor delegated this control to any other being. Preservation is the prerogative of God alone.

Creation necessitates God's preserving work. God's preservation of his creation requires both his transcendence over what he has made (the power, ability, and wisdom to effect preservation) and his immanence within his creation (his personal presence and his active, fatherly care to provide for his creation). Both God's transcendence and his immanence are essential for a faithful understanding of the Bible's teaching on providence.

God's guidance means that he has a "purposeful end" for his creation. God's providence is thus directive and purposeful. God's guidance encompasses the entirety of creation—it is his purposeful directing of all of reality and the course of history. God's guidance means he governs his creation toward the purposes he devised in eternity. He is directing his creation in such a way that the created order fulfills his plans for it.

The ultimate end of God's governing activity is the manifestation of his own glory in creation and redemption, fully expressing God's holiness in righteousness and love. God's ultimate purpose encompasses human creation as well as nonhuman creation, both animate and inanimate. Although the unfolding of this purpose incorporates exceedingly complex and mysterious processes that transcend human comprehension, God's governing actions ultimately cohere in the one divine purpose—his glory.

Biblical Teaching on Providence

The Natural Order

God rules all natural forces (Ps 147:8), all wild animals (Job 38–41), and all happenings in the world, great and small, from catastrophic storms (Job

37; Ps 29) to the falling of a sparrow (Matt 10:29). Physical life in humans and animals are his to give and to take away (Gen 2:17; 1 Sam 1:27; 2 Sam 12:19–22; Job 1:21; Pss 102:23; 104:29–30; 127:3; Ezek 24:16–18; Dan 5:23), as well as health and sickness (Deut 7:15; 28:27, 60). Even prosperity and adversity fall under his providential work (Isa 45:7; Amos 3:6). The Bible presents God's preservation and guidance in nature both as matter for praise (Psalms 104; 147) and as a guarantee that he is Lord of creation, fulfilling his gracious promises according to his redemptive purposes (Jer 31:35–37; 33:19–26).

History

Since the fall, God has been executing a plan of redemption. This plan is fulfilled in Christ's coming and culminates in his return. God's plan includes the creation of a worldwide church in which Jew and non-Jew share in God's grace on equal terms (Eph 3:3–11). At the second coming of Christ, he will glorify the cosmos (Rom 8:19–21) and bring all things under the rule of his lordship (1 Cor 15:24–26; Eph 1:9–12; Phil 2:9–11; Col 1:20).

The Old Testament prophecies of God's Messianic kingdom are fulfilled in Christ's present reign and future triumph (Isa 11:1–9; Dan 2:44; 7:12–27). A unifying theme of the Bible is God's exercise of his kingship in establishing the messianic kingdom. No enemy can thwart his plans (Ps 2:2, 4). He even uses the efforts of his foes to achieve his purposes (Acts 4:25–28). The climax of human history will be the overthrow of those who fight against God and oppose his kingdom (Revelation 19).

Theodicy

Reconciling a world where there is an all-good and all-powerful God with the reality of evil is one of the most difficult challenges Christians must address. Human existence often brings serious questions related to the preservation and governance of a good God. How does our understanding of God's providence shape our understanding of the prosperity of the wicked, even when they are oppressing and harming the just? Why do disaster and pain so often come to the righteous?

Regarding the former issue, the wicked may prosper, but only for a season—God will soon come to them and execute his justice (Pss 37; 50:16–21; 73:17–19). Until that time, God may allow them to persist in order to give them time for repentance (Rom 2:4–5; 2 Pet 3:9; Rev 2:21). The New Testament identifies a coming time when God will vindicate himself at the final judgment (Rom 2:3–5; 12:19; Jas 5:1–8).

Regarding the latter issue, the righteous will be vindicated when the day of judgment for the wicked comes (Psalm 37; Mal 3:13–4:3). In the meanwhile, suffering is understood as a means of God's care and discipline of his people (Ps 119:67, 71; Prov 3:11–12). Even when we do not understand our suffering, God can use this for our good and his glory (Job 1–2; 42; Rom 8:28–30). In the New Testament, the suffering of believers is understood as part of our fellowship in Christ's sufferings and, for some, is considered a calling of witness to the gospel (Matt 10:24–25; John 15:18–20; 16:33; Acts 9:16; 14:22; Phil 3:10–12; 1 Pet 4:12–19).

God is keeping and sustaining believers through their sufferings unto his ultimate, glorious hope (2 Pet 3:1–13). Christ's power now strengthens and sustains his followers (2 Cor 1:3–5; 12:9–10), eliciting a confidence to face all situations (Phil 4:11) and to rejoice in all adversities (Rom 8:35–37). Followers of Christ can be confident that suffering is used by God as one means of working sanctification, including his fatherly, loving discipline of his children (Heb 12:5–11), developing their character into the image of his Son (Rom 5:2–4; Jas 1:2–4; 1 Pet 5:10).

In all things, God works for the spiritual welfare of his people (Rom 8:28), supplying them with whatever is needed for their life of service to him in this present age (Matt 6:25–33; Phil 4:19).

Because of God's preservation and governance, Christians should not grow despondent or embrace despair (Psalms 42–43). Instead, God's providential work should instill courage and hope (Psalms 60; 62).

God's Sovereignty and Human Free Will

Providence is the unceasing activity of the Creator whereby his bounty and goodwill overflow to his creation (Ps 145:9; Matt 5:45–48). God upholds his creatures in ordered existence, guiding and governing all events, circumstances, and free acts of angels and men (Gen 45:5–8; Job 1:12; 2:6; Ps 107; Acts 17:28; Col 1:17; Heb 1:3), directing everything toward his glory (Eph 1:9–12). God is King over all, doing what he wills (Pss 103:19; 135:6; Dan 4:35; Eph 1:11).

Numerous verses highlight the relationship between God's guidance of his creation and the presence and power of sin. Although this is undoubtedly a complex matter, Millard Erickson provides four observations gleaned from Scripture that help us understand how God operates in our world regarding human sin:[2]

God can prevent sin. At times he deters or precludes people from performing certain sinful acts (Gen 20:6; Ps 19:13).

God does not always prevent sin. At times he simply wills to permit it (2 Chr 32:31; Ps 81:12–13; Matt 19:8; Acts 14:16). These were concessions by God to let individuals perform sinful acts.

God can direct sin. Although God does permit some sins to occur, God nonetheless directs them in such a way that good comes out of them (Gen 45:7–8; 50:19–21; Acts 2:36; Rom 11:13–15, 25). The all-powerful, all-knowing God is able to allow evil humans to do their worst and still accomplish his purposes.

God can limit sin. There are times when he does not prevent evil deeds, but he nonetheless restrains the extent or effect of what evil humans and the demonic can do (Job 1:12; 2:6; 1 Cor 10:13). Even when God permits sin to occur, he imposes limits beyond which it cannot go.

History of the Doctrine of Providence

Patristic theologians universally affirmed the doctrine of providence. Rejecting both fatalism and indeterminism, they proclaimed God is the Master of the universe who rules over all things. Human beings might not be privy to the inner workings of God's plan, but his providential power can be observed through the "economy" (*oikonomia*) he exercises over his creation. The church fathers also agreed that God may permit evil but never causes it. Evil is never morally chargeable to God. Whereas theologians of the East emphasized human freedom and responsibility, the Western fathers

---

[2] Erickson, *Christian Theology*, 2nd ed. (Grand Rapids: Baker, 2013), 424–26.

highlighted the human propensity toward sin human beings have inherited from Adam.

Augustine (AD 354–430) offered the most fully developed account of the relationship between divine providence, human freedom, and moral evil in the patristic era. The Manicheans claimed goodness and evil were two contrary but equal forces in the universe. In response, Augustine insisted evil is not itself a thing but the absence or rejection of what is good from God. He asserted that human beings were created with the freedom to obey or disobey God but lost that liberty after the fall. Although they retain their free wills, they will always act according to their sinful desires. Consequently, they cannot choose obedience apart from the gracious work of God in their hearts. Augustine also maintained that there is no contradiction between human free will and exhaustive divine foreknowledge. God exercises providential control without causally determining human action. God knows all creatures thoroughly and knows how they will act in their own free wills in response to his sovereign activity.

Thomas Aquinas (AD 1225–1274) underscored two dimensions of divine providence: preservation by which God sustains the existence of all things and governance by which he moves all things to the ends and purposes he has for them. Because God is the first cause of all things, Aquinas reasoned it is impossible for anything to occur outside the order of the divine government. Although he believed that God governs all things, he denied God is the author of evil. He reasoned that evil is the absence of good. God is responsible for creating a world in which it is possible for creatures to rebel, but he is not the direct cause of their evil and fallen actions.

Much of late medieval theology can rightly be described as semipelagian, a view that affirms salvation is initiated by God but dependent upon human cooperation. In response to this, the magisterial Reformers' emphasis on God's meticulous providence was a revival of Augustinian ideas. Luther, Zwingli, and Calvin fully embraced the monergism incipient in Augustine. Luther maintained that God works through human sinfulness to achieve his ends, but he insisted evil is only attributable to secondary agents and causes. Calvin shared this sentiment: "Satan and all the impious are so under God's hand and power that he directs their malice to whatever end seems good to him and uses their wicked deeds to carry out his judgments."[3]

---

[3] John Calvin, *Institutes of the Christian Religion* 1.16.1.

In the post-Reformation era, Jacobus Arminius (1560–1609) sought to maintain the Reformed doctrine of providence while contending for a libertarian understanding of the free will of the individual to choose his own course of action in every situation. Working within the Arminian tradition, John Wesley asserted that God maintains all as omnipresent participator in and omniscient discerner of all that is. For Wesley, providence was God working synergistically amid complex layers of causality. God works within the free dynamics of human self-determinism to elicit free responses to offers of grace.

German Protestant liberals in the nineteenth century tended to reject the classical Creator-creation distinction maintained in orthodox expressions. For Friedrich Schleiermacher, providence only describes the initial purposes God had in creating the world, not his ongoing care and governance of the world. Existentialist and neoliberal theologians in the twentieth century deemed the idea of God's ongoing providential care and direct, miraculous intervention as mythological elements that needed to be excised from Christian belief and practice.

In addition to ongoing reaffirmations of orthodox understandings of providence, the twentieth century saw the rise of process theology. Process theists tended to posit another reality alongside God by which he is necessarily limited, thus denying classical expressions of providence. A softer form of process thinking developed in recent years is open theism. This view denies that God has exhaustive knowledge of the future because, so the theory runs, the future is not really "there" to be known even by God. Although pretending to protect God against a false view of sovereignty that would exclude him from meaningful interaction within the realm of space and time, this so-called "open" view of God actually reduces him to the creaturely level by closing off both the reality of predictive prophecy and the urgency of petitionary prayer. Process theology, in all its forms, remains a dangerous deviation from historic Christian orthodoxy.

Challenges to the Christian Doctrine of Providence

The Christian doctrine of providence provides an apologetic against ideological threats to the belief of God's provision and guidance of his creation. For example, *pantheism* ("all is God") teaches God is an impersonal being to which all things belong. Everything is one and everything is god. This view denies the biblical teaching of the ontological distinction between God and his creation. Another challenge to providence is *deism*. According to this view, God allows the world to operate under its own immanent laws without his ongoing involvement. God is, in a sense, an "absentee landlord." This belief denies God's direct involvement and presence in his creation.

Determinism asserts there are no secondary causes. God is the direct cause of everything that happens in the universe—including the wicked and depraved actions of human beings. This belief denies the biblical witness to human creatures having free will and genuine moral agency. *Chance* denies God's providence by asserting that everything in the world is indeterminate—there is no guiding, intelligent, personal control of creation, thus denying God's personal and all-wise direction of his creation. Whereas the Bible teaches that human actions and decisions are meaningful parts of God's guidance of history, *fatalism* is the belief that in every situation, regardless of what we do, the outcome will be unaffected by our efforts. Fatalists believe in the strong inevitability of certain outcomes. Another rejection of biblical providence is *dualism*. Dualism contends that the universe is controlled by dueling powers of good and evil. Neither is all-powerful or sovereign. In dualism, there is no omniscient, omnipotent, omnibenevolent God preserving and guiding creation with wisdom, love, goodness, and justice.

The Mystery of Providence

God has a certain end or ends in view for creation that will be accomplished. For human creation, God's governance is often extremely difficult to understand. How do the realities of human existence contribute to these ends? As noted previously in our definition, these purposeful ends often exceed our understanding. Numerous passages speak in some way to God's providential work of preservation and guidance.

The biblical witness on this matter is descriptive. We are told what God has done, what God is doing, and what God will do. The intricacies and complexities of how God preserves and governs are not revealed to us. This underscores the great mystery of God's all-encompassing providential work. We see this especially in God's governance and how that relates to human free will and moral responsibility. If God is truly sovereign and governs all creation in accordance with his divine purposes, how can human beings be said to be true moral agents with genuine free will?

Foremost, we must remember that God's providence is the convergence of his omniscience, his omnibenevolence, and his omnipotence. God is omnipotent and omniscient—he is able to do all things in accordance with who he is and what he purposes. He is also omnibenevolent—he is the all-loving, all-wise, all-good God. The God of the Bible is not a God of brute force or arrogant self-will. The God whom Jesus taught us to call Abba is kind and generous. In his utter holiness, he is a God of never-failing mercy and compassion. We are amazed at his forbearance, his extravagant grace, and his inexpressible love.

We must keep this in mind when we acknowledge that God's works of providence are his most holy, wise, and powerful preserving and governing of all his creatures and all their actions. The Bible undoubtedly teaches divine sovereignty, but the Bible also clearly teaches human freedom and moral accountability. Just as many Bible verses teach human responsibility as those that teach divine sovereignty.

Again and again through the prophets, God pleaded for his people to repent, to turn from their wicked ways, and to seek his face. Many times, the children of Israel were confronted to turn from their sin and to follow the Lord (2 Chr 15:2). In the New Testament, Jesus wept over the city of Jerusalem and exclaimed, "How often I have longed to gather your children together, as a hen gathers her chicks under her wings, but you were not willing!" (Luke 13:34). The sin and rejection of Jerusalem's people could not thwart Christ's saving mission, but their free moral agency was not extinguished by Jesus's march to Calvary.

The Bible affirms both God's sovereignty and human free agency in the course of events. Sometimes God fulfills his purposes by intervening directly, immediately, and miraculously. More often, God fulfills his purposes by interweaving his guidance and rule with the intentions and freely chosen acts of human beings.

The Bible contains numerous examples of God's intervention in the lives of his people and in the course of nature. He sent the flood as an expression of his judgment (Gen 6–9). He visited Egypt with plagues and rescued Israel from the clutches of Pharaoh (Deut 7:8). He defeated the army of the Assyrians, leaving thousands dead. He healed the sick and raised the dead.

He engineered Peter's miraculous escape from prison and rescued Jonah from a seafaring death.

The Bible clearly reveals occasions when God miraculously intervened to fulfill his providential purposes, but more frequently, we see the hand of God interweaving divine and human activity.

After years of letting them languish in exile, God allowed the children of Israel to return to their homeland through the intervention of Cyrus, the ruler of Persia. Their release was Cyrus's idea. Under no compulsion or constraint, he freely chose to liberate the Israelites and send them home. Yet when the prophet Isaiah prophesied about this momentous event, he ascribed it to God: "Who has done this and carried it through? . . . I, the LORD . . . I am he" (Isa 41:4 NIV). God used Cyrus, including his freely chosen decisions, to accomplish what God had intended (and promised) to do beforehand.

The death of Christ is another example of how God's providence works in and through freely chosen human acts. Jesus was the Lamb of God who was slain from the foundation of the world. The shadow of the cross fell over every event of his life from Bethlehem to Calvary. For centuries the prophets had predicted the sacrificial atoning death of the Messiah, as Jesus himself acknowledged (Luke 24:26). Clearly, Jesus was put to death at the hands of cruel men who tortured and crucified him outside the gates of Jerusalem. Those who crucified Jesus were free moral agents fully accountable for their heinous deeds (Acts 2:23).

The Bible never explains how the sinful acts of wicked men coalesced with God's sovereign purpose, but somehow, mysteriously, they do work together. Our finite human minds cannot comprehend the mystery of providence. We are tempted to resolve it either by qualifying God's sovereignty or by denying human free agency. Although neater logically, this solution could never be acceptable biblically. To be faithful to what God has revealed about how he works in the affairs of this world, we must say both/and, not either/or.

Summary of Beliefs on Providence

Nothing exists except in some relationship to God. At the heart of biblical faith stands the doctrine of creation "out of nothing" (Genesis 1). God created all things. Belief in God as Creator denies self-existence to things.

Things are dependent upon God not only in their origin but also in their continuation and consummation. The action of God in the preservation of creation is his work.

Nothing happens apart from God's purposeful activity. God decrees or permits all things that come to pass. The Psalms are filled with affirmations of God's comprehensive providence (Pss 103:19; 135:5–7). There are no accidents with God (Eph 1:11).

Nothing can thwart God's gracious design in Christ. We cannot think of providence apart from Jesus Christ. Through him, God made everything in heaven and on earth (John 1:3; Col 1:16). He continually upholds the universe by the power of his word (Heb 1:3). Jesus remains the eternal divine agent in both creation and providence, subjecting all things under his feet (Col 1:17; Heb 2:8). Amidst all the ambiguities of history, he is guiding the world and everything within it toward its divinely appointed end, including and culminating in the confession of every sentient being from heaven down to hell that "Jesus Christ is Lord" (Phil 2:9–10).

Value of the Doctrine of Providence

Confidence for human existence. The biblical doctrine of providence should instill a sense of confidence and trust in Christians that God cares for and sustains his creation in general, and for his people in particular. God will preserve what he has made. God's work of preservation is no justification for foolhardiness or imprudence. It is a guard against terror and anxiety.

Reliability of creation. God's providential work instills confidence in the reliability of the created order. Because God perseveres and governs his creation in accordance with his purposes, human beings can exist and function with meaningful, purposeful lives. Human existence would be impossible without God's preserving and guiding activity.

History has purpose. The doctrine of providence reminds us that God is the sovereign lord of history. The God of the Bible is a "hands-on" God, intimately concerned with the smallest details of our lives. He is also the Creator and Judge of the world, which he is infallibly guiding toward the goal of the glorification of the final state, the complete vanquishing of Satan and sin, and the exaltation of Jesus Christ as Lord.

Providence in retrospect. When we are overcome by grief or confronted with a tragic event, either in our own lives or that of a loved one, we seldom see how these experiences fit into God's plan for us. But when we look back over our lives from the perspective of five, ten, or twenty or more years, we understand more clearly how some of those things that brought only tears and questions at the time God used for our good.

Christian living. Providence is central to the conduct of the Christian life, assuring us that God is present and active in our lives. We are in his care and can therefore face the future confidently, knowing that things are not happening merely by chance. We can pray, knowing that God hears our prayers, cares about our lives, and acts upon our petitions. We can face danger, knowing that God is aware and involved.

Throughout history, Christians who have embraced traditional conceptions of God's preserving and governing activity have found great comfort in it. A biblically faithful understanding of providence should fill Christian hearts with assurance and joy. The Belgic Confession (1561) asserts that Christians can find encouragement and assurance in God's providence, for this doctrine

> affords us unspeakable consolation, since we are taught thereby that nothing can befall us by chance, but by the direction of our most gracious and heavenly Father, who watches over us with paternal care, keeping all creatures so under his power that not a hair of our head (for they are all numbered), nor a sparrow, can fall to the ground, without the will of our Father, in whom we do entirely trust (Article 13).

For Additional Study

Berkouwer, G. C. *The Providence of God.* Grand Rapids: Eerdmans, 1952.

Calvin, John. *Institutes of the Christian Religion.* 2 Vols. Edited John T. McNeill. Philadelphia: Westminster, 1960.

Carson, D. A. *How Long, O Lord? Reflections on Suffering and Evil.* Grand Rapids: Baker, 1990.

Erickson, Millard J. *Christian Theology.* 2nd ed. Grand Rapids: Baker, 2013.

Keathley, Kenneth. *Salvation and the Sovereignty of God: A Molinist Approach.* Nashville: B & H Academic, 2010.

Luther, Martin. *The Bondage of the Will.* Translated J. I. Packer. Grand Rapids: Baker Academic, 2012.

Oden, Thomas C. *Systematic Theology.* Vol. 1. San Francisco: Harper Collins, 1987.

Piper, John. *Providence.* Wheaton: Crossway, 2021.

Spiegel, James S. *The Benefits of Providence: A New Look at Divine Sovereignty.* Wheaton: Crossway Book, 2005.

Tiessen, Terrance. *Providence and Prayer: How Does God Work in the World?* Downers Grove: IVP, 2000.

Wesley, John. *John Wesley's Teachings: God and Providence.* Vol. 1. Edited by Thomas Oden. Grand Rapids: Zondervan, 2012.

Also see these articles: God's Existence, The Trinity, Creation, Last Things

23

Humanity

Jacob Shatzer

Introduction

Who are we? Or, perhaps nearer to our experience, Who am I? Identity issues remain central in American society and culture, with various descriptors vying for relevance and dominance. We define ourselves by race, ethnicity, sex, gender, region, and favorite sports teams. While each of these aspects may have a place in describing a person, the Christian doctrine of humanity, or theological anthropology, pushes into the depths of what it means to be human. We can see these different aspects by seeing how humans relate to God, to ourselves (or to "the self"), to one another, and to the rest of creation.

The first step in understanding the Christian doctrine of humanity is to understand what it means to believe that humans are created "*imago Dei*," or in the image of God.

Relating to God—*Imago Dei*

The idea of the "image of God" comes from three Old Testament passages, all in the beginning of the book of Genesis. The first one is the fullest, and it sets the foundation for the others. It reads, "Then God said, 'Let us make man in our image, according to our likeness. They will rule the fish of the sea, the birds of the sky, the livestock, the whole earth, and the creatures that crawl on the earth.' So God created man in his own image, he created him in the image of God; he created them male and female" (Gen 1:26–27). Thus, the creation of humans is rooted in this decision to make humans in God's image.

Next, Genesis refers back to this creation of man "in the likeness of God" (Gen 5:1) before listing a genealogy from Adam to Noah. The statement serves as a preface to the genealogy to remind the reader that this line shares the "image of God" in which God created Adam and Eve. Finally, in Gen 9:6, the fact that humans are made in the image of God serves as the justification for prohibiting murder. It is wrong to kill humans because to do so is an assault on the divine image and, thus, an assault upon God. Significantly, since these last two references occur after the fall, they demonstrate that this "image of God" in humans was not entirely lost when humans sinned.

These three passages make the significance of the "image of God" clear in our understanding of what it means to be human. But they do not make immediately clear what it exactly *means* for humans to be created in God's image, or what "part" of humans is the image. Christians have wrestled with how to answer this question. "What is it about being human that reflects God's own identity?"

Typically, there are three answers: the image as a substantial likeness to God, the image as a function in relation to creation, and the image as relational to other human beings. We will look at each of these briefly. In the first option, human likeness to God means a connection to something substantive about God's nature. This image resides in some feature or capacity of human existence and enables us to relate to God in ways that animals cannot. Candidates for this feature include the soul, rationality, the ability to pursue "the good," the ability to love, or some innate sense of God. The second option turns the focus to the unique function that humans have in relation to creation. God gave Adam and Eve dominion (Gen 1:26), and the divine image is reflected when humans exercise their God-given authority and responsibility. Third, many contemporary theologians advocate a relational approach to the image of God. This view starts with God's triune nature, his perfect life as Father, Son, and Holy Spirit. We are relational beings and cannot be truly alone.

Along with these three approaches to the image of God, Christian theologians have also regularly pointed to Jesus Christ as the perfect image of God and the repairer of our broken image, damaged in the fall. Theologian

Richard Lints explains that Paul's Adam-Christ typology from Romans 5 lays the foundation for his arguments in Romans 6 and 8. In those chapters, Paul explains that Christians must be identified with Christ in his death to share his resurrection. In fact,

> The gospel finds itself in seed form, then, all the way back in Genesis 1 when God created humankind in the divine image. As the perfect image, Christ completes the original vocation of humankind and thereby shows humankind who they were originally intended to be. This does not happen, however, without experiencing the cross wherein the power of the idols was broken, and death lost its sting. The perfect image not only reveals what redeemed humans will eschatologically be but also loosens the bonds of their present enslavement to the idols they have created.[1]

We see clearly here in the work of Lints both Christ as example and Christ as "repairer." Jesus Christ—as the perfect, sinless One—gives us a picture of the image unbroken. He also, by his death on the cross, makes repair possible. In other words, Jesus gives us a picture of what the image of God should be, and he also offers to fix it in us. Our broken images can be mended because of his example and work.

Our understanding of what it means for humans to be made in the image of God, then, must begin with the Old Testament references but also take into account the way Christ displays this image and remakes fallen humans into it. These different ways of exploring the image of God must be brought together with the other element that God reveals early in Genesis: humans are created for the purpose of serving God as co-rulers. God makes humans in his image and gives them a task to do (the dominion mandate). The image is not the task, but it is not unrelated. The image, then, makes the task necessary and possible. And it is a task not just for Adam alone, but for Adam, Eve, and their descendants. Here we see the various angles for considering the image come together: something substantial aimed at a particular function to be carried out in relationship, all perfected in Christ.

---

[1] Richard Lints, *Identity and Idolatry: The Image of God and Its Inversion* (Downers Grove: IVP, 2015), 126.

Relating to the Self—The Human Constitution and Free Will

Next, we turn to how the human relates to the self. Or, put another way, what constitutes or makes up the human self, and how does that impact what humans can do? In classical terminology, we are dealing with the heady ideas of human composition (soul, spirit, mind, body, etc.) and free will.

At the simplest level, there have been three options for the human composition, depending on how many "things" or "parts" are involved. Monism argues that humans are one thing, typically defined as physical beings. This view is also called "physicalism." Dualism views humans as two things, a soul and a body, that are related in different ways depending on the type of dualism. Trichotomy, finally, inserts a third "part," leading to body, soul/spirit, and mind. In other words, dualism speaks of material and immaterial aspects, while trichotomists argue for body, soul, and spirit (1 Thess 5:23).

Trichotomy might initially seem to be a biblical view because the Bible refers to (at least) three. Even Jesus affirmed the idea that loving God with all the heart, soul, strength, and mind is the greatest commandment (Luke 10:27), so he must have believed in trichotomy. Yet, it is not that simple, because upon more careful examination the Bible refers to the whole human being from various angles. Take the word "flesh," for example. At first glance this might just be a "body" word, but that quickly creates problems. If the problem is the flesh and the body is the flesh, then what humans need is for the soul to escape the body. This is not the picture the New Testament provides. Instead, "flesh" is better understood as referring to the human as creature and other times the human as a corrupted being.

Where does this leave us then? Christians have used a few different options for emphasizing the unity of the human person while acknowledging the reality of both the spiritual and the physical. Some do this via a dualism that emphasizes the necessary unity between the two "parts" such that neither the human body nor the human soul is properly "at home" without the other. Others pursue this unity via monism, or a weak physicalism that identifies higher-order spirituality emerging out of physical elements and processes but not merely reducible to them. Millard Erickson calls his position "modified monism," emphasizing that we are not bodies *plus* something, but we are also not *merely bodies*. Others use the terminology of "compound unity" to highlight that the "soul" and the "body" are united in an irreducible way, and their separation at death is a tragic break, a break that God will heal.

But why does this even matter? First, if to be human means to be a compound unity, then we should expect salvation to heal the whole human. Thus, Christians care about the body and we expect an embodied eternity. Second, the promise of eternity with God is revealed to us in terms of resurrection and the continuity of personal identity. Any explanation of the relationship of the soul and the body that claims to be Christian must take account of this resurrection hope, embodied eternity, and continuity of identity.

The next major aspect of the human's relationship to the "self" is the notion of free will. In his recent work on theological anthropology, Marc Cortez helpfully highlights five areas where Christians generally agree.[2] First, humans have free will. Second, humans exercise their free will in ways that make them morally responsible. Third, not all human actions and decisions are meaningfully free. Fourth, free will and divine sovereignty are compatible. And fifth, free will is related in key ways to preceding factors. Of course, different people nuance and explain these elements in diverse ways.

To determine the perfect explanation of the workings of free will is beyond the scope of this chapter, but we can come to grips with two major ways of approaching the problem. (Few Christians truly believe in a complete hard determinism, which would reject free will entirely, so we will not concern ourselves with that here.)

Compatibilists believe that all human actions are completely determined by antecedent causes *and* humans are free and thus morally responsible for those actions. Some believe this perspective because contemporary science has continued to show that creatures are governed by causal laws, so there must be causes that explain the operation of the will. Others appeal to specific biblical and theological arguments supporting this position, such as nothing happening outside the power of God (Ps 103:19). Still others have philosophical reasons for rejecting other options. For example, those who believe in libertarian free will can find difficulty in relating any causation to the act of the free will, thus making it seem random.

---

[2] Marc Cortez and Michael P. Jensen, eds., *T&T Clark Reader in Theological Anthropology* (New York: T&T Clark, 2018), 99–100.

In order to explain how causation and freedom can go together, compatibilists of different stripes take different tracks. The classic position is that a human person is free insofar as they can choose to do what they want. Our desires, however, are caused. In this rendering, God can still control the desires of the heart, we can operate according to our deepest desires, and thus we are morally responsible. Hierarchical compatibilism, on the other hand, argues free actions come from our deepest, truest desires. Hierarchical interpretations want to leave room for humans not being morally responsible for actions based on compulsive desires or psychological disorders, and a hierarchy helps make those distinctions. Others say that actions that respond properly to rational considerations are truly free. Thus, free actions have rational reasoning behind them.

Libertarians, on the other hand, believe that determinism is incompatible with free will, and because everyone knows free will exists, determinism must be false. To some degree, libertarians begin with a notion of free will that is both argued for and assumed by many people, and they use that definition to reject determinism. Along with hard determinists, they see no reconciliation of determination and freedom. While hard determinists reject freedom, libertarians reject determinism. The thinking behind Christian versions of libertarianism relies not only on philosophical reasoning about the definition of freedom but also on biblical texts. For example, some make statements about people needing to choose to follow God (e.g., Josh 24:15). Others show God commanding people to make choices and expecting them to respond (Matt 3:2).

Just as there are varieties within compatibilism, different libertarians explain how a libertarian free will actually works in various ways. Some argue that a free will cannot have any cause at all other than itself. Most libertarians, however, acknowledge that choices are caused in some way but are not determined. In other words, there are past elements (events, character traits, etc.) that can impact a freely operating will. Those past events or traits of the person, however, do not render the choice certain or determined.

This debate is not one that will likely be resolved soon. And it is one that touches on other important doctrines: the doctrine of God (especially his providence) and the doctrine of salvation (how do people choose God?), to name two. Understanding the human constitution and how a human actually operates freely raise confusing questions, but we must not let those questions distract from the basic theological concepts. Humans are not basically souls stuck in physical bodies, but a compound unity of body and soul. We live in a world created by God and under his care and providence, and we make meaningful choices for which we are responsible.

Relating to the Other—Sexuality

Perhaps one of the most controversial elements of the Christian doctrine of humanity today is traditional teaching on Christian sexuality. While on the surface this seems to relate most clearly to legislation on gay marriage and various antidiscrimination laws related to that narrow topic, the controversy is actually deeper than that. In fact, in some ways, a traditional Christian understanding of sexuality is rooted in more fundamental beliefs about what it means to be human, beliefs that also contradict those in the prevailing Western culture.

Sexuality is present from the very beginning of the biblical account of humanity. Genesis 1:27 tells us that God creates humans "male and female," even before Genesis 2 explains in more detail. There we learn that God created Adam first. It was quickly obvious that it was not good for the man to be alone, and neither God nor the animals could solve that issue. Therefore, God created the woman to be the man's helper (a word sometimes used of God, so certainly not implying inferiority by necessity). While sexual complementarity is in view, the story is about more than Adam needing a counterpart to reproduce. Creating humans as "male and female" would not be remarkable or noted if it only meant "male and female for reproductive purposes, just like the rest of the animals." Creating humans as male and female receives special attention as something that defines humanity. So, while we find maleness and femaleness in the rest of creation, humans "as male and female" seems to be about more than just reproduction. Adam needs help in more than just that department.

To begin to understand the role of sexuality in the doctrine of humanity, we first must define some terms. By "sex," scholars typically refer to biological features associated with the designation "male" or "female." While many are used to thinking primarily about external features, more than that is in view here. These features include a person's chromosomes, the hormones that were dominant while they were *in utero*, the kinds of internal and external organs that are developed, and the relative amounts of hormones produced during puberty.[3] "Gender," on the other hand, typically refers to cultural expectations associated with each sex. These performances vary from culture to culture, and are often related to biological differences between the sexes.

At this point it might seem that we've drawn up a simple distinction: biologically determined "sex" is socially shaped into "gender," which is the socially acceptable way for members of a given sex to live and act. For some, this is as far as we need to go. But various problems creep up and make this basic understanding less than satisfactory. First, there are a miniscule number of biologically ambiguous cases in which one or more of the biological determiners of sex does not line up with the others. For example, Cortez gives the example of Maria Patiño, who had female genitalia and sought to compete in the Olympics as a female. She underwent testing in 1985, which determined that she had XY chromosomes instead of the female-typical XX chromosomes, and thus was unable to compete as a female.

Next, we must resist that biological sex creates gender differences, full stop. Social and environmental influences impact cultural expectations associated with each sex, and they impact how particular individuals do or do not line up with those expectations. Some aspects of gender are driven by biological considerations, but even those aspects are also socially and environmentally influenced. What I am arguing for here is often called "weak constructivism," in that I want to leave space for social and environmental factors impacting not only our conceptions of proper gender roles but also the ease with which particular individuals fit those roles. However, the Christian doctrine of sexuality seems to stop short of "strong constructivism," which contends that there is no biological foundation for sexuality beyond language and culture. Instead, I think it is important to recognize that biology does influence gender, but the ways in which it does are always impacted by culture. In other words, there is a biological givenness to sex, but our reception and interpretation of that givenness always happens within particular cultures.

But what does sexuality mean from a theological perspective? Cortez helpfully provides a few options. First, some see sexuality as primarily aimed toward procreation. The purpose of sex is reproduction. However, this view

---

[3] Cortez and Jensen, *T&T Clark Reader in Theological Anthropology*, 47.

fails to see human sexuality as any different from the rest of creation and fails to account for the value of nonprocreative sex and the full humanity of human persons who are unable to reproduce. Second, others see sexuality as pointing to the "fecund nature of God." In other words, God is creative, and sexuality is one way that humans "create" by producing offspring. This position makes human reproduction different from the rest of creation but still fails to see the fundamental importance of sexuality. It also runs into issues with possibly making God's creation necessary to his being. Third, some view sexuality as expressing something about humans as relational beings. These views see sexuality expressing something about humans as relational beings. However, these types of views tend to make sexuality a secondary element of what it means to be human, which does not fit well with the importance it is given in the Bible.

Cortez prefers to see sexuality as "bonding," by which he intends to include the strengths of a relationality/marriage view while emphasizing the significance of humans as sexual beings. He explains, "The sexual human being finds within itself a desire for another in whom there is both difference and identity." He continues, "This drive toward bonding, then, forms the basis of the connection between human sexuality and the broader importance of relationality and community for humanity in general."[4] This approach emphasizes the centrality of sexuality to what it means to be human while also including space for insights from the previous views as expressions of human sexuality (though not necessarily the basic essence of it).

Relating to Others—Friendship

The openness to and need for the other does not mean that human sexuality is the only needed expression of it. The human need for relationship finds expression in sexuality but must also find expression beyond it. In short, we all need friends.

David and Jonathan's friendship in 1 Samuel is an excellent illustration of this need. Jonathan's soul was "knit" to David's, and Jonathan loved David as himself (1 Sam 18:1 ESV). When David laments Jonathan's death, he says that Jonathan's love surpassed the love of women (2 Sam 1:26). While some

---

[4] Cortez and Jensen, *T&T Clark Reader in Theological Anthropology*, 59, 65.

homosexual advocates argue that these verses point to a homosexual rela-tionship between David and Jonathan, it is much more faithful to the per-spective of the original text—never mind the entire biblical canon—to see it instead as emphasizing the significance of friendship and the heights to which friendships can attain. David and Jonathan sacrificed for one another, gave gifts, and remained loyal. They liked each other and enjoyed being together. This is but one famous biblical example of what friendship can be.

Friendship provides a category for human relationality that does not include sexual expression but is not deficient because of that fact. While a proper understanding of sexuality sees its unique role in human bond-ing and openness to the other (as argued above), humans can still relate to one another in other significant ways. Friendship is often taken for granted or ignored, but the need for nonsexual relationships remains an important expression of human relationality and need for community.

Relating to the Rest of Creation— Humans as the "Crown of Creation"

Last, we turn to the relationship between humans and the rest of creation in order to better understand the Christian doctrine of humanity. Scripture gives us clear statements on the place of humans in creation. God has made humans a little lower than the angels, as Ps 8:5 puts it. Paul reminds us in Eph 2:10 that humans are God's masterpiece. And as we have already seen in Genesis 1, God created humans in his image and placed them over all of the creation.

Yet, as humans have become more and more aware of the value of the rest of creation and humanity's ability to cause harm to it, some secular scholars have hesitated to define humans so highly. Concern for the environment has led in some cases to elevating the rest of the created order to the same level as humanity.

The key with this element of the doctrine is to accept the elevated description of humanity's place in creation, which Scripture gives, but to like-wise accept the elevated role and responsibility given as well. Christians must grapple with what faithful stewardship of a beautiful creation looks like, not because it is of equal status as humans but because God has entrusted us with that task. The same goes for animal rights: the answer is not in lowering humanity or elevating the animal kingdom to the same status as those created in God's image. But the treatment of these fellow creatures does matter. Both environmentalism and the animal rights movement can help Christians see past abuses and potential temptations, but the best answers for a way forward do not lie in rejecting the plain sense of the verses we looked at above.

Summary of the Doctrine of Humanity

Now that we have seen the major issues in the doctrine of humanity, we will conclude by summarizing the main points.

1. Humans are the only part of the creation that is made in the image of God. While theologians have struggled to understand exactly what this image is, it is at the root of what it means to be human.
2. Humans are not composed of two separable parts, the body and the soul. Scripture speaks of humans holistically. There are different ways of proposing the way this unity is achieved, but the root issue is the significance of embodied spirituality for what it means to be human.
3. Humans make free choices, but God is sovereign. Christians have struggled to make sense of how these two elements can be true and held in tension. Some do so by emphasizing the way choices can be free but influenced, and others do so by defining true freedom as outside of such influences.
4. Human sexuality is not an add-on element or primarily an aspect of self-definition. Instead, it demonstrates the need for human bonding, the need for the other that is like but different. This does not mean that all human relationships require sexual expression.
5. Friendship is an important expression of this human need for bonding as well.
6. Christians should not abandon the idea of humanity as the pinnacle of God's creation, but we must not abandon the responsibility that comes with such a role, either.*

* Portions of this article were previously published as "A Limited Image? Practitioners, Patients, and Playing God" in *Ethics & Medicine* 34:1 (2018) 21–29.

For Additional Study

Burns, J. Patout. *Theological Anthropology*. Philadelphia: Fortress, 1981.

Cortez, Marc, and Michael P. Jensen, eds. *T&T Clark Reader in Theological Anthropology*. New York: T&T Clark, 2018.

————. *Resourcing Theological Anthropology*. Grand Rapids: Zondervan, 2017.

————. *Theological Anthropology*. New York: T&T Clark, 2010.

Farris, Joshua R. *An Introduction to Theological Anthropology*. Grand Rapids: Baker, 2020.

Hoekema, Anthony A. *Created in God's Image*. Grand Rapids: Eerdmans, 1986.

Jones, Beth Felker, and Jeffrey W. Barbeau. *The Image of God in an Image Driven Age*. Downers Grove: IVP, 2016.

Lints, Richard. *Identity and Idolatry*. Downers Grove: IVP, 2015.

Sherlock, Charles. *The Doctrine of Humanity*. Downers Grove: IVP, 1996.

Strachan, Owen. *Reenchanting Humanity*. Fearn, UK: Mentor, 2019.

Also see these articles: Creation, Sin, Gospel, The Sanctity of Life

24

Sin

MATTHEW J. HALL

> *Of man's first disobedience, and the fruit*
> *Of that forbidden tree, whose mortal taste*
> *Brought death into the world, and all our woe,*
> *With loss of Eden, till one greater man*
> *Restore us, and regain the blissful seat*
>
> JOHN MILTON, *PARADISE LOST*

There is something deeply broken in the world and in each one of us. Every human being seems to possess some innate awareness of this reality, and yet humanity has always been afflicted with a seeming inability to rightly diagnose the problem. The wrong diagnosis can be deadly. Not only does one risk missing out on an available cure through a correct prescription, but a failure to accurately diagnose a threat to our health can be devastating, even lethal.

The same holds true of even greater eternal realities. Getting our understanding of sin right, according to biblical truth, is absolutely essential. In large measure, it will overlap with how we come to understand the gospel itself. If we are confused about the nature of sin, we will inevitably be confused about the nature of salvation. Truly, the stakes could not be higher.

Defining Sin

As with all theological topics, Christians are required to operate according to certain "first principles" in any attempt to define sin. The grave peril to us is that we would construct a definition of sin that is not only lacking or deficient, but one that is unmoored from the right and true standard. Inevitably, those kinds of definitions seem to be exercises in self-indication and self-righteousness, allowing us to think better of ourselves than we ought.

The reality is that our doctrine of sin is grounded in our doctrine of God. God himself is the standard by which all are measured. His absolute holiness, his sovereign authority over his creation, and the reality of his self-revelation frame what we mean by sin and why it is that human beings are indeed liable for their sin. To put it another way, who God is and what he requires are essential in making clear to us what sin is.

At the risk of being too simplistic, we might think of sin as that which is contrary to God's will. Of course, we will need a more robust definition than that to begin to capture the totality of biblical revelation on the subject. But it seems to be a good starting point. Baptist theologian Millard Erickson has defined it this way: "Sin is any lack of conformity, active or passive, to the moral law of God. This may be a matter of act, of thought, or of inner disposition or state."[1]

Let us first consider how a number of theological traditions have defined sin in recent centuries. A naturalist explanation would propose that what we call sin is the evolutionary byproduct of our evolution as a species. In this telling, the program of Christianity is to aid modern people in bringing these ancient human impulses under control through the moral consciousness now available to us. Liberation theologies locate sin within the framework of social oppression and exploitation, claiming that whether due to class or race, sin is most evident in the attempt of individuals and social structures to promote and preserve inequalities of power. And yet each has hollowed out the central dynamics of a biblical understanding of sin and thus undermined the essence of the gospel itself.

---

[1] Millard Erickson, *Christian Theology*, 3rd ed. (Grand Rapids: Baker Academic, 2013), 596.

Sin in Scripture

There are several terms used in the Old Testament to refer to sin. The most common of these is *hattat*, simply translated in our English Bibles as "sin." In general, it means to "miss the mark" or fall short of a target. In fact, the word is often used in the Old Testament in a very literal sense when describing nontheological actions including the expert marksmanship of soldiers. But when referring to sin, it becomes clear that the Old Testament conceives of sin fundamentally as falling short of a standard, of failing to hit a mark. Of course, this presumes that there is an objective standard of holiness that is universal for all human beings. And while we might think that such language sounds almost as though sin is accidental, or something we fall into not by decision, the Old Testament's usage makes very clear that it is indeed a willful and culpable act.

Along these lines, the Old Testament also uses the term *awon*, often translated as "iniquity" or "guilt." This word speaks of the perversion of sin—a twisting of things so that they are distorted or misshapen. Another common term is *awel*, translated most commonly as "wickedness," "injustice," or "unrighteousness." Similarly, the term *pesa*, along with a number of Hebrew synonyms, speaks of sin as "rebellion." This makes clear in vivid language that sin is fundamentally a treasonous rebellion against the one true and living God.

The Old Testament also uses words such as *resa* to speak of the wickedness of sin, thus bringing about guilt among sinners. Similarly, it uses *ra* to speak of evil in general. For example, this term becomes something of a constant in describing the sinful kings of Israel, who did evil in the sight of the Lord. Thus, the Old Testament gives us a multidimensional understanding of sin in all of its horror. But most fundamentally, it frames our understanding of sin as willful rebellion against the sovereign Lord who made us.

The New Testament is entirely consistent with this picture of sin. Using terms such as *hamartia, anomia, parabasis, paraptoma, adikia,* or *asebeia,* we are confronted with sin as "transgression," "rebellion," "lawlessness," "unrighteousness," and "godlessness." In all of these, they are framed against the backdrop of the entire biblical account of a holy God who has created all things for his glory, who has given his law, and against whom all human beings have rebelled by violating his commands.

However, the Bible does not merely shape our understanding of sin by the specific words it uses but also by the broader story it tells. For example, the account in Genesis 3 makes clear to us that sin is not some external force, nor an impersonal act. Rather, sin is committed against God himself. The consequences of our first parents' sin make clear that it brought with it alienation from our Creator, as well as from one another. And one has only to read a few chapters further to see how sin afflicts the entire human race. In increasingly horrific ways, it brings about such a level of wickedness that God determines to bring about a righteous judgment on the planet that will obliterate all humanity, save one family who will be delivered by his saving grace.

Sin's Origin

For centuries, Christians have spoken of "original sin" in trying to put together a coherent and biblical explanation for our human nature. This understanding is deeply rooted in the events described in Genesis 3 and the reality of the fall. The rest of the Pentateuch and the entire Bible tells of the unfolding horrific consequences of this event, describing constant themes of violence, idolatry, immorality, and injustice. Jesus spent much of his ministry teaching about the nature and dynamics of sin, making clear that sin is not only a matter of behavior but of the heart. And the apostle Paul's writings continually paint a picture of the world that sees human depravity and corruption as comprehensive.

Writing in the sixteenth century, John Calvin's proposed definition of original sin is still remarkably helpful, identifying it as that "hereditary depravity and corruption of our nature, diffused into all parts of the soul, which first makes us liable to God's wrath, then also brings forth in us those works which Scripture calls 'works of the flesh.'"[2]

The early church wrestled deeply with these questions, trying to articulate where sin came from and how it first infected not only the creation but human beings in particular. Since the early years of Christianity, theologians have understood the connection of our current experience of sin with the fall of Adam and Eve. But precisely how one defines that connection has been a subject of significant disagreement.

---

[2] John Calvin, *Institutes of the Christian Religion* 2.1.8.

The Baptist Faith and Message (2000) is somewhat imprecise in its definition of sin. It clearly affirms man's innocence before the fall and the realities of original sin, even defining that first sin as transgression "of the command of God." Furthermore, it affirms that all humanity inherits from Adam both "a nature and an environment inclined toward sin." At the same time, the Baptist Faith and Message (2000) suggests that humans become guilty before God as transgressors as soon as they are capable of moral action. While this definition does not reject the historic idea of the imputation of Adam's guilt to all humanity, neither does it affirm it. It seems the formulation allows for Baptists to arrive at a variety of convictions on the matter. An earlier Southern Baptist confession, the Abstract of Principles (1858), provides a slightly more focused formulation, explaining all Adam's offspring inherit not only a corrupted nature, but are also "under condemnation" even prior to their capacity for moral action. The difference between the two confessions is slight, but not insignificant.

Nonetheless, historic Christianity has rightly understood the biblical emphasis on the fall of all humanity in Adam. As an old children's primer put it, "In Adam's fall we sinned all." All humanity is indeed counted guilty in him as our federal or representative head. Paul speaks of this dynamic by claiming that "sin entered the world through one man, and death through sin, in this way death spread to all people, because all sinned" (Rom 5:12).

The Effects of the Fall upon Humanity

First, all of creation was cursed. When our first parents fell, the implications were far graver than we might naturally assume. Their sin brought immediate consequences, as made clear in the pronouncements of the curse in Genesis 3. But the implications of their sin reverberated long after their own death. For one, the entire creation would be afflicted. There is not a molecule in the universe that operates untouched by the corruption of the fall and sin. We might speak of this as the ecological or cosmic consequence of the fall, whereby all of the created order now functions in ways that are disordered, deficient of their original perfection captured so well in God's assessment of their goodness in Genesis 1–2. In fact, the apostle Paul contended that even now the entire creation "was subjected to futility" and has been "groaning together with labor pains until now" (Rom 8:18–22).

Second, death is a consequence of the fall. Human beings were made for eternity. God's good design in the garden was for our first parents to know, glorify, and enjoy him forever. But their sin brought about the judgment God had promised (Gen 2:17). Disobeying his word and eating of the tree of the knowledge of good and evil brought with it death. In fact, when God pronounced his righteous judgment on Adam, he made clear that death—a returning to dust—would be a consequence of sin, one that would be passed to all of his descendants (Gen 3:19). The apostle Paul directly tied Adam's disobedience to the entrance of sin into the world, bringing with it death for all (Rom 5:12; 1 Cor 15:21–22).

Third, all human beings inherit a corrupted nature from Adam and Eve. While Christians have often debated the extent of this corruption, virtually all have affirmed that humans are born with something less than the nature of our first parents before the fall. In Protestant theology this is often articulated as "human depravity." This proposition does not contend that all human beings are as evil as they could be—thankfully, God's common restraining grace is evident all around us. Rather, it concludes from Scripture that there is no part of ourselves that is untouched by sin—that apart from divine grace humans are always bent toward sin.

Fourth, all human beings are guilty in Adam. Theologians refer to this as the imputation or crediting of Adam's sin to all of his offspring. Here we see again the connection to the specific doctrine of original sin. In particular, theologians have debated whether original sin necessarily denotes original guilt. In other words, is it right to conclude that while Adam's first sin might indeed have brought about a fallen nature for all of humanity, it also brought universal guilt? This question has taken on particular weight when raised about the state of children, particularly those that die in infancy. Are they counted guilty in Adam and therefore liable to God's eternal wrath and judgment?

We dare not rush past this casually. In most of Christian history, it has been an urgent question for families and churches, particularly when we consider the child mortality rates that were common before the advent of modern medicine. One particularly helpful and biblically responsible argument is made by Albert Mohler and Daniel Akin. They contend that there are good biblical grounds to conclude that infants who die are indeed among the elect. By framing it this way, they avoid any claim that infants are somehow exempted from the guilt of original sin. At the same time, they conclude that they are indeed the beneficiaries of God's saving grace in Christ.[3]

Another helpful way to summarize the nature of sin may be to speak of its penalty, its power, and its presence. Sin renders us guilty before a holy God, thus incurring his righteous judgment and the penalty of death. Sin exerts a corrupting power over every dimension of our humanity as well as the entire cosmos. And sin is always near to us, crouching at our door (Gen 4:7).

How Sin Works

Augustine's formulation of sin as *privatio boni*, a "privation of good," has had a shaping influence on centuries of Christian theology, and for good reason. If God is the Creator of all things as Scripture plainly teaches and he is absolutely holy, then sin and evil cannot be in themselves created substances. All that God made was truly good in the beginning. Thus, sin is the absence or the corruption of the good.

This merits further reflection on the part of Christians since it seems to have profound devotional implications. Practically, it might remind us that sin often presents itself to us in immediately attractive ways. Of course, there are times when sin is overtly ugly and heinous, and in our fallen nature, human beings are still drawn to it for that very reason. But the nature of temptation throughout Scripture seems to suggest a far more insidious reality—that sin often masquerades before our fallen eyes and consciences, deceiving and seducing us by its own false beauty. Consider for a moment the warnings of Proverbs 5, as Solomon warns his son of the allure of sexual sin in particular: "Though the lips of the forbidden woman drip honey and her words are smoother than oil, in the end she's as bitter as wormwood and as sharp as a double-edged sword" (Prov 5:3–4).

We can think of sin in terms of commission, omission, or imperfection. Sins of commission are those acts we commit, doing what God has

---

[3] Albert R. Mohler and Daniel L. Akin, "The Salvation of the 'Little Ones': Do Infants Who Die Go to Heaven?" *Fidelitas*, July 16, 2009, https://albert mohler.com/2009/07/16/the-salvation-of-the-little-ones-do-infants-who-die-go-to-heaven.

prohibited. Think for a moment of the various negative commands in Scripture. Perhaps none are more familiar to us than the "thou shalt nots" of the Decalogue. In these Ten Commandments, God expressly forbids certain things. For example, we are forbidden from committing adultery.

Sins of omission are failing to do what God has commanded. Indeed, when Jesus was asked to identify the greatest commandments, he cited two positive commands: first, to love the Lord our God with our whole heart, soul, and mind, and second, to love our neighbor as ourselves (Matt 22:37–39). Even as Christians, our consciences are perhaps especially pricked by our sins of commission when we transgress God's commands and willfully do that which he has forbidden. But are we so tenderhearted toward our failure to live up to his positive commands? Of course, our attempts at self-righteousness crumble entirely when we consider this dimension of sin. None of us has lived up to these commands. We have all fallen short of the glory of God (Rom 3:23). Sin dulls our love of God and neighbor so that we fail to render praise and thanks to the One who has made us, redeemed us, and sustained us. We fail to love one another as we ought. We are not generous toward one another, we resist forgiving others, we do not treat one another in consistently just and righteous ways, and we shrink back from compassion and mercy.

Sins of imperfection are doing what God has commanded but doing it for the wrong reasons. This category is absolutely critical in a fully orbed theology of sin. We might be tempted to assess ourselves and think we have evaded the clutches of sin. But the heart is exceptionally wicked and deceptive. This is yet another reminder from the biblical witness that behavior alone is not what matters to God. Instead, he looks to the heart and sees our very motives.

It is worth noting at this point that the Bible makes interesting connections between knowledge, sin, and guilt. On the one hand, the Bible does seem to make clear that with greater knowledge comes greater accountability. For example, Israel was given God's law and thus subjected to an even more severe standard of judgment. However, the Bible presses against our modern assumption that ignorance is universally exculpatory. In fact, Paul assures us that humanity is left without excuse because of the reality of general revelation (Romans 1). Furthermore, he speaks of a darkened understanding and an exclusion from the life of God that is due to ignorance of the heart (Eph 4:18).

Of course, one might be tempted to despair in navel-gazing introspection when it comes to this dynamic of sin. Left to interrogation, there is thus virtually no act we undertake that is completely righteous or immune from the corruption of sin. Indeed, our righteousness is like filthy rags before a holy God. The point of this truth is not to lead the Christian to despair. Rather, it points us outside of ourselves, constantly reminding us of our inability to justify ourselves according to our own righteousness and forcing us to cling to Jesus Christ afresh in faith and repentance. That is why in the hymn "The Solid Rock," we sing, "I dare not trust the sweetest frame, but wholly lean on Jesus's name."

Sin's Effects

By now, the multifaceted evil of sin becomes all too apparent to us. We might be prone to try to minimize its ugliness, but the Scriptures simply will not permit that. As we have seen, sin is objectively defined by God's revealed standards and is deeply personal, committed against him. Ever since the fall, sin has disrupted *shalom*, the wholeness of God's good creation and his fellowship with his image-bearers. But the effects of sin are diverse and broad.

Theologians speak of the *noetic* effects of sin. That is to say, our thinking is distorted by the fall. And we should not assume that this is confined merely to the exercise of our reason, although it certainly does include that. Rather, sin has compromised our affections and our loves. Before the fall, human beings had the innate and uncompromised ability to know God directly, to accurately interpret his general revelation in the world he had made, and to render back to him the praise and thanks he deserved, all in the context of a relationship of immediate fellowship. But sin has warped our minds. We enter into this world spring-loaded to sin and hardwired to misinterpret what God's world is telling us. Our hearts are corrupt, and we love evil and hate righteousness. Human beings cannot reason their way out of this problem, nor can we recalibrate our loves in our own power (Romans 1).

The experience of temptation is one that merits consideration here. It is one that is universal to all human beings, even if many merely give themselves over to every whim of temptation. The New Testament commonly uses language that can mean temptation, test, or trial. We understand that Satan is active in temptation but also recognize that even our temptations are within the permissive will of God. And while God tempts no one, he does indeed send trials to test his people, propelling us to trust him more and to grow in faith. While Satan seeks to drive us from God through temptation, trials are instruments in the hands of a gracious God to draw us closer to himself.

So what is the connection between a temptation or trial and sin? There are abundant stories of temptation throughout the Old Testament, including the account of that very first sin in Genesis 3. But few have captured more attention than that of King David in 2 Samuel 11:1–27. David's sexual sin against Bathsheba; his conspiracy to arrange the murder of her husband, Uriah; and his attempted coverup serve as a remarkable example of the ways in which subtle temptation can bloom into the most insidious and evil expressions of sin.

Christians have often spoken of three forces that account for temptation: the world, the flesh, and the devil. Our environment, our own sinful nature, and the spiritual powers of Satan and his fallen demons are all conspiring against our obedience to God. But when does temptation actually become sin? This question has profound implications for each one of us, particularly for those called to serve in pastoral care or counseling ministries. As David Calhoun has pointed out, "The church fathers attempted to distinguish the presence of corrupting thoughts from the harboring of them."[4]

The biblical narrative presents a multifaceted portrayal of the horror of sin. Sin is fundamentally an act of individual rebellion against the one true and living God. The Bible thus portrays sin as a reality for which we will each give an account as individuals before the righteous judge. And yet, the Scripture is also clear that sin has corporate dynamics, implicating whole communities and shaping societies. Whenever sinful individuals gather together, sin takes on an even more powerful and hideous strength. Some have referred to this as systemic sin or structural evil, referring to the aggregating power of sin within social groups and the ways in which "principalities and powers" (Eph 6:12) distort the world.

---

[4] David B. Calhoun, "Sin and Temptation," in *Fallen*, ed. Christopher W. Morgan and Robert A. Peterson (Wheaton: Crossway, 2013), 256–57.

The Remedy for Sin

This volume will explore in greater and more glorious detail the infinite wonders of our redemption in Jesus Christ. But the diagnosis of our condition helps us better appreciate the wonder of our prescribed remedy. Sin brings death, alienation, enmity, shame, and judgment. It shatters the good wholeness or *shalom* of God's world so that we are now alienated from our Creator and from one another.

Indeed, we are assured that Jesus Christ was offered up as an atoning sacrifice for our sins (Rom 4:25; 1 Cor 15:3; 1 John 2:2). We are also assured that the reigning Christ is even now "making everything new" (Rev 21:5) so that there is no part of the cosmos that will not be renewed by Jesus's saving work. We often sing it at Christmas, but there are few better lyrical phrasings of our hope than those penned by Isaac Watts in "Joy to the World": "No more let sins and sorrows grow, nor thorns infest the ground; He comes to make his blessings flow far as the curse is found."

Far as the curse is found. The good news for Christ's people in all ages is that, as horrific and far-reaching as the power of sin is in this world, the risen Christ has already conquered sin and death. His coming kingdom will bring the full consummation of that victory. No part of the creation is beyond the reach of his redemptive power.

For Additional Study

Calvin, John. *Institutes of the Christian Religion.* Edited by John T. McNeil. Philadelphia: Westminster, 1960. Book II, chapters I–VI.

Erickson, Millard. *Christian Theology.* 3rd ed. Grand Rapids: Baker Academic, 2013.

McCall, Thomas H. *Against God and Nature: The Doctrine of Sin.* Foundations of Evangelical Theology. Wheaton: Crossway, 2019.

Mohler, Albert R. Jr., and Daniel L. Akin. "The Salvation of the 'Little Ones': Do Infants Who Die Go to Heaven?" *Fidelitas.* July 16, 2009. https://albertmohler.com/2009/07/16/the-salvation-of-the-little-ones -do-infants-who-die-go-to-heaven.

Morgan, Christopher W., and Robert A. Peterson. *Fallen: A Theology of Sin.* Wheaton: Crossway, 2013.

Plantinga, Cornelius. *Not the Way It's Supposed to Be: A Breviary of Sin.* Grand Rapids: Eerdmans, 1995.

Also see these articles: Creation, Humanity, Gospel, Justification, Evangelism and Missions

25

The Person of Christ

Daniel L. Akin

The Biblical Witness

Christology is the study of the person and work of Jesus Christ. It examines who he is (his person) and what he does (his work). When doing Christology, theologians talk about where to begin. Some follow what is called a "Christology from above" and begin with Jesus's divinity and preexistence, as taught in texts such as John 1:1–18; Phil 2:6–11; and Col 1:15–20. Others follow a "Christology from below" and begin with the earthly life of Jesus. This is basically the approach of the Synoptic Gospels. There is also a third approach that should be considered: "Christology from behind." Here, one starts with the Old Testament and what it has to say about the coming of a Jewish Messiah, a Savior. There were hopes and expectations on the part of Israel that God's kingdom would come through a deliverer. Numerous texts reveal the developing portrait of this Savior who would fulfill the offices of prophet, priest, and king. Such passages include Gen 3:15; 12:1–3; 49:9–10; Deut 18:15–20; 2 Sam 7:12–16; Psalms 2; 16; 22–24; 45; 110; Isa 7:14; 9:6–7; 42:1–9; 49:1–12; 50:4–9; 52:13–53:12; Dan 7:13–14; 9:24–27; Mic 5:2. Step by step God reveals who the deliverer will be. He will be a special-born son in the line of Abraham, Judah, and David, who will fulfill the hopes, promises, shadows, and types of the Old Testament.

The New Testament's Witness to Christology

The New Testament affirms that God became one of us in the person of Jesus Christ. The Old Testament promised he would come, and the New Testament testifies he has come. The New Testament records a varied and complementary witness to the God, the Word, who became flesh (John 1:14). Four texts, in particular, stand out: John 1:1–18; Phil 2:5–11; Col 1:15–23 (2:9–10); and Heb 1:1–4.

John 1:1–18 emphasizes the deity of the Word (Gk. *Logos*) and the incarnation (John 1:14). He is God's agent in creation. Though there is significant philosophical and theological weight in the term *Logos*, John effectively uses it for the purpose of evangelism as a bridge word to the Hellenistic world. It served well in evangelizing both Jews and Gentiles. The *Logos* is affirmed as being 1) *coequal*, 2) *coeternal*, 3) *coexistent*, and 4) *consubstantial* with the Father.

Philippians 2:5–11 is a hymn that gives attention to the cross and the humiliation/exaltation of Christ. "Christ hymns" of the New Testament provide insight into the theology and worship of the early church. (See also Col 1:15–20; Eph 2:14–16; 1 Tim 3:16; 1 Pet 3:18–22; Heb 1:1–3.)

Philippians 2 is noted for two important aspects of Christology: (1) the *kenosis* doctrine or "emptying of Christ" as God the Son became a man, and (2) the "hypostatic union" (the uniting of two natures in one person).

Jesus did not surrender his deity when he became man, but he did surrender his glory (see John 17:5). He voluntarily forfeited, for a time, the free use of his divine attributes in taking to himself a human nature and dying on the cross.

Colossians 1:15–20 gives special attention to the issue of creation (see also John 1:3; Heb 1:1–3). Here we also find one of the strongest statements of the deity of Jesus Christ in all of Scripture. Christ is the perfect representation of the invisible God. He is the source-agent and preserver of creation. Verse 19 explains that in Christ we see the very essence of God (cf. Col 2:9–10). Christ lacks nothing of what it means to be God.

Hebrews 1:1–4 draws attention to Jesus as the climax of revelation. Jesus is the best that God could send and the best that God could give. In the coming of Christ, (1) God speaks, (2) he speaks clearly, and (3) he speaks with finality. Hebrews 1:1–4 affirms in a single and superlative sentence these essential truths.

The Witness of the Gospels to Christology

A number of crucial moments in Jesus's brief life of approximately thirty-three years are important for Christological reflection. They are historically important and theologically significant.

The Virgin Birth

Several key texts address the issue of the virgin birth:

1. Isa 7:14 (see also 9:6–7; 11:1–16)
2. Matt 1:18–25
3. Luke 1:26–38
4. Gen 3:15 (a veiled reference, to be sure)

The birth of Jesus is the fulfillment of the prophecy of the virgin birth in Isa 7:14. The biblical record reveals that Jesus Christ was born without the aid of a human father, conceived by the Holy Spirit, and born of the virgin Mary. The virgin birth impacts our understanding of the incarnation. The incarnation teaches that God became man in the person of Jesus of Nazareth. The virgin birth emphasizes both the reality of Jesus's humanity and his divinity as God's Son. Jesus Christ did not enter the world like any other human. His birth was utterly unique.

The Early Years of Jesus

The time from Jesus's early childhood to the beginning of his public ministry has rightly been referred to as "the silent years." The only record we have of any specific event is a trip to Jerusalem when Jesus was about twelve (Luke 2:41–50). Even at a young age the things of God were of supreme importance to him. Already he is aware of his unique relationship to the heavenly Father.

The Baptism of Jesus

This event is recorded in all three of the Synoptic Gospels, and it is also alluded to in John (Matt 3:13–17; Mark 1:9–11; Luke 3:21–22; John 1:31–34). Jesus said his baptism would "fulfill all righteousness" (Matt 3:15). During Christ's baptism the heavens open and the Spirit of God descends upon Jesus like a dove. A voice from heaven says, "This is my beloved Son, with whom I am well-pleased" (Matt 3:17)—a revelation of the Trinity. Jesus's baptism is the inauguration of his public ministry, and it is a public declaration of his submission to the will of the Father. Jesus is the anointed Son (Psalm 2) and Suffering Servant of the Lord (Isaiah 42; 49; 50; 53). Jesus's baptism defined and set the course for the type of Messiah he would be. Jesus is the Messiah, but his messiahship would be realized by suffering service.

The Temptation of Jesus

This event is recorded in each of the Synoptic Gospels, with Matthew and Luke providing the most extensive accounts (Matt 4:1–11; Mark 1:12–13; Luke 4:1–13). This testing of Jesus (the Greek verb "tempted" can also be rendered "tested") was divinely intended. The Spirit led him into the wilderness. There is also a clear comparison to Adam and Eve in the garden. Adam and Eve failed their test in a perfect environment and plunged the whole world into sin (Genesis 3). By contrast, Jesus was faithful in the barren wilderness and proved his qualifications to become the Savior of the world. Jesus was declared by God the Father at the baptism to be his Son and to be the Messiah. However, it is a servant-Messiah role that he would fulfill, a role that would involve suffering and death.

The Miracles of Jesus

One of the pieces of evidence put forward by Scripture for the messiahship and deity of Jesus is his miracles. The Gospels record 35 separate miracles performed by Christ. Matthew mentions 20 of them; Mark, 18; Luke, 20; and John builds his Gospel around 7 signs/miracles. These, however, are not all the miracles performed by Jesus (see John 21:25).

John focuses on seven particular miracles performed by Jesus that witness to his deity and that should cause us to put our faith in him in order that we "may have life in his name" (John 20:31). John's seven signs/miracles include the following:

1. Jesus turns water into wine (2:1–11).
2. Jesus heals a nobleman's son (4:46–54).
3. Jesus cures a paralytic (5:1–16).
4. Jesus feeds 5,000 men (6:1–15; the only miracle recorded in all four Gospels besides the resurrection).
5. Jesus walks on water (6:16–21).
6. Jesus heals a blind man (9:1–42).
7. Jesus raises Lazarus from the dead (11:1–57).

All of these are "signs" or witnesses to his deity and a confirmation of John 1:1, 14, 18.

The Transfiguration of Jesus

The theological significance of the transfiguration is often neglected. The event is recorded in each of the Synoptics (Matt 17:1–8; Mark 9:2–13; Luke 9:28–36). Peter also alludes to the event in his second letter (2 Pet 1:16–18). This outward manifestation of the inward reality of Christ allowed the disciples to catch a glimpse of his preincarnate glory (John 1:14; 17:5; Phil 2:6–7) and to anticipate his coming exaltation (2 Pet 1:16–18; Rev 1:16). The heavenly declaration of Matt 17:5 is crucial to the whole dramatic scene. The language is reminiscent of Jesus's baptism (Matt 3:13–17). God the Father again speaks and says, "This is my beloved Son, with whom I am well-pleased. Listen to him! (Matt 17:5).

The Ascension of Jesus

The ascension of our Lord is only recorded in the two-volume work of Luke (Luke 24:50–53; Acts 1:9–11). It is a particular aspect of Christ's ministry that is seldom mentioned in theologies. It is alluded to in Eph 4:8–10 and 1 Pet 3:22.

The ascension of Jesus Christ is inseparably linked to his incarnation and exaltation. The Son came down in incarnation that he might in ascension return to heaven in exaltation. In heaven there is now glorified humanity, the God-man Jesus Christ.

As *king*, Jesus sits enthroned at God's right hand. As *priest*, he has atoned for sin and now prays for us. As *prophet*, he is the final spokesman for God. This is the clear and consistent witness of Scripture to the person of Christ.

The Church's Confession

The church has consistently affirmed certain basic tenets concerning the person and work of Jesus Christ. Two issues greatly influenced the church's understanding: the monotheism that Christianity inherited from Judaism and the New Testament's clear affirmation of Jesus as God. How these competing truths could be reconciled was a significant challenge the church had to face, especially during the patristic period.

The Road to the Four Great Christological Councils

Several heretical doctrines challenged proper biblical teaching about Christ and needed to be confronted.

1. Docetism

First John was written, in part, to confront a heresy known as *docetism*. This teaching did not confess Jesus of Nazareth as the Christ (1 John 2:22) and denied the Son had come in the flesh (1 John 4:2–3; 2 John 7). It is likely these false teachers were influenced by incipient Gnosticism. Though Gnosticism developed into many forms, two teachings were basic: 1) salvation is by mystical knowledge and 2) matter is inferior or evil. Docetists denied the reality of Jesus's body as well as his sufferings and death. They argued Christ cannot be incarnate because this would involve his taking on sinful and evil flesh (matter). Christ only appeared to have a body (docetism), something John refutes in John 1:1, 14, 18 and 1 John 1:1–4.

2. Ebionism

Ebionism, an offshoot of the Judaizers, denied the essential deity of Jesus. Ebionites argued Jesus was the prophet predicted by Moses in Deuteronomy 18:15, but he was not the preexistent Son of God. Jesus was made the anointed one at his baptism, a form of adoptianism. He was chosen because of his perfect obedience to the law, something highly esteemed by the Ebionites. Similar to Ebionism, another movement and form of adoptianism argued that Christ temporarily adopted the man Jesus (Cerinthianism). In this view "the Christ" came upon the man Jesus at his baptism (Matt 3:13–17) but left him prior to his death on the cross (Matt 27:46). John refutes this heresy in 1 John 5:6–8.

3. Sabellianism

Debate concerning the person of Christ, his nature, and his relationship to the Father would continue in the second–fourth centuries, eventually leading to the four Great Christological Councils:

325 Nicaea

381 Constantinople

431 Ephesus

451 Chalcedon

Origen (c. 185–c. 254) argued for the eternal generation of the Son but held to his essential subordination. The dynamic monarchianists or adoptionists (such as Theodotus of Byzantium and Paul of Samosata [c. 260]) continued to argue that God adopted Jesus as a unique and special man on whom his power would rest.

There were also those who wanted to maintain radical monotheism and yet affirm the deity of Jesus Christ. This movement is known as modalistic monarchianism, patripassionism, or sabellianism (each of which are variations of the same view). This false teaching affirms that the three persons of the deity are simply three ways (or "modes") in which the one God has revealed or manifested himself.

The Council of Nicaea (AD 325)

The Roman emperor Constantine convened the Council of Nicaea. Arius (c. 250–336) had adopted the theology of Paul of Samosata (adoptianism or dynamic monarchianism). Arius argued that Jesus, having the Holy Spirit poured out on him at his baptism, became God-like. He was not the eternal Son equal in essence to the Father. God created Christ, a creature that had a beginning. The Arian party had two main points of contention going into the council of Nicaea: Jesus is not coeternal with God the Father, and he is created from nothing.

Arius was opposed by Alexander (c. 326) and also by Alexander's young protégé Athanasius (c. 296–373). Approximately 318 bishops gathered in Nicaea in AD 325. Arianism was rejected. The result of the first Church Council is the Nicene Creed. It reads,

The Nicene Creed

We believe in one God, the Father All Governing, Creator of all things visible and invisible;

And in one Lord Jesus Christ, the Son of God, begotten of the Father as only begotten, that is, from the essence of the Father, God from God, Light from Light, true God from true God, begotten not created, **of the same essence [*homoousion*]** as the Father, through whom all things came into being, both in heaven and earth; Who for us men and for our salvation came down and was incarnate, becoming human. He suffered and the third day he rose, and ascended into the heavens. And he will come to judge both the living and the dead. . . .

But, **those who say,** once he was not, or he was not before his generation, or he came to be out of nothing, or who assert **that he, the Son of God, is of a different hypostasis or ousia**, or that he is a creature, or changeable, or mutable, **the Catholic and Apostolic Church anathematizes them.**[1] [emphasis added]

The Council of Constantinople (AD 381)

This council was called by Emperor Theodosius. It put Arianism to an end. It reaffirmed the decision of the Council of Nicaea and completed the

---

[1] John H. Leith, ed., *Creeds of the Churches: A Reader in Christian Doctrine from the Bible to the Present*, 3rd ed. (Louisville: Westminster John Knox Press, 1982), 30–31.

final version of the Nicene Creed by adding words on the Holy Spirit and the church. It also condemned the teachings of a man named Apollinaris (c. 310–390). While Arius erred by denying the eternal deity of the Son, Apollinaris erred by deemphasizing his full humanity. He argued Jesus had a human body but a divine mind or soul.

The Council of Ephesus (AD 431)

This council condemned a man named Nestorious (451). There is debate as to whether Nestorious was truly a Nestorian. He was accused of saying that there are *two separate persons* in Christ, a human person and a divine person. Within a single body resides two persons. The council insisted that Jesus was one person, possessing both a human nature and a divine nature.

The Council of Chalcedon (AD 451)

This is the last of the four great Christological Councils. In many ways it solidified and established what the church believed the Bible teaches concerning the person of Christ. It incorporated the major components of the three previous councils. Its affirmations would not be attacked until the time of the Enlightenment, when the rejection of supernaturalism would call for a redefining of the person of Christ.

A man named Eutyches (c. 378–454) was condemned, excommunicated, and deposed. He held a view called monophysitism, meaning "one nature." Eutyches taught that the human nature of Christ was taken up and absorbed into the divine nature so that both natures were changed. A new third kind of nature resulted. The problem here is that Christ is neither truly God nor truly man. In response the following statement was adopted:

> Following, then, the holy fathers, we unite in teaching all men to confess the one and only Son, our Lord Jesus Christ. This selfsame one is perfect both in deity and also in humanness; this selfsame one is also actually God and actually man, with a rational soul and a body. He is of the same reality [*homoousion*] as we are ourselves as far as his humanness is concerned; thus, like us in all respects, sin only excepted. Before time began, he was begotten of the Father, in

respect of his deity, and now in these "last days," for us and on behalf
of our salvation, this selfsame one was born of Mary the virgin, who
is God-bearer [*theotokos*] in respect of his humanness.

[We also teach] that we apprehend this one and only Christ—
Son, Lord, only-begotten—in two natures: without confusing the
two natures, without transmuting one nature into the other, without dividing them into two separate categories, without contrasting them according to area or function. The distinctiveness of each
nature is not nullified by the union. Instead, the "properties" of
each nature are conserved and both natures concur in one "person"
[*prosopon*] and in one hypostasis. They are not divided or cut into
two "persons" [*prosopa*], but are together the one and only and only
begotten *Logos* of God, the Lord Jesus Christ. Thus have the prophets of old testified; thus the Lord Jesus Christ himself taught us;
thus the symbol of the Fathers has handed down to us.[2]

The creed of Chalcedon sought to summarize and address every problem that had plagued the church with regard to the person of Christ. It
argued against

1. Docetism: it affirmed that the Lord Jesus was perfect in his humanity
and truly human, consubstantial with us according to his humanity and born
of the Virgin Mary.

2. Adoptionism: it affirmed the eternality of the *Logos*, "begotten of the
Father before the ages." He has always existed as the Son.

3. Modalism: it distinguished the Son from the Father both by the titles
of "Father" and "Son" and by the reference to the Father having begotten the
Son before time began. The Father is not the Son.

4. Arianism: it affirmed that the Lord Jesus was perfect in his deity,
truly God.

5. Apollinarianism: it confessed that the Lord Jesus Christ was "truly
man of a reasonable soul [spirit] and body . . . consubstantial with us according to his humanity; in all things like unto us."[3]

---

2 Leith, *Creeds of the Churches*, 35–36.
3 Henry Bettenson and Chris Maundder, ed., *Documents of the Christian Church*,
3rd ed. (Oxford: Oxford University Press, 1999), 56.

6. Nestorianism: it affirmed Jesus's full deity and humanity in a real incarnation. It also spoke throughout of *one* and the *same* Son and *one* person and *one* subsistence, not parted or divided into two persons and whose natures are *in union* without division and without separation.

7. Eutychianism: it confessed that in Christ there were *two* natures without confusion and without change, the property of each nature being preserved and concurring in the one person.

Chalcedon taught that Jesus Christ is "one person with two natures," with the person being that of the Son of the triune God. The eternal Son of God took to himself a truly human nature, and Christ's divine and human natures remain distinct and retain their own properties. Yet, they are eternally and inseparably united together in one person. Jesus Christ is fully God and fully man.

Modern Attacks on the Christ of the Bible

Christological thinking went basically unchallenged in the Middle Ages and through the Reformation period (sixteenth century). With the dawning of the Enlightenment and the Age of Reason, all of that changed. The Christ revealed in the Bible and the Christ confessed by the church came under fierce assault. Attacks came from several directions, and yet, virtually each attack has two common characteristics: (1) a denial of Christ's eternal deity and (2) a rejection of his work on the cross as the sufficient provision for salvation. With the advent of classical liberalism, redefinitions of the person of Christ exploded.

The Jesus of the Liberal Theologians

In this movement, Friedrich Schleiermacher (1768–1834) helped launch the theological attacks on the Jesus of the Bible, offering an adoptionist understanding of Jesus that rejected his preexistence. For Schleiermacher, what distinguished Jesus from other humans was "the constant potency of his God-consciousness, which was a veritable existence of God in him." He presented Jesus as a God-filled man, a God-intoxicated man.

At a later date (c. 1880–1920), the history-of-religions school would dominate. It argued that Christ's preexistence and incarnation were only myths intended to give him a stature equal to that of other heroic figures of his day. A distinction was created between the *Jesus of history* (the man who actually lived) and the *Christ of Faith* (the mythical Christ created in the minds of the early church). The "Quest for the Historical Jesus," with its post-Enlightenment skepticism and alleged use of a rigorous scientific methodology, began in earnest in the latter part of the nineteenth century. Three phases of the modern quests can be identified.

The First Quest

David Friedrich Strauss wrote *The Life of Jesus* in 1835–1836. He questioned the Gospel accounts as accurate historical records of Jesus's words and deeds. The first quest for the historical Jesus—the Jesus **behind** the embellished Gospels—moved forward until Albert Schweitzer halted its progress with his bombshell book *The Quest for the Historical Jesus* (1906). Schweitzer demonstrated that these questers ignored the eschatological and apocalyptic dimensions of Jesus's life, teachings, and actions, noting that their Jesus looked suspiciously like themselves.

The Second Quest

A new quest launched around 1950. In 1953 Ernst Käsemann, a student of Rudolf Bultmann (1884–1976), who demythologized the Gospels, suggested that even though the Gospel traditions reflected the perspectives of Jesus's followers, they could not be completely discounted as historical witnesses. However, the Jesus of this second group also was distorted, looking very much like an existentialist philosopher. The New Quest experienced something of a setback in the early 1970s when existentialism waned. It did not completely vanish, but it did encounter new opposition.

The Third Quest

A period of reevaluation, methodological refinement, and new archaeological and manuscript evidence created a renewed sense that historians could get back to the historical Jesus—the Jesus behind the Gospels. Since the 1980s the number of scholars who have written major works on the historical Jesus has multiplied. First, there are those looking for a Jewish Jesus in a first-century context. Second, there is the infamous "Jesus Seminar" that is essentially an extension of the second questers. It sees limited historical value in the Gospels of the New Testament.

In the early twenty-first century there are multiple competing portraits of Jesus, portraits that picture him as a first-century Jew, a revolutionary, a cynic-like sage, a reforming teacher of Judaism, a prophet, a restorer/reformer of Israel, and/or a messianic claimant. However, several observations need to be made in response to these schools of Christological thought.

The biblical evidence demands that Jesus be a first-century Jew who spent his life in Israel. Further, the Jesus of history and the Christ of faith cannot be separated. They are one and the same. The worship of Jesus as God was there from the beginning. The Gospels were written from the standpoint of faith. This is honestly admitted in the biblical texts. Numerous eyewitnesses were alive when the Gospels were written. They most certainly would have functioned as protectors of the testimony concerning Jesus. The Gospels give us the Jesus of Scripture. This is the same Jesus confessed by the believing and orthodox church throughout two thousand years of church history.

Systematizing the Doctrine

Providing a coherent picture of the biblical and historical witness to Jesus Christ is not easy. Finite humans are attempting to describe the infinite and eternal. Still, there are at least seven bedrock affirmations. Each highlights a particular aspect of Christology.

1) There is a true incarnation of the *Logos*, the second person of the Triune God. The Son of God assumed the whole of human nature. The humanity of Jesus was exactly like that of Adam and Eve prior to the fall: it was a sinless humanity. The truest and most genuine expression of humanity is made manifest in Jesus Christ.

2) There is a necessary distinction between the natures of Jesus Christ and his person. He is a single person who possesses the totality of both the divine and human natures.

3) The God-man is the result of the incarnation, and the virgin birth is the means by which God chose to accomplish this. John Owen said it well: "He is God and man in one person. In him are two distinct natures, the one

eternal, infinite, immense, almighty, the form and essence of God; the other having a beginning in time, finite, limited, confined to a certain place, which is our nature."[4]

4) In the incarnation there is no qualification or diminution of either Christ's deity or his humanity. Each nature retains its own integrity and genuineness. Whatever it is that constitutes God as God, the Son is this in all of its fullness (Col 2:9–10). Further, whatever it is that constitutes man as man, Jesus of Nazareth is this in all of its fullness.

5) There is a genuine hypostatic union in which the divine nature and the human nature come together and are present in the one person Jesus Christ. This union is real, supernatural, personal, inseparable, and permanent. The permanence of the union should be firmly maintained. There is today in heaven a God-man who is "at the right hand of the Majesty on high" (Heb 1:3) and who "always lives to intercede for [us]" (Heb 7:25).

6) The whole of Christ's work—that is, all that he does—is to be attributed to his person and not to one or the other nature exclusively. Anselm (1033–1109) argued in *Cur Deus Homo* that it is necessary that Christ be both God and man. It was only as man that he could be a redeemer for humanity and only as a sinless man that he could die in the place of another. It was only as God that his life, ministry, and redeeming death could have infinite value and satisfy the demands of God so as to deliver others from sin. We need a God-man.

7) Jesus Christ exists only by means of the incarnation. There is no Jesus of Nazareth who possesses an independent life of his own.

Conclusion

The apostle Paul wrote,

And most certainly, the mystery of godliness is great:
He was manifested in the flesh, vindicated in the Spirit,
seen by angels, preached among the nations,
believed on in the world, taken up in glory. (1 Tim 3:16)

---

[4] Owen, *The Glory of Christ*, 28.

Jesus of Nazareth is the Christ, the fulfillment of Old Testament promises and prophecy, the Son of God and the Savior of the world. He is *Lord*, the Messiah, the risen, ascended, and exalted King of kings.

Christology is the focal point and essence of Christianity. From Genesis to Revelation, Jesus is the Bible's great theme. Scripture provides an incomparable portrait of the Word who "became flesh and dwelt among us" (John 1:14).

The Bible must be the fundamental way to see Jesus, and the witness of church history should be carefully weighed. Jesus is the God-man, complete in his deity and perfect in his humanity. He is God's Son who came into this world to save sinners, and he is the only way to God, as Jesus himself declares (John 14:6). The God-man who died on a Roman cross outside the city of Jerusalem made a perfect sacrifice and atonement for the sins of the whole world (1 John 2:2). On the Sunday following his crucifixion, God raised his Son from the dead. Jesus's resurrection is not fable or fiction. It truly happened, establishing him as "the powerful Son of God" (Rom 1:4). It establishes Christ's Lordship over all things (Phil 2:9–11; Col 1:18). Forty days following his resurrection, Jesus ascended back to heaven as the God-man, where he was exalted at his Father's right hand (Acts 1:9–11; Heb 1:3). Scripture promises that Jesus will come again to this earth as "KING OF KINGS AND LORD OF LORDS" (Rev 19:16). This is the "blessed hope" for which Christians wait (Titus 2:13). This event will bring history to a close.

Only one who is God should be Lord in our lives. Only one who is divine should have the right to have every knee bow and every tongue confess his Lordship (Phil 2:10–11). God the Father loves to exalt his Son and magnify his Name, and so should we. Only one who is God should be granted such allegiance. This worship and service Christians gladly give to the one that they confess, like Thomas, as "my Lord and my God!" (John 20:28).

FOR ADDITIONAL STUDY

Anselm, St. "On the Incarnation of the Word"; "Why God Became Man"; "On the Virgin Conception and Original Sin." In *Anselm of Canterbury: The Major Works*. Oxford: Oxford University Press, 1998.

Blomberg, Craig. *The Historical Reliability of the Gospels.* 2nd ed. Downers Grove: IVP, 2007.

Erickson, Millard. *The Word Became Flesh: A Contemporary Incarnational Christology.* Grand Rapids: Baker, 1991.

Hurtado, Larry. *How on Earth Did Jesus Become God? Historical Questions about Earliest Christian Devotion.* Grand Rapids: Eerdmans, 2005.

Letham, Robert. *The Message of the Person of Christ.* Downers Grove: IVP, 2013.

Macleod, Donald. *The Person of Christ.* Downers Grove: IVP, 1998.

McCready, Douglas. *He Came Down from Heaven.* Downers Grove: IVP, 2005.

Witherington, Ben, III. *The Jesus Quest.* Downers Grove: IVP, 1995.

Wright, N. T. *Jesus and the Victory of God.* Minneapolis: Fortress, 1996.

Also see these articles: Scripture, The Trinity, Work of Christ, Holy Spirit

26

The Work of Christ

R. Alan Streett

The work of Christ refers to Jesus's death on the cross and its benefits for believing sinners. As the apostle Paul writes, "Christ died for our sins" (1 Cor 15:3). This statement is twofold. First, "Christ died." This is the *historical fact*. Rome crucified Jesus as an insurrectionist. He was a victim of the Roman judicial system. End of story!

Second, he died "for our sins." This is the *theological truth*. The Christian story includes more than the bare facts of his death. It infuses them with eternal significance. Something was not only done *to* him but also done *by* him (*for* us). The Christ event is the core of the good news. Paul proclaimed one message only: "Christ [Messiah] and him crucified" (1 Cor 2:2).

Jesus was not only a man. He was the God-man. His incarnation had a salvific purpose. To the ancient Roman and Jewish authorities his death was simply one among many. To Christians, however, it is the central event in salvation history. This can be seen in Gabriel's instruction for Joseph to take Mary as his wife: "She will give birth to a son, and you are to name him Jesus, *because he will save his people from their sins*" (Matt 1:21, emphasis added). Jesus's birth foreshadowed his passion.[1] He was born to die. The cradle and cross were inexorably linked.

---

[1] David DeSilva, *An Introduction to the New Testament: Contexts, Methods and Ministry Formation* (Downers Grove: IVP Academic, 2018), 223.

Since the cross has historical *and* theological significance, we must understand it from both perspectives. First, we will examine it from a "boots on the ground" point of view—the events as they occurred (c. AD 30). Second, we will see how the writers of the Gospels and Epistles, and their readers explained Christ's death years after the fact.

The Cross in Historical Perspective

Mark opens his Gospel, "The beginning of the gospel of Jesus Christ, the son of God" (Mark 1:1). This is the theme of his narrative. It centers on the good news of the kingdom. He then tells how Jesus, after the arrest of John the Baptist, "went to Galilee proclaiming the good news of God: 'The time is fulfilled, and the kingdom of God has come near'" (Mark 1:14–15). All four Gospel writers identify Jesus as a preacher of the kingdom (Matthew 5–7; Mark 12:34; Luke 4:40–43; 8:1; 12:22–32; 18:24–25; John 3:3–5) who commissioned his disciples to preach the same message (Luke 9:57–59; 10:1, 9–11; 11:20).

The good news of the kingdom offered hope to Palestinian Jews living under Roman oppression. It suggested that God was about to intervene on their behalf and restore the kingdom to Israel. Based on extracanonical literature (apocalyptic and apocryphal) written between 200 BC and the first century, many were looking for the arrival of a messianic king destined to overthrow Israel's enemies and set up God's eternal kingdom in Jerusalem.

When Jesus began to preach the gospel of the kingdom, he attracted enthusiastic followers. Some who witnessed his miracles wanted to take him by force and make him king (John 6:15). Rome and its Jewish retainers, however, viewed Jesus as a troublemaker. From their point of view, he and his band of disciples threatened the fragile *pax Romana* ("Roman Peace"). When he marched into the temple complex and interrupted the required sale of sacred sacrifices and railed against the priesthood, he sealed his fate. The Sanhedrin acted swiftly and ordered him arrested. They charged and tried him as a blasphemer, a crime punishable by death. Without authorization, they were unable to carry out the sentence, so they turned Jesus over to the Roman governor Pontius Pilate to do their bidding.

When Jesus failed to bring in the kingdom as his disciples had hoped, they abandoned him. Charged with treasonous acts against the State, Jesus did nothing to defend himself but stood in silence. Pilate declared Jesus guilty and ordered him crucified, placing above the cross the words "THIS IS JESUS, THE KING OF THE JEWS" (Matt 27:37).

From a "boots on the ground"—historical perspective—Jesus died as a convicted criminal. Roman power prevailed and the fledgling Jesus movement was crushed. His disciples ran and hid, lest they too be rounded up and executed. Their hero was a dismal and disappointing failure. These were the historical events as they unfolded prior to the resurrection of Jesus Christ, c. AD 30.

The Cross in Theological Perspective

The Gospel writers, who penned their respective narratives years after Christ died, wanted their readers—separated from the events both chronologically and geographically—to grasp not only the facts of his death but their theological meaning as well. Christ, they said, did not die as a helpless victim of the Roman judicial system. His death was central to God's grand plan of redemption. As Son of God and Messiah, he was preordained to die so that God might restore the kingdom to Israel and ultimately rescue the entire cosmos from sin and chaos.

The Kingdom of God and the Cross

Theological reflection on the meaning of the cross initially was an afterthought. Prior to Jesus's resurrection and the coming of the Spirit, no one, except Jesus, understood its significance. Only in hindsight did his followers gain theological perspective.

The death of Jesus, the Messiah, was the crux of a bigger story that stretched back to creation, moved its way forward to the founding of Israel, and will continue until the end of the age when the kingdom of God covers the earth.

It All Started in the Garden

When God created Adam and Eve in his image, he gave them dominion over the earth (Gen 1:26–27) and instructed them to be fruitful and fill the planet with their offspring (Gen 1:28). This mandate would require multiple generations to accomplish and would expand far beyond the garden. During their lives they were to rule as vice-regents over God's kingdom and represent his will to the humans worldwide.

Their encounter with the serpent (Genesis 3) led them to disobey God's voice and follow the malevolent instructions of the enemy. As a result, the creature over which Adam and Eve had been given rule gained authority over them. By default, another kingdom emerged that rivaled God's own. Thousands of years later, Jesus confirmed that people belonged to one of two camps: God's or the devil's (John 8:44). Adam and Eve's own sons, Cain and Seth, chose divergent paths (Genesis 4).

When the first rulers sinned against God, they noticed they were naked and hid in shame (Gen 3:7–10). God did not abandon his people but took the initiative to restore them. He slew an animal and clothed the couple so they might stand openly in his presence. Then, in cryptic language, he foretold the day when the woman's offspring would decisively defeat the satanic seed, suffering injury in the process (Gen 3:15). Known as the *protoevangelion*, this was the first gospel announcement and the inkling that Satan's days were numbered and his kingdom was destined to fall. Until then the two kingdoms were fated to exist side by side with each vying for the allegiance of God's people.

The OT traces the woman's seed through Seth up to Jesus. Along the way God revealed his kingdom restoration plan to Abraham (Gen 12:1–3; 15:18–21; 17:5–6, 15–16), formed Israel into a kingdom of priests (Exod 19:3–6), and raised up Moses to lead an exodus (Exod 3:10–12) and Joshua to guide his people to the Promised Land (Joshua 1–12). He also set up David on his throne (2 Sam 5:1–5), moved prophets to speak about a future Suffering Servant who would establish an everlasting covenant with his people (Isa 52:13–53:12; Jer 31:31–32; 50:5; Ezek 16:60; 37:26), and promised an end-time king like David destined to rule on God's behalf (Ezek 37:25) and defeat Satan. The prophet Daniel identified the eschatological deliverer as one like the "Son of Man" who would be given dominion over earth and reign over God's everlasting kingdom (Dan 7:14).

Jesus Inaugurates God's Kingdom

Jesus knew he was destined to die and, on several occasions, spoke of his demise (Matt 16:21–28; 20:17–19; 26:1–2; Mark 8:31–33; 10:32–45; Luke

9:22–27; 18:31–34; John 2:18–22; 10:11; 12:32–33). The night before his death, he ate a final meal with his disciples.

> And he took bread, gave thanks, broke it, gave it to them, and said, "This is my body, which is given for you. Do this in remembrance of me." In the same way he also took the cup after supper and said, "This cup is the new covenant in my blood, which is poured out for you." (Luke 22:19–20)

Jesus was prepared to shed his blood to establish a new covenant, the basis for the kingdom. The cross and the crown cannot be separated.

As Jesus faced death, he trusted God to restore his life, an event about which he spoke on several occasions (Matt 12:39; 16:21; 17:9, 23; 20:19; 26:32; 27:63; Mark 9:9, 31; 14:58; Luke 9:22). His disciples were mystified at such language. After being raised, Jesus "interpreted for them the things concerning himself in all the Scriptures" (Luke 24:13–46) and explained that redemption included both Messiah's death and his resurrection (Ps 16:10; 22:1–8; 31:5; 34:20; 110:1–2; Isa 53:5–6, 12; Zech 12:10).

Rome's use of deadly force to secure and maintain peace and justice was an utter failure. Without lifting a finger, Christ struck a deadly blow to Rome and the satanic powers behind the throne (Gen 3:15). Rome's ultimate weapon—crucifixion—did not hinder God's plan for humankind. Rather, it contributed to it! Faith trumped force. God vindicated Jesus.

For forty days after his resurrection, Jesus instructed the apostles about things concerning the kingdom of God (Acts 1:5–8). He announced, "All authority has been given to me in heaven and on earth" (Matt 28:18). The declaration was pregnant with meaning. First, his authority was delegated ("given"). It came from God. Second, his authority was comprehensive ("all")—limitless. Third, it was universal ("in heaven and on earth"), encompassing the entire cosmos. No heavenly (angels or Roman deities) or earthly powers (kings or emperors) outranks him.

On the basis of this authority, Jesus instructed his disciples to "Go, therefore, and make disciples of all nations . . . to the end of the age" (Matt 28:19–20). They were to reach all the nations under Rome's dominion and beyond, baptizing converts and calling them to pledge allegiance to a new King, the one whom Rome deemed an enemy of the state.

Jesus ascended into heaven and was installed on David's throne, from which he reigns over the world (Acts 1:9–11; see also 2 Sam 7:12–16). His path to kingship was the way of the cross. This was the message Peter preached to all gathered in Jerusalem for Pentecost (Acts 2:32–36). With this understanding, we now turn our attention to some of the more popular theories of the atonement.

Theories of the Atonement

Since the earliest days of Christianity, scholars have attempted to explain the theological purpose and meaning of Christ's work on the cross. However, only a few interpret the work of Christ in a kingdom context.

Moral Influence Theory

French philosopher Peter Abelard (c. 1079–1142) was the first to espouse the moral influence theory of the atonement. American clergyman and theologian Horace Bushnell (1802–1876) promoted it among moderns. According to this theory, humans are not defiant rebels against God who deserve punishment. Instead, they are self-centered, an attitude that separates them from God. To bridge this gap, God demonstrated his love by offering his Son on the cross. When people understand the extent of God's love toward them, many are moved to repentance. The cross does not change God's attitude toward sinful man; it changes man's attitude toward God.[2]

Example Theory

The example theory, first advanced by Faustus Socinus (1539–1604), proposes that Christ's death on the cross was not a vicarious *atonement* but a vicarious *example*. He served God and mankind selflessly even to the point of death, leaving an example for others to follow (1 Pet 2:21). In the nineteenth century, the controversial German theologian Albrecht Ritschl (1822–1889) embraced and promoted the theory in academic circles. Walter

---

[2] As affirmed by Donald Bloesch, *Essentials of Evangelical Theology: God, Authority, and Salvation*, vol. 1 (New York: Harper and Row, 1978), 156.

Rauschenbusch (1861–1918), a liberal Baptist pastor and professor at Rochester Theological Seminary, popularized the theory in the early twentieth century. He believed the cross functioned as a catalyst for believers to serve God and others in the same manner as Jesus. This theory was the inspiration for Charles Shelton's best-selling novel *In His Steps*.

Governmental Theory

The governmental theory, as taught by Arminian theologian and lawyer Hugo Grotius (1583–1645), asserts that God is holy and his government is moral and just. As such, he had a right to punish sin. While this was his prerogative, he was not obligated to do so. In fact, he chose not to punish every sin but to offer forgiveness "on the basis of his forbearance" if man humbles himself "in repentance and obedience."[3]

Grotius did not believe that Jesus's death was a full payment for sin but only a "token payment,"[4] which demonstrated God's displeasure with sin. The cross represented the *kind* of punishment that all sinners deserve. When one comes to understand the gravity of sin, he is motivated to turn back to God, thus leading God not only to forgive but to preserve his moral government.[5]

Ransom Theory

The ransom theory was popular in the early and medieval church. It holds that Adam and Eve became slaves to Satan when they sinned, leading to the bondage of the entire human race. To gain their freedom, God paid Satan a ransom (Mark 10:45). The price was the body and blood of his only Son. Keeping his end of the bargain, Satan released mankind, but then he was powerless to retain his hold on Jesus, who emerged from the grave three days later. Satan lost his prized possession.

---

[3] See discussion in Bloesch, *Essentials*, 156.

[4] Henry C. Thiessen, *Lectures in Systematic Theology* (Grand Rapids: Eerdmans, 2006), 233.

[5] See discussion in Millard J. Erickson, *Introducing Christian Doctrine* (Grand Rapids: Baker Academic, 2015), 252.

Christus Victor Theory

In 1924, Gustaf Aulén labeled the Christus victor theory the "classic" view of the atonement, which the church had embraced during its first ten centuries.[6]

As with the ransom theory, Satan plays a significant role in the Christus victor theory. Throughout his earthly ministry, Christ cast out demons, healed demonic illness, and raised the dead. With each act, he progressively broke Satan's stronghold over God's people. Through the cross and resurrection, he completed the mission. Unlike in the previous theory, God did not pay a ransom to Satan to free people. Rather, Christ and Satan fought a cosmic battle for the souls of the human race, and Christ emerged victorious (Col 1:13; 1 John 2:8).

Penal Substitutionary Theory

Embraced by most evangelical believers, this theory emphasizes that God poured out his wrath on Jesus rather than on sinners: "He was pierced because of our rebellion . . . and the LORD has punished him for the iniquity of us all" (Isa 53:5–6; Rom 3:21–31). Christ had to die in man's place because the penalty for sin was so great that humans did not have the capacity to meet its demands. While God loved mankind, he could not merely overlook their sin. As a righteous God, he required a just payment. However, his love moved him to provide the payment himself.

The incarnation and the cross were God's answer to this human dilemma. The second member of the Trinity became a man (John 1:1, 14). Jesus, the God-man, died on the cross. As man, he suffered the sinner's death. As God, his death was sufficient payment for all sins. In essence, God turned the punishment on himself; thus, the love of God and the holiness of God met at the cross. The seeds of this theory are found in the biblical authors, Athanasius, Augustine, and Anselm and further developed in John Calvin.

A Fuller Explanation of the Work of Christ

While the above theories offer creative insights into Christ's death, most present a truncated or myopic view of the atonement. The work of Christ

---

[6] Aulén, *Christus Victor*, 5–20.

encompassed more than individual salvation; it was about a much larger story—the kingdom of God. God invited humans to be part of the redemption story, but he first had to remove barriers that blocked their entrance.

Barrier No. 1—Sin

Sin separates humankind from God and his kingdom. In Hebrews we learn that God instructed the Jewish high priest to make an annual atonement for sins (Heb 9:1–4). This involved a blood sacrifice (Lev 16:17; Isa 59:2; Heb 9:22; 13:11), but it was only a stopgap measure and pointed to a future atonement by which God would permanently forgive sins and reconcile sinners to himself (Heb 2:17; 9:13–14, 22). Peter writes, "Christ also suffered for sins once for all . . . that he might bring you to God" (1 Pet 3:18; see also Gal 3:13; Heb 10:19–22). Likewise, Paul affirms, "In Christ, God was reconciling the world to himself, not counting their trespasses against them" (2 Cor 5:19).

With the sin barrier removed, believers have "peace with God" (Rom 5:1). Their status moves from being outsiders to being friends of God, even members of his family (Gal 4:4–7). Paul explains that in Christ, God reconciled "everything to himself . . . by making peace through his blood, shed on the cross" (Col 1:20). Forgiveness and reconciliation are essential for becoming citizens of God's kingdom.

Barrier No. 2—Death

Humans are sinners by nature and by choice. "The wages of sin is death" (Rom 6:23). Death separates man from life in God's kingdom (Eph 2:5); therefore, he must experience new birth (John 3:3–8). The act by which the Holy Spirit births the believer into God's family and kingdom is known as regeneration (*palingenesia*). The apostle Peter writes, "Because of his great mercy, he has given us new birth [regeneration] into a living hope through the resurrection of Jesus Christ from the dead" (1 Pet 1:3). Paul reminds Titus that God "saved us . . . through the washing of regeneration and renewal by the Holy Spirit" (Titus 3:5). Christ took our death on the cross that we might have eternal life (John 3:16). Just as the Passover lamb was slaughtered and the Jews escaped death, so Christ is our Passover (1 Cor 5:7).

Barrier No. 3—Slavery

Sin enslaves, so mankind needs deliverance. The Gospel of Mark declares, "For even the Son of Man did not come to be served, but to serve, and to give his life as a ransom for many" (Mark 10:45). Ransom and redemption in our English Bibles are translated from the same word (Gk. *lutron*) and are used interchangeably. A ransom/redemption was the purchase price of a slave. Jesus's death was the cost he willingly paid to liberate man from the slave market of sin and condemnation.

In his letter to Timothy and the believers at Ephesus, the apostle Paul reiterates this theological truth: "For there is one God and one mediator between God and mankind, the man Christ Jesus, who gave himself as a ransom for all" (1 Tim 2:5–6). The OT story of the exodus foreshadows the cross with the sacrifice of the Passover lamb and the redemption of the Hebrews from Egyptian bondage. There is also a picture of redemption in the story of Hosea. Hosea's wife, Gomer, abandons him and cavorts with many lovers. In the course of time, her health fails and beauty disintegrates. Finally, one of her paramours sells her into slavery, and God instructs Hosea to redeem his wayward wife and love her despite her being unlovable. God then explains that Hosea's life will serve as a living parable of how he (God) will redeem his people.

Christ came to set the captives free (Luke 4:18–21). On the cross he accomplished his mission. Paul declares, "In him we have redemption through his blood, the forgiveness of our trespasses, according to the riches of his grace" (Eph 1:7). On the cross we were "bought at a price" (1 Cor 6:20; 7:23). To the Colossians, Paul writes, "In him we have redemption, the forgiveness of sins" (Col 1:14). To initiate our freedom, "he entered the most holy place once for all time, not by the blood of goats and calves, but by his own blood, having obtained eternal redemption" (Heb 9:12).

Barrier No. 4—Satan

Satan is God's archenemy whose nefarious kingdom stands in conflict with God's righteous kingdom. He originated the rebellion in the garden of Eden and became the self-appointed god and ruler of this world (John 12:31;

14:30). He works in the children of disobedience and blinds people to the truth of the gospel (2 Cor 4:4; Eph 2:2). Satan offered Jesus the kingdoms of the world in exchange for worship (Luke 4:5–7). Jesus refused!

On the cross Christ defeated Satan and stripped him of power. According to Hebrews, Jesus took on human flesh "so that through his death he might destroy the one holding the power of death—that is, the devil" (Heb 2:14). The apostle Paul, speaking of Jesus, assured his readers that "he disarmed the rulers and authorities and disgraced them publicly; he triumphed over them in him" (Col 2:15). He "rescued us from the domain of darkness and transferred us into the kingdom of the Son he loves" (Col 1:13). God invites Satan's followers to repent and come into the kingdom of righteousness.

Barrier No. 5—God's Wrath

Because of sin, man deserves punishment. Propitiation (Gk. *hilasmos*) carries the idea of turning away God's wrath from the believer onto Christ.[7]

In the OT, Aaron killed the sacrifice on the brazen altar and poured its blood on the lid in the holy of holies (Lev 16:3–19). When God looked down and saw the blood of the sacrifice, his justice was satisfied, and he turned his wrath away from sinners, granting them mercy instead. The OT atoning sacrifice was a type of Christ's death on the cross.

John the apostle, drawing on this OT practice, writes, "Love consists in this: not that we loved God, but that he loved us and sent his Son to be the atoning sacrifice for our sins" (1 John 4:10). God directed his anger away from us and onto his Son as he hanged on the cross.

While Christ's propitious death is universal in scope (1 John 2:2), it is effectual only for those who believe. "The one who believes in the Son has eternal life, but the one who rejects the Son will not see life; instead, the wrath of God remains on him" (John 3:36; see also Matt 3:7; Rom 1:18; 2:5–8; Eph 5:6; 2 Thess 1:6–9; Rev 6:15–17; 14:10).

Believers not only escape judgment, but God declares them righteous in his sight. This divine act is known as justification (Gk. *dikiaosune*): "He was

---

[7] Leon Morris, *The Atonement: Its Meaning and Significance* (Downers Grove: IVP, 1983), 151–52.

delivered up for our trespasses and raised for our justification" (Rom 4:25; 5:1). The "one who did not know sin [became] sin for us, so that in him we might become the righteousness of God" (2 Cor 5:21; see also 1 Pet 3:18).

Summary

From a historical standpoint, Jesus died a criminal's death on a Roman cross. From a theological perspective, however, his death was part of God's great redemptive plan. He was "the Lamb slain from the foundation of the world" (Rev 13:8 NKJV). Throughout salvation history, God revealed his desire to reestablish his universal kingdom and make a way for sinners to enter it. Many obstacles had to be removed for that to happen. The "work of Christ" on the cross was the means to that end. His death was a vicarious, substitutionary atonement. In place of sin, he offered forgiveness and reconciliation; in place of death, life; in place of slavery, redemption; in place of Satan's kingdom, God's eternal kingdom; in place of God's wrath, his righteousness.

FOR ADDITIONAL STUDY

Aulén, Gustaf. *Christus Victor*. Translated by A. G. Hebert. New York: Macmillan, 1969.

Bloesch, Donald G. *Essentials of Evangelical Theology: God, Authority, and Salvation*. Vol. 1. New York: Harper and Row, 1978.

DeSilva, David. *An Introduction to the New Testament: Contexts, Methods and Ministry Formation*. Downers Grove: IVP Academic, 2018.

Erickson, Millard J. *Introducing Christian Doctrine*. Grand Rapids: Baker Academic, 2015.

Morris, Leon. *The Atonement: Its Meaning and Significance*. Downers Grove: IVP, 1983.

Stott, John R. W. *The Cross of Christ*. Downers Grove: IVP, 1986.

Thiessen, Henry C. *Lectures in Systematic Theology.* Grand Rapids: Eerdmans, 2006.

Torrance, Thomas. *Atonement: The Person and Work of Christ.* Downers Grove: IVP Academic, 2009.

Also see these articles: Person of Christ, Holy Spirit, Justification

27

Justification

Dongsun Cho

Justification is God's gracious and forensic declaration of a sinner as righteous. This is done before the judgment of God through the righteousness of Christ imputed to him or her by faith alone apart from the observation of the law. Justification is instantaneously completed at the very moment when a sinner repents of his or her sins and trusts in Jesus Christ, who paid all of his or her penalties in full on the cross and confirmed it by his resurrection (Rom 4:24–25).

Unlike sanctification, therefore, justification is not a transformative process but a punctiliar event. Therefore, there is no partial justification for the believer. The formal cause of justification is not the internal righteousness of the believer infused by the Holy Spirit at the moment of justification but the external righteousness of Christ. Justification cannot be separated but is distinct from sanctification because the two occur simultaneously. Consequently, the biblical doctrine of justification by faith alone *per se* is not responsible for antinomianism. This is how the Reformers and their evangelical theological descendants have formulated the biblical doctrine of justification.

Some contemporary Protestant theologians, however, have challenged the Reformational understanding of justification by faith alone in terms of the nature and means of justification. Some of them, under the influence of ecumenism, have attempted to minimize the theological differences regarding understandings of justification between Protestants and Catholics, declaring the differences to be *adiaphora* to their Protestant identity. Others argue that the Reformational concept of justification by faith alone is a product of the Reformers' misreading of Paul because of their overreaction against medieval Catholicism based on their polemical spirit. Thus, it is critical for every Protestant to reevaluate the biblical data, historical development, and theological implications of justification in light of Scripture, whose authority is infallible, supreme, and magisterial in every theological dialogue and in Christian piety.

Biblical Material

The New Testament writers base their teaching of justification by faith alone on the Old Testament canon by explicitly appealing to particular Old Testament passages or by implicitly inferring *sola fide* and the righteousness of Christ from the theology of the Old Testament. When the Hebrew word meaning "to justify" (*tsādēk*) is used in the context of a courtroom, it speaks of judicial declaration and not moral transformation: "If there be a controversy between men, and they come unto judgment, that the judges may judge them; then they shall justify the righteous [ESV "acquitting the innocent"] and condemn the wicked" (Deut 25:1 KJV). Both acquitting the guilty and condemning the just are detestable to the Lord (Prov 17:15). Justification and condemnation are mutually opposite judicial concepts. The parallel structure between justification and condemnation is followed by Paul in Rom 5:16–18 and 8:1–2. Justification does not mean the infusion or implementation of any moral righteousness into the soul of the innocent person. Neither does condemnation make the guilty person more sinful internally. The justification or condemnation rendered by the judge is not transformative but declarative.

The Old Testament speaks of justification in terms of faith alone apart from the works of the law as well as imputed righteousness long before Paul. The apostle cites Gen 15:6 ("he [Abraham] believed the LORD, and he counted it to him as righteousness" ESV) in Rom 4:3, 22 and Gal 3:6. Some argue that Paul's formulation of *sola fide* results from his isolation of Gen 15:6 from its broader contexts based on Genesis 22 and 26:5, which speak of Abraham's obedience as the cause of the fulfillment of God's promise for him. However, the faithfulness of Abraham to the commands of God comes from his faith, that is, his existential trust in the almighty and faithful God who can fulfill his promise even when it seems impossible to the human mind.

When Abraham received God's promise for his descendants, his body was as good as dead because he was almost a hundred years old. So also was the womb of Sarah (Rom 4:19). But Abraham believed that he would become a father of many nations according to God's promise even when there was no reason for hope. Likewise, God's promise of the forgiveness of sins through Christ, the true and spiritual seed of Abraham, seems impossible to the natural person. But God credits faith in his promise of Christ to all believers as righteousness. When God justified Abraham, the patriarch was ungodly (Rom 4:5). Thus, the righteousness of Abraham did not come from his meritorious works but from the grace of God through his faith.

The Septuagint (the LXX) and Paul use the same Greek verb *logizomai* for "to count," "to credit," or "to reckon" in Gen 15:6, Rom 4:3, 22, and Gal 3:6. Erasmus translated *logizomai* as *imputare* ("to impute") in Latin. Imputation has more legal sense than counting or reckoning. There are two types of imputation in relation to justification. One is the imputation of righteousness, and the other is the imputation (or nonimputation) of sins and punishments (Lev 7:18; 17:4; 2 Sam 19:19). God imputes righteousness to Abraham (Rom 4:6–8), and David extols God for not imputing the penalty and guilt to sinners (Ps 32:1–2). The nonimputation of sins means the forgiveness of sins; therefore, imputed righteousness and the forgiveness of sins constitute justification.

Prior to Paul, Jesus already provided a theological understanding for forensic and declarative justification by faith alone, which is seen in the narrative of the Pharisee and the tax collector in Luke 18:9–14. Ancient Judaism before and around the birth of Christianity presented both the grace of God and the faithful observation of the law as the conditions for divine acquittal in the eschaton and eternal life. The grace of God, however, can only be given to those who are righteous, if not perfect, in observing the law. Therefore, not the tax collector but the Pharisee must be a right person worthy of being justified before God. But the tax collector, not the Pharisee, is justified before God. Justification is about one's right standing with God through divine declaration, being forgiven and pronounced righteous based on God's mercy, not one's works. The declarative justification of the tax collector occurs by faith alone because he does not have any righteousness inherent in himself. The word "faith" does not appear in this narrative, but the tax collector's genuine repentance and complete reliance upon God for salvation are the marks of justifying faith.

Linguistically, the Greek verb *dikaioō*, "to justify," also strengthens the declarative nature of justification. The Greek verb *hagioō* means "to count holy," not "to make holy." Likewise, the Greek word *homoioō* means "to declare to be similar," not "to make similar." The *-oō* ending on these words means "to count, to reckon," or "to declare." Therefore, the verb *dikaioō* must mean "to declare righteous," not "to make righteous."

Some speak of a theological inconsistency or contradiction between Paul and James on justification. They claim that James's "grace plus works" formula (Jas 2:24–25) refutes Paul's *sola fide* one. However, Paul and James should not be pitted against one another, for they are answering different questions for their different audiences. Paul's concern is to show the way of justification of a sinner before the judgment of God. The apostle presents the imputed righteousness of Christ by faith alone, not good works, as the ground of justification. On the other hand, James's concern is to rectify the unbiblical concept of faith as mental ascent—which demons also have (Jas 2:19) but without existential trust in and commitment to God—to orthodoxy. When James speaks of the insufficiency of *sola fide*, that faith is not the justifying faith to which Paul refers but the mere confession of a so-called believer whose faith does not prove its genuineness. James accentuates good works as inevitable evidence of justifying faith. Paul and James do not contradict each other on the subject of justification (Eph 2:8–10). Their views are healthy corrections of the Judaizers and the antinomians, respectively.

Historical Development

T. F. Torrance argues that the apostolic fathers abandoned the Pauline doctrine of justification by faith alone and introduced the conception of work-based justification into the second-century Christianity. However, Brian Arnold demonstrates that some second-century Christian writers continued the Pauline doctrine of justification by faith alone apart from the observation of the moral law or personal piety in a very simple way. *One Clement* 32.3–4 and *Epistle to Diognetus* 9.3–5 explicitly present the righteousness of Christ—not our own efforts, piety, or religious acts—as the ground of justification while simultaneously highlighting the necessity of good works, as James teaches.

The concepts of forensic justification and *sola fide* are also found in some fourth-century Latin exegetes before Augustine, though not in the same way or with the same level of clarification as the Reformers. Hilary of Poitiers might be the first Latin writer to use the term "*sola fide*," but it is Marius Victorinus and Ambrosiaster who make the term a significant element in the doctrine of justification. For Victorinus, *sola fide* excludes any meritorious work as a condition of the divine acceptance of sinners. The righteousness of justification is from God and, therefore, remains God's, not ours, even after we have been forgiven.[1] Ambrosiaster's usage of *sola fide* also rejects the moral observation of the law as a condition of justification. Meritorious works, whether before or after justification, are neither a cause nor a means of justification.[2] These Latin exegetes maintain the close connection between justification and sanctification as if they are one unit because good works are necessary evidence of true faith.

For Augustine, justification means both the forgiveness of sins and "being made righteous." Despite his explicit emphasis on "being made righteous," the bishop speaks of the declarative nature of justification and the imputation of righteousness, though the two concepts are not presented in the reformational manner.[3] The bishop also preserves a conceptual—not categorical—distinction between justification as forensic declaration and justification as moral transformation. Augustine appeals to the inseparable and simultaneous nature of *duplex iustitia* ("double righteousness") in one justification.[4] The first righteousness that includes the forgiveness of sins and the imputed righteousness of Christ by faith alone is completed instantaneously at baptism. The second righteousness for moral transformation is infused into the soul of the believer by the Holy Spirit at the moment that the first righteousness is given to the believer. And this second righteousness is an ongoing process. Augustine's famous catchphrase of justification—"faith

---

[1] Marius Victorinus, *Commentary on Phil* 3:9 (CSEL 83/2:206.4–12).

[2] Ambrosiaster, *Commentary on Rom* 3:24 (CSEL81/laß:118).

[3] Augustine, *Exposition of Psalms* 51:13; 68:32; 71:2, and *On the Spirit and the Letter* 15.

[4] Augustine, *Sermon on Ps* 72:15; *Miscellany of Eighty-Three Questions* 76.1.

working through love" (Gal 5:6)—does not refer to entrance into eternal life by faith and good works; instead, it pinpoints the necessity of good works as the fruit of faith in Christ against the antinomianism of Augustine's day. Bernard of Clairvaux and Thomas Aquinas continue Augustine's double structure of justification as an instantaneous event of forgiveness of sins and progress of transformation. Their theological affinity with the Reformers on justification can be found in their mystical and personal devotions more so than their formal teachings of salvation.

Martin Luther describes justification by faith alone as the doctrine on which the church stands or falls (*articulus stantis et cadentis ecclesiae*). For Luther, the forensic declaration of justification occurs on account of the imputed righteousness of Christ appropriated by faith alone. Grace is now seen as God's favor, not a power of transformation. In *The Freedom of Christian Man* (1520), Luther conceives of justification in terms of status and relationship, not substance, by using an analogy of the marital union of bridegroom and bride. Forensic and instantaneous justification takes place through a wonderful and sweet exchange between Christ as a bridegroom and the believer as a bride. The believer's sin, condemnation, and penalty are imputed to Christ, her beloved bridegroom, whereas all blessings belonging to Christ are imputed to the believer, his beloved bride. However, imputed righteousness remains alien to the believer. Further, moral transformation is an inevitable consequence of justification. Since the bride's sanctification cannot be complete on earth, she is *simul iustus et peccator* ("righteous and a sinner at the same time").

For John Calvin, justification is the hinge of true religion and the Reformation movement. Calvin develops his doctrine of justification under the influence of Luther, but he also makes his own contribution to the development of a reformational view of justification. The Reformer of Geneva makes the idea of union with Christ central to his soteriology. In light of the theme of union with Christ, Calvin focuses on the indissolubility of and simultaneity between justification and sanctification more than Luther does. The two graces of God are theologically distinct, but they cannot be separated,[5] nor do they occur in sequence. The Spirit who applies the grace of justification to the believer also transforms his or her sinful

---

[5] John Calvin, *Institutes* 3.11.11.

humanity at the same time. Therefore, the believer experiences both "being declared righteous" and "being made righteous" simultaneously.

Luther and Calvin are not satisfied with Augustine's inclusive usage of the term "justification" as a reference to sanctification. However, German Reformer Martin Bucer finds Augustine's understanding of justification to be consistent with the teaching of the Reformers. Using the concept of double righteousness, Bucer himself does not make a categorical distinction between justification and sanctification. For Bucer, the Augustinian concept of double righteousness (cause and result) of one justification does justice to the inseparable and simultaneous nature of justification and sanctification.

The Roman Catholic Council of Trent (1543–1563) condemned the reformational elements of justification such as the forensic nature of justification, imputed righteousness, *sola fide*, and assurance of justification. The contemporary Roman Catholic Church has not officially canceled this condemnation despite her various ecumenical efforts with Protestants on justification, including the *Joint Declaration on the Doctrine of Justification*.[6] The *JDDJ* is a representative ecumenical document between Catholics and Lutherans on justification. The signers of both parties try to tone down the mutual condemnation that their sixteenth-century ancestors issued and to present the differences between Lutherans and Catholics on justification as complementary and acceptable to both parties. The Catholic theologians of the *JDDJ* still claim that justification includes not only the forgiveness of sins but also the element of "being made righteous" by the infusion of righteousness in the soul of the believer.[7] Surprisingly, however, Catholics have come to agree with Lutherans about the reformational view of the assurance of salvation. Nonetheless, more traditional Lutherans cannot endorse the *JDDJ* because there has not been much change in Catholics' fundamental positions on justification since Trent.

Theological Implications

In light of the above survey, we come to recognize that forensic justification by faith alone is certainly *a*, if not *the*, tradition among various patristic and

---

[6] *Joint Declaration on the Doctrine of Justification* (*JDDJ*), 1999.
[7] See *JDDJ*, sect. 4.3, art. 27, and Sources for sect. 4.3

medieval perspectives on justification. Therefore, one should be critical of Alister E. McGrath's thesis that there is no theological affinity between the patristic/medieval theologians and the Reformers who allegedly departed from the bishops' understanding of justification.[8] That the patristic/medieval theologians who held to a patristic tradition of *sola fide* associate justification with baptismal regeneration or holiness or deification does not mean that the ancient theologians made all of the theological concepts identical without allowing for a meaningful distinction between them. A critical reader cannot easily deny the evidence of a conceptual affinity between some patristic/medieval theologians and the Reformers on *sola fide*, although he or she cannot find an identical formula of justification between patristic/medieval writers and the Reformers.

Then why do we still need a right definition of justification and a categorical distinction between justification and sanctification as the Reformers tried to preserve? First, we should worship and glorify the triune God according to his revelation. Christian orthodoxy teaches us that all three persons of the Godhead are inseparable in all divine works but have distinct roles proper to each person in certain works such as creation, the incarnation, and sanctification. To attribute honor to a person of the Trinity in a proper manner represents an element of worship and prayer. God reveals that the objective ground of justification is the redemptive work of Christ outside and for us, not the transforming ministry of the Holy Spirit within us. The Holy Spirit as the Spirit of Christ illuminates our souls to appreciate the value of the penal substitutionary death of Christ for our justification so that we continue to trust in Christ. The Holy Spirit is not here to replace the role or position of Christ but to make his presence in us more realized. Then how can we honor the Holy Spirit who is also fully God in relation to justification? We need to acknowledge and praise what the Holy Spirit does in justification. That justification is first and foremost Christocentric does not mean that it is not pneumatological. The Holy Spirit is not the formal cause of justification but causes justifying faith in the believer, unites him or her with Christ, and imputes the righteousness of Christ to him or her. The justified believer comes to have not only a new attitude toward the law of

---

[8] See Alister E. McGrath, *Iustitia Dei*, 4th ed. (Cambridge: Cambridge University Press, 2020), 70–71, 209, 215–16.

God but also a new power to fulfill it. The imputed righteousness of Christ is the formal cause of justification, but the moral righteousness of the believer is the necessary result of justification.

Second, a biblical definition of justification and a proper distinction between justification and sanctification brings peace and confidence. That a person may define justification as "being made righteous" (instead of "being declared righteous") does not necessarily mean that that person cannot be justified. Many patristic and medieval writers define justification in a more inclusive way than the Reformers do. However, such an unbiblical definition could easily mislead a believer to experience insecurity concerning his or her salvation and fear of the condemnation of God instead of joy and the love of God. Luther confessed that he hated the righteousness of God who would condemn sinners until he understood its evangelical meaning. Without forensic pardon, therefore, a person cannot but remain in fear and anxiety concerning fulfilling the requirement of the law. Once that person receives forensic pardon, however, his or her conscience will experience freedom and assurance of forgiveness. Therefore, the forensically pardoned believer can truly enjoy the law of love and fulfill it with gratitude, not fear.

Third, the loss of a proper theological distinction between justification and sanctification will result in two undesirable things in the church: legalism and antinomianism. On the one hand, to subsume justification under sanctification will produce legalism. Legalism is likely to make us pursue perfectionism in observing the law in order to secure divine pardon. Legalism betrays the gospel in that the former promotes the self-righteousness and self-glorification of a sinner that the latter denies. Legalism also deprives a person of an opportunity to experience the power of the Holy Spirit by providing him or her instead with the pseudo-power of sinful flesh. The Pauline Epistles of Romans and Galatians respond to this legalistic approach to justification. On the other hand, to separate justification from sanctification will likely lead to antinomianism. As Paul indicates in Gal 5:6, justifying faith works through love, so good works as the fruit of justification must be present in the Christian life. And by using the analogy of the body's being dead without the soul, Jas 2:26 illustrates that faith that does not result in holiness and righteousness in the Christian life is powerless and useless. The confession of Jesus Christ as the Savior without the attendant submission to his lordship is a typical example of the abuse of *sola fide*. *Sola fide* cannot be an excuse of cheap grace without repentance and discipline. In order to avoid legalism and antinomianism, we need to reemphasize the inseparability and simultaneity of the grace of justification and that of sanctification. When God regenerates a sinner, he grants him or her both faith and the Holy Spirit at the same time. Sanctification is not the ground of justification, but the former is an inseparable outcome of the latter.

To develop our Protestant heritage of justification further in a biblical way, we also need more clarification on the imputation of righteousness. Why is the concept of the imputation of righteousness so important? The forgiveness of sins comes from the nonimputation of sins and penalty upon a sinner (Rom 4:8), which makes him or her innocent. However, innocence itself does not by itself lead to eternal life, nor can innocence be the final stage of salvation. Adam was innocent before the fall, but he did not yet have eternal life and, thus, eventually fell. Forgiveness alone does not provide us righteousness by which we pass the judgment of God and enter into eternal communion with God in heaven. Therefore, the justified one is blessed because God imputes the perfect righteousness of Christ to him or her (Rom 4:9; 2 Cor 5:21). Christ achieved perfect righteousness through his active obedience to the law. Some reject the concept of imputation because the word "imputation" implies a monetary and impersonal transaction, but they fail to realize that imputation occurs through an organic and personal union with Christ by faith alone. The imagery of clothing in Gal 3:27 ("You . . . have been clothed with Christ") is a good illustration of imputation. This imputed righteousness is not imaginary but real, although it is alien to our nature. Some take faith as a meritorious work because faith shows one's total obedience to the will of God. However, Paul makes sure to explain that faith is a means whereby one can experience union with Christ. Just as faith does not cause conversion but is a means of conversion, so also faith does not cause justification but is a means of appropriating the righteousness of Christ.

Lastly, we need to respond to the "New Perspective on Paul" that raises serious challenges to our Reformational understanding of justification. E. P. Sanders, James D. G. Dunn, and N. T. Wright are the representatives of this movement. For the brevity of this article, we focus only on Wright. He redefines the term "justification" as God's legal announcement of our covenant membership (church membership), not God's legal announcement of our salvation. However, the word "righteousness" and its cognates in the Old and New Testaments never refer to the membership of a covenantal community. The words "righteousness" and "righteous," if used with a human, always mean that he or she is either legally or morally in right standing with God as the judge. The English New Testament scholar also emphasizes the eschatological aspect of justification. God's final decision for one's justification will be determined by his or her whole life, not his or her present faith in Christ. This view, however, is not the gospel. How can a person be justified (sanctified) completely by his or her life? As Jesus, John, and Paul teach, there is no complete sanctification on earth. Eschatological justification biblically means the glorious, public, and universal manifestation of the imputed righteousness of Christ that we currently possess by faith. Therefore, justification is not a future hope about which the believer cannot be sure but a present, certain reality in Christ.

Wright is also known for his rejection of the idea of imputation. There is no judge who could impute his or her personal inner righteousness to the defendant; therefore, we should not talk about God's imputation of Christ's righteousness to us. One of Wright's problems in his rejection of imputation is his theological inconsistency. He endorses the nonimputation (or negative imputation) of sin and penalty to a sinner who is in Christ as a Pauline teaching. As a result, sin and penalty are imputed to Christ. But Wright does not want to endorse the imputation of righteousness from Christ to the believer, the opposite side of nonimputation (i.e., positive imputation). First Corinthians 1:30 and 2 Cor 5:21 are clearly not in favor of Wright's denial of the concept of the imputed righteousness of Christ. What the Reformers teach with regard to imputation is that Christ's righteousness forever remains his, not the believer's, but the believer will enjoy the legal status that results from the righteousness of Christ.

FOR ADDITIONAL STUDY

Barrett, Matthew. *The Doctrine on Which the Church Stands or Falls: Justification in Biblical, Theological, Historical, and Pastoral Perspective.* Wheaton: Crossway, 2019.

Dunn, James D. G. *New Perspective on Paul.* Grand Rapids: Eerdmans, 2007.

Horton, Michael. *Justification.* 2 vols. Grand Rapids: Zondervan, 2018.

Schreiner, Thomas. *Faith Alone—The Doctrine of Justification: What the Reformers Taught—and Why It Still Matters.* Grand Rapids: Zondervan, 2015.

Wright, N. T. *Justification: God's Plan and Paul's Vision.* Downers Grove: IVP, 2016.

Also see these articles: Person of Christ, Work of Christ, Sanctification, Glorification, Holy Spirit, Spiritual Formation, Reformation Theology

28

Sanctification

NATHAN A. FINN

Introduction

It is common for evangelicals to summarize the doctrine of salvation by referring to three "tenses" in God's saving work. Justification is the past-tense moment when the believer was initially saved, by grace and through faith. Glorification is the future-tense moment when the believer will be fully saved, transfigured into a state of eternal sinless perfection. In between these two moments is sanctification, the ongoing sequence of moments wherein the Christian is gradually being saved. Like most summaries of this sort, this one is a bit too simplistic for a theological handbook. However, it does capture an important truth: salvation is not merely a past experience or a future hope, but it is also an ongoing journey. The doctrine of sanctification describes that journey. The final destination of the journey is holiness.

Doctrinal Summary

Sanctification is the ongoing work of the triune God to communicate his holiness to the life of the Christian, by grace, in cooperation with the Christian, to make him or her increasingly holy. The Bible attributes holiness to God, who is perfectly holy (Isa 6:3; Rev 4:8), which is foundational to everything else the Scripture says about sanctification. Holiness is so essential to God's character, along with his love (1 John 4:8, 16), that one could argue God's "holy love" or "loving holiness," perfectly enacted in the inner life of the Trinity, is intrinsic to all of his other divine attributes, whether communicable or incommunicable. For anything that is not God, to be holy means it is set apart or consecrated for sacred use. The Old Testament frequently attributes holiness or sacredness to inanimate objects, particularly the materials related to the tabernacle and the ark of the covenant (Exodus 25–40; Num 4:15; 10:21). Across the Scriptures, God's people are considered holy, a status to which he elected them on the basis of his divine grace (Exod 19:5–6; Deut 7:6; 14:2; 1 Pet 2:9–10). Scripture's commands for God's people to be holy are rooted in his own holiness, meaning that sanctification is the conforming of the believer's character to the perfectly holy character of God (Lev 11:44–45; 19:2; 1 Pet 1:15–16).

In Scripture, sanctification is sometimes considered a positional status and other times described as a progressive process. In keeping with the metaphor of sanctification as a journey, positional sanctification might be thought of as the starting point. Christians are referred to as those already sanctified (Acts 20:32) or those who are holy or saints (Eph 1:1; Heb 3:1; Jude 1), which is a divine calling rooted in God's grace (Rom 1:7; Col 3:12; 2 Thess 2:13). Sanctification, as with every other aspect of individual salvation, is rooted in the believer's union with Christ (1 Cor 1:2). Sanctification is closely tied to both the atonement (Heb 10:10, 14; 13:12) and justification by faith (1 Cor 6:11). David Peterson argues that in the New Testament, sanctification "primarily refers to God's way of taking possession of us in Christ, setting us apart to belong to him and to fulfil his purpose in us."[1] Positional sanctification recognizes that holiness is a status graciously conferred upon Christians at the moment we pass from spiritual death to new life in Christ. We are holy individuals, who are part of a holy people, who have been set apart for holy purposes, for the sake of bringing glory to our holy Lord.

Though positional sanctification is foundational, progressive sanctification is the way theologians and ministers primarily speak of sanctification. Whereas positional sanctification is a monergistic action in which God sovereignly consecrates believers on account of his sheer grace, progressive

---

[1] David G. Peterson, *Possessed by God: A New Testament Theology of Sanctification and Holiness*. New Studies in Biblical Theology (Downers Grove: IVP Academic, 1995), 27.

sanctification is a synergistic process in which God takes the initiative and believers respond (Phil 2:12–13). In progressive sanctification, Christians are gradually transformed so that their thoughts, words, and deeds increasingly reflect the character of God, resulting in a disconnect between the old life of the unbelieving sinner separated from God and the new life of the believing saint set apart for God (Rom 6:6; 12:2; 2 Cor 5:17). The Christian's growth in holiness is evidence of his or her union with Christ, the one who perfectly pursued holiness in his earthly incarnation and who remains perfectly holy in his eternal exaltation (Heb 4:15; 7:26). If positional sanctification is the starting point of the journey to holiness, progressive sanctification is the pathway down which the believer travels. He or she only reaches the end of the journey in the next life when the believer is fully glorified and is forever freed from the presence of sin.

The relationship between positional and progressive sanctification is evidenced across Scripture. In the Old Testament, the Lord chooses Israel as his people and redeems them from slavery in Egypt because of sheer unmerited grace (Deut 14:2; 1 Pet 2:9–10). He also sets them apart as his holy people who are in a special covenantal relationship with him (Deut 7:6–8). The Ten Commandments that summarize God's moral law assume the redemptive relationship that Israel has with God, grounding Israel's motivation for keeping God's commands in his prior grace to them (Exod 20:1–3). God calls upon the people of Israel to commit themselves to holiness and obey him because of their special relationship with him, declaring that he is the Lord who sanctifies them (Lev 20:7–8). Israel fails repeatedly to embody the holiness for which God has set them apart, but he promises them a new covenant wherein all God's people will know him, his law will be written on their regenerated hearts, and the Holy Spirit will indwell them and enable them to obey God's commands (Jer 31:31–34; Ezek 36:26–27).

In the New Testament, Paul makes clear that those who are not righteous will not inherit God's kingdom; they will not be saved (1 Cor 6:9–10; Heb 12:14). However, he also assumes that Christians are righteous because their sins were washed away, they were positionally sanctified and set apart as God's people, and they were justified through faith in Jesus Christ by the power of the Holy Spirit (1 Cor 6:11). Ongoing patterns of unrepentant sin may well be evidence one is not really a true believer (1 John 3:6–10). Jesus says that his followers are known by the fruit of their good works

(Matt 7:16–20). He uses an arboreal analogy: diseased trees produce diseased fruit, while healthy trees produce healthy fruit. Christians are healthy trees and should bear fruit that give evidence of their healthiness. Lest the genuine believer despair that he is not holy enough to be saved, Paul promises that God is faithful to sanctify Christians and keep them blameless until the last day (1 Thess 5:23; Heb 13:20–21). Though believers still struggle with sin, they are no longer in bondage to sin (Rom 6:6) because Jesus's sacrificial death has freed them from sin's power and sanctified them as his people (Heb 10:14; 13:12). God sanctifies believers through his word (John 17:17), and he promises he will complete the work of salvation in believers, including their sanctification (Phil 1:6).

As the Christian cooperates with the Holy Spirit in the journey of sanctification, he commits himself to two postures that are evidence of his ongoing spiritual maturity. On the one hand, the believer turns from his sin in ongoing repentance (2 Tim 2:21; Jas 4:8; 1 John 1:9; Rev 2:5) and strives to mortify his sin, with the help of the Holy Spirit, gradually putting to death sinful thoughts, words, and deeds (Col 3:5). As the Puritan theologian John Owen famously argued, "Be killing sin or it will be killing you."[2] On the other hand, the Christian not only strives to mortify his or her sin, but he also seeks to cultivate godly virtues. This includes the fruit of the Spirit (Gal 5:22–23) as well as the three great theological virtues of faith, hope, and love (1 Cor 13:13). Mortification and cultivation coexist in a spiritual dialectic, representing the negative (putting off) and positive (putting on) aspects of sanctification.

The journey of sanctification might best be thought of as two complementary journeys, each of which constitutes an important element of the believer's spiritual maturity. The internal journey is the Christian's ongoing growth in personal godliness. This is sometimes equated simplistically with the entirety of sanctification. However, the external journey is the believer's outward actions that flow from his personal godliness and were ordained by God (Luke 3:8; Eph 2:10; Titus 2:7, 14; Jas 2:14–26; Rev 19:7–8). This is the outward expression of sanctification. Both the internal and external journeys are characterized by an ever-increasing love for God (Deut 6:5;

---

[2] John Owen, *Overcoming Sin and Temptation: Three Classic Works by John Owen*, ed. Kelly M. Kapic and Justin Taylor (Wheaton: Crossway, 2006), 50.

Matt 22:37–38), characterized by loving obedience to his commands (John 14:15, 21; 1 John 4:7; 5:3), as well as love for neighbor (Matt 22:39; John 15:12), characterized by loving service to others (Matt 7:12; Luke 6:27; Rom 15:2). Sanctification is thus not merely personal piety, but it expresses itself through public obedience to God's commands, such as helping the poor (Rom 12:13; Gal 2:10; 1 John 3:17–18), caring for orphans and widows (Jas 1:27), and spreading the gospel to unbelievers (Matt 28:18–20). Spiritual formation focuses upon developing the dispositions, disciplines, and habits that promote the dialectic between mortification of sin and cultivation of virtue, as well as the relationship between the internal journey of personal godliness and the external journey of holy love in action.

Models of Sanctification

Different Christian traditions have gravitated toward numerous different models of sanctification. Each of these models can be found among contemporary believers. The following list is far from exhaustive. These models should be understood as general types rather than hard-and-fast categories, since it is common for an individual Christian or even a church or group of churches to select elements from more than one model.[3]

The Catholic Model

The first approach to sanctification is the **Catholic model**. Three interrelated themes are present at the center of the Catholic understanding of holiness: the sacramental nature of Christian experience, the importance of the liturgy, and Marian devotion. Each contributes to the ultimate goal of the Catholic vision of sanctification: progress toward more intimate union with Christ, a concept that Catholics understand primarily in mystical rather than theological terms. Progressive holiness is evidenced by growth in Christian love (charity), which is attained over time as the believer renounces sin and cultivates virtue. For Catholics, justification and sanctification are frequently collapsed into each other, with the seven sacraments, and especially the

---

[3] Christopher W. Morgan, *Biblical Spirituality* (Wheaton: Crossway, 2017), 217–30.

baptism and the Eucharist, playing a key role in conferring ongoing grace to faithful believers.

These three themes transcend various Catholic subtraditions. Numerous ancient and medieval monastic orders were founded to promote this model of sanctification and continue to do so today. Many modern Catholic social justice activists are motivated by this vision of sanctification. A common variation within the Catholic model is the contemplative approach to sanctification, which focuses upon the mystical experience of the presence of God through meditative prayer and fasting. The contemplative approach incorporates all three aforementioned themes among Catholics. It has also often been exported to other traditions, though normally with less emphasis on Marian devotion. Many mainline Protestants, Quakers, and some evangelicals incorporate contemplative elements into their understandings of sanctification.

The Eastern Model

The second approach to sanctification is the Eastern model, which is identified with the orthodox church. In Eastern Orthodoxy, the entire process of salvation is conceived as *theosis*, which in English is translated as "deification." This is not a process wherein human beings become divine, contrary to uncharitable interpretations by some who do not affirm the Eastern view. Rather, in *theosis*, the Holy Spirit works through the believer's faith, expressed through faithful participation in the sacraments and good works, to gradually form godly character and virtues and an increased experience of personal communion with God. Over time, the believer is so transformed that he gains immortality, which was God's original design for his human creatures. The emphasis in the Eastern model is on gradually being conformed to the image of Christ, ideally from infant baptism to natural death, with minimal emphasis placed on personal conversion when one is raised in a Christian home. Justification and glorification are each collapsed somewhat into the larger, ongoing process of sanctification via deification.

The Classical Protestant Model

The third approach to sanctification is the classical Protestant model, which is rooted in the so-called magisterial Reformation of the sixteenth century.

This is really a cluster of similar approaches that evidence continuity and discontinuity among themselves. The continuity is found in their shared commitment to the five so-called "solas" of the Reformation: *sola Scriptura* (Scripture alone), *sola gratia* (grace alone), *sola fide* (faith alone), *sola Christus* (Christ alone), and *soli Deo gloria* (God's glory alone). This shared commitment means that the classical Protestant model is rooted in a high view of Scripture's authority and sufficiency. The Protestant model rejects the sacramentalism of the Catholic model, though many Protestants continue to affirm the sanctifying value of the sacraments, especially baptism and the Lord's Supper.

Among classical Protestants, the Lutherans focus upon the centrality of justification by faith alone, with sanctification assumed as the inevitable and ultimately eschatological result of justification. Lutherans traditionally affirm a clear distinction between the law (God's commands) and the gospel (his gospel promise), though they differ among themselves as to whether the law has three uses (civil, pedagogical, normative) or just two (civil, pedagogical). The Reformed tradition also emphasizes *sola fide* and normally affirms the law-gospel distinction but emphasizes progressive sanctification more than Lutherans do. The Reformed tradition also affirms all three uses of the law, including its normative use for framing ongoing Christian obedience. The Reformed tradition also emphasizes the mortification of sin to a greater degree than Lutherans. Anglican views of sanctification are more diverse, often drawing upon elements of the Reformed perspective and combining it with a more Catholic approach to liturgy and (at times) contemplation. Some Protestants, especially in the Reformed and Anglican traditions, have transplanted elements of deification from the Eastern model into their understanding of the Christian life, though this emphasis is combined with a clearer commitment to *sola fide* and framed within the wider context of progressive sanctification.

In the eighteenth-century, transatlantic Protestantism gave birth to a renewal impulse called "evangelicalism." The evangelicals drew upon earlier renewal movements such as the Pietists (Lutherans) and the Puritans (Reformed), each of which pushed back against an alleged overemphasis on orthodoxy at the expense of personal piety. Early evangelicals were committed to the importance of a born-again experience, the value of spiritual awakening, and a commitment to faith-based activism (especially evangelism).

They were also deeply committed to the doctrine of sanctification, though different approaches to holiness emerged within the movement in the eighteenth and nineteenth centuries.

Calvinistic evangelicals for the most part continued to affirm the classical Reformed emphasis on progressive sanctification, though they normally synthesized this with an emphasis on personal conversion and an openness to God to work in extraordinary ways through revival. Jonathan Edwards and George Whitefield exemplified this approach, which was embraced by most "New Light" (pro-revival) Presbyterians and congregationalists. The evangelical Reformed view also became the default understanding of sanctification among many evangelicals who were less consistently Calvinistic in their soteriology, such as Baptists and (later) many early Dispensationalists.

However, some Arminian evangelicals introduced a new model of sanctification that challenged the Reformed consensus. Methodist founder John Wesley argued for what he called "Christian perfection," which he defined as perfect love toward God and neighbor. This perfection was a second work of grace, received from the Holy Spirit by faith, that resulted in a deliverance from the desire to sin. However, sin remained possible due to ignorance, temptation, and other shortcomings that are inherent to human nature after the fall. Wesley did not deny progressive sanctification but rather emphasized the importance of Christian perfection as a significant milestone in the journey of sanctification. Other later evangelicals who were not identified with Methodism accepted a Wesleyan view of sanctification, most notably evangelists Charles Finney and Phoebe Palmer. By the mid-nineteenth century, there were a number of holiness denominations that held to a Wesleyan view of holiness. They were often also characterized by a strong commitment to faith-based activism that they rooted in their understanding of Christian perfection.

By the late-nineteenth century, many evangelicals appreciated the Wesleyan view of holiness but rejected key assumptions such as Arminian soteriology and the enduring absence of sinful desires. Within the so-called higher life movement, or the Keswick movement, some championed a second baptism of the Holy Spirit while others affirmed ongoing fillings of the Spirit. The Keswick movement rejected Christian perfection in favor of an emphasis on surrendering yourself to the Holy Spirit's control, which was often summarized as "let go and let God." The Keswick view was promulgated at holiness conferences in America and England, winning such noteworthy adherents as the famous evangelists D. L. Moody and R. A. Torrey. Largely through their influence, Keswick views became popular among some dispensationalists around the turn of the twentieth century.

A final model of sanctification is identified with continuanist movements that emphasize the ongoing presence of miraculous spiritual gifts such as *glossolalia* and prophecy. Modern continuationism dates to the early twentieth century, when a number of mostly Wesleyan believers began to identify speaking in unknown tongues with the baptism of the Holy Spirit. Soon many non-Wesleyans took the same view, though they divorced Christian perfection from Spirit baptism. Later continuationists, who often called themselves charismatics or claimed to be part of a "third wave" of the Spirit outpouring miraculous gifts on the church, would further modify the early Pentecostal commitment to a second Holy Spirit baptism and *glossolalia*. But all continuationists affirm that miraculous gifts continue to contribute to the progressive sanctification of individuals as well as the communal sanctification of churches wherein the gifts are practiced faithfully.

Contemporary Application

Sanctification applies to every aspect of the Christian life in some way or other. For the sake of space, this chapter will limit itself to three applications: spiritual formation, Christian ethics, and the importance of good works in the Christian life.

Spiritual Formation

Spiritual formation might best be thought of as the believer's intentional strategy for pursuing ongoing growth in holiness. Returning to the analogy of sanctification as a journey, imagine the Christian sojourner on his journey to holiness. Scripture provides his roadmap, so he wants to be very familiar with God's written words. In fact, he wants to commit as much of the map to heart so his familiarity with the trail becomes second nature. Prayer provides refreshment, so he wants to be intentional about planning regular times for prayer along the way. Fasting increases his vitality, so he periodically wants to set aside time for that practice to renew his strength for the journey. Worship reminds him that he is not the only sojourner on the trail and that he needs the accountability of fellow travelers, so he normally wants to participate in worship on at least a weekly basis during his journey.

Some Christian traditions call these and similar practices the spiritual disciplines, while others prefer to call them means of grace. Regardless of the name used, the idea is that God has ordained that certain practices, undertaken with a heart of faith and an openness to the Holy Spirit's work in our lives, become conduits of sanctifying grace that the Lord uses to grow us in godliness. There are different perspectives on spiritual formation just as there are different views of sanctification. The healthiest approaches to spiritual formation are closely rooted in Scripture as our ultimate authority for faith and practice, balance the importance of personal spiritual maturity with corporate health in the body of Christ, and address both the internal and external aspects of sanctification. The goal of spiritual formation is always increasing conformity to Christ and his character.

Christian Ethics

Sanctification is also closely related to Christian ethics. How the believer thinks about such matters as God's character, his moral commands, and the cultivation of virtue necessarily affects his or her approach to ethical questions. The doctrine of sanctification is an important part of the theological prolegomena for Christian ethics. It leads the moral theologian to navigate questions of deontological models versus virtue models, the relationship between Old Testament law and New Testament commands, and the application of biblical moral principles to contemporary challenges not addressed directly in Scripture. Ethics also relates to sanctification in a more personal way. If the believer grows in holiness by mortifying sin and cultivating virtue, then ethical integrity is one line of evidence that a Christian is advancing in progressive sanctification. The doctrine of sanctification is a root of ethical thinking, while ethical integrity is a fruit of progressive sanctification.

Good Works

A final issue to which we can apply the doctrine of sanctification is the question of good works. Christians agree that good works do not save anyone, but as noted above, good works are necessary for salvation in the sense that they are evidence of spiritual transformation. Stated differently, good works do not contribute to the believer's justification, but they are evidence of his or her sanctification. Christians have been sanctified positionally to do good works that have been ordained for them by God from before the foundation of the world. Christians are being sanctified progressively as they engage in good works that glorify God, serve others, and contribute to authentic flourishing. The doctrine of sanctification offers a compelling reason for Christians to be engaged in faith-inspired good works in every sphere of life. Our good works are evidence we are growing in holiness. And the fact that good works are a fruit of sanctification should remind believers to never hypocritically divorce piety from activism. Christian figures as diverse as John Wesley, William Wilberforce, Harriet Tubman, Charles Spurgeon, Abraham Kuyper, Mother Teresa, and Charles Colson demonstrate that deep faith in Christ, a commitment to holiness, and good works that serve others are closely connected in a seamless garment of Christian faithfulness.

FOR ADDITIONAL STUDY

Alexander, Donald L., ed. *Christian Spirituality: Five Views of Sanctification.* Downers Grove: IVP Academic, 1989.

Allen, Michael. *Sanctification.* New Studies in Dogmatics. Grand Rapids: Zondervan Academic, 2017.

Berkhouwer, G. C. *Faith and Sanctification.* Studies in Dogmatics. Grand Rapids: Eerdmans, 1952.

Davis, Andrew M. *An Infinite Journey: Growing Toward Christlikeness.* Greenville, SC: Ambassador International, 2014.

Dieter, Melvin E., et al. *Five Views on Sanctification.* Grand Rapids: Academie, 1987.

Morgan, Christopher W., ed. *Biblical Spirituality.* Wheaton: Crossway, 2017.

Owen, John. *Overcoming Sin and Temptation: Three Classic Works by John Owen.* Edited by Kelly M. Kapic and Justin Taylor. Wheaton: Crossway, 2006.

Packer, J. I. *Rediscovering Holiness: Know the Fullness of Life with God*. 2nd ed. Ventura, CA: Regal, 2009.

Peterson, David G. *Possessed by God: A New Testament Theology of Sanctification and Holiness*. New Studies in Biblical Theology. Downers Grove: IVP Academic, 1995.

Sproul, R. C. *Holiness of God*. 2nd ed. Carol Stream, IL: Tyndale, 1998.

Also see these articles: Justification, Glorification, Holy Spirit, Spiritual Formation

29

Glorification

Matt Wireman

The doctrine of glorification is the often overlooked and under-developed final link in what has been termed the "golden chain of salvation." The word "glorified" ends Paul's magisterial teaching on new life in the Spirit in Romans 8, ending with the progression of verse 30, where he says, "Those he predestined, he also called; and those he called, he also justified; and those he justified, he also glorified." Volumes have been written on predestination, effectual calling, and justification. Very little has been written in recent generations on glorification.

This neglect has not often been the case, however, in the history of the teaching of the church. The doctrine was cherished and reflected on by the early church, and with great warrant as believers endured persecution and understood the relationship Paul taught in that same chapter between suffering and glory. Historically, Protestant systematic theologies have treated glorification in their discussions of soteriology or eschatology. In the evangelical tradition, theologians who have devoted special attention to the doctrine include Jonathan Edwards, in both his preaching and his published writings (discussed below), as well as the twentieth-century Baptist theologian Bernard Ramm in his 1960 treatise *Them He Glorified*.

Specifically, in discussing the Christian's adoption as a child of God, Paul writes, "The Spirit himself testifies together with our spirit that we are God's children, and if children, also heirs—heirs of God and coheirs with

Christ—*if indeed we suffer with him so that we may also be glorified with him*"
(Rom 8:16–17, emphasis added). The inheritance (or glory) guaranteed to
believers is conditioned upon the suffering they endure (note the conditional
eiper translated as "provided"). This relationship is brought to light in the
greater thread of the suffering and glory of Jesus. As Ramm rightly concludes in his work, the glory of the Christian is grounded in the glory of God
and his will to share that glory.

Biblical Summary

To get to this theological understanding, it is imperative to understand the
sweep of the biblical storyline. God created man and woman in his own
image, as distinct from all other creatures he made. The imprint of the divine
is upon us in such a way that our being is dependent upon and intertwined
in the life of God. This is not a merging of the human and divine essences.
Rather, it is a relationship of creature constantly depending on the essence
of the Creator (cf. Acts 17:28; so also, death is marked by a separation from
the divine presence in Gen 3:23). This image and glory are not utterly lost,
however, because we see even after the deluge through which Noah was
redeemed that humans still bear this image (Gen 9:6). In this way, then, the
story of redemption is really a story of return to the presence of God and a
restoration to the glory that was enjoyed and shared with him.

The redemptive purposes of God are particularly poignant in the messianic passage of Daniel 7. Beginning in verse 13, Daniel speaks about the
Ancient of Days giving the "one like a son of man . . . dominion and glory
and a kingdom, so that those of every people, nation, and language should
serve him" (vv. 13–14). The saints of the Most High receive that kingdom
forever and ever. To make this more explicit, Daniel is given an explanation in verses 19–27, to which verse 27 is the culmination of this glorious
bequeathing of all things: "The kingdom, dominion, and greatness of the
kingdoms under all of heaven *will be given to the people, the holy ones of the
Most High*" (emphasis added).

In the New Testament, Jesus picks up on this Son of Man language to
explain the relationship between his glory and his people's glory (cf. Matt
19:28). Understanding that all things in heaven and on earth have been
put under Jesus's feet (1 Cor 15:27; Col 1:18–20; Phil 2:9–11), the apostles

reached back to Daniel's messianic vision to give hope and perspective to the church as they suffered in Rome (see Rev 5:2; 7:9; 19:1–21).

Too often the doctrine of glorification is limited to individual soteriology, when Scripture makes it clear that individual salvation is part of a cosmological redemption. That is, glorification of the children of God is part of a larger soteriological paradigm. When Adam and Eve fell in the garden, sin entered the world (Rom 5:12). This resulted in all creation being subjected to bondage to decay and disintegration. That which will set the creation free is the "revealing of the sons of God" (Rom 8:18–25 ESV). And this apocalypse of the sons of God entails an apocalypse of their glory.

This glory of God and the glory shared with them is provocatively explained by Paul in Ephesians 1, where he speaks of the already/not-yet of the inheritance already given but not yet enjoyed by God's people. This concept is reiterated in Phil 3:20–21: "Our citizenship is in heaven [inherently meaning the perfection toward which Paul strains in verses 12–16], and we eagerly wait for a Savior from there, the Lord Jesus Christ. He will transform the body of our humble condition into the likeness of his glorious body, by the power that enables him to subject everything to himself." And finally, consider the apostle Peter's admonition to the Dispersion. In his first Epistle he links God's mercy with the hope of the Christian's resurrection as the imperishable, undefiled, and unfading inheritance in Christ (1 Pet 1:3–5).

The glorification enjoyed by the redeemed is bound up in the glory that is revealed to them in Jesus Christ. Christian glory is both moral and ontological.[1] That is to say, *glory* is both the Christian ethic of glorifying God as well as a transformation of the human being. This is preeminently seen in Jesus's prayer in John 17 for his believers where he links his glory to his authority to his crucifixion and resurrection (vv. 1–5). This glory is then shared with his people (vv. 20–26). The glory experienced by God's people is enjoyed already in the revelation of Christ's glorious crucifixion and salvific resurrection and yet to be enjoyed in all its fullness at the consummation of all things. At the consummation of all things, the believer is swept up into and enjoys the triune life of God.

---

[1] Clifford Barbarick, "'You Shall Be Holy, For I Am Holy' Theosis in 1 Peter," *Journal of Theological Interpretation* 9, no. 2 (Fall 2015): 297.

This enjoyment is not a loss of the individual. That is, glorification does not mean believers are incorporated into the Godhead. They remain distinct from it, but in beholding the triune glory unhindered by sin, Christians are made more than they were. In other words, the perishable is transmuted into the imperishable. The weak is sown and then harvested in power. To the natural body is added the spiritual. In the most extensive treatment of what the glorified state of the believer is, Paul teaches in 1 Cor 15:35–58 that the glorification believers enjoy is not merely spiritual but also physical.

Biblical teaching on the resurrection of believers is clear that full redemption is not merely spiritual but also in a physical body—albeit a body that does not experience the effects of the fall with corruption. This incorruptible state is guaranteed in the first fruits resurrection of Jesus (cf. Acts 2:27; Ps 16:10). The glorified body is not entirely different in its substance. There will still be flesh and blood. The deforming of the body by the agency of sin is reformed by grace and transformed in the new heavens and new earth.[2] Unlike early Gnosticism, Scripture never views the material world as undesirable. *Flesh* is simply used to distinguish one constituent part of the essence of humans from the other, such as *spirit* or *soul*.[3]

The glory yet to be revealed is nothing less than the reforming (i.e., conforming) into the image of its Creator (Rom 8:29; 1 John 3:2)—a restoring to the image that was marred by sin. As Augustine famously said, we are so transformed that we are not able to sin.[4] So Augustine writes, "For just as the first immortality which Adam lost by sinning was the ability not to die, and the last will be the inability to die, so the first free-will was the ability not to sin, the last the inability to sin."[5]

Glorification in the Christian Tradition

Historically, this metamorphosis of the believer to a renewed state of grace has been called "deification," "divinization," or "theosis." Unfortunately, the

---

[2] Herman Bavinck, *Reformed Dogmatics*, ed. John Bolt, trans. John Vriend (Grand Rapids: Baker Academic, 2004), 2.5.13.

[3] Herman N. Ridderbos, *Paul: An Outline of His Theology*, trans. John Richard de Witt (Grand Rapids: Eerdmans, 1975), 548–51.

[4] *Non posse peccare*; see Augustine, *Enchiridion* 118.

[5] Augustine, *City of God* XXII.

terminology has been imbued with contemporary understanding of new age or Eastern religions where the human becomes divine in the same sense. Historically, however, the term is more informed by the biblical testimony of what has been demonstrated above.[6] In glory, humans are not subsumed or absorbed into the Godhead. Church fathers Irenaeus (in the West) and Maximus (in the East) both pointed to the goal of human redemption to be a restoration, better reclamation, of the divine image at the culmination of salvation history.

Of the individual, Athanasius famously wrote, "God became man that man might become God."[7] Augustine echoes this sentiment: "He has called men gods, that are deified of his Grace, not born of his Substance . . . [humans] are *made gods*, are made by his own Grace, are *not born of His Substance*, that they should be the same as He, but that by favor they should come to Him, and be fellow-heirs with Christ."[8] Maximus locates the fall of Adam and Eve not in their wanting to be like God, but in the desire to be like God without God.[9] Glorification, then, is a "transcendence of the human but not an abandonment of the human. It is both an ecstasy out of human nature and a fulfillment of its proper destiny."[10]

Because glorification is eschatological, it is hard to conceive what this state will be like comprehensively. Upon death, people enter what is termed the intermediate and less preferred state to the glorified state, where the body and soul are separated (2 Cor 5:8). At the resurrection, physical bodies will rise from the graves and be judged. Those who are not clothed in the righteousness of Christ will be eternally separated (i.e., damned) from God's presence. Those who not only are clothed in Christ's righteousness but have been given (or sealed) with the promised Holy Spirit will be reunited with their imperishable body to forever be in the spiritual and physical presence of God in the new heavens and new earth.

---

[6] See Constantine R. Campbell, *Paul and Union with Christ: An Exegetical and Theological Study* (Grand Rapids: Zondervan, 2012).

[7] Athanasius, *On the Incarnation* 54.3.

[8] Augustine, *Exposition on Psalm 50*, emphasis added.

[9] Maximus, *Ambigua* 91.

[10] Eugenia Torrance, "Acquiring Incorruption: Maximian Theosis and Scientific Transhumanism," *Studies in Christian Ethics* 32, no. 2 (May 2019): 180; cf. Pseudo-Macarius, *Fifty Spiritual Homilies* II.12.14.

Glorified believers will enjoy "a happiness and rapture that can never end"[11] because they will have undergone a complete healing of their physical bodies.[12] The believer experiences in this life raptures of divine love and enjoyment, but only in part. At the end of all things, believers will see God unfettered and unhindered by the shackles of sin.[13] The Catechism of the Roman Catholic Church summarizes *glorification* as, "This consummation will be the final realization of the unity of the human race, which God willed from creation . . . [The Church] will not be wounded any longer by sin, stains, self-love, that destroy or wound the earthly community. The beatific vision, in which God opens himself in an inexhaustible way to the elect, will be the ever-flowing well-spring of happiness, peace, and mutual communion (1045)." The beatific vision spoken of is the beholding of God's glory, which effects a subsequent effulgence of glorious light.[14]

The glorious ones Peter speaks of are the angels who fell because they, like Adam, sought to be glorious in themselves and not in relation to God. As Moses's face was transfigured, as Jesus's body was transfigured on the Mount, so also the believer will be transfigured into glorious brilliance as he or she ever beholds God's resplendent light in growing degrees.[15] As the Second London Confession puts it, believers "behold the face of God in light and glory, waiting for the full redemption of their bodies" (Chapter 31). The already/not-yet of salvation is made clear. We behold the face of God in Christ (2 Cor 3:18), but only partially as we see through a glass dimly (1 Cor 13:12). In the beholding we are conformed into Christ's image and glory. We become what we worship.

As the believer beholds God's infinite glory, he or she enjoys that glory, and God's glory is infinitely manifest and experienced.[16] "To go to heaven, fully to enjoy God, is infinitely better than the most pleasant accommodations here: better than fathers and mothers, husbands, wives, or children, or the company of any or all earthly friends. These are but shadows; but

---

[11] Teresa of Avila, *Excl.* 15.3.

[12] Augustine, *De Trinitate* 4.3.6.

[13] Irenaeus, *Adv. Her.* 5.32.1.

[14] Gregory Palamas, *Philokalia* 4.376.

[15] R. Lucas Stamps, "Baptizing Theosis: Sketching an Evangelical Account," *Perichoresis* 18, no. 1 (March 2020): 102.

[16] See Jonathan Edwards, *The End for Which God Created the World.*

God is the substance. These are but scattered beams; but God is the sun. These are but streams; but God is the fountain. These are but drops; but God is the ocean."[17]

As the Belgic Confession succinctly puts the glorified state, "And as a gracious reward the Lord will make them possess a glory such as the human heart could never imagine" (Article 37). The glory experienced by the believer is always dependent upon the glory of the Creator. The many lamps are lighted by the Everlasting Light.[18] "For as the body of the Lord was glorified when he climbed the mount and was transfigured into the divine glory and into infinite light, so also the bodies of the saints are glorified and shine like lightning. Just as the interior glory of Christ covered his body and shone completely, in the same way also in the saints the interior power of Christ in them in the day will be poured out exteriorly upon their bodies."[19] So also the Heidelberg Catechism teaches that the resurrection body will be "made like Christ's glorious body" (Answer 57). The London Confession of 1644 makes this even more explicit in saying that believers are "one with him in his inheritance, and in all his glory; and that all believers by virtue of this union and oneness with God, are the adopted sons of God, and heirs of Christ, co-heirs and joint heirs with him of the inheritance of all the promises of this life, and that which is to come" (Article 27). All that the believers have and are in the life to come, they have by virtue of their union with Christ through the Holy Spirit.

The Canons of Dort tightly link the doctrine of glorification (or realized redemption) with perseverance and assurance. In the Fifth Main Point, Article 1, it says, "Those people whom God according to his purpose calls into fellowship with his Son Jesus Christ our Lord and regenerates by the Holy Spirit, God also sets free from the dominion and slavery of sin, though not entirely from the flesh and from the body of sin as long as they are in this life." Glorification is guaranteed based upon God's working in the hearts

---

[17] Edwards, "The True Christian's Life a Journey Towards Heaven," *WJE* 17: 437–38.

[18] Andrei A. Orlov and Alexander Golitzin, "'Many Lamps Are Lightened from the One': Paradigms of the Transformational Vision in Macarian Homilies," *Vigiliae Christianae* 55, no. 3 (2001): 281–98.

[19] Pseudo-Macarius, *Hom.* II.15.38.

and obedience of Christians because of the gift of his Holy Spirit. Without glorification, salvation is impotent.[20]

Many evangelical theologians, especially in more reformational traditions, have also closely identified glorification with the doctrine of progressive sanctification. Simply put, the sanctification of the Christian is fully consummated at the moment of glorification, when every vestige of sin and its effects is purged for all eternity. As Bavinck argues, "Sanctification in the New Testament consists fully in believers being conformed to the image of the Son (Rom 8:29; Gal 4:19). To that extent sanctification coincides with glorification. The latter does not just start in the afterlife but is initiated immediately with the calling."[21]

Conclusion

As the Baptist Faith and Message (2000) says, "The righteous in their resurrected and glorified bodies will receive their reward and will dwell forever in Heaven with the Lord" (Section 10). Individual glorification (as distinct from the effect of cosmic glorification) is the completion of the transformation that began the moment the believer was regenerated by the power of the Spirit. This longing experienced by the Christian as he or she struggles with indwelling sin is analogous to the longing of creation as it also longs to be free from the travails of its new birth—free from thorn and thistle that sprouts from the cursed ground. The curse that resulted from the first rebellion in the garden caused death and decay to enter God's good creation. This is why the ecstasy of Peter and Paul is heightened in considering the imperishable seed that will sprout from the ground of the new heavens and new earth. So also the believer finds solace and hope in the full redemption of the body and soul. Caught up in that glorious existence is a transformed earth that is also glorified under the rule of Christ as he shares that glory with his people.

---

[20] See John 10:28–29; cf. Refutation VI and VII.
[21] Bavinck, *Reformed Dogmatics*, 4:253.

For Additional Study

Barbarick, Clifford. "'You Shall Be Holy, For I Am Holy': Theosis in 1 Peter." *Journal of Theological Interpretation* 9, no. 2 (Fall 2015): 287–97.

Barth, Karl. *Epistle to the Romans.* London: Oxford University Press, 1933.

Bavinck, Herman. *Reformed Dogmatics*, 4 volumes. Edited by John Bolt. Translated by John Vriend. Grand Rapids: Baker Academic, 2003–2008.

Cortez, Marc. *Christological Anthropology.* Grand Rapids: Zondervan Academic, 2016.

Franks, B. E. "Full Redemption: The Puritan Doctrine of Glorification." *The Confessional Presbyterian* 15 (2019): 108–14.

Gorman, Michael. *Inhabiting the Cruciform God.* Grand Rapids: Eerdmans, 2009.

Horton, Michael. *Covenant and Eschatology.* Louisville: Westminster John Knox, 2002.

Maloney, Francis J. "Reform: Spirituality and the Person of Jesus: Christian Holiness and Deification (Theosis)." *Pacifica* 30, no. 1 (2017): 56–71.

Maximus the Confessor. *Amb. 31.8* in *Constas II*: 49.

Orlov, Andrei. "Glorification through Fear in 2 Enoch." *Journal for the Study of the Pseudepigrapha* 25, no. 3 (2016): 171–88.

Ramm, Bernard. *Them He Glorified: A Systematic Study of the Doctrine of Glorification.* Grand Rapids: Eerdmans, 1963.

Stamps, R. Lucas. "Baptizing Theosis: Sketching an Evangelical Account." *Perichoresis* 18, no. 1 (March 2020): 99–115.

Torrance, Eugenia. "Acquiring Incorruption: Maximian Theosis and Scientific Transhumanism." *Studies in Christian Ethics* 32, no. 2 (May 2019): 177–86.

Also see these articles: Justification, Sanctification, Last Things

30

The Holy Spirit

KATIE J. MCCOY

F ew doctrines in the Christian faith seem more misunderstood than the doctrine of the Holy Spirit. Yet, consider the richness of his person and presence, and few doctrines will prove more precious to the Christian's soul. That God would desire to be so united to his children that he would live within them is an unmitigated wonder. To the extent that we neglect the Holy Spirit, we are all the poorer.

The Holy Spirit: Lord and Life-Giver

From the first moments of creation to the final visions of the eschaton, the Holy Spirit is present and active. We meet the Third Person of the Godhead in Genesis 1, preexistent and shrouded in mystery: In the beginning, there was nothing, "a formless and desolate emptiness" that covered "the deep," ". . . and the Spirit of God was hovering over the surface of the waters" (Gen 1:2 NASB).

The Holy Spirit is a person in the same way the Father and the Son are persons. He is not, as Paul Tillich claimed, a "symbol for divine life," or as Friedrich Schleiermacher suggested, "the common Spirit of the Christian society."[1] No, the Spirit is neither idea nor impression. He is a person, a point

---

[1] As noted in Donald G. Bloesch, *The Holy Spirit: Works and Gifts* (Downers Grove: IVP, 2000), 51.

the apostle John took pains to make clear when he identified the Spirit by a masculine pronoun, thus disregarding the rules of Greek grammar.[2]

Sin against the Spirit is likewise personal (Gen 6:3; Isa 63:10; Acts 7:51; Heb 10:29), and the effects are severe and fearsome (Acts 5:3). Blasphemy against (or profaning) the Holy Spirit reveals a perversity of spirit unmoved by God's self-revelation in Christ and is unforgiveable (Matt 12:31–32). During Christ's incarnation, blasphemy against the Holy Spirit meant attributing to Satan the works of the Lord Jesus. Such a claim was a "heinous, absurd rejection and slander of the work of the Holy Spirit," a spiritual posture characterized today by "persistent unbelief."[3] To sin against the Holy Spirit is to sin against God.

As a person of the Godhead, the Spirit exists (or, more precisely, subsists) equally with the Father and the Son. Early church fathers acknowledged the Holy Spirit's equality in the Godhead. Gregory of Nazianzus called the Spirit consubstantial (*homoousios*) with the Father and the Son.[4] St. Basil defended the Spirit's deity, noting the "unity and indivisibility" of his work from the Father's and the Son's.[5] In Hebrew, he is the *ruah* of God; in Greek, the *pneuma* of God. Both terms carry multiple meanings depending on their context, but when *ruah* or *pneuma* depict divine activity, they refer to the Spirit of God (Ps 51:11; Isa 63:10–11; Rom 15:13; Acts 2:3–4). The *ruah* of God breathed life into man at creation (Gen 2:7). The *pneuma* of God miraculously conceived the Lord Jesus (Luke 1:34–37) and gives new birth to all who believe in his name (John 3; Titus 3:5).

As a person of the Godhead, the Spirit shares, completely and continuously, every attribute essential to divinity. As the Father and Son are eternal, timeless, and omnipotent, so is the Spirit. As the Father and Son are kind, merciful, and loving, so is the Spirit. And, as with the Father and the Son, we discover who the Spirit is by what the Spirit does.[6] Within the Godhead,

---

[2] See the discussion in Michael Green, *I Believe in the Holy Spirit* (Grand Rapids: Eerdmans, 1989), 49.

[3] Gregg R. Allison and Andreas J. Köstenberger, *The Holy Spirit*, Theology for the People of God Series (Nashville: B&H Academic, 2020), 344.

[4] As noted in James Leo Garrett Jr., *Systematic Theology: Biblical, Historical, and Evangelical*, vol. 2, 2nd ed. (North Richland Hills, TX: BIBAL, 2001), 149.

[5] Basil the Great, *On the Holy Spirit* 70.

[6] Karl Rahner, *The Trinity* (London: Bloomsbury, 2001), 22.

the Spirit applies that which the Father initiates and the Son accomplishes. Or, as Phillip Ryken summarizes, our salvation was "planned by the Father, procured by the Son, and presented and protected by the Spirit."[7]

Whereas the Son is begotten of the Father, the Spirit proceeds or comes forth from the Father.[8] This procession was not an event that occurred in time; being God, the Spirit is uncreated. Rather, the Spirit's procession characterizes his relationship within the Godhead. Just as the Son is characterized by eternal generation from the Father, the Spirit is characterized by eternal procession. Gregory Allison and Andreas J. Köstenberger observe that the "Son is sent, while the Spirit is given."[9]

The procession of the Spirit was no small matter in Christian history. This is seen particularly in the *Filioque Controversy* of the eleventh century. In the West, trinitarianism was formed and informed by the writings of Augustine, who described the Spirit as the Love between the Father and the Son (Rom 5:3). Western Christians emphasized the equality among the persons more than the relational differences between the persons. Consequently, they concluded from John 15:26 that the Spirit proceeded from the Father *and the Son* (Latin: *filioque*). In the East, trinitarianism had been formed and shaped by the Cappadocian fathers, who emphasized the monarchy of the Father and, consequently, the relational differences between the persons. They described the Spirit's relationship as processing *from* the Father *through* the Son. As Malcolm Yarnell III summarizes, "The Holy Spirit is sent economically by both the Son and the Father, the latter of whom sends the Spirit at the Son's request."[10]

The Holy Spirit: Agent of the Godhead

As the person of the Trinity who applies God's initiating and redemptive work, we may say the Holy Spirit is the divine agent of the Godhead. By this,

---

[7] Philip Graham Ryken and Michael LeFebvre, *Our Triune God: Living in the Love of the Three-In-One* (Wheaton: Crossway, 2011), 21.

[8] Gregg R. Allison and Andreas J. Köstenberger, *The Holy Spirit*, Theology for the People of God Series (Nashville: B&H Academic, 2020), 256.

[9] Allison and Köstenberger, *The Holy Spirit*, 271.

[10] Malcolm B. Yarnell III, *Who Is the Holy Spirit? Biblical Insights into His Divine Presence* (Nashville: B&H Academic, 2019), 89.

we do not mean that he is subordinate to the Father or the Son but rather that he administers that which God wills. These ministries express both the Spirit's equality in, and relationship to, the divine persons.

God the Spirit is the means by which God the Father reveals God the Son.[11] The agent of revelation, the Spirit inspired the Word of God (*theopneustos*, cf. 2 Tim 3:16) with a "superintending influence" on the Bible's human authors.[12] Second Peter 1:21 reveals the Spirit of God "carried along" God's spokesmen so that their prophecies came from him. No biblical author spoke of his own will; rather, the Spirit guided the very words he chose. The Spirit and the Word are continuously and inextricably linked, as the Spirit works through the Word to accomplish his purpose.[13]

It has been said that the Holy Spirit is the first person of the Godhead that we meet, a paradox, since the Spirit does not seek to reveal himself but Christ.[14] Our redemption, willed by the Father and procured by the Son, is administered by the Spirit. Conviction of sin, recognition of one's need for salvation, and reception of the gospel by faith are his ministries (John 16:8–11). There is no conversion without the Holy Spirit's work;[15] even our confession that Jesus is Lord comes from his enabling (1 Cor 12:3).

The creating Spirit is also the recreating Spirit. He gives new birth to all who believe in Christ (John 3:5–8; Titus 3:5). This regeneration is the instantaneous, spiritual rebirth of the Christian, imbuing him or her with eternal life.[16] It is entirely by God's grace and power. Upon regeneration, Jesus himself baptizes us with the Holy Spirit (Matt 3:11). And we receive the baptism of the Holy Spirit fully and finally at the point of our

---

[11] Green, *I Believe in the Holy Spirit*, 110.

[12] David S. Dockery, *The Doctrine of the Bible* (Fort Worth: Seminary Hill Press, 2020), 64, 67.

[13] Eph 6:17; Calvin, *Institutes of the Christian Religion*, ix. 3; Walter Klaassen, "Some Anabaptist Views on the Doctrine of the Holy Spirit," *The Mennonite Quarterly Journal* 35, no. 2 (1963): 134.

[14] Walvoord, "Contemporary Issues in the Doctrine of the Holy Spirit," *Bibliotheca Sacra* 130, no. 519 (Jul-Sep 1973): 216; Garrett Jr., *Systematic Theology*, 169.

[15] Donald V. Madvig, "Baptism in the Holy Spirit: The Doctrine of the Holy Spirit in the New Testament," *The Covenant Quarterly* 32, no. 3 (Aug 1974): 22.

[16] Walvoord, "Contemporary Issues," 135–36.

conversion.[17] The Spirit's baptism is "the active joining of a soul to the body of Christ in a point of time."[18] That we are individually baptized into the body of Christ (1 Cor 12:13) also identifies us with a "communal event" that first occurred at Pentecost, thus initiating us into the church.[19] Our redemption through Christ and our identification among the redeemed take effect by the Spirit.

Finally, as the agent of the Godhead, the Holy Spirit inaugurates the new covenant and empowers the church.[20] Before Pentecost, the Holy Spirit came *upon* particular people for particular tasks and times (Judg 3:10; 6:34; 11:29; 13:25; 1 Sam 11:6; 16:13). Michael Green explains, "The gift of God's Spirit was on the whole to special people for special tasks. It was not generally available, nor was it necessarily permanent."[21] In Christ, however, we receive the new covenant inaugurated by the Spirit.[22] Now he dwells *within* all believers in permanent union. The manifestation of the Spirit at Pentecost and among the Samaritans and Gentiles (Acts 2, 8–10, respectively) fulfilled the prophecy of Joel 2:28: God would pour out his Spirit on all humanity, without distinction, and his sons and daughters would prophesy.[23]

The Holy Spirit is, as Jesus promised, another helper (*paraklete*; John 14:16). Even more, the Lord said that it was better for us that he went to the Father so that we would receive the Spirit. Upon the Son's ascension, the Spirit's administering work had just begun.

The Holy Spirit: Our Indwelling Power

Those in Christ are the temple of the Holy Spirit (1 Cor 6:19); he is both with us and in us (John 14:17). The Creator who made the heavens makes his home in the redeemed. Truly, the kingdom of God is within us (Luke 17:21).

---

[17] Garrett Jr., *Systematic Theology*, 178–79; Michael Bird, *Evangelical Theology: A Biblical and Systematic Introduction*, 2nd ed. (Grand Rapids: Zondervan), 702–3.

[18] Walvoord, "Contemporary Issues," 145.

[19] Yarnell III, *Who Is the Holy Spirit?*, 61–62.

[20] John 20:22; Acts 1:8; Allison and Köstenberger, *The Holy Spirit*, 260.

[21] Green, *I Believe in the Holy Spirit*, 28.

[22] Allison and Köstenberger, 419; Klaassen, "Some Anabaptist Views," 132.

[23] Garrett Jr., *Systematic Theology*, 177.

His presence is a seal, a permanent mark identifying us with the One to whom we rightfully belong.[24] Thus, we are Christ's. And his presence is a down payment, the "first fruit" signifying our rightful claim to the future promises of God.[25] Thus, Christ is ours.

The Spirit's empowerment permeates the Christian life. Apart from his ministry, we could not comprehend Scripture, much less apply its truth to our lives (John 16:13; 1 Cor 2:12). We would not have assurance of salvation without him testifying to our sonship (Rom 8:16; Gal 4:6; 1 John 3:24; 4:13). He sanctifies us, both positionally as those set apart for the Lord and progressively in our Christian experience (1 Cor 6:11; Phil 2:13). He intercedes for us to the Father, aching with us where words fail (Rom 8:26). He even inspires our own prayers.[26]

Scripture tells us to walk by the Spirit (Gal 5:16, 25), thereby appropriating in our experience that which Christ accomplished for us in our place. This is no passive osmosis; to walk by the Spirit requires deliberate effort to conform one's life to God's commands.[27] We yield our will to his, surrendering our whole selves on the altar of his service (Rom 12:1–2). We submit to his leading, "consciously and continually" in dependence, obedience, and honor.[28] We obey the Word of God, through which his Spirit chastens and directs.[29]

To walk in the Spirit, we must be filled with the Spirit (Eph 5:18). Unlike the Spirit's baptism—an unrepeated event at conversion—the Spirit's filling is continuous. We are filled with "the immediate presence of God himself" such that he empowers and works through us.[30] The result is the Spirit-filled life, free *from* bondage to sin and free *to* fulfill the law of God (Rom 13:8; 1 Cor 3:17; Gal 1:4; 5:22–23; 1 John 4:18). As we walk by the Spirit, our lives

---

[24] Eph 1:13; see Gordon D. Fee, *God's Empowering Presence: The Holy Spirit in the Letters of Paul* (Grand Rapids: Baker Academic, 2012), 383; Green, *I Believe in the Holy Spirit*, 96.

[25] Eph 1:14; see Garrett Jr., *Systematic Theology*, 191–92; Green, 97.

[26] Eph 6:18; see Green, 115.

[27] Fee, 433.

[28] Allison and Köstenberger, *The Holy Spirit*, 253; Fee, 430.

[29] Walvoord, "Contemporary Issues," 216.

[30] Wayne Grudem, *Systematic Theology: An Introduction to Biblical Doctrine* (Grand Rapids: Zondervan, 1994), 649.

increasingly express the fruit of the Spirit (Gal 5:22–23). Scripture warns against resisting his leading. We quench, or extinguish, the Spirit (1 Thess 5:19) when we "suppress, stifle, or otherwise obstruct [his] ministry of the Spirit."[31] We grieve the Holy Spirit (Eph 4:30) when we ignore him, neglect God's Word, elevate ourselves, or persist in unbelief.[32]

Indwelt by the Spirit, we are his instruments. He endows us with spiritual gifts (*charismata*) according to his choosing and "varied grace" (1 Pet 4:10). These gifts are diverse (Rom 12:6–8; 1 Cor 12:4–11, 28; Eph 4:11; 1 Pet 4:10–11), but they come from the same Spirit and are given to build up the body of Christ. The Spirit has also given to some what we call "sign gifts," spiritual gifts that, in some way, miraculously proclaim the reality of God. These include the gifts of healing, miracles, speaking in tongues (an unknown language), and the interpretation of tongues. The sign gifts were especially prevalent in the apostolic era when the Word of God had not yet been fully written.

No small debate surrounds the sign gifts, particularly speaking in tongues. Viewed differently than the event at Pentecost, this gift is understood by some to be "unintelligible speech" (*gloassalalia*) to both the speaker and hearer that is directed toward God.[33] Paul himself spoke in tongues and called it a true and valid gift to the church, one that served as a sign to unbelievers.[34] Those who spoke in tongues were not in some trance-like state of ecstasy.[35] Their speech required interpretation and orderly expression, for the Spirit of peace is not the author of confusion (1 Cor 14:33). This gift was neither normative nor required of all believers to confirm conversion, and it should never be confused with the baptism of the Holy Spirit as our Pentecostal brothers and sisters erroneously claim.[36]

Some Christians believe the sign gifts belonged only to the early church, a view known as cessationism. Cessationism contrasts with continuationism,

---

[31] Walvoord, "Contemporary Issues," 215.

[32] D. Martyn Lloyd-Jones, *Growing in the Spirit: The Assurance of Our Salvation*, ed. Christopher Catherwood (Westchester: Crossway, 1989), 104–10.

[33] Fee, *God's Empowering Presence*, 173.

[34] Garrett Jr., *Systematic Theology*, 233.

[35] Fee, 173.

[36] Thomas L. Holdcroft, *The Holy Spirit: A Pentecostal Interpretation* (Clayburn, BC: Western Pentecostal Bible College, 1979), 135.

which holds that the Spirit still dispenses the sign gifts and that they remain in effect today.[37] On this point, Gordon Fee's assessment of sign gifts in the contemporary church is especially poignant when he says, "Perhaps the greater tragedy for the church is that it lost touch with the Spirit of God in its ongoing life, and as a result it often settled for what is only ordinary."[38] Scripture lacks a clear demarcation to support cessationism. From the witness of Scripture, we may be open to the Spirit's endowment of the sign gifts yet with cautious commitment that their expression be according to God's Word and with the Spirit's fruit.[39]

Finally, at the resurrection, the Holy Spirit will raise us to life as he raised the Lord Jesus from the dead (Rom 8:11; 1 Cor 6:14), giving us spiritual bodies (1 Cor 15:42–49). Scripture closes as it began—with the Spirit of God revealing the power and authority of God and calling humankind to salvation in his Name: "Both the Spirit and the bride say, 'Come!'" (Rev 22:17).

For Additional Study

Allison, Gregg R., and Andreas J. Köstenberger. *The Holy Spirit.* Theology for the People of God Series. Nashville: B&H Academic, 2020.

Basil the Great. *On the Holy Spirit.* Yonkers, NY: St Vladimir's Seminary Press, 2011.

Bird, Michael F. *Evangelical Theology: A Biblical and Systematic Introduction.* 2nd ed. Grand Rapids: Zondervan, 2020.

Bloesch, Donald G. *The Holy Spirit: Works and Gifts.* Downers Grove: IVP, 2000.

Bray, Gerald. "The Double Procession of The Holy Spirit in Evangelical Theology Today: Do We Still Need It?" *JETS* 41, no. 3 (September 1998).

---

[37] Allison and Köstenberger, *The Holy Spirit*, 430.

[38] Fee, *God's Empowering Presence*, 175.

[39] Allison and Köstenberger, 432.

Calvin, John. *Institutes of the Christian Religion.* Translated by Henry Beveridge. Peabody, MA: Hendrickson, 2008.

Dockery, David S. *The Doctrine of the Bible.* Fort Worth: Seminary Hill Press, 2020.

Fee, Gordon D. *God's Empowering Presence: The Holy Spirit in the Letters of Paul.* Grand Rapids: Baker Academic, 2012.

Garrett, James Leo, Jr. *Systematic Theology: Biblical, Historical, and Evangelical.* Vol. 2, 2nd ed. North Richland Hills, TX: BIBAL, 2001.

Green, Michael. *I Believe in the Holy Spirit.* Grand Rapids: Eerdmans, 1989.

Grudem, Wayne. *Systematic Theology: An Introduction to Biblical Doctrine.* Grand Rapids: Zondervan, 1994.

Harink, Douglas. "Spirit in the World in the Theology of John Calvin: A Contribution to a Theology of Religion and Culture." *Didaskalia* 9, no. 2 (Spring 1998).

Holdcroft, Thomas L. *The Holy Spirit: A Pentecostal Interpretation.* Clayburn, BC: Western Pentecostal Bible College, 1979.

Klaassen, Walter. "Some Anabaptist Views on the Doctrine of the Holy Spirit." *The Mennonite Quarterly Journal* 35, no. 2 (1963).

Lloyd-Jones, D. Martyn. *Growing in the Spirit: The Assurance of Our Salvation.* Edited by Christopher Catherwood. Westchester, IL: Crossway, 1989.

Madvig, Donald V. "Baptism in the Holy Spirit: The Doctrine of the Holy Spirit in the New Testament." *The Covenant Quarterly* 32, no. 3 (Aug 1974).

Rahner, Karl. *The Trinity.* London: Bloomsbury, 2001.

Ryken, Philip Graham, and Michael LeFebvre. *Our Triune God: Living in the Love of the Three-In-One.* Wheaton: Crossway, 2011.

Walvoord, John F. "Contemporary Issues in the Doctrine of the Holy Spirit." *Bibliotheca Sacra* 130, no. 519 (July-September 1973): 213–22.

———. *The Holy Spirit: A Comprehensive Study of the Person and Work of the Holy Spirit.* Grand Rapids: Zondervan, 1958.

Yarnell, Malcolm B., III. *Who Is the Holy Spirit? Biblical Insights into His Divine Presence.* Nashville: B&H Academic, 2019.

Also see these articles: Scripture, The Trinity, Person of Jesus Christ, Sanctification, Spiritual Gifts, Spiritual Formation

31

The Church

JEREMY KIMBLE

When thinking of theology as a discipline, people often think of particular topics as being most important, such as the doctrine of the Trinity, Christ's person and work, or salvation by grace through faith alone. Indeed, these are crucial doctrines to consider, giving shape to our thinking in important ways. However, one topic that often gets overlooked is the doctrine of the church, otherwise known as *ecclesiology*. While ecclesiology is not a doctrine of the highest importance in the usual understanding of doctrinal rank, it is of greater importance than many first assume. This is because the church itself is a necessary reality, in an instrumental and derivative sense. In other words, ecclesiology is connected to the doctrine of God—specifically the Trinity—as well as salvation and, as such, must be factored into our understanding of theology and redemptive history in a pronounced way. Thus, this doctrine is significant not only for proper theological understanding but also for health and vitality in the life of local churches.

Basic Summary

Many prefer to focus primarily on what the church does and how it should operate. These are important matters; however, the doctrine of the church must be understood essentially before it can be understood functionally. That is to say, what the church *is* must be discussed before one ventures into what the church *does*. With this in mind we will begin with the essence of the church and then proceed to its various functions.

Essence

To know the essence of the church means that one must understand something of God himself. The God of the universe is a trinitarian God, existing as one being in three persons. The perfectly blessed life that God lives is a life as the Father who always has his only begotten Son and the Holy Spirit in fellowship with him. Focus on God's intratrinitarian life is often referred to as the "immanent Trinity," pointing to the fact that God is in himself Father, Son, and Holy Spirit eternally before time and creation existed. More specifically, the immanent Trinity refers to God in himself and concerns the internal relations of the members of the Godhead. Our all-glorious God eternally loves, rejoices, and delights in himself as Father, Son, and Spirit (John 17:3–5, 21–24).

Whereas the immanent Trinity deals with the inner life of the triune God, the "economic Trinity" deals with the self-disclosure of the Godhead in the members' work in the world through creation and redemption. In other words, God did not remain as a Being merely relating to himself; he also created for his glory and is relationally involved with his creation. In holy love and grace God creates humanity as his image-bearers and the pinnacle of creation (Gen 1:26–28). However, due to the fall, humanity needs saving grace since we are sinners by nature (Eph 2:1–3) deserving of eternal death (Rom 3:23; 6:23). The holy triune God works in redemptive history on behalf of sinners to save and reconcile them to himself through the work of his Son, Jesus Christ (Rom 3:21–26). God calls a people to himself, elected, redeemed, adopted, and sealed for his purposes (Eph 1:3–14). And thus, the doctrine of the church—God's people called out by him, saved by grace through faith to be his workmanship (Eph 2:8–10)—is grounded in the perfections of God and the grace of the gospel. The gospel produces the church, and the church protects and promotes the gospel.

People of God

"I will be their God, and they will be my people" (Gen 17:7; Exod 6:7; 29:45; Lev 26:12; Jer 7:23; 24:7; 30:22; 31:33; Ezek 11:20; 34:24; 36:28; 37:26–27;

Hos 2:23; Zech 2:10–11; 8:8; 2 Cor 6:16; Heb 8:10; Rev 21:3). This phrase is seen throughout Scripture as a key theme, declaring that God has initiated a work of redemption to the end that he would have a people who know, love, and worship him. There was no want or lack with God; he chose to create and call out a people for his own possession (Deut 7:6–8; 1 Pet 2:9–10) to the praise of his glory (Eph 1:3–14).

The people of God as seen in Scripture can be understood in a broad sense as including both Israel and the church. God made covenants with his people in Scripture. This includes the covenant made with Abraham, who is promised a land, offspring, and blessing (Gen 12:1–3), as well as the Mosaic covenant, wherein the physical offspring of Abraham, Israel, are redeemed by God and called upon to be a kingdom of priests and a holy nation amongst all other nations (Exod 19:1–6). While God covenants with David to establish an everlasting kingdom through his offspring, Israel ultimately fails in their commission and is sent into exile and later brought back into the land by God. They await the day when the true seed of Abraham, the promised Davidic king who would reign forever (1 Chr 17:11–14), would establish a new covenant for his people, which would include not just Israel, but the nations (Deut 30:6; Jer 31:31–34; Ezek 36:25–27; 2 Cor 3:5–6; Heb 8:1–13).

The new covenant people of God are known as the church (Matt 16:18), originating in the day of Pentecost after Christ's ascension (Acts 2:1–47), indwelt by the Spirit (1 Cor 3:16–17; 6:18–20). Both Jew and Gentile have been made into one new man in Jesus Christ (Eph 2:11–22). As such, the doctrine of the church, when thinking of the people of God, must consider the similarities and differences that exist between Israel and the church in accordance with the progression of the covenants in Scripture. Concerning continuity between Israel and the church, there is a linguistic link concerning the terminology used to describe the church in that the Hebrew term for "assembly" (*qahal*) is rendered as *ekklesia* in the Septuagint, the word used to depict the church in the New Testament. Secondly, language used for Israel is also used for the church, including Abraham's seed (Rom 4:16; Gal 3:6–9, 29), as well as "royal priesthood" and "holy nation" (1 Pet 2:9; cf. Exod 19:5–6). These connections demonstrate our link to the true seed of Abraham, the new Adam, and fulfillment of all Israel was called to be, Jesus Christ. Finally, the new covenant made with Israel and Judah (Jer 31:31–34) is also applicable to the church (Hebrews 8–10).

However, we should also note some distinct differences between Israel and the church. First, Israel was under the Mosaic law as a covenant, whereas the church is not under this law but rather the new covenant. Secondly, Israel was an ethnically distinct people group, whereas the church is comprised of nations and peoples. Third, the signs of the varying covenants differ, as well as who receives them (circumcision for Jewish infant boys; baptism for believers). The work of Jesus and the indwelling of the Spirit also mark a contrast between Israel and the church. And finally, a future is spoken of for ethnic Israel just prior to Christ's return (Rom 11:25–26). Thus, in thinking of the people of God, one must consider both Israel and the church as similar yet different as God works in redemptive history with one people manifested in differing covenantal frameworks.

Nature of the Church

When referring to "the church" (i.e., the assembly) one can think of this concept in two distinct ways: the universal church and the local church. The universal church consists of the whole number of the elect, who have been, are, or shall be gathered under Christ; in short, it is the church as God sees it, the redeemed throughout history and throughout the world. The local church is an eschatological, new covenant assembly of baptized (water and Spirit) believers on mission to make disciples for the glory of God, who meet together regularly under the preaching of the Word and the observance of the ordinances for the purpose of the exaltation of God and the edification of the saints with the corporate aim of being both the sign and agent of the kingdom of Christ. Our focus, like that of the New Testament (114 occurrences of the word *ekklesia*; 109 denoting "church" as a local reality), will be on the local church.

The local church comes together in agreement on the content of the gospel (doctrine) and renders judgment on who is believing in the gospel (membership and discipline). It has been characterized since the Reformation era as a gathered assembly of believers who come under the right preaching of the Word, the right administration of the ordinances, and the right practice of discipline. A contemporary author (Gregg Allison, *Sojourners and Strangers*) also helpfully speaks of the local church being marked out in the following ways: doxological (oriented to the glory of God), logocentric

(Word-centered, both Christ and Scripture), pneumadynamic (Spirit-empowered), covenantal (new covenant people of God, in covenant with one another), confessional (adhering to doctrinal convictions), missional (committed to making disciples of Jesus), and spatio-temporal/eschatological (here in the present, oriented to the future). These are the kinds of things that characterize a people who commit to assemble together regularly as disciples of Jesus in a local church.

Beyond the marks of the church there are also biblical images that give further understanding of the nature of the church. These would include the people of God (1 Pet 2:9–11), the body of Christ (1 Cor 12:12–27), and the temple of the Spirit (1 Cor 3:16–17; 6:19; 2 Cor 5:1; 6:16; Eph 2:13–22; 1 Pet 2:5). All of these images convey the relationship we have with God and how we as a people are to live before him, by his empowering, for his glory.

Membership and Discipline

Understanding the nature of the local church as described in Scripture with its various marks and images calls one to conceive of how one might be included in such a people. Jesus has established local churches to exist throughout the world; therefore, we should commit to a local church, submit to biblical church leadership (Heb 13:17) who serve as undershepherds to the Chief Shepherd (1 Pet 5:1–4), and oversee and be overseen in our discipleship. Church membership, thus, is a commitment between an individual and a local church to oversee and be overseen in their discipleship.

The term "church membership" may not be found in Scripture (much like the term "Trinity"), but the concept is seen clearly. From the beginning, there is a keeping of numbers of those who believe and join the church (Acts 1:15; 2:41, 47; 4:4). Members are involved in choosing table servants (Acts 6:1–6), sending out missionaries (Acts 13:1–3), and settling doctrinal disputes (Acts 15:1–31). Most of the letters Paul wrote were written to various churches. Christians collectively identify themselves as churches (Acts 8:3; 11:22; 12:1, 5; 14:27). The pattern in Acts of entering church life is belief in Jesus, baptism, and joining a community of believers (Acts 2:38; 8:12; 9:18; 16:33). Christian pastors/elders are made responsible for specific sheep (Heb 13:17; Acts 20:28; 1 Pet 5:2). Christians are responsible to submit to specific leaders (Heb 13:17; 1 Tim 5:17). Christians are called to exclude unrepentant people from the fellowship (Matt 18:15–20; 1 Cor 5:13; Titus 3:10; 1 John 2:19). And the local church is where members express their spiritual gifts and service to others (Eph 4:11–16, 25–32; "one another" commands). All these imply that joining a church and committing as a member should be the normal pattern.

The church constantly seeks to formatively disciple their members, but at times, when sin becomes blatant, repeated, with no presence of repentance, they must enact corrective discipline. Discipline serves as a warning to the offender of their potential eschatological judgment, should they continue to refuse to repent, and is a means by which other church members are called to persevere in their faith. Jesus calls for discipline to be exacted after attempts are made to seek reconciliation through one-on-one interaction, two or three witnesses, and, if necessary, the whole church. If they refuse to repent at that point, they are to be put out of membership (Matt 18:15–20). Likewise, Paul wants to see the church in Corinth kept pure, and thus he advocates for discipline and removal (1 Cor 5:1–13; cf. 2 Cor 2:5–11; Rom 16:17; Gal 6:1–3; Eph 5:11; Titus 3:10; 2 Thess 3:14–15). The goal of discipline, it must be remembered, is always love and restoration. Ultimately, discipline is done to warn the sinner to repent and avoid eschatological judgment, to protect the church and maintain purity, and to present a gospel witness.

Polity

The term "polity" speaks of the concept of church governance. Different forms of polity are observed throughout church history, including polity that is episcopalian (a hierarchy of leadership, going from priests to bishops to archbishops, etc.; authority resides outside the local church), presbyterian (authority resides within the local church with the session of elders), and congregational (various forms; pure democratic, pastor-led, deacon-led, led by plurality of elders; primary characteristic is that authority resides with autonomous local churches in their membership).

While there are different understandings of church polity even within the free church tradition, we can affirm that Christ is the head of the body (Eph 1:22–23), the Chief Shepherd (1 Pet 5:4), exercising authority by means of his Word, and he has appointed undershepherds, also referred to as pastors/elders/overseers (these terms all refer to one office; Acts 20:17–28; 1

Tim 3:1–7; Titus 1:5–7; 1 Pet 5:1–4), to lead the congregation (Heb 13:17). Deacons are called to serve and care for the needs of the church (1 Tim 3:8–13; cf. Acts 6:1–7), and the congregation engages in designated decision-making (e.g., membership, discipline, doctrine, missions, budget, appointing of leadership). Thus, pastors lead by biblical persuasion, not coercion, and the final court of appeal on significant matters in the church resides in its members, who work in and watch over the temple of God (1 Cor 3:16; 2 Cor 6:16; cf. Gen 2:15; Num 3:7–8; 8:26; 18:5–6), that is, the members of the church.

Ordinances

The ordinances serve as a key means of remembering all that Christ accomplished on the cross, celebrating new life through faith in him, and anticipating the day when we will commune with him face to face. Among the majority of Protestants, two ordinances are celebrated: baptism and the Lord's Supper. These two practices are crucial in that the church consists of its membership, and that membership is made visible by a people committed to Christ and one another, submitting to his Word and celebrating the ordinances together.

As such, baptism (which means "to dip or immerse under water"; Mark 1:5, 10; John 3:23) is the initiating sign of the new covenant. It is an enacted vow whereby a person formally submits to the triune Lord of the new covenant by repentance and faith and joins the new covenant community (Matt 28:19–20; Acts 2:38, 41; 8:4–13; 10:34–48; 16:15, 30–33). Because the new covenant is for a people who know the Lord (Jer 31:34), this signifies that baptism is for those who have placed their faith in Jesus Christ for salvation. Baptism pictures identification with Christ because we are baptized into Christ (Rom 6:3; Gal 3:27) and become identified with his death, burial and resurrection (Rom 6:4). Baptism is a public declaration of a new association with Christ and thereby his church. Thus, the new covenant creates a visible people, and one becomes a visible member of that people through baptism, the sign of the new covenant signifying heart circumcision (Deut 30:6; Rom 2:25–29; Phil 3:3).

The Lord's Supper is the renewing sign of the new covenant, where we repeatedly ratify the new covenant, renewing our trust in Christ, as well as our commitment to his people. Jesus instituted the Lord's Supper in the midst of his observance of Passover with his disciples (Matt 26:17–30; Mark 14:12–26; Luke 22:7–30). It anticipates the inauguration of the new covenant (Luke 22:20) as Christ, our Passover lamb, is sacrificed (1 Cor 5:7). Paul affirms that the church should continually partake of the Lord's Supper (1 Cor 11:17–34; cf. Acts 2:42; 20:7; 1 Cor 10:14–22) for the purposes of remembering what Christ has done and reminding ourselves of the gospel, strengthening Christian community, and anticipating the marriage supper of the Lamb. Thus, the Lord's Supper gives opportunity to confess sin and to celebrate, enhance unity and fellowship, reassure of God's promises in Christ, and continually shape believers as God's people.

Mission and Ministries

Finally, the church is engaged in a specific mission and various ministries that spring from that mission. Jesus accomplished our salvation, and the salvation Jesus accomplished as his mission would be announced by the disciples as their mission. Thus, the mission of the church is to go into the world and make disciples by declaring the gospel of Jesus Christ in the power of the Spirit and to then gather these disciples into churches to worship the Lord and obey his commands to the glory of God the Father.[1] The church is for the world, encouraging its members to faithfully obey the cultural mandate to build civilization while loving neighbors and making disciples, and against the world, helping its members to be compassionately critical of and justly opposed to all in this fallen world that is tainted by sin and in rebellion against Jesus Christ.

The ministries of the church flow out of this mission. They include worship (singing, praying, proclamation, giving, celebrating the ordinances, fellowship, and everything else we do; Psalm 95; 1 Cor 10:31; Rom 12:1–2), preaching and teaching the Word of God (Rom 10:14–17; 2 Tim 4:1–4; cf. 1 Tim 3:2; Titus 1:9; Col 3:16), discipleship and training (large classes, small groups, counseling, intentional discipleship; Matt 28:19–20; Acts 2:42; Heb

---

[1] Matt 28:18–20; Luke 24:45–49; John 20:21; Acts 1:8; see Kevin DeYoung and Greg Gilbert, *What Is the Mission of the Church? Making Sense of Social Justice, Shalom, and the Great Commission* (Wheaton: Crossway, 2011).

3:12–13; 10:23–25), fellowship (having a common gospel focus and purpose and thus living together around that commonality; the "one another" commands), and service (praying for others, giving to fellow Christians and others in need of sustenance, especially widows and orphans: Acts 2:44–45; 1 Tim 2:1–2; 5:3–16; Jas 1:27; cf. Gal 6:9–10).

Brief Survey of Key Thinkers and Developments

In the patristic era (100–500) the church was conceived of as one (i.e., unified), holy (i.e., consecrated to God and his purposes), catholic (i.e., universal), and apostolic (i.e., conforming to the apostle's doctrine). Ignatius, an early bishop of Antioch in the first decade of the second century, was the first to separate the office of bishop from that of pastor, or priest, and advocate three offices in the church: bishop, priest, and deacon. He elevated the bishop as the key to the church's unity. Nothing, especially no sacraments, could go on without his supervision. He should be respected, regarded, and followed as the Lord himself. Irenaeus continued to support the importance of the bishops in the mid-second century. In direct response to various controversies (i.e., Donatism), Augustine insisted that the church is made up of both genuine believers and false members. As such, membership in the church eventually became associated with being a citizen of Rome itself, and the authority of the church grew as it became increasingly characterized by its hierarchy, with substantial authority vested in the pope.

The medieval era (500–1500) saw the continued ascendancy of the bishop of Rome, who eventually operated as supreme pontiff of the Roman Catholic Church. Another important ecclesiological idea to trace in the medieval church is the rise of sacramental theology. Augustine gave the famous definition of a sacrament as a visible form of an invisible grace, or a sign of a sacred thing, communicating benefit to those who participate in it (and to do so in an axiomatic manner called *ex opere operato* [i.e., grace is bestowed by the elements, regardless of the one who oversees and dispenses it]). Peter Lombard was the first to insist on a list of seven sacraments: baptism, confirmation, eucharist, penance, extreme unction, ordination, and marriage. This list was officially ratified in 1215 at the Fourth Lateran Council. Protestants limited sacraments to those clearly instituted by Christ and directly related to the gospel, namely, baptism and the Lord's Supper.

Beginning in the Reformation period (1500–1750) and becoming even more distinct in the modern era (1750–present day), while unity around the doctrines of grace was evident, ecclesiological differences became more pronounced as Protestants stood in unity against the teachings of the Roman Catholic Church (to which the Catholic Church responded at the Council of Trent). Variances amongst the Reformers regarding church life became entrenched doctrinal convictions and ecclesial distinctives, bringing about agreement in certain core theological areas (e.g., justification by faith alone) but disagreement over other matters (e.g., baptism, Lord's Supper, church government, forms of church worship, etc.). Some, for example, advocated for infant baptism but from differing theological vantage points (Martin Luther and John Calvin). Others argued for believer's baptism (Balthasar Hubmaier). The Lord's Supper was viewed as consubstantiation (Luther), spiritual presence (Calvin), or as a memorial (Huldrych [or Ulrich] Zwingli). This led to various splintering movements within Protestantism.

Ecclesiology increasingly became a place for demonstrable doctrinal distinctives in the modern era (1750–present). The First (1730–1740s; key figures include Jonathan Edwards, John Wesley, and George Whitefield) and Second Great Awakenings (1800–1840s; key figure is Charles Finney), for example, brought about ongoing debate in the nineteenth century and beyond regarding the purpose and method of preaching, the rapidity with which members are brought into a church, and how one conceives of salvation along both Arminian and Calvinist lines. This was due in large measure to the differing views that existed regarding the essence and purpose of the church as a whole. To cite this trajectory, by the mid-twentieth century, many evangelical churches had shifted from viewing themselves preeminently as baptized, covenanted, local assemblies to functioning primarily as outreach centers and corporate worship services as catalysts for revival.

Theologically speaking, one observed such movements as dispensationalism, offering a contrast to covenant theology, the Roman Catholic Church and Vatican II (1962–65), the ecumenical movement of the twentieth century, and Pentecostalism. Each of these movements brought their own particular approach to ecclesiology, some dealing exegetically with the relationship of Israel and the church, others dealing with the Christian church in relation to other religions, and the way in which a church should be structured and ordered in their worship. Among evangelical churches today there is agreement on orthodoxy, but often our differences are manifest in the realm of ecclesiology, showing forth various denominational distinctives.

Suggestions for Contemporary Application

The universal church, which is believers across the world throughout history, is certainly a valid understanding of how to comprehend the term "church" in certain contexts. However, the New Testament most often speaks of local churches, which are gatherings of believers to hear the Word preached and celebrate the ordinances, functioning as autonomous entities while also cooperative in ministry endeavors. This is true in the early church as one can observe local churches being planted (Acts 2:42–47; 13:1–3; 14:21–27; 15:1–30; 16:5; 20:17, 28), as well as the letters that were written to distinct local churches (Rom 1:7; 1 Cor 1:2; 5:1–13; Phil 1:1; Revelation 2–3).

Local churches should operate under the Lordship of Christ in obedience to his Word (1 Pet 5:4) and be led by qualified men (1 Tim 2:12–14) who work as pastors/elders (Acts 20:17–28; 1 Tim 3:1–7; Titus 1:5–9; 1 Pet 5:1–4), served by deacons (1 Tim 3:8–13), and governed by the congregation (Matt 18:15–20; Acts 15:1–30; 1 Cor 5:1–13). The church, comprised of local gatherings of believers, is on a mission to make disciples that we might see followers of Jesus from every tribe, tongue, nation, and language (Rev 5:9–10). We should love the church as Christ does and give ourselves to its work in the world.

Looking specifically at two areas, churches must make membership and discipline meaningful and devote themselves to discipleship. First, pastors must teach the biblical warrant for and the importance of joining a church in membership and, if necessary, the reality of church discipline. The church is its membership. Pastors oversee members, members oversee one another, and members partake of the ordinances together. As such, there must be commitment called for and oversight of one another's lives such that the church grows in maturity (Col 1:28–29; Eph 4:11–16).

There is an essential ingredient in a church that embraces biblical membership and discipline, and that is discipleship. This is our task, to go and make disciples of Jesus Christ, baptizing them and teaching them to observe all he commanded (Matt 28:19–20). Discipleship includes evangelism, seeing people hear the gospel and come to faith in Christ. It then involves teaching and modeling so as to help individuals, small groups, and classes of people grow in their faith. Discipleship includes preaching as a means of hearing and applying God's Word. And it includes missions, the sending out of disciples to the nations so that people from every tribe, tongue, nation, and language can know the living God (Rev 5:9–10). Discipleship is the heartbeat of the church, and the church is made up of members committed to this task for the glory of God. Thus, it is essential that churches focus their efforts on such matters to be faithful in God's purpose for them.

For Additional Study

Allison, Gregg. *Sojourners and Strangers: The Doctrine of the Church*. Wheaton: Crossway, 2012.

Dever, Mark, and Jonathan Leeman. *Baptist Foundations: Church Government for an Anti-Institutional Age*. Nashville: B&H Academic, 2015.

Easley, Kendall H., and Christopher W. Morgan. *The Community of Jesus: A Theology of the Church*. Nashville: B&H Academic, 2013.

Hammett, John S. *Biblical Foundations for Baptist Churches: A Contemporary Ecclesiology*. Grand Rapids: Kregel Academic, 2019.

Kimble, Jeremy M. *40 Questions about Church Membership and Discipline*. Grand Rapids: Kregel Academic, 2017.

Leeman, Jonathan. *Political Church: The Local Assembly as Embassy of Christ's Rule*. Downers Grove: IVP Academic, 2016.

Also see these articles: Holy Spirit, Church Membership, Baptism, Lord's Supper, Worship, Preaching, Pastoral Theology

32

Last Things

CRAIG A. BLAISING

The doctrine of last things, or eschatology (from *eschatos* [Greek] meaning "last"), addresses aspects of God's consummation plan for all things as narrated by Scripture.

In New Testament eschatology, these last things all relate to the return of Jesus to earth. Consequently, the doctrine of the second coming of Christ is the focal doctrine of Christian eschatology. In evangelical theology, the Second Coming is the personal, visible, bodily return of Jesus Christ to earth in glory. It is the hope and prayer of the New Testament church (1 Thess 1:10; Phil 3:20; Titus 2:13; Heb 9:28; 1 Pet 1:13; 1 Cor 16:22; Rev 22:20), predicted explicitly by Jesus himself (Matt 16:27; 24:29–31; 25:31–46; John 14:3) and by angels at his ascension (Acts 1:11).

The New Testament hope of the second coming of Christ connects with the Old Testament expectation of an eschatological coming of God. In both Testaments, the coming of God, the Lord, takes place in a day of the Lord, a time of trouble or tribulation that is an expression of divine judgment and wrath against sin and evil, extending even to the point of judgment for each individual person. However, the Lord who comes will also bring to completion the salvation of his people and usher them into an everlasting kingdom in a new creation that the Lord himself will establish forever.

Eschatology, then, is the study of this consummation sequence—the coming of the Lord in the day of the Lord, with its features of wrath and judgment, and the establishment of the everlasting kingdom in God's new creation.

Two specific challenges to understanding biblical eschatology relate to (1) its *scope* and (2) its *complexification* through progressive revelation and historical fulfillment.

The scope of eschatology is as wide as the scope of God's creation. However, many treatments of eschatology are limited to what may be called "personal eschatology." This concerns what happens to individual persons at or as a consequence of the coming of Christ. It includes such things as resurrection from the dead, personal judgment, and the allotment of eternal destinies to the saved and unsaved (traditionally spoken of as heaven or hell). Some include here a theological discussion of death and the state of the dead (see remarks under "Personal Eschatology" below).

Biblical eschatology, however, extends beyond the personal dimension to what may be called *political (and communal) eschatology*. Here the scope widens to include the corporate aspects of human life, its political, social, and communal features. Prophecies in Scripture portray the day of the Lord as an eschatological judgment upon the nations of the earth and the societies established by them. The eschatological kingdom is God's establishment of a messianic reign over the peoples and nations of the earth, including the particular people and nation of Israel. The blessing of Israel as a nation together with Gentile peoples and nations is a repeated theme among the prophets.

The New Testament, however, reveals another feature of this eschatological kingdom. In spite of its corporate ethnic and national diversity, the kingdom exhibits a spiritual unity never before seen in human corporate life. This unity comes through the indwelling, sanctifying presence of God in the lives of kingdom peoples crossing all ethnic, tribal, and national differences. It is a communion of the Holy Spirit given to all in Christ without distinction (both Jew and Gentile), and it is presently revealed in inaugural form as the chief characteristic of the church.

The relation of this transnational, transethnic, communal aspect of kingdom reality (revealed presently in the church) to its particular, multiethnic, and multinational features (the prophesied distinctions of Israel/Gentile Nations; Jews/Gentile peoples) is addressed differently by different theological systems and has a direct bearing on how the order and structure of the consummated kingdom is perceived. A variety of replacement (supersessionist or fulfillment) theologies (for example, various forms of covenantalism) envision the church replacing (by supersession or fulfillment) Israel in the consummation of the biblical story, thereby reducing the nationally diverse eschatological kingdom to a singular order of individuals united to Christ by the Holy Spirit. Traditional dispensationalism envisions a consummation in which the church, internally indistinct, exists separately alongside a distinct Israel, each with its own inheritance. Redemptive kingdom theology, or progressive dispensationalism, rejects both of these options and sees one consummate kingdom-order of multiple nations and polities whose different peoples are all directly united to Christ and equally indwelt by the Holy Spirit. The same consummate order can be viewed (1) in its ethnic and national pluralism (in which we find Israel in a state of particular promissory fulfillment) and (2) as a singular spiritual communion of individuals (Jews and Gentiles) without distinction in Christ. The church in this view neither replaces nor stands alongside Israel and Gentile nations but finds its fulfillment as the spiritual union that pervades the multinational, multi-peopled kingdom (in which we find national Israel together with Gentile peoples and nations), making them all together people(s) of God.

The scope of biblical eschatology may be widened further to include *cosmic (or territorial) eschatology*. This concerns what happens to the earth and the heavens in the eschatological consummation. The day of the Lord is described in Scripture in terms of cosmic travail that leads to a new creation, a new heavens and new earth (2 Pet 3:4–10, 13; Rev 21:1–2; cf. Isa 65:17–25; 66:22–23) as the dwelling place of God and Christ together with the redeemed. Some think that the present creation will be annihilated to make way for a new creation *ex nihilo*. However, it is more likely, and more in keeping with redemption generally, that the new creation is a renewal of the old brought about by the presence of God's glory (Rom 8:19–21). The present order does not merely continue as is into eternity but is glorified by the presence of God so that divine promises made in and about this present creation may be fulfilled. Included here are predictions concerning Jerusalem, Zion, glorified as the center of the new creation, and the territorial promises given to Israel, the everlasting fulfillment of which is a repeated theme in biblical prophecy.

A grasp of its holistic scope is necessary to appreciate a second challenge to understanding biblical eschatology: the phenomenon of *complexification* through progressive revelation and historical fulfillment.

Complexification is making a simple thing complex. This sometimes happens in the fulfillment of prophecy. Take for example the promise God gave to David in 2 Sam 7:12–13, which simply states, "I will raise up after you your descendant . . . and I will establish the throne of his kingdom forever." This simple promise to raise up David's descendant and establish his kingdom forever has been *complexified* in its fulfillment through the introduction of (1) a line of Davidic kings; (2) a suspension of Davidic rule for several centuries; (3) the incarnation of the Son of God as a later Davidic descendant, Jesus of Nazareth; (4) the crucifixion, death, burial, and resurrection of Jesus; (5) the ascension of Jesus into heaven for a period of two millennia and counting; and (6) inaugurated aspects of the promised kingdom manifested during the time of Jesus's ascension, with (7) the still remaining expectation that Christ's kingdom will be established at his coming—thus bringing to final fulfillment the original (simple) promise. The various "raisings up" that took place through this complexification were all seen in Scripture to be related to that original simple promise, but they progress toward a final and complete fulfillment through a complexity that was not specifically revealed in the original simple pronouncement.

Three areas of complexification much discussed in evangelical eschatology are *inaugurated eschatology, millennialism,* and *tribulationism.* Inaugurated eschatology and millennialism both have to do with a complexification of the eschatological kingdom into successive phases tied to the post-resurrection history of Christ. Tribulationism is a complexification of the rapture and the return of Christ to earth as distinguishable phases in a patterned, time-sequenced day of the Lord, or tribulation.

Inaugurated Eschatology

The term "inaugurated" is used here to mean that at least some realities belonging to the eschatological era of Christ's return have already been initiated, at least in part, during this time of Jesus's ascension into heaven. Complete fulfillment awaits his return. This is sometimes referred to as an *already/not-yet* fulfillment, a view popularized in evangelicalism by

G. E. Ladd but reflective of broader New Testament scholarship. Two views of inaugurated eschatology can be identified:

1. Wholly inaugurated eschatology would hold that all eschatological realities are presently inaugurated. This would seem to be contradicted by Paul's insistence that certain realities, namely the resurrection (other than Christ's resurrection) and the day of the Lord, have not yet begun (2 Tim 2:16–18; 2 Thess 2:1–3). The Second Coming clearly has not been *inaugurated* (Matt 24:23–28).

2. Partially inaugurated eschatology would hold that only features specifically identified in the New Testament as inaugurated are present today. These primarily have to do with spiritual, communal aspects of the eschatological kingdom. Accordingly, the New Testament speaks of the eschatological kingdom as both present (Col 1:13–14; Rev 1:6) and future (Matt 25:31–46; Acts 14:22; 2 Pet 1:11; Rev 5:10; 11:15; 19:15; 20:4–5; 22:3–5). This already/not-yet description is not a contradiction but a complexification of the coming of the kingdom into phases (at least, a present phase of partial, inaugural fulfillment and a future phase of final fulfillment) tied to the complexification of the coming of Christ (due to a previously unrevealed inter-advent ascension).

Millennialism

Millennialism concerns the complexification of the coming future eschatological kingdom to include a prefinal judgment phase. Crucial to millennialism is the interpretation of John's visions of a millennium (one thousand years) recorded in Revelation 20.

Amillennialism

This is the denial of any future millennial complexity. "Amillennial" literally means "no-millennial." As a label, it gained currency in twentieth-century fundamentalist and evangelical debates about millennialism. However, it promotes an eschatology that has been quite traditional in Christian thought at least since the third century. Contemporary amillennialism affirms the simple eschatological pattern of the Lord's coming in the day of judgment followed by eternal conditions, allowing only for the complexity of inaugurated eschatology.

The case for amillennialism rests typically on the following lines of argument:

1. The observance of a simple eschatological pattern in various passages of Scripture (see for example Dan 12:2; Matt 12:32; 25:31–46; Mark 10:30; Luke 18:30; 20:34–36; John 5:28–29; Acts 24:15; Eph 1:21; 2 Thess 1:6–10; 2 Pet 3:10–13).

2. Exegetical, hermeneutical proposals for Rev 20:1–6, in which (a) the verb "come to life" in Rev 20:4–5 alternates in meaning from spiritual regeneration to resurrection, (b) the descriptions of Satan in Rev 20:1–3 are construed as present inward personal realities, and (c) the narrative sequence of Revelation 19–20 in which a millennial kingdom follows the coming of Christ and precedes the final judgment is denied.

3. The justification of forms of spiritual interpretation (appealing to allegory or typology) for the reduction of political and cosmic eschatology to a personalist consummation, thereby excluding the possibility of millennialism.

The "post" in *postmillennialism* places the second coming "post," that is, "after" a future millennium. The millennium to come is envisioned as a Christian world order to be brought into existence through the missionary endeavors of the church and/or the civilizing impact of Christian nations prior to the coming of Christ. Although popular in the eighteenth and nineteenth centuries, postmillennialism declined as a viable option in evangelical theology after the collapse of Christendom in the early twentieth century. The attempt by some to revive it in the late twentieth century within the framework of inaugurated eschatology is difficult to distinguish from inaugurated amillennial eschatology.

The argument for postmillennialism is similar to that for amillennialism yet altered to make room for a future "millennial" society (not necessarily literal in its duration) on earth prior to the coming of Christ. For that, postmillennialism typically

1. Highlights Jesus's parables of a mystery form of the eschatological kingdom (Matthew 13).
2. Argues for a societal, political dimension and future aspect to the binding of Satan in Rev 20:1–3 while still discounting the narrative sequence of Revelation 19–20.
3. Adds a revivalistic and/or civilizational aspect to the first "come to life" in Rev 20:4 but otherwise accepts the exegesis of attributing radically different meanings to the two uses of the verb.

Premillennialism

Premillennialism argues that Christ will come before the millennium. The millennium is the thousand-year reign of Christ on earth after his return and prior to the final judgment. At the second coming of Christ, the dead in Christ will rise first and will reign with him over the nations of the earth for one thousand years, during which time the devil is "bound and imprisoned" so as to remove him temporarily from influence over the nations. After the consequences of his postmillennial release, Satan is then punished by being permanently cast into hell. The rest of the dead are then raised, the final judgment takes place, and the everlasting order of the new heavens and earth is brought into existence under the rule of God and his Messiah forever.

Early Christian premillennialism, or Chiliasm (from *chiliad*, "thousand"), can be found in the writings of second- and third-century writers such as Justin Martyr, Irenaeus, and Tertullian. However, due to the influence of Origen and Augustine, premillennialism waned. It was revived in the seventeenth century, became popular again in the nineteenth and twentieth centuries, and is widely represented in evangelical theology today.

Distinctions are sometimes made between historicist, historical, dispensational, and charismatic renewal premillennialism. These mostly have to do with differing perspectives on tribulationism, particularly the relation of the church to the rapture and the tribulation.

The case for premillennialism is based essentially on the following:

1. Scripture contains prophecies of a messianic reign on earth (Isa 9:6–7; 11:1–10; Luke 1:32–33).

2. The reign is expected to follow the Messiah's coming in glory (Dan 7:13–14; Matt 25:31–46; Rev 5:10).

3. The reign is sometimes described with mortal features and punitive measures, which could only be prior to the final judgment (Isa 11:1–10; 65:17–23; Zech 14:16–20).

4. Revelation 19–20 explicitly reveals a kingdom to be set up on earth for one thousand years (a millennium) after the second coming of Christ between two stages of resurrection prior to the final judgment (thus under mortal conditions).

5. The binding and imprisonment of Satan in Rev 20:2–3 and the movement of the narrative plot to the effects of his release and subsequent punishment in Rev 20:7–10 is explained in the text in terms of his future influence over nations and societies, not the present personal struggles of individuals.

6. Two stages of resurrection involving (1) a selected group of the dead and (2) all the rest of the dead mark the beginning and end of the millennial kingdom, necessarily making that kingdom a future period of time associated with the coming of Christ (the one who raises the dead at his coming) and prior to the final judgment (which can only take place after all the dead are raised).

   a. The use of the same word (*ezesan*, "came to life") for both groups of people in Rev 20:4–5 together with the sense of reversal signaled by "until" necessarily attributes the same experience to both groups. Both "came to life" but at different times. This cannot be *spiritual life* lest the passage be promoting universalism.

   b. Revelation 20:5b–6 interprets "came to life" (Rev 20:4–5a) with the word *anastasis*, which consistently means bodily resurrection. *Anastasis* is never used in Scripture to refer to regeneration.

Tribulationism

This concerns the complexification of the patterned structure and duration of the tribulation, or day of the Lord, and its relation to the rapture and the return of Christ to earth. The structure of the tribulation draws from the patterns of several day of the Lord prophecies (Jer 30:7), the "time of the end" patterns in Daniel 7–12, the Olivet Discourse of Jesus as well as some of his parables, the day of the Lord pattern relayed by Paul in 1–2 Thessalonians, and the patterned sequence and chronology given in the visions of the book of Revelation. The *rapture* refers to the "snatching up" of living believers together with resurrected saints to meet Christ in the air at the time of his coming (1 Thess 4:15–17), which involves the transformation of the living into the immortal glory of the resurrected (1 Cor 15:51–56; cf. 2 Cor 5:4–5; Phil 3:20–21; 1 John 3:2). Tribulationism debates not the fact of the rapture but its timing in the tribulation pattern.

There are three distinguishable views on the patterned structure and duration of the tribulation:

1. The church-age or historicist view in which the tribulation is identified with the troubles experienced by the church throughout the time of Christ's ascension. Advocates of this view appeal to Jesus's words in John 16:33 (ESV): "In the world, you will have tribulation," as well as descriptions in the Olivet Discourse that seem typical of historical realities. Historicism mostly downplays the sequential pattern or chronology of the tribulation emphasized in futurism.

2. The futurist view sees the tribulation as a future time of world trouble distinguishable from the general troubles of the church age. The future tribulation is the eschatological trouble referenced in Dan 12:1 and Matt 24:21 (ESV): "Then there will be great tribulation, such as has not been from the beginning of the world until now; no, and never will be." Futurism sees the tribulation as a structured pattern and chronology, especially the seven-year pattern of Dan 9:27, which is coordinated with the three-and-a-half-year patterns elsewhere in that book and in the book of Revelation.

3. Partially historicist, partially futurist: Tribulation prophecies refer to both the troubles of the church in the present age (a historicist view) and a yet future tribulation associated with the coming of Christ (a futurist view, though often without the seven-year chronology typical of futurism).

Tribulational Positions on the Relationship of the Rapture to the Return of Christ

Pretribulationism

Pretribulationism holds to a futurist view of the tribulation (typically seven years in duration) and is the belief that the rapture will precede or begin the tribulation that will in turn be concluded by the return of Christ to earth. Some pretribulationists have spoken of the rapture and the return to earth as different comings of Christ, but it is better to consider them as beginning and end points in *a complex Second Coming event* structured by the tribulation, the whole of which is best seen as the day of the Lord. Futurism sees the signs of Christ's return as tribulation elements, and since the Rapture precedes the tribulation, the rapture is then considered an imminent eschatological event (that is, not preceded by any signs of Christ's return). Pretribulationism finds its support in the relationship of the rapture to the beginning of the day of the Lord in 1 Thess 4:13–5:11 (cf. 1 Thess 1:10) and is inferred from passages such as Rev 3:10. Pretribulationism was popularized by traditional dispensationalism, which further supports the view by its theological distinction of Israel and the church as exclusive people groups, the latter of which must be excluded from the tribulation by definition (an argument not made by progressive dispensational pretribulationism). Finally, pretribulationists argue that pretribulationism is the most coherent view of the complex eschatology associated with the Lord's coming.

Midtribulationism

This view, which is not very popular today, says that the rapture will take place in the middle of a futurist tribulation, which will then be concluded by the return of Christ to earth. Some midtribulationists viewed the ascension of the two witnesses of Rev 11:11–12, resurrected after three and a half days, as a prophecy for a midtribulational rapture (after three and a half years). Since the rapture, in this view, is preceded by a portion of the tribulation pattern, it is not considered an imminent event.

Pre-Wrath Rapture Tribulationism

This type of tribulationism depends on a successful distinction between the tribulation and the day of the Lord, with the latter being a limited period of divine wrath and the former being mostly a time of human wrath. The rapture is expected to occur before the day of the Lord (in accordance with 1 Thess 1:10; 4:13–5:11) but in the latter part of the tribulation (supposedly in accordance with 2 Thess 2:1–12). Again, the rapture is not an imminent event in this view because a portion of the tribulational pattern precedes it.

Posttribulationism

This is the view that the rapture will occur together with the return of Christ to the earth viewed as a more or less singular Second Coming event at the end of the tribulation. Posttribulationists stress the use of the same *coming* vocabulary in rapture and return texts (*parousia, epiphania, apocalupsis*) and (contra the theological argument of traditional dispensationalism) point to Jesus's expectation that the church will experience some of the elements of the tribulation. The rapture is typically characterized by posttribulationists as a welcoming delegation for the returning Christ, whereas pretribulationists stress the element of rescue (1 Thess 1:10). Posttribulationists differ on their conception of the tribulation ranging from historicist to futurist views. Futurist posttribulationists would not see the rapture as imminent; historicist postribulationists, however, would see the rapture/return as essentially imminent since they view the tribulation as mostly past. The label "historical premillennialism," which was used by George Ladd to designate a futurist position distinct from dispensational pretribulationism, is used today by some who take a partially historicist, partially futurist view.[1]

---

[1] See Douglas Moo, "A Case for the Posttribulation Rapture" in *Three Views on the Rapture: Pretribulation, Prewrath, or Posttribulation*, ed. Alan Hultberg (Grand Rapids: Zondervan Academic, 2018) and Craig Blomberg, "Why I am a Historic Premillennialist," *Criswell Theological Review* 11, no. 1 (Fall 2013): 71–87.

Final Comments on Personal Eschatology

Physical death. In Scripture, physical death is described as the departure of one's soul or spirit from one's body (see for example Gen 35:18–19; 37:35). The body decays and the soul or spirit endures apart from the body in what theologians call the intermediate state of the dead (intermediate between physical [mortal] life and resurrection [immortal] life).

Intermediate state of the dead. Against various historical and modern secularist views of annihilation (the cessation of personal existence), Scripture teaches the continued existence of the dead in a place apart from life on earth.

Heaven. The New Testament teaches that when believers die, their souls go to be with Christ in paradise (Acts 7:55, 59; Phil 1:23; 2 Cor 5:1–9; Rev 6:9–11). When Christ appears, we will appear with him in glory (Colossians 3).

Sheol/Hades. Prior to Christ's ascension into heaven, the Old Testament typically placed both the righteous and unrighteous dead in *Sheol* (Hebrew), translated into Greek as *Hades* (Gen 37:35; Job 14:13; Pss 9:17; 139:8; Isa 14:9–10; Ezek 32:17–32). The righteous maintained the hope of deliverance from Sheol (Pss 16:10; 49:15; 86:13) and anticipated the presence of God with them there (Pss 23:4; 139:8). However, Scripture speaks of the anger of God on the unrighteous in Sheol (Amos 9:2; Job 14:13; Deut 32:22). The New Testament continues to speak of the unrighteous in Hades under punishment from God (2 Pet 2:9; see Luke 16:19–31). It is from Hades that they come before God at the final judgment (Rev 20:13).

The intermediate state a conscious state? Doctrines of soul sleep deny the consciousness of the dead without fully denying their existence (annihilation). They often cite the biblical use of the word "sleep" to describe the dead (1 Thess 4:13–14). However, this is best understood as a metaphor rather than a literal description. Biblical descriptions of the dead give clear evidence of consciousness (see especially Luke 16:19–31; Rev 6:9–11). Old Testament wisdom passages describing the dead as inactive are best understood in contrast to life on earth (Eccl 9:4–6, 10; Pss 115:17; 88:12), not as absolute lack of consciousness (cf. Isa 14:9–10; Ezek 32:17–32).

The intermediate state an embodied state? Some of the descriptions of the dead are bodily (see 1 Sam 28:13–19; Matt 17:3; Luke 16:19–31), which has led to speculations about an intermediate body. However, one needs to note that whatever this embodiedness is, it is not the same as resurrection embodiedness. Only the latter is true deliverance from physical death.

Resurrection of the dead. Resurrection is the reversal and removal of physical death by the restoration of embodiment to human souls. While there are some examples of resurrection to mortal life (1 Kgs 17:17–24; 2 Kgs 4:18–37; Matt 9:18–26; Luke 7:11–17; 8:49–56; John 11:14, 38–44), in Christ is revealed resurrection to immortality (not capable of physical death; 2 Tim 1:10; Heb 7:16, 25). The Scripture teaches a future resurrection of all the dead by Christ, though this comes in stages with the resurrection of the just preceding the resurrection of the unjust (separated by a millennium in John's vision in Revelation 20). The former is called the "better resurrection" (Heb 11:35), and its embodiment with glory and power is described in 1 Corinthians 15. It accords with the renewal of creation in the glory of God, the mode of everlasting life for the saved (Rom 8:19–23). The resurrection of the unjust without glory is to "eternal contempt" (Dan 12:2). While no longer capable of physical death, they experience the "second death" (Rev 20:14–15), which is separation from the blessedness of new creation life.

Final judgment. Scripture is clear that all must face judgment (Heb 9:27; Rom 14:10–12) at the coming of Christ, but that judgment is not the same for the saved as for the unsaved.

The judgment seat of Christ refers to a judgment of believers at the coming of Christ. The designation is used by Paul in 2 Cor 5:10 (cf. Rom 14:10–12, the judgment seat of God), where he indicates that it applies to all believers and that it concerns their works. First Corinthians 3:13–15 also addresses this judgment where he makes clear that it is not a matter of salvation but of reward. It takes place on the day of the Lord (1 Cor 3:13; cf. 1 Pet 4:7, 17; Jas 5:8–9), although it is difficult to be more precise than that. (Some argue that it occurs at the time of the rapture.)

The Great White Throne judgment is the descriptive phrase given to the final judgment of the unsaved. The designation appears in Rev 20:11–15, where all the unsaved dead (those not part of the "first resurrection"; Rev 20:6) are judged according to their works and absence from the "book of life." Their punishment is confinement to hell. Scripture is clear that believers do not face this judgment, having already been justified by faith in Christ (Rom 5:1; 8:1; John 5:24), although they do stand before the judgment seat of Christ for the determination of reward (see above).

Final Destiny—Everlasting Death / Everlasting Life

Everlasting death in hell. The Bible speaks of being cast into hell as the second death. In this case, death is not a separation of body and soul but a separation of resurrected persons from God's everlasting and blessed new creation, the place of everlasting life.

Hell is described in Scripture by a group of terms. The word *Gehenna* (from *gehinnom*, the valley lying to the south of Jerusalem, a site of refuse, desecration, and abomination in OT times) was used by Jesus, interchangeably with the word "fire," the phrase "lake of fire," or even "fiery furnace" to refer to the final punishment (Matt 5:29–30; 10:28; 13:40–42; 18:9; Mark 9:43–48; Luke 12:4–5). In the book of Revelation, hell is described as the "fire" or "lake of fire" (Rev 14:10–11; 19:20; 20:10, 15). Other descriptions of hell include *eternal destruction* and exclusion *from the presence of the Lord* (2 Thess 1:9), *the outer darkness* where there is *weeping and gnashing of teeth* (Matt 8:12; 22:13; 25:30), *eternal punishment* (Matt 25:46), and *wrath* (John 3:36; Rom 2:3–9).

In contrast to annihilationist or universalist views, Scripture teaches that hell is a place of eternal, conscious suffering (Matt 8:12; 22:13; 25:30, 46; Rev 14:10–11; 20:10). Furthermore, hell is punitive not remedial. Nevertheless, there are degrees of punishment in hell (Mark 12:40; Luke 12:47–48; Rom 2:6; Rev 20:12).

Everlasting life. Whereas heaven, apart from the earth, is the blessed habitation of the dead in Christ, the setting of everlasting life is in the new creation where heaven "comes down" to extend the unfading light of God's glory to a renewed earth (Rev 21:2–3, 22–23; 22:3–5; cf. Isa 60:1–3) where righteousness dwells (2 Pet 3:13). God abides in and with all the redeemed personally but also among them in a New Jerusalem, which secures the place of redeemed Israel and grants undiminished access to the nations of the resurrected who serve him and glorify him forever (Dan 7:14; Rev 21:2–3, 23–26; 22:5). The "former things" of "death, mourning, crying, and pain" will have passed away and be forgotten (Isa 25:7–9; 65:17–19; Rev 21:1–4). The best is yet to come (2 Cor 4:17–18)!

For Additional Study

Archer, Gleason, et al. *The Rapture: Pre-, Mid-, or Post-tribulational?* Grand Rapids: Zondervan, 1984.

Bingham, D. Jeffrey, and Glenn R. Kreider, ed. *Eschatology: Biblical, Historical, and Practical Approaches.* Grand Rapids: Kregel, 2016.

Blaising, Craig A. "A Theology of Israel and the Church," in *Israel, the Church, and the Middle East Conflict.* Edited by Darrell L. Bock and Mitch Glaser. Grand Rapids: Kregel, 2018.

————. "The Day of the Lord." *Bibliotheca Sacra* 169 (2012): 3–19, 131–42, 259–70, 387–401.

————, and Darrell L. Bock. *Progressive Dispensationalism.* Grand Rapids: Baker, 1993.

Bock, Darrell, ed. *Three Views on the Millennium and Beyond.* Grand Rapids: Zondervan, 1999.

Clouse, Robert G. *The Meaning of the Millennium: Four Views.* Downers Grove: IVP, 1980.

Crockett, William, ed. *Four Views on Hell.* Grand Rapids: Zondervan, 1992.

Hultberg, Alan, ed. *Three Views on the Rapture: Pretribulationism, Prewrath, or Posttribulationism.* Grand Rapids: Zondervan, 2010.

Ladd, George E. *The Prescence of the Future.* Grand Rapids: Eerdmans, 1974.

Wellum, Stephen J., and Brent E. Parker, eds. *Progressive Covenantalism: Charting a Course between Dispensational and Covenantal Theologies.* Nashville: B&H, 2016.

Also see these articles: God's Covenants, Glorification, Church

PART V

THEOLOGY AND THE CHRISTIAN LIFE

33

The Gospel

ROBERT B. SLOAN

This article will look at the biblical notion of the gospel. We will begin our study by looking closely at the main Greek word for "good news," *euangelion,* to see where it occurs, its immediate context, and what it means in those given contexts. But after that, we will also have to look broadly at the whole of Scripture because the idea of good news implies a context, especially a backstory, and therefore an appreciation for the long story of the Bible—the narrative of paradise, disaster, despair, and the promise of restoration—in which the announcement of good news makes sense.

First Corinthians 15:1–8 is a good place to start for the word "gospel." Paul refers to the gospel as the central message that he preached, the one in which the Corinthians stand and by which they are saved as they continue to faithfully believe. Paul then provides a narrative definition of it using four "that" clauses, at least two of which have extensive subpoints.

First, he refers to the death of the Messiah—a surprising assertion itself since, until the coming of Jesus, the Messiah's premature death was not anticipated. This unexpected demise is "for our sins" and "according to the Scriptures" (1 Cor 15:3). To be sure, both the death of the Messiah and its significance as occurring "for our sins" were dug out of ancient Scripture, but it was no doubt the teaching of Jesus, his actions and words, and his post-resurrection explanations that led the disciples to search the Scriptures more intently after he was raised and reevaluate them (see Luke 24:25–27, 44–45).

The teaching of Jesus and the disciples' Spirit-led reflections included not least the stone passages (Isa 8:14; 28:16; Ps 118:22; cf. Matt 21:42; Rom 9:32–33; 1 Pet 2:6–8), where the chief cornerstone was rejected, though God's kingdom nonetheless prevailed (Dan 2:34, 44–45; cf. Matt 21:44), but also the servant song of Isa 52:13–53:12, where a singular individual, as a representative of Israel, perhaps Israel's king, is called a "man of sorrows" (Isa 53:3). The servant is disfigured, rejected, scourged, chastened, afflicted, and otherwise suffers and dies on behalf of the "many" (Isa 53:11; see Mark 14:24; Rom 4:25; 1 Pet 2:21–24).

Second, the Messiah (Jesus) who died did not swoon on the cross. He truly died as evidenced by his burial, which both confirmed his death and established the location for the corpse and the subsequent resurrection.

Third, Israel's hopes for a day of resurrection were accomplished both surprisingly and microcosmically in the singular person of the Messiah. His resurrection was in keeping with the Scriptures, but here it is more likely a general reference to the long story of Scripture instead of certain specific texts. That is, the resurrection of the Messiah fulfills the scriptural promises of the final victory of God and his people. Except for Dan 12:1–3 and an allusion in Isa 25:7–8 to a future swallowing up of death for all time (a promise that Paul definitively points to as a scriptural support for the resurrection of the dead at the return of Jesus, 1 Cor 15:54), references to the resurrection of the dead are not specifically detailed in the Old Testament. However, there are many references to the suffering of God's people—including the griefs associated with death and Sheol (many examples in the Psalms: cf. 16:10–11; 18:5–6; 49:14–15; 86:13; 88:3–13; 89:46–52; 116:3–11; 139:8), which will be overcome by the covenant mercies of God. These promises of restoration are retained in the New Testament and also sharpened to refer to the resurrection of the dead as initiated by the Messiah.

The resurrection of Jesus occurred as a matter of historical fact on the third day, counting inclusively from the day of his death. That once again confirmed the reality of his death but also memorialized—because of its simultaneously shocking and joyous nature—the specific day of death's reversal via the new creation power of God. God thereby not only vindicated Jesus and his intentional laying down of his life by taking up a Roman cross but also confirmed Jesus's understanding of his mission from the Father.

Fourth, the repeated phrase "that he appeared to" in reference to the numerous resurrection witnesses who saw Jesus on multiple occasions serves to verify the truth of his bodily resurrection.

The two central moments for defining the gospel, moments that are most commonly referred to in other New Testament texts, are the death and resurrection of Jesus, clauses one and three. Clause two's reference to his burial confirms the Messiah's death, and clause four's listing of witnesses confirms the resurrection.

There are many other references to the early Christian story of the gospel, especially in Acts and the Epistles, which typically do not refer in their immediate context to the cross or the resurrection, though these no doubt take for granted the message of the cross and resurrection as presented in 1 Cor 15:1–8. There are also many references to the cross and resurrection that do not have the word "gospel" in their immediate context. Note, for example, the explanation of the significance of baptism in Rom 6:1–11, which points to the central events of the death, burial, and resurrection of Christ, without the use of the word "gospel" (see also Col 2:11–12).

There are also other highly developed treatments of the death of Jesus and its significance that lack in the immediate context a verbal reference to the gospel: for example, Rom 3:21–26. But the larger context makes clear that Paul understands his narrower arguments in Romans to come under the broad heading of "the gospel of God," for which he was set apart (1:1; see also 1:9, 15, 16; 2:16). Put another way, the theological arguments that are developed in Romans regarding the faithfulness of God as disclosed in Jesus, such as the justifying nature of his death and resurrection, and his loving power over sin, death, and the Law, are introduced in 1:1–4 as the "good news of God." It was prophetically promised in the Scriptures and culminates in Jesus, who by physical descent is a son of David and by virtue of the resurrecting power of the Spirit is the enthroned Son of God—that is, Jesus, Messiah, our Lord.

Similarly, there is a lengthy development of the meaning of "the word of the cross" in 1 Cor 1:18–25, which includes only a single reference to the gospel in 1 Cor 1:17, and there are multiple references in the broader context (1 Cor 2:1–5) to Paul's apostolic preaching, but likewise no use of the word "gospel." These variations of expression simply reflect the commonly understood meaning and use of the word "gospel" and its content and are a function of the situational arguments and stylistic features of a given document.

The word "gospel" also has other meanings, related but different, including an important usage outside the New Testament, namely, where the term refers to a literary genre, something akin to a life of Jesus. Our four canonical Gospels are often referred to simply as the Gospels, and when that happens, the term "gospel" is being used in reference to a literary genre.

But that use is not found in the New Testament, and it is important to note that even the titles of the Gospels do not point to four gospels but to a single gospel. The first book of the New Testament is called The Gospel According to Matthew. The second, The Gospel According to Mark. And so on for all four, and thus the phrase *according to* is very important. Each title refers to *the* gospel, a single gospel as told *according to* four historically reliable witnesses. The titles reflect the early Christian conviction that there is but one gospel, and it is, even when told by different witnesses, the one message about Jesus as reflected particularly in those great turning-point moments related to the cross and the resurrection, moments that draw the greatest amount of emphasis in the four narratives we call "Gospels."

This consideration of the titles of the Gospels, however, brings to mind one other important point, specifically that the word "gospel" as it occurs in the four Gospels is not used in the technical sense that we see used in Acts or the Epistles: that is, in reference to the saving death and resurrection of Jesus.

The word "gospel" is used within the four Gospels to refer to "the gospel of the kingdom" or "the gospel of God" or "the gospel of the kingdom of God" (see Matt 4:23; 9:35; 11:5; 24:14; Mark 1:14; Luke 4:18). As such, it's likely an echo of the "good news" of Isa 40:9 or 52:7, where the reference is to the long-awaited news that Yahweh is coming soon and will assert his royal power over all the earth, and especially so in his restoration of his people from exile.

And even without the word "gospel," the references in the Gospels to John and Jesus preaching the coming kingdom of God (usually "the kingdom of heaven" in Matthew) echo the same long-standing hope of Yahweh's return to rescue Israel and thus assert his kingship over all the earth. That hope also informs the climactic future envisioned in the long story of Scripture, to which we now turn.

It is this longer story of Scripture that provides the necessary context for understanding what the gospel is and means in the New Testament. The required context is nothing less than the whole biblical account of a good creation, spoiled by the fall, and a plan of redemption that is promised to Abraham, preserved in the morally checkered history of Israel and eventually inaugurated with the coming of Jesus. To be sure, this good news is specifically enacted and in greater detail worked out by the surprising death and resurrection of Jesus in keeping with the Scriptures. But the gospel of God in the ministry and preaching of Jesus, as well as in this latter, technical sense in reference especially to his death and resurrection, has a long backstory full of hope, failure, and surprising twists, and behind it all the merciful faithfulness of the one true creator God who is acting to rescue his world.

The story of the gospel begins in Genesis 1 when God blesses the man and the woman, made in his image, with stewardship over the entire creation. They are his agents to extend the rule of God in the garden to all the earth. They are kings and priests who enjoy the presence of God and are commissioned to represent his ways to all the world and promote the praise of God back to him.

But their stewardship over the creation is spoiled by their rebellion. In Genesis 3, after they disobey the commandment and fail to be the stewards and agents they've been commissioned to be, they are exiled from God's presence, and a curse is placed on them and the rest of creation. Things then go from bad to worse in the narrative of Genesis. The behavior of the people produces as judgment a flood that, except for the grace of God, would have destroyed the whole earth (Genesis 6–10). Then God, by scattering the nations, thwarts an arrogant attempt to build a tower that could reach into the heavens (Genesis 11). Finally, there emerges a figure constituting hope and rescue, Abraham, to whom God makes promises of restoration.

This plan of rescue is then set in motion when Abraham (Genesis 12–13, 15, 17) is promised a son from whom a nation would come and that, further, all the earth would be blessed through this offspring, making Abraham the father of many nations. The promises were repeated to Abraham and later extended to his son Isaac, and to Isaac's son Jacob, and from there to Israel at Mount Sinai and reiterated prior to their entry into the Promised Land.

But Israel came under the stipulated curse of the very covenant that they took upon themselves (see Deuteronomy 27–29). Failing to be obedient to the Lord alone, they worshipped idols and were ultimately sent into exile, as God had, in his righteousness, ordained (cf. Dan 9:1–19).

Nonetheless, the Lord also promised, through many Old Testament witnesses, that he would not destroy his people, that he would be faithful to the covenant promises he made to Abraham and restore a remnant, and that they would return from exile. The Lord would write his law upon their hearts, establish a new covenant with them, rebuild the temple, and dwell forever in their midst. Moreover, through a son of the great king David, they would conquer their enemies, and God would be king over all the earth. The creation would then spring to life, and the curse would be lifted, including the curse of death (cf. Deut 30:1–6; Isa 11; 25:6–9; 40:1–11; 61:1–11; Jer 31:31–34; 33:14–18; Ezek 36:22–28; Mal 3:1).

The New Testament begins with various announcements of the good news. When John appeared on the scene, followed by Jesus, and they preached to a beleaguered Israel that the kingdom of God was at hand, invoking the words of the prophets, the people were stirred, even though these hopes had been deferred for many centuries. The miracles of Jesus and his startling new teaching reinforced his announcement of the coming reign of God. But controversy about the miracle-working prophet—whom some said to be the Messiah, but others denied—quickly emerged, and the story of Jesus took a violent turn. The political leaders of Israel and the ruling authority of Rome, though usually at odds, worked together in the case of the controversial figure, and he was crucified.

Then, likewise unexpected by all, on the third day after his death and continuing for a period of forty days, Jesus was seen alive again. Not only was he bodily raised, but he appeared in a new kind of physical body, one that could eat but also appear and vanish at will, seemingly unbound by physical barriers or geographic place. The good news spread rapidly that he was alive. The resurrection was God's vindication of Jesus and a complete reversal of the earlier disastrous rejection of the Messiah. It was soon realized that the death of Jesus, though morally abhorrent, was not providentially haphazard. It was a central feature of the plan of God. Indeed, Paul later claimed that if the rulers of this age had plumbed the depths of God's hidden wisdom, they would not have crucified the Lord of glory (1 Cor 2:6–8).

His death had in retrospect a massive significance of its own. Though the pain and humiliation of it could never be forgotten, it fulfilled the saving purposes of God. It was soon proclaimed, in keeping with Jesus's own interpretation of his death as set forth at the Last Supper, as a redemptive, sin-forgiving, new-covenant-establishing, sacrificial, substitutionary death. It removed the curse of God's judgment from Israel and the world since Messiah, the Son of God, had acted on behalf of his people.

The long story of restoration was thus enacted in a microcosm by God's Son, the singular representative of Israel, the son of David, who was also the promise-fulfilling seed of Abraham. Through his obedience to the Father, his death also completed the curse of corruption brought on by sin, and thus he restored his people. By his resurrection, he was vindicated by his heavenly Father, became the firstborn of those who rise from the dead, rebuilt the temple of God, and inaugurated the new creation. In Jesus, the resurrection had begun (1 Cor 15:21), and at his ascending accession to the right hand of God—his coronation as king—he defeated the monstrous powers of darkness that attacked him just as they wreak havoc in this world, and thus he subjugated the spiritual forces of wickedness (cf. Acts 2:24; 1 Cor 15:24–26; Eph 1:19–22; 6:12; Phil 2:9–11; Col 1:12–20; 2:15; 1 Pet 3:21–22; Rev 12:5–9).

And this story of Jesus, of his death, resurrection, and exaltation above the powers to the right hand of the Father, is the message of good news now preached to the nations. In specific reference to Jesus, this is the good news that highlights the longer story of the Bible, the gospel of God: that the promises to Abraham have been fulfilled and that with the coming of Jesus, God has inaugurated the new creation, the restoration of heaven and earth. Already the blind receive their sight, the lame walk, the deaf hear, and the poor have the good news preached to them (Luke 7:22), for the Spirit of God has now been poured out on all God's people (Acts 2:16–21, 33).

But the very end is not yet. Though its restoration has begun, the creation continues to groan during this age of the church. In spite of the affirming witness of the Spirit that we are the children of God, empowered to know and do the will of God, even we who have the seal and firstfruits of the Spirit, who experience already the beginning of the new creation life, nonetheless groan and suffer affliction and distress, persecution, plague, poverty, danger, and war (Rom 8:18–35).

The end has begun, but the fulfillment of this newly inaugurated age of restoration will be accomplished only when Christ returns, when Death the final enemy is defeated and the rest of the dead are raised, evil is judged, the curse on the creation is lifted, and all is restored (Rom 8:20–23; 1 Cor 15:50–58; Phil 3:20–21).

All of that is good news, and even now in our sufferings we can rejoice (Rom 5:1–5) because the long-awaited plan of rescue has begun through the death, resurrection, and enthronement of Jesus our Lord, and we, with courage, hope, and perseverance, await its completion.

For Additional Study

Conyers, A. J. *The Eclipse of Heaven.* Downers Grove: IVP, 1997.

Greear, J. D. *Gospel: Recovering the Power that Made Christianity Revolutionary.* Nashville: B&H, 2011.

Lewis, C. S. *Mere Christianity.* New York: MacMillan, 1955.

Packer, J. I., and Thomas C. Oden. *One Faith.* Downers Grove: IVP, 2004.

Stott, John R. W. *The Cross of Christ.* Downers Grove: IVP, 1986.

Also see these articles: Work of Christ, Justification, Evangelism and Missions, Preaching

34

Church Membership

Jonathan Leeman

C hurch membership is a topic that draws mixed reviews among Christians. Some claim it is biblical, while others deny it. Some say it is essential to evangelism and growth, while others view it as exclusivist. According to the "State of the Church 2020" Barna study, 71 percent of "practicing Christians" who attend church at least once a month have joined their church, meaning almost 30 percent of attenders do not think it is worthwhile. When pollsters do not measure for attendance, but only for whether one identifies as an evangelical Christian, that percentage drops dramatically. This raises important questions. What should Christians make of church membership? Is membership biblical? Is it important? Why join a church?

Is Church Membership in the Bible?

If given only thirty seconds on an elevator to answer the question above, one could point to biblical passages on church discipline. For instance, Paul writes to the church in Corinth, "Shouldn't you be filled with grief and *remove* from your congregation the one who did this?" (1 Cor 5:2, emphasis added). Also, "For what business is it of mine to judge *outsiders*? Don't you judge those who are *inside*? God judges *outsiders*. *Remove* the evil person from among you" (1 Cor 5:12–13, emphasis added; see also Matt 18:17; Titus 3:10). A church cannot "remove" a person from the "inside" unless there is an inside from which one can be removed.

One could also point to any number of passages in the book of Acts that describe people being added to a church or gathering as a church:

- "So those who accepted [Peter's] message were baptized, and that day about three thousand people were added to them" (Acts 2:41).
- "Then great fear came on the whole church . . . They were all together in Solomon's Colonnade. No one else dared to join them, but the people spoke well of them" (Acts 5:11, 12b-13).
- "The Twelve summoned the whole company of the disciples" (Acts 6:2).

Who is the "them" in Acts 2? It is the church in Jerusalem, who gathered in Solomon's Portico and could be summoned by the twelve apostles. Church leaders may not have had a printed roll, but they knew who "they" were. They could number them, which means they could name them.

The rest of the New Testament identifies specific, concrete groups of people as a church. John writes to "the church in Ephesus" and "the church in Smyrna" and "the church in Pergamum" (Rev 2:1, 8, 12). The members of the church in Ephesus were not the members of the church in Smyrna, while the members of the church in Smyrna were not the members in Pergamum, and so forth. Paul, likewise, writes the "church of God in Corinth" and offers them instructions for when "you are assembled" or tells them "to wait for one another" when taking the Lord's Supper (1 Cor 1:2; 5:4; 11:33 ESV). Again, they knew who "they" were. So it is with every named church in the New Testament.

Are We Looking for the Right Thing?

Sometimes Christians observe that the Bible says nothing about membership packets, classes, or interviews, thus concluding membership must not be biblical. They might even suggest such "exclusivist" structures hinder the Great Commission.

This charge confuses biblical *elements* with cultural *forms*—the thing with the form of a thing. By analogy, a kitchen must have a stove to be a kitchen, but whether a gas, electric, or wood-burning stove works best will vary from place to place. Likewise, an underground house church in a Muslim nation that outlaws Christianity will have members, but it might not adopt many forms common in Western cities. For security concerns it might not even list the names of members. Yet so long as the members of this house church have self-consciously committed themselves to one another in a manner described in the next section, they share in the biblical element with Western churches.

That said, the skeptic's charge "but membership is not in the Bible" might have merit, depending on what one means by membership. If a church adopts business strategies and treats members like religious consumers, the criticism makes sense. Membership will approximate a shopper club's form of membership, or even a gas station rewards program. Join them and fill your spiritual tank every Sunday! This is not biblical church membership, and consumeristic programs will indeed work against the Great Commission in the long run, even as they grow their customer base in the short run.

Admittedly, the word "membership," as it is commonly used in twenty-first-century English, possesses a programmatic and voluntaristic resonance. Yet understanding the nature of church membership in the New Testament means appealing to the host of images that the biblical authors use to describe the church, such as family, body, temple, or flock. Membership will look and feel like family membership, as when Paul tells Timothy to treat older men and women as fathers and mothers and younger men and women as brothers and sisters (1 Tim 5:1–2). It will look and feel like membership in a body, with some playing the part of a hand, others an arm, other an eye, others an ear, and all parts mutually dependent (1 Cor 12:12–26). It will look and feel like living stones together comprising a temple (1 Pet 2:5). And so forth.

In short, critics who claim church membership is not in the Bible might be right, but they may be looking for the wrong thing. How then should we understand the essence of this biblical element?

What Is Church Membership?

Throughout Scripture, God marks off a people for himself by drawing a line between his people and the rest of humanity. The garden of Eden has an inside and an outside, as does Noah's ark, as do the people of God in the wilderness, as do the people of Israel in the land. The Lord even uses plagues to distinguish the people of Israel from the Egyptians, as with the plague of flies and hail (Exod 8:22–23; 9:26). He wants the identity of his people distinct and known.

God also identifies himself with a people: "I will take you as my people, and I will be your God" (Exod 6:7)—so they might in turn display his glory before all the earth, which they do by obeying his law and being conformed to his image (e.g., Deut 4:6–8; Ezek 36:22–23; Eph 3:10). More than flies or hail, he identifies himself with his Old Testament people through the covenantal signs of circumcision and Sabbath-keeping, and eventually their presence in the land. These signs and borders make God's people "visible" or public. They enable the nations to see Israel and their life together and so to know what God himself is like.

God further identifies Israel as his own by granting them a kind of his presence. He walks with Adam and Eve in the garden. And he dwells specially in Israel's tabernacle and temple. Since God dwells and rules in heaven (e.g., Ps 2:4), the Bible eventually treats these places where God dwells on earth as points of intersection and overlap between heaven and earth, as later seen in Matthew's Gospel momentarily (Matt 17:1–13) or as when the author of Hebrews says Israel's tabernacle offered "a copy and shadow of the heavenly things" (Heb 8:5).

All this, at least, was the design. A key lesson of the Old Testament is that all these outward signs and shadows and laws do not make a people righteous. Through his prophets, therefore, God promises a new covenant. It would work internally and invisibly through the forgiveness of sin and the regeneration of the heart (Isaiah 53; Jer 31:31–34; Ezek 36:24–27). And this invisible and internal work would occur through the preaching of God's Word and the power of God's Spirit (Isa 55:3–11; Ezek 37:1–14; cf. Rom 10:9–17).

Yet the promise of a new covenant leaves a crucial question unanswered: How will this invisibly forgiven and regenerated people become visible or public—both to each other and the nations? How does a kingdom patrol its borders when there are no borders? And who has the authority to do so?

Against this Old Testament backdrop, Jesus shows up in Matthew's Gospel promising to establish his heavenly kingdom on earth once again, and to do this he will build his church (Matt 16:18). Along these lines, New Testament church membership is at least three things:

1. Church membership is an earthly declaration of heavenly citizenship in Christ's kingdom

Matthew's Gospel presents a fascinating dynamic between heaven and earth. The Gospel opens with Jesus promising the kingdom of heaven is at hand (Matt 4:17). He explains the poor in spirit will inherit the kingdom of heaven (5:3). They will seek the Father's glory in heaven through their good deeds (5:16). They will pray for earth to become like heaven (6:10). They will store up treasure in heaven (6:19). And they will follow the one with all authority in heaven and earth (28:18). The word "heaven" is used seventy-five times in Matthew, and "heaven" and "earth" are used together twelve times. It is a defining theme.

In the Old Testament, ethnic Israel and its leaders represent heaven. But, says Jesus, Israel's leaders "shut the kingdom of heaven in people's faces" (Matt 23:13), and now the "sons of the kingdom" or Israel will be cast out while "many will come from east and west" to "the kingdom of heaven" (Matt 8:11–12). Who exactly, then, will represent heaven on earth now?

First of all, Jesus Christ will. Heaven affirms Jesus: "Behold, a voice from heaven said, 'This is my beloved Son'" (3:17; see also 11:27). But Christ's church and churches will also represent heaven on earth. To this end, Jesus gives Peter and the apostles, as well as local churches, the keys of the kingdom for binding on earth what is bound in heaven and loosing on earth what is loosed in heaven (16:19; 18:18).

The gathered local church possesses the authority to stand in front of a confessor of faith in Christ, to consider that confession, to consider his or her life, and to announce an official judgment on heaven's behalf: "This is/is not a true confession" and "This is/is not a true confessor." This is exactly what Jesus does with Peter in Matthew 16 and what a church is commanded to do in reverse in Matthew 18. The keys are this authority to pronounce heaven's judgments on the *what* and the *who* of the gospel.

A key-wielding declaration does not make a person a Christian, just like a judge's declaration "guilty" or "not guilty" does not make a person innocent or guilty (for courtroom themes, see Deut 19:15 and Matt 18:16, 19–20). But from a public standpoint, that key-wielding declaration, like a judge's declaration, formally recognizes an individual to be one thing or another. It *binds* or *looses* the individual.

Consider another metaphor: local churches act as embassies of heaven. Like the U.S. Embassy in Brussels, Belgium, speaking for the U.S. State Department by renewing my expired passport, so churches publicly speak for heaven by affirming a person's citizenship there. These heavenly embassies also affirm what the gospel is or is not, as when an ambassador says "this, not that" is his government's position.

Christians possess this power when they formally assemble together and agree with one another, teach Jesus and Paul. Right after giving churches the keys, Jesus remarks, "If two of you on earth *agree* about any matter that you pray for, it will be done for you by my Father in heaven. For where two or three are *gathered together* in my name, I am *there* among them" (Matt 18:19–20, emphasis mine). By saying he is "there," Jesus does not mean he hovers like a mystical fog in the room. He means this key-wielding gathering—when they "gather" and "agree" with each other on who Jesus is and what they are pronouncing—possesses a courtroom and ambassadorial authority for representing him on earth. Paul later invokes this power when he tells the Corinthian church to remove a man from membership when they are assembled in the name of the Lord "and the power of our Lord Jesus is present" (1 Cor 5:4 NIV). At the white-hot center of church authority is a legal or binding/loosing agreement. It is an authority conducive to the new covenant, where no separate class of priests or kings plays mediator (see Jer 31:33–34). The earliest Baptist confession, the 1644 First London Confession, astutely observed that churches form and members are recognized "by mutual agreement" (Article 33). Baptists often refer to these agreements as church covenants.

In the opening book of the New Testament, church membership starts here, as a gathered church's agreement and declaration of heavenly citizenship. To draw out the principles at play, church membership is a relationship between a church and a Christian characterized (1) by the church's affirmation and oversight over the Christian's profession and discipleship and (2) by the Christian's submission to that church's oversight. One could also call all this a "covenant," as many Christians have. All of this suggests that Christians do not "join" churches like they might join a club. They "submit" to them. It is an act of heavenly citizenship. Joining a church is a voluntary decision from the state's standpoint, and membership is voluntary insofar as a Christian is free to pick which church to join, or to leave one church and join another. But Christians must join churches.

Jesus's purpose in these membership structures concerns his name—his witness and reputation. Where Israel's disobedience and idolatry functioned as a kind of anti-evangelism, telling the nations that the Lord was no different than their gods, the new covenant places God's law on the heart. It depends upon being "born again" or "regenerate." Yet it also depends upon being properly identified with Jesus. Jesus therefore charged these new covenant assemblies with baptizing in his name and gathering in his name. Regenerate church membership, which marks off a forgiven, poor-in-spirit, and heaven-shaped people, serves the purpose of the church's witness and making disciples. It is part of Jesus's evangelism program.

2. Church membership is enacted and recognized through the ordinances

Churches exercise the keys of the kingdom by preaching the gospel, which formally affirms the *what* of the gospel. They also do so by celebrating the ordinances, which formally affirms the *who* of the gospel. Baptism is the front door of membership. The Lord's Supper is the regular family meal. Both reveal *who* the church is, even as they declare *what* the gospel is.

Christians often read Jesus's command to baptize in Matthew 28 in isolation from Matthew 16 and 18, as if the responsibility to baptize belongs to individuals. But Matthew ties the three texts together by invoking the language of heaven and earth, Jesus's name, and his presence (Matt 16:19; 18:18–20; 28:18–20). Those who gather in his name possess the authority to baptize in his name. Those with whom he now dwells he will always dwell. The lesson: churches possess the authority to baptize, and baptism ordinarily occurs into church membership. Acts 8 and the Ethiopian eunuch's baptism might offer a gospel-frontier exception, but Acts 2 and the baptism of the three thousand is the norm.

The Supper, then, belongs to church members. One could even say church membership simply means membership at the table. The Supper reveals and publicizes who the church is. Paul writes, "Because there is one bread, we who are many are one body, since all of us share the one bread" (1 Cor 10:17). Who is the one body? It is those who partake of the one bread. Members should therefore only receive the Supper while "discerning the body," and members should "welcome one another" (1 Cor 11:33). The

Supper is not a private or individual meal. It is not for kids at summer camp or for wedding ceremonies. It is a church meal and a sign of membership in the new covenant (see also Matt 26:28).

The ordinances make the invisible church visible, the universal church local, and Christ's forgiven and born-again people on earth identifiable and public, both to themselves and the nations. They are the signs of membership, which means they publicly constitute membership.

3. Church membership is an office

Christians have a long tradition of referring to elders and deacons as church "officers." The nomenclature rightly recognizes the role and responsibilities that Scripture gives to church leaders, as well as the unique honor due to pastors (1 Tim 5:17). But church membership, too, is an office. One does not make a general any less an officer by referring to a lieutenant as an officer. Herman Bavinck remarked: "And just as all believers have a gift, so also they all hold an office. Not only in the church as organism but also in the church as institution, they have a calling and a task laid on them by the Lord."[1]

Presbyterian theologian Charles Hodge defined an office like this: "The ministry is properly an office, because it is something which cannot be assumed at pleasure by any and everyone. A man must be appointed thereto by some competent authority. It involves not only the right, but the obligation to exercise certain functions, or to discharge certain duties; and it confers certain powers or prerogatives, which other men are bound to recognize and respect."[2] What Presbyterians ascribe uniquely to the elders, Baptists ascribe in some measure to every member, since Baptist ecclesiology builds more decisively on membership in the new covenant. Membership does not belong to everyone but to baptized believers. And every member must "exercise certain functions," "discharge certain duties," and possess "certain powers."

---

[1] Herman Bavinck, *Reformed Dogmatics: Holy Spirit, Church, New Creation*, vol. 4., ed. John Bolt, trans. John Vriend (Grand Rapids: Baker Academic, 2008), 375.

[2] Charles Hodge, *Discussions in Church Polity* (New York: Westminster Publishing House, 2001), 346.

Membership is a new covenant office, but it is rooted in Adam's original role as a priest-king. God commanded Adam to be fruitful, multiply, and rule over the earth like a king (Gen 1:28; see also Psalm 8). Yet he also commanded him to "to work it and to watch over it," the same responsibilities later given to priests (Gen 2:15; Num 3:7–8; 8:26; 18:5–6). Since God dwelled in the garden, Adam was to keep it holy unto the Lord. Of course, Adam failed at this job. He let the serpent inside. Noah, Abraham, and the nation of Israel failed too. Christ eventually came and perfectly fulfilled the job of priest and king. He then assigned us the job of being priest-kings too. "You are . . . a royal priesthood" (1 Pet 2:9). Like Adam, therefore, every member is charged with pushing back the borders of the garden like kings while simultaneously watching over the garden like priests.

As kings, church members strive to make disciples and be ambassadors of reconciliation. They work to bring more hearts into subjugation to God's rule and more of the earth under the gospel's dominion. As priests, church members must watch over the place where God dwells, the church, the new covenant temple (1 Cor 3:16). They work to keep holiness separated from unholiness in their individual and corporate lives by speaking the truth in love and practicing personal and public church discipline (2 Cor 6:14–7:1; Eph 4:15–16, 29).

Every member must work to protect the gospel, as Paul exhorted the members of the Galatian churches (Gal 1:6–9). They must work to protect gospel confessors, as he exhorted the Corinthians (1 Corinthians 5). And they must work to make disciples by evangelizing and discipling other believers (Matt 28:18–20; Eph 4:12–16, 29). Church leaders who "fire" church members from this job, whether through formal church structures or by turning members into consumers, undermine the members' sense of gospel responsibility and kingdom ownership. Such leaders cultivate complacency, nominalism, and eventually theological liberalism.

A pastor or elder's job is to equip church members to do their jobs (Eph 4:11). The weekly church gathering is a time of job training. Those in the office of pastor work to teach those in the office of member to know the gospel, to live by the gospel, to protect the church's gospel witness, and to extend the gospel's reach into one another's lives and among outsiders. If the pastors do not do their jobs well, neither will the members. If pastors do, members do. When the pastor's office is rightly aligned with the member's office, the result is Jesus's discipleship program.

Summary: Frequently Asked Questions

To summarize, what is church membership? It is how Jesus intends for visible churches to formally recognize and affirm the invisibly born-again, law-indwelt members of the new covenant. It is how gatherings of Christians agree or covenant together and declare, "Here are heaven's citizens on earth." In that sense, church membership is part of Christ's evangelism program. It also works as Christ's assurance-of-salvation program, where Christians receive assurance of salvation from their congregation's affirmation.

Church membership is also an office. It assigns each member with (1) the priestly task of keeping the place where God dwells, the temple, consecrated to the Lord as well as (2) the kingly task of pushing out the boundaries of Eden by making disciples. Both tasks require training and leadership from pastors. And putting the pastors' and members' work together yields Jesus's discipleship program.

What role do the ordinances play? Church membership is recognized and enacted by the ordinances. They designate who the church is—who the members are.

Who can join a church? Anyone who repents of their sins, trusts in Christ, and obeys Jesus's command to be baptized. Church membership is not for unbelievers, for the children of believers, or for any believer who has not been baptized. It is for baptized believers—members of the new covenant who submit to being formally recognized in Jesus's name.

How can a person join a church? Different cultural settings allow for different practices. In a Western context beset by Christian nominalism and many false Jesuses, a wise church will probably include practices such as membership classes and interviews. These allow a church to know what an individual believes and the individual to know what a church believes. At the very least, the biblical minimum involves (1) a conversation that asks those questions, like Jesus asking the apostles, "Who do you say that I am?" (Matt 16:15); and (2) a commitment or agreement or covenant by which individuals bind and are bound (Matt 18:18–20).

How can a person leave a church? The short answer is by death, by joining another gospel-preaching church, or by church discipline. From the kingdom perspective, church membership is not voluntary. Christians must join churches. The Bible leaves no room for fading away or resigning "into the world," as an older generation of Baptists put it.

Finally, what are the responsibilities of membership? Members must work to make disciples. This includes sharing the gospel, protecting the gospel from false versions of it, recognizing new members in the gospel, protecting and correcting one another in the gospel, and building one another up in the gospel.

Christians who remain unattached to a church at best weaken their faith. At worst, they deceive themselves about whether they are Christians. Christians join churches not merely because it is good for personal growth, but because it is what Christians *are*—members of Christ's body and family. Just as those declared righteous in Christ will "put on" deeds of righteousness (Col 3:10, 12; Jas 2:14–16), so members of Christ's universal body will "put on" that membership locally. And just as a failure to put on righteousness calls into question one's positional righteousness in Christ, so with the failure to join a church. It calls into question one's membership in Christ's people. A person cannot claim to love God but then want nothing to do with other Christians (1 John 4:20). Membership in the universal church cannot remain an abstract idea. If it is real, it will show up on earth.

Membership offers the safety of the sheep pen, where Christ is shepherd. It offers the nourishment of being attached to a body, like an arm to a torso, where Christ is the head. It offers the love of a family, where Christ is the firstborn of many heirs. It offers the obligations and duties of citizenship in a holy nation, where Christ is the King.

For Additional Study

Barna Group. "Introducing the State of the Church 2020." https://www .barna.com/research/state-of-the-church-2020/.

Bavinck, Herman. *Reformed Dogmatics: Holy Spirit, Church, New Creation*, vol. 4. Edited John Bolt. Translated John Vriend. Grand Rapids: Baker Academic, 2008.

Hodge, Charles. *Discussions in Church Polity.* New York: Scribners, 1878. Reprint, New York: Westminster Publishing House, 2001.

Kimble, Jeremy M. *40 Questions about Church Membership and Discipline.* Grand Rapids: Kregel Academic, 2017.

Leeman, Jonathan. *Church Membership: How the World Knows Who Represents Jesus.* Wheaton: Crossway, 2012.

———. *The Church and the Surprising Offense of God's Love: Reintroducing the Doctrines of Church Membership and Discipline.* Wheaton: Crossway, 2010.

Also see these articles: Baptism, The Lord's Supper, Worship

35

Baptism

CHRISTOPHER CHUN

Depending on the particular Christian tradition, baptism may be administered by either immersing the baptismal candidate in water or, alternatively, sprinkling or pouring water on the head. When the apostle Paul wrote to believers about "one baptism" in Eph 4:5, he was teaching them that regardless of their background or nationality, they all served the same Lord and encouraged them to be unified by the faith expressed in baptism. Yet in the history of Christianity, the issue of baptism has been one of the fault-lines that runs between denominations and goes all the way back to the early church. There are many variations on how this sacrament or ordinance is understood. For the sake of simplicity, this study has reduced them down to three models: 1) the Sacramental model as exemplified by Roman Catholics (e.g., orthodox and Anglican, especially its high-church and Anglo-Catholic forms); 2) the Covenantal model as exemplified by Presbyterians (e.g., various reformed traditions that practice infant baptism); and 3) the Declaratory model as exemplified by Baptists (e.g., Anabaptist and Puritan traditions as well as various restoration, Pentecostal, and dissenting movements).

The Nature of Baptism

The Catholic model is best represented by the Council of Trent, which convened in 1545 and ended in 1563. This meeting was one of the most

significant Councils in the Roman Catholic tradition. The catechism that
it produced defines baptism as "the Sacrament of regeneration by water in
the word."[1] The act of baptism was seen as the means of salvation *ex opere
operato*; thus, salvation was inconceivable in the sixteenth century apart from
infant baptism because it eradicated both original and venial sins.

Protestants in general, and Presbyterians in particular, denied this
Catholic model of baptismal regeneration. The Westminster Confession of
Faith (1647) states while it is a "great sin" to neglect baptism, "grace and salvation are not so inseparably annexed unto it." The Westminster-Presbyterian
model sees baptism as a sign of the covenant:

> Baptism is a *sacrament* of the New Testament, ordained by Jesus
> Christ, not only for the solemn admission of the party *baptized into
> the visible church*, but also to be unto him *a sign and seal of the cov-
> enant of grace*, of his ingrafting into Christ, of regeneration, of remis-
> sion of sins, and of his giving up unto God, through Jesus Christ, to
> walk in newness of life. (28.1)

Baptism is the act of faith by which people are brought into the covenant and
admission to the visible church.

It is interesting that the 1689 London Baptist Confession of Particular
Baptists, which has enormous overlaps with and the same genetic pool as
Westminster, differs on a few key concepts:

> Baptism is an *ordinance* of the New Testament, ordained by Jesus
> Christ, to be unto the party baptized, a *sign* of his *fellowship* with
> him, in his death and resurrection; of his being engrafted into him;
> of remission of sins; and of giving up into God, through Jesus Christ,
> to live and walk in newness of life. (29.1)

While particular Baptists in London started with a similar trajectory as their
Westminster-Presbyterian counterpart, they preferred the word "ordinance"
rather than "sacrament" and omitted entirely the language of the "sign of
the covenant." London Baptists instead used the phrase "sign of fellowship
with Christ." This is because sacramental and covenant verbiages are necessary components for the infant baptism incorporated into the Presbyterian

---

[1] *Catechism of the Council of Trent for Parish Priests*, 2:2.

model. In the Baptist tradition neither sacramental nor covenant language is typically used. While some Baptists appreciate covenantal language in association with baptism, a majority of Baptists do not feel the need to use it. Presbyterian and Baptist models differ on the candidate of baptism. The former baptize infants as well as adults, whereas the latter baptize professing believers only. This practice is often called "credobaptism." Nonetheless, both Presbyterian and Baptist models agree in their common denunciation of the Catholic version of Baptismal regeneration.

The Baptismal Candidate, Believers' Church, and Credobaptism

Who shall receive baptism? Patristic scholar Everett Ferguson observes, "There is general agreement that there is no firm evidence for infant baptism before the latter part of the second century."[2] Ferguson examines the origin of baptism and how the practice of infant baptism developed in the first five hundred years of Christianity. The first explicit reference to infant baptism seems to have been made by Tertullian in AD 206 and is a sign of increasing acceptance of the concept of baptismal regeneration. The most plausible explanation for the origins of infant baptism is found in the practice of "emergency baptism" where the rite was administered to sick children who were expected to die soon. This "emergency" infant baptism gave hope to grieving parents that their offspring would be saved. This practice continued throughout the Middle Ages.

The genesis of the Baptist tradition, according to British historian David Bebbington, "lie in the maelstrom of the sixteenth-century Reformation,"[3] and, as such, discussions of Anabaptists in Switzerland deserve attention. Conrad Grebel and George Blaurock were disciples of the great Swiss Reformer, Ulrich Huldrych (or Ulrich) Zwingli. However, Grebel and Blaurock believed that the reform ought to progress faster. Zwingli was moving faster than Martin Luther in Germany but still not rapidly enough to

---

[2] Everett Ferguson, *Baptism in the Early Church: History, Theology, and Liturgy in the First Five Centuries* (Grand Rapids: Eerdmans, 2009), 856–57.

[3] David W. Bebbington, *Baptists through the Centuries: A History of a Global People*, 2nd ed. (Waco, TX: Baylor University Press, 2018), 7.

satisfy these Anabaptists. Grebel and the radicals came into harsh conflict with Zwingli over the issue of infant baptism. A public debate was held on January 17, 1525, when Zwingli argued against his former followers. The city council, however, sided with Zwingli, and they ordered infant baptism to be administered to Grebel's group. The council mandated any unbaptized infants to be submitted for baptism within eight days; failure to comply with the order would result in exile. But Grebel refused to baptize his daughter Isabella. On January 21, 1525, Grebel baptized Blaurock, who then baptized some other people in the lake. With this dramatic insistence that baptism be connected with personal faith, the Anabaptist movement began.

Readers today may take this as a cause for celebration; namely, that somebody had been baptized. But, according to the state church in the sixteenth century, this was a provocative act and was seen as an act of rebellion. As far as the state church was concerned, this group was being "rebaptized" (hence the name *Anabaptist*) and undermining the civil authority. All Christians had already been baptized as infants. Anabaptists decided that what happened to them as children prior to a profession of faith was not a true baptism. They did not view themselves as being rebaptized; instead, they saw themselves as people who were following the Lord for the first time as believers in true Christian baptism. Anabaptists were persecuted by those on all sides. Catholics often burned them. Magisterial Protestants usually drowned them.

Many Anabaptists were persecuted and lost their lives in the sixteenth century because in performing "rebaptism" they were believed to be guilty of blasphemy. Felix Manz was executed by drowning, and the execution was called the "third baptism" because it was considered an antidote to the "second baptism." Rebaptism was not only branded a heresy, it was also illegal. Despite this, Anabaptists rejected infant baptism and did so with strong words. The Schleitheim Confession (1527) was drafted in a meeting of the Swiss Brethren on February 24, 1527. It declared that infant baptism was "the highest and the chief abomination of the pope." The Confession's principal author, Michael Sattler, was burned at the stake for his views less than three months later.

Baptists can trace their origins to seventh-century England. Although Baptists do not have a single historical figure like Martin Luther or John Wesley as their founder, present-day Baptists are the result of two historical forces: English Puritanism and continental Anabaptism. English Puritanism was spurred on by the desire to purify the Church of England. Anabaptists in Europe, much like the Puritan separatists, also wanted to purify the church, especially concerning the establishment of a regenerate membership marked by baptism. When English separatists and continental Anabaptists came together, they gave rise to Baptists.

Whether this amalgamation in England took place only among general Baptists (John Smyth's congregation in 1609 and Thomas Helwys's congregation in 1612) or also impacted the particular Baptists (the Jacob-Lathrop-Jessey church, 1616) is still debated among historians. That said, whether one espouses the Anabaptist kinship theory or the English separatist descent theory, what is unmistakable is the fact that seventeenth-century Baptists rejected infant baptism and consequently suffered terrible persecution under the established church. John Smyth, the founder of the general Baptist movement, was not shy about his criticism when he published *Character of the Beast* (1609), in which he argued that infant baptism was Satan's way of keeping his hands on the Church of England, making it into a "worldly" church. He called members of the established church "harlots" in that they shared with Rome the "mark of the beast" of infant baptism. Both general and particular Baptists in seventeenth-century England were tortured for their view of baptism. Many Puritans, congregationalists, and Baptists left "Old England" for America's "New England" in order to escape the persecution.

The immigration to America was a symbolic Puritan dream: a New England, set on a hill for others to see. In 1620 the first group of Puritans, the "pilgrims," set sail to the New World on the *Mayflower* and started the Plymouth Plantation in America. In the 1630s immigration reached its highest peak, as nearly fourteen thousand settlers came to Massachusetts. The vision was for a purified church to be established. The settlers put the Massachusetts Bay Colony on a pedestal for the Church of England and the rest of Europe to see as a model community of Christian charity. They believed the Bay Colony was God's chosen New Israel. This was God's high calling for the New World. A brand-new society was to be built from the ground up, a new community that John Winthrop famously envisioned as the "City upon a Hill."

This vision of the new world did not last forever. It became increasingly difficult to maintain this American utopian dream. By the third generation of settlers in New England, the early eighteenth century saw a spiritual decline set in and affect the American churches. For example, when Jonathan Edwards arrived to assist his grandfather, Solomon Stoddard, in Northampton parish in 1727, Edwards was affected by what he saw happening, particularly with the young people in that congregation. To address this issue, Stoddard and the leadership found it necessary to redefine citizenship through the establishment of a halfway covenant that created partial church membership.

It was primarily driven by the fact that as the first generation of Puritan settlers in the New World began to fade away, their children and grandchildren often did not have as much religious fervency and piety. The halfway covenant allowed parents to bring their children to the church for baptism, even though the parents themselves did not have credible professions of faith. In fact, people were even encouraged to come to the Lord's Table, since this sacrament was viewed as a "converting ordinance" rather than as a time of fellowship among believers. This could lead to second, third, and even fourth generations of unconverted church members through the vehicle of the halfway covenant. Edwards had a problem with this view. When he eventually opposed his grandfather's halfway covenant, Edwards was dismissed from his congregation. But Edwards was not alone. Many congregationalists, as it turns out, were dissatisfied with the halfway covenant. This ultimately became the catalyst for many congregationalist clergies, such as Isaac Backus and Shubal Stearns, to convert to become separate Baptists during the Great Awakening.

Backus's upbringing was in old Congregationalism, yet his mother influenced the young Isaac with her robust "conversionist" theology. She insisted that the church should be formed only by those who had experienced a true conversion. Consequently, we know Backus had been exposed to the concept of the believer's church early on in his life. In 1741, he experienced a personal conversion under the preaching of George Whitefield and Edwards during the Awakening. Later Backus felt the call to preach, and in 1748 he started to pastor a separate church. It was called "separate" because it had adopted conversionist theology from the Awakening. Unlike churches that adopted halfway covenants, the separate congregations did not admit people to the Lord's Supper unless they professed conversion.

In 1749, two of Backus's church members adopted credobaptism, and Backus was temporally convinced they were right. Backus thought that the halfway covenant was a strange practice in that it allowed unconverted parents to bring their children to the church for infant baptism. Due to social pressure and stigmatism, Backus later retracted this concern and went back to the old position of affirming infant baptism. Upon his resumption to the practice of infant baptism, however, Backus immediately began to see a palpable decline in the spiritual health of the church. He noticed that the practice of infant baptism tended to diminish the fervency of people about conversion. Once again, the issue was halfway covenant, the same problem that Edwards had with his grandfather's position. Two years later, in 1751, Backus finally revisited, once again, his ideas about baptism, and "after agonizing prayer and intense study of Scripture, he became convinced that no scriptural warrant for infant baptism existed."[4] Backus concluded that he could not baptize infants. From Backus's preaching and counseling, all the church members became convinced of his view. In 1756, this congregational church became a Baptist church. Unlike Edwards, Backus went a step further and became a separate Baptist, but he certainly was not alone in making that pilgrimage.

Although "rebaptism" was not illegal, like in sixteenth-century Europe, still, even in America, social pressure to conform was immense. Adoniram and Ann Judson are a famous case in point. Ann Hasseltine married Adoniram Judson on February 5, 1812. Just a few weeks afterward, on February 19, the newlyweds sailed for Calcutta, India. Both Ann and Adoniram, having been raised in congregationalist families, were aware that upon their arrival they would be ministering alongside the famous English Baptist missionaries of Serampore, led by William Carey, Joshua Marshman, and William Ward. As one of the first American missionaries, Adoniram wondered how they could work together with their differences concerning infant baptism. Supposing that all of their first converts would be adults, he wondered if he should also baptize the children of these new believers in a heathen land. To solve these theological and practical issues, the Judsons launched an intense study of Scripture during their four-month voyage to India. As a result of this endeavor, the Judsons drastically changed their views on baptism. Had

---

[4] Pamela R. Durso and Keith E. Durso, *The Story of Baptists in the United States* (Brentwood, TN: Baptist History and Heritage Society, 2006), 48.

they known that the Baptist missionaries of India had a policy to avoid such controversies, they might never have started this investigation.

At any rate, in describing her husband, Ann wrote, "The more [Adoniram] examined, the more his doubts increased; and unwilling as he was to admit it, he was *afraid* the Baptists were right and he wrong." Ann added, "But as his mind was still uneasy, he again renewed the subject. I felt afraid he would become a Baptist, and frequently urged the unhappy consequences if he should." Modern readers might not be able to fathom these fears associated with being Baptists. Ann, who was also from an aristocratic congregational family, wrote to her closest friend back home, "Can you, my dear Nancy, still love me, still desire to hear from me, when I tell you I have become a Baptist?" Her apologetic tone captures this difficult dilemma. In spite of Ann's initial denial of the views of credobaptism, she finally came to the same biblical conviction as did her husband. At much personal cost, Ann finally decided to leave her respectable social standing, and much to her shame and pride, she told her friend, "My dear Nancy, we are confirmed Baptists, not because we wished to be, but because truth compelled us to be. . . . We anticipate the loss of reputation, and of the affection and esteem of many of our American friends."[5] Ann and Adoniram Judson essentially left America as congregationalists but arrived in India as Baptists.

This idea of obeying whatever the Bible teaches, in spite of whatever persecution or social ostracization might follow, is also stirringly affirmed by the nineteenth-century Victorian Baptist preacher, Charles Spurgeon:

> If I thought it wrong to be a Baptist, I should give it up and become what I believe to be right . . . If we could find infant baptism in the word of God, we would adopt it. It would help us out of a great difficulty, for it would take away from us that reproach which is attached to us—that we are odd and do not as other people do. But we have looked well through the bible [*sic*] and cannot find it, and do not believe it is there; nor do we believe that others can find infant baptism in the Scriptures, unless they themselves first put it there.[6]

---

[5] Ann Judson, "Letter to a Friend about Becoming a Baptist," in *A Sourcebook for Baptist Heritage*, ed. H. Leon McBeth (Nashville: Broadman, 1990), 207–8.

[6] Charles H. Spurgeon, *C. H. Spurgeon's Autobiography: Compiled from His Diary, Letters, and Records by His Wife and His Private Secretary* (London: Passmore &

Not a single instance of unambiguous infant baptism is mentioned in the entire Scriptures unless paedobaptists can successfully see infant baptism in places like the book of Acts where allusions to the baptism of a "household" can be found. Although nineteenth-century rhetoric from Spurgeon is not nearly as harsh as sixteenth- and seventeenth-centuries' wordings, i.e., calling infant baptism as "the highest and chief abomination of the pope" or "mark of the beast," it still criticizes adherents of infant baptism for interpreting biblical texts in a way that merely enshrines their own needs and biases—a practice commonly referred to as *eisegesis* or reading things "into" the text.

The Mode of Baptism: Sprinkle or Immerse?

The general lexical definition for the word *baptizo* is "to dip, immerse, plunge, wash." This does not have to mean exclusively "immerse," but lexical sources note that this is the standard meaning of the word as it is used in both the New Testament and the Septuagint. This being the case, it suggests the burden of proof should be on the shoulders of those who would rather sprinkle than immerse. Many paedobaptists who practice sprinkling as their primary mode of baptism would often point to *Didache* 7:1–3 as their earliest precedent of the early church as well as advocate freedom in the mode of baptism:

> (1) Now concerning baptism, baptize as follows: after you have reviewed all these things, baptize in the name of the Father and of the Son and of the Holy Spirit in running water. (2) But if you have no running water, then baptize in some other water; and if you are not able to baptize in cold water, then do so in warm. (3) But if you have neither, then pour water on the head three times in the name of Father and Son and Holy Spirit.[7]

From this passage, proponents of the sprinkling method often conclude that the author of the *Didache* had a much broader understanding of the mode of baptism than just being immersed. Baptists, however, frequently dismiss

---

Alabaster, 1897), 1:115.

[7] W. Michael Holmes, ed., "The Didache" in *The Apostolic Fathers: Greek Texts and English Translations*, 3rd ed. (Grand Rapids: Baker Academic, 2006), 166–67.

this argument by observing that the *Didache* is not the Bible (i.e., canonical Scripture) and, therefore, does not have to be accepted as authoritative. That said, those Baptists who find value in Christian tradition could still see the *Didache* as important since this is one of the earliest Christian discussions outside of the New Testament regarding the method of baptism, i.e., circa late first or early second century.

A careful examination of the *Didache* text, however, indicates that even if so-called "freedom" in the mode has a specific priority, the instruction for baptism is explicit: baptize in the trinitarian formula in the "running water," probably referring to a lake or river. This demands the question: why would anyone need a river in order to sprinkle? The text seems to suggest immersion is clearly the preference. The author of the *Didache* unmistakably prioritizes immersion over all other modes. The stipulation: if there is "no running water" only because the water is scarce in this region, only out of necessity should one consider baptizing in "some other water." Unable to baptize in "cold water"? Only then, "in warm." There is a hierarchy insofar as the mode is concerned. Only if there is neither running water or some other water may the administrator consider "pouring water on the head three times," which also requires more ounces of water than mere sprinkling. If the *Didache* carries credence, then immersion should be the normative practice. Other modes should be considered only when sufficient water is not available.

Perhaps the clearest picture of immersion is established by the New Testament itself, especially Rom 6:3–5:

> Or are you unaware that all of us who were baptized into Christ Jesus were baptized into his death? Therefore we were buried with him by baptism into death, in order that, just as Christ was raised from the dead by the glory of the Father, so we too may walk in newness of life. For if we have been united with him in the likeness of his death, we will certainly also be in the likeness of his resurrection.

In this scriptural passage, the most natural reading denotes immersion. Baptism is a symbol that the believers are united with Christ in his death, burial, and resurrection. Death and burial are signaled when the baptismal candidate is immersed under the water, and when the candidate comes up from the water, it symbolizes believer's resurrection. Immersion baptism is an outward symbol of the inward reality, which indicates the change that has been made from an unbeliever to a believer in Christ.

Final Thoughts and Application

A familiar pseudo-Augustinian sentiment—"In essentials, unity; in non-essentials, liberty; in all things, charity"—has served the church well in our time. When it comes to tolerance, the church has come a long way since the sixteenth and seventeenth centuries. In church history, many of the Baptists and Anabaptists have lost their lives because of their views on baptism. Evidently, the state church thought that baptism issues were more important than life itself. Those who "rebaptized" were banished from society or even sentenced to death. On the other side, the leaders of the nonconforming movements were not exactly charitable, calling infant baptism the "chief abomination." Today, the church rightly understands that the topic of baptism is neither a doctrine over which to kill nor a practice that defines the essence of Christian faith. While this is a positive development, it is not without a downside. In the name of "charity," the pendulum has swung the other way. The church today, perhaps unwittingly, has often made baptism into something unimportant and even frivolous. Surely just because the baptism issue is "nonessential" does not mean it is insignificant.

The three issues that underpin this practice are first, the nature of baptism (baptismal regeneration or not); second, the candidate of baptism (infant or credobaptism); and third, the mode of baptism (sprinkling or immersion), all of which are often met with an attitude of indifference from the average believer today. If a person actually cares about these issues, he or she will quickly realize that unless the conversation is between Protestants and Catholics, the problem of baptismal regeneration is a moot point. If, however, the discussion is between Presbyterians and Baptists on the candidates of baptism, the debates revolve around intricacies of the meaning of circumcision as well as continuity and discontinuity between the Old and the New Testaments. Presbyterians will likely defend the infant baptism issue on the ground of covenant theology. Contrary to popular misbelief, Baptists still may work within the general covenantal framework while still maintaining credobaptism. In other words, Baptists neither have to affirm dispensationalist hermeneutics nor devalue Christian tradition in order to be Baptist.

Under the Presbyterian model, infants will not be baptized unless the parent(s) give a credible profession of faith and will not allow children to participate in the Lord's Supper until the child is old enough to make their own profession credible. However, the notions of a "believers' church," or "conversionist theology," or "regenerate church membership," are at the very core of what drove early Anabaptists, general Baptists, particular Baptists, and separate Baptists to break away from the established church in their respective settings.

The internal inconsistencies within the Presbyterian model of infant baptism (as opposed to Roman Catholic) cause one to wonder if the practice of the Presbyterians is mere leftover residue from the sixteenth-century magisterial reformers. From a Baptist viewpoint, Christendom, including the Reformation era, is characterized by failure to make a distinction between the church and the state. If infant baptism is merely an old tradition from an epoch when living as a law-abiding citizen meant baptizing infants, much like registering one's child for a state census today, there is no reason to observe this outdated practice, especially when infant baptism undercuts the biblical distinction between the church and the unbelieving world.

In the post-denominational era, baptism is often not seen as that important. Perhaps the mode of baptism, i.e., "how much water to use," is more trivial than the discussion on the nature and candidate of baptism. That said, unless there is compelling evidence to argue otherwise, the assumption is that Jesus was immersed at John's baptism. As mentioned above, Romans 6 also uses the metaphor of immersion; twentieth-century theologian Karl Barth, who was a lifelong member of the Swiss Reformed church, a denomination that practices infant baptism, comments on this passage with observations that accord with the Baptist theology:

> The Greek word βαπτίζω and the German word *Taufen* (from *Tiefe*, "depth") originally and properly describe the process by which a man or an object is completely immersed in water and then withdrawn from it again. Primitive baptism carried out in this manner had in its mode, exactly like the circumcision of the Old Testament,

the character of a *direct threat to life*, succeeded immediately by the corresponding deliverance and preservation, *the raising from baptism.* One can hardly deny that *baptism carried out as immersion*—as it was in the West until well on into the Middle Ages—showed what was represented in far more expressive fashion than did the affusion which later became customary, especially when this affusion was reduced from a real wetting to a sprinkling and eventually in practice to a mere moistening with as little water as possible.[8]

Unless there are problems with health or the church facility, says Barth, are there any "important reasons for doing otherwise?" For Barth, Romans 6 describes a critical happening in the life of a Christian and that of a believer. Baptismal candidates ought to be immersed since "Baptism vividly symbolizes our identification with Jesus Christ in his death, burial, and resurrection." Barth's point can be seen to concur with the instruction found in the *Didache.*

In the early church, there is a clear preference concerning how much water should be used involving baptism. Hence, both the biblical text and early church tradition prescribe immersion as the preferred mode. Unless there is a scarcity of water or a health limitation, immersion ought to be the normative practice for the church, even in our twenty-first century post-denominational milieu.

FOR ADDITIONAL STUDY

Barth, Karl. *The Teaching of the Church Regarding Baptism.* Translated by A. E. Payne. London: SCM Press, 1948.

Bauer, Walter, Frederick W. Danker, and William F. Arndt, eds. *Greek-English Lexicon of the New Testament.* 3rd ed. Chicago: University of Chicago Press, 2000.

Bebbington, David W. *Baptists through the Centuries: A History of a Global People.* 2nd ed. Waco, TX: Baylor University Press, 2018.

---

[8] Barth, *The Teaching of the Church Regarding Baptism,* 9.

Catechism of the Council of Trent for Parish Priests. Translated by John A. McHugh and Charles J. Callan. New York: Joseph H. Wagner, 1934.

Durso, Pamela R., and Keith E. Durso. *The Story of Baptists in the United States.* Brentwood, TN: Baptist History and Heritage Society, 2006.

Ferguson, Everett. *Baptism in the Early Church: History, Theology, and Liturgy in the First Five Centuries.* Grand Rapids: Eerdmans, 2009.

Grenz, Stanley. *Isaac Backus—Puritan and Baptist: His Place in History, His Thought and Their Implications for Modern Baptist Theology.* Macon, GA: Mercer University Press, 1983.

Holmes, W. Michael, ed. "The Didache." In *The Apostolic Fathers: Greek Texts and English Translations.* 3rd ed. Grand Rapids: Baker Academic, 2006.

Jewett, Paul K. *Infant Baptism and the Covenant of Grace.* Grand Rapids: Eerdmans, 1978.

Judson, Ann. "Letter to a Friend about Becoming a Baptist (1812)." In *A Sourcebook for Baptist Heritage.* Edited H. Leon McBeth, 207–8. Nashville: Broadman, 1990.

Schreiner, Thomas, and Shawn Wright, eds. *Believer's Baptism: Sign of the New Covenant in Christ.* Nashville: B&H Academic, 2006.

Smyth, John. "Character of the Beast (1609)". In *Baptist Roots: A Reader in the Theology of a Christian People,* eds. Curtis W. Freeman, James Wm McClendon, and C. Rosalee Velloso da Silva, 76–82. Valley Forge, PA: Judson Press, 1999.

Spurgeon, Charles H. *C. H. Spurgeon's Autobiography: Compiled from His Diary, Letters, and Records by His Wife and His Private Secretary.* London: Passmore & Alabaster, 1897.

Also see these articles: Gospel, Church, Church Membership, Lord's Supper, Evangelism and Missions

36

The Lord's Supper

MARK DEVINE

Five components of Christian worship stand apart as the most ancient, fundamental, and ubiquitous—the sermon, prayer, baptism, the Lord's Supper, and song. Twenty centuries after their institution, the meanings of baptism and the Lord's Supper remain the most controverted and elusive of consensus within the global church.

Yet where the authority of the Bible still obtains, even the lowest of low church traditions—those most wary of ritual—retain both. Lutherans expressed the Protestant acknowledgment of the central importance of baptism and the Lord's Supper in the Augsburg Confession, Article VII (1530) where the true church is defined as the place where the word is rightly preached and the sacraments are rightly administered. Sadly, the long history of contention and even warring over the Supper tends to obscure vast areas of agreement among orthodox, Catholic, and Protestant Christians around the table of the Lord. The church celebrates the Lord's Supper as a dominical ordinance that memorializes the death of Jesus until he returns to earth (1 Corinthians 11). The elements of bread and wine symbolize the broken body and shed blood of the Savior who gave his life for the forgiveness of sins. Most Christians acknowledge that Christ is somehow present in the Supper and that the bonds between believers are somehow strengthened in the shared partaking of the elements.

The Supper occupies a unique place in Christian worship as the one ordinance believers are to enjoy repeatedly through their lives culminating in the promised messianic banquet where the Lord himself shall once more, and in person, serve as host (Isa 25:6; Matt 8:11). At the inaugural Supper Jesus said to his apostles, "I will not drink of this fruit of the vine from now on until that day when I drink it with you, new, in My Father's kingdom" (Matt 26:29 NASB).

Jesus presided over a smaller gathering of disciples after his resurrection but before he ascended to the right hand of the Father. During the Emmaus Road encounter, the risen Jesus, while yet unrecognized by his followers, "took the bread, blessed and broke it, and gave it to them. Then their eyes were opened, and they recognized him, but he disappeared from their sight." Later his followers "began to describe what had happened on the road and how he was made known to them in the breaking of bread" (Luke 24:30, 31, 35). Christians around the world partake of the bread and the cup again and again on this side of the return of Jesus according to their Lord's own Maundy Thursday directive: "Do this (*mandatum*) in remembrance of me" (1 Cor 11:24), even as they await with happy anticipation that future partaking in their eternal home.

The Lord's Supper also discloses the inextricable unity between the New Testament and the Old. By inaugurating the Supper at the Passover meal, Jesus confirmed the deep, beautiful, and essential unity between the passing over of the Death Angel at the sight of the blood of sheep and goats in ancient Egypt and the passing over of sin forever secured by the spilling of his own blood at Calvary. The ancient central festival of Israel that memorialized temporary deliverance from earthly bondage through the sacrifice of unblemished animals in Egypt foreshadowed, as type to antitype, the perfect and eternal deliverance from sin, death, hell, and the devil through the sacrifice of the spotless Lamb of God in the central festival of the global church.

Before the Reformation

Matthew recorded Jesus's words of institution in the Upper Room:

> While they were eating, Jesus took some bread, and after a blessing, He broke it and gave it to the disciples, and said, "Take, eat; this is

My body." And when He had taken a cup and given thanks [*eucharistesas*], He gave it to them, saying, "Drink from it, all of you; for this is My blood of the covenant, which is poured out for many for forgiveness of sins." (Matt 26:26–28 NASB)

The four accounts of the Supper's institution in the Bible—followed by the prominent place given to it in the *Didache* and by saints Justin, Ignatius, Irenaeus, Cyprian and many others—show that the Eucharist has featured as a central component of Christian worship since its institution by the Lord himself. Jesus instituted it on the first Maundy Thursday. But what did the church believe took place in the Lord's Supper? Was Jesus Christ really present in it? Precision in doctrine often follows controversy, which, for the Lord's Supper, did not emerge in earnest until the Middle Ages.

In the ninth century Paschasius Radbertus expressed doubts that the presence of Christ in the elements could be identified with the body of Jesus in heaven. Berengarius opposed the real presence of Christ in the Supper for a short time in the eleventh century. At the Fourth Lateran Council of 1215, the doctrine of the real presence became the dogma of transubstantiation in the Roman church: "The body and the blood of Jesus Christ are truly [*substantia*] contained in the sacrament of the altar under the outward appearances (*accidents*) of bread and wine, the bread having been transubstantiated into the body and the wine into the blood."[1] More than three centuries after Christ, John Chrysostom (c. 347–407) spoke of "the Lord being sacrificed and laid upon the altar and the priest standing and praying over the victim."[2] The Council of Trent (1545–1563) consolidated early church teaching on the real presence, the Eucharist as a sacrifice, and the theologizing of Thomas Aquinas on the Supper resulting in the doctrine of the sacrifice of the Mass against which Martin Luther and others had protested. As Jaroslav Pelikan aptly puts it, Roman doctrine asserts that "Christ sacrificed himself on Calvary once, but the Mass re-presents that sacrifice."[3]

---

[1] Jaroslav Pelikan, *The Christian Tradition: A History of the Development of Doctrine* (Chicago: University of Chicago Press, 1978), 3:203–4.

[2] Pelikan, *The Christian Tradition*, 1:2.

[3] Pelikan, *The Melody of Theology: A Philosophical Dictionary* (Cambridge: Harvard University Press, 1988), 79.

Reformation Voices

Of the seven sacraments affirmed in the Roman church, Martin Luther retained only the dominical ordinances he found in the Bible—baptism and the Lord's Supper. Both serve as channels of divine blessing, but neither does so "in itself" (*ex opera operato*) "by mere partaking."[4] Faith alone finds the promise of Christ alone by grace alone in the visible word of the Lord's Supper. For Luther, believers obtain salvation without the sacraments, but baptism and the Supper provide assurance of the promise of God in Christ to forgive sinners and save them unto eternal life.

Protestants reject the Roman Catholic sacrifice of the Mass according to the testimony of Rom 6:10, Heb 7:27, and 1 Pet 3:18 that Christ died "once for all." To imagine otherwise involves an attempt to crucify Christ afresh. Thus, Luther wrote,

> For through [Christ's] one death and sacrifice he has taken away and swallowed up all sins. Yet [the Roman priests] go ahead every day and offer him up a thousand times throughout the world. . . . This is such an abomination. . . . The blasphemy is so great that it must wait for eternal hell fire.[5]

Martin Luther believed the doctrine of transubstantiation was an absurd attempt to reduce the mystery of Christ's presence in the Supper to a rational event. Jesus Christ's actual body is present in, with, and under the properties of the elements of bread and wine without any transformation of the substance of either. Sometimes called "consubstantiation," this view asserts the actual bodily presence of Christ in the Supper by virtue of the communication of properties (*communicatio idiomatum*) between the divine and human natures of the God-man, Jesus Christ. Christ's body participates in the omnipresence of the divine nature so that his body is truly, though mysteriously, present everywhere, including in the Supper. Christ is present bodily in the Supper, owing to divine omniscience, not rational comprehension of the mode of that presence.

---

[4] See Martin Luther, *The Annotated Luther*, vol. 3, ed. Hans J. Hillerbrand, Kirsi I. Stjerna, Timothy J. Wengert (Minneapolis: Fortress, 2015), 38–59.

[5] Martin Luther, *Luther's Works*, 36:320.

Huldrych (or Ulrich) Zwingli, the Swiss Reformer, objected. If Christ was somehow present *at* the Lord's Supper by virtue of the divine omnipresence, his body was certainly not present *in* the Supper. For Zwingli, the location of Christ's body was no mystery. X marks the spot—Jesus Christ is seated at the right hand of the heavenly Father. Holy Communion for Zwingli involved the deployment of divinely provided symbols that serve as "a memorial of the suffering of Christ."[6] This view came to be known pejoratively as "mere symbolism."

Because the fierce tensions between Luther and Zwingli over the Supper threatened to explode into open conflict, Landgrave Philip of Hesse called a summit meeting to be held at Marburg in October of 1529. Consensus was reached on fourteen points of doctrine, but on the Lord's Supper the delegations had to admit, "We have not agreed together at this moment whether the body and blood of Christ be corporeally present in the bread and wine."[7] At the climax of the meeting, Zwingli lamented that Luther defended a doctrine but was "unable or unwilling to cite a single Scripture passage to prove it." Luther, having anticipated Zwingli's well-known objection to the real presence, had secretly etched in Latin Jesus's words of institution into the wooden tabletop and had covered them with an inscription. In response to Zwingli's challenge, Luther uncovered his etching—*hoc est corpus meum* ("this is my body") and declared, "Here is our Scripture passage."[8] Zwingli insisted that *est* (is) be read as *significat* (signifies), but Luther pointed to the little three-letter word etched in the table before them, *est*, and refused to budge.

Children of the Reformation

Variations on Zwingli's non-sacramental, minimalist view of the Supper would be shared by many of the radical Reformers, including the Anabaptists. In order to emphasize their convictions about what was and was not present in the Supper, Swiss Anabaptists, in the Schleitheim Confession of 1527,

---

[6] See Alister E. McGrath, *Christian Theology: An Introduction*, 6th ed. (Newark: John Wiley & Sons, 2017), 400.

[7] See Timothy George, *Theology of the Reformers*, rev. ed. (Nashville: B&H, 2013), 155.

[8] George, *Theology of the Reformers*, 151.

speak not of the Eucharist or of the Lord's Supper but of the "breaking of bread" and of "the Lord's table."

> All those who wish to break one bread in remembrance of the broken body of Christ, and all who wish to drink of one drink as a remembrance of the shed blood of Christ, shall be unified beforehand by baptism in one body of Christ which is the church of God. . . .[9]

For these Swiss Anabaptist forebearers of the Mennonites, both baptism and the Lord's Supper served as instruments of the separation of believers from the world and of discipline within the church, not as means of saving grace. Baptismal pools and tables of the Lord belonged not to unbelieving infants and the unconverted children of church members but to publicly confessing disciples of Jesus Christ separated from the world unto him.

> For as Paul points out we cannot at the same time be partakers of the Lord's table and the table of devils; we cannot at the same time drink the cup of the Lord and the cup of the devil.[10]

A century later, Mennonites at Dordrecht (1632) called the Supper "a sacrament" but kept to the language of remembrance and signification in its confession of what the Supper is. For them, the Lord's Supper was

> to be observed to [Christ's] remembrance . . . to be observed by believers in commemoration of the suffering and death of the Lord . . . So is the observance of this sacrament also to remind us of the benefit of the said death and sufferings of Christ . . . [in the Supper] we endeavor to maintain and keep alive the union and communion which we have with God, and amongst one another; which is thus shown and represented to us by the . . . breaking of bread.[11]

The Christian traditions deeply influenced by the so-called "mere symbolist" and "mere memorialist" views of the Supper that trace back to Zwingli have fought hard against any notion of "carnality" in the Supper

---

[9] John H. Leith, *Creeds of the Churches*, 3rd ed. (Louisville: Westminster John Knox, 1982), 285.

[10] Leith, *Creeds*, 285.

[11] Leith, *Creeds*, 302.

whereby Christ's body is supposed in any way to be present. And they have mainly resisted affirmation of any "sacramental" component in the Supper, especially where consumption of the elements holds out the promise of converting grace. Some, such as the Anabaptists at Schleitheim, even hesitate to affirm the possibility that communicants might lay hold of "benefits" in the Supper, speaking instead only of how the elements might "remind us of the benefit" of the death of Jesus.

But must rejection of carnality, converting grace, or some automatic sacramentalism inherent in the elements and available to whoever partakes (*ex opera operato*) require denial that God the Holy Spirit might use the Supper to "benefit" communicants? Would this be so even if such benefits are reduced to those derived from a divinely mandated "reminding"?

In time, some of the streams of Christianity most closely associated with the Zwinglian minimalist views of the Lord's Supper would retain but also supplement Zwinglian symbolism and memorialism with the language of "benefit." The chief source of that supplementation was the theology of John Calvin.

A Spiritual Banquet

The second-generation Reformer John Calvin (1509–1564) advanced his own version of the real presence of Jesus Christ in the Lord's Supper. He was convinced his reading of Scripture on this point was both more faithful to the biblical text than that of Rome, Luther, or Zwingli and that it offered a viable mediating position he desperately hoped might heal the breach among Protestants over Holy Communion. Calvin taught that the Supper is a spiritual banquet in which believers, by faith, partake of Jesus Christ, who is truly present, not physically or carnally, but spiritually. As bread and wine "nourishes, sustains, and preserves the life of the body," so the bread and wine offered in Holy Communion, if received by faith, "benefits us spiritually . . . confirms, comforts, refreshes, and makes us joyful."[12] Communicants do truly "feed upon Christ by faith" spiritually and so benefit spiritually in the Supper.

---

[12] John Calvin, *Institutes of the Christian Religion* 4.17.3.

The Supper, for Calvin, held the power to nourish the faith and the communal bonds of fellowship among the faithful but also to make sick or even result in the death of those who partake "in an unworthy manner," those who eat and drink "without recognizing the body" (1 Cor 11:27–29). How might approach to a table packing such power ever merit the appending of the word "mere" to modify its meaning? For Calvin, Christians approach the Lord's Table not hoping to chew on Christ or to secure their conversion unto salvation. But believers do, as baptized disciples, expect to meet their Lord at the banquet table in the bread and the cup and to lay hold of real spiritual benefits there.

The Baptists

Many nineteenth and twentieth century Baptists who trace their roots more to English separatism than to Anabaptism would also reflect dependance upon a minimalist understanding of the Lord's Supper. The distinctive marks of Zwingli's teaching weave through confessional history of the believers' churches with their focus upon the symbolic nature of communion that memorializes the death of Jesus Christ on the cross. That influence is on display in the Baptist Faith and Message adopted by the Southern Baptist Convention in 1963:

> The Lord's Supper is a symbolic act of obedience whereby members of the church, through partaking of the bread and the fruit of the vine, memorialize the death of the Redeemer and anticipate his second coming.

Communicants act in the Supper. God does not. A mere thirty-eight years earlier, in the Baptist Faith and Message 1925, the same Southern Baptist Convention had adopted fuller and richer language in their confession. The Supper is by no means a sacrifice but is designed to commemorate his death, to confirm the pledge and renewal of their communion with him and of their church fellowship. But still, the commemorating, confirming, and renewing mark the human acts of believers in the Supper, not the divine delivery of benefits through it.

Though Baptists of the last two centuries have taken or tended toward nonsacramental views of both baptism and the Lord's Supper, many Baptists of the seventeenth and eighteenth centuries did not. In the year 1600, almost all English Christians understood the sacraments of baptism and the Lord's Supper according to article 25 of the 39 articles of the Church of England and thus as not

> only badges of Christian men's profession, but also as effectual signs of grace and God's good will toward us, by which he doth work invisibly in us, and doth not only quicken but also strengthen and confirm our Faith in Him.

Baptists, having emerged from English Separatism, put forth in 1612 their *Propositions and Conclusions* wherein they taught a doctrine of the sacraments that integrated both baptism and the Lord's Supper with the preached word:

> The outward baptism and supper do not confer and convey grace and regeneration to participants or communicants: but as the word preached, they serve only to support and stir up repentance and faith of communicants till Christ come . . .

By the nineteenth century the settling of Baptists into minimalist and nonsacramental language to express their views of baptism and the Lord's Supper had greatly advanced on both sides of the Atlantic. But the founding president of the Southern Baptist Theological Seminary, James Petigru Boyce, employs remarkable sacramental language in this 1864 catechism:

> 7. Does the mere partaking, either of Baptism or the Lord's Supper confer spiritual blessings?
> No; they are worthless, if not injurious, to those who do not exercise faith.

> 8. But how is it when they are partaken of by those who do exercise faith?
> The Spirit of God makes them, to such persons, precious means of grace.

Charles Haddon Spurgeon spoke of baptism and the Lord's Supper as ordinances, not as sacraments. He employed the then familiar Baptist formula regarding the ordinances as outward and visible signs of inward and invisible graces. But Spurgeon's accounting of the inward grace of which the Supper was a sign was anything but bare or spare. In the Supper, Spurgeon believed, "Jesus Christ comes to us and refreshes us, and in that sense, we eat his flesh and drink his blood."[13] The Supper was "more than a memorial, it is a fellowship, a communion."[14]

To deny that communion offers spiritual benefits to partakers does not evacuate the Supper of meaning. Jesus said, "Do this in remembrance of me," and the apostle Paul said, "For as often as you eat this bread and drink the cup, you proclaim the Lord's death until he comes" (1 Cor 11:23–26). The obedient remembering and proclaiming resonate with deep biblical meaning and purpose. One of the most frequently issued divine reprimands Holy Scripture records is that God's people "forget" the Lord's faithfulness, commands, and their covenant privileges and responsibilities. And the church across the ages recognizes that proclamation of the death, resurrection, and promised return of Jesus belong to most urgent, precious, and happy duties of discipleship. Must the same Christians who know they meet Christ in prayer and preaching insist that they do not in the bread and the cup of communion? Must believers who seek and find help in sermons and hymn-singing deny finding any assistance at all at the table of the Lord?

After two thousand years since the Lord Jesus inaugurated the Supper on that first Maundy Thursday, its place in Christian worship remains secure. Surely pastors and theologians of every denomination find sufficient incentive in Holy Scripture for the deepening of our comprehension of the sacred meal instituted by our Lord and to the retrieval of faithful understandings that our forbearers might bequeath to us if only we heirs would but claim that inheritance. The painful history of disagreement around the Lord's Table surely stands as one of the most scandalous and shameful stains on the long story of people of God. May the Lord grant to us more enjoyment of the fellowship within the body of Christ, and may we find more of that enjoyment around the table of remembrance he set for us.

---

[13] Anthony R. Cross and Philip Thompson, *Baptist Sacramentalism* (Eugene, OR: Pickwick, 2020), 71–72.

[14] Cross and Thompson, *Baptist Sacramentalism*, 75.

For Additional Study

Cross, Anthony R., and Philip Thompson. *Baptist Sacramentalism.* Eugene, OR: Pickwick, 2020.

George, Timothy. *The Theology of the Reformers.* Rev. ed. Nashville: B&H, 2013.

Leith, John H. *Creeds of the Churches.* 3rd ed. Louisville: Westminster John Knox, 1982.

Lumpkin, William L. *Baptist Confessions of Faith.* 2nd rev. ed. Edited by Bill J. Leonard. King of Prussia, PA: Judson, 2011.

Schreiner, Thomas R., and Matthew Crawford, eds. *The Lord's Supper.* Nashville: B&H, 2011.

Waters, Guy P. *The Lord's Supper as the Sign and Meal of the New Covenant.* Wheaton: Crossway, 2019.

Also see these articles: Reformation Theology, Church, Church Membership, Baptism

37

Spiritual Formation and Discipleship

STEFANA DAN LAING

Introduction and Overview

Christian spiritual formation is the gradual and holistic shaping of a believer by the triune God into the fullness of the image of Christ through the Holy Spirit's facilitation of union with Christ and, through him, union with the Father (John 14:20–23). This sanctified and sanctifying union results in spiritual growth that flows out in works of loving mission, effected through spiritual disciplines that believers practice both privately and corporately. Spiritual formation is not the same as Christian spirituality, which is more of a generic umbrella term. Formation implies that there is a subject to be formed, a formative agent (or agents), a program of formation, and a formational goal toward which one strives.

Biblical Overview

The Old Testament speaks clearly and frequently about the need for the people of God to be formed into a holy nation and a royal priesthood, reflecting the nature and character of their God (Exod 19:6; 1 Pet 2:9). The Israelites were formed by hearing, memorizing, and fulfilling the Torah and were obligated to pass it on to their children, forming the next generation

473

to know and obey God. Aside from continuously teaching Torah ("when you sit in your house, and when you walk along the way, when you lie down and when you get up," Deut 6:7), Israel would be formed by incorporating God's truth into facets of daily life, binding small token reminders onto their bodies, doorframes, and gates (Deut 6:8–9). Rituals (like sacrifices), festivals (like Passover), and creedal affirmations (like the Shema) throughout the year were instructive and formative to their faith and identity, as was regular recounting of historical narratives, a kind of national testimony of God's deliverance and faithfulness (Deut 6:20–25; Psalm 105). Virtually all the relevant passages about Israel's spiritual life speak in corporate terms, underscoring the critical importance of the community as a formative context for growing spiritually and connecting to God. The New Testament continues these established formative structures, structures within which even Jesus operated. While they speak in individual terms about each disciple's sacrificial response to the calling of Christ, the Gospels and the early apostolic message spoke unitedly in corporate terms about spiritual formation in and through the church with a missional, extramural *telos*. Believers grew in their understanding of faith and spiritual maturity, in holiness and the practice of Christian virtue. Together they were fitted into a structure that resembled a family, a household, and a temple of the living God (Ephesians 2; 1 Peter 2).

Historical Overview

The concept of personal spiritual formation and of official formation for clerical ministry has a long history among Catholic and orthodox Christians with respect to priestly formation and an even longer history in Christian monasticism with respect to the training and instruction of novices in communal institutions. Their training involved biblical and doctrinal knowledge and character formation under the tutelage of a spiritual director or mentor. In the tradition of the desert fathers, there is frequent reference to a spiritual father or mother (*abba* or *amma*), spiritually mature practitioners to whom younger monks would come, begging them, "Speak a word!" From the sayings and teachings of the desert fathers, certain teachers such as Evagrius Ponticus (known as a psychologist of the soul) gathered and systematized the desert's wisdom. One of his students, John Cassian, transmitted his teachings to the West and dispensed them to his own monastic community of brothers at Marseilles. In time, these teachings and the monastic model of formation within community influenced Benedict, who called monastic life a "school for the Lord's service." Through him, the teaching has come down to the present. Each member practiced the virtues of humility, chastity, obedience, and vibrant love for God and one another, understanding that for ongoing and lasting growth, formation must be holistic, involving heart (emotion), soul (will/desire), mind (intellect/understanding), and strength (actions), and it must extend love to the neighbor (social dimension). In the contemporary Catholic Church, contributions to spiritual formation come from writers such as Father Richard Rohr (OFM), a Franciscan, and Sister Mary Margaret Funk (OSB), a Benedictine. Orthodox contributors to this field include John Chryssavgis, John Zizioulas, Kallistos Ware, and Benedicta Ward.

Outside the monastic tradition, the church offered its own program of formation as catechetical instruction to baptismal candidates. The extensive catechetical process formed a critical part of discipleship in areas where people came to faith without any prior knowledge of the Old Testament or of Christian doctrine. Other means of formation included liturgy, celebrations of seasons in the Christian calendar, and observance of rituals through the sacraments/ordinances of the church. The Reformed tradition shone a spotlight on robust biblical preaching and also encouraged formation in the home through family worship and study of catechisms. The Wesleyan and Pietist traditions emphasized formation through frequent and regular small group meetings (such as the Wesley brothers' "Holy Club") in which members studied and prayed together and held each other accountable for practicing the spiritual disciplines.

Contemporary Context

Current literature abounds in this field, and it is burgeoning with abundant resources for evangelicals. In about the 1960s, evangelicals took an intentional interest in spiritual formation, and several theological institutions incorporated principles and practices of this discipline into their curricula of training ministers. Asbury, Wheaton, Biola, Moody, Fuller, Dallas Theological Seminary, and Southern Baptist seminaries offered courses on spiritual formation for Christian ministry within their curricula. Some schools eventually established degrees and entire departments dedicated to spiritual and pastoral formation.[1]

An early and enduring writer on formation was Richard Foster, whose classic book *Celebration of Discipline* (1978) marked the clear entry of Protestant evangelicals into this arena. Foster, a Quaker, was profoundly influenced by the prolific Dallas Willard, a Southern Baptist minister and philosopher, whose books *Spirit of the Disciplines* (1988), *The Divine Conspiracy* (1999), and *Renovation of the Heart* (2002) promoted holistic spiritual growth through the practice of classic Christian disciplines. Together they founded Renovaré, an institute promoting resources for "intentional Christian spiritual formation." Books by Willard, Foster, Christopher Hall (who writes on formation from the patristic tradition), Jan Johnson (on *lectio divina*), Evan Howard (Vineyard minister and founder of Spirituality Shoppe), and others have created robust offerings for students and laypersons alike. Other writers who have contributed to the field include Southern Baptist Donald Whitney, who focused on pursuing sanctification through biblical spiritual disciplines, and Methodist Richard Mulholland, who envisioned formation as a life-long journey with a communal goal.[2] Increasingly, theological institutions not only offer classes in Christian formation but also integrate formational elements into each course in their ministerial degree programs. This strategy mitigates against the bifurcation of the devotional and intellectual life of future ministers and instead encourages a spiritual synthesis of heart, head, and practical ministry within an ecclesial context.

Theological and Biblical Foundations

Spiritual formation is an integral part of sanctification, located and grounded in this doctrine. It is a vital aspect of soteriology that facilitates a believer's transformation into Christlikeness. Many would consider sanctification chiefly the work of the Holy Spirit, but in truth, it is the work of the triune

---

[1] Evan Howard, *A Guide to Christian Spiritual Formation* (Grand Rapids: Baker, 2018), 6–8.

[2] See M. Robert Mulholland Jr. and Ruth Haley Barton, *Invitation to a Journey: A Road Map to Spiritual Formation*, rev. ed. (Downers Grove: IVP, 2016).

God. This trinitarian activity becomes apparent when spiritual formation is viewed through a systematic theological lens.

We can think of spiritual formation in theological terms from creation through to transformation. Genesis 1 clearly indicates that humanity was initially formed by God's own hands, fashioned in the divine image and likeness, and enlivened by God's own breath as it was breathed into the first human's nostrils. This creation act constituted a literal *formation* of humanity by a good, communal God who created the first humans to be communal and good, able to relate to God and to each other. God's enlivening breath points forward to the reception/infilling by the Holy Spirit at regeneration, which begins the process of sanctification. Biblical spirituality is body-affirming from the beginning and teaches that God's physical creation is revelatory of the nature, character, and glory of God (Psalms 8, 19). Genesis declares that the material creation and embodied existence are good, underscoring the importance of the doctrines of creation and theological anthropology (*imago Dei*) for understanding humans' ability to walk in holiness with their Creator God.

Human nature experienced *deformation* of the *imago Dei* as it became marred because of sinful disobedience and its consequences. Disobedience brought about the fall of human nature and the corruption of flesh, intellect, and soul/desire/will. Humanity's fall impacted the created order as the entire creation became vulnerable to forces of deterioration, decay, and death (Romans 8). Sin entered the world, and our human nature became susceptible to its power to harm ourselves, others, and the created order. The negative dynamics in play at the time of the fall—demonic temptation, misguided and selfish desire, pride, blame, shame, guilt, pain—as well as the resultant struggle between humans at intimate family levels and in broader society, remain in play as long as the world is under the sway of the "prince of the powers of the air" who is "at work in those who are disobedient" (Eph 2:1–3; Genesis 3–4). In addition, there is spiritual and physical conflict within each human being because each still bears God's image yet lives out of a fallen human nature. The fact of these struggles can be discouraging (Romans 7), but believers do not struggle without hope.

Because of the Creator's mercy and great love for his fallen creatures, God made possible a *re-formation* and initiated the process himself. Through the incarnation of the agent of all creation, God revealed himself to humankind through Christ the "last Adam" (Romans 5; 1 Corinthians 15), who demonstrated how to live a life pleasing to God. By Christ's atoning death in humans' place, justification is effected as their ransom is paid, their sin is covered, and the offer of salvation is extended to humans by grace through faith. Thus, the process of re-creation (regeneration) is initiated, and the marred *imago Dei* begins to be restored as, through Christ, who is the very image of the Father (2 Cor 4:4; Heb 1:3), God "condemned sin in the flesh" (Rom 8:3). By Christ's resurrection, God who raised him has triumphed over death and sin, opening the possibility for human beings to be indwelt by the Holy Spirit and live a resurrected life, putting "to death the deeds of the body" (Rom 8:13) even in the present life, not just at the eschaton.

Victory over sin does not mean that believers never sin anymore, but rather that they receive the strength to disallow sin to "reign" in their mortal bodies, considering themselves "dead to sin and alive to God in Christ Jesus" (Rom 6:11), as the Spirit's restoring and sanctifying work of *conformation* to Christ takes place in them. Spiritual formation as a topic of study concentrates mostly on the conformation process, for which we may also commonly use the term "sanctification" interchangeably. In sanctification, regenerate believers continue to grow by both inward and outward processes as they are shaped and refined into the image of Christ. Amid these inner and outer influences, questions of sin, grace, and agency abound with regard to rooting out sin and how God's grace empowers the believer to do so. Because sin can never be fully eradicated from human nature in this life, sanctification always involves struggle. This process distinguishes itself in that—unlike justification—it involves human action/agency in order to make progress. In justification, which Protestants understand as a punctiliar, completed action performed by God alone, the triune God acts for us on the basis of our faith in the message of salvation and the sacrifice of Christ. Our justification involves no other action on our part, nor do we receive any merit whatsoever. It is an action effected purely by God's sheer grace.

In sanctification and spiritual maturity, however, God involves regenerate believers in their own growth in holiness, as demonstrated by imperatives such as "adopt the same attitude as that of Christ Jesus" (Phil 2:5); "walk worthy of the calling you received" (Eph 4:1); "grow in every way into him who is the head—Christ" (Eph 4:15); "take off . . . the old self . . . be renewed in the spirit of your minds . . . put on the new self" (Eph 4:22–24);

"be imitators of God, as dearly loved children, and walk in love, as Christ also loved us" (Eph 5:1–2). Internally, the Holy Spirit indwells believers, empowering them to learn and obey God's Word, uniting them to the Spirit of Christ, and through Christ to the Father (John 16). Externally, believers engage in spiritual disciplines (termed in some traditions "means of grace") as aids toward holiness. These disciplines are based in Scripture and modeled by Christ and our faith predecessors in both Old and New Testaments. They encourage and effect a continuing process of conformation, which can lead to gradual *transformation* of a person's life. The operative agents are the trinitarian God and human free will, although the latter remains fallen.

The earthly journey of sanctification is accomplished by the Spirit's indwelling and enlivening activity, transforming believers from within and aligning their minds, hearts, and wills to the mind and character of Christ. Believers therefore can choose to live obediently and walk in holiness, thus pleasing God and fulfilling his will (Rom 12:1–2). As believers grow in spiritual maturity through God's inner work "into the measure of the stature and fullness of Christ," they also grow through their own outward exercise of works of faith, accomplishing Paul's admonition to "work out your own salvation with fear and trembling," even though "it is God who is working in you both to will and to work" (Phil 2:12–13). There is still no merit in works of faith, and any fruit that a believer may bear is due solely to the sanctifying work of God (Galatians 5). Transformation is a continuing, lifelong process and not a completed stage until glorification. It does indicate progress and is the fruit of constant and intentional conformation to Christ—to his "mind," his way of thinking about God and the world, his perspective on spiritual realities, his priorities, actions, habits, and mission. Transformation is frequently marked by a life of peace and self-mastery, of deep spiritual joy and a fervent love for God and others. The struggle against sin seems less intense, and one's life is spiritually stable and fruitful. In Christian works of spiritual devotion (such as biographies [*vitae*] of holy men and women), this stage is often characterized by expressions of loving intimacy with Christ, who is pictured as the heavenly Bridegroom, and of earnest and even painful longing for consummation at the heavenly banquet (Song of Songs 2; Revelation 21–22). Other typical literature illustrating spiritual growth and the long path of transformation includes stories of journey like *Pilgrim's Progress*. Transformation looks toward glorification after the resurrection, hoping for the full restoration of the *imago Dei* in humans so that we can behold God in his light, being fully alive at the beatific vision, as described by Irenaeus of Lyon: "The glory of God is a living human being and human life is the vision of God."[3]

Dynamics and Practices of Formation

How does formation happen, and how can Christians be spiritually formed? Before these questions can be adequately answered, we must acknowledge that formation of various kinds takes place continuously. Surrounding influences, both internal and external, constantly shape human minds, hearts, desires, and actions. Some formation is intentional and chosen, while other influences are unintentional and even undesirable.

External Factors in Spiritual Formation

External shaping through stimuli from the people and culture surrounding us appeals to our desires and forms a particular mindset and character. These stimuli can be positive or negative. For example, absorbing worldly messages that focus largely on self-love and leave no room for God-minded kingdom priorities will shape a person who absorbs these messages *away* from God. These external messages appeal to the sinful flesh, and humans carry out their associated actions and make decisions based on worldly discernment. Conversely, godly and edifying messages from a context of the worshipping community and Christian fellowship will shape a person thus surrounded *toward* God. This shaping happens when believers intentionally and expectantly seek to study and hear God's Word (Psalm 1).

In each case, the context can be intended or unintended, which will also have shaping consequences. *Unintended* formation passively accepts, absorbs, and integrates positive or negative influences and messages into one's mindset and resulting actions; sometimes these actions (especially from a mindset that has absorbed negativity) are surprising, and the thoughts and impulses behind them might not be fully realized or understood. It is particularly important to think about unintended external formation because frequently

---

[3] Irenaeus of Lyon, *Against Heresies* 4.20.7.

they result in unintended negative consequences that take time to identify, understand, and root out. These might include bad habits (of engagement or neglect), self-directed negativity including self-harm and addiction, depression, and other psychosocial and spiritual suffering/woundedness. *Intentional* formation implies agency wherein a person chooses her context so that she will be formed in a particular spiritual direction, as when, for example, one attends church or chooses to surround oneself with other encouraging believers. One may also intentionally resist conforming to the surrounding "age," both ethically (offering one's body as a living sacrifice) and theologically (discerning truth about God and his perfect will), while also intentionally seeking the renewal of one's mind for transformation (Rom 12:1–2).

The intentional rejection of negatively shaping forces leads one to rely on the Holy Spirit's work from within. Believers are shaped *internally* by the Spirit, who works to conform and transform believers. We may intentionally place ourselves in a position to be renewed, conformed, and transformed, but the Spirit sovereignly works according to his good pleasure. In this way he works both when we open ourselves to his work through spiritual disciplines and holy obedience, and also in mysterious and unexpected ways when we have reached the limit of our own efforts, or when we are disabled by suffering or wearied by our struggle with sin (John 3:8; Rom 8:26–27).

Psalm 1 wonderfully exemplifies the spiritual shaping of two kinds of people—blessed and wicked. Two formative influences appear in the text: the negative external influence of bad company (wicked scoffers) should be intentionally avoided, while the positive internal shaping influence of the Torah/Word should be cultivated and allowed to shape and nurture one's life as the law is regularly and constantly read, studied, and lived out. The person thus formed is spiritually stable, prosperous, righteous, and fruitful and walks the path of blessing and abundant life, while the path of the wicked leads to instability, condemnation, ruin, and disaster.

Shaping the New Self: Agency in Spiritual Formation

The Bible clearly expresses dual agency in formation: the triune God and each individual disciple. God has effected our liberation from sin and given new life in Christ for continued growth in holiness. This holiness is not something God alone maintains in us, as Paul encourages active steps toward holistic sanctification. "Do not offer any [of your members] to sin as weapons for unrighteousness, but . . . offer yourselves . . . and all the parts of yourselves to God as weapons for righteousness" (Rom 6:13). This intentional self-preservation from sin and self-presentation for righteousness involves all aspects of our humanity, and this passage especially emphasizes the "members of" our bodies, the external locus of sin (Rom 7:14–24). The believer's responsibility for sanctification is to "put to death the deeds of the body" and to walk in step with the Spirit (Rom 8:13). Similarly, Paul urges believers to "take off" the corrupted old self and "put on the new self . . . created according to God's likeness in righteousness and purity of the truth" (Eph 4:22–24). Although God's Spirit gives grace and strength to accomplish this, there remains a constant struggle between flesh and spirit, between a worldly mindset hostile to God and a spiritual indwelling that longs for God and for the fulfillment of his will for the created order. The struggle stems from our own sinfulness, as sinful tendencies and desires are lodged in our very members, as well as from the pull of the "rulers and authorities" around us (Eph 3:10; 6:12), which never stop opposing God's kingdom work of re-creation. The spiritual disciplines are a beginning point to engage in the struggle.

Killing Off the Old Self: Purpose of Spiritual Disciplines

A key component of spiritual formation is practice of the Christian spiritual disciplines. Many believers do not understand how the disciplines fit into the spiritual life because they either view the disciplines as optional or, worse, eschew them as meritorious works. However, the disciplines are an essential means of sanctification and are integral to spiritual growth. They are not a system or a bonus module one inserts into the spiritual life; rather, the disciplines are compulsory exercises for training in righteousness (1 Timothy 4) to effect personal and social change. Discipleship begins with self-denial, and disciplines are multiple ways to "put to death" (or mortify) aspects of sin in the body. Disciplines exercise and nurture the spiritual life by holistically addressing, strengthening, and refining areas of spiritual weakness, thereby strengthening the believer through struggle. Disciplines place believers in a position of availability before God, yielded and open to him to do transforming work in and through them. Therefore, through the disciplines, believers can fulfill the call to love both God and neighbor with the whole self.

Process of the Disciplines

The human body is a main vehicle through which the disciplines take hold and become effective, but Paul also teaches about another "body" he calls "the body of sin" (Rom 6:6) or "body of death" (Rom 7:24). This "body" is made up of sinful habits and attitudes;[4] it constitutes the points of unlikeness to Christ, places in which humans are de-formed by sin. Because of Christ's atoning death and our putting to death the "old self," the body of sin is rendered ineffective. Through the "new self" we are made alive in Christ and can freely walk in righteousness, "which results in sanctification" (Rom 6:19). When believers offer themselves to God through the spiritual disciplines stirred up by the Holy Spirit, who moves their mind and will in a Godward direction, then God gradually transforms them at every level. The disciplines gradually "re-form" thoughts, desires, and habits, which "con-form" us to Christ's mind and a life directed toward and in alignment with God.[5] Disciplines must be offered out of unconditional obedience, and as they are offered consistently and perseveringly—in spite of struggle—they become a means of grace and transformation.[6]

The disciplines have the effect of gradually breaking the hold of sin in human life. By practicing disciplines of active engagement (e.g., fellowship, prayer, worship, service, stewardship, hospitality, manual labor, Bible study), as well as of renunciation or private practice (e.g., fasting, chastity, solitude, silence, simplicity, meditation, discernment), believers are systematically and gradually trained to act, react, or respond to life situations in godly ways. Intentional engagement in these practices forms rhythms within believers, cuts against the grain of sinful tendencies, and "breaks the iron-clad grip of sin over human personality" as some disciplines treat sins of the mind, others sins of the affect, and others sins of the body.[7] The challenge to believers is the integration of disciplines into all of life, leaving no room for compartmentalization between life in the world and life in God, so that all of life is brought into conformity and "harmony with the will of God and the Kingdom of God," even as Jesus intended through his Sermon on the Mount (Matthew 5–7).[8]

---

[4] Mulholland and Barton, *Invitation to a Journey*, 145.

[5] Dallas Willard, *Renovation of the Heart* (Colorado Springs: NavPress, 2002), 71.

[6] Mulholland and Barton, 153.

[7] Willard, *Renovation*, 75.

[8] Willard, *Renovation*, 93.

For Additional Study

Athanasius. *On the Incarnation.* Translated by John Behr. Yonkers, NY: St. Vladimir's Seminary Press, 2011.

————. *Life of Antony.* Translated by Tim Vivian and Rowan A. Greer. Kalamazoo, MI: Cistercian Publications, 2003.

Augustine. *Confessions.* Translated by Maria Boulding. The Works of Saint Augustine, pt. 1, vol. 1. New York: New City Press, 2001.

Benedict. *The Rule of Saint Benedict.* Translated by David Parry. Cistercian Studies Series, no. 99. Leominster, England: Gracewing, 1992.

Bunyan, John. *Pilgrim's Progress.* Edited by W. R. Owens. Oxford Word's Classics. Oxford: Oxford University, 2003.

Cassian, John. *Institutes.* Translated by Boniface Ramsey. Ancient Christian Writers, no. 58. New York: The Newman Press, 2000.

————. *Conferences.* Translated by Colm Luibheid. New York: Paulist Press, 1985.

Chryssavgis, John. *In the Heart of the Desert.* Bloomington, IN: World Wisdom, 2008.

Evagrius. *On the Eight Thoughts.* Translated Robert E. Sinkiewicz in *Evagrius of Pontus: The Greek Ascetic Corpus.* Oxford: Oxford University Press, 2003.

Foster, Richard. *Celebration of Discipline.* 1978. Reprint, San Francisco: Harper Collins, 1998.

Funk, Mary Margaret. *Discernment Matters.* Collegeville, MN: Liturgical Press, 2013.

Gregory of Nyssa. *Life of Moses.* Translated by Abraham J. Malherbe and Everett Ferguson. New York: Paulist Press, 1978.

————. *Life of Saint Macrina.* Translated by Kevin Corrigan. Toronto: Peregrina, 1987.

Hausherr, Irenee. *Spiritual Direction in the Early Christian East.* Translated by Anthony P. Gythiel. Kalamazoo, MI: Cistercian, 1990.

Howard, Evan. *A Guide to Christian Spiritual Formation*. Grand Rapids: Baker, 2018.

Irenaeus of Lyon. *Against all Heresies* 1–5. In *The Ante-Nicene Fathers, vol. I: The Apostolic Fathers with Justine Martyr and Irenaeus*. Edited by Roberts, Alexander, James Donaldson, and Arthur C. Coxe. New York: Cosimo Inc, 2007.

Mulholland, M. Richard, with Ruth Haley Barton. *Invitation to a Journey*. IVP, 2016.

Scorgie, Glen, ed. *Dictionary of Christian Spirituality*. Grand Rapids: Zondervan, 2011.

Whitney, Donald. *Spiritual Disciplines for the Christian Life*. Colorado Springs: NavPress, 1991.

Willard, Dallas. *Spirit of the Disciplines*. San Francisco: HarperCollins, 1988.

———. *Renovation of the Heart*. Colorado Springs: NavPress, 2002.

Also see these articles: Holy Spirit, Sanctification, Worship, Prayer, Pastoral Theology

Worship

Preben Vang

Often, at least in modern American and Western European contexts, the word "worship" has become a reference to an event or a service, lasting a good hour and usually happening at some point during the weekend. In some contexts, it has even become a synonym for a special kind of music played and sung during those services/events. To correct such a narrowly defined notion of worship, others have claimed that "everything is worship."

The thinking that causes such a statement seems easy enough to follow when it suggests that 1) worship cannot and should not be limited to a weekly event and 2) everything we do as human beings automatically expresses our true priorities and allegiances and is therefore an expression of what we assign true worth (what we worship). However, in real life, when statements about worship become sweeping and all-inclusive, they often translate into the exact opposite of their original intention. If everything is worship, then nothing is worship, or, at least, worship is nothing in particular. Moreover, when rather undefined and diffused notions of worship are coupled with Western individualism, "worship" easily loses its substance and direction and turns into a matter of mere private devotion.

At the core of the word "worship" is the old English word "worthship," a word referencing that to which humans attach the highest worth. Put differently, worship speaks to the *what* and the *why* of the direction of human reverence. Historically, the word has been used in relation to God alone, as people considered him the only Being worthy of ultimate adoration, homage, praise, allegiance, thanksgiving, sacrifice, etc. From this it follows that the essence of worship is to express that God alone is the center of human life and the only true place for humans to find meaning and direction for their life. To worship, then, is to articulate and communicate one's pledged awareness that everything else in life (relationships, work, enjoyment, desires, goals, et al.) gains significance and achieves purpose from its rootedness in one's desire to honor God.

In much of the popular conversation among Christians about worship, focus has remained on the style and liturgy of a service—or the evangelistic/ missional focus and potential and purpose of such services. The underlying questions seem to be either "What do I prefer?" or "How can we use it to attract more people?" Both of these thoughts militate directly against the description of *worthship* above. Further, in the biblical perception, the term "worship" speaks to the exact opposite of events carefully designed to please the worshipper rather than the One being worshipped. Worship, rather, is to reflect on who God *is* and what God *does* (and has done) for human beings and rightfully express gratitude and submissiveness to him because of it.

There is, of course, a deep and persistent call in Scripture for the gospel to be preached and communicated at all times to all people of all cultures and nations. Yet even good, necessary, and God-honoring events, whose main aim is to attract new (and more) people, can too easily come to confuse the purpose of worship. While many Christian activities are both good and essential, *worship alone is the supreme and indispensable activity of the Christian church*. For example, Christians do not worship for the purpose of evangelism; it is the other way around. Christians evangelize in order to bring people back into fellowship with God so they can and will worship their Creator. Worship is the end! Other Christian efforts and activities—including evangelism, discipleship, healing, social engagement, et al.—are the means to that end, to bring creation back to the worship of their Creator.

The aim of this article is to explore the relationship between worship and theology. How does what we believe about God impact our worship? In particular, how does worship become Christian? Christian worship must by definition focus on a response to what God has done through Christ; or, more fully, Christian worship is the human communicative response to God's communication of his love for his creation in Christ.

Strikingly different from the worship of other religions in the Roman Empire—filled as these were with statues, temples, sacrifices, and cultic rituals—early Christian worship had a decidedly verbal character, one that was deeply rooted in its expression of gratitude for God's revelatory acts in history as expressed most climactically in Christ. Centered as it was, therefore, in the experience and awareness of God's love, mercy, and grace, early Christian worship was a place of gathering and sending. Worship was a movement beginning with awe-filled gatherings centering around the risen Lord, who by his Spirit would empower his people to imitate his acts of love, mercy, and grace (Matt 16:24; Luke 9:23; 1 Cor 4:16; 11:1; 1 Thess 1:6; cf. 1 Thess 2:14; Heb 6:12; 13:7; 3 John 11) as they were sent to a life of witness in the world.

Early Christians clearly understood themselves as worshippers in the tradition of Abraham (Gal 3:6–7). Moreover, they were *the people of the new covenant* promised by the prophets (Jer 31:33–34; Ezek 36:26–27); indeed, they were the very people who had come to know the presence of God through the evident indwelling of God's Holy Spirit (Joel 2:28–29; Acts 2:1–4, 16–18; 1 Cor 3:16; cf. John 4:23–24). With the assurance and experience of the presence of God's living Spirit in their gatherings (worship), they were moored to God's story and God's deeds rather than to location and/or sacred buildings.

Even the timing for their gatherings declared their understanding of God's revelation in history—the resurrection of Christ on a Sunday morning became the time that symbolically gave evidence to the focus of their worship (Mark 16:4–6; Luke 24:1–7; Matt 28:5–6; Acts 20:7; 1 Cor 16:2). Their call (Acts 2:42) was fivefold, including 1) to gather for worship (Acts 1:15; 2:46; 5:12; 1 Cor 14:26; Heb 10:25; cf. plural pronouns about church), 2) to focus on the teachings of Christ, 3) to share their new life, 4) to remember Christ's sacrifice (the breaking of bread), and 5) to pray (Acts 2:42). When they did, they would come to know the resurrected Christ who remained with them (Matt 18:20).

Who Is God and Why Should He Be Worshipped?

That theology, one's view of God, has a profound impact on every aspect of Christian worship goes without saying. Historically, specific theological

convictions have directly shaped not only worship styles and specific liturgical expression, but even church architecture and furniture are shaped by
the same. Differences in style and content of worship services between
various denominations' worship, along with the architecture of their buildings and furnishings, speak directly to convictions about God and about
worship. Put succinctly, *semiotics is semantics*—the signs we use express our
convictions. While such a statement is a truism of life in general, it becomes
a theological statement when it relates to worship. That is, the "signs" we
use in a worship service (language, movement, books, architecture, furniture, dress, liturgy, lights, time-priorities, etc.) are ultimately theological
expressions.

This reality, however, never flows in just one direction—rather, it's
a dance. Just as much as theological convictions have a decidedly shaping
effect on worship pattern and content, the worship experience itself has a
shaping effect on people's theological convictions. This latter reality is true
not only because the act of worship itself communicates a formative quality
unto the participants, but it is true also because of the direct work of God's
Spirit upon the participants. The formative acts of worship as expressed, for
example, in Acts 2:42, become vehicles for the Spirit.

Even a quick glance at "worship" as described in Scripture reveals that
patterns do not follow the unavoidably reductionist explanations set by modern and systematized expressions of theological exploration. Great, helpful,
and astute as the best of these are, the scriptural impetus for worship comes,
as expressed above, from the awareness of the full sweep of God's story as
God reveals his loving presence from the time of creation to the fulfilment of
his purpose at history's end. Moreover, rather than being cosmological (ahis-
torical confrontation between God and other powers), biblical worship has a
distinctly narrative quality. When God's Holy Spirit opens people's eyes, and
they come to stand in awe of his loving and merciful involvement past and
present, worship becomes their only natural reaction. The transcendent God
is known through his immanence and worshipped as "God with us" and for
us (*pro nobis*).

Related to worship, Christians read the biblical narrative to know God,
to know themselves, and to know the world they live in. In the biblical narrative, the last two of these points are understood as a reflection upon the
first—who God is as the creator and sustainer of his creation.

Several significant points come to the fore for a brief overview. God's name does not arrive from people's prognoses of his qualities, nor does he give himself a descriptive label ("the Mighty One" or "the Powerful One"). Rather, he allows only one name for himself, *Yahweh*—"I AM—the one you need for me to be to you." This biblical emphasis on God's self-disclosure (Exod 3:14) accentuates that the God of the biblical narrative is both self-defining and self-communicating. Humans do not get to define him; rather, they come to know him only through his relationship with them.

God is knowable precisely because he is a *living and acting* God. That is, he is not dead, not even quiescent. Again, this speaks to fellowship. Just like another person cannot truly be known outside of an active relationship with that person, knowledge of God cannot be separated from a commitment to Christ as he is revealed through the biblical narrative. As church fathers such as Augustine and Anselm put it, *I believe in order to understand.* In other words, God illuminates our reading of his narrative by his Holy Spirit that we may come to know him. Genuine Christian worship presumes a personal relationship with God in Christ.

God's relational character is an expression of his very being. The God who is worshipped as ONE (*Hear, O Israel, Yahweh is our God, Yahweh is one,* Deut 6:4) also reveals himself as Father, Son (Rom 9:5), and Spirit. The three are distinct yet not separable. In God's self-revelation, neither of the three persons can be understood apart from the two others. God's very being finds definition by the relationship among the Father, Son, and Spirit. God is relational within himself and should be worshipped as triune!

The emphasis on God being the Creator of all that exists (Genesis 1–2; 14:19c; Ps 89:11; Rom 11:36; Rev 4:11), including the individual human (Ps 139:14–15; Eccl 12:1), highlights not only the human dependence upon her Creator but the depth of human relationships. Put differently, for worship of the triune creator God to be acceptable and meaningful, it must include a vehement rejection of the sin-caused divisions that surround diversity. As Christians root their self-understanding, their identity, in their relationship to God, worshipping and celebrating the very God who created them in his triune image brings awareness to a relational reality where all belong as siblings under his care and provisions. Since providence in biblical terms speaks to God's purpose and destiny for his creation, it follows that to worship in the light of God's providence is to reject the omnipotence of sin.

Christian Worship and Participation in the Story of God

Since *Christian* worship is both Christocentric (Matt 9:8; Acts 13:32–33; Rom 9:5; Col 1:15–19; Heb 1:2–3) and trinitarian (Matt 28:19; John 14:1–4, 16–17, 26; Gal 4:6; 1 Cor 12:4–6; 2 Cor 13:14), it invites people to stand in awe before the God whose redemptive work happened on the scene of history—"in remembrance of me."

Beyond these broader considerations of who God is in his self-revelation, the narrative focus of early Christian worship springs from a self-understanding among the disciples that identified them as the people God invited, and continues to invite, to be his messengers to the world. Their identity was/is shaped by their connection to God's story as revealed climactically in Christ. Like how the Passover towers above other events as an identity marker for Israel and calls them to remembrance in the Mosaic covenant (e.g., *I am the God who brought you out of Egypt* [Exod 13:3, 8, 14, 16; 20:2; 29:46, etc.]), so Jesus's charge to his disciples during the Last Supper (*Do this in remembrance of me*) turned the celebration of the Lord's Supper into their defining mark of identity. Remembrance is not a mere "don't forget"; rather, it is a story-telling moment that gives identity to those who are defined by the same—a moment that places "my story" on the canvas of God's story.

Luke's summary of Peter's sermon in Acts 2:14–39 highlights how the experience at Pentecost defined the disciples' self-understanding as the people of the new covenant anticipated by the prophets. This perception of their identity as those who were called to worship in Spirit and truth (John 4:23) forged their understanding of the relationship between worship and identity. It might be briefly summarized like this:

1. They understood themselves as an elected people, not as individually elected persons. In line with the full story of God's dealing with his people through history, worship was corporate. God revealed himself in their midst; God's Spirit called people together to hear his voice, to see his power, to submit to his Lordship, and to offer thanks for his grace.

2. By establishing Jesus's identity through powerful genealogies, the Gospels of Matthew and Luke connect the Christians' experience to

the story of Israel and transform their Gospels into defining identity statements for the new covenant community.

For example, in Matthew, the genealogy of Jesus Christ can be reduced to two key connections—he is the son of David and the son of Abraham. Seeing Jesus's direct connection to Abraham, the father of Israel's faith and the recipient of God's promise of blessing (Gen 12:3), allows Matthew's readers to conclude that Jesus and his followers are the fulfillment of these promises from God. Similarly, Jesus's direct relation to David, a man after God's own heart who brought the promise to Abraham as close to its fulfillment as Israel had ever known, positions him as the one sent to establish God's kingdom among the people.

Broadly speaking, Luke does the same but connects Jesus's genealogy back through Abraham to God himself, thereby removing any possible doubt about the divine origin of Jesus and the purpose of his followers.

3. Mark begins his Gospel with John the Baptist and his explicit pronouncement of Jesus as the "one to come." From his opening line, the stage is set for the unavoidable conclusion that the story of Jesus and his followers inseparably connects to God's promises for his people. As C. H. Dodd helpfully concludes, Mark desires to describe the significance of the gospel for the whole event of God.[1] Further, the connection between Mark's opening and Isaiah 40 intimates that the prophetic restoration motif is fulfilled in Jesus and through the people following him.

4. Jesus's own worship and proclamation likewise followed the narratival pattern of promise and fulfilment. In Mark's summary of Jesus's preaching (1:15—the good news of God [*euangelion tou theou*] is that the Kingdom of God has come near), nearness does not refer to time as if to say "it's coming soon" but to space; it is here—Jesus brought it! It can be felt and seen—the anticipated "age to come" has now broken through (Matt 12:28; Luke 14:20; Matt 11:4–5/Luke 7:22; cf. Isa 35:4–5), albeit not in full.

---

[1] C. H. Dodd, *The Apostolic Preaching and Its Developments* (New York: HarperCollins, 1939), 8.

God's story is approaching its point of fulfillment, and his new covenant people participates in its arrival. Jesus's proclamation of the kingdom speaks less about the time of the kingdom and more about the character of the kingdom (cf. Luke 4:16–21).

5. The worship scene on the Mount of Transfiguration (Mark 9:1–7), which follows Peter's confession of Jesus as the Messiah (Mark 8:27–29; Matt 16:13–19), brings the Christian sense of identity and worship to a point of climactic heights. While seeing Jesus in his divine glory, God the Father speaks words echoing the three-part revelatory statement from Jesus's baptism with an important change to the third part of the statement: "This is my son, whom I love . . . listen to him" (Matt 17:5 NIV).

   The disciples are now included in the Father's revelatory statement about Jesus. Simultaneously, God confirms their confession and places them as Jesus's apprentices. Indeed, the whole scene functions as a declarative event parallel to Sinai and illustrative of eschatological fulfillment. The mountain is high and enveloped in a cloud (Exod 24:25–26; 19:9) symbolizing the power and glory of God's presence (Exod 40:34–8; Num 9:15–6; Isa 4:5).

6. As if to remind Christian readers that their worship must remain focused on God and his presence among them, Mark unmistakably highlights this by tersely connecting three defining worship events. Following immediately after what arguably was the greatest point of Jesus-worship by the Jewish crowds (Mark 11:1–11), Mark sandwiches the temple cleansing into the midst of the "cursing of the fig tree" story. In the flow of Mark's narrative, the withering fig tree incident showcases the necessity for acceptable worship to be closely moored to God's plan and purposes.

7. Like a crescendo to the good news about God's purpose for his creation, Jesus's resurrection establishes his teaching about himself and on the presence of God's kingdom as indisputably true. God's new covenant people are to worship as those who live in the time of fulfillment. God's eternal purpose of using his people as witnesses of his salvation to all nations has been made clear. When the resurrected Lord calls them to the mountain for worship and commission (Matt

28:17–20), their identity as God's people is now clear and ready to be
sealed by the Spirit (Acts 2; cf. 2 Cor 1:22; Eph 1:13; 4:30).

That the outpouring of God's Spirit at Pentecost as described in Acts 2
concludes with a description of new covenant worship is hardly incidental.
Acts 2:42–47 succinctly captures the reversal of the prophetic charge of the
Mosaic covenant. Their collective indictment can be summarized in three
categories that Luke here portrays as having been reversed by the new covenant people—by those filled by the Spirit of Jesus (e.g., Phil 1:19).

The three prophetic charges against the Mosaic covenant people were
1) idolatry, 2) social injustice, and 3) religious formalism. These were the
three issues that had destroyed their relationship with (and worship of)
God, and these were the points of rebellion from which they were called to
repent. Luke addresses each of these head on in Acts 2:42–47 as he exposes
how the early Christians worshipped in Spirit and truth. They were 1) no
longer idolatrous; rather, they were faithfully devoted to, not straying from
(*proskartereo*), God's purposes for his creation (Acts 2:42–43); 2) no longer
allowing social injustice; rather, they were taking care of the poor and the
needy (Acts 2:44–45); and 3) no longer merely formal and external in their
worship; rather, they met every day in the temple and in their homes with
sincere hearts (Acts 2:46–47).

Christian worship, then, without being pedantic in detail, is linked
to all the major themes of theology as these express God's revelation of
himself—creation, rebellion (sin), covenant, redemption, kingdom, and
eschatology. While it refuses the reduction to personal devotion, it does
point to the inseparability of worship and faithful living. In this way,
Christian worship holds together the time set aside for planned and
directed worship (the celebration of Jesus's Lordship, the awe-filled adoration of the God who makes his goodness known on the scene of history,
and the anticipation of his empowering presence) with the daily commitment to live life as a reflection of God's involved presence by his Spirit
(Mark 12:23; John 4:23; Rom 12:1–2; 15:16; 2 Cor 8:12; Phil 4:18; Heb
12:28; 13:21; 1 Pet 2:5). Biblical worship makes no room for a separation
of external action from internal attitude and claim of commitment (cf. Isa
1:11–17; Amos 5:21–24).

Christian Worship as Trinitarian

In both testaments, acceptable worship is about responding in appropriate ways to God's initiative in revelation and salvation. Although the emphasis is on God as the one who calls and causes his people to worship, the response remains theirs. In other words, the experience of the truth of God's story, and the Christians' awareness of their participation in it awakens a desire to voice the same in a self-surrendering adoration toward the King who made it happen (cf. John 3:30). Again, genuinely life-transforming vitality among God's people is inseparably moored to the acknowledgment that Christian worship must center around God's comprehensive plan and purpose for his people and his creation.

The depth and width of such acceptance has far-reaching consequences for Christian worship. For example, that God created men and women as an integral part of his creation and uniquely made them in his own image places humans as those who are called to bring praise to God on behalf of all creation. That is, they function as ministers (or priests) of and to creation, so to speak. Their worship, then, is never just local, narrow, or limited to self; rather, it conveys the worship of a creation that eagerly yearns for the revelation of God's glory (Rom 8:19–24; cf. Pss 8:2–9; 19:1). In the midst of this, the good news is that even when humans fail and the image of God in and among them becomes blurred, God meets his people in Christ and offers renewal and restoration of his image by his Spirit (2 Cor 3:18; Col 3:10).

Naturally, the prayer Jesus taught his disciples (Matt 6:9–13) has a direct and shaping influence on the Christian understanding of worship. The Lord's prayer summarizes Jesus's teaching on the kingdom and is as such a kingdom prayer—Let your kingdom come!

Unfortunately, this second clause of the prayer has often been (mis) understood in temporal terms, suggesting that the main focus for Christians is to pray for the speedy arrival of God's presence. However, the text itself suggests that Jesus taught his disciples to pray for the kingdom to become visible in their midst. The first three petitionary verbs are aorist passive imperatives. The flow of the prayer runs something like this:

Cause your name to be made holy (among us).

Cause your kingdom to come (i.e., be visible among us).

Cause your will to be done (among us).

The rest of the prayer is driven by active verbs that communicate what kingdom presence looks like in practice (bread for all, forgiveness, removal of temptations, deliverance from evil).

Nothing in these parallel statements suggests that the second clause should point to the future while the references in the first and the third are present. In other words, Jesus is teaching his disciples to worship in light of God's kingdom presence even as they experience themselves as participants in the same.

Understanding Christian worship in light of God's story and eschatological purpose centers it in the very nature of the God who has revealed himself as triune, and it rescues it both from a narrow therapeutic emphasis designed to serve the attendees and an aloof emphasis on deistic transcendence. When worship focuses on God's story as it pivotally climaxes in the event of Jesus, it naturally gains a solid trinitarian focus.

A trinitarian worship service will by its very nature include an emphasis on, and a celebration of gratitude toward, God the Father as both Creator and Provider—the one who not only created out of the overflow of his love but also continues to provide for the needs of his creation.

At the same time, trinitarian worship will by its very nature include an expression of awe and amazement toward God the Son as Redeemer and Revealer—the one who came both to reveal the true character of God for all to see (John 1:18) and to make possible the very redemption that enables humans to approach their Creator and experience his loving presence. The Son who not only tore down the wall that separated people from God but also the one that separates us from each other (Eph 2:14).

Finally, trinitarian worship will by its nature give space to seek and to experience the presence and joy of God the Spirit as Sustainer and Enabler—the one who fills his people with his sustaining presence (Acts 9:17; Rom 8:14–16; Gal 3:14; 4:6) and guidance (John 16:13–15; 1 Cor 2:10–15; Eph 1:17; cf. Gal 5:22–26) and the one who enables our relationship with God

(Rom 5:5; 8:2; 2 Cor 3:3–6; Eph 1:13) and empowers our lives and witness to others (1 Cor 12:4–13).

In summary, Christian worship that is deeply rooted in God's story from Genesis to Revelation will not only become a celebration and a declaration of a church's commitment to God's plan and purpose for his creation; it will also avoid being pulled in a variety of directions by the currents of the contemporary world. It will refuse to be transformed into something that is nontrinitarian and foreign to biblical text. Concurrently, it will avoid confusing trinitarianism for Christomonism and thereby miss celebrating the Father and the Spirit. Further, it will overcome the temptation to confuse trinitarianism with a mere therapeutic spirituality that focuses on how the Spirit benefits "me" and forgets that it is the Father and the Son who send the Spirit.

FOR ADDITIONAL STUDY

Block, Daniel. *For the Glory of God: Recovering a Biblical Theology of Worship.* Grand Rapids: Baker, 2016.

Forrest, Benjamin, Walter C. Kaiser Jr., and Vernon Whaley, eds. *Biblical Worship.* Grand Rapids: Kregel, 2021.

Okholm, Dennis. *Learning Theology through the Church's Worship.* Grand Rapids: Baker, 2018.

Oliphant, Scott. *The Majesty of Mystery: Celebrating the Glory of an Incomprehensible God.* Bellevue, WA: Lexham, 2016.

Peterson, David G. *Engaging with God: A Biblical Theology of Worship.* Downers Grove: IVP, 2002.

Also see these articles: Church, Preaching, Prayer, Lord's Supper, Pastoral Theology

39

Preaching

ROBERT SMITH JR.

Helmut Thielicke, the German theologian from Hamburg, Germany, was convinced that preaching is always permeated with theological reflection. One hears the gospel and, through the prevenient, enabling Spirit of God, believes the gospel and has a saving experience. Following this saving experience, the believer through some form of catechesis acquires the ability to theologize the saving experience and give a defense for the hope that resides within (1 Pet 3:15). Anselm, the Archbishop of Canterbury, spoke of faith seeking understanding. So the biblical sequence is not understanding seeking faith.

There is an inextricable relationship between preaching and theology. The word "preaching" has fallen on hard times. Without preaching, the church is on life support and cannot effectively minister to a critically ill world. The church might have a form of godliness, but without preaching, the church denies its source of power. George Whitefield was requested by his hearers to furnish a copy of his sermon for publication. He reportedly said that he had no problem as long as the lightning, thunder, and rainbow was printed with it. If preaching retires, then theology is unemployed. Thielicke's massive *Theological Ethics* (four volumes in German and three volumes in English) is a work extending to more than three thousand pages, which he began when he was banished from his professorship by the Nazi government and finished after twenty-one years. As he looked back on what he had done, he recognized that what he was basically trying to do was to lay a new foundation for Christian preaching.

This theological compendium served as a reservoir out of which his preaching was drawn. This made Thielicke a theological preacher. In this regard, Thielicke confronted the believer with the question, "Why do you believe what you believe?" and not simply with the question, "What do you believe?" So Thielicke resisted merely preaching his theology—he preached out of the wealth of his theological labor.

Theology is the discipline of "God talk." It enables us to talk about God. Preaching is designed to proclaim the verities and attributes of God in a message that never changes and also in fresh and relevant ways that do change. This is an audacious enterprise and is why Thielicke was persuaded that theology that could not be preached was no theology at all. Preaching needs theology and theology needs preaching. Theology serves as a monitor, an arbiter, to discipline preaching, keeping it on course and calling it back to its center, Christ. Preaching is the precursor or announcer of the eternal truths of God.

Maintaining Balance in Theological Preaching

There is a great chasm between theology and preaching today. It is a great divorce at best and abandonment of theology from preaching. Vows need to be renewed, and unity needs to be restored between the two. Sandy F. Ray, venerable pastor-preacher of the Cornerstone Baptist Church in Brooklyn, New York, recalls an incident when he was working in a hospital. The head nurse became desperately ill. I was informed by the surgeon that she was suffering from what he diagnosed as intestinal cohesion. Some of the intestines had flattened, and no nourishment could pass through her system. She was losing weight and becoming extremely weak. The surgeon had to correct the adhesion of the intestines so that food could pass through. There is the problem today of theological and homiletical cohesion, which is preventing the nourishment of the Word of God from passing through so that the unsaved can be initiated into salvation by faith and can grow into sanctification. Paul Scherer provides an accurate prognosis for preaching:

Nothing can do them good without disturbing them. And nothing will disturb them to any lasting effect unless it disturbs them deeply. It is therefore of less value than is commonly supposed week in and week out simply to address those needs which lie around on the surface of human life, needs of which everybody is conscious: how to keep from feeling lonely; what it takes to be brave; the way to bear up under disappointment; the secret of success. Jesus said astonishingly little about any of that. Instead, he addressed himself to those needs so often unconscious which lie at the root of a man's sense of bewilderment, alienation, and anxiety. He was forever getting farther in and deeper down; and that is never likely to be painless.[1]

Theology and preaching are experiencing a blockage, needing redemptive surgery so that the truth of God's Word can surge through and meet the needs of the spiritually hungry congregations. The joints and marrow, the soul and spirit, of preaching are composed of theology. Theological preaching appears to be a distant reality. So how is theological preaching properly done? Preachers assume that if "too much" theology is inserted in the sermon, it will reduce space for application, thus causing the congregants to check out of the sermon before the conclusion.

There is a great temptation for preachers to sparingly include theological principles in their sermons; the result is sermons that are nearly theologically bankrupt and anemic. Some pastors are of the wrongheaded opinion that the preacher who delivers a consistent diet of theology in sermons can kill a church. To preach theologically is to consistently marry theology and preaching in every sermon. What God has joined together, let no one put asunder. It is a mistake to separate theology from preaching or to play one against another. It is not an either/or matter; rather, it is both/and. Theology prepares the preacher to preach the good news of the gospel.

To properly preach theologically is to preach with a sense of the whole counsel of God. The whole counsel of God can be defined as that broad and overarching concept that unites and ties together every passage of Scripture so that it relates to the overall plan and comprehensive purpose of

---

[1] Paul Scherer, *The Word God Sent* (New York: Harper and Row, 1965), 70.

God revealed in the Scriptures by the Holy Spirit in order to magnify Jesus Christ. Theological preaching is *trinitarian*—"revealed in the Scriptures by the Holy Spirit." There is a tendency in today's preaching to be binarian— emphasizing God the Father and the Son only. The Holy Spirit is often neglected, and if recalled at all, the Holy Spirit is considered a stepchild of the Trinity. At best, the Holy Spirit is a divine footnote in the revelation of God. Our preaching tends to be untheological, and our theology tends to be unpreachable.

Greg Heisler put his finger on the pulsating heartbeat of our preaching predicament when he wrote, "My conviction is we have failed to connect the discipline of homiletics with the doctrine of pneumatology, and as a result we find ourselves 'surprised by the Spirit' when he does move."[2] The valley of dry bones of our preaching needs the empowering of the Spirit. In this definition of the whole counsel of God, a Christological connection is drawn as a necessity for preaching theologically. Preaching exists for the purpose of magnifying Jesus Christ. It is the bridge that transports the hearer to Christ with biblical integrity. David asked, "How shall the ark of the Lord come to us?" (2 Sam 6:9). The ark of God, which represented the presence of God in the midst of the people of God, came a thousand years after David in a human body (the incarnate Christ) and not in a wooden box. Theological preaching always points the hearer to God, who is the hero of every text. Theological preaching through intertextuality elucidates the overarching redemptive purpose of God seen in the redemptive drama of salvation history. It "relates to the overall plan and comprehensive purpose of God." Joseph is sold into slavery in Egypt by his brothers. God uses their betrayal of Joseph to save Joseph's brothers from famine and eventual extinction in order that in the final analysis Judah is spared and, eighteen hundred years later, Christ our Savior is born through the line of Judah. A theology of preaching answers the questions, "What is the place of theology in the pulpit? What is the minister doing when preaching? What is the role and place of preaching in the life of the church? How does the pulpit answer the question of theology—What shall I say? How does the pulpit answer the question of homiletics or proclamation—How shall I say it?" In the first homiletics textbook in church history, *De Doctrina Christiana*, Augustine of Hippo in the fifth century devoted

---

[2] Greg Heisler, *Spirit-Led Preaching* (Nashville: B&H Academic, 2018), 3.

hermeneutics/theology to books 1–3. He then devoted homiletics to book 4. Theology serves as the foundation for preaching.

The Place of Personal Witness in Theological Preaching

In her book *When Life and Beliefs Collide,* Carolyn C. James uses the metaphor of a war zone to stress the importance of doctrine and theology as the serious Christian engages in spiritual warfare. The serious Christian makes an effort to advance the kingdom of God through personal witness. She writes,

> When faith is stripped to the bone and all our props and crutches are gone, our knowledge of God—that he is good and is still on the throne—is the only thing that keeps us going. . . . Soft theology won't sustain us on the battlefield. Marching into battle with superficial, false, and flimsy ideas of God is like going to war with a pop gun tucked under your arm. When fatigue hits and still the battle rages, it makes all the difference in the world to know that God's plan is in place, even here. The thought that he has temporarily surrendered his sovereignty to someone else undermines our confidence, drains us of courage, and weakens our hope. None of us can afford a theology that cannot withstand the pressures of the war zone that fits only within a world of comfort and pleasure, where all our ducks are in neat rows and the pieces fit neatly together. We are called to be soldiers, to enter the war zone, to feel the heat of battle for ourselves and for each other, and to see God more clearly within the context of our struggle.[3]

Even though we ourselves do not preach, we preach Christ through ourselves. No wonder Phillips Brooks stated in his Lyman Beecher Lectures on Preaching that "preaching is the communication of truth by man to men."[4] For Brooks, it was the transference of truth from human personality to human personalities. Our congregants need to hear the implications of scriptural verities—Daniel in the lions' den and the woman at the well. But

---

[3] Carolyn C. James, *When Life and Beliefs Collide: How Knowing God Makes a Difference* (Grand Rapids: Zondervan, 2002), 95.

[4] Phillips Brooks, *Lectures on Preaching* (New York: E. P. Dutton, 1877), 5.

they also want to know whether the preacher's personal experience mirrors the biblical story. Has the preacher ever been in a lions' den and can testify of God's rescue? Has the preacher ever been spiritually thirsty and experienced the refreshing fullness of living water? Can preachers join with the blind man in John 9 in praise and thanksgiving and say, "One thing I do know, I was blind and now I can see!" (John 9:25).

Much of our gospel promulgation is spent in personally addressing those gathered in the sanctuary to hear the Word of God. We need to remember that a past experience with God will give us present confidence, we ought to know that God can be trusted in turbulent times to give us tranquility in the midst of it all, and we must bear our burdens in the heat of the day. Personal witness must stand alongside personal address. "*I* know that *my* Redeemer lives. . . . Even after my skin has been destroyed, yet I will see God in my flesh. I will see him myself; my eyes will look at him, and not as a stranger" (Job 19:25–27, emphasis added). Hearers want to know if those who preach to them experientially relate to the text they are preaching. Helmut Thielicke was persuaded that

> the aim in proclamation is to press through to basic issues by counterquestioning. Behind all other questions lies the question of humanity itself and, deeply concealed behind that, the question of God. . . . For most people in Thielicke's world, the concept of God might seem to be of little relevance or necessity. . . . by working through the immediate problems of individual and social life, raising probing counterquestions, Thielicke hopes to show that all these problems lead by different routes to the question of something unconditional that constitutes the ground of human life. Thielicke identifies this element as the God whom we may know through Jesus Christ and the knowledge of whom is the answer to every underlying question. . . . What does it mean to be human? How does one achieve authentic humanity?

For Thielicke, of course, this question cannot be divorced from the question of God. It is in relation to God that one perceives and achieves true human identity.[5]

---

[5] Martin Marty and Dean Peerman, eds., *A Handbook of Christian Theologians* (Nashville: Abingdon, 1987), 547–48.

A sign of an effective preacher/teacher of the gospel narrative is seen in the ability to turn what the preacher hears in the biblical text into what the hearer sees in life's situations. Theological preaching is not a discourse of abstraction. The hearers become mirrors of identity with the biblical text, often through the preacher's willingness to put his/her autobiographical disclosure on display. Thielicke was quite effective in this regard, and it provided him with a personal touch in his preaching.

The Role of Imagery in Theological Preaching

These are difficult times for preachers to accept the reality that words, particularly abstract words, are oftentimes not enough. Some things cannot be fully explained or expressed with words only. Dietrich Bonhoeffer noted, "The time when people could be told everything by means of words, whether theological or pious, is over."[6] There are deep abiding truths that need the benefit of images to capture reality. Propositional truths speak to the head. They are taught, reflected upon, systematized, and organized. But images are caught. Propositional truths reinforce the theological experience that is being imaged. When words fall exhausted at the feet of futility, another medium has to be used to translate the theological experience. This medium is that of the "silent pictures" of imagery. A theological image properly used gives people the right message, which causes them to respond appropriately. The crossing of Jacob's hands speaks of God's sovereignty in bypassing human tradition and custom so that the divine design and plan may be executed. This image encourages believers to trust their future and destiny to the God who turns interruptions into invitations. Some truths are too deep for words and require images. For example, in his *Cotton Patch* paraphrase, Clarence Jordan takes 2 Cor 5:19, "That is, in Christ, God was reconciling the world to himself," and paraphrases it to say, "God was in Christ *hugging* the world back to himself." Theology is the scaffold that forms the building of proclamation. Once a building is up and the construction is completed, the scaffold is taken down, and the building alone is seen. However, even though the scaffold is removed, the building is still silently and invisibly influenced by

---

[6] Dietrich Bonhoeffer, *Letters and Papers from Prison*, trans. R. Fuller et al. (New York: Simon and Schuster, 1997), 279.

the scaffold. The scaffold of theology shapes and influences the building of proclamation.

The preacher does not stand and preach undigested and untranslated theology or pile up abstract mountains of theology in the preaching moment. Rather, a theological preacher goes to the mountain of abstract theology during the week of sermon preparation. The preacher cannot take the entire mountain of theology to the church on Sunday and serve it to the congregation just as it is. The mountain of theology is untranslated, undigested, and unbroken. It has to be broken up by the bulldozer of the preacher's mind into "bite-sized" pieces. The preacher then puts the bite-sized theological pieces in the dump truck of proclamation and delivers it to the congregation for spiritual nourishment. Theological preaching is not an abstract theological discourse that ignores the real needs of the congregation. It is the needed combination of exegeting the biblical text and the contemporary audience. It is the merger of interpreting the passage of the "then and there" and applying it to the "here and now" of contemporary times. Application is very significant. In Bryan Chapell's thought, there is no expository preaching without application. Yet there is the temptation on the part of the preacher to rush to applying the passage for the contemporary congregation without deeply inserting biblical theological principles into the sermon. Biblical theology is the *aurality* that puts its ear to the pavement of the text, and biblical preaching is the *orality* that vocalizes what it has heard from the biblical/theological text. Biblical theology is the hinge that swings the door of preaching open for the Christian to behold the wondrous works of the Lord.

It seems to me that John Stott brings together the anatomy of theological preaching in his definition of biblical preaching. Here, then, is his definition: "To expound Scripture is to open up the inspired text with such faithfulness and sensitivity that God's voice is heard, and his people obey him."[7] The definition contains six implications that are dynamically transferrable to theological preaching. Stott writes,

---

[7] Cited in John Stott, "A Definition of Biblical Preaching," in *The Art and Craft of Biblical Preaching*, ed. Haddon Robinson and Craig Larson (Grand Rapids: Zondervan, 2005), 24.

I. Two Convictions about the Biblical Text

(1) **It is an inspired text.** God has spoken through the Bible. The Bible is not *a* word of God but *the* Word of God. "All Scripture is inspired by God . . ." (2 Tim 3:16).

(2) **The inspired text to some degree is a closed text.** The Bible is a closed book, and its message must be given to the congregation by the minister who is led by the Holy Spirit to open up the text and reveal its meaning. "Weren't our hearts burning within us while he was talking with us on the road and explaining the Scriptures to us?" (Luke 24:32).

II. Two Obligations in Expounding

(1) **The first obligation is faithfulness to the biblical text.** The first order of responsibility in the preaching enterprise is to say what the text says and not what the preacher or the congregation wants it to say.

(2) **The second obligation is sensitivity to the modern world.** After explaining the meaning of the ancient texts, the preacher moves to applying its meaning to the modern world.

III. Two Expectations in Consequence

(1) **We can expect God's voice to be heard.** Jesus told the disciples, "Whoever listens to you listens to me" (Luke 10:16). In other words, when preachers say what Jesus said, they become the voice box of Christ, speaking on his behalf.

(2) **God's people will obey him.** The word of God demands a response. The proper response to the word of God from the people of God must be, "Speak [Lord], for your servant is listening" (1 Sam 3:10).

Since preaching is an act of worship, the goal of every preacher should be to preach so that the congregation will preach the pastor's Sunday morning message in beauty salons, barber shops, employment circles, recreational facilities, at home, and abroad. Peter Taylor Forsyth poetically depicts preaching as "the organized hallelujah of an ordered community."[8]

---

[8] Peter Taylor Forsyth, *Positive Preaching and the Modern Mind* (New York: A.C. Armstrong & Son, 1907), 95.

For Additional Study

Achtemeier, Elizabeth. *Preaching as Theology and Art.* Nashville: Abingdon, 1984.

Clowney, Edmund P. *Preaching and Biblical Theology.* Grand Rapids: Eerdmans, 1961.

Edwards, O. C. *A History of Preaching.* Nashville: Abingdon, 2004.

Evans, James H. *We Have Been Believers: An African-American Systematic Theology.* Minneapolis: Fortress, 1992.

Forde, Gerhard O. *Theology Is for Proclamation.* Minneapolis: Fortress Press, 1990.

Lischer, Richard. *A Theology of Preaching.* Nashville: Abingdon, 1981.

Roberts, James Deotis. *The Prophethood of Black Believers.* Louisville: Westminster/John Knox, 1994.

Taylor, Edward, ed. *The Words of Gardner Taylor.* Philadelphia: Fortress, 2000.

Wedel, Theodore Otto. *The Pulpit Rediscovers Theology.* Greenwich, CT: Seabury, 1956.

Also see these articles: Scripture, Hermeneutics, Church, Spiritual Gifts, Evangelism and Missions, Prayer, Pastoral Theology

40

Theology for Evangelism and Missions

David S. Dockery

If anything has disappeared from modern thought in the twenty-first century, it is the belief in an eternal heaven and an everlasting hell. Even those who retain some vague idea of heavenly bliss beyond this life are slow to acknowledge the reality of final judgment and condemnation. Modern men and women live with the mindset that there is no heaven, no hell, and therefore no guilt.

Much confusion exists concerning the gospel and the need for evangelism and missions in our contemporary context. The church has added to this confusion by focusing on evangelistic methodologies and mission strategies, as important as these might be, rather than prioritizing an understanding of the meaning, transformational power, and veracity of the message of evangelism and missions, which is foundational for developing a theology of evangelism and missions. What has been lost, or at least misplaced, is the recognition that at the heart of genuine evangelism and missionary outreach must be a firm theological foundation. In this article, we will seek to explore the basic themes that help us grasp the biblical and theological aspects of the gospel message. Based on a commitment to the full truthfulness of the Bible with a dependency on the role of the Holy Spirit in enabling the work of evangelism and missions, we will look at (1) the meaning of God as creator and the place of men and women in God's creation; (2) the fall of humanity into sin; (3) God's provision for sinners in the redemptive work of Jesus Christ; and (4) God's salvation of men and women from their estranged, guilty, and dreadful plight with implications for the church's task of personal evangelism and global missions.

We acknowledge that the message of and commission for the work of evangelism, which involves the communication of the good news of God's saving grace in Jesus Christ in word and in deed, as well as the work of global missions, which involves communicating this good news in cross-cultural contexts, is found in the Bible, God's truthful and inspired Word (2 Tim 3:16). The work of evangelism and missions rests on the authority of God's written Word. Furthermore, it is understood that the work of evangelism and missions cannot be done in our human frailty; it requires the empowering of God's Spirit (Acts 1:8). While the work of evangelism and missions is broad in its scope, including the mandate to make disciples of all nations (see Revelation 5, 7) and teaching others to do all that Jesus commanded (Matt 28:19), this article will focus on a theological foundation of the gospel message. Apart from this theological grounding, evangelism and missions risk losing their message and their power.

Men and Women in God's Creation

Men and women are the highest forms of God's earthly creation. All other aspects of creation are for the purpose of serving men and women; men and women are created to serve God and are thus created with what has been referred to as a vacuum that only God himself can fill. Men and women are complex creatures of God, composed of not only physical bodies but also immaterial selves, called souls or spirits. In the present life men and women function as whole persons, though it is a type of conditional unity because the material and immaterial aspects interact with and upon each other in such intricate ways that they are not easily distinguished. Yet as has been expounded by many others throughout the history of the church, the characteristics of the immaterial (soul/spirit) cannot be attributed only to the physical. Humans were a unity at creation and will once again be a complete unity at glorification, but during this present age we can affirm a type of conditional unity brought by the entrance and effects of sin.[1]

---

[1] See Millard J. Erickson, *Christian Theology*, 3rd ed. (Grand Rapids: Baker, 2013), 451–95.

God has created us in his image and likeness (Gen 1:26–27). Because men and women are created in the image of God, they have rationality, morality, spirituality, and personality. They can relate to God and other humans while rightly exercising dominion over the earth and the animals (Gen 1:26–28; Psalm 8). Nothing in us or about us is separable, distinct, or discoverable as the divine image. Each person individually and the entire race corporately are the image of God. Yet no single aspect of human nature or behavior or thought pattern can be isolated as the image of God.[2]

Sin and the Fall

Even though men and women are created in God's image, the entrance of sin into the world has had great and negative influences upon God's creation, especially for humans created in God's image. As a result of sin, the image of God, though not lost, was affected by sin. The role of exercising dominion (Gen 1:28) has been drastically disturbed by the effects of sin on humans and the curse on nature (Genesis 3). The ability to live in right relationship with God, with others, with nature, and with ourselves has been corrupted. All attempts at righteousness fall short (Isa 64:6; Rom 3:23). Humans are ultimately spiritually dead and alienated from God (Eph 2:1–3). Men and women are unable to reflect properly the image and likeness as a result of the entrance of sin into the world (Rom 1:18–32). Evangelism and missions are necessary because men and women in every country and every context, throughout every period of history, are separated and alienated from God.

The sin of Adam and Eve (Genesis 3) was not just a moral lapse but a deliberate turning away from God and rejection of him. The day they disobeyed God, they died spiritually, which ultimately brought about physical death (Gen 2:17). Spiritual death points to the state of alienation and separation from God as a result of sin. Both spiritual and physical death are the result of sin. All die because all have sinned (Rom 3:23; 6:23), a message echoed in the Old Testament and the New (Josh 23:14; Eccl 9:5; Ezek 18:4; Rom 5:12; Heb 9:27). After sin's entrance, death became a universal physical and spiritual reality. Death is so pervasive that the New Testament points to death as a realm

---

[2] See John F. Kilner, *Dignity and Destiny: Humanity in the Image of God* (Grand Rapids: Eerdmans, 2015).

where the devil reigns (Heb 2:14; Rev 1:18; 20:13) as a ruler (Rom 5:14, 17) and as an enemy or a destructive warrior (1 Cor 15:26; Rev 20:14).

Whatever else Gen 2:17 means, it certainly teaches that physical death in the human world is the result of human sin. Death in this passage points to the disruption of human fellowship with God. Because of Adam's sin, every human being is now constituted as a sinner (Rom 5:19). When Adam and Eve sinned, they passed into a new state, one dominated and symbolized by death. While spiritual death and physical death can be differentiated, they cannot be separated. After Adam and Eve sinned, they died immediately in the spiritual sense and became subject to separation from God's loving presence. At that time, the door opened for all humans to enter a state in which bodily death was inevitable (Rom 5:12–19). Each person who has ever lived, apart from Jesus Christ, has been affected by sin and has followed in Adam's footsteps (Rom 3:23; 5:12). Death is not merely something that happens to people at the conclusion of life; it is the definition and description of life apart from fellowship with God.

Spiritual death is expressed in several ways, including active antagonism toward God and rejecting his manifestation through his creation (Rom 1:18–32). Instead of loving God, people are indifferent toward him. Instead of seeking forgiveness, humans seek to rationalize their guilt. Instead of seeking to please God, men and women seek to please themselves. Apart from God, there is no hope for humans. They are under divine condemnation and excluded from relationship with God for all eternity. The apostle Paul portrays humans apart from Christ as foolish and disobedient; that is, they are mentally and morally depraved (Rom 3:9–20; Eph 2:1–3). Men and women need salvation because we are in a desperate condition without Christ (Titus 3:3–4). The grace of God has provided our restoration and brought about a right relationship with God, with one another, with nature, and with ourselves. Apart from understanding the vast impact of sin, we will never fully appreciate the good news of the gospel.[3]

---

[3] See David L. Smith, *With Willful Intent: A Theology of Sin* (Wheaton: Bridgepoint, 1994); Erickson, *Christian Theology,* 513–99.

God's Provision in Jesus Christ

The message of evangelism and missions is found in the gracious redemption that God provided in the person of Jesus Christ. It was necessary that Christ should be both God and man (see Anselm, *Cur Deus Homo: Why God Became Man*). Only as man could Jesus be a redeemer for humanity, and only as a sinless man could he fittingly die for others. Yet it was only as God that his life, ministry, and redeeming death could have infinite value and satisfy the wrath of God to deliver others from it. Unless the work of evangelism and missions, the telling of the good news of the gospel, is focused on the person and work of Jesus Christ, it is misguided.

Inherent in the gospel message is the recognition that Christ has a human nature, but he is not merely a human person. The person of Christ is the God-man, the second person of the Trinity. In the incarnation, Jesus did not change into a human person nor adopt a human personage. He assumed a human nature in addition to his divine nature. With the assumption of his human nature, he is a divine-human person possessing all essential qualities of both the human and divine nature, which is a mystery beyond full comprehension.[4]

At the heart of the evangelistic message is the amazing news that Christ's death provided for sinners a sinless substitutionary sacrifice that satisfied divine justice. This incomprehensively valuable redemption delivered sinners from enslavement and reconciled and restored believers from estrangement to full fellowship and inheritance in the household of God. The basis of our salvation is totally in God himself and in Christ's atoning, redeeming, and reconciling work on the cross. Atonement was realized when God took upon himself, in the person of Jesus, the sinfulness and guilt of humankind so that his justice might be executed and the sins of men and women forgiven. P. T. Forsyth powerfully stated, "The word of Christ stands not simply for God's sorrow over sin but for God's wrath on sin."[5] As redeemer, Jesus broke the power of

---

[4] See Millard J. Erickson, *The Word Became Flesh* (Grand Rapids: Baker, 1991); Daniel Akin, *Christology: The Study of Christ* (Nashville: Rainer Publishing, 2015).

[5] Peter Taylor Forsyth, *The Work of Christ* (London: Hodder and Stoughton, 1910), 169.

sin and created within his followers a new and obedient heart by delivering sinners from the power of sin, guilt, death, and Satan, bringing about a people who have been bought with a price (1 Cor 6:19–20; 1 Pet 1:18). Jesus, as reconciler, healed the separation and brokenness created by sin and restored communion between God and humankind. Reconciliation is an act by which we are delivered from estrangement to fellowship with God. Because of Christ's accomplishment on the cross, God has chosen to treat sinful men and women as children rather than transgressors (2 Cor 5:18–20; Eph 2:12–16; Col 1:20–22). Paul, in 2 Cor 5:14, points us to the motivation for sharing the good news of the gospel in a local context or in a cross-cultural one: it is the love of God made known in Jesus Christ and his work on the cross.[6]

Fallen sinners also need to recognize that the resurrection verifies these truths (Acts 2:27–35; 1 Cor 15:3–4). The resurrection establishes the lordship and deity of Jesus while guaranteeing the justification of sinners, which was accomplished at the cross (Rom 1:3–4; 4:24–25; 5:9–10). We cannot miss that the resurrection of Jesus Christ is also a pledge of our future resurrection (1 Cor 6:14) and of God's final judgment for those who reject Christ as Lord and Savior (Acts 17:31). Following his resurrection, Christ ascended into heaven (Acts 1:9–11), where he is now exalted at God's right hand (Heb 1:3), a position of great honor. Having sat down, Christ demonstrated that his earthly work was completed (Phil 2:9–11; Heb 1:3; 7:25). Indeed, this is good news for sinful men and women.[7]

God's Salvation of Men and Women

There is a biblical urgency for God's people to do the work of evangelism and missions. Theologian Carl F. H. Henry (1913–2000) puts this in theological and missiological context when he says, "The Gospel is only good news if it gets there in time."[8] The Bible maintains that faith in Christ alone is the only means by which we receive and appropriate the good news of the gospel. Salvation is a gift of God, which cannot be merited by good works

---

[6] See John R. W. Stott, *The Cross of Christ* (Downers Grove: IVP, 1986).

[7] See Carl F. H. Henry, *The Identity of Jesus of Nazareth* (Nashville: B&H, 1992).

[8] Daniel Akin et al., *40 Questions about the Great Commission* (Grand Rapids: Kregel, 2020), 115.

(Rom 3:22–24; Eph 2:8–9; Titus 3:5–6). Grace comes to us while we are still in our sins and brings spiritual transformation based on the accomplished work of Jesus Christ. For the recipients of grace, the promise holds that Jesus Christ delivers us from the wrath to come (1 Thess 1:10; 5:9). Those who believe the message of the gospel need not fear future condemnation because believers have been justified by grace through faith (Rom 8:1). As Martin Luther said, "This is the mystery of the riches of divine grace for sinners, for by a wonderful exchange our sins are not ours but Christ's and Christ's righteousness is not Christ's but ours."[9]

Grace comes to us while we are still in our sins and brings spiritual transformation based on the accomplished work of Jesus Christ and the power of God's Spirit. When men and women receive the grace of God, it is a testimony to the impact of grace itself, but when grace is rejected, it is attributable to the hardness and sinfulness of the human heart. As many theologians have affirmed, grace is the free and loving favor to the ill-deserving.[10] The Bible pictures God coming into our lives, taking us just as we are because he is abundantly merciful (Eph 2:1–10). Those involved in the work of evangelism and missions must recognize that salvation is of God, yet men and women must respond to God's grace. Only persons who have heard the good news and who have been enabled by God's Spirit to respond to this good news are transformed by grace. We affirm the priority of God's initiating grace while emphasizing both the human responsibility to share the good news of Jesus Christ and the need for men and women to believe the good news (Rom 10:5–17). The work of salvation is the work of the majestic trinitarian God; its origin is in God the Father, its basis is in the grace of God in Christ, and it comes to us through the work of God's Spirit.[11]

The work of evangelism and missions calls for a human response to this good news. Far from violating our wills or personalities, God's grace appeals to our deepest yearnings, and therefore, when we are exposed to grace, intrinsically we are drawn toward God. Initiation of this gracious gift

---

[9] Martin Luther, *Works of Martin Luther* (St. Louis: Concordia, 1973), 5:68.

[10] See Benjamin B. Warfield, *The Plan of Salvation* (Grand Rapids: Eerdmans, reprint 1975).

[11] See Charles C. Ryrie, *Basic Theology* (Chicago: Moody, 1999), 358–66.

remains with God but is experienced from the human side as a choice. God releases the depraved and sinful wills of humans, bringing about believing responses. By God's grace, our alienated and stubborn wills are turned in a completely new direction.[12]

When God extends his grace to us, he is the active agent, but he always extends grace through means, such as the preached word, the written Word of God, the prayers of other believers, the invitation to respond to grace, and the faith of the respondent. This was the contention of William Carey in the late eighteenth century when he urged the church leaders of his day to send missionaries to other contexts around the globe in obedience to the commission of the resurrected Christ (Matt 28:18–20; Luke 24:45–47; John 20:21). A theology of evangelism and missions affirms God as the source of salvation while recognizing the importance of human means in this glorious work. Thus, we see the imperative of evangelism and missions, the necessity of proclamation, and the need for responding faith. Faith is the means by which men and women receive and appropriate salvation (Eph 2:8–9). Faith includes a full commitment of the whole person to the Lord Jesus, a commitment that involves knowledge, trust, and obedience. Faith is not merely an intellectual assent or an emotional response but a complete inward spiritual change confirmed to us by the Holy Spirit. Faith is altogether brought by God, and it is the human response bringing about trust in God's redemptive work of salvation in Jesus Christ, resulting in full liberation from the penalty of sin. The object of faith is Jesus Christ himself. Though faith is more than doctrinal assent, it must include an adherence to the truths made known in Scripture regarding the person and work of Christ. In our commitment to Jesus Christ, we acknowledge him as Savior from sin and Lord of our lives, even Lord of creation (Rom 10:9). Still, we must be mindful that it is possible to affirm a knowledge of Christ without a living and active faith in him (Jas 2:19).

God's grace brings about conversion, which signifies our turning to Christ initiated by God. It is a great work of God's Spirit, changing the

---

[12] See E. Y. Mullins, *Baptist Beliefs* (Valley Forge, PA: Judson, 1912), 26–28; W. T. Conner, *The Gospel of Redemption* (Nashville: Broadman, 1945), 51–75; and Timothy George, *Amazing Grace: God's Pursuit, Our Response*, 2nd ed. (Wheaton: Crossway, 2011).

human heart and bringing life to sinful and separated people. A key aspect of thinking theologically about the work of evangelism and missions is the recognition that the response to the evangelistic message manifests itself differently in each person who experiences conversion. Not all have a Damascus road experience like the apostle Paul as recounted in Acts 9:1–31. Some are converted quietly like Lydia (Acts 16:14) and others dramatically like the Philippian jailer (Acts 16:30–34). Yet, for everyone who trusts in Jesus Christ as Lord, it involves a turning away from sin to righteousness and issues both in service to the world and separation from it. The turning away from sin is what is meant by repentance. It is a changing of our minds and hearts about our sinfulness as well as the offer of the gospel. Repentance involves a forsaking of our sins and a turning toward the things of God. It is a turning right about, and the work of evangelism and missions involves announcing that God commands all people everywhere to turn to him. True conversion brings about the impartation of a new nature.[13]

God's work of salvation takes place when we are united with Christ, placed in union with him. God's regenerating and justifying work must be understood in light of who we are in Christ (John 15; Rom 6:1–11; Eph 1:3–14). Personally, our union with Christ presents us in a new position before God. Experientially, the union of believers with God is one of the most tender concepts expressed in Scripture. This marvelous union, which the Bible refers to as a mystery (Col 1:27–28), cannot be dissected or denied.

Regeneration is the most frequently discussed term within popular Christianity. It is a spiritual change by which the Holy Spirit imparts divine life to those who place their trust in Christ. The idea is familiar in the New Testament writings of John, Peter, and Paul, and is not without Old Testament precedent (Ezekiel 36–37; John 3:3–8; Titus 3:5–7; 1 Pet 1:23). From John 3 comes the popular term "born again" or "born from above," whereby God imparts righteousness to believing men and women. It is the experiential picture of our entrance into God's family whereby adoption refers to our position in this family (Gal 3:23–4:7). Adoption is not entirely a past event, for the consummation of our adoption awaits the redemption

---

[13] See Erickson, *Christian Theology*, 825–946, as well as Donald G. Bloesch, *Essentials of Evangelical Theology*, 2 vols. (San Francisco: Harper and Row, 1978–79), 1:181–247.

of our bodies (Rom 8:15–27). It is something hoped for as well as something already possessed.

Concerning our adoption, J. I. Packer says, "It is the highest privilege that the gospel offers: higher even than justification. . . . To be right with God the Judge is a great thing, but to be loved and cared for by God the Father is greater."[14] Salvation is more than just inward renewal; it also includes being justified by grace through faith. Predominantly a Pauline concept, the justification of rebellious sinners is accomplished at the cross of Christ (Rom 5:10), guaranteed by his resurrection (Rom 4:24–25), and applied to us when we believe (Rom 5:1). While regeneration pictures an experiential imparting of righteousness, justification is a declaration of our righteousness. Experientially we still sin, but God views believers as totally righteous (Rom 4:1–8). Because of Christ's vicarious sacrifice, God no longer counts our sins against us (2 Cor 5:19–21). Justification is more than pardon; it is a granting of positive favor in God's sight (Rom 3:21–26). We are not justified to become regenerated, and we are not regenerated to become justified. We must not confuse these two marvelous truths, separate them, or comingle them. God never justifies us without regenerating us, and he never regenerates us without justifying us.

Salvation involves the forgiveness of our sins, the putting away of sin and its penalty. It includes a gracious forgetting (Eph 4:32), a sending away of our sins (Matt 26:28), and a putting aside or disregarding of all sin (Rom 3:25). The Bible is the only religious book that emphasizes complete and total forgiveness (Heb 10:10–17), as pictured in the account of the prodigal son (Luke 15:11–32). Scripture presents the basis of forgiveness as the shedding of blood (Heb 9:22–26) and the means of our forgiveness as our faith and repentance. God is the author and finisher of our faith (Heb 12:2). Salvation is from sin, for the world has primarily a need of a sin bearer (John 1:29), which involves disarming believers from the rulers and authorities of this world (Col 2:14–15). Salvation, which is found only in Jesus Christ (John 14:6; Acts 4:12), is imperishable (1 Pet 1:3–4) and is the source of all spiritual blessing (Eph 1:3). Apart from Jesus Christ, there is no hope; sinners would be doomed to a Christless eternity. We thus give thanks for this blessed salvation, which is secured in Christ, knowing that nothing

---

[14] J. I. Packer, *Knowing God* (Downers Grove: IVP, 1993), 206–7.

can separate us from the love of Christ (Rom 8:31–39). While believers are responsible to persevere and hold on to God, ultimately our security in Christ comes because he has a hold on us (John 10:27–30).

The work of evangelism and missions must be understood within God's overall redemptive work, for God is not just saving individuals, but he is saving a people for himself. The plan of salvation includes not only the redemption of individuals but also the redemption of all creation (Rom 8:18–27; Rev 20:11–15), the redemption of people from every tribe and language and people and nation (Rev 5:9; 7:9). At the consummation, the old order will pass away, and the new order, described as the new heaven and new earth (Revelation 21–22), will come.[15] Our evangelistic and missionary message must also reflect awareness of our context, a lesson to be learned from the apostles in the book of Acts (see Acts 2:14–36; 3:11–26; 13:16–41; 17:22–31; 22:6–21; 24:10–21; 26:12–23).

Conclusion

A firm theological foundation is important for faithful evangelistic proclamation and missionary service. Followers of Christ must work harder at closing the gap between theology and the work of evangelism so that our theology is done for the church and proclamation and service is grounded in a scripturally formed theology. Our evangelistic message need not include every point in this article, but a faithful messenger of the gospel must ground the message firmly in biblical and theological foundations while understanding the need for the Spirit's enablement, especially when encountering spiritual opposition (Eph 6:10–17). We affirm that our evangelistic proclamation and commitments to global missions must be shaped by the truths regarding creation, fall, and redemption. In grace, God takes the initiative in bringing sinners to Christ through the evangelistic proclamation of the gospel and the human response of faith. All of salvation is of God, yet recipients of this salvation must respond in faith and commitment to the crucified and resurrected Christ. We gladly acknowledge Jesus Christ as Lord, our prophet, priest, and king who has completely revealed God, has reconciled men and women to

---

[15] See James Leo Garrett, *Systematic Theology*, 2 vols (Grand Rapids: Eerdmans, 1995), 2:432–54.

God, and who now sits enthroned as ruler of God's kingdom and head of his church. In him we place our trust and hope, offering our thanksgiving, praise, and worship for the gift of salvation he has provided for us by grace through faith (Eph 2:8–9). Like the apostle Paul, let us pray for opportunities to proclaim the gospel message with all boldness and without hindrance among the nations (Acts 28:31). Let us be moved and motivated by the words of the great missionary to China, Hudson Taylor (1832–1905): "The Great Commission is not an option to be considered; it is a command to be obeyed."

For Additional Study

Akin, Daniel L., and Benjamin L. Merkle and George G. Robinson, *40 Questions about the Great Commission*. Grand Rapids: Kregel, 2020.

Carson, D. A. *Telling Truth: Evangelizing Postmoderns*. Grand Rapids: Zondervan, 2000.

Erickson, Millard J. *Does It Matter That I'm Saved?* Grand Rapids: Baker, 1996.

Green, Michael. *Evangelism in the Early Church*. Grand Rapids: Eerdmans, 2004.

Oden, Thomas C. *The Transforming Power of Grace*. Nashville: Abingdon, 1993.

Ott, Craig, Stephen J. Strauss, and Timothy C. Tennent. *Encountering Theology of Missions*. Grand Rapids: Baker, 2010.

Packer, J. I. *Evangelism and the Sovereignty of God*. Rev. ed. Downers Grove: IVP, 2012.

Wright, Christopher J. H. *The Mission of God: Unlocking the Bible's Grand Narrative*. Downers Grove: IVP, 2006.

Also see these articles: Humanity, Sin, Person of Christ, Work of Christ, Gospel, Justification, Holy Spirit, Spiritual Gifts, Prayer, Global Theology

41

Spiritual Gifts

CHUCK LAWLESS

In 1972, Ray Stedman, pastor of the Peninsula Bible Church in Palo Alto, California, published the book *Body Life*, a work that emphasized training laypersons to use their spiritual gifts. As much as any other book in that time, that work became a popular resource for evangelicals discussing the topic of gifts. Stedman views spiritual gifts as gifts of the Holy Spirit given to believers for service in the church when they become Christians. Indeed, he emphasizes the point that God gives every believer at least one such gift—and believers are to identify and exercise their gifts in the ministry of the church. No believer has legitimate reason not to serve God through his church, for God gives each believer at least one gift to serve him.

Several years later, Fuller Theological Seminary professor C. Peter Wagner published *Your Spiritual Gifts Can Help Your Church Grow*, a resource that affirmed Stedman's book as highly influential. Wagner called a spiritual gift a "special attribute" the Holy Spirit gives to every member of the body of Christ.[1] These gifts are graces of God, unearned and undeserved, given for use within the local church. Working cooperatively within the local congregation, believers help each other determine their gifts, exercise them, and complement the efforts of one another through various gifts in the body.

---

[1] C. Peter Wagner, *Your Spiritual Gifts Can Help Your Church Grow* (Ventura, CA: Regal Books, 1979), 42.

Wagner is perhaps best known for his "Wagner Modified Houts Questionnaire," a spiritual gifts inventory he adapted from an inventory created by professor Richard Houts of Ontario Bible College. First published in 1979, the inventory consisted of 125 questions connected to twenty-five spiritual gifts. Following that publication, other spiritual gifts inventories like the "Team Ministry" inventory first published in 1985 by Church Growth Institute in Lynchburg, Virginia, gained in popularity. This resource includes 108 questions connected to nine gifts.

That one inventory includes twenty-five gifts and another includes only nine gifts is a reminder that the topic of spiritual gifts has often led to debate and controversy. This reality, though, is not new. The apostle Paul wrote in 1 Cor 12:1, "Now concerning spiritual gifts: brothers and sisters, I do not want you to be unaware"—at least suggesting a need to tackle this topic. The Corinthian believers had apparently asked Paul about gifts in their previous correspondence with him, and they were battling over spiritual gifts in their present context. Some believed their gifts were more significant than others, and that belief had led to division in the church (1 Corinthians 12–14). The "gifts" God had given—by definition, something believers had not earned or deserved—had become a source of pride and controversy. Some of the members, in fact, felt they were less significant in the body of Christ.

Regrettably, this topic still leads to division at times today. Some church leaders debate which spiritual gifts are still available for believers today. Others question if the lists of gifts in the Bible are exhaustive. Some practically treat particular gifts as more important than others, even if they would claim otherwise about the equal validity of all gifts; indeed, some churches and denominations can connect historical debates and disagreements to this controversial topic. Thus, the goal of this brief article is to introduce this topic, consider its significance, and discuss its application in the local church.

Defining "Spiritual Gifts"

The apostle Paul used several words that describe spiritual gifts. For example, he used *pneumatikon* in 1 Cor 12:1 and 14:1, translated as "spiritual gifts" in some versions (e.g., ESV, CSB). Some scholars prefer "spiritual things" or "spiritual persons" in 1 Cor 12:1, but either option emphasizes the Holy Spirit as the source of such gifts. Paul most often employed *charismata* (1 Cor

12:4; 12:31; Rom 12:6), from the root word *charis* meaning "grace," when speaking of gifts; thus, these "gifts" are abilities God has granted rather than something the believer has earned. *Domata*, the word Paul used in Eph 4:8 to describe persons/positions God has given to the church, is likewise translated "gifts." Other words connected to spiritual gifts are *diakoniai* ("ministries" in 1 Cor 12:5 CSB) and *energemata* ("activities" in 1 Cor 12:6 CSB). Both words situate the use of spiritual gifts within the church and remind believers that God grants gifts in his power for the purpose of ministering to others.

The Scriptures are also clear that God has given each believer at least one spiritual gift. Again, Paul's writings are informative. Believers may have "different gifts" (Rom 12:6), but a "manifestation of the Spirit is given *to each person*" (1 Cor 12:7, emphasis added). The Spirit grants gifts to all believers, "distributing *to each person* as he wills" (1 Cor 12:11, emphasis added). Those gifts are given "for the common good" (1 Cor 12:7). The apostle Peter similarly wrote of both the individual and corporate nature of gifts: "Just as *each one has received a gift*, use it to serve others, as good stewards of the varied grace of God" (1 Pet 4:10, emphasis added). No one believer has all the gifts (1 Cor 12:14–21, 28–30), but all believers have at least one.

A review of definitions of "spiritual gift" leads to the following conclusions: The Holy Spirit is instrumental in granting the gift; thus, a spiritual gift is supernatural in nature. That gift is also given rather than earned. It is often related to a particular ability or ministry responsibility such as teaching. Whatever the gift is, the Holy Spirit grants it for edifying the church; gifts are for serving others, not for building up oneself. Based on these understandings, a spiritual gift may be defined as "an ability the Holy Spirit graciously grants to each believer to build up the church."

Laying the Groundwork

The Scriptures include four key passages that identify spiritual gifts: 1 Corinthians 12–14; Rom 12:3–8; Eph 4:7–13; and 1 Pet 4:10–11. Some scholars include 1 Cor 7:7, with particular reference to the gift of celibacy, in this list as well. Others also refer to 1 Cor 13:1–3, 8–10, though the gifts listed there are included in other lists.

Several caveats are in order prior to examining the gifts lists in Scripture. First, the lists show some overlap, but each is also distinct. No single list includes all the other gifts in the remaining lists. That reality suggests these lists are not exhaustive; they instead offer examples of the wide variety of gifts God grants his followers. One point of the writers might have been not only to show the vast array of gifts in the church but also to demonstrate the miraculous unity in diversity God creates in his body. Should the specific situation and needs warrant it, it seems altogether possible the Spirit may provide believers with other gifts not listed in the Scriptures.

Second, some gifts such as "service" should be evident among all believers, but those gifted in that area likely show an uncommon ability in that aspect of the Christian walk. Likewise, the Scriptures do not fully define the relationship between spiritual gifts and natural abilities or talents. Spiritual gifts are unique from talents, but it seems God may take "a natural talent in an unbeliever and transform it into a spiritual gift when the person enters the Body of Christ" in some cases.[2] For example, a nonbeliever with a long-term interest in, clear aptitude for, and university training in teaching may well determine he has the spiritual gift of teaching when he chooses to be a Christ-follower. His gift of teaching might then be most evident when he effectively and powerfully teaches the Word of God—and that ability is, as with all spiritual gifts, a grace from the Lord. One might thus consider gifts as miraculous (e.g., tongues, interpretation of tongues, healing, miracles) or nonmiraculous (e.g., teaching, helps, leading, giving), though the distinction must not be forced since all gifts are from God.

Third, believers are to "desire the greater gifts" (1 Cor 12:31; cf. 14:1). The Spirit of God gives gifts as he wills (1 Cor 12:11), but believers are nevertheless commanded to seek them, even with great earnest. They are to seek the *greater* gifts, that is, those most helpful in edifying the church. Those who are "zealous for spiritual gifts" should "seek to excel in building up the church" (1 Cor 14:12). Thus, they seek prophecy more than unintelligible and uninterpreted tongues, for "the person who prophesies speaks to people for their strengthening, encouragement, and consolation" (1 Cor 14:3). Likewise, God gives gifts of persons to the church "to equip the saints for the work of ministry, to build up the body of Christ" (Eph 4:12). All use of gifts, though, is to be governed by the pursuit of love for others (1 Cor 14:1).

---

[2] Wagner, *Your Spiritual Gifts Can Help Your Church Grow*, 87.

Fourth, scholars debate whether all gifts remain available today. In other words, they wrestle with the question of whether gifts are temporary (no longer available today) or permanent (still available today). The "cessationist" position argues that miraculous gifts such as prophecy, tongues, and healing are no longer available today. They were available until the end of the apostolic age, and they particularly validated the preaching of the apostles in the early days of the church. That church was built "on the foundation of the apostles and prophets" (Eph 2:20), but their teaching is now found in the Scriptures. The gifts and miracles that built up the early church are therefore no longer necessary.

The "continuationist" position, on the other hand, contends that all gifts remain available today and are still operative in the church. These gifts were not limited to the time of the apostles; as Sam Storms writes, "nowhere does the New Testament ever suggest that certain spiritual gifts were uniquely and exclusively tied to them [the apostles] or that with their passing came the passing of such gifts."[3] Pentecostals, for example, emphasize baptism in the Holy Spirit, a subsequent event to one's conversion marked by speaking in tongues. Charismatics debate among themselves the timing of baptism in the Holy Spirit and the necessity of speaking in tongues, but they nonetheless affirm the availability of all the miraculous gifts. Third wave continuationism, often associated with C. Peter Wagner and John Wimber, accepts the ongoing working of the miraculous gifts but does not emphasize a baptism in the Spirit subsequent to conversion.

The "open but cautious" position reflects those who fully accept neither the cessationist nor the continuationist position. "Open but cautious" proponents accept the possibility of miraculous gifts today, but they are particularly apprehensive about perceived misuses and abuses of gifts by some who still affirm these gifts. Concern about error or divisiveness regarding the gifts results in caution, though not denial of the miraculous gifts.

Fifth, as noted previously, the list in Ephesians 4 focuses more on persons given to the church than on particular gifts that individuals possess. At the same time, however, one cannot separate the position from the gift; for example, the pastor-teacher would have unique ability to teach, the prophet would have the gift of prophecy, and the evangelist would be especially gifted

---

[3] Sam Storms, *Understanding Spiritual Gifts: A Comprehensive Guide* (Grand Rapids: Zondervan, 2020), 106.

at leading others to follow Christ. Each of these persons may have additional spiritual gifts in the gift lists, but it is not invalid to talk of role and gift in the same conversation when discussing apostles, prophets, evangelists, and pastor-teachers in Ephesians 4.

Of the four roles listed in Ephesians 4, the roles of apostle and prophet may be the most debated ones. This article will address the role of prophet in the next section, but some attention must here be given to the role of apostle. Though many scholars argue that apostles must have been eyewitnesses to the ministry of Jesus, Paul used the term "apostle" throughout his writings in a broader sense than only one of Jesus's original twelve disciples. He refers to others by this "sent one" term—e.g., Titus (2 Cor 8:23); Epaphroditus (Phil 2:25); Andronicus and Junia (Rom 16:7); and James, the brother of the Lord (Gal 1:19)—and it seems he spoke generally of those sent on a mission in Ephesians 4. Stedman thus calls those with this gift today "secondary apostles," and both he and Tom Schreiner conclude that "apostle" may refer to pioneer missionaries.[4]

Identifying the Gifts

Scholars have offered various attempts to classify the gifts listed in the New Testament. Some have reduced the gifts to the two categories Peter described in 1 Pet 4:11—gifts of speaking and gifts of serving. Though he questions the use of such categories in general, Sam Storms points out that some speak of *manifestation* gifts in 1 Cor 12:7–10, *ministry* gifts in Eph 4:11, and *motivational* gifts in Rom 12:6–8.[5] Wayne Grudem likewise speaks of *prophetic* gifts that include "anything that involves teaching, encouraging, exhorting, or rebuking others"; *priestly* gifts that focus on extending mercy, care, and intercession; and *kingly* gifts related to administration in the church.[6]

Schreiner summarizes the spiritual gifts lists with the following chart:[7]

---

[4] Ray C. Stedman, *Body Life* (Grand Rapids: Discovery House), 74; Schreiner, Kindle loc. 324.

[5] Sam Storms, *Understanding Spiritual Gifts*, 28.

[6] Wayne Grudem, *Systematic Theology: An Introduction to Biblical Doctrine* (Grand Rapids: Zondervan, 1994), 1021.

[7] Schreiner, Kindle loc. 225.

Romans 12:6–8	1 Corinthians 12:7–10	1 Corinthians 12:28	Ephesians 4:11
Having gifts that differ according to the grace given to us	*To each is given the manifestation of the Spirit for the common good*	*And God has appointed in the church*	*And he gave*
		Apostles	Apostles
Prophecy	Prophecy	Prophets	Prophets
			Evangelists
	Ability to distinguish between spirits		
Teaching	Word of wisdom and word of knowledge	Teachers	Pastors and teachers
Exhorting			
	Working of miracles	Miracles	
	Gifts of healing	Gifts of healing	
Serving		Helping	
Leading		Administrating	
	Various kinds of tongues	Various kinds of tongues	
	Interpretation of tongues		
Giving			
	Faith		
Mercy			

Schreiner affirms the unlikelihood that this list is exhaustive, though he questions what other gifts might have been listed. At the same time, his arrangement of this chart illustrates some of his own conclusions about these gifts. For example, he equates "word of wisdom" and "word of knowledge" with the gift of teaching in all of Paul's other lists. Others view these gifts as Holy Spirit-inspired knowledge and wisdom to speak into a situation or as insights revealed miraculously to a believer who would not have otherwise known the information.

Schreiner also connects the gift of leadership with administration and the gift of serving with helping, recognizing the overlap of these responsibilities, respectively. Further, he concludes that believers with the gifts such as giving, mercy, and evangelism are uniquely able to do these tasks required of all believers. Every Christ follower, for example, must give to support God's work and minister to others, but some believers give most sacrificially.

Among the various gifts, prophecy and tongues have likely created the most controversy among believers. For some, the gift of prophecy is simply preaching the Scriptures. It is the ability to open the Word, interpret it properly, and teach it with power and authority. Thus, those who preach often also give evidence of the gifts of teaching and exhortation (likely, the ability to come alongside others to urge them toward righteous living and comfort them in times of difficulty). In addition to foretelling the future, prophets also "speak forth" the Word of God already revealed.

For others, prophecy is communicating an immediate message from God; that is, the prophet almost unexpectedly receives and speaks a divinely anointed revelation for a particular person or situation (e.g., 1 Cor 14:26, 30). Unlike teaching based on the study of the written Word, prophecy is a more spontaneous act directed by the Spirit. At the same time, though, some who hold this position assert that this gift is not a guarantee of an infallible message. Grudem, for example, states that prophets spoke "not with absolute divine authority, but simply to report something that God had laid on their hearts or brought to their minds."[8] He thus concludes that although the gift of prophecy is still available today, prophecies should not be equated with Scripture. Rather, believers must test every prophecy (1 Thess 5:19–21).

Schreiner, on the other hand, contends New Testament prophets were the equivalent of Old Testament prophets, and they spoke inerrantly and infallibly as they and the apostles laid the foundation of the church (Eph 2:20). That foundation was completed with the New Testament apostles and

---

[8] Grudem, *Systematic Theology*, 1051.

prophets, and the written Bible now serves as the foundation—not prophets who speak without error today. If the gift of prophecy were available today, the church would need to wrestle with whether the inspired words of the prophets somehow stand equivalent to the already-revealed Word of God.

Emphasis on the gift of tongues gained steam in North America with the Los Angeles Azusa Street Revival in the early 1900s. Under the influence of Charles Parham of Topeka, Kansas, whose followers had received baptism of the Holy Spirit and spoken in tongues in 1900, African-American preacher William Seymour was the tool for revival in Azusa Street. Seymour preached about tongues, and a revival began in 1906 that led to the beginnings of the Pentecostal movement. Almost sixty years later, the emphasis on tongues moved into mainline churches, and the charismatic movement began. Both movements have, however, had their critics—especially regarding abuses of the gift of tongues.

Controversy surrounding tongues, of course, was not unknown. Some in the church in Corinth were emphasizing tongues as a greater gift, and the spectacular nature of speaking in a previously unknown tongue was surely captivating to them. Paul, though, corrected that position by emphasizing the value of all gifts and by elevating prophecy that others would understand (1 Cor 12:29–31; 14:1–3). He did not forbid speaking in tongues (1 Cor 14:39), but he did put parameters around the use of this gift in a worship service. Without an interpreter, believers were to keep silent and speak only to themselves and God (1 Cor 14:27–28). Apparently, one could control when he or she would exhibit the gift of tongues, and it was acceptable to speak in tongues privately rather than cause commotion in the church.

Debates continue today as to whether tongues are messages spoken in a known language, ecstatic expressions, or both in different settings. Some argue that the gift results in believers speaking another human language they did not previously know, as in Acts 2:5–11. In this case, the hearers heard the message in their own language. Proponents of this position contend that even in 1 Corinthians 14, the language is apparently a known language because someone must interpret it so the message is understood.

Others take the position that tongues are ecstatic utterances, at least in some instances. Paul, for example, indicated that believers speaking in tongues were speaking to God, not to men, and they spoke "mysteries in the Spirit" (1 Cor 14:2). He also spoke of "different" and "various" kinds of tongues (1 Cor 12:10, 28), which could imply tongues different from human language. The reference to "tongues of angels" (1 Cor 13:1 ESV) might also suggest a language that is not human. This gift of tongues is a means of singing and offering praise to God even though the speaker might not understand the language (1 Cor 14:2; 14–17).

Amid these differences and discussions, one must remember Paul's final words to the Corinthians regarding these matters: "But everything is to be done decently and in order" (1 Cor 14:40). The use of the gifts in Corinth had been disorderly and divisive, and Paul countered that tendency with these words. Everything was to be done for the purpose of edifying the church.

Applying Spiritual Gifts

Believers must be careful not to fall into extremes regarding spiritual gifts. On one hand, they must not overemphasize them to the point they overshadow love and create division. Such excessive attention can lead to spiritual elitism not unlike that found in the church in Corinth. On the other hand, they must not underemphasize gifts out of fear of the opposite concern. To do so would be to ignore Paul's call to seek the gifts and to fail to see how God has created his people for his work. Finding proper balance is imperative in leading believers to identify and use their gifts. Following, then, are several suggestions for employing gifts in the local church.

First, the process of discovering and utilizing gifts cannot be separated from the local church. God has created his body in such a way that every member matters (1 Corinthians 12), regardless of his or her role or giftedness. No division is to exist in the body; members weep and rejoice with each other (1 Cor 12:25–26). The Scriptures thus leave little room for an individualistic approach to spiritual gifts discovery apart from the people of God. Indeed, it is often the affirmation of others that convinces a believer of his or her giftedness.

Second, church leaders must teach about spiritual gifts. Not only does their inclusion in the Scriptures require pastors to explain them, but doing so will also help members avoid developing a faulty understanding of the gifts. It will also help edify and encourage the church; avoiding the topic because of potential controversy is simply not an option.

Third, actually serving in a church is a significant way to discover one's gifts. Believers do not determine gifts solely on the basis of a spiritual gifts inventory, but they identify them best through the practice of ministry. In some ways, this process is investigation marked by discovering ministry needs in the church, serving fully in a particular role, and evaluating with the help of others what gifts one might have. Effectiveness in a ministry role and confirmation from other believers thus become indicators of one's giftedness.

Fourth, do not place final weight on a spiritual gifts inventory. Given the varied debates about spiritual gifts, every spiritual gifts inventory reflects the bias of the one who created it. If the creator believes the miraculous gifts are no longer available, they are not likely options on the inventory. Someone who believes the gifts lists are not exhaustive will produce an inventory different from someone who limits the gifts to those listed in the New Testament. In addition, simply relying on an inventory might grant permission for a believer to be less than obedient to God's commands. Someone who apparently does not have the gift of mercy may, for example, give too little attention to being compassionate toward others. At the same time, some who discover their giftedness through an inventory alone might see no need to develop that gift after they have already identified it.

Fifth, involve church members early in some aspect of ministry. Everyone will not be immediately prepared and equipped for certain positions, but a church should offer "entry-level" positions to engage members soon after they commit to a church. Doing so early connects the new member to the church through involvement, one of the necessities for assimilating members into a church. Involved members will then have opportunity to test their gifts and connect with other members who can help assess their giftedness. This process teaches new members early that the congregation expects its members to use their gifts to edify the church.

Finally, be aware of potential problems when members serve long-term outside their giftedness. Many church members will serve in any open position simply because they love the church. Often they are serving in multiple roles—not all of which will allow them to serve according to their spiritual gifts. Serving outside of one's giftedness may be necessary in some settings, but doing so long-term can become both frustrating and exhausting. Additionally, it usually eliminates an opening for someone else who *is* more gifted in that arena. It is thus best to help believers find their giftedness, continually grow in that area, and focus their energy toward using their own gifts.

For Additional Study

Berding, Ken. *What Are Spiritual Gifts?* Grand Rapids: Kregel, 2006.

Grudem, Wayne. *Systematic Theology: An Introduction to Biblical Doctrine.* Grand Rapids: Zondervan, 1994.

————. ed. *Are Miraculous Gifts for Today? 4 Views.* Grand Rapids: Zondervan, 1996.

Hemphill, Ken. *You Are Gifted: Your Spiritual Gifts and the Kingdom of God.* Nashville: B&H, 2009.

Keener, Craig S. *Gift Giver: The Holy Spirit for Today.* Grand Rapids: Baker, 2001.

Schreiner, Thomas R. *Spiritual Gifts: What They Are and Why They Matter.* Nashville: B&H, 2018.

Storms, Sam. *Understanding Spiritual Gifts: A Comprehensive Guide.* Grand Rapids: Zondervan, 2020.

Wagner, C. Peter. *Your Spiritual Gifts Can Help Your Church Grow.* Ventura, CA: Regal Books, 1979.

Also see these articles: Holy Spirit, Sanctification, Spiritual Formation and Discipleship, Preaching, Evangelism and Missions

42

Prayer

SUSAN BOOTH

P rayer is human communication and communion shared with God. It is both a wrestling for kingdom purposes and an experience of fellowship with God.

Prayer in the Old Testament

The Bible explains that God created humans in "the image of God" (Gen 1:27). Whatever else this remarkable phrase communicates, it includes relationship. We were made to know and love God, to walk and talk with him. God's first recorded words to humans were a commission—to spread the praise of his glory to the ends of the earth. Tragically, we have only the barest hint of what that initial spiritual intimacy with God may have looked like since the only description of it follows on the heels of Adam and Eve's disobedience (Gen 3:8).

Humanity's first recorded words specifically addressed to God were not a prayer, but rather an expression of fear, blame, and broken relationship (Gen 3:10–13). The second set of words spoken to God reveal just how quickly sin escalated: Cain's angry defense—"Am I my brother's keeper?"—failed to conceal he was his brother's killer (Gen 4:9 ESV). The downward spiral continued, broken only by the brief mention that some men from Seth's line "began to call on the name of the LORD" (Gen 4:26).

In the account of the Patriarchs, divine-human interchanges record primarily the words of the Lord and surprisingly few human statements. The patriarchs' responses include immediate obedience, worship, falling prostrate, or a subservient "Here I am" (Gen 12:4, 7, 8; 17:3, 17; 22:1, 11). Occasionally, the patriarchs asked for clarification, expressed hesitancy, or even pressed for stipulations to be met (Gen 15:2–3, 8; 17:17–18; 28:20–22). With the appearance of the Lord in Genesis 18, the record of these verbal exchanges shifted more to conversation when Abraham humbly pleaded that the Lord spare the citizens of Sodom (Gen 18:23–33). The first time the verb "to pray" (Hebrew: *pālal*) appears in the Old Testament is when the Lord gave instructions for Abraham to intercede on behalf of Abimelech and his family: "He is a prophet, and he will pray for you and you will live" (Gen 20:7; cf. 17). This Hebrew word for "intercession" typically occurs in the context of sinners needing pardon.

Later leaders interceded on behalf of the nation. Moses, with whom the Lord spoke "face to face, just as a man speaks with his friend," repeatedly interceded on behalf of the wayward Israelites (Exod 33:11). After the golden calf debacle, Moses refused to go another step without the Lord's presence and boldly pled to see his glory. God rewarded him with a glimpse of his goodness and the classic definition of his character (Exod 34:6–7). Samuel, who learned to hear the Lord's voice as a child, committed to pray without ceasing on Israel's behalf (1 Sam 12:23; cf. 7:5; 12:19).

The first occurrence of the noun *tephillah* ("prayer," from *pālal*) surfaces in David's extended prayerful response to the Lord's declaration of the Davidic Covenant (2 Sam 7:27). About half of the other occurrences appear in the Psalms as laments calling on the Lord to hear the requests and intercessions of individuals (e.g., Ps 17:1 [two times]). Even a brief sampling of Psalms reveals the broad range of David's influence on our understanding of prayer (e.g., Psalms 19, 23, 51, 69, 139, 145). Solomon's dedication of the temple illustrates how supplications were also communal and directed toward the temple (1 Kings 8 [seven times]). The Lord promised that when his people would repent and pray, he would hear, forgive, and heal their land (2 Chr 7:14).

When Israel forsook the living God to worship lifeless idols, the Lord refused to listen to their empty prayers (Isa 1:15). After centuries of patience, God set judgment in motion, and no amount of prayer would forestall it

(Jer 15:1). He even commanded Jeremiah to stop interceding on the nation's behalf (Jer 7:16; 11:14; 14:11). At the close of the exile, however, Daniel's sincere pleadings and confessions on behalf of the nation were accompanied by fasting, sackcloth, and ashes (Dan 9:3–19). Similar expressions of self-abasement appear in Ezra's intercession for the returned exiles (Ezra 9:5–15) and the corporate confession of sin by the Levites as recorded in Nehemiah (Neh 9:1, 5–37).

A brief survey of Psalms illustrates the wide range of Old Testament prayers. They include not only intercession, but also cries for deliverance from trouble (Psalm 57), confession of personal sin (Psalm 51), calls for destruction of enemies (Psalm 59), laments over the injustice and immorality of the wicked (Psalm 73), and complaints bemoaning the Lord's apparent silence or inaction (Psalm 13). Alongside these kingdom-work struggles appear prayers expressing deep communion: jubilant hymns of thanksgiving and corporate praise (Psalm 100, 103) as well as meditations on God's character, works, and word (Psalm 27, 104, 119).

Prayer in the New Testament

Prior to the New Testament period, life in Second Temple Judaism revolved around both regular seasons of prayer and spontaneous prayer. The yearly calendar began with prayer at Rosh Hashanah and Yom Kippur, and liturgies accompanied the three annual festivals. The daily rhythms of life included mealtime prayers, as well as morning and evening prayers that coincided with the offering of incense at the temple. The announcement of the Messiah's forerunner came during evening prayer (Luke 1:10), and the revelation of the Messiah's arrival produced spontaneous celebrations of praise (Mary: Luke 1:46–55; Zechariah: Luke 1:67–79; Simeon: Luke 2:29–32).

Though he was God in flesh, Jesus modeled reliance on prayer during his time on earth. The Gospels record the Lord demonstrating a habitual pattern of praying often and in solitude, before sunrise and sometimes all night (Luke 5:16; 6:12; 9:18, 28). Jesus prayed when he broke bread, and he publicly voiced praise and thanksgiving to the Father (Luke 9:16; 10:21; 22:17, 19; 24:30). He interceded for others, including children, the disciples, and those present when he raised Lazarus (Mark 10:16; Luke 22:32; John 11:41–42).

Even though the disciples lived in a culture steeped in religion, they witnessed something in the power and efficacy of Jesus's prayer-life that compelled them to ask, "Teach us to pray." His answer to their request—commonly called "The Lord's Prayer"—is not a rote incantation, but rather a template or model for them and subsequent generations (Matt 6:9–13; Luke 11:2–4). Jesus invited his followers to address Almighty God with both shocking intimacy and deep respect: "Our Father in heaven." Recalling that God alone is holy, they are to enter his presence with worship and align their lives to his kingdom. Once they have focused on God himself, they may express their utter dependence on him for his daily provision, mercy, and deliverance.

Jesus also taught about prayer. He urged his disciples to pray for their enemies, to request laborers for the harvest, and to ask for strength in the face of peril and persecution (Luke 6:28; 10:2; 21:36). Jesus used parables to illustrate boldness and persistence in prayer (Luke 11:5–8; 18:1–8). He warned his followers not to babble empty words or to seek public recognition while praying (Matt 6:5–8). Instead, they were to confess their sin with humility (Luke 18:9–14). They should ask with the confidence of a child petitioning an earthly father because the heavenly Father graciously gives good things to those who ask (Matt 7:7–11).

Prayer characterized the final week of Jesus's earthly life. He displayed zeal for his Father's "house of prayer" and offered thanks for the Last Supper's cup and bread (Luke 19:45–46; 22:17–19). He interceded fervently for his disciples (John 17). With "loud cries and tears" he pled passionately to know the Father's will and to be able to surrender to it fully (Heb 5:7; Luke 22:39–46). On the cross, Jesus prayed for his enemies and committed his spirit to God (Luke 23:34, 46). After the resurrection he broke bread with prayer at Emmaus, and he blessed his disciples as he ascended into heaven (Luke 24:30, 51).

The rest of the New Testament continues to underscore the significance of prayer for believers. Continual united prayer preceded the outpouring of the Holy Spirit and the birth of the church (Acts 1:14). Devoted prayer sustained the early church through growth and persecution alike (Acts 2:42; 4:24–31; 7:59–60). Believing prayer resulted in miracles (Acts 9:40; 12:12–17; 16:25–26; 28:8). Prayer, fasting, and laying on of hands confirmed conversion, commissioned for ministry, and gave birth to mission (Acts 1:24; 6:6; 8:17; 9:11–12; 10:9–13; 13:2–3; 14:23).

The centrality of prayer in the early church finds further support in the thanksgiving and praises that well up in Paul's letters. The apostle frequently shifts from addressing his recipients to praying on their behalf (e.g., Eph 1:15–19; 3:14–21; Phil 1:9–11; Col 1:9–14; 2 Thess 1:11–12). His epistles record dozens of instances where he thanks God for believers, pronounces blessings on them, and reports his fervent prayer for them. Paul likewise requested that they, in turn, pray for him—that he might be rescued from wicked unbelievers, that he might visit them, and that he might have an open door to proclaim the gospel clearly and fearlessly (Rom 15:30–33; Eph 6:19–20; Col 4:2–4; 2 Thess 3:2–3). The apostle heeded his own exhortation to intercede unceasingly with thanksgiving on behalf of all the saints and those in authority over them (Phil 4:6–7; 1 Thess 5:17; 1 Tim 2:1–3).

The restoration of all things pictured in Revelation 21–22 shows redeemed humanity once again dwelling in the unmediated presence of God, enjoying unbroken communication and communion with God. The redeemed will see his face and worship him (Rev 21:3–4, 22; 22:4). Not surprisingly, the Bible concludes with a prayer for the Lord's return in anticipation of this fully restored relationship—"Amen! Come Lord Jesus!"

Theology of Prayer

Prayer is based on the nature and character of God. Because God is relational, he created humanity in his image, and he initiates communication with them. Because he is a God who reveals himself, he speaks to his people, and they are able to recognize his voice and respond. Because God is everywhere, knows all things, and has all power, he hears the petitions of all who call upon his name. Because of his compassionate nature and steadfast love, he is inclined to answer and extend forgiveness. Because of his providence and sovereign activity in the world, he sets answers in motion before lips even voice requests (Isa 65:24).

Prayer is an essential part of the nature of humanity. People are created beings, dependent on the God who made them in his image. Because that image was fractured in the fall, people by nature address their petitions to god(s) made by their hands or conceived in their minds. The Lord in his mercy, however, made a way for sinful people to receive forgiveness through the symbolism of animal sacrifice. Old Testament saints eventually directed their prayers toward the temple as the place of both sacrifice and intercession (2 Chr 7:12; Isa 53:12). This focus on sacrifice and intercession anticipated the coming of the Messiah.

Prayer is made possible by the person and work of Christ. The book of Hebrews explains that believers are able to pray because of Jesus's work as both mediator and atoning sacrifice. As the Son of God, Jesus is "the radiance of God's glory and the exact expression of his nature" (Heb 1:3). In the incarnation he became like humans in every way—tempted as we are yet not yielding to sin—so that he might become a faithful high priest and make atonement for our sins (Heb 2:17–18). Unlike a human high priest, our mediator entered into the heavenly inner sanctuary by means of his own blood—a "once for all time" sacrifice (Heb 9:12). Christ offered himself through the eternal Spirit to God the Father so that our sins might be removed (Heb 9:14). The blood of Jesus thus makes it possible for believers to enter the sanctuary through prayer, boldly approaching the throne of God in order to "receive mercy and find grace to help us in time of need" (Heb 4:16; cf. 10:19). Because Jesus's priesthood is eternal, "he is able to save completely those who come to God through him, since he always lives to intercede for them" (Heb 7:25). Christ not only makes prayer possible, but he also prays for us.

The Spirit of God, who indwells believers, likewise plays a distinct role in prayer. The Spirit gives life to our mortal bodies; he leads us, and he enables us to put to death the deeds of the body (Rom 8:11, 13). He is the "Spirit of adoption, by whom we cry out, 'Abba, Father!'" (Rom 8:15). Like Jesus, the Spirit intercedes to God on our behalf. When we do not know what to pray or how to pray appropriately, he helps us in our weakness, interceding "with inexpressible groanings," aligning our prayers to the will of God (Rom 8:26–27). As believers walk in step with the Spirit, so they are to pray in the Spirit (Gal 5:16; Eph 6:18).

To whom then should we pray? Jesus himself always prayed to God the Father and taught his followers to do the same while still maintaining the distinction between himself and his disciples ("my Father and your Father," John 20:17). In his time on earth, Jesus also encouraged people to trust him and ask him for help (John 14:1, 13–14). Thomas expressed adoration to Christ, Stephen committed his spirit to him, and believers called on his name (John 20:28; Acts 7:59; 9:21). Although the New Testament does not record prayers addressed to the Spirit, he is our "Counselor" (John 14:16), so occasional prayers to the Holy Spirit are appropriate—particularly in view of his roles to teach and guide, to convict us of sin, and to empower and gift us for ministry (John 14:26; 16:7–14; Acts 1:8; 1 Cor 12:11). The typical New Testament pattern, however, is to address prayer to the Father, through the work of the Son, by means of the Spirit (Eph 2:13–18). The Trinity is thus an integral part of the biblical teaching on prayer as the three distinct persons of the Godhead work together in perfect unity as one in the context of prayer (Eph 3:14–21).

How does prayer work in conjunction with the sovereignty of God? Included in God's sovereign purposes for his creation is the participation of people who pray according to his will. We can be confident that the Father delights in hearing and answering such prayers (Ezek 36:37; 1 John 5:14–15). We discern the will of God as we immerse ourselves in his Word and ask him for wisdom (Jas 1:5). When we still do not know how to pray, the Spirit aids our prayers by aligning them to the Father's will (Rom 8:26–28). Jesus himself modeled framing even deeply heartfelt petition in conditional terms: "Father, if you are willing, take this cup away from me—nevertheless, not my will, but yours, be done" (Luke 22:42; cf. Matt 6:10). In matters where God's will is not clearly addressed in Scripture, we should follow his example of humble submission to the Father's sovereign purposes.

What does it mean to pray "in Jesus's name"? On the eve of his crucifixion, Jesus taught his followers to pray in his name and promised to answer them (John 14:13–14; 15:16; 16:23–24). Later, his followers did miracles in his name—as his representatives, under his authority (Acts 3:16; 9:27; Jas 5:14). The phrase is not a simple tagline to signal the end of a prayer. Praying in Jesus's name is a reminder that the only approach to a holy, almighty God is through the perfect sacrifice of his Son. Because believers are now "in Christ," we share in Jesus's access to the presence of God (Eph 2:13, 18).

What does it mean when prayer offered in faith goes unanswered? God is active in this world and has chosen to move in concert with those who pray in faith. The Lord indeed answers the prayers of his people (Ps 106:23; Amos 7:1–6; Jas 5:16–18). God is not bound, however, to grant every request made to him. Certain conditions must be met, such as praying in the Spirit, in the name of Jesus, according to the Father's will, as well as in agreement with other believers and the word of God (Matt 18:19; John 15:7). The prayer must be offered in faith, with humility, persistence, proper motives, and a clean conscience (Matt 21:21–22; Luke 11:8; Jas 4:3; Ps 66:18). Even when these conditions are met, still the answer is sometimes "not yet," sometimes "no." Abraham waited decades for Isaac; Israel prayed centuries for the Messiah. Paul pled three times for the Lord to remove his "thorn in the flesh," but God allowed the thorn to remain as a guard against pride and a testimony to Christ's sufficiency in weakness (2 Cor 12:7–9). Jesus himself beseeched the Father to take away the cup of suffering, but he yielded to his Father's ordained plan for redemption (Luke 22:42). Even when the answer to a petition is "no," God encounters his people and ministers to them through prayer.

Doctrine of Prayer in Christian History

Early Church

One of the first writings on prayer in the early church was Origen's *Treatise on Prayer*. Origen (c. 185–254) concluded that all believers should organize prayer around four elements he observed throughout Scripture: adoration, thanksgiving, confession, and petition, ending with a return to adoration. Neoplatonic influences appear in Origen's beliefs that prayer should concern only spiritual benefits and the highest form of prayer is contemplation.

Monastic asceticism began by the fourth century as the first monks retreated into the desert to focus on prayer and meditation, supplemented by Bible reading and fasting. These desert fathers and mothers abandoned society and family in hopes of attaining deep communion with God. Their prayers sometimes included short repetitive formulas.

Augustine, addressing the subject of prayer in response to a young widow (Letter 130, AD 412), wrote that a person must first desire to behold the Lord and to dwell with him (Ps 27:4). Thereafter, one may pray to live a happy life, asking for no more or less than is necessary. Augustine noted that petitions require words and the Lord's Prayer provides the model for petitions. Unceasing prayer, however, does not require a multiplicity of words, but rather the prolonged warmth of desire for God himself.

John Cassian's writings on monasticism drew many into the communal monastic movement in the West. Cassian (c. 365–435) taught that petitions should be limited to only those included in the Lord's Prayer.[1] As a means to achieve unceasing prayer, he recommended using Psalm 70:1 as a formula, chanting it from first to last waking thought.[2] Cassian believed this continual prayer paved the way for a more sublime prayer that transcended thoughts and words and infused the mind with heavenly light.[3]

Middle Ages

Benedict of Nursia (c. 480–547) founded a monastic order characterized by silence and strict obedience. Community life revolved around seven daily prayer services and one at night. The influence of Benedict's rule shaped monastic life in the West throughout the Middle Ages, as did the continued emphasis on mystical union with God.

The father of scholasticism, Anselm of Canterbury (1033–1109), wrote theological treatises and composed prayers for devotional use. Included among these are prayers that both venerated and called for help from the Virgin Mary and canonized saints—a practice consistent with the teachings of the Catholic Church.

The center of monastic life in the East was prayer and spirituality. The Hesychasts continually repeated the "Jesus Prayer": "Lord Jesus Christ, Son of God, have mercy on me." As mind and heart merged, the supplicant might receive a beatific vision of divine light. Though some attacked this practice as superstitious, the Councils of Constantinople (mid-1300s) adopted hesychasm ("quietness") into the orthodox tradition.

Reformation and Early Modern Eras

The Reformers shifted the focus of prayer from mysticism to petition. In a small booklet, *A Simple Way to Pray* (1535), Martin Luther recommended the discipline of morning and evening prayers after preparing the heart by recitation of Scripture. Luther described how he meditated through each petition of the Lord's Prayer and advised listening for the "preaching" of the

---

[1] John Cassian, *Conference* 9.24.
[2] Cassian, 10.10.
[3] Cassian, 9.25.

Holy Spirit. The longest chapter in John Calvin's *Institutes* (1536) indicated the importance of prayer as "the principal exercise of faith" (Bk. 3, Ch. XX). He noted God graciously desires to give but waits for believers to ask with confident hope. Because Christ alone is the sole mediator, Calvin argued strongly against praying to departed saints.

The Puritan holiness movement began in 1564 in opposition to certain rituals included in the *Book of Common Prayer*. The Puritans' high regard for Scripture contributed to their recognition of the prominence of petition and intercession. They prayed morning and evening, devoting their entire lives to prayer. Puritan theological literature also reflected an experiential spirituality where prayer was the primary avenue for intimate communion with God.

Intercession for kingdom purposes led to great missionary movements as well. In 1727, Count Zinzendorf and the Moravians launched an around-the-clock prayer vigil in Germany that continued unbroken for a century. Pietistic prayer resulted in the deployment of hundreds of missionaries around the world. Similarly, intercessory prayer played a crucial role in the Great Awakenings and subsequent mission movements in the modern era.

Twentieth Century

Donald Bloesch observed two distinct patterns of prayer in the twentieth century that remain with us today.[4] Influenced by Neoplatonism and Eastern philosophy, Christian mysticism views prayer as ascending through successive stages—meditation, contemplation, ecstasy—with the goal of receiving a vision or achieving union with God (deification). In contrast, biblical personalism (akin to Friedrich Heiler's "prophetic prayer") verbalizes petitions in order to receive help from above, the goal being God's transformative power displayed in a broken world. Though neoorthodox theologians disparaged mysticism, the dominant trend of recent decades has been contemplative prayer as an individual, inner experience of God's presence. Synthesizing these two disparate patterns is impossible, but Bloesch contends that biblical piety, as it has in history, should include both meditation

---

[4] Donald G. Bloesch, *The Struggle of Prayer* (San Francisco: Harper & Row, 1980), 97–130.

(on Scripture and on Christ) and devotional contemplation—but never as replacements for prayer.

Contemporary Application

An evangelical perspective properly grounds the understanding of prayer in the teachings of Scripture. As dependent beings, we voice our requests to the Father, who helps us based on the redeeming work of his Son. We struggle in prayer, seeking the will of God and his kingdom purposes for the world around us. At the same time, as we pray, we experience sweet fellowship with God through his indwelling Spirit. Rightly understood, prayer is both conversation and encounter with the Lord.

Prayer glorifies God and deepens our individual and corporate communion with him. Our petitions remind us of our dependence on God and help us express our trust in him. Prayer aligns us to God's will and allows us to participate in his kingdom activity around the world.

Prayer is essential for missional living. We intercede for the advance of the gospel among the nations. We request opportunities to share Christ with sensitivity and boldness. We pray for the Spirit to direct conversations, to remove the veil that darkens people's understanding, and to convict them of sin. We plead that God brings them to salvation.

Prayer is also critical for personal discipleship. We implore God to search our hearts and cleanse us. We strap on spiritual armor and stand against the enemy's schemes. We trade in our tangled knots of anxiety for his peace that passes understanding. Through prayer, we abide in Jesus and delight in his presence; we meditate on God's Word and walk in his Spirit. As we do, he transforms us. We begin to absorb his priorities and passions. We start to see the world and people through his eyes. We obey him. Over time, we even become more like Jesus. The world can tell when we have spent time with the Lord in prayer.

For Additional Study

Bloesch, Donald G. *The Struggle of Prayer.* San Francisco: Harper & Row, 1980.

————. "Prayer" in *Evangelical Dictionary of Theology.* Edited by Daniel J. Treier and Walter A. Elwell. Grand Rapids: Baker Academic, 2017, 690–91.

Carson, D. A. ed. *Teach Us to Pray: Prayer in the Bible and the World.* Exeter, UK: World Evangelism Fellowship and Paternoster, 1990.

Foster, Richard J. *Prayer: Finding the Heart's True Home.* New York: HarperSanFrancisco, 1992.

Garrett, James Leo, Jr. *Systematic Theology: Biblical, Historical, & Evangelical.* Vol 2. Grand Rapids: Eerdmans, 1995, 393–410.

Keller, Timothy. *Prayer: Experiencing Awe and Intimacy with God.* New York: Dutton, 2014.

Millar, J. Gary. *Calling on the Name of the Lord: A Biblical Theology of Prayer.* New Studies in Biblical Theology. Vol. 38. Downers Grove: IVP Academic, 2016.

Spear, Wayne R. *The Theology of Prayer: The Systematic Study of the Biblical Teaching on Prayer.* Grand Rapids: Baker, 1979.

Also see these articles: Trinity, Holy Spirit, Worship, Spiritual Formation and Discipleship

43

Stewardship

Evan Lenow

S tewardship, at the mere mention of the word, often conjures up images of building campaigns and appeals for money in the church. For years, I opened a series of lectures on stewardship in my classes by asking what immediately came to my students' minds when they heard the term. Most answers revolved around money, budgets, fundraising, and questionable manipulation of people to give of their financial resources. Unfortunately, many of my students had not been exposed to the positive side of stewardship—the side that promotes a biblical understanding of the management of resources for the glory of God. Stewardship encompasses far more than many people realize because it is built upon the idea of managing all aspects of God's creation. In this essay, we will explore a basic understanding of stewardship, survey developments in the field of stewardship, and make application to contemporary issues.

What Is Stewardship?

Stewardship is the management of resources by an individual or group of people on behalf of the owner. In an ideal stewardship relationship, both the steward and the owner benefit from the faithful management of the owner's resources. The key management component of stewardship is evident in the very term itself. A steward is a manager; therefore, stewardship must relate to management of some type of resource. The owner places his or her resources under the care of the steward with an expectation that the resources will be cared for with the same level of attention that the owner would provide on his or her own.

Biblical Foundations

In order to grasp the theological significance of stewardship, we need to begin by looking at the owner. In Ps 24:1–2, David writes, "The earth and everything in it, the world and its inhabitants, belong to the LORD; for he laid its foundation on the seas and established it on the rivers." Calling the attention of his readers back to creation, David declares that every aspect of this world belongs to God because he created everything. Not only do the natural resources of the earth and sea belong to the Lord, but all the earth's inhabitants are also possessions of the Lord. Thus, we belong to God in the same way that the rest of creation does. Certainly, humans represent the pinnacle of creation and are the only part of creation made in God's image (Gen 1:26–27); however, God still exercises a form of ownership over all humans because he created us as well.

Since God functions as the owner over all things in this world, humans are then left to exercise a stewardship role over creation. This stewardship is first introduced in the creation narrative as God gives the first man and woman instructions: "Be fruitful, multiply, fill the earth, and subdue it. Rule the fish of the sea, the birds of the sky, and every creature that crawls on the earth" (Gen 1:28). The command to subdue the earth and rule over the fish, birds, and creatures speaks to humans' unique role in creation—one of stewardship. We can expand this stewardship responsibility corporately to all aspects of creation, including our own selves. Thus, we need to consider how best to manage God's creation in such a way that it benefits God, through bringing him glory, and benefits the human stewards by drawing us into closer relationship with our Creator.

Moving beyond the creation narrative, both the Old and New Testaments offer examples of stewardship that help us to understand the concept more fully. The most prominent example of stewardship in the Old Testament comes from the life of Joseph. He functioned in the role of a steward on two different occasions and had his own steward who managed his household (Gen 44:1, 4). In Genesis 39, the story of Joseph picks up with him being purchased by Potiphar, the captain of Pharaoh's bodyguard. Upon seeing how everything under Joseph's control prospered (Gen 39:3), "Potiphar also put him in charge of his household and placed all that he owned under his authority. From the time that he put him in charge of his household and of all that he owned, the LORD blessed the Egyptian's house because of Joseph. The LORD's blessing was on all that he owned, in his house and in his fields. He left all that he owned under Joseph's authority; he did not concern himself with anything except the food he ate" (Gen 39:4–6). The idea communicated in this passage is that Joseph became the household manager for Potiphar and oversaw everything in his possession. Joseph was quite capable in his management of Potiphar's resources, and the Lord blessed Potiphar's household on account of Joseph. After his demise in Potiphar's house, Joseph once again rose to the place of a prominent steward in Pharaoh's government (Gen 41:38–45). Pharaoh declared, "Since God has made all this known to you, there is no one as discerning and wise as you are. You will be over my house, and all my people will obey your commands. Only I, as king, will be greater than you" (Gen 41:39–40). In both circumstances, Joseph oversaw the property, resources, and responsibility of the owners (Potiphar and Pharaoh). His skillful management reflected the blessings of the Lord on his life and resulted in the continued success of his masters.

In the New Testament, we see a more formal description of stewardship. The technical term *oikonomos* ("steward") appears ten different times in the New Testament corpus. The two most common uses of this term are both significant for our discussion of stewardship. First, the basic use of steward relates to a household manager who oversees the daily operation of a house for the owner. This common usage appears in Jesus's parables and their descriptions multiple times (Luke 12:42; 16:1, 3, 8) as well as in Paul's description of a child living under the supervision of a guardian until he is mature enough to be responsible for himself (Gal 4:2). The stewards in these occurrences function in much the same way as Joseph did in the households of Potiphar and Pharaoh. The second common use of "steward" relates to managing the eternal things of God. Paul uses the term to describe himself as a trustworthy manager "of the mysteries of God" (1 Cor 4:1–2) and as a requirement for church leaders (Titus 1:7). Peter also uses the term as an admonition for his readers to employ their gifts "as good stewards of the varied grace of God" (1 Pet 4:10). While there are significant spiritual connotations in these occurrences, they still communicate the basic idea of one person managing a resource that belongs to someone else.

After exploring some of the scriptural uses of the terms and concepts for stewardship, we can glean that stewardship is an important biblical concept that applies to both everyday life and eternal matters. The next aspect of stewardship that warrants our attention is the relationship between the steward and the owner. This relationship can best be analyzed through one of Jesus's parables on stewardship.

The Relationship between Owner and Steward

The parable of the talents in Matt 25:14–30 gives the most extensive description of stewardship in all of Scripture and helps us see the importance of the relationship between an owner and his or her steward. Before we begin to analyze the text, we need to remember that this parable is part of a series of parables on the kingdom of heaven. Therefore, any application we make to stewardship in everyday life must also be filtered through the lens of the importance of the kingdom of heaven.

In this familiar parable, Jesus describes a man who is about to go on a journey, so he distributes varying amounts of talents to three different servants (five talents, two talents, and one talent). The master then leaves on a journey of unspecified length, and the servants are on their own to manage the resources that have been entrusted to them. Two of the servants trade with the talents and double the money. The third servant buries the one talent until his master returned. "After a long time," the master returns and asks his servants to make an account of their efforts. The first two servants are commended for their faithfulness, while the third servant is scolded for his laziness. The talent is taken from him and given to the one who now has ten talents, and "this good-for-nothing servant" is thrown out of the master's presence.

What do we learn about the relationship between the owner and the steward from this passage? First, we see that the relationship between the owner and steward is one of trust. Jesus tells us that the master "entrusted his possessions" to the servants (Matt 25:14). A relationship had already been built between the owner and his stewards, and trust had been established. Stewardship, thus, requires trust on the part of the owner to turn over any portion of his or her possessions to another person to manage.

Second, we see that the owner entrusts his possessions on the basis of ability. The relationship is strong enough that the owner has evaluated the abilities of the various stewards and decides on the amount of money to entrust to each one on that basis. When looking at this parable, we might often focus on the failure of the third servant and warn against being lazy like him. However, it is interesting to note that this lazy steward was the one whom the owner deemed as the least capable. A wise owner is not going to entrust his or her possessions into the hands of an incapable steward. In this case, we see the result of the inability of the third servant to steward well.

The third characteristic of the relationship between owner and steward is that the steward is held accountable by the owner. As Jesus depicts in his parable, "After a long time the master of those servants came and settled accounts with them" (Matt 25:19). The stewards were not left to manage the owner's resources in perpetuity. Instead, the owner called them to account for their stewardship once he returned from his journey. A good steward knows that his or her master will return and works to reach a pleasing outcome when he or she is held accountable.

The Eternal Significance of Stewardship

The application of the parable of the talents is easy to make in the world of financial stewardship—the steward is responsible to the owner to provide faithful management of his or her financial resources so that they are returned with investment gains when the owner requires accountability. At the same time, we must recognize that this parable points to an eternal principle related to the kingdom of heaven. God places his followers in the position of stewards of the kingdom. It is the responsibility of the Christian to "invest" eternal resources into the growth of the kingdom so that when our master returns from his "journey," we will be prepared to give an account for what we have done with his resources.

Paul specifically employs this concept in 1 Cor 4:1–2 as he describes his own role as a steward of "the mysteries of God" (1 Cor 4:1). In this sense, Paul has been entrusted with the gospel message and tasked to manage it well by sharing it with others and keeping his message true to what had been entrusted to him. This is further emphasized by Paul's statement that "it is required that managers be found faithful" (1 Cor 4:2). As we saw in the previous section, a lazy and unfaithful steward is worthless. A true steward of the mysteries of God will remain faithful to his or her task. This is the same idea that Paul further communicates to Titus as a requirement of church leaders to be blameless and "holding to the faithful message as taught, so that he will be able both to encourage with sound teaching and to refute those who contradict it" (Titus 1:7–9, specifically Titus 1:9). Thus, a steward of eternal matters must be faithful, blameless, and committed to sound teaching. To neglect these characteristics is to fail in the eternal aspect of stewardship.

Developments in the Discipline of Stewardship

The discipline of stewardship is different than other academic disciplines in that the concept is often called upon across various fields, but its own development is not particularly unified. We see stewardship addressed as a serious topic in disciplines as wide-ranging as business and creation care, theology and government. Therefore, much of what we see in the development of the discipline relates to stewardship as a subdiscipline within a larger field. That being said, it is interesting to note a few of these disciplines to see where the ideas have developed.

Stewardship and Wealth

The most common area to see discussions of stewardship is within the larger discussion of wealth and poverty. Much has been written in this area, and it has been an important theme from biblical days until now. Justo González has provided a helpful volume on the history of the church's views on wealth in his work *Faith and Wealth: A History of Early Christian Ideas on the Origin, Significance, and Use of Money*. Beginning with the intertestamental period and moving through the first four centuries of the church, González notes the various positions on the role of money. González believes this to be an important question in the development of doctrine, but he acknowledges, "Unfortunately, this aspect of Christian doctrine has usually been ignored by historians of theology, and it is even less known by the church at large."[1]

---

[1] Justo L. González, *Faith and Wealth: A History of Early Christian Ideas on the Origin, Significance, and Use of Money* (San Francisco: Harper & Row, 1999), xiii.

In more recent days, there has been a significant number of volumes addressing the idea of wealth in the church. Significant theological works on the topic include Craig Blomberg's *Christians in an Age of Wealth: A Biblical Theology of Stewardship*, Anne Bradley and Art Lindsley's *For the Least of These: A Biblical Answer to Poverty*, Ronald Sider's *Rich Christians in an Age of Hunger*, and Wayne Grudem and Barry Asmus's *The Poverty of Nations: A Sustainable Solution*. These more theological works address matters of giving, wealth accumulation, and poverty relief. They offer differing solutions to the problems of poverty and the role of government. Such a contrast is most clearly seen between the work of Sider and the volume by Grudem and Asmus.

From a pastoral and practical perspective, the work of Randy Alcorn is likely the most familiar to lay readers. He has written several works on the topic of financial stewardship, including *Money, Possessions, and Eternity* and *Managing God's Money: A Biblical Guide*. David Platt also generated significant conversation over his book *Radical*. Platt challenged American Christians to rethink the significance they place on wealth in their own lives in light of the struggles of people in other parts of the world. In an attempt to strike a balance between unyielding accumulation of wealth and complete sacrifice, John Cortines and Gregory Baumer have offered two recent contributions to the field: *God and Money: How We Discovered True Riches at Harvard Business School* and *True Riches: What Jesus Really Said about Money and Your Heart*.

Stewardship and Creation

Another area of significant development in the field of stewardship comes in the realm of creation care. Discussion about environmental stewardship often lends itself to policy decisions regarding pollution, endangered species, and climate change. However, there is a body of literature that attempts to look at creation care from a theological perspective. Evangelicals first began to wade into the waters of creation care with Francis Schaeffer's *Pollution and the Death of Man*. Since that time there have been numerous works that address environmental stewardship while still maintaining a robust theological grounding. These works include Douglas and Jonathan Moo's *Creation Care: A Biblical Theology for the World* and Mark Liederbach and Seth Bible's

True North: Christ, the Gospel, and Creation Care. In the larger realm of stewardship, creation care does not receive the same level of treatment as financial stewardship; however, it is an important topic of discussion for Christians to engage in order to fulfill the original creation mandate of Gen 1:28.

Whole-Life Stewardship

Whole-life stewardship is the recognition that every aspect of life deserves to be stewarded faithfully. There is no part of life that does not belong to God, and there is no part of life that does not deserve to be managed well. In 1 Cor 10:31 Paul tells us, "So, whether you eat or drink, or whatever you do, do everything for the glory of God." We must live every aspect of life to God's glory, and the only way to do this is through stewardship of our whole lives. Gerard Berghoef and Lester DeKoster summarize this idea well as they write, "The basic forms of stewardship are twice defined: (1) by the opportunities for doing good that we learn to become aware of, and (2) by the gifts God has on deposit with us designed to meet such opportunities."[2]

The literature that promotes this approach to stewardship is continuing to grow as part of a connection between vocation and discipleship. Berghoef and DeKoster's older volume that was reprinted in 2013 under the title *Faithful in All God's House* is a good example of using the model of stewardship to speak to issues beyond (while still including) finances. Greg Forster offers an even larger perspective on stewardship as a model for engaging the entire culture in *Joy for the World: How Christianity Lost Its Cultural Influence and Can Begin Rebuilding It.* In the specific realm of vocation, the Theology of Work Project (www.theologyofwork.org) provides an interesting dynamic to the broader conversation of whole-life stewardship. These contributions just scratch the surface of the larger conversation of stewardship.

Applying Stewardship to Life

As evidenced by the immediately preceding section, there are virtually limitless areas to which the concept of stewardship can be applied in contemporary

---

[2] Gerard Berghoef and Lester DeKoster, *Faithful in All God's House: Stewardship and the Christian Life.* (Grand Rapids: Christian's Library Press, 2013), 9–10.

life. There are several specific areas in which believers should particularly pay attention to how they steward the resources God has entrusted to them. Without a doubt, stewardship of financial resources is a priority to the Lord. Jesus addressed matters of money and possessions regularly in his teaching, often calling on his hearers to rethink the way they related to finances (Matt 6:24; Mark 10:17–35; 12:41–44; Luke 12:31–34). Jesus's warning in Matt 6:24 is perhaps the most important to the discussion of stewardship. He admonishes his followers, "No one can serve two masters, since either he will hate one and love the other, or he will be devoted to one and despise the other. You cannot serve both God and money." According to Jesus, money is the resource, not the master. We are the stewards of all the financial resources God has granted to us; therefore, we serve our Lord, not the resource.

Stewardship of creation is probably the area that receives the most skepticism among evangelicals, but it is also the first task that mankind was given at creation. As noted above, God commanded the first man and woman to subdue the earth and rule over the created animals (Gen 1:28). The type of creation care that fits a stewardship model is a theocentric model that views all of creation as having inherent value. Humans as bearers of God's image (Gen 1:26–27) have the highest inherent value, but we must not forget that God called his creation "good" (Gen 1:4, 12, 18, 21, 25, 31). Viewing all of creation as having worth then helps us to steward what God has created and owns with God's glory in mind. Instead of approaching our management of creation as something that should simply be used to advance short-term human interests, a focus on stewardship of creation will keep God's glory at the forefront.

The final application of stewardship is the most important one—stewardship of the kingdom. Going back to the parable of the talents, Jesus's intent was to draw the attention of his hearers to their stewardship of the kingdom while awaiting his return. Such stewardship falls to all believers in every age. There are at least two important components of the stewardship of the kingdom. First, it is the responsibility of all believers to share the good news of the kingdom of God to those who need to hear it. The Great Commission is a command to steward the kingdom. Jesus declares, "Go, therefore, and make disciples of all nations, baptizing them in the name of the Father and of the Son and of the Holy Spirit, teaching them to observe everything I have commanded you" (Matt 28:19–20a). Combined with Jesus's parting words immediately before he ascended (Acts 1:8), the disciples were commissioned to take the good news of the gospel to every corner of the earth. This same commission extends to believers today as we await the return of our Savior.

The second component of stewardship of the kingdom is doctrinal faithfulness. This is the emphasis that Paul references when he refers to himself as a steward of the mysteries of God in 1 Cor 4:1–2. He further states that such stewards should be faithful. Paul's goal was to be a faithful manager of the gospel that God entrusted to him, and he also knew that such stewardship would extend beyond just himself. He instructed Timothy, "What you have heard from me in the presence of many witnesses, commit to faithful men who will be able to teach others also" (2 Tim 2:2). We now stand in this long line of faithful stewards who have been entrusted with kingdom-centered resources to proclaim and teach so that others will be brought into the kingdom.

At the end of the day, all stewardship is kingdom-centered because all stewardship reflects God's ownership of creation. He is the master, and we are the managers that use his resources to bring him glory. Just as Paul noted in 1 Cor 10:31, "So, whether you eat or drink, or whatever you do, do everything for the glory of God," every action we take should be an act of stewardship that brings glory to the owner of all things.

For Additional Study

Alcorn, Randy C. *Money, Possessions, and Eternity*. Carol Stream, IL: Tyndale House, 2003.

Berghoef, Gerard, and Lester DeKoster. *Faithful in All God's House: Stewardship and the Christian Life*. Grand Rapids: Christian's Library Press, 2013.

Blomberg, Craig. *Christians in an Age of Wealth: A Biblical Theology of Stewardship*. Grand Rapids: Zondervan, 2013.

Forster, Greg. *Joy for the World: How Christianity Lost Its Cultural Influence and Can Begin to Rebuild It*. Wheaton: Crossway, 2014.

González, Justo L. *Faith and Wealth: A History of Early Christian Ideas on the Origin, Significance, and Use of Money*. San Francisco: Harper & Row, 1999.

Liederbach, Mark, and Seth Bible. *True North: Christ, the Gospel, and Creation Care*. Nashville: B&H, 2012.

Moo, Douglas J., and Jonathan A. Moo. *Creation Care: A Biblical Theology for the World*. Grand Rapids: Zondervan, 2018.

Also see these articles: Creation, Providence, Humanity

PART VI
THEOLOGY AND CULTURE

44

Religious Liberty

Hunter Baker

O ne of the surprises of the twenty-first century is that religious liberty has become a controversial concept in American politics. Once largely dwelling in the domain of American constitutional jurisprudence, it now receives the attention of our politicians, media, and social media. To some it is a cherished right. To others it is simply a respectable-sounding concept employed to cloak crude discrimination in the language of law. What cannot be denied is that religious liberty is important and may be the most essential of freedoms.

A Summary of the Idea

What do we mean when we talk about religious liberty? How can we understand it? Still more specifically, how should Christians and the church think about religious liberty?

One of the great Greek tragedies posed the timeless questions of whether human beings always follow the laws of the state or there are other, higher, laws that are more important. Antigone, daughter of Oedipus, decided to bury her brother's body even though her uncle the king had declared the body should molder in public, thus accruing shame. When Antigone confessed the crime, which occasioned the king's rage, she declared that she did not suppose his laws to be superior to those of the gods.

It is along similar lines that heroes of the Old Testament such as Daniel, Shadrach, Meshach, and Abednego refused to cede their full loyalty to an earthly ruler who commanded them to follow a course at odds with their faith. Martin Luther King Jr. would further memorialize them and the strength of their cause in his soaring *Letter from Birmingham Jail.*

Jesus Christ offered a brief but powerful meditation upon the question of faith and government authority when he was challenged by Pharisees to answer the question of whether it was right to pay taxes to Caesar. Considering the image of Caesar on a coin, he responded, "Render unto Caesar what is Caesar's and to God what is God's." Jesus's answer to the question seems to indicate that Caesar (the government or the state) does have a legitimate zone of authority. That is, of course, bolstered by what Paul wrote later in Romans 13. So, we render unto Caesar. But do not miss the second part of the statement: Render unto God what is God's. The clear implication is that Caesar's domain is not coextensive with God's. There are some things that God reserves to himself, such as worship and obedience to his law. When Caesar acts within his mandate, by all means give him his due. But do not mistake his lesser rule for God's greater one. Martin Luther King Jr.'s famed letter is a masterful text differentiating the claims of human and divine law.

All of this flies in the face of what has been the experience of human beings throughout most of history as we understand it. Religious and political power have often been united. Being a citizen or subject has typically been the same as to be a member of a cult or religion. The religious and political power reinforced each other. To introduce the idea that religious obligations could lead to a challenge of the reigning political authority is to disrupt an ancient power relationship. Indeed, the charge that Jesus was a king was a way to encourage the secular authority to execute him.

Pagan rulers of the Roman Empire found themselves vexed by the seemingly hardheaded refusals of Christians to accept what they viewed as their tolerant reign. Roman leaders largely allowed adherents of a variety of religions to continue in their normal practice as long as they would also worship the emperor. There was no need for searching doctrinal discussions because pagan religion was not so much about truth as it was about participation and performance. What a person believed was not terribly important if they honored the public cult. But Christians felt that they could not render even the performance. To them, it was nonnegotiable to insist that Jesus is Lord, not Caesar. The result was persecution that ended with Constantine in the early fourth century, even though the Empire did not become Christian until the latter part of the fourth century.

When the Roman Empire fell, the church survived and became a powerful source of cultural memory and civilization as it evangelized Europe and built upon its growing power and authority. In time the Christian church largely entered into an alliance with the state to once again consolidate social and political power. Kings and popes argued over who was really in the driver's seat, but there was little question of religious liberty for the people. Eventually, though, change would come from within the church and from within Christendom. Religious liberty, over the course of centuries, would become a widely acknowledged human right. In the next section, we will discuss how that development occurred.

But what is this religious liberty that has developed out of our history? Boiled down to its essence, to have religious liberty means that there is no church established by the state to which citizens must belong or pay taxes to support. The church and the state are institutionally separated so that bishops are not bureaucrats and elected officials do not dictate doctrine. Citizens decide whether they participate in any faith or no faith. The church and the state communicate and can help each other, but they are not the same thing and maintain an important independence. Indeed, the separation of the church and state is an important part of protecting religious liberty. (Whenever we speak approvingly of the separation of church and state, it is important to be clear that separation is not a synonym for the kind of secularism that pushes faith out of the public square. Secularism is a more extreme step and can add up to real coercion and marginalization from the state.)

To sum up, in a society with respect for religious liberty, religion is a voluntary matter and generally not a suitable subject for regulation by the state. Religious liberty means that the government takes special account of the faith and conscience of citizens and places a priority on protecting them.

Survey of Key Thinkers and Developments

Constantine is often pilloried for having tied Christianity to the state through his conversion and subsequent involvement in church affairs. The reality is that he stopped the persecution of Christians and was probably more lenient in his treatment of faith than other emperors had been. He rejected coercion in religion, though he did favor the Christian church over paganism.

After the fall of Rome, the Catholic Church came to dominate Europe for approximately a millennium. For the most part, major controversies had to do with whether the state or church was supreme and not the question of whether adherents of different faiths would be free to preach, teach, and practice their beliefs. Freedom of religion wasn't even on the table. To the extent that challenges to the Catholic doctrines and way of doing things arose, they could often be sublimated into specific religious orders.

The challenge to the Catholic Church brought by Martin Luther and the other Reformers fractured Christianity into different camps of faith and practice that were not simply subsumed within the Catholic network of orders. Instead of having essentially all Western Christians under Catholicism, substantial numbers of people became Calvinists, Lutherans, Anabaptists, etc. Some of these groups formed major political alliances with states and cities such as Luther's Germany and Calvin's Geneva, while others forcefully rejected such combinations. The Anabaptists, for example, believed it was important to preserve the church's purity against the various compromises forced by political religion.

Although Luther's Germany featured a Protestant German church in the place of the Catholic one as the established body, it is important to note that Luther wrote against force in matters of faith. He complained that the state had little business coercing people regarding religion. Both he and Calvin tried to set out distinctive roles for the church to avoid the problem of popes and kings jockeying for position and power. They thought of God at the top and then the church and state as having separate tasks under God in their ministry to the people. Greater clarity of responsibilities did not end the strong commitment to legally established churches in Europe, though. Protestants in Catholic nations lived dangerously, as did Catholics in Protestant countries. Anabaptists and related movements were largely unwelcomed and often persecuted because of the radical nature of their challenge to existing arrangements. Their total rejection of church-state alliances, while normal to us, seemed destabilizing and irresponsible to many at the time.

How did religious liberty come about in the wake of the fractured Christian church that existed after the Reformation? There are several answers to this question.

In practical terms, the wars of religion that followed the Reformation had taken the lives of millions. Ultimately, there had to be some practical resolution as the cost of conflict was too high. The Peace of Westphalia in 1648 reiterated the idea that the sovereign could choose the religion of the state, but it also included provision for private freedom of worship for others and for some public freedom under regulation. Pragmatism has played a significant part in the development of religious liberty as an answer to growing pluralism.

To some degree, the further evolution of religious liberty in America was also due to practical considerations. American churches were far away from the centers of religious authority in Europe. It was harder to control religion in the frontier country. The less settled conditions and the more individualistic spirit combined to increase religious pluralism and mitigated against religious control. While we often think of the U.S. in terms of its propositional role in the philosophic debate in favor of religious liberty, the situation on the ground must be part of the picture.

Technology played a role too. The development of the printing press around the time of the Reformation led to an explosion in the available reading material and to a powerful movement among Protestants to make the Scriptures available to church members to read. A necessary part of the change was a massive campaign for literacy. Thanks to efforts by people such as Martin Luther and, later, the team behind the King James Bible, literacy vastly expanded in Europe. Almost necessarily, the combination of increased literacy and greater availability of texts (especially the Bible) led to a democratization of access and interpretation of Scripture. Laypeople were thus able to argue with some confidence and conviction against high status individuals by pointing to the actual text of the Bible. Certainly, a scripturally informed individual would be less likely to passively accept existing orders, religious or otherwise.

The same sort of effect pushed things along in America. We have already considered the lack of centralized authority and the fertile ground for religious pluralism in the colonies, but we also need to consider events such as the Great Awakening in the early to mid-eighteenth century. Many Christians in America became convinced of the primary importance of the individual's relationship to God unmediated by the existing power structures and hierarchies. The Awakening was surely bolstered by the availability of Bible texts and the ability to read them. It should be clear that moving toward an emphasis on the individual's relationship to God is also to move away from trust in the kind of legally established churches that were often entangled with politics and state power.

This article began with some of the historic, practical, technological, and sociological contributors to the development of religious liberty to avoid giving the impression that it is only great thinkers who make history through their arguments. However, in the case of religious liberty, there is little doubt that both religious and secular thinkers presented compelling reasons to escape the old practice of legally establishing religious faiths while suppressing or marginalizing others.

The Reformation is often separated into the magisterial Reformation and the radical Reformation. The magisterial Reformation is what most people think of when they think of the Reformation. It includes headline figures such as Martin Luther and John Calvin. While the magisterial Reformation successfully broke the near religious monopoly of the Catholic Church in Europe, it continued the practice of churches and governments working hand in hand. Thus, the magisterial Reformation resulted in national churches throughout Europe aligned with various crowns. The radical Reformation, best typified by the Anabaptists, thought the magisterial Reformation didn't go nearly far enough. The Anabaptists insisted that the church, like the early Christian church, should not be caught up in the power, violence, money, and compromises inherent in state religion. Better to be despised and persecuted than to be corrupted by worldly power such as that which Satan offered Jesus. So, their thinking went.

There is an important step to be noticed in the Anabaptist approach. Within the magisterial Reformation, the pattern continued of human beings simultaneously joining the political and religious community at birth. To be a subject (or a more exalted citizen) was also to be a church member. We could think of a church that operates in this way as a *comprehensive* church. Everyone is within the church whether out of conscious decision or not. The Anabaptists were determined to move away from that kind of assumption of church membership based on simply being born into a particular community. Instead of the *comprehensive* church, they pointed to the need for a *regenerate* church body. In other words, the only members of the church would be those people who had decided to put their sinful selves to death and to follow Jesus.

The famed religious scholar Ernst Troeltsch categorized the comprehensive bodies as "churches" and the regenerate ones as "sects." His characterization, though meant to be scientific, clearly favored the magisterial style over the radical. But the problems of the comprehensive churches and the benefits of the regenerate ones should be obvious. There will always be pressure for comprehensive churches to adhere to social consensus rather than shaping it. They are likely to sanction the status quo. In addition, the energy of the church will tend to be sapped by the large number of members who are largely indifferent to its activities. For the Anabaptists and their descendants, it was tremendously important that the church and its members be utterly sincere and free in their pursuit of holiness and their dedication to Christ.

Unsurprisingly, the free churches following in the footsteps of the Anabaptists (such as the more recognizable Baptists), shunned religious coercion and state connections, and pursued religious liberty through the separation of church and state. For the purpose of clarity, it is important to understand that the institutional separation of church and state is not a synonym for secularism, though many wrongly interpret the concept that way. Rather, separation maintains the independence of the church from the state (which many Christians emphasize) and of the state from the church (which some Christians as well as secular people tend to underscore).

Baptists such as John Leland and Isaac Backus were pioneers of religious liberty in the American colonies and then in the new republic. Their beliefs paired well with the growing democratization of the young nation and the increased emphasis on a person's direct relationship with God. In addition, there was a nice correspondence between the concerns of the regenerate person and that of the secular political thinkers of the time.

The common threads, whether we look to Baptist figures such as Leland and Backus or John Locke, John Stuart Mill, Thomas Jefferson, and James Madison, are readily recognizable. At the core of the case for religious liberty is the simple fact that no one can be made to believe anything. They can be made to *say* that they believe something, but then their unbelief would only be compounded by the lie they are forced to tell when the government forces them to profess that which they do not hold to be true. Such an approach would simply multiply sin. In addition, forcing people to confess and/or participate in religion runs the risk of turning faith into a cynical exercise through which large numbers of people render a minimum performance simply to get by.

Further, anyone interested in missionary activity, religious liberty advocates argued, should be wary of giving the state the power to dictate religion. How many non-Christian parts of the world would be still more securely closed off to hearing the gospel if we continued to reinforce the idea that the religion of the state is the religion of the people. We would doom many millions to continue as Hindus, Buddhists, pagans, and the like. Believers with confidence in their message should be against legal control of religion, not for it. Let the search for religious truth be a free one to maximize the chances that it will actually be found.

At the heart of the case for religious liberty is the principle that one's most valuable personal possessions are one's faith and conscience. To coerce people in those sacred preserves is a form of violence done to the soul. Roger Williams memorably compared coercion of the soul to rape. Along similar lines is the idea that God himself would be offended by such an offering and that forced religion would be the opposite of the sweet aroma of sincere prayer.

America was really the place where religious liberty made its earliest and greatest advances. The First and Second Great Awakenings resonated with the spirit of the regenerate rather than the comprehensive church. Over time it came to be the case that the United States developed a generally constructive combination of voluntary religion along with something like an informal establishment of Christianity in the broader culture. Chesterton once referred to the U.S. as "a nation with the soul of a church."

The colonies and then the states had their different approaches to church establishment. We could categorize them broadly into the two camps of the Virginia and Massachusetts approaches. Virginia developed a strong religious liberty framework with the guidance of James Madison and Thomas Jefferson, along with the influence of John Leland. Massachusetts, on the other hand, embodied the light establishment preferred by John Adams. The constitution of the new nation did not take a side but recused the federal government from establishing any faith and promised not to interfere with the free exercise (not only worship) of religion. In the various states, the Virginia approach would prevail within a few decades, and the federal government's policy toward itself was eventually construed to apply uniformly against all governments in the United States.

Although devout Christians often bristle at the phrase "the separation of church and state," the simple fact is that American churches have thrived far more than their European counterparts that performed their work throughout most of the last two centuries under some form of legal establishment. In particular, the free church upstarts such as Baptists and Methodists grew at astonishing rates through much of the nineteenth and twentieth centuries.

It should be noted, however, that the Catholic Church, despite its tendency to prefer establishment, also found the American church-state regime conducive to its flourishing, which is something the American Catholic scholar John Courtney Murray pointed out as he tried to encourage his church to embrace religious liberty more fully. In particular, he thought the official indifference of the American state toward religion was a far superior situation for the church relative to the hostile policies of other nations that purported to be secular but were in fact aggressively antireligious. Murray wrote of a papal nuncio shocked to find early in American history that the Congress denied any right to approve the founding of a new bishopric. The church had long struggled with secular authorities who wanted to control such matters. This lack of jurisdiction in America, Murray thought, was a very good thing for the church.

During the final four decades of the twentieth century, American religious liberty reached its apex. The Supreme Court, in a period of expanding its protection of constitutional rights, interpreted religious liberty so strongly as to require accommodation when hindered by even generally applicable statutes and regulations. The court in that period appropriately valued religious liberty and understood the great need to protect faith and conscience because of the tremendous damage done when they are violated.

It is important to note that requiring an accommodation for religious objectors is not lawless as some have suggested. Rather, the First Amendment is itself, as Steven D. Smith has written, law of a high order. Accommodating free exercise of religion is clearly lawful in the American system. The logic of constitutional rights is that they are values we prize so highly we seek to

protect them even over against shifting majority passions because we recognize that the majority is not, as Tocqueville wrote, always right or moral.

Requiring accommodation for religious liberty was a critical step because
of the extraordinary growth of government during the modern era. As the
scope and reach of laws and administrative regulations has vastly increased,
the potential for collisions with the free exercise of religion has likewise
expanded. As long as the Supreme Court upheld the logic of accommodation, citizens had a chance to protect their religious liberty against encroach-
ments by ambitious and omnicompetent governments.

Contemporary Application

The kinds of official establishments that would require citizens to be members of a state church, to pay tithes as taxes, to have pastors working as agents
of the government, to have doctrine be subject to various officials, these
things have largely faded into history. Unfortunately, those positive developments do not mean that religious liberty has been secured.

We live in an era where the vanguard of opinion often does not value a
quintessential American right such as freedom of speech, so it should not be
surprising that religious liberty is even less esteemed. Thanks to a confluence
of events, the fate of religious freedom is in some doubt.

First, in 1989 the Supreme Court revised its free exercise jurisprudence
by strengthening the deference due to generally applicable statutes and regulations even when free exercise rights are infringed upon. Second, the court
rebuffed Congress's nearly unanimous passage of the Religious Freedom
Restoration Act (RFRA)—which sought to restore the earlier high level of
protection—by limiting its reach to the federal government and not to the
state and local authorities. Third, a second attempt to achieve the objective
set out by RFRA resulted in a weak law (RLUIPA—The Religious Land
Use and Institutionalized Persons Act) amid a clash over the impact of the
law on discrimination against gays and lesbians.

We saw RFRA provide a path for Hobby Lobby and a variety of
Christian nonprofits to successfully seek free exercise accommodation from
the federal mandate that employers provide insurance coverage for abortifacient and contraceptive drugs, but the reaction to the court's decision was
hot. In addition, we have seen various wedding merchants (such as florists,

photographers, and bakers) attempt to gain relief from anti-discrimination laws that would force them to ply their trade in same-sex weddings even when they have a sincere religious objection to participating. That controversy, which could easily grow more heated as the gulf between Christian orthodoxy and the new view of human sexuality expands, is still largely undetermined at this writing.

What should the people of God do in response to the current situation? Many Christians have lived in times and places where they had no avenue for influencing law and government other than simply being martyred. We have the right to speak, to gather, to vote, and to share our views with friends and fellow citizens. We should do those things. And we should do them wisely and fearlessly. Some of the fallout from changes in our current culture will not affect many Christians. They will be tempted to stand by and simply be glad that new laws and attitudes don't affect them directly. The better answer is to exercise faithful stewardship over the blessings God has given and to demonstrate solidarity with brothers and sisters in Christ. Alexis de Tocqueville wrote of the sad plight of the person of conviction who is persecuted by majority opinion so sure of its own righteousness. Those who might come to that person's aid all too often remain aloof and allow the person under attack to simply wither into a sad civil nonexistence. We must have the courage and fellow feeling necessary to protect religious liberty for the sake of faith and conscience.

FOR ADDITIONAL STUDY

Baker, Hunter. *The End of Secularism*. Wheaton: Crossway Academic, 2009.

Murray, John Courtney. *We Hold These Truths: Catholic Reflections on the American Proposition*. New York: Sheed and Ward, 1960.

Locke, John. *Letter Concerning Toleration*, 1689.

Madison, James. *Memorial and Remonstrance against Religious Assessments*, 1785.

Smith, Steven D. *Pagans & Christians in the City: Culture Wars from the Tiber to the Potomac*. Grand Rapids: Eerdmans, 2018.

Walker, Andrew T. *Liberty for All*. Grand Rapids: Brazos, 2021.

Williams, Roger. *The Bloody Tenet, of Persecution for Cause of Conscience*, 1644.

Also see these articles: Humanity, Church and State, Sanctity of Human Life, Marriage and Sexuality

45

Church and State

JONATHAN LEEMAN

To summarize the relationship between church and state in a sentence, we could say that God has given the *power of the sword* to governments and the *power of the keys* to churches, and he intends for them to work separately but cooperatively toward the greater end of worship. Both fail often and miserably in their jobs. Yet we need to first understand the blueprint in order to better identify departures from it. Let's therefore unpack that summary sentence one phrase at a time.[1]

God

As the Creator of all things, God rules all things comprehensibly. God, as author, by definition, possesses author-*ity*.

The nations may rage against him now (Ps 2:1). Yet God's future judgment will overrule. Judgment tomorrow means rule today. He will judge every judge and president by his standards, not theirs. Therefore, the Psalmist declares, "Say among the nations, 'The LORD reigns!'" and "He judges the peoples fairly" (Ps 96:10). Elsewhere, the psalmist warns, "So now, kings, be wise; receive instruction, you judges of the earth" (Ps 2:10). The warning

---

[1] An earlier version of this chapter appeared at https://www.thegospelcoalition .org/essay/the-relationship-of-church-and-state/. Used with permission.

addresses not just the kings and rulers of the biblical world but the presidents and prime ministers, voters and opinion-makers of today.

God is not the king of two kingdoms, as some writers put it. Two kingdoms imply two kings. God is the one king of all the nations: "Who should not fear you, King of the nations?" (Jer 10:6–7).

The story of the Bible is the story of God making his rule, which has been hidden since expelling Adam and Eve from Eden, visible at different times in different ways. He made his rule visible through mighty acts of salvation or judgment and through covenantal signs such as circumcision and Sabbath keeping and baptism. Most clearly, his rule became visible in the person and work of his Son, who possesses all authority in heaven and earth (Matt 28:18–20). The coming of Jesus's kingdom does not mean God now rules in places where he did not rule before. It means that God's rule becomes visible and acknowledged in places where it was not before.

All the earth divides between those places where Christ's rule is accepted and places where it is resisted (see Ps 2:1–3). There are no "neutral" spaces— not in the public square, not elsewhere, as popular as the idea of religious "neutrality" may be in the democratic West. The public square, in fact, is nothing more than a battleground of gods, which everyone enters on behalf of their God or gods, whether the god's name is Jesus or Allah, sex or the stock market.

Therefore, the psalmist, again addressing the nations and their kings, warns, "Pay homage to the Son or he will be angry and you will perish in your rebellion" (Ps 2:12).

Has Given the Power of the Sword to Government

If Jesus is king over all the earth, does that mean Christians should use the power of government to bring all things into subjection to him? Should they criminalize all sin and force people to worship him with the power of the government, like Charlemagne did in the ninth century?

No. Jesus rules over every square inch, as has been said, but he does not rule over every inch in the same way. He grants different authorities to different parties. To parents he gives the power of the rod. To governments he gives the power of the sword. To churches he gives the power of the keys. Yet to none of the parties does God give the authority to coerce true worship or criminalize false worship. Nor does he give governments the authority to criminalize all sin.

Paul called the government's power the power of the sword (Rom 13:4). Yet the original authorization for coercive action occurred right after the flood. God had just repeated the charge he had given to Adam: "Be fruitful and multiply and fill the earth" (Gen 9:1, 7). Yet now in this post-fall world, to keep the Cains from killing the Abels, God included this proviso:

> And for your lifeblood I will require a reckoning: from every beast
> I will require it and from man. From his fellow man I will require a
> reckoning for the life of man.
> "Whoever sheds the blood of man,
> by man shall his blood be shed,
> for God made man in his own image." (vv. 5–6)

God did not establish a particular form of government in these verses, whether monarchy, aristocracy, or democracy. Rather, he handed human beings the basic ingredient necessary for gathering together and forming governments in this fallen world: the ability to use morally legitimate coercive force for his purposes in justice.

Several further things are worth noticing in Romans 13. First, the government's authority comes from God. The U. S. Declaration of Independence might say that governments "derive their just powers from the consent of the governed," as if to say any powers *not* derived from the people's consent is unjust. Government's just powers derive from God, whether or not people consent to it. Paul would later say, "So then, the one who resists the authority is opposing God's command, and those who oppose it will bring judgment on themselves" (Rom 13:2). Paul does not mean God approves of everything any given government does, nor that we should obey governments no matter what. He does mean their authority comes from him, and that we should obey them, at least when they act within the jurisdiction he gave.

Second, God does not authorize governments to do whatever they wish. He does not authorize them to redefine marriage or the family, to tell churches what they must believe or who their members are, or to use force unjustly or indiscriminately, lest the force of these verses boomerang back and indict the government itself. No government is "above" the demands of these verses. Finally, he does not authorize governments to prosecute crimes against

him (such as blasphemy or false worship) or to criminalize every sin imagin-
able (such as adultery, homosexuality, lust, or gluttony). Indeed, it would seem
governments must tolerate false religions, so long as they cause no direct
harm to human beings: "whoever sheds the blood of *man*," not "of God."

Third, God authorizes governments to protect the life of God-imagers.
He grants them the ability to establish a basic form of justice. The word
"justice" can be defined biblically as *rendering judgment according to what's
right*. The specific rights and wrongs to be adjudicated by the government
fall under the banner of what can be called "Noahic justice." Noahic justice
is not a maximalist, perfectionist form of justice of the kind God required
of old covenant Israel or the new covenant church: "Be perfect, therefore, as
your heavenly Father is perfect" (Matt 5:48). It is not every conceivable right
and wrong the government must adjudicate. Rather, it's a narrowly defined
preservative or protectionist form of justice. God intends *all* governments
in *all* nations to establish this more limited form of life-preserving justice
on their citizens, whether they acknowledge God or not. "By justice a king
builds stability to a land" (Prov 29:4). Such justice ensures peace and order
(1 Tim 2:2).

Everything a government does—every law it makes, every courtroom
ruling it declares, every executive agency code it enforces—it should do for the
purpose of protecting and affirming its citizens as God-imagers. Anything
that harms, hurts, oppresses, exploits, hinders, tramples upon, degrades, or
threatens human beings as God-imagers arguably becomes a target of the
government's opposition. And, by implication, anything that aids, abets, promotes, or encourages a set of conditions that contributes to the ability of
God-imagers to live out their vocation of imaging God should be considered
as a candidate for possible governmental encouragement. Punish the bad,
reward the good, as Paul put it in Romans 13.

Christians will disagree over how far the demands of justice warrant
such activity. Does protecting and affirming the *imago Dei* warrant universal health care, or a progressive tax structure, or a ceiling on carbon dioxide
emissions, or national math standards for eighth graders? The answers often
belong to the category of Christian freedom and prudence. The point here is
we have a basic standard by which to assess our answers and arguments: what
protects and establishes the platform on which God-imagers can fulfill their
divine calling as divine imagers?

Martin Luther King Jr. captured the basic idea in his *Letter from Birmingham Jail* when he said, "Any law that uplifts human personality is just. Any law that degrades human personality is unjust."[2]

And the "Power of the Keys" to Churches

If God has given the power of the sword to the state, he has given the power of the keys to churches.

The Bible first talks about the keys in Matthew 16. Jesus first gave the keys to Peter, and by extension all the apostles, immediately after Peter confesses Jesus as the Christ, the Messiah. Jesus promises to build his church and then says, "I will give you the keys of the kingdom of heaven, and whatever you bind on earth will have been bound in heaven, and whatever you loose on earth will have been loosed in heaven" (Matt 16:19).

Two chapters later, Jesus gives the keys to local churches. Addressing the scenario of a Christian wandering into sin, Jesus encourages the disciples to address a person privately, but eventually before the whole church. If the sinning member refuses to listen to the church, then they should collectively remove him or her from the church. In case someone wonders by what authority a church might remove one of its members, Jesus repeats the line about the keys: "Truly, I tell you, whatever you bind on earth will have been bound in heaven, and whatever you loose on earth will have been loosed in heaven" (Matt 18:18). While the "you" in chapter 16 is singular, here it is plural, as in "Whatever y'all bind on earth. . . ."

What does it mean for a church to exercise the keys by binding and loosing on earth what is bound and loosed in heaven? The short answer is that churches exercise the keys by rendering judgments on the *what* and the *who* of the gospel, confessions, and confessors. Practically, they do this in preaching and in administrating the ordinances. Through preaching, a church says, "This is a right gospel confession." Through the ordinances, it declares, "This is a true gospel confessor." To put it programmatically, the keys allow churches to write statements of faith and receive and remove members.

The work of wielding the keys is a judicial activity like the work of a judge in a courtroom. A judge does not make the law. He or she interprets it.

---

[2] Martin Luther King Jr., "Letter from Birmingham Jail" (April 16, 1963).

Then, based on that interpretation, a judge does not make a person actually innocent or guilty, but when he or she declares "guilty" or "not guilty," the whole legal system swings in action and treats the person as such. A judge's judgments bind. They are publicly effectual.

Similarly, by virtue of the keys of the kingdom, churches don't "make" the gospel, nor do they "make" people Christians. But they possess an authority the individual Christian does not possess: the ability to represent the kingdom of Christ in formally recognizing people as members of the church or in removing them. They formally represent Christ.

And He Intends for Them to Work Separately

Placing the institutions of church and state side by side, what can we say about their relationship? To begin with, the two institutions should remain *separate* in the sense that neither should wield the authority God has given to the other. Pastors should not wield the sword. Presidents should not wield the keys. And generally, those separate authorities come with separate jurisdictions or fields of activity. Churches generally should not delve into the intricacies of trade policy, while Congress should not offer counsel on which Bible translations are best or who to receive as members.

For instance, Emperor Constantine should not have involved himself in the Council of Nicaea's deliberations on the doctrine of the Trinity, at least not in his capacity as emperor. Likewise, the government has no business telling nongovernmental organizations, especially churches, that they must be willing to hire gays or lesbians, as a recent candidate for U.S. president argued.

On the flip side, John Calvin, in his capacity as a pastor, should not have participated in the execution of Michael Servetus for heresy. Likewise, Christian Scientists should not be allowed to deny medical care to their children on behalf of "religious freedom." Barring governments from protecting the lives of their citizens is to usurp the sword. In general, evangelical preachers should be slow to address issues of public policy unless those issues are explicit in Scripture or clear "by good and necessary consequence" (Westminster Confession).

In short, nowhere does the New Testament envision the wedding of church and state that characterized the Western world from the fourth century to the American Revolution in what's called "Christendom" or the "Constantinian settlement." Under this settlement, the emperor and pope or the king and archbishop together ruled a so-called "Christian" empire or nation, a label made possible by infant baptism and the fact that every child born into national citizenship could simultaneously be baptized into church membership.

That said, the jurisdictions of church and state do overlap. When Emperor Theodosius massacred seven thousand Thessalonians in response to the assassination of a military officer, the bishop Ambrose may well have been entirely within his rights to excommunicate "church member" Theodosius for the excessive and unjust manner in which "Emperor" Theodosius was doing his job of wielding the sword. Likewise, some Roman Catholic bishops refused to give the Lord's Supper to senators Edward Kennedy and Joe Biden for their active support of abortion. By the same token, a government would be entirely within its right to prosecute a pastor or church who is breaking the law and harming people, as with a church that refused to pay payroll taxes for staff or that failed to report child abuse.

The challenge today is most people, including most Christians, misconstrue the separation of church and state. They treat it as being about the origin of ideas, as if to say, when an idea originates in someone's religion, we should not bring it into the public square and impose it on others. Yet the separation of church and state applies not to individual Christians, as such, but to churches in their authority-exercising capacity. Furthermore, every claim of justice originates in someone's religion, someone's worship, including the worship of atheists and idolaters. Ironically, it's Bible readers who limit themselves with limits on the imposition of their religion through the mechanisms of the state. Christians should impose what God says about murder or theft because that falls within government's jurisdiction as defined above. Yet they will not impose what it says about the worship of Christ or belief in his resurrection because that does not fall within the government's jurisdiction. The gods of secularism and paganism, however, have no self-imposed limits as when they require idolatry, such as the worship of the goddess of sex, through the courts, public schools, and marketplace. No one ever seems to talk about the separation of idolatry and the state.

In short, a biblically conceived separation of church and state is not about where an individual's convictions come from. It is about jurisdictional authority. God has given one kind of authority to governments (the sword) and another kind to churches (the keys), and neither should usurp the other.

But Cooperatively

While the Bible formally separates the powers of church and state, it also envisions, at least in the ideal, an underlying foundation of cooperation. God calls both institutions to enact his righteousness, each for its part. Governments should do so within the narrow lane of protection. Churches should do so with a broader lane of perfection.

The apostle John offers a glimpse of what the day of judgment will look like for all institutional authorities who adopted their own standards of righteousness and not God's:

> Then the kings of the earth, the nobles, the generals, the rich, the powerful, and every slave and free person hid in the caves and among the rocks of the mountains. And they said to the mountains and to the rocks, "Fall on us and hide us from the face of the one seated on the throne and from the wrath of the Lamb, because the great day of their wrath has come! And who is able to stand?" (Rev 6:15–17)

God will hold every ruler and leader, and everyone in every place of the political hierarchy, from slave to free, accountable to the standards of his righteousness.

Too often, however, Christians interpret Jesus's words about rendering to Caesar what is Caesar and to God what is God's (Mark 12:17) as if Caesar was somehow outside of God's jurisdiction. They envision two separate circles—one for Caesar's things and one for God's things.

Caesar's Things:
Politics,
Government, Etc.

God's Things:
Worship, Faith,
Church, Etc.

Yet the context of these verses is worth noticing. Jesus asked whose image was on the coin. The people replied, "Caesar's." Yet every member of Jesus's largely Jewish audience would have known that Caesar himself was created in God's image. Really, what Jesus offered was a big circle with a smaller circle inside of it:

This is why Jesus would later tell Pilate he would have no authority if God had not given it (John 19:11). God intended Caesar—and every government in the history of the world—to do his job in obedience, not rebellion. And there is no third way. Ideally, church and state will cooperate, not continually work against one another.

A right understanding of the God-intended cooperation between churches and the government requires a slightly sharper definition of their God-intended jurisdictions. Past thinkers, like Martin Luther, or John Locke following him, divided the inner and outer person and then assigned the inner person to the church and the outer person to the government—calling them two kingdoms. Better than dividing up the work of church and government between two kingdoms, I believe, is dividing them between two ages. The institutions of government and family belong to the present age of creation. They serve everyone who has been born. The church and its officers belong to the age of new creation, which began at Pentecost and embraces all who have been born again. The institutions of the present age must rely on coercive authority, whether rod or sword. The institutions of the age to come rely on the indwelling work of the Spirit, the Word of God, and the declaration-pronouncing keys.

What is important to recognize is that the age of creation and new creation presently overlap. They operate simultaneously. The whole person (inner and outer) lives within the legitimate but fallen institutional structures of creation (family, state). And the whole born again person (inner and outer) lives by the power of the Spirit within the institutional structures of the new creation (church, ordained elders). Governments serve to protect this present age of creation, while churches serve to present and proclaim the age of new creation. And God *intends* for the institutions of both ages to serve one another, at least until he returns, concludes this present age, and ushers in the fullness of the age to come. At that time the institutions of this present age will pass away or at least be transformed beyond imagination (see Matt 17:24–27; 22:30). For now, however, the state exists to provide a platform for the church's work of redemption, while the righteousness and justice of the church serves as a prophetic witness for the state. When both church and state behave in justice and righteousness, they can affirm and reinforce one another. They can cooperate.

Toward the Greater End of Worship

Ultimately, both governments and churches serve God's purpose of calling all people to worship him, the former indirectly, the latter directly. The government's work is a prerequisite to the mission of the church and salvation, just as learning to read is a prerequisite to reading the Bible. Common-grace platforms are meant to serve special-grace purposes.

Indeed, this is what we see in Scripture. First, God grants a charter for governments. Then he calls Abraham out of Ur. Genesis 9 precedes Genesis 12 for a reason. Just like God promises to lay down his bow of war and not destroy the earth by a flood, so he means for governments to provide the peace and safety necessary for the storyline of redemption to get under way.

Paul reaffirms this point when he tells us that God established the boundaries of the nations so "that they might seek God, and perhaps they might reach out and find him" (Acts 17:27). Similarly, he tells us to pray for kings and authorities so that we may live peaceful lives pleasing to God, "who wants everyone to be saved and to come to the knowledge of the truth" (1 Tim 2:4).

Governments finally exist, then, to serve the purposes of worship. People need to be able to walk to church without getting mauled by marauders.

They cannot get saved if they are dead. The work of government provides the platform. Protecting religious freedom doesn't just serve Christians; it serves everyone.

Looking at the actual biblical record of governments gives Christians reasons to be both discouraged and encouraged. Some governments in the Bible sheltered God's people: Abimelech, Pharoah in the time of Joseph, the late Nebuchadnezzar, Cyrus, and the Roman proconsul Festus. Yet many governments sought to devour God's people: Pharaoh in the time of Moses, Sennacherib, Pilate, and the Beast of Revelation. Romans 13 calls governments servants; Psalm 2 calls them imposters. Most governments contain both. But some are better than others.

Therefore, Christians should not put too much hope in government, but they should not give up on it either. Churches need good governments. They enable churches to do their work in peace. A culture and its political institutions might turn against Christianity, but Christians should strive to make an impact for as long as they have opportunity. It may get worse. Just ask Christians in North Korea, China, or Iran.

Who Should We Vote For?

Perhaps we can summarize this entire essay by answering the question: So who should Christians vote for in the next election?

Christians should vote for the candidate, the party, the legislation, or the ballot measures with a limited but clear view of what the government has been authorized and ordered by God to do: to exercise judgment and establish justice; to build platforms of peace, order, and flourishing; and to make sure people are free and not hindered from knowing God and being redeemed.

We do not want a government that thinks it can offer redemption but a government that views its work as a prerequisite for redemption for all of its citizens. It builds the streets so that you can drive to church, protects the womb so that you can live and hear the gospel, insists on fair-lending and housing practices so that you can own a home and offer hospitality to non-Christians, works for education so that you can read and teach your children the Bible, treats all people and races equally so that Christians can join the same churches and present a picture of heaven's diversity, protects marriage and the family so that husbands and wives can model Christ's love for the church, and polices the streets so that you are free to assemble as churches unmolested and to make an honest living so that you can give money to the work of God. In sum, government renders judgment to establish peace, order, and prosperity *so that* the church might do what God calls it to do— make disciples.

For Additional Study

Dockery, David S., and John Stonestreet, eds. *Life, Marriage, and Religious Liberty: What Belongs to God, What Belongs to Caesar.* Nashville: Fidelis, 2019.

Finn, Nathan A. "Church and State." *Southwestern Journal of Theology* 64, no. 2 (Spring 2022).

Joireman, Sandra F. *Church, State, and Citizens: Christian Approaches to Political Engagement.* Oxford: Oxford University Press, 2009.

Kereney, P. C. *Church, State, and Public Justice: Five Views.* Downers Grove: IVP, 2007.

Wilken, Robert Louis. *Liberty in the Things of God.* New Haven, CT: Yale University Press, 2019.

Wilson, John F., and Donald Drakeman. *Church and State in American History.* London: Routledge, 2019.

Also see these articles: Creation, Providence, Humanity, Religious Liberty

46

The Sanctity of Human Life

C. BEN MITCHELL

Introduction

No moral issue has done more to galvanize Christians in the late twentieth and early twenty-first centuries than the sanctity of human life. Contemporary debates about abortion, euthanasia, and other biomedical and life issues often invoke the terms "the right to life" and "the sanctity of human life." Although neither of these expressions is found in the Bible, the biblical witness testifies throughout to the uniqueness of human life. Specifically, the Bible maintains that only human beings are made in the image of God (the *imago Dei*).

Carl F. H. Henry, one of the leading theologians of the evangelical movement in the twentieth century, believed that "[t]he importance of a proper understanding of the *imago Dei* can hardly be overstated. The answer given to the imago-inquiry soon becomes determinative for the entire gamut of doctrinal affirmation. The ramifications are not only theological, but [for] every phase of the . . . cultural enterprise as a whole."[1] Every human life is made sacred by God. (This is what is meant by "the sanctity of human life." It is probably not coincidental that Henry's comment was published in 1973, the same year as the United States Supreme Court's decision in *Roe v. Wade*

---

[1] Carl F. H. Henry, "Man" in *Baker's Dictionary of Theology*, ed. Geoffrey W. Bromiley and Carl F. H. Henry (Grand Rapids: Baker, 1973), 339.

(1973), which changed the abortion debate in America. Together with *Doe v. Bolton* (1973), the decisions made it unlawful for government to interfere in an abortion decision where the "health" (broadly defined) of the mother was at risk.

The Doctrine

Two primary biblical texts are generally appealed to as clearest descriptions of the sanctity of human life: Genesis 1 and Genesis 9. Genesis 1 declares that the apex of God's creative activity was the creation of Adam, a "living soul" (Gen 1:24) in God's own "image" and "likeness" (Gen 1:27). While other animals are soulish as well, only humankind is made in God's image. The image of God, then, is the source of the sanctity of life or human exceptionalism, the notion that human beings occupy a unique place in the created order.

The early verses of Genesis 9 include a prohibition against murdering humans (i.e., homicide) found in the Noahic covenant. After the devastating flood, God renewed the creation covenant he had made with Adam and Eve, this time with Noah and his children (Gen 9:1–6). Several features of this covenant renewal are notable. First, the covenant is identical to the creation covenant with respect to the positive commands to be fruitful, procreate, and be good stewards over the earth and its resources. Second, permission to kill animals for food and presumably other uses is added. Third, the covenant prohibits the unjust killing of another human being. Finally, animal life is thereby tacitly distinguished from human life by the prohibition of homicide. The rationale given for this prohibition is that humankind is made in God's own image. "Whoever sheds human blood, by humans his blood will be shed, for God made humans in his image" (Gen 9:6). The conclusion follows that since only members of the species *Homo sapiens* are imagers of God, human life deserves greater, or a different kind of, respect than animal life does.

Interpreters have varied widely in their opinions about what exactly constitutes the *imago Dei*. Numerous options have been offered: (1) humankind's erect bodily form, (2) human dominion over nature, (3) human reason, (4) human pre-fallen righteousness, (5) human capacities, (6) the juxtaposition between man and woman, (7) responsible creaturehood and moral conformity to God, and (8) various composite views. One thing seems clear from the history of interpretation of these texts; namely, that the *imago Dei* is the most salient characteristic of human beings. What it means to be human is to image God, and what it means to image God is to be human, just as Jesus Christ is both human and the image of God.

Another important text that evokes the notion of the sanctity of human life is Psalm 139. Verses 13–16 provide a glimpse of what God knows about every individual. Here God is portrayed as a knitter who carefully, meticulously, and lovingly creates a human being in the nurturing environment of his or her mother's womb. Job echoes the knitting motif when he says, "You clothed me with skin and flesh, and wove me together with bones and tendons" (Job 10:11).

According to the psalmist, God formed the "inward parts" of his being (Ps 139:13, literally "kidneys," usually a reference to the emotional self). Likewise, his body, his "frame" (Ps 139:15 ESV), was not hidden from God when he was being fashioned. Thus, God creates the whole person—both physical and emotional—and he or she is "fearfully and wonderfully" made. The psalmist uses extraordinarily vivid language to describe God's intricate handiwork in human creation. The words "intricately woven" (Ps 139:15 ESV) can be translated "colorfully embroidered." Embroidery or tapestry provides a vivid picture of the detailed craftmanship God exercises in creating human beings. "Depths of the earth" is likely a reference to human origins. Adam was made originally "of the dust from the ground" (Gen 2:7), and to dust all humans shall return. This form of parallelism is found especially in Job: "Naked I came from my mother's womb, and naked I will leave this life" (Job 1:21). God even saw the psalmist's "unformed substance" or "unshapen mass" in the womb. In other words, from the earliest stages of development God knows every one of his unborn human creations intimately and personally.

Both the Jewish and Christian communities in antiquity affirmed human dignity and opposed abortion and infanticide. As Michael J. Gorman has shown, despite the lack of a specific prohibition against abortion in the Hebrew Bible, the Jewish witness against the practice is fairly consistent. "Though rare cases of abortion may have occurred in Judaism," observes Gorman, "the witness of antiquity is that Jews, unlike pagans, did not practice deliberate abortion."[2] For instance, the first-century historian and apologist

---

[2] Michael Gorman, *Abortion and the Early Church* (Downers Grove: IVP, 1982), 34.

for Judaism, Josephus, wrote in *Against Apion* that "the law orders all the offspring to be brought up, and forbids women either to cause abortion or to make away with the fetus; a woman convicted of this is regarded as an infanticide, because she destroys a soul and diminishes the race."[3]

In his *Plea for Christians* (AD 177) the apologist Athenagoras offers an illustration of Christian respect for human life against the charge that Christians practiced murder because they "ate the flesh and drank the blood of Christ" in the Eucharist: "What reason would we have to commit murder when we say that women who induce abortions are murderers, and will have to give account of it to God?"[4] Similarly, Tertullian provided a defense against the charge that Christians sacrificed their children in his *Apology to Emperor Septimus Severus* (AD 197): "In our case, murder being once for all forbidden, we may not destroy even the fetus in the womb, while as yet the human being derives blood from other parts of the body for its sustenance. To hinder a birth is merely a speedier man-killing."[5] Tertullian clearly used the repudiation of abortion as a symbol of the virtue of the Christian community.

The Didache (AD 50–70), or *The Teaching of the Twelve Apostles*, was an early church handbook and among other uses was a guide for new converts to Christianity. In the second section of the document, *The Didache* states straightforwardly, "Do not kill a fetus by abortion, or commit infanticide." Other examples from the early Christian movement could be multiplied. Suffice it to say that beyond merely a consensus opposing abortion and infanticide, early Christians were instrumental in building orphanages and hospitals as a way of celebrating and protecting the sanctity of every human life.[6]

The Implications

Most Catholic, orthodox, and evangelical Protestants affirm the biblical teaching about the sanctity of human life and follow the example of the

---

[3] Josephus, *Against Apion* 2.202.

[4] Athenagoras, *A Plea for the Christians* 35; see Gorman, *Abortion and the Early Church*, 54.

[5] Gorman, *Abortion and the Early Church*, 55.

[6] See Gary B. Ferguson, *Medicine and Health Care in Early Christianity* (Baltimore: Johns Hopkins University Press, 2009).

early Christians. According to historian David Bebbington, evangelicalism is characterized by four elements: Biblicism, crucicentrism, conversionism, and activism. That is another way of saying that evangelicals tend to believe in (1) the authority of the Scriptures of the Old and New Testaments, (2) the reality and importance of the atonement of Jesus Christ on a cross, (3) the necessity of regeneration through saving faith, and (4) the requirement to live out in one's private and public life the entailments of this gospel of the risen Lord. Evangelicals, therefore, often engage contemporary social and ethical issues such as abortion.

Abortion

According to a recent survey conducted by the Pew Research Center, about six in ten U.S. adults believe abortion should be legal in all or most cases. On the other side of the issue, while the same poll found that only 28 percent of U.S. Catholics favored overturning *Roe vs. Wade*, 61 percent of white evangelicals and 28 percent of black Protestants believe *Roe v. Wade* should be overturned.[7]

In 2010, the National Association of Evangelicals (NAE), an organization representing forty denominations and thousands of churches, passed a resolution on abortion affirming that "all humans, male and female, are made in the image of God (Gen 1:27) and, therefore, have intrinsic dignity that should be respected and honored. Indeed, the breath of life in all human beings is a gift from God (Gen 2:7) and thus inherently holy. The National Association of Evangelicals (NAE) has pledged to protect the sanctity of human life and to safeguard its nature. In light of our respect for the precious gift of life, the NAE continues to speak on the sensitive subject of abortion."

Southern Baptists, the largest non-Catholic religious denomination in the U.S., has done an about-face on abortion since the 1970s. In 1970, a poll conducted by the Baptist Sunday School Board found that 70 percent of Southern Baptist pastors supported abortion to protect the mental or physical health of the mother, 64 percent supported abortion in cases of fetal deformity, and 71 percent in cases of rape. By 1982, the minds of Southern Baptists had

---

[7] Pew Research Center, May 2022, "America's Abortion Quandary," 7–11, https://www.pewresearch.org/religion/2022/05/06/americas-abortion-quandary/.

changed. In the resolution *On Abortion and Infanticide*, passed at the annual meeting of the Southern Baptist Convention, the messengers affirmed that (1) "Both medical science and biblical references indicate that human life begins at conception"; (2) "Southern Baptists have traditionally upheld the sanctity and worth of all human life, both born and preborn, as being created in the image of God"; (3) "Current judicial opinion gives no guarantee of protection of preborn persons, thus permitting the widespread practice of abortion on demand, which has led to the killing of an estimated four thousand developing human beings daily in the United States"; and (4) "Social acceptance of abortion has begun to dull society's respect for all human life, leading to growing occurrences of infanticide, child abuse, and active euthanasia."

Since that time, Southern Baptists have passed a number of resolutions opposing abortion on demand, including partial birth abortions. In 2015 messengers passed what might be characterized as an omnibus resolution on the sanctity of human life. It is quoted below in its entirety:

On the Sanctity of Human Life 2015[8]

Biblical revelation clearly and consistently affirms that human life is formed by God in His image and is therefore worthy of honor and dignity (Gen 1:27; 9:6); and

WHEREAS, God alone is the Author of life and He alone numbers our days, from the moment of conception until natural death (Job 14:5–7; Ps 39:4); and

WHEREAS, The Bible commands us to honor our parents and the aged (Exod 20:12; Lev 19:32; Eph 6:2); and

WHEREAS, The Baptist Faith & Message (2000) affirms that "children, from the moment of conception, are a blessing and heritage from the Lord" and calls us to "speak on behalf of the unborn and contend for the sanctity of all human life from conception to natural death"; and

---

[8] SBC Resolutions, "On The Sanctity Of Human Life," June 1, 2015, https://www.sbc.net/resource-library/resolutions/on-the-sanctity-of-human-life/.

WHEREAS, An estimated fifty-seven million unborn babies have been aborted since the legalization of abortion in 1973 (Roe v. Wade); and

WHEREAS, Legislation or court rulings have effectively legalized physician-assisted suicide in several states and additional states are considering similar action; and

WHEREAS, Recent federal directives seek to compel religious organizations to provide coverage for abortifacient technologies and services; now, therefore, be it

RESOLVED, That the messengers to the Southern Baptist Convention meeting in Columbus, Ohio, June 16–17, 2015, affirm the dignity and sanctity of human life at all stages of development, from conception to natural death; and be it further

RESOLVED, That we reaffirm our repudiation of the genocide of legalized abortion in the United States and call on civil authorities to enact laws that defend the lives of the unborn; and be it further

RESOLVED, That we welcome and commend legislation that ensures that all mothers will be fully informed by medical providers of the life development of their unborn children; and be it further

RESOLVED, That we call on our fellow citizens of good will to collaborate with us on behalf of justice, the protection of protection of human life, and the cause of human flourishing; and be it further

RESOLVED, That we encourage Southern Baptists to continue and to expand their local ministries that care for and protect the unborn, the vulnerable, and the aged; and be it further

RESOLVED, That we call on Southern Baptist churches and entities to show the love of Christ through appropriate means to those women most vulnerable to the victimization of the abortion industry, and to show grace and mercy to those individuals who grieve with repentance over past abortions; and be it further

RESOLVED, That we call on our churches and all believers to care for the elderly among us, to show them honor and dignity, and to prayerfully support and counsel those who are providing end-of-life care for the aged, the terminally ill, and the chronically infirmed; and be it further

RESOLVED, That we commend the efforts of our denominational entities, especially The Ethics & Religious Liberty Commission, in the defense and protection of human life at every stage; and be it finally

RESOLVED, That we pray and work for the repeal of unjust laws and inhumane practices that degrade human life, all the while looking toward the day when our Lord will make all things new and "Death will be no more; grief, crying, and pain will be no more, because the previous things have passed away" (Rev 21:4).

Human Embryo Research

During the early days of the abortion debate in America, the controversy focused on the question "When does human life begin?" Today, anyone who is honest with the scientific evidence believes that human life begins at conception. When living human sperm unite with a living human ovum, a living human embryo is generated. At least one human life begins at conception (twinning could occur, resulting in two or more individuals). They are not potential human beings; they are human beings with potential. Therefore, the question now is, "What do we owe these nascent human beings?" Are we morally obligated to protect them, or may we use them for embryo-destructive research?

In 1999 Southern Baptists meeting in Atlanta at their annual meeting passed a resolution *On Human Embryonic and Stem Cell Research.*[9] This resolution followed a recommendation from The National Bioethics Advisory Commission appointed under President Bill Clinton that Congress remove its ban on tax-funded human embryo research. The resolution acknowledges

---

[9] SBC Resolutions, "On Human Embryonic and Stem Cell Research" (1999 Annual Meeting), https://www.sbc.net/resource-library/resolutions/resolution-on -human-embryonic-and-stem-cell-research/.

that (1) "The Bible teaches that human beings are made in the image and likeness of God (Gen 1:27; 9:6) and protectable human life begins at fertilization," (2) "Efforts to rescind the ban on public funding of human embryo research rely on a crass utilitarian ethic which would sacrifice the lives of the few for the benefits of the many," and (3) "Current law against federal funding of research in which human embryos are harmed and/or destroyed reflects well-established national and international legal and ethical norms against misusing any human being for research purposes" because "Some forms of human stem cell research require the destruction of human embryos in order to obtain the cells for such research and Southern Baptists are on record for their decades-long opposition to abortion except to save the physical life of the mother and their opposition to destructive human embryo research."

Southern Baptist views on embryo-destructive research had not changed by 2005, when messengers meeting in Nashville approved the resolution *On Stem Cell Research*.[10] The resolution is predicated on the view that "the Bible teaches that all human life is sacred (Gen 1:26–27)" and was prompted by a vote by the U.S. House of Representatives to fund research using embryos left over from fertility treatments using in vitro fertilization. The resolution strongly supports "stem cell research that does not require the destruction of human embryos or put them at risk in obtaining human stem cells" and decries "embryo-destructive research, since it kills human beings in their earliest stages of development."

By extension, the SBC resolutions include opposition to so-called abortion pills in *On RU-486, the French Abortion Pill* (1994) and to efforts to require churches and other entities to provide insurance coverage that includes contraception distribution and abortion-causing drugs in *On Protecting Religious Liberty*.

End-of-Life Issues

The sanctity of human life has clear implications at the other end of life. With a host of countries with legalized euthanasia and a growing number of states in the U.S. with legalized physician-assisted suicide, there are good

---

[10] SBC Resolutions, "On Stem Cell Research" (2005 Annual Meeting), https://www.sbc.net/resource-library/resolutions/on-stem-cell-research/.

reasons for Christians not only to resist the euthanasia juggernaut but to redouble efforts to support palliative care and hospice.

Southern Baptists recognized this dual responsibility in the resolution *On Human Organ Donations* (1988).[11] The messengers at the annual convention encouraged physicians and nurses "to request organ donation in appropriate circumstances," acknowledging that the decision to donate one's organs is a personal matter to be considered voluntarily "in the spirit of stewardship, compassion for the needs of others, and alleviating suffering." At the same time, messengers cautioned against seeing support for organ donation as support for ending human life. "[N]othing in the resolution [is to] be construed to condone euthanasia, infanticide, abortion, or harvesting of fetal tissue for the procurement of organs."

Even more directly, in 1992 Southern Baptists passed a resolution *On Euthanasia and Assisted Suicide*[12] that begins with the affirmation that "the Bible teaches that God created all human life in his own image and declares human life to be sacred from conception until death" and that "Southern Baptists have historically affirmed biblical teaching regarding the sanctity of human life." Messengers understood that the implications of the sanctity of human life include awareness "of the fact that the end of life may be painful," and therefore the resolution urges "scientists and physicians to continue their research into more effective pain management" and encourages "hospitals, nursing care facilities, and hospices to increase their efforts to keep dying persons as comfortable as possible and call on Christians to help provide companionship and appropriate physical and spiritual ministry to persons who are dying." The resolution continues by opposing "efforts to designate food and water as 'extraordinary treatment,'" asserting that "nutrition and hydration continue to be viewed as compassionate and ordinary medical care and humane treatment" and rejecting "as appropriate any action which, of itself or by intention, causes a person's death." Finally, the messengers voted to "call upon federal, state, and local governments to prosecute under

---

[11] SBC Resolutions, "On Human Organ Donations" (1988 Annual Meeting), https://www.sbc.net/resource-library/resolutions/resolution-on-human-organ-donations/.

[12] SBC Resolutions, "On Euthanasia and Assisted Suicide" (1992 Annual Meeting), https://www.sbc.net/resource-library/resolutions/resolution-on-euthanasia-and-assisted-suicide/.

the law physicians or others who practice euthanasia or assist patients to commit suicide."

In 2001, Southern Baptists extended their concern about euthanasia in a resolution *On Euthanasia in The Netherlands*.[13] Grounded in the doctrine of the sacredness of human life from conception through natural death, the resolution expresses "moral, spiritual, and social concern for all of the nations of the globe." Resisting quality of life judgments, the messengers stated their "belief that every human life, including the life of the terminally ill, disabled, or clinically depressed patient, is sacred and ought to be protected against unnecessary harm."

The Future

There are few reasons to think that debates about abortion, embryo-destructive research, euthanasia, and assisted suicide are going away any time soon. Christians need to be vigilant in their defense of the sanctity of human life from conception to natural death. This must include careful attention to emerging biotechnologies and changes in health care policy.

For instance, in 2020, Jennifer Doudna was awarded the Nobel Prize for Chemistry for her pioneering work in the gene editing technology, CRISPR, an acronym for clustered regularly interspaced short palindromic repeats.[14] Although human gene editing technology may have very beneficial applications, Christians will have to address the means proposed to get to the ends of good medicine. Namely, some research in gene editing will require the use and destruction of human embryos. Belief in the sanctity of human life will require faithful Christians to continue to resist embryo-destructive research.

Furthermore, Christians must also think carefully about who decides what are *good* genes and what are *bad* genes. Gene editing should not discriminate, for example, against people with disabilities. In 2017, news stories appeared across the world reporting that Iceland has nearly eliminated Down syndrome from its population. In fact, Iceland has reduced the

---

[13] SBC Resolutions, "On Euthanasia in The Netherlands" (2001 Annual Meeting), https://www.sbc.net/resource-library/resolutions/on-euthanasia-in-the-netherlands/.

[14] See Jennifer A. Doudna and Samuel H. Sternberg, *Crack in Creation: Gene Editing and the Unthinkable Power to Control Evolution* (New York: Houghton Mifflin, 2017).

number of children born with Down syndrome by using prenatal genetic tests and aborting unborn children diagnosed with the syndrome. Icelandic law permits abortion of fetuses with deformities after sixteen weeks, including abortion of children with Down syndrome.

Bible-believing Christians around the world are committed to the celebration and protection of the sanctity of human life. A faithful theological anthropology grounds the doctrine in the Scriptures of the Old and New Testaments and in the God/Man, Jesus of Nazareth, the Son of the living God. Every human being, regardless of age or ability, is made in God's image and likeness and has a life worth respecting. Every human life has been made sacred by God himself.

FOR ADDITIONAL STUDY

Doudna, Jennifer A. and Samuel H. Sternberg. *A Crack in Creation: Gene Editing and the Unthinkable Power to Control Evolution.* New York: Houghton Mifflin, 2017.

George, Robert P. *The Clash of Orthodoxies: Law, Religion, and Morality in Crisis.* Wilmington, DE: ISI, 2001.

George, Robert P., and Christopher Tollefsen. *Embryo: A Defense of Human Life.* Princeton, NJ: Witherspoon, 2014.

Gorman, Michael. *Abortion and the Early Church.* Downers Grove: IVP, 1982.

Harrison, Everett, Geoffrey Bromiley, and Carl F. H. Henry, eds. *Baker's Dictionary of Theology.* Grand Rapids: Baker, 1973.

Kilner, John F. *Dignity and Destiny: Humanity in the Image of God.* Grand Rapids: Eerdmans, 2015.

————, ed. *Why the Church Needs Bioethics.* Grand Rapids: Eerdmans, 2011.

————, and C. Ben Mitchell. *Does God Need Our Help? Cloning, Assisted Suicide, and Other Challenges in Bioethics.* Wheaton: Tyndale House, 2003.

Also see these articles: Creation, Humanity, Religious Liberty, Stewardship

47

Racial Reconciliation

WALTER R. STRICKLAND II AND BRIAN DAVIS

The problem of racial division is a symptom of a much larger issue—sin. Sin vandalizes God's good creation through distortion, corruption, perversion, and pollution. The scope of sin is both vertical (Genesis 1–3) and horizontal (Genesis 4), bringing about estrangement with God and one another. Sin's impact on God's design for ethnicity and culture illuminates the problem that racial reconciliation engages (Acts 10:9–48). Scripture testifies to the goodness of ethnicity—a biological reality—featured in the Great Commission (Matt 28:19) and in God's kingdom vision comprised of all peoples (Rev 7:9). The Bible also affirms the dignity of cultures around the globe reflected in norms that elucidate humor, clothing, food preferences, and social interaction. Despite the goodness of ethnicity and culture, the process of racialization sinfully warps them both.

Theological Foundations

Racialization contradicts God's intended design by socially constructing negative or positive meaning and attributing it to biological characteristics and cultural traits. This process results in artificial divisions within humanity. Racialization dishonors God by fabricating "in" and "out" groups, a hierarchy that tragically deviates from the oneness humanity is intended to share (as a united race). Despite racialization's social origins, Christians must bear witness to the gospel's restorative power amid the rotten fruit of social stigmas and broken systems produced by racism.

Reconciliation is a significant theological theme to describe Christ's work on the cross (Rom 5:10–11; 2 Cor 5:18–20; Col 1:19–22) that has immediate implications for the sin of racialization. In Ephesians 2, God reconciled Jews and Gentiles—two groups with historical animosity—creating one new humanity in place of the two (Eph 2:15). Jesus's sacrificial death for sin is God's provision for racial reconciliation.

Racial Reconciliation Defined

A consensus on a definition for racial reconciliation is elusive, but a biblical definition considers the full scope of Christ's redeeming work—restoring sin's vertical and horizontal consequences. Some definitions are entirely vertical in scope and others are exclusively horizontal, but no aspect of the gospel must be jettisoned in pursuit of reconciliation. A biblical definition is:

> An ongoing multiethnic process involving forgiveness, repentance, and justice, that works to repair broken relationships and systems marred by sin, for the purpose of unity within the body of Christ.[1]

This definition contains three aspects that are essential to racial reconciliation. First, reconciliation is an ongoing process for God's people, not an event. Second, unity requires individual responsibility, namely, restoring broken relationships that were estranged by sin. Third, racial justice requires restoring social systems because they reflect human sinfulness and finiteness (intentionally or unintentionally) and cause the marginalized to be further disenfranchised (see Jas 2:1–9).

---

[1] See Brenda Salter McNeil, *Roadmap to Reconciliation 2.0* (Downers Grove: IVP, 2020), 26.

Race and Space (with particular attention to the American context)

Although America is statistically diverse, it is largely segregated into racialized "spaces."[2] In actuality, spaces do not have race or ethnicity, but communal environments are forged by the expectations, patterns, and customs of the predominant culture who occupy a space. Decisions such as programming, clothing expectations, music, and preaching style reflect the culture in mind when a space was created as well as how it is sustained. In Christian contexts, a calloused normalization of a single culture is challenged by a gospel whose *telos* is every tribe, tongue, people, and language worshipping the Savior together (Rev 5:9).

The comfortable assumption of cultural myopia in American ecclesiastical spaces is a sinful implication of American history and requires God-honoring intervention. The efforts of people in different contexts will be distinct despite having the same goal of reconciliation in mind. Despite the uniqueness of unifying efforts in each space, those making proactive strides toward reconciliation are allies. The following sections identify five spaces—and the distinct work within them—that serve as starting points to work toward unity.

Minority in a Majority Space

George Yancey serves as a Christian sociologist and professor at Baylor University. His work is shaped by a desire to influence majority culture spaces as a minority. Yancey promotes a mutual responsibility approach between minority and majority cultures to foster unity.[3] His model is less about direct answers and more about a correct theological posture that facilitates understanding and healing.

---

[2] See John W. Frazier and Florence M. Morgai, *Multicultural Geographies* (Albany, NY: Global Academic, 2010), 279.

[3] See George Yancey, *Beyond Racial Gridlock: Embracing Mutual Responsibility* (Downers Grove: IVP, 2006).

Yancey presents human sinfulness as the source of all racial tension. Like others, he understands reconciliation to involve addressing structural and institutional concerns. In the mutual responsibility model, people of color pursue reconciliation by creating an environment where sincere friendship emerges, helping those in the majority culture to understand racism's impact on their friends' lives. Then Christians can work together to pursue racial justice and to show the non-Christian world what a biblical solution to racism looks like.

Yancey's mutual responsibility model helps avoid a white-savior or black-savior fallacy. The white-savior approach often reflects paternalism, viewing white people as bearing the primary responsibility to "fix the problem." This occurs, often unintentionally, when initiatives are launched to help impoverished minority communities but fail to address their own racial shortcomings. Paternalism is common when a church's only significant interaction with black and brown people is when they are in the position of benevolence. Rather, Yancey calls for majority culture Christians to intentionally diversify their social networks and place themselves in minority contexts as learners.

Similarly, the black-savior approach heaves the responsibility to Christians of color. Delegating the pursuit of reconciliation to people of color is common when an organization hires or promotes a minority (qualified or not) to appear inclusive (i.e., tokenism). Yancey's mutual responsibility approach resists both extremes. He outlines that racial reconciliation requires a multiethnic Christian coalition working together in humility to embrace their unique roles in racial healing. To that end, a mutual responsibility approach values multiracial churches because it fosters numerous opportunities for cross-cultural dialogue and partnership.

The mutual responsibility model's potential notwithstanding, not every majority culture space is hospitable to this pursuit. Encouraged by the Word of God, well-intended believers in majority contexts are prone to enthusiastically sprint toward solutions without preparing the environment for a person of color to lead in a reconciling manner. In majority contexts, reconciliation efforts do not begin by appointing a minority leader, but they are initiated by existing leadership—at times at great personal cost. The leadership's task is to underscore the biblical necessity for reconciliation and implement a thoughtful action plan. Over the years the longstanding commitment of existing leadership can transform a toxic space into a place where minorities can help facilitate real change.

Minorities in a majority space bear a unique burden that cannot be ignored. One tension is the pressure to assimilate to the dominant culture. This often results in the emotional crisis caused by assimilation or doubling down on a home culture only to be shunned by the dominant group. This dynamic is intensified by bearing the emotionally taxing burden of being "different" and continually explaining cultural customs and contemporary racialized issues while negotiating personal emotions. To avoid burnout, minorities need majority culture advocates to champion issues of concern when they are weary and have pastoral care and relational support that accounts for this emotional toll. Working within a majority culture space has unique challenges but also produces real fruit that is indispensable for the American church to pursue racial reconciliation in a meaningful way.

Minority in a Minority Space

J. Deotis Roberts is an African-American theologian who has served at various black churches and historically black universities. His theological project features the concepts of liberation and reconciliation that must be considered in tandem and in relation to one another.[4] For Roberts, a true black theology fosters a Christian experience characterized by freedom for blacks and whites alike. As a result, nothing can be done to pursue liberation (freedom from oppression) that jeopardizes the possibility of reconciliation. Ultimately, Roberts insists that believers who take the gospel message seriously affirm that whites must repent of racial bias and apathy and blacks must forgive. While Roberts's paradigm emphasizes a black/white binary because of his context, the principles are similar for other dominant/nondominant contexts.

With blacks as his primary audience, he rightly emphasizes liberation first because genuine reconciliation between humans only occurs between equals. He insists that African Americans understand their image-bearing

---

[4] See J. Deotis Roberts, *Liberation and Reconciliation: A Black Theology* (Philadelphia: Westminster Press, 1971).

capacity, and whites recognize the same in order to work toward genuine reconciliation. His theological project is an effort to reclaim the full humanity of blacks as equal persons under God and then unto each other.

Roberts's understanding of sin involves three concepts: the individual, social, and structural. In response to the multifarious nature of sin, Roberts proposes the twin virtues of love and justice that are inherently interconnected. He contends that justice is love in public and laments an overly individualized understanding of the gospel that carries no public or ethical implications.

Roberts contends that faith in God confronts collective evils and reconciliation requires mutual action. He calls black churches to "internal prophecy"—addressing individual sins and their collective shortcomings as a slumbering giant regarding social change. He also insists that black churches engage in "external prophecy"—being outspoken in word and deed in the face of injustice.

Beyond his primarily black audience, Roberts contends that whites also bear responsibility in reconciliation. He argues that love is "costly grace" and calls white believers to recognize their responsibility to awaken other whites so that racism may be overcome, root and branch. In sum, white individuals must personally repent, socially recruit others, and contribute to systemic change that makes life more human for black people. For Roberts, reconciliation requires both parties to take responsibility for what they can and must do. As such, he envisioned blacks and whites working together for reconciliation, albeit commensurate with their social and cultural contexts.

For some minorities in minority spaces, there is a hesitancy toward racial reconciliation efforts because segregation and oppression were the impetus that necessitated minority majority environments. Historically, racial reconciliation for minorities is associated with being required to give up the culture that nurtured their families and carried a people through racial hatred. Empathetically, Roberts asserts that black assimilation to pursue reconciliation is not biblical mutuality:

> Black-white reconciliation, in Christian terms, cannot be based upon the superordination-subordination pattern of whites over blacks. . . . Reconciliation must be based upon a oneness in nature

and grace between all people upon the principle of equality. Equity belongs to the time of integration.[5]

Roberts argues that the church is a Spirit-filled fellowship that is unified without being uniform. Christ's reconciling love liberates each of his children and transforms them into agents of reconciliation.

Multicultural Space

Mark DeYmaz, pastor of Mosaic Church in central Arkansas and cofounder of the Mosaix Global Network, challenges monoethnic churches of any ethnicity. For DeYmaz, a multiethnic church is more equipped to reach a diverse community in the twenty-first century. He argues that the church's inability, unwillingness, and lack of intentionality regarding racial reconciliation has rendered her impotent in the eyes of society on matters of race, class, and injustice.[6] Christian unity speaks profoundly to a watching world, communicating a oneness of purpose, passion, and love, particularly in contexts and countries where centuries of racism and cultural division has existed.

For DeYmaz, racism is a spiritual problem requiring a spiritual solution. In his writing he highlights Scripture as a unified starting point to bring God's people together. His gospel-centered multiethnic passion emerges most clearly from Acts and the Pauline epistles, serving as a multiethnic mandate for churches.

DeYmaz argues that gospel proclamation at Antioch was a pivotal moment in the church's development because Jews and Gentiles were united in Christ. He also notes the importance of Acts 13 because the leadership team was called by name and ethnicity—underscoring the importance of diverse leadership. For DeYmaz, the church's success in Antioch was in part due to the gospel's ability to reconcile estranged groups to one another—only a "Prince of Peace" can bring unity to historically estranged peoples.

---

[5] J. Deotis Roberts, *Liberation and Reconciliation: A Black Theology*, 2nd ed. (Louisville: Westminster John Knox Press, 2005), ix.

[6] See Mark DeYmaz and Bob Whitesel, *ReMIX: Transitioning Your Church to Living Color* (Nashville: Abingdon, 2016), 10.

In practice, DeYmaz is convinced that a spirit of unity amid diversity is most effectively established at the inception of a local church. Throughout church life, a vision for multiethnicity requires intentional decisions relating to worship style, pastoral leadership, and engaging issues of injustice. Furthermore, DeYmaz suggests that monoethnic churches take intentional steps, including creating a document that clearly articulates a purpose and vision for multiethnic ministry.

Multicultural spaces are not without their challenges because diverse cultures give way to a diversity of opinions. Diverse communities navigate these ongoing tensions by encouraging congregants to hold their personal preferences with open hands, keenly aware that they gather with people who might think, feel, and vote differently than they do. These tensions reveal that multicultural spaces also have a dominant culture—which emphasizes that multiethnicity is not inherently multicultural. The presence of the former without the latter results in a church that "looks" diverse while being a haven for one particular cultural normativity. The dominant culture in a multiethnic context bears the unique responsibility of being sensitive to the needs, thoughts, and feelings of others. Humility is essential in any church, but it is particularly relevant in a multicultural environment where giving up personal preferences is required. The gospel, and genuine diversity, creates spaces where believers of different ethnicities and cultures come together by raising Christ high enough to unite the body while eliminating unnecessary cultural assimilation.

Majority in a Majority Space

Pursuing racial reconciliation is not the property of minorities—it requires a multiethnic coalition. Daniel Hill, pastor of River City Community Church in Chicago, reflects this sentiment. He encourages majority Christians to be aware of their ethnic and cultural background and to understand how it impacts public and ecclesial settings. The essence of Hill's admonition is rigorous introspection and social analysis to understand racialization and determine how majority culture members contribute to this multifaceted phenomenon.

For Hill, white supremacy is the author of racial difference and must be dismantled. Following Ken Wytsma, this approach draws an appropriate distinction between "hard" white supremacy upheld by intentionally racist people and "soft" white supremacy that subconsciously standardizes white cultural norms, yet both forms are upheld in individual sentiment, groups, and social structures. Hill notes that in American majority culture churches, white culture is normalized, and other cultures are judged based upon those norms.

Hill laments that more than any racial demographic, majority culture Christians tend to deny racial injustice most commonly. He argues that corporate denial sustains individual apathy, which demonstrates the importance of corporate confession and repentance. Hill also warns majority culture Christians of personal righteousness that views life solely through individual moral actions, which inhibits the progress of pursuing racial justice individually and systemically as a united effort.

Hill particularly calls on white Christians to have the sociological imagination to locate where they are in society and use their cultural power to contribute to the important work of changing social structures. While Hill identifies a comprehensive social problem, he encourages white Christians to stand in solidarity with believers of color, seeking to become change agents within their sphere of influence. This includes resituating the necessity of identical political convictions in relationships, giving up preferences, having your motives questioned, and receiving unfounded accusations of being a liberal or a Marxist from longtime friends or family for voicing concerns about racial injustice.

Majority in a Minority Space

There is too often a grievous gap in popular Christian thought about whites intentionally participating in minority spaces. The two primary reasons for this vacuum are conscious (and subconscious) paternalism and white cultural normativity. These dynamics repress intentional consideration of whites attending church or participating in a ministry that is majority minority before it calls for serious consideration.

If inhabiting a minority space reaches the level of conscious engagement for majority Christians, another challenge to overcome is the stigmatization of minority men. Widely perpetuated stigmas of black and brown men require intentional effort for whites to overcome. Such stigmas are especially

difficult to supplant when considering the shepherd's role of spiritual authority and oversight.

Kingdom diversification must include whites populating minority-
led ministries. When inhabiting a new space, it is imperative to listen and
understand the celebration and anxieties of a community. Whites could also
participate in the new space both relationally and structurally. Lastly, there
is a call for service in the context alongside those who are accustomed to
that environment. Each step brings about self-awareness and energizes this
crucial—and often overlooked—avenue of pursuing racial reconciliation.

Characteristics of Reconciliation

While various spaces present unique challenges to pursue the united goal of
racial reconciliation, every Christian effort to bring people together shares several common traits. In addition to common Christlike characteristics such as
love, humility, passion, forgiveness, and conviction, the following are characteristic of productive reconciliation work no matter the context.

Identity

In reconciliation efforts, it is common to diminish personal uniqueness to
mitigate the challenge of coming together. Two negative consequences that
emerge from counterfeit unity are colorblindness and the centering of unity
on something other than our fundamental identity as Christ-followers.
Colorblindness asserts that the best way to cure racial strife is to ignore race
and its negative consequences. Yancey suggests that for some whites, a colorblind philosophy stems from the fear of being called racist no matter what
they say or do. Colorblindness ignores how race and racism play a role in
churches and society today. Furthermore, a colorblind philosophy overlooks
the creativity of God who made people differently.

Moreover, affirming colorblindness does not mean that unity is forged
on biblical grounds; too often, Christ is diminished as the unifier, and
another characteristic fuses a group together. The addition to the gospel that
unifies people becomes a stumbling block for those who do not meet the
criterion (be it social, cultural, or economic). Counterfeit unity diminishes
the Savior's ability to bring his children together. While each God-given

personal characteristic is a gift, only the foundation of our identity as children of the Lord Jesus serves as a foundation for unity.

From Privilege to Stewardship

In contemporary culture, the word "privilege" is commonly used to silence people—especially when the adjective "white" modifies the term. While every person has a varying degree of privilege, the biblical example of Boaz presents a man with significant influence leveraging it, not purely for himself, but on behalf of another (see Ruth 1–4). In particular, the story explains that Boaz demonstrated the love of God to a foreigner, Ruth. The admonition from Boaz's example is not to feel guilty about privileges but to honor Christ as a steward who meets the needs of those around them.

Empathy and Compassion

Paul instructed Christians to bear each other's burdens (Gal 6:2). Miroslav Volf argues that reconciliation is not the absence of conflict but communion between former combatants.[7] Only the gospel produces such radical empathy and compassion, particularly across racial lines. Likewise, Christians should be sensitive to the emotions of their brothers and sisters in Christ. Minority Christians often lament that their white brothers and sisters have rejoiced with them collectively but rarely weep at the tragic consequences of living in a racialized society (Rom 12:15). Racial reconciliation invites Christians to put on compassionate hearts since they have been raised together with Christ (Col 3:1–12).

Lament and Confession

Lament is a passionate response to pain, and in Scripture it leads to petition and gives way to praise. Lament and corporate confession go hand in hand. As John Perkins stated, it is un-American to admit shortcomings and publicly humble ourselves, but this is the way of Christ.[8] Numerous examples

---

[7] Miroslav Volf, *Exclusion and Embrace* (Nashville: Abingdon, 1996), 126.

[8] John Perkins, *One Blood: Parting Words to the Church on Race and Love* (Chicago: Moody, 2018), 83.

of corporate confession can be found in Scripture (Ezra 9; Amos 2:6–16; Mal 1:6; Neh 1:6–7; Dan 9:5–6). Lament and corporate confession are two important ways for a church to express sorrow for historic and contemporary racialization.

Conclusion

The challenge of overcoming racialization is staggering, but despite the historic baggage and complexity, the gospel holds out hope (Gal 3:28; Eph 2:11–22). The call for every Christian to participate in applying the gospel to sinfulness is undeniable, and unique consideration must be given to how God is calling us to engage one of the longest-standing strongholds in American history—racism. May God raise up allies, joining together with a renewed eschatological vision (see Rev 7:9), in reconciliation, commissioning all of us to a variety of spaces to work faithfully toward the unity of God's people.

FOR ADDITIONAL STUDY

Darling, Daniel, ed. *Ministers of Reconciliation*. Bellingham, WA: Lexham, 2021.

Perkins, John. *One Blood: Parting Words to the Church on Race and Love*. Chicago: Moody, 2018.

Williams, Jarvis. *One New Man: The Cross and Racial Reconciliation in Pauline Theology*. Nashville: B&H, 2010.

Williams, Thaddeus. *Confronting Injustice without Compromising Truth*. Grand Rapids: Zondervan, 2020.

Yancey, George. *Beyond Racial Gridlock: Embracing Mutual Responsibility*. Downers Grove: IVP, 2006.

Also see these articles: Creation, Humanity, Gospel

48

Marriage and Sexuality

Mark D. Liederbach

Questions related to marriage and sexuality always linger near the center of cultural concern and social debate. One needs only to look at recent legal recognition of same-sex unions as "marriages" and the rising cultural, moral, and legal pressures affirming ideas about gender fluidity and the acceptance of LGBTQ+ lifestyle choices to recognize this truth.

The manner in which one addresses these questions will always reflect, and arise from, some underlying worldview assumptions about the nature of reality and the foundations of morality. No point of view is spiritually or morally neutral. For this reason, it is always important that Christians have a clear sense of the biblical and theological convictions that ought to ground and drive their perspectives on any moral or ethical issue. Given the perennial concern for issues related to marriage and sexuality, it is all the more imperative that Christians understand and cling to the deeper faith convictions that will enable them not only to live out God's good design in these areas but also be able to give a defense for the hope that is in them.

The purpose of this article is to discuss the biblical and theological foundations that ought to shape our understanding and practice of marriage and sexuality. First, it will lay out elements of a biblical ethic centered on the worship of God as the starting point from which to engage any topic in ethics. Having done so, it will then identify and highlight ten biblical and theological principles that ought to shape a Christian's view of marriage and sexuality in light of the previously developed ethic of worship. It will close with a brief word about singleness.

Biblical Foundations

A biblically and theologically sound foundation for understanding any topic in the area of ethics or morality must always give priority to the question of *Who* over *how*. Indeed, the best and most proper way to understand *how* we ought to live must be determined in light of the *Who* it is that created our universe, designed our natures, and gave us sufficient instruction on how to live maximally in the universe according to our design. The first step, therefore, in discovering the richest meaning of both marriage and sexuality from a distinctly Christian point of view must begin where all good theology and ethics begin—with an inquiry about God and his purposes for the world.

From the very first words of the Bible—"In the beginning God"—the reader is oriented to the fact that not only is God the ground of all existence, but what follows is a grand narrative that displays the wonders of the Creator. Properly understood, the first two chapters of the Bible place God, the Creator, as the focus of the story. This simple reality ought to shape our understanding of the Bible in a manner that transforms our reading of it from an anthropocentric perspective where human experiences and needs are central to one in which humans (indeed, all things) are meant to exist for the purposes and glory of God.

The creation account that follows in the remainder of Genesis 1, then, is meant to offer a panoramic view of creation that displays in general terms how God pieced into existence each vital component of what was to be a faultless world. And as the narrative in the first chapter moves toward its summit, one discovers that it is the creation of man and woman that emerges as the crowning jewel of the masterpiece of God's glory.

What we learn from Gen 1:26–31 is that God set human beings apart from the rest of creation in at least two significant ways. First, he gave them a special nature distinct from all other parts of the creation as *image-bearers*. Second, God gave to Adam and Eve a distinct blessing and task. They were to be *fruitful and multiply* in order to fill creation, and they were to *subdue* the creation *and rule* it as benevolent stewards. The clear implication from the passage is that it would be in the fulfilling of God's agenda for them that they would experience the promised blessing and its accompanying joys. They would maximally flourish as human beings as they lived 1) in accord with God's design and 2) for his purposes and glory.

In Genesis 2, the scene moves from a panoramic view of all creation to a close up of the creation of Adam and Eve as well as the marriage relationship. In zooming in on this final element of creation, God allows the reader to get a more particular look at the finer details of *how* humans were created as well as the reason *why* he created the marriage relationship and human sexuality as he did. Genesis 2:7, 15, and 18 are most helpful for this purpose.

First, regarding the nature of human beings, Scripture indicates that God initially created the "dust" and "ground" as "land" and that he declared the land to be good. Genesis 2:7 tells us that God used that good earth to purposefully design, form, and bring to life a human being. Adam is literally made of the earth (dust, ground) that God declared to be good. From this small point we see an important idea in Christian theology. God created all physical matter, and because God created it, we know it is good. From this we can see that God not only affirms the physical nature of the world but also of the physical body of human beings. Scripture indicates that God intended the human body to be enjoyed and celebrated as a part of his creative grace.

Human beings, however, are more than simply physical bodies. Genesis 2:7 also indicates that God breathed the breath of life *into* the human body and thereby transformed the mere body into a "living being." As such, human beings are composed of both a material part (the body) and an immaterial part (the soul). The body and soul become integrated into a unified whole sometimes described by theologians and philosophers as a *psych-somatic unity* or *dualistic holism*. Christian ethicists normally describe the united nature of human beings with the terms "embodied selves" or "embodied souls." The important part for our discussion is to understand that Scripture rejects any form of dualism like those present in ancient Greek philosophies, where the immaterial soul was considered to be good while the body is evil. Instead, the human person is a unified whole that includes both body and soul.

A second point we gather from these verses relates to the particular and special purpose God had for creating Adam and putting him in the garden. It should come as no surprise that a human being's purpose would be directly related to his or her nature. That is, God designs the human person such that what he or she *is* perfectly coincides with what he or she *ought* to do. A closer look at Gen 2:15 helps us see this beautiful link between our nature and our purpose.

After creating Adam as an embodied soul, God then took him, placed him into the garden in Eden, and gave him a task. Because of the way most English versions translate the original Hebrew words in this verse, it is possible to conclude that Adam's primary task was to be a gardener. Indeed, in a manner of speaking this would be an accurate understanding. There is no question that God wanted him to cultivate the garden, look after it, and cause it to flourish. However, keeping in mind what we have learned above about the nature of God and how he designed his image-bearers, it should come as no surprise that when we take a more nuanced look at this verse and the passage it sits within, a richer meaning and understanding springs forth. Adam's cultivating and keeping of the garden was meant to be a part of—and means to—a life fully on mission, rightly ordered to God in worshipful obedience so that the whole earth ultimately offers to God maximally all the glory that he is due.

To understand this, consider the phrase "cultivate it and keep it" in Gen 2:15 (NASB1995). The Hebrew words translated into English are *abad* ("cultivate") and *shamar* ("keep"). There are several very interesting things about these words as they appear in relation to each other in the Old Testament. In regard to the word *abad*, depending on both the immediate context as well as the larger context of the passage in which it falls, it can be translated as "cultivate," "work," "serve," or "worship." The word *shamar*, again depending on context, can be rendered "keep," "watch," "preserve," "care for," or "obey." When these words appear together in the text, they form a grammatical pair that is known as a *collocation*. In simplest terms, a collocation is a grouping of words that appear together consistently, and which convey a greater meaning when they appear together than they might otherwise convey when the words are used separately. For example, one might find the words "precious" and "stone" placed together in Hebrew to give the meaning of a "piece of jewelry."

Therefore, while it is plausible to think of God placing Adam into the garden "to work it and take care of it," given the theocentric nature of the created order and nature of Adam as a psychosomatic unity, it is best to see that God placed Adam in the garden to "worship and obey." God designed Adam to obey his commands in the physical realm as an act of worship rightly ordered spiritually. That is, from both the linguistic perspective and the context of the larger Genesis 1 & 2 setting, it becomes clear that God did not give Adam the role of farmer as his primary calling. Rather, he made him as a worshipper with the primary task of doing all things as worship. His nature, design, and calling were to worship the Creator and fully express proper worship through obedience to his commands and purposes as he took care of the world in which he lived (see Rom 11:36; 1 Cor 10:31; Col 3:17).

Third, this point is of particular importance when we consider that Gen 2:18 (NASB1995) indicates that Adam was *alone* in the garden and God declared that this condition was "not good." And because Adam's "alone" status was "not good," God decided to create a "helper suitable" for Adam, which is important because it highlights the reality that God wanted Adam to have a partner uniquely created and gifted to complement Adam's own nature and assist him in God's purpose. As his "helper," the woman is both uniquely similar to Adam in comparison to all other beings in creation and yet particularly different: she is female, he is male. And as such, she can partner with Adam and join with him in pursuing the existence for which he was created in a manner that no other being in creation could do.

Having looked at Gen 1:26–28 and Gen 2:7, 15, and 18 separately, we are now in a position to piece these ideas together and discover the profound nature of God's design for both the marriage relationship and our human sexuality. We know from Gen 1:26–28 that a central element of God's purposes in creating Eve was to help Adam "be fruitful and multiply." It would certainly be difficult for him to fulfill this task alone! Thus, as Gen 2:18 tells us, his "aloneness" was "not good." He needed a companion—a "suitable helper"—with whom he could accomplish God's desires. God remedied Adam's aloneness not simply (or even primarily) because he was "lonely" but because remaining "alone" would make it impossible to complete the task of filling and subduing the earth.

Consider the following line of reasoning. If God created Adam and Eve and placed them in a garden of perfect safety and peace in order to worship and obey, and if that worshipful obedience transcended the realm of duty and was instead the highest form of fulfillment and thus joy, and if God created Eve as Adam's perfectly complementary helper so that together they could fulfill his agenda to be fruitful and multiply and fill the earth and subdue it, then one has to wonder what the world would have been like if

Adam and Eve had never given in to Satan's temptations in Genesis 3 and plunged the world into sin.

What would have happened if they had remained pure, obeyed God, and fulfilled the task to be fruitful and multiply and to rule the world and subdue it? What kind of people would have filled creation? What would Adam and Eve's sexual and fruitful oneness have accomplished? The answer is a world filled with God-honoring, sinless worshippers united under one purpose: to subdue and rule the world for the glory of God. From the point of creation on, human beings were created not only to worship but also to be about the mission of spreading that worship to the ends of the earth. God created Adam and Eve and gave them in marriage one to another so that together they could be the worship leaders of all creation. The purpose of *all* human life is to bring glory to God. As Rom 11:36 puts it, "For from him and through him and to him are all things. To him be the glory forever. Amen." And it is in fulfilling that purpose that we will find ultimate value and ful-fillment in *all* venues of life (including sex). Marriage and sex are ultimately about worshipping God and bringing him glory.

Biblical Principles Regarding Marriage and Sexuality

Having grounded the purposes for which God created the whole cosmos (including marriage and sexuality) in a comprehensive ethic of worship, we can now assert key theological principles about both the nature of marriage and human sexuality that ought to in turn guide our thinking and behavior.

God Designed the Difference between the Male and Female Binary

As for the nature of human sexuality, Gen 1:26–27 indicates that God cre-ated human beings in his image, and then more specifically in verse 27 it is stated that maleness and femaleness are both designed to bear God's image.

The text indicates that the *imago Dei* is foundational to humanness and that each human being—by God's design—was created to bear the image of God according to an assigned gender. Maleness and femaleness are written into our very nature. This does not suggest that the *imago Dei* is defined by maleness and femaleness, but rather that one can only bear the *imago Dei* as either a male or a female and that being male or female expresses the *imago Dei*. Thus, because human sexual identity is a gift from God closely linked to the *imago Dei*, we can unabashedly state that sexual identity is an inherent quality of humanness and not a social construct. A man is male not only because his body has male parts and his society then constructs a pattern for how he is to behave. Rather, he is male and has male parts and ought to behave a certain way because God made him a man and desired for him to reflect his image as a male and then gave instructions about how to function as a male. The same is true for women. God created them female with female parts and made them so that they ought to behave as women in accordance with the instructions he gave regarding womanhood. Our sexual identity, then, finds its ultimate grounding in God's creation order and is an inherent part of our makeup as image-bearers. It is not a construction of societal norms or ideas.

The first principle of sexuality is that God created only two genders: male and female. While modern behaviorists and postmodern social constructionists would want to suggest that many genders exist, we know this to be not only an assertion based on faulty worldview assumptions about the nature of human beings and human sexuality but also a misapplication of fact and value categories. That is, the mere fact that many people *do* act homosexually or bisexually or trans and perhaps even claim an enduring orientation based on experience does not make it *right*, *good*, or *moral*. Rather, God built each human with a particular nature: male or female. The irregularities that may come in various desires or even the variant bodily or genetic markers (i.e., cisgender) are the devastating effects of the fall that come to life in our desires, our bodies, and even our social structures and ideas.

God Designed the Male and Female Binary to Be Complementary

God made male and female to correspond to one another. Thus, as the full context of Genesis 1–2 (and the entire Bible) indicates, the clear default position is that sexuality is designed by God to be heterosexual in nature. Therefore, it is proper to find members of the opposite gender as attractive, but one ought not to be aroused sexually by persons of one's own gender. Neither should one be aroused by the viewing of two other people of the same gender engaged in sexual behavior as much pornographic material and an increasing number of television shows and movies portray. Simply put, homosexuality and homosexual behaviors are *never* attractive or right.

God Designed the Equal Value of Each Gender (Masculinity and Femininity)

Because males and females are both image-bearers, men and women also carry an equal dignity or inherent value before the Lord. The fact that they will display the *imago Dei* differently does not negate this fundamental equality of value. Likewise, because God gives both the task to be fruitful and multiply, fill the earth, and subdue it, we ought to understand that while the part they will play in the grand design will be different, the value of each part is equally important to God. It is good and right when a person understands their inherent value, is comfortable in his or her gender-related tasking or role, and is confident in the importance of living within these differences before God—in the manner God describes—as an act of worship.

God Designed the Physical Part of Our Selves to Be Good

In addition to these three principles, Gen 2:7 gives added insight into the constitution of men and women as sexual. As we have seen, this text reveals that human anthropology involves both a material/physical element and an immaterial/spiritual or soul element. What sets humans apart from other living creatures is not that we have physical life but that our life is "God breathed" in a way that gives us a unique "soul" that bears the image of God. The immaterial and the material elements are integrally and necessarily linked in each of us as embodied selves.

God made bodies with a sexual nature, and if God declared these sexual bodies to be "good," then God must intend for us to appreciate it as good and celebrate a rightly ordered expression of our bodily sex and sexuality. When we (in appropriate ways) appreciate the physical qualities of the complementary gender and (in appropriate contexts) enjoy the physical pleasure that God built to accompany the proper expressions of our sexuality, we can rejoice in the goodness of our Maker's design. The question, then, is not *if* we can appreciate the body and bodily pleasures but *how* and *when* it is right to do so.

God Designed the Spiritual Part of Our Selves to Be Good

There is a nonphysical component to our sexual nature that it is also good and right to appreciate. Because humans are one integrated whole of body and soul, it is good and right to think of our souls as also "sexed." That is, if I have a male body, it is because I have a male soul. Likewise, if a person has a female body, it is because she has a female soul. Therefore, all elements of a person such as spirituality and holiness, character and virtue, personality and disposition, are all related in an important way to our sexuality. Each person's expression of godliness (1 Tim 4:8) should accord with his or her own being as a male or female. Following this, then, because godliness is of such great value, we ought to find the expression of godliness in and through gender-appropriate behavior to be very appealing. One of the great fringe benefits of this reality is that even as our physical bodies decay in a fallen world through age or disease, our attractiveness can still increase to others in a very real and important way in spite of the decline of our physical body. While this concept is almost completely lost on an overly physicalist culture, Christians should embrace the good hope of this concept as we age.

God Designed Heterosexual Marriage to Be Good

In addition to these elements, the Gen 2:24–25 narrative of God's creation of Eve and the establishment of the marital union indicates several additional characteristics of God-honoring sexual expression and human sexuality. A "man" is to leave his father and mother and join with his "wife." Thus, another important element of human sexuality is that sexual coitus is meant—by its very nature—to take place within a heterosexual marital context. In fact, the only context in which God describes physical genital sexual expression to be "good" is in a marriage covenant between one man and one woman. Put simply, there is in reality no such thing as a "same-sex marriage." Stated positively, God-honoring sex will only be truly maximized in the context of a permanent heterosexual marital context.

God Designed Monogamy to Be Good

God designed sexuality to be monogamous. Not only does Deut 17:17 (NASB1995) indicate that it was wrong for the kings to "multiply wives," but throughout both the Old and New Testaments we see a number of prohibitions on adultery, fornication, prostitution, divorce, and remarriage after a divorce. The fact that Old Testament patriarchs had multiple wives does not mean it was God's perfect will for them to do so. Therefore, it is good, right, and maximally glorifying to God for a man to remain married to one woman all of his life and likewise for a woman to stay married to the same man as long as they both shall live. Further, and by direct implication, the only proper viewing of nakedness in a sexual context is between the two heterosexual partners within this marital covenant. Pornographic exposure is a form of adultery.

God Designed Childbearing and Childrearing to Be Good

Sexual intercourse or "becoming one flesh" is an element of sexuality designed by God and given as a gift to a man and his wife. Directly related to this is the fact that sexual intercourse is designed to lead to both procreation and begetting of children in the God-given task to fill the earth and subdue it. Having and raising godly offspring is a designed end of marriage and something every marriage should desire, not as an ultimate end, but as a part of God's greater plan for a marriage. While tragically not all married couples can have biologically related children, adoption and meaningful discipleship of other believers in the faith can be beautiful expressions of God's plan to fill the earth with worshippers.

God Designed Unashamed Nakedness to Be Good

Another implication from the Genesis 1 & 2 accounts of creation is that unashamed nakedness is a good gift God intends a husband and wife to enjoy. Here the reference is not only to the joy of seeing one another naked physically but doing so in an unashamed manner. This implies rather clearly the comfort of a trusting friendship with both God and with each other. In the context of marriage, these two friendships (with God and with spouse) are meant to be the foundation for a willingness to bare the *entire* self to one another: body and soul. From a biblical point of view, the naked lives and bodies of a husband and wife together is good in the eyes of God (Song 4:1–5:1).

God Designed Marriages to Be Evangelistic and Missional

Finally, it is important to recognize that all of these principles are meant to be understood and enjoyed within a theocentric frame of reference. Remember that Gen 1:28 places marriage within the context of God's mission to see the earth filled with worshippers. While humans are meant to follow these preceding nine principles and find freedom and joy in and through them, each of these principles will only find their ultimate expression and fulfillment when they are pursued for the glory of God and in accord with the mission of God. Scripture is clear that marriage (and, therefore, sexual expression) is designed and meant by God to depict something about the relationship of Christ's love for his bride the church (Eph 5:18–33). When properly understood and beautifully lived, a Christian marriage is meant to be an evangelistic witness and a missional platform so that a watching world can know something of the love God intends to show his church.

A Brief Word on a Biblical Understanding of Singleness

Every follower of Christ is called to love and worship God and to love and serve others (Matt 22:36–40). It is also the case that some have been called to singleness for the purpose of kingdom work (1 Corinthians 7). In Matthew 19 singleness and celibacy are seen not as a curse but as a blessing and calling, allowing for greater opportunities to serve both church and society. Even those who find themselves in involuntary singleness need to leverage the opportunity for expanded service to others.

For Additional Study

Heimbach, Daniel. *Fundamental Christian Ethics.* Nashville: B&H Academic, 2022.

Keller, Timothy, with Kathy Keller. *The Meaning of Marriage.* New York: Penguin, 2013.

Liederbach, Mark D., and Evan Lenow. *Ethics as Worship: The Pursuit of Moral Discipleship.* Phillipsburg, NJ: P&R Publishing, 2021.

Magnuson, Ken. *Invitation to Christian Ethics.* Grand Rapids: Kregel, 2020.

Marshall, Jennifer. *Now and Not Yet: Making Sense of the Single Life in the Twenty-First Century.* Portland, OR: Multnomah, 2007.

Tripp, Paul David. *Marriage.* Wheaton: Crossway, 2021.

Yuan, Christopher. *Holy Sexuality and the Gospel.* Portland, OR: Multnomah, 2018.

See also these articles: Creation, Humanity, Worship, Religious Liberty

49

Theology, the Arts, and Literature

KAREN SWALLOW PRIOR

Amid the urgency of the church's call to share the gospel, make disciples, build the church, and minister to people in need and distress, should we make time for art? Do the works of human hands and mortal minds really matter in the face of eternity? I respond with a resounding yes. Not only do the works of human culture and imagination matter, but they matter more than and in ways that differ from what we are often taught. It's easy to think of the arts and humanities as frivolous pursuits, the domain of the cultural elite and, for the rest of us mere mortals, occasional fodder for leisurely indulgence during vacations or holidays.

Modern attitudes toward art and the humanities often fall into one of two extremes, aestheticism or utilitarianism. Notably, both of these ideologies developed in the nineteenth century. Utilitarianism is a philosophy that measures all human activities and institutions based on their usefulness, specifically, their ability to bring the greatest "happiness" to the greatest number of people. On the surface, such a worldview might seem practical, helpful, and good. However, utilitarianism makes no room for the excesses of grace or even the inherent value or dignity of human life or human works apart from their usefulness. On the other extreme is aestheticism, which emerged as a reaction against the prevailing utilitarian and didactic attitudes toward art that characterized the Victorian era. Aestheticism, or "art for art's sake," advocates that art needs no justification for itself and need not serve any "use" whatsoever. This view was most famously expressed by Oscar Wilde in his preface to *The Picture of Dorian Gray*, where he proclaimed, "All art is quite useless." What Wilde means by this odd quip is that in order for a work of art to be truly art, it cannot serve any useful function at all. Its utter uselessness is, in Wilde's view, its greatest value. It's important for the Christian to understand that both aestheticism and utilitarianism represent extreme views, each in opposition to the other. Neither is biblical, but both views have deeply influenced the disordered and opposite understandings of both art and the humanities that our culture has today.

This cultural division between the art aficionados and the so-called philistines, between highbrow and lowbrow, has not always been the state of things. Christians in particular can and should have a different way of thinking about the arts and humanities altogether. Both Scripture and Judeo-Christian history offer a more balanced and holistic approach than that which characterizes our contemporary culture. It helps, first, to think about what we mean when we talk about art and the larger field of the humanities that includes the arts.

When we today think of "art," we usually have in mind the "fine arts." But this distinction of "fine arts" from the rest of art (like the extreme views of aestheticism and utilitarianism) is also a modern development. In ancient times, the works produced by artisans—*art*—included a wide range of objects. That included what we might today call *crafts,* as well as functional goods such as dishes and clothes, and, of course, purely decorative items. This earlier understanding of art—as something made by human hands and therefore "artificial" rather than natural—was expansive and sweeping. Human beings were understood to be as creative and imaginative as God (or the gods, as the case may be). After all, the divine creations found in nature are nearly infinite in variety and range, from the obviously useful (plants for food) to the seemingly extraneous (like the colors of coral in deep seas). No wonder the psalmist exclaims, "How countless are your works, LORD! In wisdom you made them all; the earth is full of your creatures" (Ps 104:24). Indeed, it is. And this abundance seen in God's creation is reflected in the abundance displayed in the works of human hands. At the most fundamental level, human creativity reflects the work and the very nature of our Creator.

Of course, that doesn't mean that the works we make are automatically good or God-honoring. Like all our human faculties, our creativity is fallen.

It's not hard to look around and find, in either history or our current day examples, the ways in which the human creations—from the Tower of Babel to the modern entertainment industry—have been elevated to undue worth, valued more than God, as disordered loves. Yet, at the same time, to undervalue human achievement is to undervalue the image-bearers of God. A God-honoring understanding values human works in proper order, neither too much nor too little. So how then do we properly assess and value creative works and human ideas, those things that have no immediate practical use?

What we call the humanities is the field of inquiry that encompasses human creativity and culture. The humanities offer a staging ground where human creativity, imagination, and ideas can be explored, developed, and tested. In the medieval universities, the term was used to distinguish the academic disciplines that centered on studies of human accomplishment from those that centered on divinity, or God. A comprehensive definition of the humanities, as we understand the discipline today, is given by Douglas Jacobsen and Rhonda Hustedt Jacobsen:

> The humanities seek to understand human existence, and especially human creativity, in all of the different times, places, cultures, and circumstances in which people have lived. The humanities explore how human beings have suffered, survived, prospered, thrived, and influenced the non-human world around them, seeking to identify and encourage better ways of being human while acknowledging that what constitutes "better" will always be contested.[1]

The unfortunate decline in recent decades of humanities programs in higher education, including Christian institutions, reflects the larger culture's increasingly utilitarian approach to learning. This decline represents a failure of the culture—and the church—to strive toward more and better understandings of human existence, human meaning, and human creativity. These are abstract pursuits that defy quantification or measure, and in this way, they work against all the practicality, efficiency, and pragmatism that drive our age. Yet nowhere more than in Christian theology and imagination is there room—even the necessity—for the gratuitousness, for the things that have

---

[1] Douglas Jacobsen and Rhonda Hustedt Jacobsen, "Can Christianity Save the Humanities?," *The Cresset* LXXXI, no. 1 (Michaelmas 2017): 11–20.

no immediate use or application—yet are the very things that express our humanity. As the Jacobsens write,

> The humanities do not engage in the disinterested study of human existence. To the contrary, the humanities seek to encourage and sustain human flourishing in all of its diversity. In this task, the virtues of honesty and humility may be necessary, but it is the virtue of hope that gets humanities scholars out of bed in the morning and that sustains them in their work. Without hope, the humanities can easily become nothing more than intelligent voyeurism. Informed by hope, however, scholars in the humanities have the power little by little, one person at a time, to remake the world.
>
> And, of course, the same virtues apply to Christian life. Christian faith demands honesty in evaluating personal strengths and weaknesses (and the strengths and weaknesses of others), and it requires humility about what Christians claim to know. Apart from authentic hope, Christianity can easily become nothing more than escapism that has little if anything good to say about the world as it presently exists. When Christians lose touch with honesty, humility, and hope, history has shown that Christianity can easily become inauthentic, oppressive, and even evil.[2]

As one branch of the humanities, art, too, is an attempt at understanding, as well as expressing, human existence. And just as creating a work of art is an expression of God's image-bearers reflecting his nature, so, too, the entire field of the humanities—which today includes literature, language, history, philosophy, and art (and once included mathematics and logic, as they, too, expressed human understanding of the natural order)—reflects the divine nature of our humanity.

If we understand human creativity and understanding to be a reflection of God's nature reflected by those who bear his image, then we must look first to his example.

God is many things: Father, Provider, Shepherd, Lord. Yet God chose to begin the revelation of himself to us in his Word with an account of him as Creator. When he created the world, God declared it to be "good," and

---

[2] Jacobsen and Jacobsen, "Can Christianity Save the Humanities?", 11–20.

when he made humankind, he declared it as "very good." The magnificent beauty of God's creation is evident everywhere: in azure skies, in the glow of the morning sun, in the glistening of fish, in dew drops on blades of grass, in the red flames of a tulip. Even in its fallen state, the created world is good because God made the world good. Likewise, our ability to create is good because it reflects our Creator's goodness. We were created for good works, and our good works give God glory.

The Bible makes clear God's own care for beauty and craftsmanship. When God directed the building of his holy tabernacle, he called two skilled artisans, Bezalel and Oholiab, to follow his specifications in constructing a place adorned by beauty that would make its sacred nature manifest (Exod 31:2–6). In a small classic work *Art and the Bible*, Francis Schaeffer describes in delightful detail the way in which the God of the Bible makes his love of beauty and art known:

> While Moses was on Sinai, God gave him specific instructions concerning the way in which the tabernacle should be made. He commanded Moses to gather from the Israelites gold and silver, fine cloth and dyed ram skins, fine wood, and precious gems, and so forth. Then God said, "According to all that I shew thee, the pattern of the tabernacle, and the pattern of all the furniture thereof, even so shall ye make it" (Exod 25:9). Where did the pattern come from? It came from God. This is reaffirmed a few verses later, where God said, "And see that thou make them after their pattern, which hath been shewed thee in the mount [or, as the Hebrew says, 'which thou wast caused to see']" (Exod 25:40). God himself showed Moses the pattern of the tabernacle. In other words, God was the architect, not man. Over and over in the account of how the tabernacle is to be made, this phrase appears: "And thou shalt make . . ." That is, God told Moses what to do in detail. These were commands, commands from the same God who gave the Ten Commandments.[3]

Schaeffer goes on to recount the various kinds of artistic works displayed in the worship spaces of the Israelites: gold cherubim, ornate candlesticks, adorned robes, precious stones, decorative pomegranates, statues of oxen, a

---

[3] Francis A. Schaeffer, *Art and the Bible* (Downers Grove: IVP, 2006), 20–21.

lily-shaped pool, and carvings of trees and flowers. Such a catalog is magnificent in its lavish abundance, inspiring in its sheer gratuitousness.

The building of the tabernacle and the description for the ornamentation of that holy place is but one extended example in Scripture of God's delight in beauty. The many ways in which the Bible describes God as a creator and his world as his creation is deeply instructive for how we as believers should think about art and human creativity. For example, Isaiah 64:8 describes the Lord as a potter and humans as his clay, the work of his hands. In his long lament, Job appeals to the Lord using similar imagery: "Your hands shaped me and made me. Will you now turn and destroy me? Remember that you molded me like clay. Will you now turn me to dust again?" (Job 10:8–9 NIV). Ephesians 2:10 says that "we are [God's] workmanship," created in Christ to do good works of our own. Even our own sanctification is cast in terms of creative process in Rom 12:2 NIV): "Do not conform to the pattern of this world, but be transformed by the renewing of your mind. Then you will be able to test and approve what God's will is—his good, pleasing, and perfect will." Perhaps one of the most beautiful images of God as artisan is in Ps 139:13–16, which describes God as a knitter, weaver, and writer:

> For it was you who created my inward parts; you knit me together in my mother's womb. I will praise you because I have been remarkably and wondrously made. Your works are wondrous, and I know this very well. My bones were not hidden from you when I was made in secret, when I was formed in the depths of the earth. Your eyes saw me when I was formless; all my days were written in your book and planned before a single one of them began.

Finally, it is significant that we who receive Christ are described as a new creation (2 Cor 5:17).

It's easy for such language to become so familiar that we lose some of its power and significance. But in *Art and Faith*, Christian artist Makoto Fujimura offers a profound reflection on what it means that God promises a new creation rather than merely "fixing" the old. Too often, Fujimura says, we adopt what he calls a "plumbing theology," one in which we only hope for God to fix the pipes. God isn't in the fixing business, however. Rather, Fujimura argues, "God does not just mend, repair, and restore. God renews and generates, transcending our expectations of even what we desire, beyond what we dare to ask or imagine."[4]

The principles of beauty and art can also be seen as reflecting the concept of the Trinity, one of the doctrinal distinctives that sets Christianity apart from all other major religions. The classical triumvirate—the transcendentals of goodness, truth, and beauty—while developed apart from the Judeo-Christian tradition, offer intriguing parallels to Father, Son, and Holy Spirit. In considering beauty specifically, Thomas Aquinas gives a formulation of the classical components of the beautiful that is threefold: integrity, proportion, and illumination (more on this below). Even the universal proportion associated with balance and beauty in nature, architecture, mathematics, and human faces—known as Fibonacci's sequence or the golden ratio (a common principle applied in painting and photography)—manifests, roughly, in thirds. In literature and film, the pattern of creation, fall, and redemption is a nearly universal feature of good stories. In *The Mind of the Maker*, Dorothy Sayers evaluates the success of a book based on its balance of qualities she identifies as associated with the Father, Son, and Holy Spirit, namely, idea, energy, and power. Duke Divinity professor and theologian Jeremy Begbie finds a connection between the doctrine of the Trinity and the three-note chord of many musical compositions, saying,

> To experience a three-note chord is to experience a kind of space in which three things (heard notes) can occupy the same space (the space you hear) while being perceived as different. That is not possible with the eye. We can't see three different colors in the same space *as different*. They will hide each other, or merge into something else. Hearing a chord can change our mental categories, and in ways that allow the Bible's witness to the Trinity to be heard far more clearly. I have used this example in hundreds of places: schools, colleges, universities, churches; with believers, agnostics, and atheists.[5]

---

[4] See Makoto Fujimura, *Art and Faith* (New Haven, CT: Yale University Press, 2021).

[5] See Kathleen L. Housley, "A Conversation with Jeremy Begbie," *Image* 85, 2021, https://imagejournal.org/article/a-conversation-with-jeremy-begbie/.

Of course, the Bible itself is a rich, beautiful literary text that employs various genres that partake of the long legacy of literature. If God had inspired the Bible to be written along utilitarian lines, it would consist of and be intended merely as a simple how-to manual, like the instructions that come with a new kitchen gadget or a math textbook. But it is significant that the Bible consists of books of history, poetry, song, prophecy, proverbs, letters, narratives, and even sharp and shocking jeremiad, a genre so named based on the book of that appellation. Yes, the Bible has plenty of instructions too. But it is so much more than simply a list of instructions. The Bible—like all good art—invites us into human history, beckons us into God's divine design, and points us toward ultimate redemption and renewal.

It's important to note that the Bible does this—like all good art—not by presenting a sanitized, Pollyanna view of life. Rather, the Bible juxtaposes grit with grace, sin with salvation, and doubt with faith. It offers the whole picture, not only of God's divine plan, but of humankind's fallenness too. As is often noted in discussions of the works of human minds, Philippians 4:8 admonishes believers to think on "whatever is true, whatever is honorable, whatever is just, whatever is pure, whatever is lovely, whatever is commendable." It continues to exhort Christians that "if there is any excellence, if there is anything worthy of praise, think about these things" (ESV). This verse is sometimes used as justification to avoid the darker realities of life and art. Yet if we consider the whole counsel of this passage and all of Scripture, we recognize that what is "true" is not always sweet, what is "just" requires acknowledging what is unjust, and what is truly excellent must be tied to reality. Indeed, the Bible itself does not shy away from presenting a true picture of fallen humanity. We do well when we measure human artistic expression against God's standard, judging as lacking those works that provide too easy or cheap a picture of either human experience or human redemption. Thomas Aquinas's formulation of the classical conception of beauty—integrity, proportion, and illumination, as mentioned above—is helpful here. We perceive integrity in light of the fall. We perceive proportion in light of distortion. And we perceive illumination against darkness.

These principles can help Christians better understand and appreciate modern art, which often presents a stumbling block to those of us who see and know the goodness that is so often lacking in contemporary creations. It is easy to look at abstract, modern, or "found" art and judge that it lacks any creativity or meaning at all. But often there is a great deal of meaning behind these puzzling works. Indeed, the "anti-aesthetic" aesthetic of many contemporary works and movements (in other words, their clear denial of any sense of beauty) is deeply expressive of the worldviews that define our times.

In his insightful and moving essay "How Art Became Irrelevant," Michael Lewis offers a thoughtful explanation about the turn toward the dark, morbid, and meaningless that art took in the early twentieth century. In Lewis's account, the distorted and disfigured human portraits that overtook art a century ago reflect the horrors the World Wars wreaked on the bodies of soldiers. He explains,

> Christianity had introduced the motif of beautiful suffering, in which even the most agonizing of deaths could be shown to have a tragic dignity. But things had now been done to the human body that were unprecedented, and on an unprecedented scale. The cruel savagery of this art can be understood only as the product of collective trauma, like the babble of absurd free associations that tumble from our mouths when in a state of shock.[6]

Later developments in art and architecture took various turns, Lewis shows, toward playfulness, irony, and political and cultural critique—and often against beauty. We might not find this kind of modern art or literature pleasant, but that does not mean that it lacks meaning or significance. For the Christian, even what Phillip Rieff terms "deathworks" (because they tend toward a spirit of destruction rather than creation) tell us things about the culture that we as Christians must know in order to be salt and light where God has placed us.[7]

In 1 Thess 5:21–22, the Christian is exhorted, ". . . test all things. Hold on to what is good. Stay away from every kind of evil." Through literature, art, and other cultural artifacts, Christians can be exposed to worldviews that oppose the biblical worldview and see pagan philosophies fleshed out and

---

[6] Michael Lewis, "How Art Became Irrelevant: A chronological survey of the demise of art," *Commentary Magazine,* July/August 2015, https://www.commentary.org/articles/michael-lewis/how-art-became-irrelevant/.

[7] See Philip Rieff, *My Life among the Deathworks: Illustrations of the Aesthetics of Authority* (Charlottesville, VA: University of Virginia Press, 2006).

enacted in the lives of those who have followed them, both in history and in literature, and thus put these ideas to the test.

Testing all things includes—indeed, depends, in large part—on the imagination. The worldviews and ideologies embodied in works of litera-ture, for example, offer a staging ground to test out the consequences of their ideas. This often involves negative consequences. But the imagination is also what allows us to envision something better than this fallen reality. Walter Brueggemann characterizes imagination as "the capacity to host and voice a world other than the one that is in front of us."[8] A healthy, strong, and bibli-cally informed imagination is one that is better equipped to perceive, weigh, apply the truths of both special and general revelation to our own faith and our witness to the world.

This has implications not only for our own personal faith and growth but for our culture as well. For, as James Davison Hunter says, "Culture is far more profound at the level of *imagination* than at the level of argument."[9] This makes Fujimura's insights compelling:

> Imagination, like art, has often been seen as suspect by some Christians who perceive the art world as an assault upon traditional values. These expectations of art are largely driven by fear that art will lead us away from "truth" into archaic forms of expression. Yet after many decades of the church proclaiming "truth," we are no closer as a culture to truth and beauty now than we were a century ago.[10]

Jeremy Begbie, in the same interview cited earlier, explains that "the arts give expression to a metaphorical way of perceiving the world—a bodily, emo-tionally charged outlook which reminds us there is always more to the world than we can name, control, and grasp." He continues,

---

[8] Walter Brueggemann, "Slow Wisdom as a Sub-Version of Reality," in *Educating for Wisdom in the 21st Century*, ed. Darin H. Davis (South Bend, IN: St. Augustine's Press, 2019), 111.

[9] James Davison Hunter, "Faithful Presence: James Davison Hunter says our strategies to transform culture are ineffective, and the goal itself is misguided," interview in *Christianity Today*, May 14, 2010, https://www.christianitytoday.com /ct/2010/may/16.33.html.

[10] Fujimura, *Art and Faith*, 5.

The Christian imagination, I suggest, needs to be disciplined first of all not by scientific method (valid as that is within limits), but by the Scriptures, which means listening to the heart of what these texts actually tell us about the world we live in: that the entire universe, with space and time, depends on God at every point for its existence—for its origin, purpose, and goal. . . .

. . . I think, we need to see that the artist has a crucial role to play in helping us perceive and believe this grand vision. The artist can help us to see the world as the creation of the God of Jesus Christ. There are all sorts of possibilities here. The arts can help us see (and feel) that the world can never be captured by one level of explanation (by, say, the physical sciences). As Rowan Williams has recently argued, the artist reminds us that there's always more to what we perceive. Because the arts . . . remind us that the world is always more than we make of it. And that very naturally pushes in a theological direction.

What's more, the artist can help us imagine the ultimate future of the world—its re-creation by God—something the natural sciences are not equipped to demonstrate. Christian art, I believe, whatever else it evokes, will surely have a dimension of promise about it, a flavor of hope.[11]

Christians know that our hope is tied to the future, to things unseen but imagined. Art is a training ground for creating, cultivating, and encouraging visions of the good, the true, and the beautiful—all of which point us to their one true source, the Creator God. And this is good.

For Additional Study

Fant, Gene. *The Liberal Arts: A Student's Guide.* Wheaton: Crossway, 2012.

Fujimura, Makoto. *Art and Faith.* New Haven, CT: Yale University Press, 2021.

---

[11] See Housley, "A Conversation with Jeremy Begbie."

Munson, Paul, and Joshua Farris Drake. *Art and Music: A Student's Guide.* Wheaton: Crossway, 2014.

Prior, Karen Swallow. *On Reading Well: Finding the Good Life through Great Books.* Grand Rapids: Brazos, 2018.

Ryken, Leland. *The Liberated Imagination: Thinking Christianly about the Arts.* Eugene, OR: Wipf & Stock, 2005.

Schaeffer, Francis A. *Art and the Bible.* Downers Grove: IVP, 2006.

Worley, Taylor. *Memento Mori in Contemporary Art: Theologies of Lament and Hope.* London: Routledge, 2019.

Also see these articles: The Trinity, Creation, Humanity, Stewardship

CONTRIBUTORS

Daniel L. Akin, President, Professor of Preaching and Theology, Southeastern Baptist Theological Seminary

Jonathan Arnold, Associate Professor of Church History and Historical Theology, Director of Research Doctoral Studies, Southwestern Baptist Theological Seminary

Hunter Baker, Dean, College of Arts and Sciences, Professor of Political Science, Union University

Craig A. Blaising, Senior Professor of Theology, Southwestern Baptist Theological Seminary

Susan Booth, Professor of Evangelism and Missions, Director of Student Learning Assessment, Canadian Baptist Theological Seminary and College

Dongsun Cho, Associate Professor of Historical Theology, Korea Baptist Theological University and Seminary

Christopher Chun, Professor of Church History, Director of the Jonathan Edwards Center, Gateway Seminary

Brian Davis, Lead Pastor, Plaza Baptist Church, Charlotte, NC

Mark DeVine, Associate Professor of Divinity, Beeson Divinity School, Samford University

J. Andrew Dickerson, Assistant Archivist and Digitization Specialist, Southeastern Baptist Theological Seminary

David S. Dockery, President, International Alliance for Christian Education, Distinguished Professor of Theology and Interim President, Southwestern Baptist Theological Seminary

J. Scott Duvall, Senior Professor of New Testament, Southwestern Baptist Theological Seminary

Stephen B. Eccher, Associate Professor of Church History and Reformation Studies, Southeastern Baptist Theological Seminary

Nathan A. Finn, Provost and Dean of the University Faculty, Professor of Christian Studies and History, North Greenville University

Timothy George, Distinguished Professor of Divinity, Beeson Divinity School, Samford University

W. Madison Grace II, Associate Professor of Theology, Director of the Oxford Studies Program, Southwestern Baptist Theological Seminary

Matthew J. Hall, Provost and Senior Vice President, Biola University

John S. Hammett, John L. Dagg Senior Professor of Systematic Theology, Southeastern Baptist Theological Seminary

Adam Harwood, McFarland Chair of Theology, Director of the Baptist Center for Theology and Ministry, New Orleans Baptist Theological Seminary

R. L. Hatchett, Professor of Theology, Houston Baptist University

Jeremiah J. Johnston, President, Christian Thinkers Society and Dean of Spiritual Development, Prestonwood Christian Academy

Kenneth D. Keathley, Jesse B. Hendley Endowed Chair of Biblical Theology, Senior Professor of Theology, and Director of the L. Russ Bush Center for Faith and Culture, Southeastern Baptist Theological Seminary

Jeremy Kimble, Associate Professor of Theology, Cedarville University

Stefana Dan Laing, Associate Professor of Divinity, Beeson Divinity School, Samford University

Chuck Lawless, Vice President for Spiritual Formation and Ministry Centers, Dean of Doctoral Studies, Richard & Gina Headrick Professor of Evangelism and Missions, Southeastern Baptist Theological Seminary

Jonathan Leeman, Editorial Director, 9 Marks Ministries

Evan Lenow, Director, Church and Ministry Relations, Mississippi College

Mark D. Liederbach, Vice President for Student Services, Dean of Students, Senior Professor of Theology, Ethics, and Culture, Southeastern Baptist Theological Seminary

Katie J. McCoy, Director, Women's Ministry, Baptist General Convention of Texas

Oren R. Martin, Associate Professor of Christian Theology, Boyce College, Southern Baptist Theological Seminary

C. Ben Mitchell, Former Graves Professor of Moral Philosophy, Union University

R. Stanton Norman, President, Williams Baptist University

J. Matthew Pinson, President, Welch College

Harry L. Poe, Charles W. Colson Professor of Faith and Culture, Union University

Karen Swallow Prior, Research Professor of English and Christianity and Culture, Southeastern Baptist Theological Seminary

Rhyne R. Putman, Associate Vice President for Academic Affairs, Director of Worldview Formation, Professor of Christian Ministries, Williams Baptist University

Jacob Shatzer, Assistant Provost and Director for Curriculum and Program Development, Associate Professor of Theological Studies, Union University

Robert B. Sloan, President, Houston Baptist University

Robert Smith Jr., Charles T. Carter Baptist Professor of Divinity, Beeson Divinity School, Samford University

Luke Stamps, Chair, School of Theology and Ministry, Dickinson Chair of Religion, and Professor of Biblical and Theological Studies, Oklahoma Baptist University

Owen Strachan, Provost, Research Professor of Theology, Grace Bible Theological Seminary

Andrew Streett, Associate Professor of Biblical Theology, Southwestern Baptist Theological Seminary

R. Alan Streett, Senior Distinguished Professor Emeritus of Biblical Theology, Criswell College

Walter R. Strickland II, Assistant Professor of Systematic and Contextual Theology, Southeastern Baptist Theological Seminary

Christy Thornton, Assistant Professor of Christian Thought and Associate Director of PhD Studies, Southeastern Baptist Theological Seminary

Preben Vang, Professor of Christian Scriptures, Director of the Doctor of Ministry Program, George W. Truett Theological Seminary, Baylor University

M. Justin Wainscott, Director of Professional Doctoral Studies and Assistant Professor of Pastoral Ministry, Southwestern Baptist Theological Seminary

Matt Wireman, Associate Dean of the School of Ministry, Professor of Theology and Church History, North Greenville University

Malcolm B. Yarnell III, Research Professor of Theology, Southwestern Baptist Theological Seminary

NAME INDEX

SUBJECT INDEX

A

abbots, 187–88
abortion, 50, 568, 577, 583–90, 593
   pills, 591
absolution, 191–92
Abstract of Principles, 315
ABTEN (African Baptist Theological
   Education Network), 227
activism, 371, 375, 587
addiction, 481
administration
   gift of, 527–28
adoptianism, 177, 329–30, 332
adultery, 318, 574, 616
adversities, 288–89
aestheticism, 619–20
African Baptist Theological Education
   Network (ABTEN), 227
African Religions and Philosophy (Mbiti),
   225
afterlife, 384
Against Apion (Josephus), 586
Against Eunomius (Gregory of Nyssa),
   176
Against Heresies (Eusebius), 169
Against Marcion (Tertullian), 173
Against the Arians (Athanasius), 176
aged, the, 589. *See* elderly, the

Age of Lights, 59. *See also*
   Enlightenment, the
Age of Reason, 333
agnosticism, 140, 625
American Revolution, 576
amillennialism, 413–14
Anabaptists, the, 197, 200, 202–3, 265,
   447, 449–51, 465–67, 562, 564–65
   persecution of, 450
analogy, 136–37
anastasis, 416–17
angels, 21–22, 32–33
   fallen, 382
   of the devil, 99
   of the Lord, 16, 19
Anglican Church, 200
Anglicanism, 200, 371
   high church, 91
Anglo-Catholics, 447
animal rights, 308–9
animals, 300, 305, 553, 584
anthropology
   Augustine, 196
   Pauline, 199
antinomianism, 199, 356, 358, 361
apocalyptic literature, 73, 340
apocryphal literature, 48, 340
Apollinarianism, 89, 178, 180, 332

SCRIPTURE INDEX

39:4–6 *547*
40:4–8 *32*
41 *100*
41:38–45 *547*
41:39–40 *547*
44:1 *546*
44:4 *546*
45:5–8 *290*
45:7–8 *290*
49:9–10 *323*
50:19–21 *290*
50:20 *29*

Exodus

3:1–4:17 *100*
3:2–3 *16*
3:2–6 *32*
3:5 *250*
3:6 *16, 18, 236*
3:10–12 *342*
3:14 *491*
4:2–9 *32*
6:7 *398, 438*
6:7–8 *101*
8:22–23 *438*
9:26 *438*
13:3 *492*
13:8 *492*
13:14 *492*
13:16 *492*
13:21 *17*
13:21–22 *32*
14:24 *17*
15:11 *250*
19:1–6 *399*
19:3–6 *32, 342*
19:5–6 *366, 399*
19:6 *473*
19:9 *494*
19:18 *17*
20:1–3 *367*
20:1–17 *35*
20:2 *492*
20:3 *237*
20:11 *27*
20:12 *588*
20:19 *19*

24:3–8 *32*
24:17 *17*
24:25–26 *494*
25:9 *623*
25–40 *366*
25:40 *623*
28:30 *32*
29:45 *398*
29:46 *492*
31:2–6 *623*
33:11 *18, 32, 534*
33:18 *18*
33:20 *16, 18*
34:6–7 *534*
34:29–30 *18*
34:35 *18*
40:34 *17*
40:34–8 *494*
40:38 *17*

Leviticus

7:18 *355*
11:44–45 *366*
16:3–19 *349*
16:17 *347*
17:4 *355*
18:21 *258*
19:2 *366*
19:32 *588*
20:2–6 *258*
20:7–8 *367*
20:13 *35*
26:4 *27*
26:12 *398*

Numbers

3:7–8 *403, 443*
4:15 *366*
8:26 *403, 443*
9:15–6 *494*
9:15–16 *17*
10:21 *366*
11:1b–3 *17*
14:14 *17–18*
15:26 *35*
16:35 *17*
18:5–6 *403, 443*

Mark

Acts

1 Corinthians